Lecture Notes
in Business Information Processing   43

Series Editors

Wil van der Aalst
Eindhoven Technical University, The Netherlands
John Mylopoulos
University of Trento, Italy
Norman M. Sadeh
Carnegie Mellon University, Pittsburgh, PA, USA
Michael J. Shaw
University of Illinois, Urbana-Champaign, IL, USA
Clemens Szyperski
Microsoft Research, Redmond, WA, USA

Stefanie Rinderle-Ma   Shazia Sadiq
Frank Leymann (Eds.)

Business Process Management Workshops

BPM 2009 International Workshops
Ulm, Germany, September 7, 2009
Revised Papers

 Springer

Volume Editors

Stefanie Rinderle-Ma
Ulm University, Germany
University of Vienna, Austria (since 1.1.2010)
E-mail: stefanie.rinderle-ma@univie.ac.at

Shazia Sadiq
University of Queensland, St Lucia, Australia
E-mail: shazia@itee.uq.edu.au

Frank Leymann
IAAS, University of Stuttgart, Germany
E-mail: leymann@iaas.uni-stuttgart.de

Library of Congress Control Number: 2010923102

ACM Computing Classification (1998): J.1, H.4, D.2, J.3

ISSN   1865-1348
ISBN-10   3-642-12185-3 Springer Berlin Heidelberg New York
ISBN-13   978-3-642-12185-2 Springer Berlin Heidelberg New York

springer.com

© Springer-Verlag Berlin Heidelberg 2010
Printed in Germany

Typesetting: Camera-ready by author, data conversion by Scientific Publishing Services, Chennai, India
Printed on acid-free paper   06/3180   5 4 3 2 1 0

Preface

Business process management (BPM) constitutes one of the most exciting research areas in computer science and the BPM Conference together with its workshops provides a distinct platform for presenting the latest research and showing future directions in this area. These proceedings contain the final versions of papers accepted for the workshops held in conjunction with the 7th International Conference on Business Process Management (BPM 2009). The BPM 2009 conference and workshops took place in Ulm, Germany. We received many interesting workshop proposals, eight of which were selected. Ultimately the workshops ran on September 7, 2009 featuring highly interesting keynotes, inspiring scientific presentations, and fruitful discussions. The history of five years of BPM workshops in a row proves the continued success of the workshop program.

The workshops held in 2009 included one new workshop on empirical research in business process management and seven well-established workshops.

First International Workshop on Empirical Research in Business Process Management(ER-BPM 2009). The ER-BPM 2009 workshop addressed the demand for empirical research methods such as experimental or case studies to BPM and invited fellow colleagues to investigate both the potential and the limitations of BPM methods and technologies in practice. The ER-BPM workshop aimed at closing the gap in knowledge on process management and at discussing empirical research in the space of BPM and associated phenomena.

12th International Workshop on Reference Modeling (RefMod 2009). Although conceptual models have proven to be a useful means to support information systems engineering in the past few years, creating and especially maintaining conceptual models can be quite challenging and costly. Using reference models provides promising means to reduce costs because of their explicit aim of being reused. The RefMod 2009 workshop aimed at reference modeling research, i.e., the question of how to design conceptual models in order to make them notably reusable and how to apply them efficiently without any loss of quality.

5th International Workshop on Business Process Design (BPD 2009). The BPD 2009 workshop was dedicated to the design, evaluation, and comparison of process design or process improvement techniques, tools, and methods. It aimed to provide a snapshot of the current research dedicated to process design and to comprehensively cover process enhancement approaches such as TRIZ, reference (best practice) models, process innovation, or resource-based approaches to process improvement.

Third International Workshop on Collaborative Business Processes (CBP 2009). The CBP 2009 workshop focused on collaborative business processes and the specific challenges throughout their lifecycle including business process strategy, design, execution, and control. Specifically, collaborative business process settings provoke an extended demand for flexibility, decentralization, and interoperability. Within the CBP 2009 workshop, conceptual and technological approaches to solve those collaborative problems were presented and discussed.

5th International Workshop on Business Process Intelligence (BPI 2009). The goal of the BPD 2009 workshop was to provide a better understanding of techniques and algorithms to support a company's processes at design time and the way they are handled at runtime. It aimed at bringing together practitioners and researchers from different communities such as business process management, information systems research, business administration, software engineering, artificial intelligence, and data mining who share an interest in the analysis of business processes and process-aware information systems.

Second International Workshop on Business Process Management and Social Software (BPMS 2009). The objective of the BPMS 2009 workshop was to explore how social software and social production interact with business process management, how business process management has to change to comply with social production, and how business processes may profit from social techniques. In particular, the workshop discussed the following topics: (1) new opportunities provided by social software for BPM, (2) engineering the next generation of business processes: BPM 2.0? and (3) business process implementation support by social software.

Second International Workshop on Event-Driven Business Process Management (edBPM 2009). The main goal of the edBPM 2009 workshop was to create awareness about the role of event processing for business process management, define the challenges, and start establishing a research community around these two areas. As loosely coupled event-driven architecture for BPM provides significant benefits such as responsiveness, agility, and flexibility, the importance of this topic is growing due to the need of future service systems (part of the so-called Internet of Services) for context-awareness and reactivity, which can be achieved by introducing event-driven awareness.

Third International Workshop on Process-Oriented Information Systems in Healthcare (ProHealth 2009). The ProHealth 2009 workshop dealt with different facets of process-oriented healthcare information systems, and gave insights into the social and technological challenges, applications, and perspectives emerging for BPM in this context. Specifically, the ProHealth 2009 workshop focused on research projects which aim at closing the gap between the potential and the actual usage of IT in healthcare.

We would like to thank all the people who contributed to making the BPM 2009 workshops a success. First of all, we thank the Chairs of the workshops for defining, preparing, and conducting workshops that show how broad and exciting BPM research can be. Furthermore, we thank the reviewers of all workshops who contributed to the quality of their workshops with their high-quality reviews and everyone who submitted papers for the different workshops. Without their effort and spirit it would have been impossible to set up such an interesting scientific program for the BPM 2009 workshops. We are specifically grateful to the local organizing team of the BPM 2009 conference and workshops who provided a professionally organized setting in Ulm. Finally, we thank the keynote speakers for complementing the scientific program with their highly interesting presentations.

September 2009

Stefanie Rinderle-Ma
Shazia Sadiq
Frank Leymann

Organization

Workshop Organizing Committee

Stefanie Rinderle-Ma   Ulm University, Germany
Shazia Sadiq   University of Queensland, Australia
Frank Leymann   University of Stuttgart, Germany

Fifth International Workshop on Business Process Design (BPD 2009)

Michael Rosemann   Queensland University of Technology, Australia
Selma Limam Mansar   Carnegie Mellon University, Qatar
Hajo Reijers   Eindhoven University ot Technology, The Netherlands

Fifth International Workshop on Business Process Intelligence (BPI 2009)

Malu Castellanos   Hewlett-Packard Laboratories, USA
Ana Karla de Medeiros   Technische Universiteit Eindhoven, The Netherlands
Jan Mendling   Humboldt-Universität zu Berlin, Germany
Barbara Weber   Universität Innsbruck, Austria

Second International Workshop on Business Process Management and Social Software (BPMS2 2009)

Selmin Nurcan   University Paris 1 Panthéon Sorbonne, France
Rainer Schmidt   Aalen University, Germany

Third International Workshop on Collaborative Business Processes (CBP 2009)

Chengfei Liu   Swinburne University of Technology, Australia
Dirk Werth   DFKI, Germany

Marek Kowalkiewicz   SAP Research, Australia
Xiaohui Zhao   Swinburne University of Technology,
                          Australia

Second International Workshop on Event-Driven Business Process Management (edBPM 2009)

Rainer von Ammon   CITT Regensburg, Germany
Opher Etzion   IBM Research Lab in Haifa, Israel
Heiko Ludwig   IBM TJ Watson Research Center, USA
Adrian Paschke   Corporate Semantic Web, Free
                          University Berlin, Germany
                          and RuleML Inc., Canada
Nenad Stojanovic   FZI Research Center for Information
                          Technologies at the University of
                          Karlsruhe, Germany

First International Workshop on Empirical Research in Business Process Management (ER-BPM 2009)

Bela Mutschler   University of Applied Sciences
                          Ravensburg-Weingarten, Germany
Roel Wieringa   University of Twente, The Netherlands
Jan Recker   Queensland University of Technology,
                          Australia

Third International Workshop on Process-Oriented Information Systems in Healthcare (ProHealth 2009)

Mor Peleg   University of Haifa, Israel
Richard Lenz   University of Erlangen and Nuremberg,
                          Germany
Paul de Clercq   Medecs BV, Eindhoven,
                          The Netherlands

12th International Workshop on Reference Modeling (RefMod 2009)

Jörg Becker   ERCIS, Münster, Germany
Patrick Delfmann   ERCIS, Münster, Germany

Table of Contents

BPD Workshop

BPI Workshop

BPMS2 Workshop

CBP Workshop

edBPM Workshop

ER-BPM Workshop

ProHealth Workshop

RefMod Workshop

BPD Workshop

Introduction to the Fourth Workshop on Business Process Design (BPD 2009)

The conscious (re)design of business processes is a powerful means for the improvement of process performance and process conformance. However, despite its popularity and obvious pay-offs, process design is still more art than science. In contrast to the dense academic expertise that has been developed in the area of business process modeling, theoretical sound and empirically validated business process design methodologies are still not available. Many methodologies on this subject remain relatively vague about how to actually derive superior process designs. The practice of business process design tends to largely rely on the creativity of business professionals to come up with new process layouts. However, the lack of a reliable methodology means that the outcomes of such efforts are hard to predict. This is an unsatisfying situation for the academic and practical BPM community as process design plays an essential role in the overall business process lifecycle.

The aim of this workshop series is to initiate, develop, continue and summarize high quality discussions that further nurture a relevant body of knowledge on the disciplined, well-understood and appropriately evaluated design of business processes. The BPD09 workshop has been dedicated to the design, evaluation and comparison of process design or process improvement techniques, tools and methods. It's aim was to provide a snapshot of the current research dedicated to process design and to comprehensively cover process enhancement approaches such as TRIZ, reference (best practice) models, process innovation or resource-based approaches to process improvement. Diversity in the underlying research methodologies and papers along the entire Design Science-Behavioral Science continuum were explicitly encouraged.

The BPD workshop has an established track record as a credible event and is since five years affiliated with the BPM conference series. It attracted this year 15 submissions of which 6 papers were selected for presentation after a highly competitive review process. The event was opened by a keynote from Rob Davis, IDS UK and highly successful book author on process modeling and design.

Like in the previous four years, we are very grateful for the timely, critical and constructive reviews and the overall ongoing support of the member of our workshop program committee. We trust that all involved authors, reviewers, presenters and workshop attendees benefited from this workshop and that we collectively keep on making progress towards better process designs.

Eindhoven/Doha/Brisbane, July 2009

Michael Rosemann
Selma Limam Mansar
Hajo Reijers

S. Rinderle-Ma et al. (Eds.): BPM 2009 Workshops, LNBIP 43, p. 3, 2010.
© Springer-Verlag Berlin Heidelberg 2010

Diagnosing and Repairing Data Anomalies in Process Models

Ahmed Awad[1], Gero Decker[1], and Niels Lohmann[2]

[1] Business Process Technology Group
Hasso Plattner Institute at the University of Potsdam
{ahmed.awad,gero.decker}@hpi.uni-potsdam.de
[2] Institut für Informatik, Universität Rostock, 18051 Rostock, Germany
niels.lohmann@uni-rostock.de

Abstract. When using process models for automation, correctness of the models is a key requirement. While many approaches concentrate on control flow verification only, correct data flow modeling is of similar importance. This paper introduces an approach for detecting and repairing modeling errors that only occur in the interplay between control flow and data flow. The approach is based on Petri nets and detects anomalies in BPMN models. In addition to the diagnosis of the modeling errors, a subset of errors can also be repaired automatically.

Keywords: Business Process Modeling, Data Flow Anomalies, BPMN.

1 Introduction

Process models reflect the business activities and their relationships in an organization. They can be used for analyzing cost, resource utilization or process performance. They can also be used for automation. Especially in the latter case, not only the control flow between activities must be specified but also branching conditions, data flow and preconditions and effects of activities.

The Business Process Modeling Notation (BPMN [1]) is the de-facto standard for process modeling. It provides support for modeling control flow, data flow and resource allocation. For facilitating the handover of BPMN models to developers or enabling the transformation of BPMN to executable languages such as the Business Process Execution Language (BPEL [2]), data flow modeling is an essential aspect. This is mainly done through so called *data objects* that are written or read by activities. On top of that, it can be specified that a data object must be in a certain state before an activity can start or that a data object will be in another state after it was written by an activity. This allows to study the interplay between control flow and data flow in a process.

When using process models for automation, correctness of the process models is of key importance. Many different notions of correctness have been reported in the literature, mostly concentrating on control flow only [3,4,5,6]. These techniques reveal deadlocks, livelocks and other types of unwanted behavior of process models. Although data flow modeling is as important regarding automation, only few corresponding verification techniques can be observed [7,8].

In this context, the contribution of our paper is three-fold. (i) We provide a formalization of basic data object processing in BPMN based on Petri nets [9], (ii) we define

S. Rinderle-Ma et al. (Eds.): BPM 2009 Workshops, LNBIP 43, pp. 5–16, 2010.

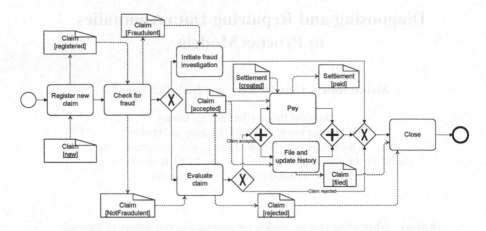

Fig. 1. A process model regarding data object handling adapted from [10]

a correctness notion for the interplay between control flow and data flow that can be computed efficiently, and (iii) we provide a technique for automatically repairing some of the modeling errors. While we use BPMN as main target language of our approach, it could easily be applied to other languages as well.

The paper is structured as follows. The next section will provide an example that will be used throughout this paper. Section 3 introduces the mapping of BPMN to Petri nets. Different types of data anomalies are discussed in Sect. 4. The formalization of such anomalies along with resolution strategies are in Sect. 5. Section 6 reports on related work, before Sect. 7 concludes the paper and points to future work.

2   Motivating Example

Figure 1 depicts a business process that handles insurance claims. The circles represent the start and end of the process, the rounded rectangles are activities and the diamond shapes are gateways for defining the branching structure. Data objects are represented by rectangles with dog-ears.

First, the new claim (the data object under study) is registered. It is checked whether the claim is fraudulent or not. In case it is fraudulent, an investigation is initiated to reveal this fraud. Otherwise, the claim is evaluated to be either accepted or rejected. Accepted claims are paid to the claimer. In all cases claims are closed at the end.

From the control flow perspective, the process model is correct according to several correctness notions from the literature. In particular, the process is *sound* [11], i.e., the process will always terminate without leaving running activities behind. This can be proved by translating the BPMN model to a Petri net as described in [12]. The result of this transformation is shown in Fig. 2.

On the one hand, we can conclude that the control flow of the given BPMN model is sound. On the other hand, the BPMN model also contains information about data flow. We want to make sure that the data flow is also correct.

The use of data objects with defined states can be interpreted as preconditions and effects of activities. For instance, a registered claim exists after activity "register new

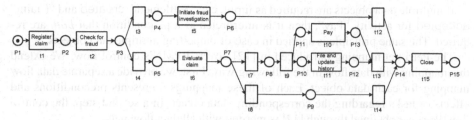

Fig. 2. Petri net representation of the example (considering the control flow only)

claim" has completed. Activity "pay" can in turn only be executed if an accepted claim is present. Also branching conditions can be specified, as it is the case for distinguishing accepted and rejected claims for deciding to take the upper or lower branch.

The example contains a number of anomalies that only appear in the interplay between control flow and data flow. For instance, "pay" and "file and update history" are specified to run concurrently, while executing "file and update history" before starting "pay" would lead to a problem: The claim needs to be in state accepted but it was already set to filed. Further discussion about data anomalies is deferred to Sect. 4.

3 Mapping of Data Objects to Petri Nets

The BPMN specification considers data objects as a way to visualize how data is processed. The semantics of data objects remain unspecified and even left to the interpretation of the modeler (see [1, page 93]). However, the BPMN specification defines the notion of *input sets* for activities. Where each input set is a conjunction of data conditions that must hold to *perform* the activity. If more than one input set are defined for an activity, one of them is sufficient to execute that activity. Similarly, output sets can be defined. Therefore, we introduce a particular semantics of BPMN data objects in this paper, as a necessary precondition for formal verification, that is inspired by the notion of input/output sets.

First of all, we assume a single copy of the data object that is handled within the process. This single copy is assumed to exist from the moment of process instantiation. Multiple data object shapes with the same label are considered to refer to the same data object. For instance, all shapes labeled "claim" refer to the same claim object (cf. Fig. 1). Exactly one claim object is assumed to exist for each instance of that process.

On the other hand, each data object is in a certain state at any time during the execution of the process. This state changes through the execution of activities. BPMN offers the possibility to specify allowed states of a data object. Moreover, it can be specified which state a data object must be in before an activity can start (precondition) and which state a data object will be in after having completed an activity (effect). This is represented via associations in BPMN. A directed association from a data object to an activity symbolizes a precondition and an association leaving an activity towards a data object symbolizes an effect.

While it is often required that a data object is in exactly one state before being able to execute an activity, e.g. "Claim" in state new required for starting activity "Register new claim", it might also be allowed that the data object is in either one of a set of states, like activity "Close" which accepts the "Claim" object in state either filed or rejected.

If multiple data objects are required as input, e.g. "Settlement" created and "Claim" accepted for activity "Pay", then it is interpreted as a precondition that *both* are required. The same principle is applied in case of outputting multiple data objects.

The Petri net mapping introduced in [12] covers BPMN's control flow. We extend this mapping with data flow in the following way: First, we provide a separate data flow mapping for each data object. Each of these mappings represents preconditions and effects of tasks regarding the corresponding data object. In a second step, the control flow Petri net obtained through [12] is merged with all data flow nets.

Figure 3 illustrates the data flow mapping.[1] Each data object is mapped to a set of places. Each place represents one of the states the data object can be in. Activities with preconditions or effects are modeled as transitions. Depending on the kind of preconditions and effects, an activity can be represented by one or a set of transitions in the data flow model. Arcs connect these places with transitions, again depending on the preconditions and effects.

The simplest case is represented as case a). Here, an activity A reads a data object in a certain state and changes it to another state. This is represented as consuming a token from place [*Data object, state*] and producing a token on [*Data object, other_state*]. In case b), executing activity A does not have any effect on the data objects. However, it requires the data object to be in a certain state. This is modeled using a bi-flow in the data flow Petri net: The transition consumes and produces a token from the same place.

All other patterns require multiple transitions per activity. Case c) displays that the data object is changed to a certain state (*other_state*) when executing activity A. Multiple transitions are used as the data object can be in a number of previous states. For each previous state a transition models the change to the new state. In this case, it does not make any difference if the data object is used as input (without constraint on the state) or not at all.

Case d) shows how it is represented that the data object must be in either state n or state m, before activity A can start. While the state is not changed, it must still be ensured that activity cannot execute when the data object is in a different state, say x. If an activity takes a data object as input but does not impose any constraint on its state, we normally would need to represent this by enumerating all states. However, as we know that the data object is guaranteed to be in one of the states, this would not realize any restrictions. Therefore, we simply do not reflect this case at all in the mapping.

Case e) shows that a number of different outcomes of activity A is also modeled using multiple transitions. Here, for each combination of input state and valid output state, a transition must be introduced.

Case f) illustrates how data object states can also be used in branching conditions. This case is actually quite similar to case d).

Figure 4 shows the resulting data flow Petri net for the claim in our example. In addition to the control flow model we have already seen and this first data flow model, we need to generate a third Petri net covering the data flow regarding the settlement.

In a next step, the control flow and data flow Petri nets are composed. Composition of two Petri nets is done through transition fusion, i.e. for each pair of transitions from the two models that originate from the same activity in the BPMN model a transition is

---

[1] Places with white background represent control flow places, we have added them to help understand the mapping.

BPMN	Description	Petri Net
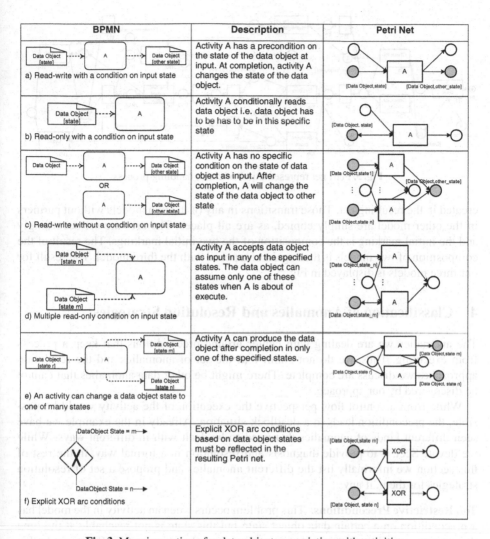 a) Read-write with a condition on input state	Activity A has a precondition on the state of the data object at input. At completion, activity A changes the state of the data object.	
b) Read-only with a condition on input state	Activity A conditionally reads data object i.e. data object has to be has to be in this specific state	
c) Read-write without a condition on input state	Activity A has no specific condition on the state of data object as input. After completion, A will change the state of the data object to other state	
d) Multiple read-only condition on input state	Activity A accepts data object as input in any of the specified states. The data object can assume only one of these states when A is about of execute.	
e) An activity can change a data object state to one of many states	Activity A can produce the data object after completion in only one of the specified states.	
f) Explicit XOR arc conditions	Explicit XOR arc conditions based on data object states must be reflected in the resulting Petri net.	

Fig. 3. Mapping options for data objects association with activities

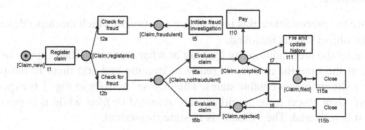

Fig. 4. Claim data object flow representation

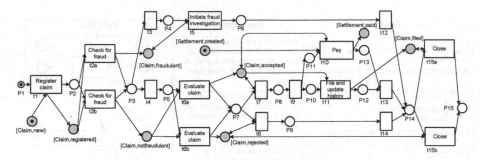

Fig. 5. Petri net representation of claim handling process

created in the resulting net. Those transitions in any of the two models without partners in the other model are simply copied, as are all places. The arcs are set accordingly and the initial marking is the composition of the two initial markings. The result of the composition of two models is then again composed with the third model. The result for our three models is displayed in Fig. 5.

4   Classification of Anomalies and Resolution Strategies

The anomalies we are dealing with center around preconditions that keep a process from executing. Thus, we do not claim that the set of anomalies and the resolution approaches we discuss are complete. There might be other data anomalies that cannot be discovered by our approach.

While from a control flow perspective the execution of the activity would be possible, the precondition leads to a deadlock situation. Already in the example we have seen different kinds of anomalies that need to be dealt with in different ways. While we devote Sect. 5 to provide diagnosis and resolution in a formal way, in the rest of this section we informally list the different anomalies and propose a set of resolution strategies for them, if any.

Too Restrictive Preconditions. This problem occurs when an activity in the model has a precondition on a certain data object state but this state is not reachable at the time the activity is ready to execute — from the control flow perspective. Solutions to this situation could be:

- Remove the precondition: this is the naive solution in which the dependency on this specific object state is removed.
- Loosening the precondition: by looking at what are the available states of the data object at the time the activity is ready to execute and add them to the preconditions as alternative acceptable states. The "Close" activity in Fig. 1 is expecting the "Claim" data object to be in either state *rejected* or *filed* while it is possible that when it is activated. The "Claim" is in state *fraudulent*.

Implicit Routing. This could be seen as a special case of the *too restrictive preconditions* anomaly where the data precondition is missed for some activity due to improper selection of the path to go. For instance, in Fig. 1 activity "Check for fraud" could produce the "Claim" in state *not fraudulent* but still the control flow could be routed by the XOR-Split to activity "Initiate fraud investigation". This happened because the branches of the XOR-Split did not have explicit conditions, i.e. the control flow is not in synchronization with the data flow. The solution for this problem is to *avoid* this unwanted routing by discovering the branching conditions of the XOR-Split and updating the model with them.

Implicit Constraints on the Execution Order. Whenever there are two concurrent activities share precondition(s), the anomaly occurs when at least one of these activities updates the state of the data object. The best solution to the problem could be to force sequentialization among such activities. Making local changes by forcing sequentialization between these activities can lead to other problems. Thus, human intervention might be required in such case.

5 Resolution of Data Anomalies

5.1 Notations and Basic Definitions

To formally reason about the behavior of a BPMN model with data objects, we use classical Petri nets [9] with their standard definitions: A *Petri net* is a tuple $[P, T, F, m_0]$ where P and T are two finite disjoint sets of *places* and *transitions*, respectively, $F \subseteq ((P \times T) \cup (T \times P))$ is a *flow relation*, and $m_0 : P \to \mathbb{N}$ is an *initial marking*. For a node $x \in P \cup T$, define $^\bullet x = \{y \mid [y, x] \in F\}$ and $x^\bullet = \{y \mid [x, y] \in F\}$. A transition t is *enabled* by a marking m (denoted $m \xrightarrow{t}$) if $m(p) > 0$ for all $p \in {}^\bullet t$. An enabled transition can *fire* in m (denoted $m \xrightarrow{t} m'$), resulting in a successor marking m' with $m'(p) = m(p) + 1$ for $p \in t^\bullet \setminus {}^\bullet t$, $m'(p) = m(p) + 1$ for $p \in {}^\bullet t \setminus t^\bullet$, and $m'(p) = m(p)$ otherwise.

Let $N_c = [P_c, T_c, F_c, m_{0_c}, final_c]$ be the Petri net translation of the control flow aspects of the BPMN process under consideration (using the translation from [12], cf. Fig. 2). Similarly, let $N = [P, T, F, m_0, final]$ be the Petri net translation including control flow and data flow (using the patterns from Fig. 3, cf. Fig. 5). We assume that the set of places P is a disjoint union of *control flow places* P_c and *data places* $P_d \subseteq \mathcal{D} \times \mathcal{S}$; that is, a data place is a pair of a data object and a data state thereof. Furthermore, there is a surjective labeling function $\ell : T \to T_c$ that maps each transition of N to a transition of N_c. For two transitions $t_1, t_2 \in T$ we have $\ell(t_1) = \ell(t_2)$ iff t_1 and t_2 model the same activity, but t_1 is connected to different data places as t_2, i.e. ${}^\bullet t_1 \cap P_c = {}^\bullet t_2 \cap P_c$ and $t_1{}^\bullet \cap P_c = t_2{}^\bullet \cap P_c$.

We further extend the standard definition of Petri nets by defining a finite set *final* of *final markings* to distinguish desired final states from unwanted blocking states. We use the term *deadlock* for a marking $m \notin final$ which does not enable any transition.

Example. For the net N_c in Fig. 2, the marking $[p_{15}]$ is the only final marking. When also considering data places for net N in Fig. 5, any marking m with (i) $m(p_{15}) = 1$, (ii) $m(p) = 0$ for all other control places $p \in P_c \setminus \{p_{15}\}$, and (iii) for each data object $d \in \mathcal{D}$, marks exactly one place $[d, s]$. For instance, the marking $[p_{15}, [\text{Settlement, paid}], [\text{Claim, filed}]]$ is a final marking of N.

As a starting point of the analysis, we assume that the control flow model N_c is *weakly terminating*. That is, from each marking m reachable from the initial marking m_{0_c}, a final marking $m_f \in final_c$ is reachable. A control flow model that is not weakly terminating can deadlock or livelock, which is surely undesired. Such flaws need to be corrected even before considering data aspects and are therefore out of scope of this paper. Weak termination is closely related to soundness. The latter further requires that the net does not contain dead transition. This requirement is too strong in case transitions model state changes of data objects.

5.2 Resolving Too Restrictive Preconditions

If the model of both the control flow and the data flow deadlocks, such a deadlock m of N marks control flow places that enable transitions in the pure control flow model N_c. These transitions can be used to determine which data flow tokens are missing to enable a transition in m.

Definition 1 (Control-flow enabledness). *Let m be a deadlock of N and let m_c be a marking of N_c with $m_c(p) = m(p)$ for all $p \in P_c$. Define the set of* control-flow-enabled transitions *of m as $T_{cfe}(m) = \{t' \in T \mid m_c \xrightarrow{t}_{N_c} and \ell(t') = t\}$.*

As N_c weakly terminates, $T_{cfe}(m) \neq \emptyset$ for all deadlocks of N. We now can examine the preset of control-flow enable transitions to determine which data flow tokens are missing.

Definition 2 (Missing data states). *Let m be a deadlock of N and $t \in T_{cfe}(m)$ a control-flow-enabled transition. Define the* missing data states *of t in m as $P_{mdi}(t, m) = ({}^\bullet t \cap P_d) \setminus \{p \mid m(p) > 0\}$.*

For a control-flow-enabled transition t in m, $P_{mdi}(t, m)$ consists of those data places that additionally need to be marked to enable t. This information can now be used to fix by either (1) changing the model such that these tokens are present; (2) adding an additional transition t' with $\ell(t) = \ell(t')$ that can fire in the current data state.

Example. Consider the deadlock $[p_{14}, [\text{Claim}, \text{fraudulent}], [\text{Settlement}, \text{created}]]$ of net N in Fig. 5. The transitions t_{15a} and t_{15b} are control flow enabled. The missing data inputs are $[\text{Claim}, \text{filed}]$ and $[\text{Claim}, \text{rejected}]$, respectively. The deadlock can be resolved by either relaxing a transition's input condition (e.g. by removing the edge $[[\text{Claim}, \text{filed}], t_{15a}]$ or to add a new "Close" transition t_{15c} to the net with ${}^\bullet t_{15c} = \{p_{14}, [\text{Claim}, \text{fraudulent}]\}$ and $t_{15c}{}^\bullet = \{p_{15}, [\text{Claim}, \text{fraudulent}]\}$.

5.3 Resolving Implicit Routing

In this section, we introduce the notion of data equivalence which can be used to classify occurring deadlocks. The classification then can be used to propose resolution strategies for these deadlocks.

Definition 3 (Data invariance, data equivalence). *A transition $t \in T$ is data invariant, iff $({}^\bullet t \cup t^\bullet) \cap P_d = \emptyset$. Let m_1, m_2 be markings of N. m_1 and m_2 are data equivalent, denoted $m_1 \sim_d m_2$, iff (i) $m_1(p) = m_2(p)$ for all $p \in P_d$ and (ii) there is a data invariant transition sequence σ such that $m_1 \xrightarrow{\sigma} m_2$ or $m_2 \xrightarrow{\sigma} m_1$. For a marking m of N, define the* data equivalence class *of m as $[\![m]\!] = \{m' \mid m \sim_d m'\}$.*

It is easy to see that $\sim_d$ is an equivalence relation that partitions the set of reachable markings of N into data equivalence classes. These equivalence classes can be used to classify deadlocks of N.

Definition 4 (Unsynchronized deadlock). *Let m be a deadlock of N. m is an* unsynchronized deadlock *if there exists a marking $m' \in [\![m]\!]$ such that $m' \xrightarrow{*} m''$ with $[\![m'']\!] \neq [\![m]\!]$ or $m'' \in$ final.*

Let $m^* \in [\![m]\!]$ be a marking such that the transition sequence $m^* \xrightarrow{\sigma} m$ is minimal and $m^* \xrightarrow{*} m''$. m^* enables at least two mutually exclusive transitions t_1 and t_2. Let t_1 be the first transition of σ. To avoid the deadlock m, this transition must not fire in the data state of $[\![m]\!]$. Hence, the BPMN model has to be changed such that the XOR-split modeled by t_1 is refined by an appropriate branching condition.

Example. Consider the deadlock $[p_5, [\text{Claim}, \text{fraudulent}], [\text{Settlement}, \text{created}]]$ of the net of Fig. 5. There exists a data-equivalent marking $[p_4, [\text{Claim}, \text{fraudulent}], [\text{Settlement}, \text{created}]]$ which activates transition "Initiate fraud investigation". To avoid the deadlock, transition t_4 must not fire in this data state $[\text{Claim}, \text{fraudulent}]$. This can be achieved by adding explicit XOR split branching conditions.

Branching conditions are realized on the Petri net level using bi-flows, as already illustrated in Fig. 3. Refining branching conditions means in this context that certain combinations of data object states should be excluded. We need to distinguish two cases in this context. Either there is currently no restriction on the data objects in question or there is one. The latter case is easier as we can simply delete the corresponding transition from the Petri net. If no transition is left for the XOR-split we know that we cannot find any branching condition that would guarantee proper behavior. In the first case, we need to enumerate all combinations of data object states except for the current combination.

5.4 Resolving Implicit Constraints on the Execution Order

The case of "implicit constraints on the execution order" occurs when a deadlock is reached from a point where two or more transitions can run concurrently, but have common input data places.

Definition 5 (Implicit Constraints on the Execution Order). *Let m be a deadlock of N. m is called a* data-flow/control-flow *conflict iff there exists a marking m' with $m' \xrightarrow{t_1} m$, $m' \xrightarrow{t_2} m''$, $({}^\bullet t_1 \cap P_c) \cap ({}^\bullet t_2 \cap P_c) = \emptyset$, $({}^\bullet t_1 \cap P_d) \cap ({}^\bullet t_2 \cap P_d) \neq \emptyset$, and $({}^\bullet t_1 \cap P_d) \cap (t_2{}^\bullet \cap P_d) = \emptyset$.*

Example. The deadlock $[p_{11}, p_{12}, [\text{Claim}, \text{filed}], [\text{Settlement}, \text{created}]]$ of net N in Fig. 5 is reachable from the previous marking $[p_{10}, p_{11}, [\text{Claim}, \text{accepted}], [\text{Settlement}, \text{created}]]$ where both t_{10} and t_{11} are enabled. This situation meets the requirements of Def. 5: t_{10} and t_{11} are concurrent (from the control flow perspective), but share a common data place $[\text{Claim}, \text{accepted}]$.

Resolving implicit constraints on the execution order requires the modification of the control flow logic of the process. On a reachability graph level, state transitions from "good" states to "bad" states need to be removed. "Good" states would be those states from where a valid final state is still reachable whereas from "bad" states no valid final state is reachable. While the problematic state transitions are identified in the combined model for control flow and data flow, corresponding state transitions would then be removed from the control flow model.

While this is feasible on reachability graph level, projecting a corresponding change back to Petri nets (and finally back to BPMN) is very challenging. This is due to the fact that one transition in the Petri net corresponds to potentially many state transitions in the reachability graph. Therefore, removing individual state transitions from the reachability graph typically results in heavy modifications of the Petri net structure rather than just removing individual nodes. There exist techniques for generating Petri nets for a given automata [13]. However, this clearly goes beyond the scope of the paper. Projecting the modification of the Petri net back to a modification of the initial BPMN model is then the next challenge that would need to be tackled.

Therefore, our approach simply suggests to the modeler that the execution order must be altered in order to avoid a certain firing sequence of transitions. It is then up to the modeler to perform modifications that actually lead to a resolved model.

In a recent case study [14], we showed that the soundness property of industrial process models can be checked in few microseconds using the Petri net verification tool LoLA [15]. We claim that the the the diagnosis for data anomalies can be integrated into this soundness check without severe performance loss, because it is also based on state space exploration.

6 Related Work

To the best of our knowledge, there is no research conducted to formalize the data flow aspects in BPMN. On the other hand, data flow formalization in process modeling has been recently addressed from different points of view.

The first discussion of the importance of modeling data in process models is in [7]. They identify a set of data anomalies. However, the paper just signaled these anomalies without an approach to detect them. A refinement of this set of anomalies was given in [8]. In addition, authors provide a formal approach that extends UML ADs to model data flow aspects and detect anomalies.

Van Hee et al. [16] present a case study how consistency between models of different aspects of a system can be achieved. They model object life cycles derived from CRUD matrices as workflow nets and later synchronized with the control flow. Their approach, however, does not present strategies how inconsistencies between data flow and control flow can be removed.

Verification of data flow aspects in BPEL was discussed in [17]. The authors use a modern compiler technology to discover the data dependency between interacting services as a step to enhance control-flow only verification of BPEL processes. Later on, the extracted data dependency enriches the underlying Petri net representing the control flow with extra places and transitions. The approach maps only those messages that affect the value of a data item used in decision points. Model checking data aware message exchange with web services was discussed in [18] where authors have extended the Computational Tree Logic (CTL) with first order quantification in order to verify that sequence of messages exchanged will satisfy certain properties based on data contents of these messages.

In [19], object life cycles are studied in the context of inter-organizational business processes implemented as services. The synchronization between control flow and data flow not only confines the control flow of a service, but also its interaction with other services. It is likely that the results of this paper can be adapted to inter-organizational business processes.

Dual Workflow Nets [20] DWF-net is a new approach that enables the explicit modeling of data flow along with the control flow. As DWF-net introduces new types of nodes and differentiates between data and control tokens, specific algorithms for verification of such types of nets is developed. Compared to our approach, we can model the same situations DWF-net is designed to model using only Petri nets.

A very recent approach to discover so-called data flow anti patterns in workflow was discussed in [21]. The approach depends on the data anomalies discussed in [8] to discover such anomalies in annotated workflow nets. Each anti pattern is formally described using temporal logic. Yet, the approach is still limited to verification. Unlike our approach, it does not provide remedy suggestions.

7   Discussion

An approach to detect and resolve data anomalies in process models was introduced. Based on the notion of data objects and their states, we extended the formalization of BPMN using Petri nets. Also, we could identify a set of modeling errors that appear at the interplay between data flow and control flow. Moreover, resolution strategies to some of these anomalies were discussed.

The handling of multiple copies of the same data object is still an open question for future work. In that case, we need to distinguish between the different instances and the state of each. Then, place transition Petri nets would fall short for the task of reasoning. However, colored Petri nets would be an alternative.

Although we formalized the case of different data objects read by an activity as a *conjunction* of these data states, it might be the case that if data object $d1$ is not present then activity takes $d2$ as an alternative input (disjunction). Reflecting this requirement on the formalization is straightforward. However, BPMN needs to introduce new modeling (visual) constructs to help the modeler express his intention explicitly.

The proposed resolution of deadlocks coming up from the different data anomalies by loosening preconditions/discovering routing conditions by introducing/removing a set of transitions and flow relations do not prohibit a backward mapping from the modified control and data flow Petri net to a modified BPMN model.

The contribution in this paper can be seen as a step forward in verification of process models. Moreover, automated remedy of anomalies is possible. In case that the anomaly is not automatically resolvable, the modeler is aware of the part of the model where the problem is so that corrective actions can take place.

Finally, the approach provided in this paper can be extended to reason about data anomalies in communicating processes.

References

1. OMG: Business Process Modeling Notation (BPMN) version 1.2. Technical report, Object Management Group (OMG) (January 2009), http://www.bpmn.org/
2. Alves, A., et al.: Web Services Business Process Execution Language Version 2.0. Technical report, OASIS (2007)

3. van der Aalst, W.M.P.: Verification of workflow nets. In: Azéma, P., Balbo, G. (eds.) ICATPN 1997. LNCS, vol. 1248, pp. 407–426. Springer, Heidelberg (1997)
4. Puhlmann, F., Weske, M.: Investigations on soundness regarding lazy activities. In: Dustdar, S., Fiadeiro, J.L., Sheth, A.P. (eds.) BPM 2006. LNCS, vol. 4102, pp. 145–160. Springer, Heidelberg (2006)
5. Sadiq, W., Orlowska, M.E.: Applying graph reduction techniques for identifying structural conflicts in process models. In: Jarke, M., Oberweis, A. (eds.) CAiSE 1999. LNCS, vol. 1626, pp. 195–209. Springer, Heidelberg (1999)
6. van Dongen, B.F., Mendling, J., van der Aalst, W.M.P.: Structural patterns for soundness of business process models. In: EDOC 2006, pp. 116–128. IEEE Computer Society, Los Alamitos (2006)
7. Sadiq, S., Orlowska, M., Sadiq, W., Foulger, C.: Data flow and validation in workflow modeling. In: ADC, pp. 207–214. Australian Computer Society, Inc. (2004)
8. Sun, S.X., Zhao, J.L., Nunamaker, J.F., Sheng, O.R.L.: Formulating the data-flow perspective for business process management. Info. Sys. Research 17(4), 374–391 (2006)
9. Reisig, W.: Petri Nets. EATCS Monographs on Theoretical Computer Science edn. Springer, Heidelberg (1985)
10. Ryndina, K., Küster, J.M., Gall, H.C.: Consistency of business process models and object life cycles. In: Kühne, T. (ed.) MoDELS 2006. LNCS, vol. 4364, pp. 80–90. Springer, Heidelberg (2007)
11. van der Aalst, W.M.P., van Hee, K.M.: Workflow Management: Models, Methods, and Systems (Cooperative Information Systems). MIT Press, Cambridge (2002)
12. Dijkman, R.M., Dumas, M., Ouyang, C.: Semantics and analysis of business process models in BPMN. Inf. Softw. Technol. 50(12), 1281–1294 (2008)
13. Cortadella, J., Kishinevsky, M., Kondratyev, A., Lavagno, L., Yakovlev, A., England, N.R.: Petrify: a tool for manipulating concurrent specifications and synthesis of asynchronous controllers. IEICE Transactions on Information and Systems 80, 315–325 (1997)
14. Fahland, D., Favre, C., Jobstmann, B., Koehler, J., Lohmann, N., Völzer, H., Wolf, K.: Instantaneous soundness checking of industrial business process models. In: Dayal, U., Eder, J., Koehler, J., Reijers, H.A. (eds.) Business Process Management. LNCS, vol. 5701, pp. 278–293. Springer, Heidelberg (2009)
15. Wolf, K.: Generating Petri net state spaces. In: Kleijn, J., Yakovlev, A. (eds.) ICATPN 2007. LNCS, vol. 4546, pp. 29–42. Springer, Heidelberg (2007)
16. van Kees, M., Sidorova, N., Somers, L.J., Voorhoeve, M.: Consistency in model integration. Data Knowl. Eng. 56(1), 4–22 (2006)
17. Moser, S., Martens, A., Görlach, K., Amme, W., Godlinski, A.: Advanced verification of distributed WS-BPEL business processes incorporating CSSA-based data flow analysis. In: SCC 2007, pp. 98–105. IEEE Computer Society, Los Alamitos (2007)
18. Hallé, S., Villemaire, R., Cherkaoui, O., Ghandour, B.: Model checking data-aware workflow properties with CTL-FO+. In: EDOC 2007, pp. 267–278. IEEE Computer Society, Los Alamitos (2007)
19. Lohmann, N., Massuthe, P., Wolf, K.: Behavioral constraints for services. In: Alonso, G., Dadam, P., Rosemann, M. (eds.) BPM 2007. LNCS, vol. 4714, pp. 271–287. Springer, Heidelberg (2007)
20. Fan, S., Dou, W.C., Chen, J.: Dual workflow nets: Mixed control/data-flow representation for workflow modeling and verification. In: Chang, K.C.-C., Wang, W., Chen, L., Ellis, C.A., Hsu, C.-H., Tsoi, A.C., Wang, H. (eds.) APWeb/WAIM 2007. LNCS, vol. 4537, pp. 433–444. Springer, Heidelberg (2007)
21. Trčka, N., van der Aalst, W.M.P., Sidorova, N.: Data-flow anti-patterns: Discovering data-flow errors in workflows. In: van Eck, P., Gordijn, J., Wieringa, R. (eds.) Advanced Information Systems Engineering. LNCS, vol. 5565, pp. 425–439. Springer, Heidelberg (2009)

Designing Generic Business Processes Based on SOA: An Approach and a Use Case

Krishnendu Kunti, Ujval Mysore, and Apeksha

Infosys Technologies Limited, Hosur Road, Bangalore, India - 560100
{Krishnendu_Kunti,Ujval_Mysore Apeksha_Apeksha}@Infosys.com

Abstract. In an enterprise, it is quite common to find related business functions not only in the same domain but also across other domains. However, often these business functions are implemented in isolation primarily because they were developed independent of one another and in the absence of process centric approach towards implementation. In the recent years, developments in business process modeling [3][4] and support for executable syntax for business process models coupled with architectural paradigms like Service oriented architecture (SOA) [1] have made it easier to design and implement reusable process for generic business functions. Many approaches[7][8] have been proposed for identifying and designing common business processes but are limited to designing the Business process model and do not examine the challenges in propagating the same principles on to the implementation. Here, we propose an approach which covers the design & implementation to ensure reuse & flexibility while maintaining the other benefits of cost of ownership.

Keywords: Business functions, Generic sub functions, Generic business process, SOA, Process modeling, Data definitions, SOA based deployment.

1 Introduction

In enterprises, it is common to come across similar business functions. Business functions represents very high-level unit of business e.g. managing loans, managing purchases etc. Business processes supporting these business functions often display commonalities in terms of the activities performed as part of the process. These common activities across business functions can be seen as generic sub-functions and can be implemented using generic business process definitions.

However, often business functions are mostly implemented individually using one or more applications, where the process is ingrained in the application logic. The existing approach often leads to higher cost of ownership, process replication, slower time to market and difficulty of usage on the part of an end user. In such scenarios, the solution lies in creation of generic process for related business functions and mechanism to extend such business process. Until now, we have found literature validating the idea of generic business process [14][7][8] and modeling variation of business process[13]. These findings provide a good starting point for understanding the constitution of similar business process and techniques to model such business process. We also found good literature on classification of differences in similar

S. Rinderle-Ma et al. (Eds.): BPM 2009 Workshops, LNBIP 43, pp. 17–28, 2010.
© Springer-Verlag Berlin Heidelberg 2010

business process [12], these findings highlight the manner in which similar business process can differ from one another and more importantly provide insights on what can be considered similar business process in spite of apparent differences.

From an implementation point of view the work on workflow patterns [10][11], depicting different technical patters required to implement workflows is relevant. These patterns provide a bottom up view i.e. starting with technical capability and subsequently looking for business fitment. In this paper we have proposed a systematic top down approach using process modeling and SOA for creation of generic business process for related business functions. We have included a step by step design of how the business sub functions should be developed, deployed/distributed across the physical layers during implementation. Subsequently, the approach is validated by a real life case study.

2   Designing Generic Business Process Using SOA

Generic business process implements similar sub functions across different business context. These similar sub functions provide common logical capability with variations pertaining to actual implementation. Designing generic business process starts with identification of generic sub-functions by creation of process models, identification of dynamic parts in process model, identification of common services, defining generic business flows using SOA, service data definition and extension mechanism for all relevant scenarios.

SOA is an architectural paradigm [1][2], which facilitates reuse of business functions by provisioning them as services. SOA proves to be an ideal candidate for definition of logical process definition and its system specific extension mechanism due to inherent malleability in SOA centric design. BPM when used with SOA allows weaving of business processes using services and thereby does not confine a business workflow to a functional business process.

3   Steps Involved in Service Oriented Business Process Design for Generic Business Flows

A typical enterprise often has a set of business processes aimed at fulfilling requirements of associates. These business processes might serve totally unrelated fulfillment needs and hence owned by different business units catering to these needs. For instance, loans request business process might be owned by finance whereas procurement process might be owned by operations. This form of business function specific ownership of business processes often creates a notion that these processes are totally unrelated.

However, a lot of similarity emerges among these seemingly, unrelated business processes when seen in the light of coarse grain functionality provided to the end user. For instance even though loans and purchase business process might look unrelated, operations like submit, verify, approve, reject etc are common in both the business processes. Hence, there exists an opportunity of consolidation of these business process using SOA and BPM.

The following section, describes steps involved in designing generic business flows using SOA.

Identification of similar business sub functions. The first step is to identify the similar business sub functions across one or more business functions. This is done by creating process models for business functions and subsequently identifying common sub functions. In this phase, modeling techniques that captures variability in similar process [13] can be used. Using such technique will help in definition of logical generic business process.

Identification of dynamic parts in business sub functions. Dynamic parts in sub function represent differences in similar business process [12]. For example, a credentials check may be a common requirement across the processes, but this part of the process may need to interact with a security system specific to a unit to which the business process belongs. Identification of dynamic parts in business processes will help in designing configuration driven mechanisms to incorporate incremental changes. This also helps definition of separate smaller sub process which takes care of dynamic parts.

Defining generic business flows using SOA. Generic business flows do not essentially represent an end-to-end process flow. Rather it represents a generic sub function or a part of generic sub function based on usage criteria. For instance, in the given case study (refer section 4) a user first retrieves all pending requests and then views individual request details. Hence, retrieving pending fulfillment requests and accessing individual request details are segmented into two individual flows, based on general usage practice of end users. A generic flow may be as simple as containing just a single activity or set of activities occurring one after the other.

Defining services required by generic business flows. The next step is to identify services, which will be used to compose generic business flows identified in the previous step. Service granularity is an important consideration while identifying services. It is good to define a coarse-grained service rather than a fine grained one. Coarse-grained service allows better representation of process. Once a coarse-grained service is defined, multiple processes can use it without modification.

Identification of common and extended data definitions. The services identified above are generic in nature and same services are used in multiple business context. The actual implementation specific to the business process is manifested at run time depending on the data passed to it. To achieve this functionality, the interface should support generic data types that are common for all the processes and it should provision a way to define data-types specific to a particular process. One way of fulfilling this is by making use of XML schema's extension feature. This is explained in detail in the case study.

Identification of physical layers for SOA based Deployment. The identified generic processes can be deployed across three layers – process layer, ESB layer and source systems layer. Let us look at each of these layers:

Process layer. The static parts of the generic business process or the logical service definitions are deployed in the process layer. This part of the process does not need to interact with any source applications. These make calls to the services deployed on the ESB layer.

ESB layer. The Enterprise Service Bus (ESB) [5] layer holds dynamic services/parts of the processes, which interact with the source systems. Wherever a dynamic part is encountered in a process, proper routing of request to the correct endpoint and, translations between business process specific data-definitions and service specific data-definitions needs to be performed.

Source systems layer. This layer contains systems/applications specific to business processes.

The advantage of this way of deployment is that it offers us the flexibility to add a new system to the common platform by just adding routing and translation rules in ESB without affecting the process definition.

Identification of SOA Patterns for achieving correct service granularity. A coarse grain service is required to support high level business functionality, where the functionality might be realized using more than one component. SOA patterns [9] provide mechanism for realization of required service granularity using underlying components.

4   Business Case Study

The case study illustrates implementation of enterprise authorization system at the premises of a pharmaceutical major in United States. The process flows have been intentionally made simpler in this paper for two reasons; ease of understanding for readers and complying with confidentiality requirements of the enterprise under study. All the same, information required to bring out salient points has been included in the narrative.

4.1   As Is Business Scenario

In the existing business scenario, individual functional business units own specific fulfillment business process and its implementation. The present model of process and application ownership has the following impact:

- Total higher cost of ownership: Each business process owner develops, maintains and supports individual application leading to overall higher cost of ownership.
- Difficulty in usage: A typical approver accesses more than seven fulfillment application to approve all pending fulfillment requests.
- Process replication: Different applications often support similar business processes in same functional area. For instance, there are five procurement fulfillment processes/ applications owned by different sub divisions each procuring items in different category.
- Uneven adoption of technology: Each of these applications is at different level of technology adoption, leading to inconsistent end user experience.

- Slower time to market: Apart from screen flow a lot of data translation and business logic is embedded in UI layer as a result, any addition/upgrade in the present process is both effort and time intensive.

4.2 Business Process Design Based on SOA

The business process design was carried out in accordance with the steps mentioned in section 3

Identification of Similar Business Sub Functions. A set of business processes aimed at approvals of fulfillment requests were examined for identification of generic flows across these processes. In this paper we will examine two such processes.

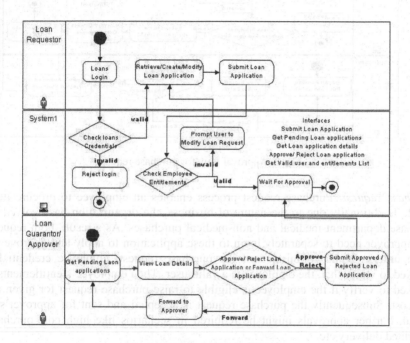

Fig. 1. Approval flow for loan request

Loans Request: Loan request process enables an employee to avail corporate loans, Fig 1. Corporate loans are provided by the organization at attractive interest rates and flexible payment duration. An Employee's job band, duration of employment and present status of availed corporate loans determines his/ her eligibility for applying a new loan. An employee is required to nominate a guarantor, who needs to approve/ vouch for employee even before the loan is submitted to approver. While submission of the loan request, employee credentials is checked to verify that, the employee is a valid user. Then employee's entitlements are checked to verify if the employee is eligible to apply for a loan. Subsequently the loan application is accepted and sent for guarantor's approval. Once the guarantor vouches/ approves loan application, it is sent to approver for final approval.

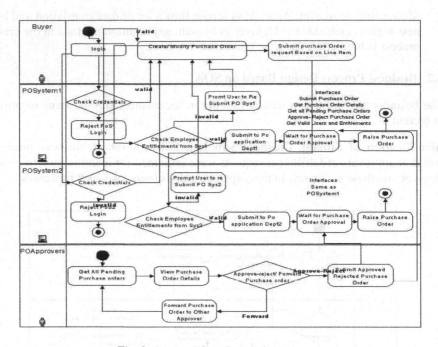

Fig. 2. Approval flow for purchase request

Purchase request: Purchase request process enables an employee to procure items, Fig 2. Traditionally due to the nature of business, the organization has evolved two purchase department medical and non-medical purchases. As a result, both requester and approver need to separately login to these application to apply and approve purchase orders. While submission of the purchase request, employee credentials is checked to verify that, the employee is a valid user. Then employee's entitlements are checked to verify if the employee is eligible to raise purchase request for given item and cost. Subsequently the purchase request is accepted and sent for approver's approval. Further approvals might be required in scenarios like high cost purchases, expedited delivery etc.

Looking at these business processes, we see the following similar business sub functions:

- User credentials validation and creation of fulfillment request.
- Submission of fulfillment request and entitlements check.
- Retrieving pending fulfillment requests and accessing individual request details.
- Approving or forwarding a fulfillment request. Please note the mentioned processes require one or more approvers even though they might call approvers by different name. For example, first approver in loans application is termed as guarantor.

Identification of Dynamic Parts in business sub functions. The following dynamic parts are identified in   the above generic business sub functions:

Table 1. Dynamic parts in business processes

Business Flow	Dynamic Part	Comment
User credentials validation and creation of fulfillment request	Credentials Validation	Credentials information is maintained in individual application supporting the process.
Submission of fulfillment request and entitlements check	All	Request are submitted to individual applications, these applications are responsible for entitlements check
Retrieving pending fulfillment requests and accessing individual request details	All	Pending Requests and request details for a given process are fetched from individual applications
Approving or forwarding a fulfillment request	All	Approved requests needs to be forwarded to application supporting the process

Defining generic business flows using SOA. The following business flows are created based on similar business sub functions and usage criteria.

- Create and submit fulfillment request flow: This process allows creation of fulfillment request, checking entitlements for request and user combination and finally submission of fulfillment request. The services used in this process are Create- Modify-Submit and Entitlements check.

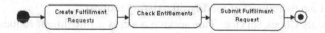

Fig. 3. Create and submit fulfillment request flow

- Get all pending requests flow: This process allows retrieval of all pending requests for requestor and approver. The service used in this process is Retrieve fulfillment request service.

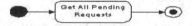

Fig. 4. Get all pending requests flow

- Get details flow: This process allows user or approver to get details of a request. The service used in this process is Get details of fulfillment service.

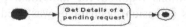

Fig. 5. Get details flow

- Alter and submit fulfillment request flow: This process allows fulfillment requestor to modify the request, perform entitlements check on modified request and resubmit the request. This process also allows approver to approve-reject-forward the request. The services used in this process are Create Modify-Submit, Entitlements check, Approve-Reject-Forward service. On the whole, this flow represents submission of a request both new and modified and captures the steps in it.

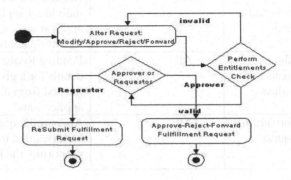

Fig. 6. Alter and submit fulfillment request

Defining services required by generic business flows. The following services are identified which will be used by generic flows:

- User login service: This service will check user credentials and login a fulfillment request creator or approver.
- Create-Modify-Submit fulfillment request service: This service will allow a user to submit a new request or modify an existing request.
- Entitlements Check service: This service accepts a fulfillment request along with user Id and performs entitlements check.
- Retrieve fulfillment requests service: For a given requestor or approver this service retrieves all pending fulfillment requests and shows fulfillment status.
- Get Details of a fulfillment request service: This service allows retrieval of details for a fulfillment request.
- Approve- reject- forward service: This service allows approval, rejection or forward fulfillment request.

Identification of common and extended data definitions. Common business services defined in previous section would require interface definitions that will cater to the two business processes.

The key criteria for designing an optimal interface is to identify data definitions that remain constant for all processes (canonical) as well as providing mechanism for extending data definitions required for individual processes. For the given scenarios XML schema's extension mechanism was used to achieve the required objective.

```
<xsd:include schemaLocation="FulfillmentSources.xsd" />
<xsd:complexType name="FulFillType">
<xsd:sequence>
<xsd:element name="Id" type="xsd:string" minOccurs="0" />
...........
<xsd:element name="Payload" minOccurs="0"
type="inf:PayloadType" />
</xsd:sequence>
</xsd:complexType>
<xsd:complexType name="UserType">
.....
</xsd:complexType>
<xsd:element name="ApprovalStatus" type="e:StatusType" />
<xsd:element name="ErrStatus" type="e:StatusType" />
<xsd:complexType name="StatusType">
.....
</xsd:complexType>
<xsd:element name="SrcAppType">
</xsd:element>.....
```

Listing 1. Fulfillment.xsd, Barebones canonical XSD

```
<xsd:complexType name="PayloadType">
<xsd:sequence>
<xsd:sequence>
  <!-- purchase -->
<xsd:element minOccurs="0" ref="po:purchaseSumry" />
<xsd:element minOccurs="0" ref="po:purchaseDetl" />
<!-- loan -->
<xsd:element minOccurs="0" ref="loan:LoanSummary" />
</xsd:sequence>
</xsd:complexType>
```

Listing 2. FulfillmentSources.xsd, Glue code XSD

Fulfillment.xsd (listing 1) depicts a barebones xsd representing canonical data for all processes whereas fulfillmentSources.xsd (listing 2) acts as a glue code that in turn refers to business process data definitions (XSDs). Using this scheme, addition of a new business data type just requires one line entry in fulfillment.xsd. This form of data definition clearly demarcates common data, source specific data and glue code combining these two. The canonical types identified in fulfillment.xsd are:

- FulFillType: This type captures data for individual fulfillment types (i.e. loans and purchase). The generic fields includes data points that are common across all processes like requestId, fulfillmentType, approvalAction etc whereas process specific data points are referred from the fulfillmentSources.xsd using "Payload-Type" element in fulfillment.xsd.

- UserType: This represents a fulfillment requestor and approver. It carries attributes needed for credentials and entitlements validations.
- StatusType: This represents status of a fulfillment request.
- SourceApplicationType: This represents pertaining to application that supports the particular business process.

Identification of physical layers for SOA based Deployment. As identified in previous sections some parts of the common business process are dynamic i.e. these functionalities are provided by individual application supporting the business process. Source application specific dynamic parts are deployed in Enterprise service bus. ESB layer manages routing and translation specific to source systems. Process layer accesses ESB layer via service interfaces. In this scheme, once generic business flows have been defined, addition of a new fulfillment system to the common platform just requires definition of routing and translation rule in ESB without affecting the process definition.

Identification of SOA Patterns for achieving correct service granularity. It is most likely that some systems still might not exactly fit the generalized flows based on SOA. There might be custom business flow involved or business process might themselves be implemented on more than one system as in case of the purchase order process etc. In such scenarios, SOA patterns should be used to achieve right granularity of service. For instance, for the purchase order process the following patterns were used to achieve service level granularity:

Service aggregator pattern for Retrieve fulfillment requests service: A custom business flow was defined that invoked both purchase system in parallel and accumulated the outputs before sending the response. ESB layer in turn called this business flow.

Service Façade for rest of the services: A service façade was created in the ESB layer that took the responsibility of routing and translating the request to required source system level service.

4.3   Results

The designed generic business processes successfully supported seven different corporate approval flows across eight approval applications with more than thirty three thousand users. In future the framework is intended to support more approval flows, however for each approval flow static and dynamic parts needs to be identified manually. Further SOA pattern or sub-process needs to be created for integrating the identified dynamic part with generic flow.

The implementation was carried out over a period of five man-years, excluding effort on part of applications owners towards development of application service interfaces and approval flow knowledge sharing. A single portal was created for all supported approval flows; as a result, a corporate user can view, approve or reject all approvals from a single portal. During implementation a large portion of time was spent on identifying an approval process in detail and subsequently finding commonalities across process, automation of these activities will result in significant reduction in time and effort. Every approval application was required to provide certain service interfaces to be used in process definition, this required buy in from all approval application owners. A decision was made to support custom approval application functionalities (e.g. compliance requirements related, custom mail formats etc) only after proper due diligence as these functionalities could not be used by other applications.

For small to medium XML payload (less than 2 Mb), the deployed processes scaled well, however there was a notable reduction in performance for large payload (around 4 to 5 Mb). Incidentally for the given process a user seldom sends more than few KB (e.g. 10 KB) of XML payload, any required large supporting documents like vouchers etc are sent using attachments or shared using URL. As a thumb rule of thumb logic or calculation intensive pieces of workflow should be kept out of process flow definition as an external service, these pieces are better addressed using programming languages like JAVA.

Adoption of SOA centric architecture required additional investments in terms software/hardware components and training costs, at the same time the system provided significantly enhanced end user experience and an overall efficiency in approvals process. The framework also provided a mechanism for supporting future approval process using the same platform hence saving on incremental time and cost.

5 Conclusions and Future Work

This paper presents a top down systematic approach for implementation of generic business process using SOA the proposed methodology is indeed effective and has been proved in a real life business scenario. The approach describes a set of steps towards realization of goal. In the described case study steps are carried out based on business consultants and architects knowledge /experience. There a good scope in terms of formalizing knowledge used during each of the mentioned steps and creating tools to aid manual work.

As a part of future work we would like to explore some mechanism to determine similarities across a set of process models in automated manner based on user defined parameters. This would greatly reduce the effort required for information elicitation by meeting multiple process owners. We would also like to formulate SOA based implementation methodology for addressing differences in similar business process. In order to achieve this objective we intend to create a SOA patterns catalogue describing, which SOA pattern to use in order to implement process specific differences. The paper on Classification of Differences between Similar Business Processes [12] can act as a good starting point for this work.

References

1. Erl, T.: Service-Oriented Architecture (SOA): Concepts, Technology, and Design. Prentice Hall, Englewood Cliffs (2005)
2. Schulte, R.W., Natis, Y.V.: SOA Definition and Principles (2003),
   http://cours.logti.etsmtl.ca/mti727/notes/
   soa-definition-and-principles-en-v10.pdf
3. Kamoun, F.: A roadmap towards the convergence of business process management and service oriented architecture. Ubiquity 8(14), 1 (2007)

4. Havey, M.: What Is Business Process Modeling (2005),
   http://www.onjava.com/pub/a/onjava/2005/07/20/
   businessprocessmodeling.html
5. Goldshlager, M.L., Zhang, B.L.-J.: Designing and implementing Enterprise Service Bus
   (ESB) and SOA solutions. In: 2005 IEEE International Conference on Services Computing, vol. 2, p. xiv. IEEE XPlore, Los Alamitos (2005)
6. ACORD XML for P&C/Surety standard,
   http://www.acord.org/standards/propertyxml.aspx
7. Koussouris, S., Tsitsanis, A., Gionis, G., Psarras, J.: Designing Generic Municipal Services Process Models towards eGovernment Interoperability Infrastructures (2008),
   http://minbar.cs.dartmouth.edu/greecom/ejeta/specialMay08-
   issue/ejeta-special-08may-3.pdf
8. Ho, C.C.: Workflow Service Provisioning: Generic Business Process Designs (1999),
   http://innovexpo.itee.uq.edu.au/1999/csabstracts/Ho_C.pdf
9. Community site for SOA design patterns, http://www.soapatterns.org
10. Keen, M., et al.: Patterns: Implementing an SOA Using an Enterprise Service Bus, IBM
    Redbooks (2004),
    http://www.redbooks.ibm.com/redbooks/pdfs/sg246306.pdf
11. Workflow patterns,
    http://www.workflowpatterns.com/patterns/index.php
12. Dijkman, R.: A Classification of Differences between Similar Business Processes. In: 11th
    IEEE International Enterprise Distributed Object Computing Conference (2007)
13. Moon, M., Hong, M., Yeom, K.: Two-level Variability Analysis for Business Process with
    Reusability and Extensibility. In: Annual IEEE International Computer Software and Ap-
    plications Conference (2008)
14. Malone, T.W., Crowston, K., Herman, G.A.: Organizing Business Knowledge: The MIT
    Process Handbook

Integrating Users in Object-Aware Process Management Systems: Issues and Challenges

Vera Künzle and Manfred Reichert

Institute of Databases and Information Systems, Ulm University, Germany
{vera.kuenzle,manfred.reichert}@uni-ulm.de

Abstract. Despite the increasing maturity of contemporary Workflow Management Systems (WfMS), there still exist numerous process-aware application systems with more or less hard-coded process logic. This does not only cause high maintenance efforts (e.g. costly code adaptions), but also results in hard-coded rules for controlling the access to business processes, business functions, and business data. In particular, the assignment of users to process activities needs to be compliant with the rights granted for executing business functions and for accessing business data. A major reason for not using WfMS in a broader context is the inflexibility provided by their activity-centered paradigm, which also limits the access control strategies offered by them. This position paper discusses key challenges for a process management technology in which processes, data objects and users are well integrated in order to ensure a sufficient degree of flexibility. We denote such technology as *Object-Aware Process Management System* and consider related research as fundamental for the further maturation of process management technology.

Keywords: Object-aware Process Management, Data-driven Processes, Process Design Methods, Access Control, Human Aspects.

1 Introduction

Contemporary application systems (e.g., ERP and CRM systems) enable access to *business data*, offer a variety of *business functions* to users, and provide an integrated view on supported *business processes*. However, in most cases underlying business process logic, business functions, and access control constraints are hard-coded within the application system. As a major drawback, even simple process changes then require costly code adaptations and high efforts for testing [1]. To cope with this unsatisfactory situation, *Workflow Management Systems (WfMS)* have been introduced. Usually a WfMS provides generic functions for modeling, executing and monitoring business processes. Contemporary WfMS, however, have not achieved the technological maturity yet for adequately supporting the processes from *Application Systems*. In particular, existing WfMS show strong limitations if a close integration of the process and data perspectives is needed. Another challenge constitutes *access control*. Many information systems rely on *Role-Based Access Control (RBAC)* mechanisms [2,3] to make

S. Rinderle-Ma et al. (Eds.): BPM 2009 Workshops, LNBIP 43, pp. 29–41, 2010.

the specification of permissions independent from concrete users and thus to ease users management. However, the basic RBAC approach does not allow to distinguish between permissions of the type and of the instance level [4]. Furthermore, a closer integration of process and data necessitates a more sophisticated approach for access control. On the one hand, access to business data and permissions for executing business functions depend on the executed processes. On the other hand, when defining actor assignments for process activities, permissions for accessing data as well as for executing functions have to be taken into account. Current WfMS do not adequately cope with such interdependencies. In [1] we have introduced an advanced paradigm for the support of *data-driven processes* and have discussed some of the challenges emerging in this context. In particular, we have elaborated the requirements for a generic process management component, which integrates the data- and function-based view, known from many application systems, with a view on the supported processes. Thereby, our specific focus has been on the integration of data and processes. This paper adds a complementary aspect to our previous discussions, namely how to integrate users in *Object-aware Process Management Systems*[1]; i.e., in addition to the challenges arising from a closer integration of process and data, we discuss fundamental requirements for access control in Object-aware Process Management Systems. Understanding these challenges is fundamental in order to integrate users in such systems. We use the following example to illustrate relevant issues for realizing an Object-aware Process Management System.

Illustrating Example. We consider the (simplified) process of a job application as typical in *human resource management*. Using an Internet online form, interested **job applicants** may apply for a **vacancy**. The overall goal of the process is to decide which applicant shall get the offered job. Different **personnel officers** are responsible for different **job applications**. They may request internal **reviews** for each job applicant. Corresponding review forms have to be filled out by **employees from functional divisions** until a certain deadline. Usually, they evaluate the application(s), **make a proposal** on how to proceed (e.g., whether or not a particular applicant shall be invited for an interview), and **submit** their recommendation to the personnel officer. Based on the reviews the personnel officer makes his **decision** on the application(s) or he initiates further steps like interviews or additional reviews. In general, different reviews may be requested and submitted respectively at different points in time.

Section 2 summarizes important aspects on application systems as well as on WfMS, and describes five key challenges for integrating data and processes in Object-aware Process Management Systems. In Section 3 we first present basic issues related to access control. Then we discuss additional challenges which specifically deal with the integration of users. Section 4 discusses existing approaches. The paper concludes with an outlook in Section 5.

---

[1] An Object-aware Process Management System denotes a process- and object-aware information system with a tight integration of the process and the data perspective.

2   Integrating Processes and Data

In [1] we have introduced the notion of *Object-aware Process Management System*. Our overall goal is to provide a generic component for enabling *data-driven processes* with an *integrated view* on process and data. On the one hand, we want to offer similar features as realized in hard-coded application systems, on the other hand we want to benefit from the advantages known from workflow technology; i.e.; to provide generic functions for realizing such applications. This section summarizes challenges for integrating processes and data in Object-aware Process Management Systems, which we elaborated in two case studies.

2.1   Backgrounds

We first provide the needed backgrounds for understanding following discussions. **Application Systems** provide features for managing business data. The latter are represented by a number of *object instances* (e.g. **job application of Luise Loop**) of different *object types* (e.g. **job application**), which may be related to each other (e.g., for a **job application** several **reviews** may exist). Object types and their relations are modeled in the (application) *data structure*. An object type consists of a set of *attributes* (e.g., **name** of an **applicant** or **decision** about a **job application**). The instances of a particular object type then differ in the values of these attributes. Using basic *functions*, object instances can be created, deleted or changed; i.e, attribute values can be read/written by authorized users. Several object instances can be displayed in a table; whose rows correspond to object instances [1]. Users may invoke specific functions (e.g. forms) on selected object instances in order to read/write its attribute values. In addition to this data- and function-centered view, existing applications often provide an integrated view on processes. Generally, a *process* is needed to reach a particular *business goal*; i.e., object instances having certain attribute values. Therefore, application systems implement *mandatory activities* which have to be performed on these object instances in a certain order and be assigned to authorized users; i.e., *mandatory activities* are executed in the context of a particular process and are added to user worklists. Users are themselves treated as entities maintained in the underlying application database. Consider **applicants**, **personnel officers** and **employees** as users of a human resource management system. Generally, for each real world entity type (e.g. **job application**), and therefore for each role (e.g. **applicant**), a specific object type exists. As a result, each user is represented by an object instance. Consequently, it is not sufficient to assign privileges only on basis of object types and roles. Instead, respective systems have to manage *permissions* at the level of individual object instances as well; e.g. a user may work on a particular process activity for process instance A, while he is not allowed to work on the same activity within another process instance B of same type. Finally, the permissions to work on a particular activity at instance level may depend on accessed data. One drawback of existing applications is the hard-coding of the process logic and the authorization constraints within the application system.

Workflow Management Systems. WfMS offer promising perspectives for realizing more flexible process implementations. Usually a *process definition* consists of a set of activities and their execution constraints (e.g., *control flow*) [5]. The latter can be defined based on a number of control flow patterns which, for example, allow to express sequential, alternative and parallel activity routing or loop backs [6]. Each single *activity*, in turn, represents a task and is linked to a specific business function of an application system. Application data is usually managed by the invoked applications themselves. Only data needed for process control (e.g. for evaluating transition or join conditions) or for supplying activity input parameters of activities are stored and managed within the WfMS. In many WfMS, only *atomic data elements* (i.e. attributes) can be handled; i.e., grouping data elements or defining semantical relations between them is not possible. Roles and users are typically captured in an *organization model* maintained by the WfMS [7]. To be able to assign human activities to the right actors, WfMS use *actor expressions* which are related to components of the organizational model (e.g. user roles). Such assignments have to be defined for each human activity. At runtime, for each business case an instance of the corresponding process definition is created and executed according to the defined control flow. A particular activity may be only enabled if all preceding activities are completed or cannot be executed anymore (except loop backs). When a human activity becomes enabled, corresponding work items are added to worklists of authorized users. Finally, when such a work item is selected by a user, the WfMS launches the associated business function of an application system.

2.2   Basic Challenges for Integrating Processes and Data

Process support in Application Systems raises challenges not adequately addressed by existing WfMS (see [1] for details):

Challenge 1 (Integrating process and data). Processes need to be tightly integrated with application data [8]; i.e.; business data should be managed based on processed objects. Another challenge is to cope with the varying and dynamic number of object instances to be handled within processes during runtime; for each `job application` a different number of `reviews` may exist, which can be instantiated at different points in time. Therefore, the relations between object instances have to be considered during process execution; e.g., to decide about a `job application` only the `reviews` for this concrete application have to be evaluated. In this context, authorized users work on *mandatory activities* needed for the progress of the process instance and offered to users in their worklists. In addition, they may optionally edit attribute values of object instances at arbitrary points in time (denoted as *optional activities*) [1]. As example consider attribute `comment` of a `review` object instance that may be changed at any point in time.

Challenge 2 (Choosing granularities for process and activities). The modelling of processes and data constitute two sides of the same coin and therefore should be compliant with each other [9]. We have to distinguish between

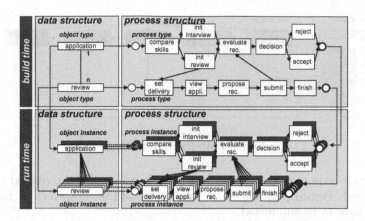

Fig. 1. Analogy between data and process structure

object level and *(data-) structure level*: A particular *process type* should be modeled in accordance with a specific *object type* (see Fig.1). Further, process activities may directly refer to attributes of this object type; e.g., in activity make decision of a job application the value of attribute decision has to filled out. Furthermore, the overall *data structure* has to be taken into account when executing a process instance. To decide on a job application the corresponding reviews have to be evaluated. Relations between process instances should therefore correspond to the ones between the corresponding data objects [10]. Finally, process instantiation needs to be coupled with the creation of related object instances [1].

Challenge 3 (Data-based modeling). *Process steps* should not be modeled in terms of black-box activities [8], but be defined as *data conditions* on the attributes of the corresponding object type (see Fig. 2); e.g., to reach the process goal of a job application, attribute decision must be set. This allows us to determine necessary attribute changes over time; i.e., to figure out what attribute changes are required for an object instance to reach the next logical process step of the corresponding process instance. Attribute changes affecting the progress of a process instance can be bound to the execution of *mandatory activities*. Simultaneously, *optional activities* can be executed on the respective object instance (e.g. changing the attribute comment of a review); but usually have no influence on the progress of the process.

Challenge 4 (Synchronizing process instances). It should be possible to execute both instances of the same and instances of different process types *asynchronously* to each other. However, due to data dependencies at object instance level, we need to be able to synchronize their execution at certain points [1,10,11]. Furthermore, to a super-ordinate process instance several sub-ordinate process instances should be assignable in accordance with the relationships between the corresponding object instances and their cardinalities [1]. Fig.1 depicts an example of synchronized process instances. Here, the process instance for a job

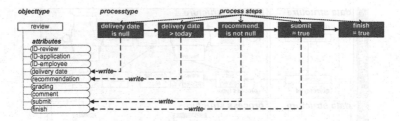

Fig. 2. Data-based modelling

application may continue while the process instances for the related **reviews** are executed. Before deciding on a **job application**, however, all requested **reviews** have to be submitted.

Challenge 5 (Flexibility). Process execution is *data-driven*; i.e., it should not be guided by activities, but be based on the state of processed object instances. This way, a more flexible execution behaviour can be realized. In addition to mandatory activities, optional ones may be performed asynchronously. Which optional activities are available at a certain point in time depends on the state of the processed object instance. For example, after submitting a **review** its attribute **comment** cannot be changed anymore. Finally, it should be possible to conjointly work on multiple activities of same type, but belonging to different process instances, i.e. to process the activities in one go [12,1]. A user should be able to change the values of certain attributes for a set of object instances simultaneously (e.g. to decide on several **job applications**).

3   Integrating Users

This section first summarizes backgrounds on access control. Following this, we discuss fundamental challenges for integrating users in *Object-aware Process Management Systems*.

3.1   Backgrounds on Access Control

Access control mechanisms (so called *authorization*) protect data from unauthorized access (*confidentiality*) and improper changes (*integrity*) [13]. Coincidently, one has to ensure that each user gets access to all required data and functions (*availability*) [13,14]. We need to consider access control at different layers of abstraction [15]: *strategies, models* and *mechanisms*. Strategies determine which components (e.g. data, functions) within a system shall be protected, and define the required kinds of privileges. A *model*, in turn, formally represents the applied strategy, whereas the used *mechanism* determines its technical implementation. Most existing systems use *Role-Based Access Control* (RBAC) as strategy. The additional layer between users and privileges allows for quicker and less cumbersome administration [3]. Furthermore, users with same positions or duties get same rights [14]. Complementary to these abstraction layers, different kinds of systems make different claims in respect to the needed strategy. Access control can be arranged in four levels, each of them depending on the functionality of the system [16].

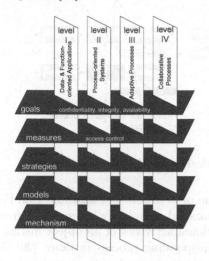

Fig. 3. Classification of access control

Application Systems are on Level 1 and WfMS are assigned to Level 2. Levels 3 and 4, in turn, are used for process-aware information systems enabling adaptive or collaborative processes [17]. Fig. 3 shows the different abstraction layers and the different levels of access control. In the following we focus on systems covering Levels 1 and 2. We only consider the abstraction layer of the strategy dimension. Technical aspects (e.g., models or concrete mechanisms) are out of the scope of this paper. Further, we limit ourselves to privileges for executing activities and for reading application data.

3.2   Challenges for Integrating Users

Challenge 6 (Horizontal and vertical user assignment). In WfMS, human activities are associated with actor expressions; e.g., based on user roles (denoted as *horizontal authorization*). Users who may work on respective activities are then determined during runtime based on these expressions. This is no longer sufficient in our case, since the selection of potential actors does not only depend on the activity itself, but also on the object instance processed by this activity [18,19] (denoted as *vertical authorization*). Consider Fig. 4, which depicts a partial view on different process instances handling `job applications`. Fig. 4a illustrates horizontal authorizations, whereas Fig. 4b shows horizontal as well as vertical authorization. While certain actors are only allowed to perform activity `make decision` for applicants whose name starts with a letter between 'A' and 'L', other ones may only perform this activity for applicants whose name starts with a letter between 'M' und 'Z'. Existing WfMS fail to deal with such data-dependent, vertical authorizations.

Challenge 7 (Consistency between data- and process authorization). For *optional activities* it does not make sense to obey a strict execution order as for *mandatory* ones. Although the progress of a process instance is based on attribute values, changes of these values should be possible outside the scope of normal process execution as well. However, when executing such *optional activities*, undesired manipulations of object attributes have to be prevented. After an employee from a functional division has submitted his `review`, for example

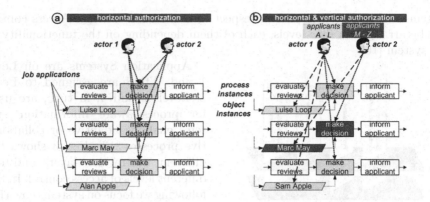

Fig. 4. Horizontal and vertical user assignment

he is no longer allowed to change the value of attribute `recommendation`. For this reason, optional activities cannot be handled completely independent from mandatory ones; i.e., authorization for optional activities of an object instance needs to consider the progress of the corresponding process instance [20]. In particular, correct executability of the process instance has to be guaranteed; i.e., it must be ensured that all mandatory activities of the process can be executed. Since a process step is defined based on attribute values, the user who is executing the mandatory activities should therefore have the permission to change corresponding attributes. Fig. 5 shows an object instance and process instance respectivley as well as the corresponding privileges for a `review`. Permissions to read / write a specific attribute value depend on the progress of the corresponding process instance. Attributes whose values have to be changed within a mandatory activity are marked with black; attributes that can be read or changed when executing optional activities are coloured white. Note that the latter may vary depending on the progress of the process instance. Users are not allowed to change attribute values used for the definition of a previous process step (except loops). These permissions are coloured grey.

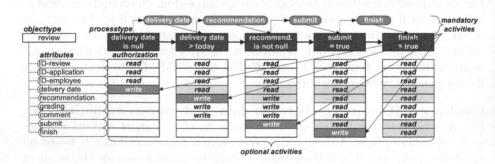

Fig. 5. Consistency between data- and process authorization

Challenge 8 (Relations between users and object instances). As motivated, *horizontal* as well as *vertical* authorizations are needed. Regarding *vertical authorizations*, permissions have to be restricted to a set of object instances or one particular object instance [21,22]. Thereby, the mapping between users and object instances (i.e., the regulation which user has which access rights for which object instances) is not arbitrary, but underlies certain conditions [23]. An `applicant` is allowed to read his own `job application`, but not the `job applications` of other `applicants`. Therefore, it is not appropriate to treat actor assignments and application data independent from each other as in existing WfMS. To achieve this, data structures (i.e., object types and their relations to each other) should also include organizational entities; i.e., roles have to be explicitly defined as object types. Each individual user is then mapped to an object instance. At runtime, a user may reference other object instances; e.g., an organisation unit. Users themselves may be referenced by other object instances; e.g., an applicant may submit several applications which then refer to this user. The different relationships between users and object instances have to be taken into account when assigning actors to activities.

Challenge 9 (User assignment and authorization). Permissions are defined based on the attributes of object types. When executing mandatory activities, attribute changes necessary for enabling the next process step have to be accomplished. In order to assign users to mandatory activities, their permissions are evaluated. Having the permission to change certain attributes does not necessarily mean that the user has to perform a mandatory activity; i.e., we have to distinguish between mandatory and optional permissions. Only for users with mandatory permissions, a respective, mandatory activity is listed in their worklist. Users with optional permissions may change the corresponding attributes when executing optional activities. This means, users may change the attribute values, relevant to enable the next process step, when executing an optional activity. Such implicit transitions may be desired in some situations, while in other cases responsible users should explicitly verify the specified attribute values; e.g., attribute `proposed action` can be entered when executing an optional activity. As effect, the next process step `filled out` can be reached without having executed mandatory activity `fill out`. By contrast, in order to `submit` a `review`, mandatory activity `submit` will have to be executed even if attribute `submitted` has been entered within an optional activity (see Fig.5).

4 Existing Approaches

In [1] we have described existing approaches in relation to Challenges 1 - 5. In particular, some of the discussed issues are addressed in Artifact-Centric Modelling [24], Product-Based Workflow-Support [9,25], Data-Driven Process Coordination [10,26], Case Handling [8], and Proclets [11]. In the following, we discuss existing work in respect to Challenges 6 - 9.

Challenge 6 (Horizontal and vertical user assignment). [27] describes an approach for realizing Applications Systems, which groups permissions for accessing data and functions. Whether a user may perform a particular activity depends on the agreement of another user at runtime. This makes it possible to manually approve the object instances relevant in the given situation. However, it is not possible to access data outside the scope of a specific activity; i.e., optional activites are not considered. Like [27], current WfMS focus on actor assignments for controlling activity executions. By contrast, permissions for accessing data and functions are mostly managed within the invoked application systems. [28] describes the concept of "instance-based user group". Each actor gets access to all object instances associated with at least one process instance he has been involved in. The opposite direction (i.e., user assignments depending on permissions for data access) is not considered. [18] enables management of specific properties for each data element relevant for the process. In addition to actor expressions, for each activity, relevant properties of the used data elements are defined. Obviously, this is done redundantly and therefore data inconsistencies might arise.

Challenge 7 (Consistency between data and process authorization). [8] distinguishes between mandatory and optional data elements of an activity; but no differentiation between mandatory and optional activities is made. Similar to [28], users get access to all data elements of the process instances they are involved in (i.e., the permission to read / write data is assigned implicitly). [27] and [20] define permissions for accessing data and functions in the context of a specific task. The other direction (i.e., the assignment of users to tasks depending on given permissions on functions) is not considered. Since all permissions are defined at the level of object types, it is not possible to assign different permissions for object instances of the same type.

Challenge 8 (Relations between users and object instances). In some approaches [29,22,30,21,23], it is possibe to restrict permissions to a selected set of object instances. However, only in few cases [22,21,23] these restrictions can be defined depending on the relationships between users and object instances. In particular, it is not possible to consider relationships already defined in the data structure. Instead, they have to be defined redundantly based on the permissions.

Challenge 9 (User assignment and authorization). Except few systems (e.g., case handling) WfMS do not support optional activities as described in sect. 3. Hence, it is not possible to differentiate between tasks users must execute and tasks they may execute. In [31], various possibilities for assigning and activating activities are described. [3] takes the hierarchy of roles into account and [32] allows to define different priorities for assigning users to activities. However, in all approaches, always at least one user has to execute an activity. Opposed to this, [8] focuses on data access rather than on assigning users to activities. Further, for each activity it is possible to differentiate between optional and mandatory data elements.

In summary, the described challenges have been partially addressed by existing work. However, a comprehensive solution for generic access control in object-aware process management is still missing.

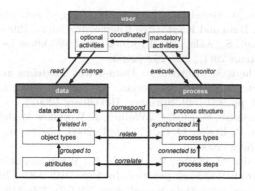

Fig. 6. Integration of processes, data and users

5 Outlook

Our overall vision is to develop a framework and enabling technology for *Object-aware Process Management*. We will tackle the described challenges in order to enable a tight integration of processes, data objects and users. Fig.6 illustrates the discussed interdependencies. This work has been conducted within the PHILharmonic Flows project. [2] In future papers we will provide detailed insights into the different components of an Object-aware Process Management system as well as their complex interdependencies.

References

1. Künzle, V., Reichert, M.: Towards Object-aware Process Management Systems: Issues, Challenges, Benefits. In: Proc. BPMDS 2009. LNBIP, vol. 29, pp. 197–210. Springer, Heidelberg (2009)
2. Osborn, S., Sandhu, R., Munawer, Q.: Configuring Role-Based Access Control to Enforce Mandatory and Discretionary Access Control Policies. ACM Trans. Inf. Syst. Secur. 3(2), 85–106 (2000)
3. Bertino, E., Ferrari, E., Atluri, V.: The Specification and Enforcement of Authorization Constraints in Workflow Management Systems. ACM Trans. Inf. Syst. Secur. 2(1), 65–104 (1999)
4. Sandhu, R., Coyne, E., Feinstein, H., Youman, C.: Role-based Access Control Models. IEEE Computer 29(2), 38–47 (1996)
5. Aalst, W., Hee, K.: Workflow-Management - Models, Methods and Systems. MIT Press, Cambridge (2004)
6. Aalst, W., Hofstede, A., Kiepuszewski, B., Barros, A.: Workflow Patterns. Distr. & Parallel Databases 14, 5–51 (2003)
7. Rinderle-Ma, S., Manfred, R.: A Formal Framework for Adaptive Access Control Models. In: Spaccapietra, S., Atzeni, P., Fages, F., Hacid, M.-S., Kifer, M., Mylopoulos, J., Pernici, B., Shvaiko, P., Trujillo, J., Zaihrayeu, I. (eds.) Journal on Data Semantics IX. LNCS, vol. 4601, pp. 82–112. Springer, Heidelberg (2007)

---

[2] Process, Humans and Information Linkage for harmonic Business Flows.

8. Aalst, W., Weske, M., Grünbauer, D.: Case Handling: A new paradigm for business process support. Data and Knowledge Engineering 53(2), 129–162 (2005)
9. Reijers, H., Liman, S., Aalst, W.: Product-based Workflow Design. Management Information Systems 20(1), 229–262 (2003)
10. Müller, D., Reichert, M., Herbst, J.: Data-driven Modeling and Coordination of Large Process Structures. In: Meersman, R., Tari, Z. (eds.) OTM 2007, Part I. LNCS, vol. 4803, pp. 131–149. Springer, Heidelberg (2007)
11. Aalst, W., Barthelmess, P., Ellis, C., Wainer, J.: Workflow Modeling using Proclets. In: Scheuermann, P., Etzion, O. (eds.) CoopIS 2000. LNCS, vol. 1901, pp. 198–209. Springer, Heidelberg (2000)
12. Sadiq, S., Orlowska, M., Sadiq, W., Schulz, K.: When workflows will not deliver: The case of contradicting work practice. In: Proc. BIS 2005 (2005)
13. Bertino, E.: Data security. Data Knowl. Eng. 25(1-2), 199–216 (1998)
14. Ferraiolo, D., Kuhn, R.: Role-based Access Control. In: Proc. 15th NIST-NCSC, pp. 554–563 (1992)
15. Samarati, P., Vimercati, S.: Access Control: Policies, Models and Mechanisms. In: Focardi, R., Gorrieri, R. (eds.) FOSAD 2000. LNCS, vol. 2171, p. 137. Springer, Heidelberg (2001)
16. Pfeiffer, V.: A Framework for Evaluating Access Control Concepts in Workflow Management Systems. Master thesis (2005)
17. Weber, B., Reichert, M., Wild, W., Rinderle, S.: Balancing Flexibility and Security in Adaptive Process Management Systems. In: Meersman, R., Tari, Z. (eds.) OTM 2005. LNCS, vol. 3760, pp. 59–76. Springer, Heidelberg (2005)
18. Rosemann, M., Mühlen, M.: Modellierung der Aufbauorganisation in Workflow-Management-Systemen: Kritische Bestandsaufnahme und Gestaltungsvorschläge. EMISA Forum 3(1), 78–86 (1998)
19. Rosemann, M., Mühlen, M.: Organizational Management in Workflow Applications: Issues and Perspectives. Inf. Technol. and Mgmt. 5(3-4), 271–291 (2004)
20. Botha, R.: Cosawoe – A Model for Context-sensitive Access Control in Workflow Environments. PhD thesis (2002)
21. Hu, J., Weaver, A.: A Dynamic, Context-Aware Security Infrastructure for Distributed Healthcare Applications. In: Proc. PSPT 2004 (2004)
22. Kumar, A., Karnik, N., Chafle, G.: Context Sensitivity in Role-based Access Control. SIGOPS 36(3), 53–66 (2002)
23. Barkley, J., Beznosov, K., Uppal, J.: Supporting Relationships in Access Control Using Role Based Access Control. In: Proc. RBAC 1999, pp. 55–65 (1999)
24. Liu, R., Bhattacharya, K., Wu, F.: Modeling Business Contexture and Behavior Using Business Artifacts. In: Krogstie, J., Opdahl, A.L., Sindre, G. (eds.) CAiSE 2007 and WES 2007. LNCS, vol. 4495, pp. 324–339. Springer, Heidelberg (2007)
25. Vanderfeesten, I.T.P., Reijers, H.A., van der Aalst, W.M.P.: Product-based Workow Support: Dynamic Workow Execution. In: Bellahsène, Z., Léonard, M. (eds.) CAiSE 2008. LNCS, vol. 5074, pp. 571–574. Springer, Heidelberg (2008)
26. Müller, D., Reichert, M., Herbst, J.: A New Paradigm for the Enactment and Dynamic Adaptation of Data-driven Process Structures. In: Bellahsène, Z., Léonard, M. (eds.) CAiSE 2008. LNCS, vol. 5074, pp. 48–63. Springer, Heidelberg (2008)
27. Sandhu, R., Thomas, R.: Task-based Authorization Controls (TBAC): A Family of Models for Active and Enterprise-oriented Authorization Management. In: Proc. IFIP 1997, pp. 166–181 (1997)
28. Wu, S., Sheth, A., Miller, J., Luo, Z.: Authorization and Access Control Of Application Data In Workflow-Systems. JIIS 18, 71–94 (2002)

29. Lupu, E., Sloman, M.: A Policy Based Role Object Model. In: Proc. EDOC 1997, pp. 36–47 (1997)
30. Thomas, R.: Team-based Access Control (TMAC): A Primitive for Applying Role-based Access Controls in Collaborative Environments. In: Proc. RBAC 1997, pp. 13–19 (1997)
31. Russell, N., Hofstede, A., Edmond, D.: Workflow Resource Patterns. In: Pastor, Ó., Falcão e Cunha, J. (eds.) CAiSE 2005. LNCS, vol. 3520, pp. 216–232. Springer, Heidelberg (2005)
32. Wainer, J., Barthelmess, P., Kumar, A.: W-RBAC - A Workflow Security Model Incorporating Controlled Overriding of Constraints. IJCIS 12 (2003)

From Requirements to Executable Processes:
A Literature Study

Andreas Gehlert[1], Olha Danylevych[2], and Dimka Karastoyanova[2]

[1] University of Duisburg-Essen, Schützenbahn 70; 45117 Essen
andreas.gehlert@sse.uni-due.de
[2] University of Stuttgart, Universitätsstr. 38, 70569 Stuttgart
{olha.danylevych,dimka.karastoyanova}@iaas.uni-stuttgart.de

Abstract. Service compositions are a major component to realize service-based applications (SBAs). The design of these service compositions follows mainly a process-modelling approach—an initial business process is refined until it can be executed on a workflow engine. Although this process-modelling approach proved to be useful, it largely disregards the knowledge gained in the requirements engineering discipline, e. g. in eliciting, documenting, managing and tracing requirements. Disregarding the requirements engineering phase may lead to undesired effects of the later service compositions such as lack of acceptance by the later users. To defuse this potentially critical issue we are interested in the interplay between requirements engineering and process modelling techniques. As a first step in this direction, we analyse the current literature in requirements engineering and process modelling in order to find overlaps where the techniques from both domains can be combined in useful ways. Our main finding is that scenario-based approaches from the requirements engineering discipline are a good basis for deriving executable processes. Depending whether the focus is on requirements engineering or on process design the integration of the techniques are slightly different.

Keywords: Requirements Engineering, Process Modelling, Use Cases, Process Fragments.

1 Introduction

Service compositions are the central element in service-based applications (SBAs) — the new paradigm in software and service development. A service composition combines a set of services according to a meaningful business goal. In the case of using a process-based approach for service compositions the services are connected by control and data flow definitions. The underlying idea of such a process-modelling approach is to step-wise refine a process model until it contains all necessary information to be executed, for instance, an executable BPEL process can be executed on a BPEL engine (cf. bottom of Fig. 1).

One of the advantages of this approach is straightforward and of great practical importance for the creation of SBAs: the same modelling paradigm (process modelling) can be used during the entire development process of the service composition. This

S. Rinderle-Ma et al. (Eds.): BPM 2009 Workshops, LNBIP 43, pp. 42–52, 2010.

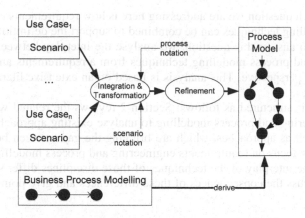

Fig. 1. Framework for Intertwining Requirements Engineering and Process Modelling Approaches

enables an automated support for the verification of the process model and its translation from the initial process model to the executable one. This modelling process, however, is a highly creative activity [e. g. 1], which can be difficult to control and plan.

Another discipline, which heavily depends on modelling, is requirements engineering (RE). Requirements engineering techniques such as prioritisation allow explicitly planning, managing and controlling modelling projects. In addition, agreement techniques allow to reason about the agreements achieved by different stakeholders. Lastly, tracing techniques allow documenting the origin and the destination of a requirements artefact [cf. 2 for a recent review on techniques of the different RE activities]. So, there is a potential to use RE techniques to structure and manage the process modelling activities.

Most interestingly, RE techniques, such as use cases based techniques share many commonalities with processes since use cases contain scenarios. A scenario is a sequence of activities, which describe a typical system interaction. Therefore, scenarios document parts of a process [3]. In particular, use case based techniques allow to model use cases in isolation and to verify and integrate those individual use cases later [4, p. 314]. Another argument for using RE techniques is based on empirical findings. Nawrocki et al. found in [5] that use cases are significantly easier to understand with respect to *error detection* than corresponding process models written in the Business Process Modelling Notation (BPMN).

Use case based approaches do not make any assumptions about the technology of the system to be built. Consequently, we are interested in answering the questions how RE techniques can help to derive process models. The starting point for this interaction is the idea to apply use case based RE techniques to derive isolated process fragments. These fragments need to be integrated and subsequently translated into an executable process modelling language. We are not only interested in the current state of the art from the two disciplines—requirements engineering and process modelling, but also to know what information can be captured by this approach and what information need to be added manually (cf. top of Fig. 1).

The research question we are addressing here is how requirements engineering and process modelling techniques can be combined to support the definition of executable workflows. To answer this question, we analyse the interplay between requirements engineering and process modelling techniques from a requirements and from a process modelling perspective. This analysis is based on an extensive literature review of both disciplines.

The paper is structured as follows: Section 2 reviews the related work in requirements engineering and process modelling to analyse existing approaches in both disciplines as well as approaches, which are bridging the gap between both disciplines. Because of the focus on requirements engineering and process modelling respectively in section 2 the interplay of the techniques of those disciplines differ slightly. In section 3 we discuss the consequences of these differences and give pointers to possible future work.

2 From Requirements to Executable Processes – Combining Techniques

The state of the art in business process modelling encompasses a variety of notations for modelling business process, ranging from declarative approaches like DecSerFlow [6] to imperative/workflow-like approaches such as BPMN and the Business Process Execution Language (BPEL). The process modelling notations have different levels of abstraction—from technology-independent graphical modelling notations like Event-Driven Process Chains (EPC) [7] or BPMN to executable process modelling notations like BPEL.

However, the design of a process model is currently based on the step-wise refinement of an initial business process. This refinement is a complex modelling activity, which is difficult to manage and control. Although very similar approaches for modelling processes, managing and controlling those modelling activities are well understood in the RE discipline, work has just started to use RE techniques for designing business processes (cf. subsection 2.1). Those approaches apply use cases to develop isolated scenarios, which are integrated later on to derive a process. This process must than be further refined in order to be executable.

Approaches originated from the process modelling discipline translate use cases into process modelling notations (e. g. EPCs or BPMN), integrate the resulting models and translate them further to executable process models (e. g. written in BPEL, c.f. subsection 2.2). In addition, those approaches introduce relevant information, which is currently not covered by traditional RE approaches such as constraints.

2.1 Requirements Engineering Perspective

One accepted requirements engineering approach is the use case approach. A use case is a structured description of the interaction between the system and its users. According to Cockburn [3], a use case description contains a primary actor initiating the use case, stakeholders influenced by the use case, the goal of the use case, guarantees (e. g. post-conditions), which hold when the use case is executed, pre-conditions and triggers determining when the use case is started, the main scenario and extensions to this main scenario describing the different use case steps. Use cases are usually documented in textual forms with the help of use case templates.

A system specification based on use cases is then a set of such use cases. Using a set of use cases for the system specification allows eliciting and documenting the system's requirements in decentralised teams. This comes at the cost of having a large number of use cases, which must be carefully managed and integrated [8]. Although UML use case diagrams [9] allow modelling the dependencies between different use cases by means of use case diagrams, their degree of formality alone is not enough to foster the integration of the embedded scenarios and, therefore, to derive a process [4].

The use case elements of interest for this paper are scenarios. Scenarios describe a sequence of steps, which lead to the fulfilment of the use case's goal. Each scenario can be extended by other scenarios in order to introduce alternatives and loops. Scenarios have particularly proven to be useful in requirements engineering projects especially when abstract modelling fails or when interdisciplinary teams work in the project [10, p. 38].

The scenarios embedded in the use case are usually expressed in natural language. Although this fosters the communication with non-technical stakeholders, it is associated with the difficulty of using the provided information in an automated manner, e. g. to automatically integrate scenarios or to automatically check scenarios for validity and consistency. One way to deal with this problem is to use a more formal notation to represent scenarios such as message sequence charts (MSCs). Automated support in deriving MSCs from textual use cases are for instance provided in [11].

Since their introduction in 1996 by the International Telecommunication Union (ITU), MSCs have a long and successful history in the RE discipline [12]. Their formal syntax and semantics allow verifying, transforming and integrating MSCs automatically. In their recent paper Uchitel et al. [8, p. 101] describe three approaches to integrate MSCs: the first approach is built on modelling the relations between the individual MSCs in a high level message sequence chart (hMSC). The introduction of hMSCs further allows re-using individual MSCs in different paths of the system's behaviour. Another approach is built on the component's states embedded in the MSC. Identical states in different MSCs are used for the integration. Lastly, a constraint-based approach [e. g. 4] can be used to integrate individual MSCs.

Each of those integration approaches comes with their distinct advantages and disadvantages. hMSCs for instance provide a good overview of the system and allow at the same time to re-use scenarios in different parts of the hMSC. This approach fosters the creation of many small scenarios, which are themselves difficult to understand. The integration with the help of scenario states allows modelling larger chunks of the system in one scenario but hinders scenario re-use and complicates the integration of the individual scenarios. Lastly, the constraint-based approach is most expressive and allows the description of arbitrary combination of individual scenarios. Since the constraints, however, are formulated in a formal language, they are difficult to understand for non-technical stakeholders.

So far, we have demonstrated that the requirements engineering discipline provides a tool-chain, which allows to elicit use cases in an informal manner, to derive more formal scenarios based on this specification and to integrate individual scenarios forming a coherent system specification (cf. Fig. 2). The missing element is a transformation algorithm, which translates the integrated scenario into an executable process model, e. g. into BPEL.

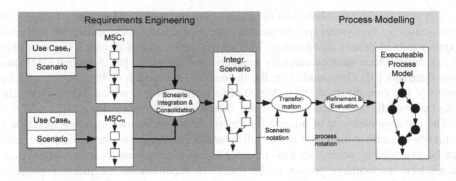

Fig. 2. Requirements Engineering Perspective of Deriving Process Models Based on Use Cases

Current transformation approaches such as [13-15] are based on an intermediate format, e. g. EPC or BPMN, which are in turn transformed into BPEL code [e. g. 16]. These approaches are discussed in more detail below. Having the focus on requirements engineering it is important to note that the individual scenarios as part of the requirements are integrated prior to their translation to a suitable workflow notation. This issue will be elaborated in more detail below.

2.2 Process Modelling Perspective

An alternative way of deriving an executable process is to translate the *individual* use-case scenarios to a process oriented language and to integrate the resulting process fragments afterwards using process-merge technologies. Lübke [15] for instance provide algorithms, which transforms a textual scenario as part of a use case specification into an EPC and integrates the resulting EPCs to a coherent model (cf. Fig. 3).

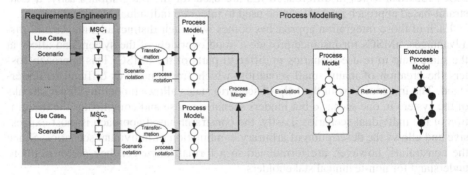

Fig. 3. Process Modelling Perspective of Deriving Process Models Based on Use Cases

Having the focus on processes, the scenarios as part of the requirements are transformed to processes and these processes are merged later on. In contrast to the requirements engineering perspective discussed above, the merging activity is performed to processes and not to scenarios. This difference is further elaborated in section 3.

The approaches presented in [13, 15] are based on merging the resulting EPCs according to their pre- and post-conditions, e. g. on the events initiating and finalising an EPC process fragment. The difference between this work and the RE approach is the point in time the use case is translated into a process model. While in RE approaches the scenarios are integrated first and translated afterwards into a process model, the process oriented approaches translate use cases to process models first and integrate them afterwards.

Although the two approaches seem to be similar in nature, merging process models allow the elicitation and the usage of additional constraints on those process models. This additional constrains guide the integration of the resulting process fragments, hence, allowing a better control over those fragments.

Although not exhaustive, the following constraints, which are typically not considered during a use case analysis, are used in the process modelling literature:

- Quality of Service related requirements for the whole system such as availability of the service composition.
- Operational properties like maximal costs for one process instance.
- Non-functional requirements of the single use cases, e. g. the use case A must be performed in at most 30 minutes.
- Extended relations between use cases such as use case A must be executed two times before use case B.

These constraints may also influence the process model itself. For instance, if use case A must be executed 10 times before use case B (extended relation between use cases) and the execution time for use case A should be small (non-functional constraint), the process designer may decide to re-organise the process according to the multiple instance pattern so that different instances of use case A can be executed in parallel to save time and to fulfil the non-functional constraint.

Specification and modelling of constraints from requirements has been extensively covered in the literature. Lu et al. [17] for instance classify constrains in strategic, operational, regulatory and contractual constraints. Gagne and Trudel [18] treat the specification of temporal logic constraints for process modelling using Allen's interval algebra [19]. Förster et al. [20] address the verification of process constraints expressed as Business Rules."

After the application of the constraints to the process fragments, there may still be more than one process, which fulfils all constraints since the integration of the different process fragments can be seen as combinatory problem. Process metrics help to chose among the possible process models fulfilling all constraints.

The metrics to be adopted depend on the important properties of the process models. On the one hand these are metrics used for prediction of the Quality of Service for a process-based service composition. This issue has been extensively treated, among others, by Marzolla et al. [21] and Rud et al. [22]. On the other hand the metrics evaluating "quality" of the model are also of interest. Such metrics may include the cohesion and coupling metrics proposed by Vanderfeesten et al. in [23]. The authors transform the well understood metrics from the software engineering discipline ([24]) to processes. Vanderfeesten et al. argue that the ratio of cohesion and coupling is an important characteristic of execution quality and maintenance and, therefore, can be used while choosing the most appropriate process model. Other metrics applicable for the evaluation of process model alternatives are the modularity metric by Reijers and Mendling [25], which is proven to be important for the understandability, and cyclic complexity of processes [cf. 26].

The conceptual difference between many process modelling techniques (e. g. EPC and BPMN) and executable process languages such as BPEL, which are mainly due to a different expressiveness and a different paradigm (graph based vs. block based) of the languages [27] lead to the need to refine processes. Process refinement has been extensively covered by both industry and academia. The goal is to iteratively and incrementally refine an abstract process model (e. g. the one obtained from use cases) into an executable one with the help of one or more semi-automated model transformations.

Born et al. [28] for instance treat the application of technologies to business process refinement, with the emphasis on goal-modelling and reuse or pre-existing business process patterns and fragments.

Markovic and Kowalkiewicz [29] also address the alignment of business goals and business processes using semantic technologies. They introduce a business goal ontology that is correlated to the already proposed business process ontology. High-level business goals (e.g. "increase company competitiveness") are hierarchical, can broken down into sub-goals (e.g. "uncover technology trends"), and are then refined into operational goals (e.g. "activate service") that are claimed to be easily mappable to concrete business process models.

3 Summary and Conclusions

We have shown in the paper that current RE techniques allow to elicit, document, verify and manage requirements, which are relevant for the design of processes. Use case based approaches contain scenarios, which can be used as process fragments when deriving processes. The key difference between RE approaches and process modelling approaches is that RE approach always aim to elicit and document a set of scenarios, which need to subsequently be integrated based on high level message sequence charts, scenario states or constraints. The resulting integrated scenarios can then be translated into process models (cf. subsection 2.1).

Approaches, which originate from the process modelling discipline, translate initial use cases into EPC or BPMN models, integrate these process models and translate them into executable process models. In contrast to RE approaches, the focus here is on the constraints, which guide the integration of different process fragments and on evaluation criteria, which help choosing between different process variants in case more than one process model fulfils all given constraints (cf. subsection 2.2).

Having analysed the requirements engineering and process modelling perspective we found a major difference: from the requirements engineering perspective the individual *scenarios are merged* before they are translated to a process modelling notation. In the process modelling perspective, the individual scenarios are translated to a process modelling notation and the resulting *process models are merged*. Although this difference seems to be a minor issue, the resulting consequences are important:

- *Merging Scenarios*: Merging scenarios is a well understood and much elaborated in the requirements engineering discipline. The overall process of designing executable processes could benefit from this maturity.
- *Merging Process Models*: comes with a couple of advantages, which are mainly due to the fact that process models are produced later in the process design lifecycle. Process models (e. g. a BPEL process) contain, among others, activities that perform message exchanges with (i. e. invocations of) other services (for instance, the invoke, receive and reply activities in BPEL).

    Moreover, the process models can be further annotated with Process Performance Metrics (PPMs) that explain how to calculate/evaluate particular performance attributes (e.g. completion time and average activity execution time). PPMs are not necessarily defined on single process executions (e. g. completion time of one instance), but their evaluation can span across multiple executions (e. g. average completion time).

    During the monitoring (either at run-time or post-mortem) of the execution of business processes and fragments annotated with PPMs, data about the processes are produced and aggregated by evaluating the PPMs.

    Notice that this information is 'linked' to executable artefacts (e. g. the particular process fragment in a Fragment Library owned by an enterprise), and not scenarios. That is, the data collected by PPMs are not known at design time, but only after the use of fragments in "production" (e. g. using them to compose business processes that are then run and monitored).

    The availability of this 'run-time' information is very relevant for the creation of merges of process fragments that are "optimal", e. g. in terms of QoS. Moreover, the additional information provides more flexibility during the process merge, allowing the consideration of criteria that span beyond the design time knowledge of the behaviour of the fragments, but also how they behaved at run-time (which is often not foreseeable at design time: for instance, you can generally never say if a process always terminates or not). Of course, this additional flexibility is not available while merging scenarios, because those data might not be available.

    Finally, the data collected and aggregated from the PPMs during monitoring can support the identification of which fragments in the business process should be explicitly modelled (for instance using activities and control flows), and which one should instead be "masked" behind an external service. This is of course related to the out- and in-sourcing of business process fragments. There is an entire branch of BPM research, called (Business Process) Gap Analysis that deals with it, and (among others) with the problem of identifying the right "granularity" for the services.

Consequently, when choosing between the two alternatives the maturity of the scenario integration activity (focus on requirements engineering) must be balanced with the possibility of re-using more information (focus on process modelling). Which approach is more effective cannot be answered on the basis of this literature review and requires a future empirical evaluation.

There are a couple of deficiencies in both approaches, which are apparent from our literature study:

- *Missing information about services*: Neither scenario based techniques nor traditional process modelling techniques capture information about the services used in an executable process model or service composition. Weidlich at al. [30], for instance, argue that the process designer and the requirements engineer should work together when specifying the service interfaces and when discovering and selecting the service. Although they do not provide a clear methodology, they speculate that typical requirements engineering techniques such as use case visualisation, glossaries and requirements tracing can foster this collaboration.Vara and Sánchez [31] provide an alternative approach. They argue that process modelling should be executed by a process expert as first step in the development of SBAs. Once the process model is defined, the requirements engineer derives use cases for each activity in the process model and, thereby, specifies the behaviour of the service. However, the link between the process model and the use case is described informally only and a clear methodology is missing.
- *Different expressiveness of process modelling languages*: As argued in [27], process modelling languages and executable process languages have a different expressiveness, which leads to information loss or information deficits when transforming conceptual process models into executable ones. While this problem can be solved by annotating process models with the respective execution information [e. g. 32], it remains unclear how this additional information affects the readability of those models.
- *Difficult translation from scenarios to process models:* Because of the conceptual differences between scenarios and process models, the translation between the two worlds is difficult and not yet well understood.

Consequently, the bridge between requirements engineering techniques and executable workflows is not yet complete, e. g. it is not yet possible to develop and design service-based applications based on traditional requirements engineering techniques. This incompleteness results in manual and, consequently, error-prone and cost-intensive model transformations.

Future research directions is fourfold: First, empirical research is needed to decide in which situation a requirements centred and in which situations a process centred perspective is beneficial. Second, requirements engineering techniques must be extended to cover important aspects for the service world such as quality of service, service selection and compliance. Third, in the process world the translation between process models and their executable counterparts need to be researched. Finally, the translation between requirements engineering and process modelling notations should be investigated in more detail.

Acknowledgements

The research leading to these results has received funding from the European Community's Seventh Framework Programme FP7/2007-2013 under grant agreement 215483 (S-Cube).

References

1. Dresbach, S.: Modeling by Construction: A New Methodology for Constructing Models for Decision Support. Lehrstuhl für Wirtschaftsinformatik und Operations Research, University of Cologne, Germany (1995)
2. Cheng, B.H.C., Atlee, J.M.: Research Directions in Requirements Engineering. In: Conference on the Future of Software Engieering (FOSE 2007), Washington, USA, pp. 285–303 (2007)
3. Cockburn, A.: Writing Effective Use Cases. Addison-Wesley Professional, Reading (2000)
4. Whittle, J., Schumann, J.: Generating Statechart Designs from Scenarios. In: Proceedings of the 22nd International Conference on Software Engineering (ICSE 2000), Limerick, Ireland, pp. 314–323 (2000)
5. Nawrocki, J.R., Nedza, T., Ochodek, M., Olek, L.: Describing Business Processes with Use Cases. In: Abramowicz, W., Mayr, H.C. (eds.) 9th International Conference on Business Information Systems (BIS 2006), Klagenfurt, Austria, vol. 85, pp. 13–27 (2006)
6. van der Aalst, W.M.P., Pesic, M.: DecSerFlow: Towards a Truly Declarative Service Flow Language. In: Leymann, F., Reisig, W., Thatte, S.R., van der Aalst, W.M.P. (eds.) The Role of Business Processes in Service Oriented Architectures, Dagstuhl, Germany, vol. 06291 (2006)
7. Keller, G., Nüttgens, M., Scheer, A.-W.: Semantische Prozeßmodellierung auf der Grundlage Ereignisgesteuerter Prozeßketten (EPK). Veröffentlichungen des Instituts für Wirtschaftsinformatik (IWi). Universität des Saarlandes (1992)
8. Uchitel, S., Kramer, J., Magee, J.: Synthesis of Behavioral Models from Scenarios. IEEE Transactions on Software Engineering 29, 99–115 (2003)
9. OMG: UML 2.0 Superstructure Specification (2003)
10. Weidenhaupt, K., Pohl, K., Jarke, M., Haumer, P.: Scenarios in System Development: Current Practice. IEEE Software 15, 34–45 (1998)
11. Miga, A., Amyot, D., Bordeleau, F., Cameron, D., Woodside, C.M.: Deriving Message Sequence Charts from Use Case Maps Scenario Specifications. In: Reed, R., Reed, J. (eds.) SDL 2001. LNCS, vol. 2078, pp. 268–287. Springer, Heidelberg (2001)
12. ITU: Message Sequence Charts. International Telecomunication Union, Telecommunication Standardization Sector (1996)
13. Lübke, D., Schneider, K., Weidlich, M.: Visualizing Use Case Sets as BPMN Processes. In: 3rd International Workshop on Requirements Engineering Visualization (REV 2008), Barcelona, Spain (2008)
14. Ouyang, C., Dumas, M., Breutel, S., ter Hofstede, A.H.M.: Translating Standard Process Models to BPEL. In: Dubois, E., Pohl, K. (eds.) CAiSE 2006. LNCS, vol. 4001, pp. 417–432. Springer, Heidelberg (2006)
15. Lübke, D.: Transformation of Use Cases to EPC Models. 5. Workshop der Gesellschaft für Informatik e.V (GI) und Treffen ihres Arbeitskreises. In: Geschäftsprozessmanagement mit Ereignisgesteuerten Prozessketten (WI-EPK). CEUR Workshop Proceedings, vol. 224, Vienna, Austria, pp. 137–156 (2006)
16. Ziemann, J., Mendling, J.: EPC-Based Modelling of BPEL Processes: A Pragmatic Transformation Approach. In: International Conference on Modern Information Technology in the Innovation Processes of the Industrial Enterprises (MITIP 2005) Genoa, Italy (2005)
17. Lu, R., Sadiq, S., Governatori, G.: On Managing Business Processes Variants. Data & Knowledge Engineering 68, 642–664 (2009)
18. Gagné, D., Trudel, A.: A Formal Temporal Semantics for Microsoft Project based on Allen's Interval Algebra. In: Abramowicz, W., Maciaszek, L.A., Kowalczyk, R., Speck, A. (eds.) Business Process, Services Computing and Intelligent Service Management, Leipzig, Germany, vol. 137, pp. 32–45 (2009)

19. Allen, J.F.: Maintaining Knowledge about Temporal Intervals. Communications of the ACM 26, 832–843 (1983)
20. Förster, A., Engels, G., Schattkowsky, T., Straeten, R.v.D.: Verification of Business Process Quality Constraints Based on Visual Process Patterns. In: First Joint IEEE/IFIP Symposium on Theoretical Aspects of Software Engineering, TASE 2007, Shanghai, China, pp. 197–208 (2007)
21. Marzolla, M., Mirandola, R.: Performance Prediction of Web Service Workflows. In: Overhage, S., Szyperski, C., Reussner, R., Stafford, J.A. (eds.) QoSA 2007. LNCS, vol. 4880, pp. 127–144. Springer, Heidelberg (2008)
22. Rud, D., Kunz, M., Schmietendorf, A., Dumke, R.: Performance Analysis in WS-BPEL-Based Infrastructures. In: 23rd Annual UK Performance Engineering Workshop (UKPEW 2007), Edge Hill University, Ormskirk, Lancashire, UK, pp. 130–141 (2007)
23. Vanderfeesten, I., Reijers, H.A., Aalst, W.M.P.v.d.: Evaluating Workflow Process Designs using Cohesion and Coupling Metrics. Computers in Industry 59, 429–437 (2008)
24. Chidamber, S.R., Kemerer, C.F.: A Metrics Suite for Object Oriented Design. IEEE Transactions on Software Engineering 20, 476–493 (1994)
25. Reijers, H., Mendling, J.: Modularity in Process Models: Review and Effects. In: Dumas, M., Reichert, M., Shan, M.-C. (eds.) BPM 2008. LNCS, vol. 5240, pp. 20–35. Springer, Heidelberg (2008)
26. Cardoso, J., Mendling, J., Neumann, G., Reijers, H.A.: A Discourse on Complexity of Process Models (Survey Paper). In: Eder, J., Dustdar, S. (eds.) BPM Workshops 2006. LNCS, vol. 4103, pp. 117–128. Springer, Heidelberg (2006)
27. Recker, J., Mendling, J.: On the Translation between BPMN and BPEL: Conceptual Mismatch between Process Modelling Languages. In: Krogstie, J., Halpin, T.A., Proper, H.A. (eds.) 11th International Workshop on Exploring Modeling Methods in Systems Analysis and Design (EMMSAD 2006), pp. 521–532. Namur University Press, Namur (2006)
28. Born, M., Brelage, C., Markovic, I., Weber, I.: Semantic Business Process Modeling: from Business Goals to Execution-Level Business Processes. Forschungszentrum Informatik, Karlsruhe (2008)
29. Markovic, I., Kowalkiewicz, M.: Linking Business Goals to Process Models in Semantic Business Process Modeling. In: 12th International IEEE Enterprise Distributed Object Computing Conference, 2008 (EDOC 2008), Munich, Germany, pp. 332–338 (2008)
30. Weidlich, M., Grosskopf, A., Lübke, D., Schneider, K., Knauss, E., Singer, L.: Verzahnung von Requirements Engineering und Geschäftsprozessdesign. 1. In: Workshops für Requirements Engineering und Business Prcess Management (REBPM 2009), Kaiserslautern, Deutschland (2009)
31. Vara, J.L.: Improving Requirements Analysis through Business Process Modelling: a Participative Approach. In: Fensel, D., Abramowicz, W. (eds.) 11th International Conference on Business Information Systems (BIS 2008), pp. 165–176. Springer, Heidelberg (2008)
32. White, S.A.: Using BPMN to Model a BPEL Process. BPTrends, 1–18 (2005)

Towards a Framework for Business Process Standardization

Christoph Rosenkranz[1], Stefan Seidel[2], Jan Mendling[3],
Markus Schaefermeyer[1], and Jan Recker[4]

[1] Information Systems Engineering, University of Frankfurt
60323 Frankfurt am Main, Germany
rosenkranz@wiwi.uni-frankfurt.de,
schaefermeyer@wiwi.uni-frankfurt.de
[2] Institute of Information Systems, University of Liechtenstein
9490 Vaduz, Principality of Liechtenstein
stefan.seidel@hochschule.li
[3] Institut fuer Wirtschaftsinformatik, Humboldt-Universitaet zu Berlin
10178 Berlin, Germany
jan.mendling@wiwi.hu-berlin.de
[4] Information Systems Program, Queensland University of Technology,
Brisbane, QLD 4000, Australia
j.recker@qut.edu.au

Abstract. Organizations increasingly seek to achieve operational excellence by standardizing business processes. Standardization initiatives may have different purposes, such as process streamlining, process automation, or even process outsourcing. However, standardization of processes is easier said than done. Standardization success depends on various factors, such as existent IT capabilities, available standard frameworks, market situation, and the processes' nature, such as their level of routine or structuredness. This paper uncovers the complex nature and relative influence of process-internal and -environmental factors relevant to process standardization, by discussing three case studies from different industries. The findings are summarized in a set of initial conjectures about successful process standardization. This exploratory research is a first step towards uncovering the characteristics of successful process standardization efforts.

Keywords: Business process management, business process design, business process standardization.

1 Introduction

Over recent decades, a broad range of management initiatives under the umbrella of *business process management* have been discussed and applied (e.g., TQM, Six Sigma, Lean, and others), with the aim of improving the design of business processes as important strategic assets of companies [1]. With the current economic climate demanding a focus on cost-cutting and operational excellence, many organizations specifically (re-) design their process with the view to reduce process costs through *process standardization*. This may be because business processes are sought to be

S. Rinderle-Ma et al. (Eds.): BPM 2009 Workshops, LNBIP 43, pp. 53–63, 2010.
© Springer-Verlag Berlin Heidelberg 2010

streamlined, automated, or outsourced: if processes are standardized then organizations can unplug one vendor and plug in another [2].

Standardization refers to the activity of establishing and recording a limited set of solutions to actual or potential problems directed at benefits for the parties involved, balancing their needs and intending and expecting that these solutions will be repeated or continuously used during a certain period by a substantial number of parties for whom they are meant [3]. Standardization, however, depends on a variety of factors, such as existing IT capabilities, available standard frameworks, existent knowledge, business strategies, market situation, and competitors.

The objective of our research is to uncover some of the factors that are relevant to the design of standardized processes. Our long-term goal is to support organizations in deciding on (a) which processes to standardize, and (b) how this can be done. In this paper, we examine three exploratory cases of organizations engaging in process standardization efforts so as to identify relevant factors that inform business process standardization. We proceed as follows. In the next section we set the scene for our research by reviewing relevant literature on process design and standardization. In Section 3 we discuss three case studies on business process standardization. We synthesize our findings in the fourth section in a set of conjectures about successful process standardization, and conclude this paper in Section 5 with a review of our contributions and an outlook to future work.

2 Background

Business processes are those value-adding activities that organizations execute to accomplish a particular objective for a particular customer [4]. Business processes can be large and inter-departmental (e.g., procurement, order management, service delivery) or relatively narrow and intra-departmental (e.g., order entry or invoice verification). Often, processes even cut across organizational boundaries [5].

Processes differ in their degree of variability. Some processes tend to be artistic [6] or creative [7], others are mass-customized [8] or automated [9]. Others distinguish manufacturing or production, and management and support processes [10]. The highly diverse nature of processes makes their management and (re-) design a cumbersome and complex challenge.

Recent years have seen the emergence of a number of initiatives to rationalize the practice of process (re-) design. For example, the *Business Process Maturity Model* (BPMM) was developed by the Object Management Group (OMG) in order to provide a framework for assessing process maturity, and to guide business process (re-) design initiatives [11]. Its general idea is to measure the process capability of an organization by examining the extent to which its processes are managed (level two maturity), standardized (level three), measured (level four), and continually innovated (level five maturity). Other noticeable initiatives include the Open Process Handbook initiative [12] or the work on design heuristics [13].

Recently, researchers have argued that not all processes fit these 'universal' approaches to design and management [6, 7, 14]. For example, highly creative processes are known to be unpredictable, even chaotic, ambiguous and consequently far from any routine or standard that could be applied to them [7], whereas some support processes (such as accounting or procurement) may be more likely to standardization. Lillrank [15] suggests a number of criteria to differentiate various types of processes (see Table 1).

Table 1. Classification of Standard, Routine and Non-routine Processes [15]

	Standard	Routine	Non-routine
Input criteria	Single variety	Bounded variety set	Open input set
Assessment	Acceptance test	Classification	Interpretation
Conversion rules	Switch, algorithm	Algorithm, habit	Heuristics
Repetition	Identical	Similar	Non-repetitive
Logic	Binary	Fuzzy	Interpretative
Downside	Defect: a critical performance variable is outside tolerance limits	Error: a faulty classification of inputs leads to wrong routine	Failure: situation is not interpreted properly and targets are not achieved
Upside	Conformance to specifications	Requisite variety	Task accomplishment
Control tools	Specifications, manuals, automation	Guidelines, repertoires, checklists	Shared values, competences, resources
Learning	Single-loop adjustment, reduction of variation	More and sharper categories, fewer categorization errors	Double-loop learning, better interpretative schemes

We contend that the *nature* of a process impacts on the standardization potential thereof, and, consequently, on the success of a process standardization initiative. We will use the attributes as listed in Table 1 in order to characterize the processes that were subject to the standardization efforts found in three case studies. Note that, due to the varying nature of processes within the case organizations (see below), Lillrank's criteria informed rather than meticulously guided our analysis. Besides the processes' nature, we will also examine environmental factors that may have impacted the cases.

3 Three Cases of Process Standardization

In our effort to exploring the factors relevant to business process standardization, we consider three exploratory case studies of companies engaging in process standardization initiatives. The case organizations were selected using convenience sampling; however, we believe that the selected sample is sufficient at this exploratory stage of our research. We conducted interviews in all cases that were recorded, transcribed and analyzed using techniques of qualitative data analysis. We also had access to online process documentations and internal process descriptions.

In the following we present each of the three cases, using a classification framework that allows us to cross-reference and compare the three cases. As indicated, we refer to Lillrank's classification (see Table 1), and also provide further detail about relevant environmental factors where appropriate. Altogether, we discuss the focus and the goal of standardization, characteristics of the initiative and the maturity level of the involved processes.

3.1 Case 1: IT Service Provider

The first case concerns a German IT service provider (ITSP, fictitious name). Eight interview were conducted with service managers responsible for overall service quality as well as employees executing the processes. ITSPs motivation to engage in process standardization efforts resulted from its strategic objective to guarantee high service quality by unifying all internal core business processes.

3.1.1 Case Overview
ITSP has approx. 3,000 employees, runs a data-processing center, and provides IT services such as development, implementation and administration of IT solutions across several industrial sectors such as logistics, media, finance, and healthcare. ITSP has several German subsidiaries and holds branches throughout sixteen different countries. During order fulfillment, ITSP often has to execute a variety of distinct business processes, in each of which the interaction of employees from geographically distant branches is necessary.

Due to the installation of several new branches, ITSP experienced severe problems with overall process accomplishment and quality of processes. Consequently, ITSP decided to standardize core business processes and underlying support processes to enable smooth process execution and process quality across all subsidiaries. The main concern was to ensure that every branch could operate the processes consistent to predefined process definitions. Existing core business processes were documented using a customized version of ARIS. This foundation was used by project members to develop and finally implement improved, standardized versions of the core business processes.

3.1.2 The Standardization Procedure
To make the core business processes obligatory for all business divisions, ITSP tried to achieve standardization by conducting a centrally managed project, which traversed through different phases: during the process definition phase, the project management team dealt with the company-wide process description and documentation of existing business processes. For each core business process, an experienced process owner was defined who was responsible for the correct definition of the process. In a top-down approach, the overall structure of the core business processes was modeled at a macro-level, followed by incremental refinement. The standardization effort resulted in a detailed business process documentation of a first part of the core business processes, divided into sub-processes at the micro-level.

Upon unification, review, and approval of process documentation, the next stage of the initiative commenced. All employees working within processes affected by the standardization project attended trainings to become familiar with the established process standards. At the end of this stage, additional training was provided. Finally, the approved business processes were implemented.

3.1.3 Assessment
ITSPs standardization effort focused on all those core business processes and corresponding sub-processes that an order has to pass through during the fulfillment cycle. Due to the high strategic importance of the project, significant monetary and human resources were invested in the design of improved, standardized processes at a very high level of detail. Our analysis reveals that many of the analyzed processes are routine rather than standard processes; processes appear similar on a macro-level but

show striking differences upon closer examination. Hence, some of the processes exhibit significant sequential or task variety at a more detailed level and therefore are rather complex and not repeatable. Employees rejected, or were unable to use, the process definitions in some cases and rather relied on their own routines and habits instead. In conclusion, the inherent process complexity was not sufficiently absorbed at the macro-level. In addition, end user acceptance of the new process designs was quite low, further hampering the initiative, and counteracting a progression in maturity as per the BPMM model.

3.2 Case 2: Visual Effects Production

The unit of analysis described in the second case is an Australian Visual Effect Company (VFXC, fictitious name). The sourcing strategy involved semi-structured interviews and the use of process modeling techniques. Two analysts were involved in the process of data collection and we interviewed a total of six people. Both creative supervisors who act as operational process managers and artists were interviewed. In the first place, the project aimed at investigating processes that rely on creativity and thus focused on the stage of process analysis. It was hoped that the results of this analysis would support VFXC in standardizing their processes. Process improvement and standardization in VFXC then became an ongoing BPM initiative. VFXC's motivation for process improvement and standardization primarily results from the objective of mitigating and avoiding risk.

3.2.1 Case Overview

VFXC processes can be characterized as highly relying on creativity, client-focused, complex, inter-dependent, but also repetitive. The organization produces visual effects; i.e., computer-generated artifacts that are combined with conventional film material. The organization has more than 100 employees and works with internationally known film studios. VFXC's core process is the so-called *production pipeline*, which comprises of a number of highly interwoven sub-processes; examples include *modeling* and *animation*. One major challenge in managing processes in visual effects production is the mitigation and avoidance of risk. Due to the involvement of different stakeholders who often cast subjective judgments over creative products, processes are linked to *creative risk*. At the same time, processes are characterized by *operational risks*, such as the potential mismatch between an organization's technical capabilities and requirements for the creative product [7].

3.2.2 The Standardization Procedion

In the stage of process analysis it became clear that VFXC's processes are characterized by high levels of uncertainty with regard to process outcome, structure, and required resources. Processes have a high demand for flexibility. Consequently, standardization in a sense of establishing and recording a limited set of solutions to actual or potential problems (compare section 1) becomes less desirable. However, it turned out that VFXC's processes comprise of both well-structured parts and highly creative parts. The latter one may be referred to as *pockets of creativity* [7].

The project thus subsequently focused on indentifying those parts that are characterized by creativity (that is, uncertainty with regard to outcome, process, and required resources) and understand how they interact with rather well-structured process parts. For example, this approach allowed VFXC to move well-structured data-handling tasks to the IT department and thus allowed creative people to spend more time on their creative work. As indicated, process improvement and standardization became an ongoing initiative supported by the top management.

3.2.3 Assessment

VFXC's processes comprise of both highly creative parts and well-structured parts. Based on the findings of the above described project we can conclude that creative parts, or pockets of creativity, should not be subject to standardization efforts. Well-structured, non-creative tasks, however, may be subject to such efforts. The challenge can thus be seen in identifying those parts of creativity-intensive processes that are characterized by high-levels of creativity and those parts that are well-structured and predictable. These sections may then become subject to process automation or out-sourcing, for example (see, for instance, the example provided in [9]). The study also revealed that higher efficiency of well-structured, predictable sections allows organizations to allocate more resources, in particular time and budget, to the processes' creative sections which, in turn, is associated with higher creative performance. Non-standardized processes (i.e., routine and non-routine "pockets of creativity") will always exist because of the organization's creative nature; therefore higher levels of BPMM in its traditional sense are also unlikely.

3.3 Case 3: Insurance Software Implementation

The unit of analysis described in this third case is an Austrian Insurance Group (AUSIG, fictitious name). We collected the facts on this case by interviewing a project team member working for an external consulting company involved in the project. The objective of this project was the development of a rapid implementation approach for the group's standard software. AUSIG was acquiring different regional insurance companies in central and Eastern Europe and faced issues associated with the implementation of standard insurance software based on the solutions developed for the Austrian market. AUSIG recognized that the differences, and commonalities, of the business processes in the different countries had to be understood in order to come up with a fit/gap analysis. The results would then be used for the implementation in a particular country.

3.3.1 Case Overview

AUSIG offers an extensive range of insurance products. The group's operations cover the different stages of the insurance value chain, including underwriting, policy administration, claims handling, payments, risk management, and accounting. Altogether the group has about 18,000 employees. The newly acquired subsidiaries in Central and Eastern Europe need to be aligned to the group's operations in order to leverage synergies. The group uses a range of standard software products that support insurance operations. The implementation of country operations based on these software solutions has proved to be unexpectedly difficult in the past, causing AUSIG to seek a more systematic approach to manage implementation projects. The group decided to adapt the ADONIS business process modeling approach [16] and have it tailored to its requirements by an external consulting company.

3.3.2 The Standardization Procedure

The project aimed at defining a so-called rapid implementation approach for the group's standard software. It started in September 2007 and completed in April 2008 and covered two major phases: first, the definition of a methodology and, second, the application of this methodology for one particular implementation project with a single country subsidiary which was running an implementation project at that time. The ADONIS business process modeling approach was considered since the tool was already in use throughout the group. The project team decided to include business processes, products, documents, roles, and software use cases in the newly designed approach. Also different extensions were introduced to ADONIS, in particular for capturing information on variants enabling the generation of reports on fit/gap analysis between standard group processes and country variants.

3.3.3 Assessment

The methodology developed in the project was found useful for approaching the challenge of software implementation processes in the different countries. AUSIG aims to use the methodology in upcoming implementation projects. The project identified one major challenge of standardization: While core insurance processes can be standardized from a business point of view, there are several national regulations that demand pockets of variability for the different countries.

4 Discussion

Table 2 and Table 3 summarize the characteristics of the standardization initiatives and their respective processes. The three cases show that the case organizations vary in the way they managed their standardization initiatives, on which level of detail they (re-) designed their processes, and what extent of resource commitment was involved.

The three cases provided examples for processes that display differing standardization potentials. For instance, while processes from ITSP (Case 1) tend to be routine, processes from VFCX (Case 2) show highly non-routine components (pockets of creativity), and are mainly characterized by uncertainty and high levels of flexibility. In contrast, AUSIG (Case 3) featured highly repetitive processes that varied only in parts across countries. Whereas most processes of AUSIG and the core processes of ITSP could be standardized, the core process of VFXC, the so-called production pipeline, turned out to be a quite creative process not amendable to standardization. However, this process also includes well-structured parts that can be subject to standardizations efforts. For instance, VFCX was enabled to move well-structured data-handling tasks to the IT department which, in turn, allowed creative people to spend more time on their creative work.

The cases further differ in the extent of end user involvement, strategic commitment, and process maturity. For instance, it is noticeable that, VFXC and ITSP were ranked level 2 "managed", while AUSIG was ranked level 3, "standardized". Thus, all three organizations have at least moderate levels of BPM maturity, indicating a positive correlation with standardization potential. However, it is unclear if the BPMM is sufficient to allow for the assessment of more "differentiated" process standardization initiatives, which necessarily focus only on those parts of routine and non-routine processes that can be standardized.

Table 2. Characteristics of the Cases (1)

Characteristics	Case 1 (ITSP)	Case 2 (VFXC)	Case 3 (AUSIG)
Focus of standardization	ITSP's standardization effort concentrated on core business processes. In order to enable smooth process execution, underlying support processes were also standardized if required.	VFXC's analysis and standardization efforts concentrate on the core process of the production of visual effects processes.	Procedural model for the implementation of standard insurance software in subsidiaries of the AUSIG group.
Characteristics of processes subject to the initiative	The processes are characterized by similarity, but are not identical (e. g., different customer solutions). Processes boundaries and involved actors are fuzzy. Guidelines and checklists are frequently used. All in all, processes can be classified as "routine".	The processes are characterized by the application of heuristics, the interpretation of involved actors, the actors' competencies, shared values and the availability of resources. These factors become critical as VFX production is characterized by uncertainty regarding both process and resources.	The processes are characterized by algorithmic decision rules.
BPMM level of processes	ITSP's overall business processes correspond to level two (*managed*) because non-standardized core business processes still exist. Only the part of the core business processes that were standardized during this first project meet level three (*standardized*) requirements.	VFXC'S overall business processes correspond to level two *"managed"* because non-standardized business processes still exist. It is assumed that, due to the organization's creative nature, non-standardized (sub-) processes will always exist.	AUSIG's overall business processes correspond to level three *"standardized"*, but show a great variety in the different countries.
Motivation / goal for standardization	To guarantee high service levels and process quality in order to enable process execution constantly throughout all subsidiaries.	Enable the mitigation and avoidance of risk and improve creative and operational process performance.	Enable a systematic and rapid implementation of the group's standard software.
Management of standardization	A central project managed by a team consisting of service and task managers as well as task operators and defined process owners.	Initially, the project focused on the analysis of existent business processes in VFXC. One analyst accompanied the organization for the period of one month. The analyst worked closely with a visual effects supervisor who coordinated process analysis within VFXC.	Central project managed by project team sponsored by board.
Level of detail of standardization	Initially, the overall structure of the core business processes was defined at a macro-level. Over time, the coarse descriptions evolved to a detailed process model reflecting sub-processes on a micro-level.	Initially, the overall structure of the core process of generating visual effects sequences was analyzed. Over time, the coarse description evolved to a detailed process model, including sub-processes at the micro-level.	Business processes and related artifacts were documented on three levels of detail.
Spent effort for standardization	No information available due to missing estimation and control techniques.	One analyst was present at a limited number of occasions. The other analyst spent 2 months full-time with VFXC in order to model and analyze processes.	No detailed information is available due to missing estimation and control techniques.

Table 3. Characteristics of the Cases (2)

Characteristics	Case 1 (ITSP)	Case 2 (VFXC)	Case 3 (AUSIG)
End user involvement	Task operators, task managers and service managers all are familiar with the business process which is the object of standardization. Additionally, the process owner ideally is the company's most work-experienced employee concerning the process s/he is responsible for.	The efforts in the analysis stage involved artist who carry out the analyzed processes as well as visual effects supervisors who have in-depth knowledge of the analyzed end-to-end processes.	No end users were involved.
Strategic commitment	Continuous top management support is attained by integrating the chief executive officer into the validation process of the *process definition phase.*	Continuous top management support is attained by integrating the chief executive officer into both process analysis and definition.	The project was sponsored by the board of the group.
Applied techniques	An extended version of the ARIS modeling technique is deployed.	An extended version of the ARIS modeling technique was used in the stage of process analysis. Semi-structured interviews were used in order to gain an in-depth understanding of the processes.	An extended version of the ADONIS modeling technique was used in the stage of process analysis.
Experience of project team	All team members, especially the service managers, are experienced process experts which operate on a daily basis within the affected business domains. They all exhibit knowledge about standardization and the management of standardization projects necessary for their daily work.	The analysts who conducted the process analysis as well as the semi-structured interviews were process experts who were familiar with the domain being investigated.	The analysts who conducted the process analysis as well as the semi-structured interviews are process experts who were familiar with the domain being investigated.
Size/complexity of standardization initiative	The complexity of this standardization project is very high because its main goal is the standardization of all core business processes which themselves are very complex and customer-specific.	The complexity of this project is moderate as it focuses on the organization's core process.	The complexity of this project is moderate as it focuses on the group's core processes and those of one subsidiary.
Scope of standardization initiative	The core processes of the entire company should be standardized in the end. Therefore, each foreign subsidiary is affected by this project.	The initiative aims at analyzing and, if possible, standardizing the organization's core processes. Based on the analysis, the organization started to move certain well-structured, non-creative tasks away from the key creative people.	Definition of the methodology and application in one country subsidiary.

Obviously, non-routine processes are less applicable to standardization than routine processes. The criteria introduced by Lillrank [15] (see Table 1) may thus be used in order to facilitate the process of deciding whether a process may be standardized or not. However, through our case studies it became apparent that even those processes that are non-routine, or even creative, may comprise sections that may in fact become subject to process standardization. Consequently, we conjecture:

> *Process analysts need to understand whether a process is amendable to standardization as a whole, or whether only sub-processes may be subject to standardization. Generally, non-routine (sub-) processes are not amendable to standardization.*

Our analysis also revealed that process standardization initiatives are carried out with quite differing objectives. While ITSP (Case 1) aimed at the rather broad objective of facilitating "smooth processes" and attaining "higher process quality", VFXC (Case 2) aimed at mitigating risk, and AUSIG (Case 3) aimed at introducing a standard software for insurance companies. Consequently, we conjecture:

> *Process analysts must consider the purpose of the initiative to decide what aspects of a process (structure, documents, resources, etc.) can be standardized.*

We argue that these two conjectures are not mutually exclusive, and need to be considered simultaneously when launching standardization initiatives. A possible implication of these conjectures is that organizations should screen their processes to pinpoint those (sub-) processes that are standard, routine, or non-routine. At the same time, they should decide, for each (sub-) process, whether process-flow, process-outcome, or required process-resources (such as documents) will be subject to standardization. It can thus be concluded, that any process standardization initiative needs to carefully consider the organizational context as well as the processes' nature.

5   Conclusions

In this paper we discussed different factors relevant to business process standardization. We have shown that processes subject to standardization efforts may differ across a set of defined attributes. Most notably, there are different parts of processes that need to remain open for creative decision making (pockets of creativity) and others that have to meet legal regulations of different countries (pockets of variability). Moreover, standardization initiatives are carried out with different purposes. While this paper discussed different process initiatives, it did not provide a final conclusion on how organizations can actually decide whether a process is amendable to standardization and what aspects of a process may be subject to this standardization. Instead, based on our insights, we provided a set of conjectures that speculate about factors pertinent to successful process standardization.

We realize that the scope of our effort to date has been limited to a restricted set of organizations, the selection of which was based on pragmatic rationale. Access to more organizations is needed to uncover further details relevant to standardization. For instance, manufacturing processes in the consumer products industry display a unique ratio between standardization and localization, epitomized in the 'line of visibility' (how much of a process is disclosed to the customer, how much is internal and standardized?). Accordingly, we will extend our research to cover a wider range of business process across different industries.

Aside from extending our case studies, our future research aims at distilling more concise guidelines on how processes can be assessed, in order to decide how organizations approach process standardization initiatives. This requires an in-depth understanding of factors that impact on the standardization of business processes. Some of these factors we suggested in this paper, with the intent of further broadening and deepening our analysis in future studies.

References

1. Chang, W.M.V., Cheng, T.C.E.: A Process Improvement Choice Model. Knowledge and Process Management 6, 189–204 (1999)
2. Tas, J., Sunder, S.: Financial Services Business Process Outsourcing. Communications of the ACM 47, 50–52 (2004)
3. Blind, K., Hipp, C.: The Role of Quality Standards in Innovative Service Companies: An Empirical Analysis for Germany. Technological Forecasting and Social Change 70, 653–669 (2003)
4. Davenport, T.H.: The Coming Commoditization of Processes. Harvard Business Review 83, 100–108 (2005)
5. Kock, N.F., McQueen, R.J.: Product Flow, Breadth and Complexity of Business Processes: An Empirircal Study of Fifteen Business Processes in Three Organisations. Business Process Re-engineering and Management Journal 2, 8–22 (1996)
6. Hall, J.M., Johnson, M.E.: When Should a Process Be Art, Not Science? Harvard Business Review 87, 58–65 (2009)
7. Seidel, S.: A Theory of Managing Creativity-intensive Processes. PhD Thesis, Muenster School of Business and Economics. The University of Muenster, Muenster (2009)
8. Feitzinger, E., Lee, H.L.: Mass Customization at Hewlett-Packard: The Power of Postponement. Harvard Business Review 75, 116–121 (1997)
9. Ouyang, C., la Rosa, M., Ter Hofstede, A.H.M., Dumas, M., Shortland, K.: Towards Web-Scale Workflows for Film Production. IEEE Internet Computing 12, 53–61 (2008)
10. Harmon, P.: Business Process Change: A Guide for Business Managers and BPM and Six Sigma Professionals, 2nd edn. Morgan Kaufmann, San Francisco (2007)
11. OMG: Business Process Maturity Model (BPMM), Version 1.0. Object Management Group (2008), http://www.omg.org/spec/BPMM/1.0/
12. Malone, T.W., Crowston, K., Herman, G.A.: Organizing Business Knowledge: The MIT Process Handbook. MIT Press, Cambridge (2003)
13. Reijers, H.A., Mansar, S.L.: Best Practices in Business Process Redesign: An Overview and Qualitative Evaluation of Successful Redesign Heuristics. Omega 33, 283–306 (2005)
14. Rosemann, M., Recker, J., Flender, C.: Contextualization of Business Processes. International Journal of Business Process Integration and Management 3, 47–60 (2008)
15. Lillrank, P.: The Quality of Standard, Routine and Nonroutine Processes. Organization Studies 24, 215–233 (2003)
16. Karagiannis, D., Junginger, S., Strobl, R.: Introduction to Business Process Management Systems Concepts. In: Scholz-Reiter, B., Stickel, E. (eds.) Business Process Modelling, pp. 81–109. Springer, Berlin (1996)

BPI Workshop

Introduction to the Fifth International Workshop on Business Process Intelligence (BPI 2009)

Business Process Intelligence (BPI) is an area that is quickly gaining interest and importance in industry and research. BPI refers to the application of various measurement and analysis techniques in the area of business process management. In practice, BPI is embodied in tools for managing process execution quality by offering several features such as analysis, prediction, monitoring, control, and optimization.

The goal of this workshop is to provide a better understanding of techniques and algorithms to support a company's processes at design time and the way they are handled at runtime. We aim to bring together practitioners and researchers from different communities such as business process management, information systems research, business administration, software engineering, artificial intelligence, and data mining who share an interest in the analysis of business processes and process-aware information systems. The workshop aims at discussing the current state of ongoing research and sharing practical experiences.

The Call for Papers for this workshop attracted 25 international submissions. Each paper was reviewed by at least three members of the program committee and the 10 best papers were selected for presentation at the workshop. The papers presented at the workshop provided a mix of novel research ideas, practical applications of BPI as well as new tool support. The paper by *Nakatumba and van der Aalst* introduces an approach to "explore the effect of workload on service times". The work by *Goel, Gruhn, and Richter* discusses "a new generalization of the Resource-Constrained Project Scheduling Problem". Motivated by the need to better support the mining of less structured process models, *Veiga and Ferreira* introduce a mining technique which "is divided in two stages: preprocessing and sequence clustering". The paper by *Heer and Außem and Wörzberger* specifies a flexible approach to "leverage OLAP technology for the processing and visualization of multidimensional project management data in the plant engineering domain". The work by *Kress and Seese* presents an approach "for the autonomous optimization of service industry's business processes". The paper by *Günther, Rozinat, and van der Aalst* describes "a new activity mining approach based on global trace segmentation". Motivated by the fact that not all possible business contexts of a process are known during its modelling, *Ghattas, Soffer and Peleg* introduces a "context learning framework". The work by *van Dongen and Adriansyah* presents "a simple clustering algorithm to derive a model from an event log, such that this model only contains a limited set of nodes and edges". The paper by *Jagadeesh Chandra Bose and van der Aalst* introduces a clustered-based approach for mining less structure process models. The work by *Awad and Weske* describe an extension of their "formal approach for efficient compliance checking based on model checking technology".

September 2009   Malu Castellanos, Ana Karla Alves de Medeiros,
                                                     Jan Mendling and Barbara Weber (Editors)

S. Rinderle-Ma et al. (Eds.): BPM 2009 Workshops, LNBIP 43, pp. 67–68, 2010.
© Springer-Verlag Berlin Heidelberg 2010

Workshop Organization

Dr. Malu Castellanos
Intelligent Enterprise Technologies Lab
Hewlett-Packard Laboratories
1501 Page Mill Rd, CA 94304, USA

Dr. Ana Karla Alves de Medeiros
Information Systems Group
Technische Universiteit Eindhoven
Postbus 513 (Paviljoen J6), 5600 MB Eindhoven, The Netherlands

Dr. Jan Mendling (contact chair)
Humboldt-Universität zu Berlin
Wirtschaftswissenschaftliche Fakultät
Institut für Wirtschaftsinformatik
Spandauer Straße 1, 10178 Berlin, Germany

Dr. Barbara Weber
Institut für Informatik
Universität Innsbruck
Technikerstraße 21a, 6020 Innsbruck, Austria

Program Committee

Wil van der Aalst, Technical University of Eindhoven, The Netherlands
Boualem Benatallah, University of New South Wales, Australia
Gerardo Canfora, University of Sannio, Italy
Peter Dadam, University of Ulm, Germany
Boudewijn van Dongen, Technical University of Eindhoven, The Netherlands
Diogo R. Ferreira, Technical University of Lisbon, Portugal
Walid Galoul, DERI Galway, Ireland
Gianluigi Greco, University of Calabria, Italy
Antonella Guzzo, University of Calabria, Italy
Joachim Herbst, DaimlerChrysler Research and Technology, Germany
Jun-Jang Jeng, IBM Research, USA
J¨urgen Moormann, Frankfurt School of Finance & Management, Germany
Michael zur Muehlen, Stevens Institute of Technology, USA
Cesare Pautasso, University of Lugano, Switzerland
Manfred Reichert, University of Ulm, Germany
Pnina Soffer, Haifa University, Israel
Hans Weigand, Infolab, Tilburg University, The Netherlands
Ton Weijters, Technical University of Eindhoven, The Netherlands
Mathias Weske, Hasso Plattner Institute at University of Potsdam, Germany

Analyzing Resource Behavior
Using Process Mining

Joyce Nakatumba and Wil M.P. van der Aalst

Eindhoven University of Technology
P.O. Box 513, NL-5600 MB, Eindhoven, The Netherlands
{jnakatum,w.m.p.v.d.aalst}@tue.nl

Abstract. It is vital to use accurate models for the analysis, design, and/or control of business processes. Unfortunately, there are often important *discrepancies between reality and models*. In earlier work, we have shown that simulation models are often based on incorrect assumptions and one example is the speed at which people work. The "Yerkes-Dodson Law of Arousal" suggests that a worker that is under time pressure may become more efficient and thus finish tasks faster. However, if the pressure is too high, then the worker's performance may degrade. Traditionally, it was difficult to investigate such phenomena and few analysis tools (e.g., simulation packages) support workload-dependent behavior. Fortunately, more and more activities are being recorded and modern *process mining* techniques provide detailed insights in the way that people really work. This paper uses a new process mining plug-in that has been added to ProM to explore the *effect of workload on service times*. Based on historic data and by using regression analysis, the relationship between workload and services time is investigated. This information can be used for various types of analysis and decision making, including more realistic forms of simulation.

Keywords: Process Mining, Yerkes-Dodson Law of Arousal, Business process Simulation.

1 Introduction

Organizations are increasingly using Process-Aware Information Systems (PAISs) to reduce costs and improve the performance and efficiency of important business processes. PAISs provide a means to support, control, and monitor operational business processes. Examples of PAISs are Workflow Management Systems (WFMSs), Business Process Management Systems (BPMSs) but also other "process-aware" systems, such as Enterprise Resource Planning Systems (e.g., SAP R/3, Oracle, JD Edwards, etc.), call-center systems, Product-Data Management Systems, and process-centric middleware (e.g., IBM's WebSphere, JBoss, etc.) [5]. While PAISs support processes they also record information about these processes in the form of so-called *event logs*, also known as audit trails or transaction logs [2]. In these logs, information is stored about activities

S. Rinderle-Ma et al. (Eds.): BPM 2009 Workshops, LNBIP 43, pp. 69–80, 2010.

as they are being executed. This information can include the times at which events were executed, who executed these events, etc. This information can be used among other things, for performance analysis,e.g., the identification of bottlenecks in a process model. Event logs provide an excellent source of information for *process mining*, i.e., extracting non-trivial knowledge from historic data. In this paper, we advocate the use of process mining in order to extract characteristic properties of resources.

Many organizations have used *simulation* at some point to analyze, for example, the performance of their business processes. In most of these simulation approaches, however, the models used are very naive and do not use the information recorded in the event logs. We refer to this kind of simulation as *traditional simulation* [1]. Traditional simulation, therefore, *rarely uses historic information* and also typically suffers from the problem that *human resources are modeled in a rather naive way*. As a result, the simulation results obtained are seldom a good reflection of what is actually happening in the organization.

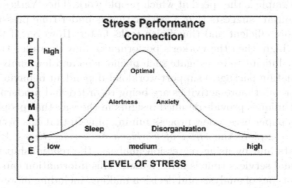

Fig. 1. Yerkes-Dodson Law modeled as U-shaped Curve. When the stress level is low, the performance is also low. This increases as the stress levels also increase up to a certain optimal level beyond which the performance drops (adapted from [12]).

In [1], we identify aspects of resource behavior that are not captured in today's simulation tools. In particular, we point out that people do not work at constant speeds and their processing speeds are usually influenced by their workload. We refer to this as *workload-dependent processing speeds* and the analysis of this phenomenon is the focus of this paper. There are a number of studies that suggest a relation between workload and performance of workers. In the literature, this phenomenon is known as the "Yerkes-Dodson Law of Arousal" [12]. This law models the relationship between arousal and performance as an inverse U-Shaped curve as depicted in Figure 1. This implies that for a given individual and a given set of tasks, there is an optimal level at which the performance of that individual has a maximal value and beyond this optimal level the worker's performance collapses. This aspect has been studied in social sciences and operations management. Until recently, there were no means for systematically observing such phenomena in the workplace. However, because human activity is increasingly recorded by PAIS technology and the availability of process mining tools such as ProM, it is now possible to better characterize resource behavior based on empirical data. Therefore, this is important for two main reasons.

First of all, a better resource characterization will help *to make simulation models that are more realistic and that are tightly coupled to PAISs* [1,9,10]. This will enable the use of process mining for operational decision making, i.e., based on a reliable model and both real-time and historic data, it becomes worthwhile to use simulation on a daily basis. This paper therefore, is a first step approach to the use of process mining as a technique for the extraction of characteristic properties of resources from event logs, i.e., the effect of changing workload on resource behavior. This information can then be incorporated in simulation models. The results of various process mining techniques can be combined as shown in [9] to yield an integrated simulation model.

Secondly, good insights into the behavior and performance of people will assist in a *better work distribution*. One of the major objectives of a PAIS is to facilitate the distribution of work amongst the group of resources involved in a process. However, today's PAIS systems use very limited understanding of resource behavior. But with better characterization of resource behavior, this can act as a basis for making work allocation decisions in real life.

In this paper, we use linear regression analysis to quantify the "Yerkes-Dodson Law of Arousal" based on empirical data. *Linear Regression Analysis* is a statistical technique used for investigating and modeling the relationship between variables [7]. We use regression because of its various purposes, i.e., it can be used to describe and summarize a dataset through the regression equations, it can be used for prediction of the response variable based on the predictor variables, the variables in a regression model are usually related in a cause-effect relationship and so regression can be used in confirming such a relationship and also regression is a useful technique for parameter estimation. Although we use linear regression in this paper, there are more powerful regression techniques that can be used to truly capture the U-shape shown in Figure 1.

The remainder of the paper is organized as follows. First, we provide an overview of event logs and process mining in Section 2. Section 3 has a discussion of workload-dependent processing speeds. We explain how to extract the workload and processing speeds based on the information available in event logs in Section 4. In Section 5, we describe the application of our approach to a case study based on real-life logs to validate our approach. Section 6 has a discussion of related work and finally Section 7 gives conclusions.

2   Process Mining: An Overview

2.1   Event Logs

Most information systems (e.g. WFM and BPM systems) provide some kind of *event log* also referred to as audit trail entry or workflow log [2]. An event log contains log entries about activities executed for a business process. We assume that it is possible to record events such that each event refers to an activity and is related to a particular case (i.e., a process instance). For any process mining technique, an event log is needed as the input. In order to understand what an event log is, we define the concept of an *event*.

Definition 1 (Event, Property). Let $\mathcal{E}$ be the event universe, i.e., the set of all possible event identifiers, and $\mathcal{T}$ the time domain. We assume that events have various properties, e.g., an event has a timestamp, it corresponds to a particular activity, is executed by a particular resource and has a particular type. For each of these properties, there are functions $prop_{time} \in \mathcal{E} \to \mathcal{T}$ assigning timestamps to events, $prop_{act} \in \mathcal{E} \to \mathcal{A}$ assigning activities to events, $prop_{type} \in \mathcal{E} \to \{start, complete\}$ assigning event types to the events, and $prop_{res} \in \mathcal{E} \nrightarrow \mathcal{R}$ is a partial function assigning resources to events. For $e \in \mathcal{E}$, we define $\overline{e}$ as a shorthand for $prop_{time}(e)$, i.e., the time of occurrence of event e.

An event e is described by some unique identifier and can have several properties. In this paper, we use these properties which are; the timestamp of an event ($prop_{time}(e)$), the activity name ($prop_{act}(e)$), the name of the resource that executed the activity ($prop_{res}(e)$) and the event type of the activity ($prop_{type}(e)$). Note $prop_{res}$ is a partial function because some events may not be linked to any resource.

An event log is a set of events. Each event in the log is linked to a particular trace and is globally unique, i.e., the same event cannot occur twice in a log. A trace represents a particular process instance and furthermore for each trace, time should be non-decreasing within each trace in the log.

Definition 2 (Event Log and Trace). A trace is a sequence of events $\sigma \in \mathcal{E}^*$ such that each event appears only once and time is non-decreasing, i.e., for $1 \leq i < j \leq |\sigma| : \sigma(i) \neq \sigma(j)$ and $\overline{\sigma(i)} \leq \overline{\sigma(j)}$. $\mathcal{C}$ is the set of all possible traces (including partial traces). An event log is a set of traces $L \subseteq \mathcal{C}$ such that each event appears at most once in the entire log, i.e., for any $\sigma_1, \sigma_2 \in L$: $\forall_{e_1 \in \sigma_1} \forall_{e_2 \in \sigma_2} \; e_1 \neq e_2$ or $\sigma_1 = \sigma_2$.

Note that $\overline{\sigma(i)} \leq \overline{\sigma(j)}$ means that time is non-decreasing (i.e., $prop_{time}(\sigma(i)) \leq prop_{time}(\sigma(j))$ if i occurs before j). The last requirement states that σ_1 and σ_2 should not have any overlapping events. This is done to ensure that events are globally unique and do not appear in multiple traces.

Table 1 shows a fragment of an event log with two traces and each trace consists of a number of events. For example, the first trace has three events ($1a$, $1b$, $1c$) with different properties. For event $1a$, $prop_{act}(1a)$ =A, $prop_{res}(1a)$ =Mary, $prop_{time}(1a)$ =20th November 2007 at 8:00am and $prop_{type}(1a)$ =start.

2.2   Process Mining

Process mining aims at the extraction of information from a set of real executions (event logs). As already stated, event logs are the starting point for any process mining technique. Before any technique can be applied to the event log, information can directly be obtained from the log through the *preprocessing* step.

Table 1. A fragment of an event log

event	properties			
	activity	resource	timestamp	type
1a	A	Mary	20-11-2007:8.00	start
1b	A	Mary	21-11-2007:8.13	complete
1c	B	John	01-12-2007:8.16	start
2a	A	Angela	08-02-2008:8.10	start

This information can include the number of traces and events in the log, the activities and resources, and the frequency of their occurrences in the log, etc. Based on this information *log filtering* can be done, for example, to remove the resources with infrequent occurrence. After this step, then process mining techniques can be applied to the log to discover three different perspectives (process, organizational, case) through the *processing* step.

The *process* perspective focusses on the control-flow, i.e., the ordering of activities and the goal here is to find a good characterization of all the possible paths, e.g., expressed in terms of a Petri net [2]. The *organizational* perspective focusses on the resources, i.e., which performers are involved in the process model and how are they related. The goal is to either structure the organization by classifying people in terms of roles and organizational units or to show relation between individual performers (i.e., build a social network [11]). The *case* perspective focuses on properties of cases. Cases can be characterized by their paths in the process or by the values of the corresponding data elements, e.g., if a case represents a supply order it is interesting to know the number of products ordered. Orthogonal to these three perspectives, the result of a mining effort can refer to performance issues. For example, information about flow times and waiting times. The discovered process model can then be enhanced with this performance information.

3   Workload-Dependent Processing Speeds

In many systems, the speed at which resources work is partly determined by the amount of work at present. This is especially true for human beings; in busy periods people tend to increase their speed in order to process more cases. However, when people are given too much work over a long period of time, their performance then tends to drop. This phenomenon is known as the "Yerkes-Dodson Law of Arousal" [12] and is illustrated by the inverse U-Shaped curve depicted in Figure 1. If the law holds, the performance of people (i.e., the speed at which they work) is determined by the workload that is currently present in the system [8]. An example would be a production system where the speed of a server is relatively low when there is too much work (stress) or when there is very little work (laziness) [3].

In this paper, we discuss a new process mining technique implemented in our Process Mining framework (ProM), to quantify the relationship between workload and processing speeds based on historic data. From the event logs

Case Id	Activity Names	Resource Names	Start Times	Completion Times	Service Times (minutes)
1	A	Mary	Tue Jun 12 08:34:56 CEST 2007	Tue Jun 12 08:40:01 CEST 2007	5
1	B	Jane	Tue Jun 12 08:35:12 CEST 2007	Tue Jun 12 11:39:06 CEST 2007	184
1	C	Jo	Tue Jun 12 08:40:19 CEST 2007	Tue Jun 12 09:30:17 CEST 2007	50
2	A	Erik	Tue Jun 12 10:20:30 CEST 2007	Tue Jun 12 10:59:16 CEST 2007	39
2	C	Brenda	Tue Jun 12 10:20:20 CEST 2007	Tue Jun 12 11:40:08 CEST 2007	80

Fig. 2. Overview of the approach. First an event log in MXML format is translated into a tabular format showing (a) case id's, (b) activity names, (c) resource names, (d) start times, (e) completion times, and (f) service times (difference between the completion and start times). This table is then used to calculate the workload and regression analysis is carried out to find the relationship between workload and processing speeds. This can be done at different levels of granularity, e.g., per activity, per resource, or per resource/activity combination.

expressed in standard Mining *XML* (MXML) format [4], we extract information about traces, the activities per trace, the resources that execute these activities, and their respective service times (this is measured in minutes and is explained in Section 4.2).

Figure 2 shows a sample table of the basic information extracted from the event logs. Based on this information, we determine the workload and processing speeds. As will be shown in the next section, multiple definitions of the workload are possible. This workload information can be compared with the actual service times (last column in the main table shown in Figure 2), i.e., the time required to execute an activity (thus denoting the processing speed). Then using linear regression analysis, we quantify the relationship between the workload and the processing speeds. In the next section, we describe in detail how the workload and processing speeds are defined and measured based on the information in the event log.

4   Relationship between Workload and Processing Speeds

4.1   Workload

As already stated, people do not work at constant speeds and their processing speeds are often influenced by the current workload.

The workload of a resource or a group of resources can be defined as either: (a) the number of work items waiting at the start of execution of an activity, i.e., the amount of work that has been scheduled for a given user or (b) the number of activities that have been executed over a particular period. In this paper, we focus on the second option, i.e., the number of activities that have been executed over a particular period defines "how busy" the resource has been. We now define the notion of workload used in this paper.

Definition 3 (Workload). Let T be the time domain, C be a set of all possible traces, $L \subseteq C$ be an event log, and $\mathcal{E}$ be a set of all possible event identifiers.

- We define the *event universe* of L as $\mathcal{E}_L = \{e \in \mathcal{E} \mid \exists_{\sigma \in L} \, e \in \sigma\}$.
- $\mathcal{E}_L$ is partitioned into two sets: $\mathcal{E}_L^s = \{e \in \mathcal{E}_L \mid prop_{type}(e) = start\}$ (i.e., all start events in L) and $\mathcal{E}_L^c = \{e \in \mathcal{E}_L \mid prop_{type}(e) = complete\}$ (i.e., all complete events in L).
- The workload calculation based on L is parameterized by the following four parameters: $\mathcal{E}_{ref}$, $\mathcal{E}_{load}$, h_{back}, and h_{forw}.
- $\mathcal{E}_{ref} \subseteq \mathcal{E}_L$ is the set of *reference events*, i.e., the events for which the workload is calculated.
- $\mathcal{E}_{load} \subseteq \mathcal{E}_L$ is the set of *load events*, i.e., the events considered when calculating the workload.
- $h_{back} \in T \rightarrow T$ is a function that defines the *start* of the time window given some reference time, i.e., for some reference time $t \in T$, the time window starts at $h_{back}(t)$ (with $h_{back}(t) \leq t$).
- $h_{forw} \in T \rightarrow T$ is a function that defines the *end* of the time window given some reference time, i.e., for some reference time $t \in T$, the time window ends at $h_{forw}(t)$ (with $t \leq h_{forw}(t)$).
- Based on L, $\mathcal{E}_{ref}$, $\mathcal{E}_{load}$, h_{back}, and h_{forw}, we define the workload function $busy \in \mathcal{E}_{ref} \rightarrow \mathbb{N}$, where $\mathbb{N}$ is the set of natural numbers $\{0, 1, 2, ..\}$ as follows: $busy(e) = |\{e' \in \mathcal{E}_{load} \mid h_{back}(\bar{e}) \leq \bar{e'} \leq h_{forw}(\bar{e})\}|$, i.e., the number of load events in the time window associated with a reference event e.

Function *busy* calculates the workload for all the reference events. An event e is a reference event, i.e., $e \in \mathcal{E}_{ref}$, if it can be associated to some service time. For example, one can take $\mathcal{E}_{ref} = \mathcal{E}_L^s$, i.e., all start events are reference events and by looking up the corresponding complete events it is possible to measure their service times. It is also possible to take $\mathcal{E}_{ref} = \mathcal{E}_L^c$ or even $\mathcal{E}_{ref} = \mathcal{E}_L$. In the later case there are two reference events for each activity. Based on the timestamp of some reference event $e \in \mathcal{E}_{ref}$, we calculate a time window that starts at $h_{back}(\bar{e})$ and ends at $h_{forw}(\bar{e})$. Note that the time window depends on the definition of the parameters h_{back} and h_{forw}. For example, if $h_{back}(t) = t - a$ and $h_{forw}(t) = t + b$, then events that occurred less than a time units before some reference event and not more than b time units after some reference event are considered. When the values chosen for a and b are long (i.e., in our approach a and b are between 1 to 24 hours), then we see a greater effect of the workload on the processing speed. Based on such a time window, function *busy* then simply counts the number of load events. The set of load events may be defined as $\mathcal{E}_{load} = \mathcal{E}_L^s$. It is also possible to take $\mathcal{E}_{load} = \mathcal{E}_L^c$ or even $\mathcal{E}_{load} = \mathcal{E}_L$.

Definition 3 looks at $\mathcal{E}_{ref}$ and $\mathcal{E}_{load}$ for the log as whole. However, it is possible to determine these sets of events *per activity*, *per resource*, or *per activity/resource combination*.

4.2 Processing Speeds

In this section, we define the processing speeds based on the information in the logs. The processing speeds can be defined as either the *flow time* (i.e., the time required to handle a case from beginning to end) or the *service times* (based on the actual processing time of individual activities). In this paper, we only consider the service times as a way of denoting the processing speeds. Given that we have the *start* and *complete* events of an activity recorded in the log, the service time is defined as the difference between the times at which these two events were executed.

Definition 4 (Service Time). Let L, $\mathcal{E}_L$, $\mathcal{E}_L^s$ and $\mathcal{E}_L^c$ be as defined in Definition 3. Function $st \in \mathcal{E}_L \rightarrow \mathcal{T}$ maps events onto the duration of the corresponding activity, i.e., the service time. We assume that there is a one-to-one correspondence between $\mathcal{E}_L^s$ and $\mathcal{E}_L^c$, i.e., any $e_s \in \mathcal{E}_L^s$ corresponds to precisely one event $e_c \in \mathcal{E}_L^c$ and vice versa. The service time of these events are equal, i.e., $st(e_s) = st(e_c) = \overline{e_c} - \overline{e_s}$.

Note that the above definition heavily relies on the assumption that there is a one-to-one correspondence between start and complete events. When reading the traces in the log, there are situations when for an activity only the *start* event is recorded and not the *complete* event or when the *complete* event is recorded and not the *start* event for the same activity. In order to avoid the recording of incorrect durations, we match the *start* and *complete* events by linking events that belong to the same trace and for which the activity names are the same. Events which can not be matched are discarded. Moreover, we have heuristics to determine when events were started based entirely on the complete events.

After obtaining the workload and the service times, we use simple linear regression analysis to find the relationship between workload (as the *independent variable*) and processing speed (as the *dependent variable*). In this case, we have one independent variable and one dependent variable, however, it is easy to add other independent variables (e.g., based on alternative definitions of workload). From the analysis we obtain parameters required for the construction of the regression equation given by: $y = \beta_0 + \beta_1 x + \varepsilon$ where: y is the dependent variable (processing speed expressed in terms of the service time, i.e., $st(e)$), x is the independent variable (workload, i.e., $busy(e)$), β_0 (intercept) is the value of y when $x = 0$, β_1 (slope) is the change in y produced by a unit change in x, ε is the error of prediction obtained using the regression equation.

Other parameters can also be obtained from the regression analysis which are; the *correlation coefficient* (r) is the degree to which two variables are linearly related ($-1 \leq r \leq 1$) and *r-square of the regression equation* (R^2, or the coefficient of determination), which is the proportion of variation in y accounted for by x ($0 \leq R^2 \leq 1$). Higher values of R^2 ($0.7 \leq R^2 \leq 1$) indicate a good fit of the regression equation to the data while the intermediate values ($0.5 \leq R^2 \leq 0.7$) show a moderate fit and low values ($0 \leq R^2 \leq 0.5$) indicate a poor fit. The approach described in this paper is implemented as a plug-in in the process mining tool ProM. In the next section, we discuss the results from the application of this approach to real-life logs.

5   Experiments

We tested our approach and the implemented ProM plug-in on a real case study based on a process that handles the getting of building contracts in a Dutch municipality.

5.1   Case Study

The case study was conducted on real-life logs from a municipality in the Netherlands. This municipality uses a workflow system and the logs used are from a process that deals with the getting of a building permit. Through the preprocessing step we obtained important information about the log. The event log contains information about 2076 cases, 67271 events, 109 resources and 11 activities. The start date of the log is "2003-01-24" and the end date is "2005-11-08". We filtered the log to remove the resources and activities with infrequent occurrence and also only considered the events with both the *start* and *complete*. The information contained in the main table (as shown in Figure 2), can be viewed based on three perspectives, i.e, the resource, activity and resource/activity perspectives.

Table 2. Linear regression results based on the resource dimension

resource names	correlation co-efficient (r)	R^2	intercept (β_0)	slope (β_1)
jcokkie	0.44	0.19	22053	7860
bfemke	0.68	0.46	-20502	38537
klargen	0.84	0.71	-585057	704292
mbree	0.68	0.47	-1264	3849
clijfers	0.22	0.05	11850	21920
pkelders	0.17	0.03	1619	115.8
bgeveren	0.73	0.53	-299007	355963

Tables 2 and 3 show the linear regression results based on the *resource perspective* and the *resource/activity perspective* respectively[1]. After filtering events from the main table, based on the resource perspective, we select the events to use for the reference and load events. In this case study, the *complete*[2] events are selected and also $h_{forw}(t) = t+23hrs$ and $h_{back}(t) = t+23hrs$ where t is the time of execution of a reference event. The result of the relationship between workload and processing speed is reflected by the r and R^2 values. For example, resource "klargen" in row three of Table 2, has high positive values for r and R^2. This implies that "how busy" this resource has been in the past affects the speed at which he executes activities. Both tables also show the slope and intercept values which are used in the regression equation. For example, the regression equation for "klargen" in Table 2 is: *processing speed* = -585057.5 + 704292(*workload*),

---

[1] The resource names in Tables 2 and 3 have been changed to ensure confidentiality.

[2] Although we selected the *complete* events for the reference and load events, we could have also chosen the *start* events or both the *start* and *complete* events.

i.e., $\beta_0 = -585057.5$ and $\beta_1 = 704292$ in $y = \beta_0 + \beta_1 x + \varepsilon$. The results obtained in Table 2 are based on all the activities that the resources executed over the whole log. We point out that in real-life resources can be involved in multiple processes yet the event log records events for one particular process in isolation that a resource may be involved in. Hence the resource utilization is low in these logs. This affects the values obtained for r and R^2 (they are not as high as they may have been expected).

Table 3. Linear regression results for the resource/activity dimension. For example, for the fifth row "jcokkie" is the resource name and "CTT" is the activity name.

resource & activity names	correlation coefficient (r)	R^2	intercept (β_0)	slope (β_1)
pbakere/Publiceren	0.99	0.99	-14559.3	25824.7
pbakere/AR03Arcdossier	0.98	0.99	-612530	742325.5
jcokkie/BV99Convdoss	0.99	0.98	-14037.7	99539
jcokkie/CTT	0.78	0.61	-139809	86795
jcokkie/AR03Arcdossier	0.99	0.99	354495	258812.5
clijfers/BV26Financion	0.65	0.43	-41275.8	46161.6
clijfers/BV24Afwerkbesch	0.99	0.99	-129321	131731.7
clijfers/BV36W0Z	0.79	0.63	-263634	266631.2
nlijslet/BV26Bouwcontrole	0.97	0.95	-97185.4	102766.2
pkelders/BV06Milieu	0.73	0.53	-21966	2059.2
pkelders/BV29Gereed	0.99	0.99	-6940	6940
pkelders/BV28Gestat	0.57	0.30	-4961	4961
hwyman/BV26Belastingen	0.97	0.94	-9544.5	10640.5
groemer/BV24Afwerk	0.77	0.59	-76566	84550.7
dtruyde/BV06CCT	0.92	0.86	-263933	273645

To obtain the results shown in Table 3, we filter the log based on the resources to get the activities that each resource executes and the events per activity are used for obtaining the workload. Several values for R^2 in this table are greater than 0.7 which is a strong indication that most of the variability in the processing speeds is explainable by the workload. For example, for "pbakere&Publiceren" in row 1 of Table 3, $R^2 = 0.99$ which implies that 99% of the variability in the processing speed is dependent on the workload for this resource. We also point out that, although for some resources there is no significant relationship when all the activities they executed are considered (see Table 2) as reflected by the low r and R^2, there is a significant relationship when the individual activities are considered as reflected by the high r and R^2 values (see Table 3). For example, resource "jcokkie" in the first row of Table 2 has values of $r = 0.44$ and $R^2 = 0.19$, whereas in Table 3, in row 5 "jcokkie & AR03 Arcdossiers" with values of $r = 0.99$ and $R^2 = 0.99$ and in row 4 "jcokkie & CTT" where $r = 0.78$ and $R^2 = 0.61$. These examples indeed suggest that the speed at which people work is indeed influenced by their workload.

6   Related Work

The work presented in this paper is related to earlier work on process mining and operations management. Recently many tools and techniques for process mining have been developed [2,11]. Note that process mining is not restricted to control-flow discovery [2]. For example, in [11] the main aim is to build organizational models from event logs and analyze relationships between resources involved in a process.

The "Yerkes-Dodson Law of Arousal" [12] illustrated in Figure 1, is one of the main motivations for this paper. In operations management, substantial work has been done to operationalize this "law" using mathematical models and simulation in order to explore the relationship between workload and shop performance [3]. In [8] queues with workload-dependent arrival rates and service rates are considered. The authors of these papers investigate what the effect on production efficiency is based on controlling the arrival rates and service rates as a result of the workload present in the system. Juedes et al. [6] introduce the concept of workload-dependent processing speeds in real-time computing. In this study, they deal with a maximum allowable workload problem for real-time systems with tasks having variable workload sizes.

The related work mentioned above does not actually measure the relationship between workload and service times. This paper has presented such an analysis technique based on linear regression analysis. This is supported by a new plug-in in ProM and has been applied to several examples. We are not aware of other studies that try to discover phenomena such as the one described by the "Yerkes-Dodson Law of Arousal".

7   Conclusion

Although organizations use various analysis techniques to analyze their business processes, the results may be very misleading if the assumptions used are incorrect. For example, in most simulation tools service times are simply sampled from a probability distribution without considering the workload. In this paper, we presented an approach to quantify the relationship between workload and processing speed. This approach is based on regression analysis and is implemented as a new plug-in in ProM.

We consider this as a first step approach in the use of process mining techniques for the extraction of useful information from event logs that characterizes resource behavior and also as an addition to the repertoire of process mining techniques. We expect that process mining techniques will focus more and more on the behavior of workers once it becomes easier to discover processes.

Experimentation shows that the relationship described by the "Yerkes-Dodson Law of Arousal" really exists. However, to truly capture the inverse U-shape depicted in Figure 1, we need more sophisticated regression techniques. In this paper, we focus on the definition of workload as the number of work items that have been executed over a particular period, but there other workload definitions that are possible and can be explored. Our future research will aim at more powerful analysis techniques and a tight coupling between simulation and operational decision making. As discussed in [1], we want to make simulation more realistic by adequately modeling resources based on empirical data. Besides workload-dependent process times, we also take into account that people are involved in multiple processes, are available only part-time, work in batches. Experiments show that these factors really influence performance [1].

References

1. van der Aalst, W.M.P., Nakatumba, J., Rozinat, A., Russell, N.: Business Process Simulation: How to get it Right? In: vom Brocke, J., Rosemann, M. (eds.) International Handbook on Business Process Management. Springer, Berlin (2008)
2. van der Aalst, W.M.P., Weijters, A.J.M.M., Maruster, L.: Workflow Mining: Discovering Process Models from Event Logs. IEEE Transactions on Knowledge and Data Engineering 16(9), 1128–1142 (2004)
3. Bertrand, J.W.M., van Ooijen, H.P.G.: Workload Based Order Release and Productivity: A Missing Link. Production Planning and Control 13(7), 665–678 (2002)
4. van Dongen, B.F., van der Aalst, W.M.P.: A Meta Model for Process Mining Data. In: Casto, J., Teniente, E. (eds.) Proceedings of the CAiSE Workshops (EMOI-INTEROP Workshop), vol. 2, pp. 309–320 (2005)
5. Dumas, M., van der Aalst, W.M.P., ter Hofstede, A.H.M.: Process-Aware Information Systems: Bridging People and Software through Process Technology. Wiley & Sons, Chichester (2005)
6. Juedes, D., Drews, F., Welch, L.: Workload Functions: A New Paradigm for Realtime Computing. In: 10th IEEE Real-Time and Embedded Technology and Applications Symposium Work-In Progress Session, pp. 25–28 (2004)
7. Montgomery, D.C., Peck, E.A.: Introduction to Linear Regression Analysis. Wiley & Sons, Chichester (1992)
8. van Ooijen, H.P.G., Bertrand, J.W.M.: The effects of a simple arrival rate control policy on throughput and work-in-progress in production systems with workload dependent processing rates. International Journal of Production Economics 85, 61–68 (2003)
9. Rozinat, A., Mans, R.S., Song, M., van der Aalst, W.M.P.: Discovering Simulation Models. Information Systems 34(3), 305–327 (2009)
10. Rozinat, A., Wynn, M.T., van der Aalst, W.M.P., ter Hofstede, A.H.M., Fidge, C.: Workflow Simulation for Operational Decision Support Using Design, Historic and State Information. In: Dumas, M., Reichert, M., Shan, M.-C. (eds.) BPM 2008. LNCS, vol. 5240, pp. 196–211. Springer, Heidelberg (2008)
11. Song, M., van der Aalst, W.M.P.: Towards Comprehensive Support for Organizational Mining. Decision Support Systems 46(1), 300–317 (2008)
12. Wickens, C.D.: Engineering Psychology and Human Performance. Harper (1992)

Mobile Workforce Scheduling Problem with Multitask-Processes

Asvin Goel[1,2], Volker Gruhn[1], and Thomas Richter[1,*]

[1] Chair of Applied Telematics / e-Business, University of Leipzig
Klostergasse 3, 04109 Leipzig, Germany
{goel,gruhn,richter}@ebus.informatik.uni-leipzig.de
[2] MIT-Zaragoza International Logistics Program, Zaragoza Logistics Center
Avda. Gómez Laguna 25, 1ª planta, 50009 Zaragoza, Spain
asvin@mit.edu

Abstract. In this work we introduce a new generalization of the Resource-Constrained Project Scheduling Problem – the Mobile Workforce Scheduling Problem with Multitask-Processes (MWSP-MP). This scheduling problem arises in mobile work scenarios and is characterized by tasks to be scheduled that are not independent from each other, but belong to structured business processes. These business processes are subject to timing and cost related properties and restrictions that have to be considered for the scheduling of resources. We fortify the relevance of the MWSP-MP by illustration with process examples from the utility industry and present an initial heuristic for the insertion of processes into solutions of the problem.

Keywords: Workforce Scheduling, Mobile Business Processes, Workforce Management.

1 Introduction

Mobile business processes can be seen as processes, of which at least one activity takes place outside the organization's physical bounds [1][2]. If we consider mobile processes in network based industries (e.g. utilities, telecommunications) we can state that indeed selected mobile processes can be seen as a combination of mobile activities, taking place at different locations. These processes consist of more than one mobile activity. The problem description in the following section introduces such a business process originating in the utility industry. The business processes in question are usually composed of different mobile activities taking place at different locations. Additionally time restrictions apply as e.g. down-times have to be minimized. In such mobile environments numerous business processes are executed in parallel by different workers / teams. Based on their respective qualifications and locations workers may perform not all but just a few activities of a process, possibly even alternatingly for two or more

---

* Corresponding author.

S. Rinderle-Ma et al. (Eds.): BPM 2009 Workshops, LNBIP 43, pp. 81–91, 2010.

processes. Additionally complexity increases by the possibility of emergencies (processes with high priorities) during operation which demand the immediate re-scheduling of closeby, adequately skilled workers.

The scheduling of workers in such environments is a challenging task. We introduce a new generalization of the Resource-Constrained Project Scheduling Problem, the Mobile Workforce Scheduling Problem with Multitask-Processes – MWSP-MP. This scheduling problem considers costs related to travel efforts, costs related to process execution by differently skilled workers, and process priority constraints. We formalize the problem and outline a method for inserting idle processes into an existing solution and an insertion heuristic for generating solutions from scratch.

The remainder of this article is organized as follows. Section 2 introduces the problem with an illustrating business process. Section 3 gives an overview of the related work. In section 4 we introduce the scheduling objectives and the resulting formulation of the problem. In section 5 we present an algorithm for inserting processes into the current solution. In the concluding section 6 we discuss further research.

2   Problem Illustration

We will illustrate the problem based on a mobile business process. The process discussed here is among the knowledge gained from a consulting project with a German gas and power supply. The project aims for the performance evaluation of the whole network maintenance department, considering workers' scheduling, assignment of assets to different regional subsidiaries, qualification gaps of working units, and the like.

Consider for instance the damage handling of the network maintenance unit of a utility. The top part of Fig. 1 shows a typical situation after a power cable is damaged, e.g. due to construction work. The damage occurs at location L3 while the cable runs from a substation at location L1 to another substation at location L2.

For the repair of the damage security concerns demand that the stations at L1 and L2 have to be turned off before and turned on again after the damage is fixed. The bottom part of Fig. 1 shows the resulting process as UML Activity Diagram. As long as the stations are turned off no energy is sold to customers connected between L1 and L2 (such customers can still draw electricity from the line if the cable ist damaged at only one point and no shortcut occurred during the damage). Thus and due to legal regulations demanding a minimum yearly uptime it is desirable to minimise the downtime of the line.

If the whole process outlined in Fig. 1 is associated to a time window (i.e. an interval defining the earliest possible start and the latest possible end of the process) or a maximum duration (as for power outages), all five tasks are closely coupled in time, while possibly far apart in space. Thus different workers may have to perform the different tasks to match the harsh time restrictions. For our example this means that different workers may turn the stations on and

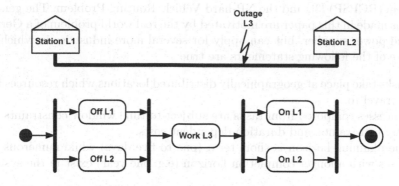

Fig. 1. Power line outage and maintenance process

off while a third team works at the site of the damage. It is thus necessary to create individual schedules (working plans) for the workers matching the time restrictions of the whole process. As a task performed by a mobile worker is part of a distinct *administrative* business process, processes with multiple mobile tasks to be performed at multiple locations by multiple workers add a new dimension by forming a cross sectional *functional* process.

If we consider the aim to reduce travel efforts while preserving the service quality of all processes (i.e. the priority-dependent accomplishment) in the system, it is obvious, that the workers have to perform tasks in both different administrative processes and different functional processes close to their respective locations (see Fig. 2; W1 – W3 denote workers). The resulting overlap of concerns of workers' schedules turns actually independent processes into interdependent processes, since both processes and traveling/working are subject to time restrictions. In this way delays that occur at a certain site may cause massive delays and thus increasing costs at completely different sites and processes.

For increasing numbers of processes and workers the generation of the worker's schedules becomes a challenging task. The problem of scheduling of mobile workers generalizes both the NP-hard Resource-Constrained Project Scheduling

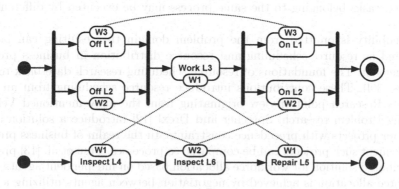

Fig. 2. Process interdependencies

Problem (RCPSP) [3], and the NP-hard Vehicle Routing Problem. The generalizations made in this paper are motivated by the real world problem of a German
gas and power supplier, but can apply for several more industries in which one
or more of the following statements are true:

1. Tasks take place at geographically distributed locations which resources have
   to travel to.
2. Processes composed from tasks are subject to time window constraints, priority constraints, and duration dependent costs.
3. The planning horizon is short term (one to five days) while numerous processes with a longer completion horizon (e.g. one year) exist in the system.

In this work we present a mathematical formulation of the Mobile Workforce
Scheduling Problem with Multitask-Processes (MWSP-MP) by adapting the way
the class of RCPSPs is usually formulated [4] and a first simple algorithm for
the insertion of processes and the generation of an initial solution.

3   Related Work

Several problems are related to our work. In the case where each process consists of exactly one task, the problem can be interpreted as a variant of the
Vehicle Routing Problem with Time Windows. Comprehensive surveys on the
Vehicle Routing Problem (VRP) and the VRP with Time Windows are given by
[5] and [6]. Different skills and qualifications of resources can be interpreted as
order/vehicle compatibility constraints which are commonly used for the Heterogeneous Fleet VRP which recently was surveyed by [7]. There are several generalizations of the VRP in which each transportation request consists of more
than one task. In the Pickup and Delivery Problem [8,9] each transportation
request consists of exactly one pickup task and one delivery task. In the General
Pickup and Delivery Problem [10] and the General Vehicle Routing Problem [11]
transportation requests may include multiple pickup and delivery tasks. These
problems have in common, that all tasks belonging to one transportation request
must be executed by the same vehicle. In the problem considered in this paper,
however, tasks belonging to the same process may be executed by different resources.

If mobility is omitted from the problem domain the resulting can be interpreted as resource-scheduling and resource distribution in business process
management. The foundations of resource scheduling research date back to the
1990ies [3,4]. These contributions introduce resource scheduling from an Operations Research point-of-view originating from the abovementioned Vehicle
Routing Problem research. Sprecher and Drexl [12] introduce a solution algorithm for projects with precedence constraints. In the realm of business process
management such projects can be compared to processes. Ursu et al. [13] present
a distributed solution for workforce allocation based on independent agents. The
workforce allocation is achieved by negotiation between agents utilizing a specialized communication protocol. Russell et al. introduce a series of 43 Workflow

resource patterns in [14]. A discussion of organizational aspects of resource management is given in [15]. Netjes et al. [16] introduce a Colored Petri Net [17] based model for the analysis of resource utilization and perform several examinations regarding the skill balancing and resource allocation order in banking processes. In-depth Petri net based modeling and analysis of work distribution mechanisms of the Workflow Management Systems Staffware, FileNet, and FLOWer is presented in [18]. Further research by Pesic and van der Aalst focuses on the development of a reference model for work distribution in Workflow Management Systems [19]. They focus on the general lifecycle of work items and introduce a CPN based approach for the distribution of work items to resources at runtime. Though most of the work depicted above had creative influence on our work none covers the properties of mobile process environments.

Resource allocation in mobile process environments has been in the focus of the following work. An automated resource management system (ARMS) for British Telecom is introduced in [20]. The system is intended for forecasting and analysis of resource demands and executes the dispatching of jobs to resources but does not handle precedence relations of chained tasks and process durations. Cowling et al. introduce a similar problem in [21]. They consider mobile processes with time window restrictions, skill demands, and precedence constraints applying to tasks. The determination of tasks to be performed is based on static priority values of the tasks with the objective to perform a maximum of highly prioritized tasks. Complex processes consisting of several tasks and implications of process durations are not considered. Our problem in opposition considers the process as a whole with related constraints.

4   The Mobile Workforce Scheduling Problem with Multitask-Processes (MWSP-MP)

In this section we will introduce the foundations and parameters of the MWSP-MP based on the properties of the processes it is suited for. We assume that numerous processes are well known in advance and have a long execution horizon (e. g. annual inspections have to be performed in the current year without further timing restrictions given). Such processes usually have a very low priority at the beginning of the year. Additionally higher prioritized processes show up dynamically and usually have a shorter execution horizon (same day to one month). An example is the repair of failed equipment. Since processes are subject to priorities we want to execute processes with higher priority first. Nonetheless, due to legal regulations all processes ultimately have to be performed during their respective execution horizon (up to one year). The planning horizon is too short (one day to one week) to plan all processes present. To avoid low processes being postponed over and over we consider to dynamically increase priorities of actually low priority processes gradually whenever the next planning horizon is due. This is subject to the preprocessing of the data before scheduling, not to the scheduling algorithm itself. For any process considered all or none tasks have to be performed.

Based on the nature of the processes in question process costs are determined by the duration of process execution. For the example in Fig. 1 this means, that the process is more expensive the longer the stations L1 and L2 and the according connected consumers are shut down. Further costs arise by the travel times and travel distances of the workforce. Accordingly we want the workforce to travel as sparse as possible.

Let us denote the set of all processes by $\mathcal{P}$. Each $p \in \mathcal{P}$ is associated with a priority value π_p. For each process $p \in \mathcal{P}$ let $\mathcal{T}_p$ denote the set of tasks belonging to process p. Each task $\tau \in \mathcal{T}_p$ may require some skills (qualifications) for performing the task. These skill requirements are represented by a vector $q^\tau := (q_1^\tau, \ldots, q_k^\tau)$, where k represents the number of different skills a resource may have. Let $\mathcal{C}_p \subset \mathcal{T}_p \times \mathcal{T}_p$ denote the set of precedence constraints associated to process p. These constraints require that for each pair of tasks $\tau, \tau' \in \mathcal{T}_p$ with $(\tau, \tau') \in \mathcal{C}_p$ task τ must be completed before task τ' may be started. For each pair $(\tau, \tau') \in \mathcal{T}_p \times \mathcal{T}_p$ let $c_{\tau,\tau'}$ denote the costs arising at each unit of time between the beginning of task τ and the completion of task τ'. In the example in Figure 1, these costs may represent the costs per unit of time during which stations L1 and L2 are shut down.

Let us denote the set of all resources (workers) by $\mathcal{R}$. Each worker $r \in \mathcal{R}$ has specific skills represented by a vector $q^r = (q_1^r, \ldots, q_k^r)$. For each resource $r \in \mathcal{R}$ let n_r denote the resource's depot. Let $\mathcal{D} := \{n_r \mid r \in \mathcal{R}\}$ denote the set of all depots. Note that for any two resources $r, r' \in \mathcal{R}$ we assume that $n_r \neq n_{r'}$, even if the depot of the two different resources is located at the same geographical position.

Let

$$\mathcal{N} := \mathcal{D} \cup \bigcup_{p \in \mathcal{P}} \mathcal{T}_p$$

and

$$\mathcal{A} := \mathcal{N} \times \mathcal{N} \setminus \{(n,n) \in \mathcal{N} \times \mathcal{N} \mid n \notin \mathcal{D}\}$$

For each resource $r \in \mathcal{R}$ and each arc $(n,m) \in \mathcal{A}$ let c_{nm}^r and d_{nm}^r denote the nonnegative costs and duration for traveling from n to m. For each resource $r \in \mathcal{R}$ and each task $\tau \in \bigcup_{p \in \mathcal{P}} \mathcal{T}_p$ let s_τ^r denote the service time resource r needs for performing task τ.

The Mobile Workforce Scheduling Problem with Multitask-Processes (MWSP-MP) is then modeled using the binary variables x_{nm}^r indicating whether resource r visits node m immediately after node n ($x_{nm}^r = 1$), or not ($x_{nm}^r = 0$), the binary variables y_n^r indicating whether resource r visits node n ($y_n^r = 1$), or not ($y_n^r = 0$), and the continuous variables t_n indicating the arrival time at node n.

The resulting (bi-objective) MWSP-MP is

minimize

$$\sum_{r \in \mathcal{R}} \sum_{(n,m) \in \mathcal{A}} x_{nm}^r c_{nm}^r +$$

$$\sum_{p \in \mathcal{P}} \sum_{(\tau,\tau') \in \mathcal{T}_p \times \mathcal{T}_p} \sum_{r \in \mathcal{R}} y_{\tau'}^r (t_{\tau'} + s_{\tau'}^r - t_\tau) c_{\tau,\tau'} \tag{1}$$

maximize

$$\sum_{p \in \mathcal{P}} \pi_p \frac{\sum_{\tau \in \mathcal{T}_p} \sum_{r \in \mathcal{R}} y_\tau^r}{|\mathcal{T}_p|} \tag{2}$$

subject to

$$\sum_{(n,m) \in \mathcal{A}} x_{nm}^r = \sum_{(m,n) \in \mathcal{A}} x_{mn}^r \text{ for all } r \in \mathcal{R}, n \in \mathcal{N} \tag{3}$$

$$\sum_{r \in \mathcal{R}} \sum_{(n,m) \in \mathcal{A}} x_{nm}^r = y_n^r \text{ for all } n \in \mathcal{N} \tag{4}$$

$$y_{n_r}^r = 1 \text{ for all } r \in \mathcal{R} \tag{5}$$

$$\sum_{r \in \mathcal{R}} y_n^r \leq 1 \text{ for all } n \in \mathcal{N} \tag{6}$$

$$\sum_{\tau' \in \mathcal{T}_p} \sum_{r \in R} y_{\tau'}^r = |\mathcal{T}_p| \sum_{r \in R} y_\tau^r \text{ for all } p \in \mathcal{P}, \tau \in \mathcal{T}_p \tag{7}$$

$$x_{nm}^r = 1 \Rightarrow t_n + s_n^r + d_{nm}^r \leq t_m$$
$$\text{for all } r \in \mathcal{R}, (n,m) \in \mathcal{A} \mid m \neq n_r \tag{8}$$

$$y_n^r = 1 \Rightarrow t_n^{min} \leq t_n \leq t_n^{max} - s_n^r$$
$$\text{for all } r \in \mathcal{R}, n \in \mathcal{N} \tag{9}$$

$$y_n^r = 1 \Rightarrow q^n \leq q^r \text{ for all } r \in \mathcal{R}, n \in \mathcal{N} \tag{10}$$

$$x_{nm}^r \in \{0,1\} \text{ for all } r \in \mathcal{R}, (n,m) \in \mathcal{A}$$
$$y_n^r \in \{0,1\} \text{ for all } r \in \mathcal{R}, n \in \mathcal{N} \tag{11}$$

Objective (1) is to minimize travel costs plus process execution costs. Note, that if resource r executes task τ', $(t_{\tau'} + s_{\tau'}^r) - t_\tau$ represents the time between the begin of task τ and the end of task τ', and that $y_{\tau'}^r = 1$ for at most one resource. Objective (2) is to maximize the sum of all priorities associated to processes performed. Equation (3) represents the flow conservation constraints forcing that each node $n \in \mathcal{N}$ will be left after being reached by a resource. (4) assures that the values of binary variables x_{nm}^r and y_n^r are well defined. (5) assures that each resource departs from its depot. (6) and (7) guarantee that each node is visited at most one and that either all tasks associated to a process are performed or none. Equations (8) and (9) represent time windows constraints. (10) represents skill constraints, imposing that only resources with appropriate qualifications can execute tasks. Note that the operator $\leq$ is defined to compare vectors element-wise. Finally equation (11) imposes that the values of x_{nm}^r and y_n^r are binary.

5   Solution Approach

This section describes a method for inserting idle processes into the current solution and outlines a solution algorithm for the MWSP-MP. For each process $p \in \mathcal{P}$ and each task $\tau \in \mathcal{T}_p$ let us define precedence indices i_τ in such a way that i_τ represents the length of the longest path from a task without predecessors to τ in the network defined by $\mathcal{T}_p$ and $\mathcal{C}_p$ (see Fig. 3). All arcs defined by $\mathcal{C}_p$ are assumed to have length 1.

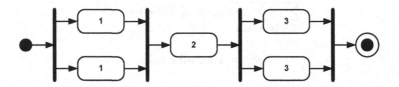

Fig. 3. Precedence of tasks

$$S := \{s\}$$
$$\textbf{for } i = 1 \textbf{ to } max\{i_\tau | \tau \in \mathcal{T}_p\} \textbf{ do}$$
$$\quad \textbf{for all } \tau \in \mathcal{T}_p \textbf{ with } i_\tau = i \textbf{ do}$$
$$\quad\quad S^* = \emptyset$$
$$\quad\quad \textbf{for all } r \in R \textbf{ with } q^\tau \le q^r \textbf{ do}$$
$$\quad\quad\quad \textbf{for all } s \in S \textbf{ do}$$
$$\quad\quad\quad\quad \textbf{for } j = 1 \textbf{ to } \lambda_r^s - 1 \textbf{ do}$$
$$\quad\quad\quad\quad\quad s^* = insert(s,r,\tau,j)$$
$$\quad\quad\quad\quad\quad \textbf{if } s^* \textbf{ is feasible then}$$
$$\quad\quad\quad\quad\quad\quad S^* \leftarrow S^* \cup \{s^*\}$$
$$\quad\quad\quad\quad\quad \textbf{end if}$$
$$\quad\quad\quad\quad \textbf{end for}$$
$$\quad\quad\quad \textbf{end for}$$
$$\quad\quad \textbf{end for}$$
$$\quad\quad S = S^*$$
$$\quad \textbf{end for}$$
$$\textbf{end for}$$

Fig. 4. Algorithm for process insertion

Given an initial solution s of the MWSP-MP let $\sigma_r^s = (\tau_1, \ldots, \tau_{\lambda_r^s})$ be the work plan of resource $r \in R$. A process $p \in P$ can be inserted into the solution using the algorithm outlined in Fig. 4.

In this algorithm $insert(s,r,\tau,j)$ inserts task τ between positions j and $j+1$ in the schedule of resource r. We assume that throughout this algorithm all time values are set to the first possible value complying with time window and precedence constraints. Under this assumption the verification whether the solution obtained by this operation is feasible is relatively easy. However, compliance with

s = empty schedule
repeat
  1. chose (previously not selected) process $p \in P$ with highest priority π_p
  2. determine cheapest insertion possibility and insert p to schedule s (if possible)
until no further feasible insertion is possible

Fig. 5. Insertion heuristic

time window and precedence constraints must be carefully verified for all succeeding tasks. This algorithm either terminates with a set of feasible solutions S or with an empty set if no feasible insertion is possible. Depending on process execution costs, the start times of certain tasks may be shifted to later points in time to minimize total costs. Among all feasible solutions in S the one with lowest costs can be chosen.

Let us now outline an algorithm (see Fig. 5) for determining solutions from scratch using above method in an iterative way. The insertion heuristic iteratively choses the idle process with highest priority value and inserts it to the current solution using the algorithm for process insertion described above.

By this the heuristic simultaneously keeps an eye on maximizing priorities and minimizing costs. The solution obtained by this insertion heuristic can be further improved by meta-heuristic approaches such as Large Neighbourhood Search [22]. Further work will evaluate the effectiveness of the outlined insertion algorithm and different improvement methods.

6 Conclusion

We introduced a new generalization of the Resource-Constrained Project Scheduling Problem, the Mobile Workforce Scheduling Problem with Multitask-Processes – MWSP-MP. We presented a formulation of the problem and outlined a method for inserting idle processes into an existing solution and an insertion heuristic for generating solutions from scratch. Nonetheless this is work in progress, and we are currently implementing the algorithms and evaluate them. For this purpose we obtained real world data in terms of the network structure from a German power and gas supply serving 500.000 customers and covering an area of 7000 km^2. Additionally the process environment in question has to deal with process interruption and the rollback of interrupted tasks. This may occur if highly prioritized processes require currently working resources to participate in the remedy of defects immediately. The according constraints will be introduced into the problem. Our research aims at a scheduling algorithm to be utilized in business process simulation [23] for the optimization of mobile process environments.

Acknowledgment

The Chair of Applied Telematics/e-Business at the University of Leipzig is endowed by Deutsche Telekom AG.

References

1. Gruhn, V., Köhler, A., Klawes, R.: Modeling and analysis of mobile business processes. Journal of Enterprise Information Management 20(6), 657 (2007)
2. Luff, P., Heath, C.: Mobility in collaboration. In: Proceedings of the 1998 ACM Conference on Computer supported cooperative work, pp. 305–314. ACM Press, New York (1998)
3. Kolisch, R.: Serial and parallel resource-constrained project scheduling methods revisited: Theory and computation. European Journal of Operational Research 90(2), 320–333 (1996)
4. Brucker, P., Drexl, A., Möhring, R., Neumann, K., Pesch, E.: Resource-constrained project scheduling: Notation, classification, models, and methods. European Journal of Operational Research 112(1), 3–41 (1999)
5. Laporte, G., Semet, F.: Classical heuristics for the capacitated vrp. In: Toth, P., Vigo, D. (eds.) The Vehicle Routing Problem. SIAM Monographs on Discrete Mathematics and Applications, Philadelphia, pp. 109–128 (2002)
6. Cordeau, F.J., Desaulniers, G., Desrosiers, J., Solomon, M., Soumis, F.: Vrp with time windows. In: Toth, P., Vigo, D. (eds.) The Vehicle Routing Problem. SIAM Monographs on Discrete Mathematics and Applications, Philadelphia, pp. 157–193 (2002)
7. Baldacci, R., Battarra, M., Vigo, D.: Routing a heterogeneous fleet of vehicles. In: The Vehicle Routing Problem: Latest Advances and New Challenges. Operations Research/Computer Science Interfaces Series, vol. 43, pp. 3–27. Springer, Heidelberg (2008)
8. Parragh, S., Doerner, K., Hartl, R.: A survey on pickup and delivery problems - part i: Transportation between customers and depot. Journal für Betriebswirtschaft 58(1), 21–51 (2008)
9. Parragh, S., Doerner, K., Hartl, R.: A survey on pickup and delivery problems - part ii: Transportation between pickup and delivery locations. Journal für Betriebswirtschaft 58(2), 81–117 (2008)
10. Savelsbergh, W.P.M., Sol, M.: The general pickup and delivery problem. Transportation Science 29(1), 17–30 (1995)
11. Goel, A., Gruhn, V.: A general vehicle routing problem. European Journal of Operational Research 191(3), 650–660 (2008)
12. Sprecher, A., Drexl, A.: Multi-mode resource-constrained project scheduling by a simple, general and powerful sequencing algorithm. European Journal of Operational Research 107(2), 431–450 (1998)
13. Ursu, F.M.: Distributed resource allocation via local choices: A case study of workforce allocation. International Journal of Knowledge-Based and Intelligent Engineering Systems 9(4), 293–301 (2005)
14. Russell, N., van der Aalst, M.P.W., ter Hofstede, H.M.A., Edmond, D.: Workflow resource patterns. In: Pastor, Ó., Falcão e Cunha, J. (eds.) CAiSE 2005. LNCS, vol. 3520, pp. 216–232. Springer, Heidelberg (2005)
15. Zur Muehlen, M.: Organizational management in workflow applications - issues and perspectives. Information Technology and Management 5(3), 271–291 (2004)
16. Netjes, M., van der Aalst, M.P.W., Reijers, A.H.: Analysis of resource-constrained processes with colored petri nets. In: Sixth Workshop and Tutorial on Practical Use of Coloured Petri Nets and the CPN Tools (2005)
17. Jensen, K.: Coloured Petri nets: basic concepts, analysis methods and practical use, 2nd edn., vol. 1. Springer-Verlag, London, UK (1996)

18. Pesic, M., van der Aalst, M.P.W.: Modelling work distribution mechanisms using colored petri nets. International Journal on Software Tools for Technology Transfer (STTT) 9(3), 327–352 (2007)
19. Pesic, M., van der Aalst, M.P.W.: Towards a reference model for work distribution in workflow management systems. Business Process Reference Models
20. Voudouris, C., Owusu, K.G., Dorne, J.H.R., Ladde, C., Virginas, B.: Arms: An automated resource management system for british telecommunications plc. European Journal of Operational Research 171(3), 951–961 (2006)
21. Cowling, P., Colledge, N., Dahal, K., Remde, S.: The trade off between diversity and quality for multi-objective workforce scheduling. In: Gottlieb, J., Raidl, G.R. (eds.) EvoCOP 2006. LNCS, vol. 3906, pp. 13–24. Springer, Heidelberg (2006)
22. Shaw, P.: A new local search algorithm providing high quality solutions to vehicle routing problems. APES Group, Dept. of Computer Science, University of Strathclyde, Glasgow, Scotland, UK (1997)
23. Gruhn, V., Richter, T.: A general model of mobile environments: Simulation support for strategic management decisions. In: Proceedings of the 2nd International Workshop on Personalization in Grid and Service Computing, PGSC 2008 (2008)

Understanding Spaghetti Models with Sequence Clustering for ProM

Gabriel M. Veiga and Diogo R. Ferreira

IST – Technical University of Lisbon
Avenida Prof. Dr. Cavaco Silva
2744-016 Porto Salvo, Portugal
{gabriel.veiga,diogo.ferreira}@tagus.ist.utl.pt

Abstract. The goal of process mining is to discover process models from event logs. However, for processes that are not well structured and have a lot of diverse behavior, existing process mining techniques generate highly complex models that are often difficult to understand; these are called spaghetti models. One way to try to understand these models is to divide the log into clusters in order to analyze reduced sets of cases. However, the amount of noise and ad-hoc behavior present in real-world logs still poses a problem, as this type of behavior interferes with the clustering and complicates the models of the generated clusters, affecting the discovery of patterns. In this paper we present an approach that aims at overcoming these difficulties by extracting only the useful data and presenting it in an understandable manner. The solution has been implemented in ProM and is divided in two stages: preprocessing and sequence clustering. We illustrate the approach in a case study where it becomes possible to identify behavioral patterns even in the presence of very diverse and confusing behavior.

Keywords: Process Mining, Preprocessing, Sequence Clustering, ProM, Markov Chains, Event Logs, Hierarchical Clustering, Process Models.

1 Introduction

The main application of process mining is the discovery of process models. For processes with a lot of different cases and high diversity of behavior, the models generated tend to be very confusing and difficult to understand. These models are usually called *spaghetti models*. Clustering techniques have been investigated as a means to deal with this complexity by dividing cases into clusters, leading to less confusing models. However, results may still suffer from the presence of certain unusual cases that include noise and ad-hoc behavior, which are common in real-world environments. Usually this type of behavior is not relevant to understand a process and it unnecessarily complicates the discovered models.

In this paper we present an approach that is able to deal with these problems by means of sequence clustering techniques. This is a kind of model-based clustering that partitions the cases according to the order in which events occurred. For the purpose of this work the model used to represent each cluster is

S. Rinderle-Ma et al. (Eds.): BPM 2009 Workshops, LNBIP 43, pp. 92–103, 2010.
© Springer-Verlag Berlin Heidelberg 2010

a first-order Markov Chain. The fact that this clustering is probabilistic makes it suitable to deal with logs containing many different types of behavior, possibly non-recurrent behavior as well. When sequence clustering is applied, the log is divided into a number of clusters and the correspondent Markov Chains are generated. Additionally, the approach also comprises a preprocessing stage, where the goal is to clean the log of certain events that will only complicate the clustering method and its results. If after both techniques are applied the models are still confusing, sequence clustering can be re-applied hierarchically within each cluster until understandable results are obtained. This approach has been implemented in ProM [1], an extensible framework for process mining that already includes many techniques to address challenges in this area.

The paper is organized as follows: Section 2 provides an overview of existing work involving clustering and process mining. Section 3 presents the proposed approach, including the preprocessing stage and the sequence clustering algorithm. Section 4 demonstrates the approach in a real-world case study where the goal was to understand the typical behavior of faults in an application server. Section 5 concludes this paper.

2   Clustering in Process Mining

When generating process models, conventional control-flow mining techniques tend to over-generalize. In the attempt to represent all the different behavior present in the log these techniques create models that allow for more behavior than the one actually observed. When a log has process instances with very different behavior the generated models are even more complex and confusing. One way to address the problem is by means of clustering techniques [2].

One such approach has already been implemented in ProM and is known as the *Disjunctive Workflow Schema* (DWS) mining plug-in [3]. According to this methodology, first the complete log is examined and a model is generated using the *HeuristicsMiner* [4]. If the model generated is optimal and no over-generalization is detected the approach stops, otherwise the log is divided into clusters using the *K-means* clustering method. If the cluster models still allow for too much behavior the clusters are repartitioned and so on until optimal models are achieved.

Trace Clustering [5] is another technique implemented in ProM that aims at partitioning the log by grouping similar sequences together. The motivation for this technique is the existence of flexible environments, where the execution of processes does not follow a rigid set of rules. This approach makes use of *distance-based clustering* along with profiles, with the purpose of reducing the diversity and the complexity of models by lowering the number of cases analyzed at once. Each profile is composed by a set of features that describe and numerically classify a case from a particular perspective. Distance metrics (like the Euclidean distance or the Hamming distance) are then used to calculate the distance between two cases. Clustering methods such as *K-means Clustering* or *Self-Organizing Maps* (SOM) can then be used to group closely related cases into the same cluster. Recent work in trace clustering includes the use of an edit distance between sequences, where the cost of edit operations can be determined by taking into account the context of an event within a sequence [6].

3 Sequence Clustering for ProM

Like the techniques described above, sequence clustering can take a set of sequences and group them into clusters, so that similar types of sequence are placed in the same cluster. But in contrast with the above techniques, sequence clustering is performed directly on the input sequences, as opposed to being performed on features extracted from those sequences. Sequence clustering has been extensively used in the field of bioinformatics, for example to classify large protein datasets into different families [7]. Process mining also deals with sequences, but instead of aminoacids the sequences contain events that have occurred during the execution of a given process. Sequence clustering techniques are therefore a natural candidate to perform clustering on workflow logs.

3.1 Sequence Clustering

The sequence clustering algorithm used here is based on first-order Markov chains [8,9]. Each cluster is represented by the corresponding Markov chain and by all the sequences assigned to it. For the purpose of process mining it becomes useful to augment the simple Markov chain model with two dummy states: the input and the output state. This is necessary in order to represent the probability of a given event being the first or the last event in a sequence, which may become useful to distinguish between some types of sequences. The use of input and output states is an extension to the work described in [10].

Figure 1 shows a simple example of such a chain depicted in ProM via the sequence clustering plug-in developed in this work. In this figure, darker elements (both states and transitions) are more recurrent than lighter ones. By analyzing the color of elements and the probability associated with each transition it is possible to decide which elements should be kept for analysis, and which elements can be discarded. For example, one may choose to remove transitions that have very low probabilities, so that only the most typical behavior can be analyzed. Although this kind of model is not as expressive as a Petri net, it can be useful to understand and apply post-processing to the generated cluster models.

The assignment of sequences to clusters is based on the probability of each cluster producing the given sequence. In general, a given sequence will be assigned to the cluster that is able to produce it with higher probability. Let ($\circ$) and ($\bullet$) denote the input and output states, respectively. To calculate the probability of a sequence $\bar{x} = \{\circ, x_1, x_2, \cdots, x_L, \bullet\}$ being produced by cluster c_k the following formula is used:

$$p\left(x \mid c_k\right) = p\left(x_1 \mid \circ; c_k\right) \cdot \left[\prod_{i=2}^{L} p\left(x_i \mid x_{i-1}; c_k\right)\right] \cdot p\left(\bullet \mid x_L; c_k\right) \tag{1}$$

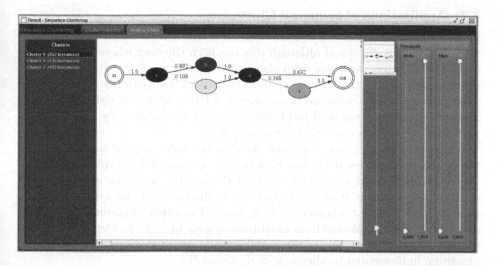

Fig. 1. Example of a cluster model displayed in the sequence clustering plug-in

where $p\left(x_i \mid x_{i-1}; c_k\right)$ is the transition probability from x_{i-1} to x_i in the Markov chain associated with cluster c_k. This formula handles the input and output states in the same way as any other regular state that corresponds to an event.

The goal of sequence clustering is to estimate these parameters for all clusters c_k (with $k = 1, 2, \ldots, K$) based on a set of input sequences. For that purpose, the algorithm relies on an Expectation–Maximization procedure [11] to improve the model parameters iteratively. For a given number of clusters K the algorithm proceeds as follows:

1. Initialize randomly the state transition probabilities of the Markov chains associated with each cluster.
2. For all input sequences, assign each sequence to the cluster that can produce it with higher probability according to equation (1).
3. Compute the state transition probabilities of the Markov chain of each cluster, considering the sequences that were assigned to that cluster in step 2.
4. Repeat steps 2 and 3 until the assignment of sequences to clusters does not change, and hence the cluster models do not change either.

In other words, first we randomly distribute the sequences into the clusters (steps 1 and 2), then in step 3 we re-estimate the cluster models (Markov chains and their transition probabilities) according to the sequences assigned to each cluster. After this first iteration we re-assign the sequences to clusters and again re-estimate the cluster models (steps 2 and 3). These two steps are executed repeatedly until the algorithm converges. The result is a set of Markov models that describe the behavior of each cluster. In this work we have implemented this algorithm as a sequence clustering plug-in for ProM.

3.2   Applications of Sequence Clustering

Sequence clustering algorithms have been an active field of research in the area of bioinformatics [7,12] and although this has been the area where it finds most applications, some work has been done with this type of algorithms in other areas as well. In [8], the authors analyze the navigation patterns on a website, where these patterns consisted of sequences of URL categories visited by users. Sequence clustering was used to identify common user profiles by placing users with similar navigation paths in the same cluster.

Sequence clustering has also been used in the field of process mining [10], where the authors described two experiments of identifying typical behavior. One experiment used an event log collected manually from the activities of a software development team, and allowed the discovery of the typical interaction patterns between members of that team. The other experiment was conducted over traces collected from a datavase system in order to identify common routines. In both experiments the authors made use of the sequence clustering algorithm implemented in Microsoft SQL Server [13].

3.3   Preprocessing

Although the sequence clustering algorithm described above is robust to noise, all sequences must ultimately be assigned to a cluster. If a sequence is very uncommon and different from all the others it will affect the probabilistic model of that cluster and in the end will make it harder to interpret the model of that cluster. To avoid this problem, some preprocessing must be done to the input sequences prior to applying sequence clustering. This preprocessing can be seen as a way to clean the dataset of undesired events and also a way to eliminate undesirable sequences. For example, undesired events can be those that occur only very rarely, and undesired sequences can be single-step sequences that have only one event.

Some of the steps that can be performed during preprocessing are described in [9] and include, for example, dropping events and sequences with low support. In this work we have extended these steps by allowing not only the least but also the most recurring events and sequences to be discarded. This was motivated by the fact that in some real-world applications the log is filled with some very frequent but unrelated events that must be removed in order to allow the analysis to focus on the relevant behavior. Spaghetti models are often cluttered with events that occur very often but only contribute to obscure the process model one aims to discover.

The preprocessing steps implemented within the sequence clustering plug-in are optional and configurable. They focus on the following features:

1. *Event type* – The events recorded in a MXML log file [14] may represent different points in the lifetime of workflow activities, such as the start or completion of a given activity. For sequence clustering what is important is the order of activity execution, so we retain only one type of event and that is usually the completion event for each activity. Therefore only events of type "complete" are kept after this step.

2. *Event support* – Some events may be so infrequent that they are not relevant for the purpose of discovering typical behavior. These events should be removed in order to facilitate analysis. On the other hand, some events may be so frequent that they too became irrelevant and even undesirable if they hide the behavior one aims to discover. Therefore, this preprocessing can remove events both with too low and too high support.

3. *Consecutive repetitions* – Sequence clustering is a means to analyze the transitions between states in a process. If an event is followed by an equal event then it should be considered only once, since the state of the process has not changed. Consecutive repetitions are therefore removed, for example: the sequence $A \rightarrow C \rightarrow C \rightarrow D$ becomes $A \rightarrow C \rightarrow D$.

4. *Sequence length* – After the previous preprocessing steps, it may happen that some sequences collapse to only a few events or even to a single event. This preprocessing step provides the possibility to discard those sequences. It also provides the possibility to discard exceedingly long sequences which can have undesirable effects in the analysis results. Sequence length can therefore be limited to a certain range.

5. *Sequence support* – Some sequences may be rather unique so that they hardly contribute to the discovery of typical behavior. In principle the previous preprocessing steps will prevent the existence of such sequences at this stage but, as with events, sequences that occur very rarely can be removed from the dataset. In some applications such as fault detection it may be useful to actually discard the most common sequences and focus instead on the less frequent ones, so sequence support can also be limited to a certain range.

The order presented is the order in which the preprocessing steps should be applied, because if the steps are applied in a different order the results may differ. For example, rare sequences should only be removed at the final stage, because previous steps may transform them into common sequences. Imagining we have the rare sequence $A \rightarrow B \rightarrow C \rightarrow D$, but in step 2 state B is considered to have low support and is removed, then it becomes $A \rightarrow C \rightarrow D$. This new sequence might not be a rare sequence and therefore should not be removed.

3.4   Implementation within ProM

The above preprocessing steps and the sequence clustering algorithm have been implemented and are available as a new plug-in for the process mining framework ProM[1]. Figure 2 shows the inputs and outputs for this plug-in.

The preprocessing stage receives an input log in MXML format [14] and also some options provided by the user, which specify the parameters to be used in the preprocessing steps described above. The result is a filtered log. This log is made available to the ProM framework, so that it may be analyzed with other plug-ins if desired. Instead of acting just as a first stage to sequence clustering, the preprocessing stage can also be used together with other types of analysis

---

[1] The ProM framework can be found at http://prom.win.tue.nl/tools/prom

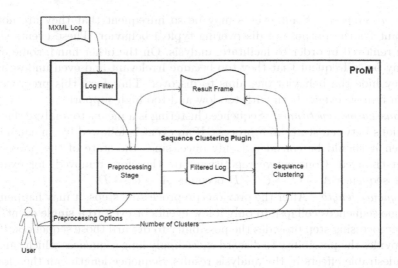

Fig. 2. Sequence Clustering plug-in in the ProM framework

available in the framework. Figure 3 presents a screenshot of this stage, depicting the options available for the user to pre-process the input log (top-right corner).

The sequence clustering stage receives the filtered log as input from the pre-processing stage and also the desired number of clusters. In general the plug-in will generate a solution with the provided number of clusters except when some clusters turn out to be empty. The plug-in provides special functionalities for visualizing the results, both in terms of sequences that belong to each cluster

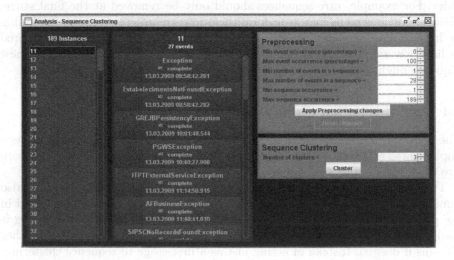

Fig. 3. Preprocessing stage for the Sequence Clustering plug-in

and in terms of the Markov chain for each cluster. Each cluster can be used again as an event log in ProM, so it becomes possible to further subdivide it into clusters, or for another process mining plug-in to analyze it. These features allow the user to drill-down through the behavior of clusters.

On one hand, sequence clustering is a mining plug-in that extracts models of behavior for the different behavioral patterns found in the event log. Figure 1 shows the type of results that the plug-in is able to present. When visualizing the results, the user can adjust thresholds that correspond to the minimum and maximum probability of both edges and nodes (right-hand side of fig.1). This allows the user to adjust what is shown in the graphical model by removing elements (both states and transitions) that are either too frequent or too rare. This feature facilitates the understanding of spaghetti models without having to re-run the algorithm again.

On the other hand, sequence clustering can also be regarded as an analysis plug-in since it generates new events logs that can be analyzed by other plug-ins available in the ProM framework. This is also useful for analyzing spaghetti models, which are hard to understand at first, but can be made simpler by dividing their complete behavior into a set of clusters that can be analyzed separately by other algorithms.

4   Case Study: Application Server Logs

Public administration and public services often have large-scale IT systems that serve thousands of users. These systems are usually backed by an infrastructure that involves replication, redundancy and load balancing. Due to the large number of replicated software applications and due to the large number of simultaneously connected users, it becomes exceedingly difficult to determine the cause for some malfunctions that produce instabilities that propagate across the system and negatively affect the experience of several users at the same time.

In this section we present one such case study based on the experience at a public institution. At the time the institution was struggling with complaints about a situation in which the applications would freeze or crash unexpectedly for several users at the same time. The applications are Java-based and were developed according to a client/server architecture where the end users had a fat client and the back-end was implemented as a set of Enterprise JavaBeans hosted in an application server that has been replicated across a server farm.

Since the root cause for this malfunction was hard to determine, we turned to the application server logs in order to study the exceptions that had been recorded for each Java thread. This proved to be quite difficult, not only for the overwhelming amount of exceptions being recorded all the time, but also for the fact that it was difficult to establish any causal relationship between those exceptions. Figure 4 depicts the result of a first attempt to analyze the application server logs using the heuristics miner [4].

Using the sequence clustering plug-in and its preprocessing capabilities, as well as the possibility of visually adjusting the cluster models according to certain

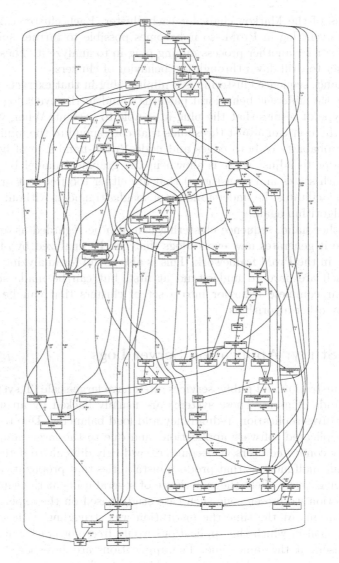

Fig. 4. Spaghetti model obtained from the application server logs using the heuristics miner

thresholds, it was possible to identify several patterns involving different types of exceptions. These patterns were found after several attempts of tuning with the preprocessing parameters, selecting the number of clusters (typically from 3 to 12) and applying thresholds to the cluster models in order to make them more understandable. Figure 5 shows a selection of four clusters from the analysis results. Each of these clusters represents about 10% of the sequences in the original event log.

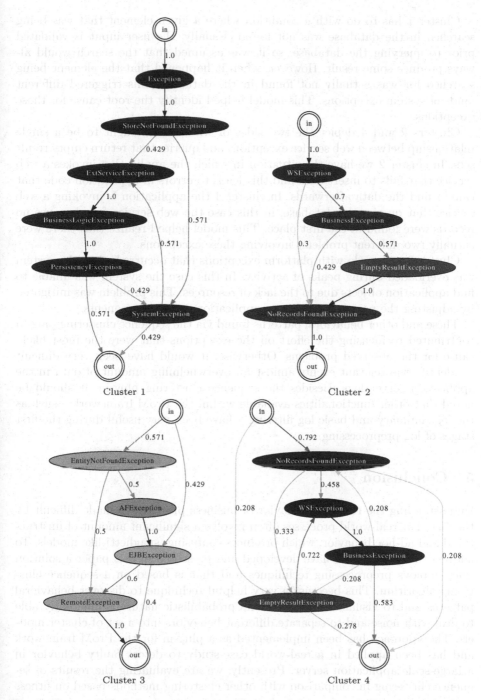

Fig. 5. Some of the behavioral patterns discovered from the application server logs using the sequence clustering plug-in

Cluster 1 has to do with a condition where a given element that was being searched in the database was not found. Usually, the user input is validated prior to querying the database, so it was assumed that the search would always produce some result. However, when it happened that the element being searched for was actually not found in the database, this triggered different kinds of system exceptions. This model helped identify the root cause for those exceptions.

Clusters 2 and 4 depict the two sides of what was thought to be a single relationship between web service exceptions and queries that return empty result sets. In cluster 2 we have the situation in which the application invokes a web service that fails to insert data and this leads to errors in application code that cannot find the data afterwards. In cluster 4 the application is invoking a web service that queries the database; in this case the web service fails because no records were found in the first place. This model helped realize that there were actually two different problems involving these exceptions.

Cluster 3 had to do with platform exceptions that occurred when the system was overloaded during peaks of activity. In this case the system was unable to find application objects due to the lack of resources. This problem was mitigated by adjusting the parameters of some application server components.

These and other behavioral patterns found via the sequence clustering plug-in contributed to focusing the effort on the exceptions that were the most likely cause for the observed problems. Otherwise, it would have been very difficult to identify the relevant events amidst an overwhelming amount of data in the application server logs. Besides the sequence clustering plug-in, it should be noted that other functionalities available within the ProM framework – such as the log summary and basic log filtering – have been very useful during the first stages of log preprocessing.

5 Conclusion

Understanding the run-time behavior of business processes is made difficult by the fact that real-world processes often involve a significant amount of unstructured and ad-hoc behavior, which produces confusing, spaghetti-like models. To address this problem we have developed and presented in this paper a solution that employs preprocessing techniques and that is based on a sequence clustering algorithm. This becomes a very helpful technique to discover behavioral patterns and to visualize them, since its probabilistic nature is inherently able to deal with noise and to separate different behaviors into a set of cluster models. The approach has been implemented as a plug-in for the ProM framework and has been applied in a real-world case-study to detect faulty behavior in a large-scale application server. Presently, we are evaluating the results of sequence clustering in comparison with other clustering methods based on fitness metrics.

References

1. van Dongen, B., de Medeiros, A.A., Verbeek, H., Weijters, A., van der Aalst, W.: The proM framework: A new era in process mining tool support. In: Ciardo, G., Darondeau, P. (eds.) ICATPN 2005. LNCS, vol. 3536, pp. 444–454. Springer, Heidelberg (2005)
2. Greco, G., Guzzo, A., Pontieri, L., Saccá, D.: Mining expressive process models by clustering workflow traces. In: Dai, H., Srikant, R., Zhang, C. (eds.) PAKDD 2004. LNCS (LNAI), vol. 3056, pp. 52–62. Springer, Heidelberg (2004)
3. de Medeiros, A.K.A., Guzzo, A., Greco, G., van der Aalst, W.M.P., Weijters, A.J.M.M.T., van Dongen, B.F., Saccà, D.: Process mining based on clustering: A quest for precision. In: ter Hofstede, A.H.M., Benatallah, B., Paik, H.-Y. (eds.) BPM Workshops 2007. LNCS, vol. 4928, pp. 17–29. Springer, Heidelberg (2008)
4. Weijters, A., van der Aalst, W., de Medeiros, A.A.: Process mining with the heuristicsminer algorithm. BETA Working Paper Series WP 166, Eindhoven University of Technology (2006)
5. Song, M., Günther, C., van der Aalst, W.: Trace clustering in process mining. In: Proceedings of the 4th Workshop on Business Process Intelligence (BPI 2008), BPM Workshops 2008, Milan, September 1 (2008)
6. Bose, R.P.J.C., van der Aalst, W.M.P.: Context aware trace clustering: Towards improving process mining results. In: SDM, pp. 401–412. SIAM, Philadelphia (2009)
7. Enright, A.J., Ouzounis, C.: Generage: a robust algorithm for sequence clustering and domain detection. Bioinformatics 16(5), 451–457 (2000)
8. Cadez, I., Heckerman, D., Meek, C., Smyth, P., White, S.: Model-based clustering and visualization of navigation patterns on a web site. Data Mining and Knowledge Discovery 7(4), 399–424 (2003)
9. Ferreira, D.: Applied sequence clustering techniques for process mining. In: Cardoso, J., van der Aalst, W. (eds.) Handbook of Research on Business Process Modeling. IGI Global (2009)
10. Ferreira, D., Zacarias, M., Malheiros, M., Ferreira, P.: Approaching process mining with sequence clustering: Experiments and findings. In: Alonso, G., Dadam, P., Rosemann, M. (eds.) BPM 2007. LNCS, vol. 4714, pp. 360–374. Springer, Heidelberg (2007)
11. Dempster, A., Laird, N., Rubin, D.: Maximum likelihood from incomplete data via the EM algorithm. Journal of the Royal Statistical Society, Series B 39(1), 1–38 (1977)
12. Enright, A.J., van Dongen, S., Ouzounis, C.: An efficient algorithm for large-scale detection of protein families. Nucleic Acids Research 30(7), 1575–1584 (2002)
13. Tang, Z., MacLennan, J.: Data Mining with SQL Server 2005, ch. 8 pp. 209–227. Wiley Publishing, Inc., Chichester (2005)
14. van Dongen, B., van der Aalst, W.: A meta model for process mining data. In: Casto, J., Teniente, E. (eds.) Proceedings of the CAiSE 2005 Workshops (EMOI-INTEROP Workshop), FEUP, Porto, Portugal, vol. 2, pp. 309–320 (2005)

Flexible Multi-dimensional Visualization of Process Enactment Data

Thomas Heer, Christoph Außem, and René Wörzberger

RWTH Aachen University, 52074 Aachen, Germany
{heer,aussem,woerzberger}@se.rwth-aachen.de
http://se.rwth-aachen.de

Abstract. The management of development processes is a challenging task and needs adequate tool support. In the course of a development project, many different engineering and management processes are enacted and have to be controlled. The management data has an inherently multidimensional character. Most project and process management systems fail to present large multidimensional datasets in an adequate way. This paper describes a flexible approach, which leverages OLAP technology for the processing and visualization of multidimensional project management data in the plant engineering domain. The management data includes the execution traces and the progress measures of all workflows in an engineering project. The aggregation and visualization of this data facilitates the analysis of a huge number of process instances which is a prerequisite for process improvement.

Keywords: Business process visualization, Data warehousing, Monitoring of business processes.

1 Introduction

The four key responsibilities of *process management* are the definition, measurement, control and improvement of processes [1]. These activities form a *continual improvement cycle*, which applies in particular to the management of development processes. In a development project, many different, *flexible, collaborative processes* are executed and the project as a whole constitutes one instance of a development process. *Process management* is a means to improve the efficiency and performance of projects in an organization. The prerequisite for *process improvement* is the *measurement and analysis* of the enacted processes [1]. In large projects, software tool-support in is needed for this task.

Plant engineering projects are a prominent example for large and complex development projects [2,3]. They comprise a huge number of tasks and subprocesses, many involved process participants with different functional roles, and a highly complex product. The project management data is inherently *multidimensional*, where dimensions are e.g. the engineering phases, the functional roles and the different parts of the chemical plant.

S. Rinderle-Ma et al. (Eds.): BPM 2009 Workshops, LNBIP 43, pp. 104–115, 2010.
© Springer-Verlag Berlin Heidelberg 2010

For that reason, *software-tools* for the monitoring and analysis of development projects in plant engineering need to be able to handle and to *visualize* multi-dimensional project data in an adequate way. Business Intelligence technologies like Online Analytical Processing (OLAP) [4] together with appropriate visualization techniques [5,6] can be applied for this purpose.

In this paper we present a novel approach for *process status analysis* which is the foundation for process improvement [7]. This paper shows how the necessary enactment data of process instances can be collected, processed and analyzed. An overview over the approach is given in Fig. 1. *Measure values* are calculated for the process management data and they are exported to a *data warehouse*. Inside the data warehouse the measure values are arranged along several dimensions of a *hyper cube*. OLAP operations on the hyper cube lead to projections, which are visualized in a flexibly configurable view. The view for process status analysis is *coupled* with the different editing views for process management.

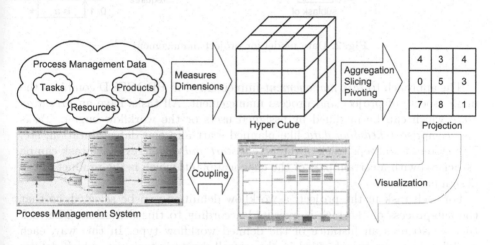

Fig. 1. Overview of the approach

The described approach is implemented in the prototype PROCEED[1] which is developed at the Department for Computer Science 3 of RWTH Aachen University. PROCEED is an extension to the commercial computer aided engineering tool Comos^TM, a product of Comos Industry Solutions GmbH [8]. The PROCEED prototype comprises project management functionality and a workflow engine for the management of recurring engineering tasks.

In Section 2 we describe the transition from the object-oriented data model for process management to the hyper cube of the data warehouse. Section 3 deals with the processing and the visualization of the data. Section 4 is concerned with the realization of the prototype. Related Work is discussed in Section 5, and Section 6 concludes the paper.

---

[1] <u>Proc</u>ess Management <u>E</u>nvironment for <u>E</u>ngineering <u>D</u>esign Processes.

2   Data Model

For PROCEED, an *object-oriented management data model* has been developed, which comprises entities and relations for process-oriented, data-driven project management in the plant engineering domain. Figure 2 shows a simplified cutout of the management data model.

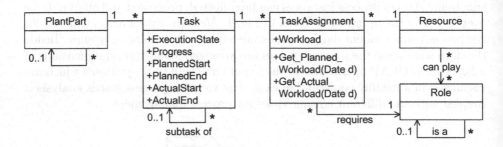

Fig. 2. Data model for project management

The approach to *task management* implemented in PROCEED combines the main aspects of project and process management. All tasks have an *execution state* which can be modified by assigned users or the workflow engine. Tasks also comprise *scheduling data* like planned start and end dates, duration, etc. The system also keeps track of the *actual start and end dates*. Each task can be associated with a certain part of the chemical plant, which is the product of the design process.

For each task in the project, a workflow definition can be selected, so that the sub-process of the task is executed according to this definition. The task then constitutes an instance of the defined workflow type. In this way, each workflow instance is embedded in the overall dynamic task net, which defines the *context* for its execution. This connection between a project plan in the form of a dynamic task net and workflow definitions has been described in [9].

Users are assigned to tasks via explicit task assignments. A *task assignment* specifies a *required role*, which the user has to hold in order to be assigned to the task. Several users can be assigned to one task. For a task assignment, the *required workload* is defined and distributed over the duration of the task. By means of a time recording system, the *actual workload* of an assigned user is recorded for the task assignment. Roles, tasks, assignments and plant parts are defined for a specific plant engineering project.

The object-oriented data model is suitable for process management, but does not meet the requirements for project status analysis. To facilitate the latter, the management data is exported to a *data warehouse* (cf. Sec. 4) and OLAP technology is applied for data processing.

2.1 Process Measures

Process measures are used to analyze a running instance of a development process. The measure values are calculated by PROCEED and exported to the data warehouse. The defined measures have been identified together with the industry partner Comos Industry Solutions. The list of measures is extendable but would require a modification of the prototype. In PROCEED, the following measures are used:

- workload
- cost
- start date
- end date
- progress
- SPI (schedule performance index)
- CPI (cost performance index)

For a task assignment, there is the planned workload and the actual workload of the assigned resource. The unit of measurement for workload is person hours. For a task, the workload values of all task assignments and subtasks are aggregated. The cost of resources and tasks is derived from the workload and the cost rate of the respective resources. Start and end dates of tasks are planned, and the actual start and end dates are logged by PROCEED. The schedule performance index (SPI) and the cost performance index (CPI) indicate for a task, whether it is on schedule and within budget limits, respectively [10]. For each resource, the available workload per day is defined.

2.2 Dimensions and Hyper Cube

The different measures can be associated with tasks, users, roles, plant parts and dates. For this reason, the data in the data warehouse is structured along several *dimensions*. These dimensions span a *hyper cube* which stores all measure values in its cells, i.e. at its coordinates. The major dimensions of the hyper cube are:

- time
- tasks
- roles
- resources
- plant parts

The coordinates of each of these major dimensions are *structured hierarchically*, e.g. by the task-subtask relation and the specialization of roles. There may even be multiple hierarchies defined for one dimension, e.g. the tasks can also be grouped by the workflow type or the activity type of which they are an instance.

Fig. 3 shows on the left an example of a three-dimensional hyper cube which holds the actual workload in person hours. The depicted cube is a sub-cube of the complete hyper cube containing all dimensions and all measure values. It is the result of a so-called *slicing operation* [11], by which the coordinates on the time dimension have been fixed to the timeframe 2009/09/08 to 2009/09/10. The values in the cube cells result from an *aggregation* over all coordinates of the remaining dimensions (e.g. plant parts) except for the time stamp dimension, where always the most recent value is used.

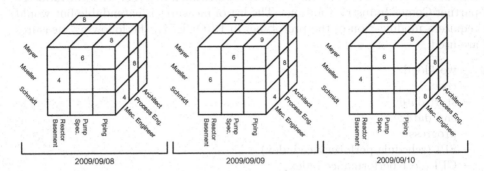

Fig. 3. Example hyper cube

3   Configurable View for Process Status Analysis

PROCEED has been developed to support the management of dynamic development processes, where the process models may continually change during enactment. In PROCEED, tasks, resources, engineering data and their interrelations are modeled in one integrated management model.

The PROCEED prototype provides several views for project planning and controlling. The *task net view* allows for the creation, execution and change of dynamic task nets [12]. A hierarchically structured *task list view* is used to give process participants an overview over their tasks. In the *resource management view*, roles can be defined for the project, the project team can be assembled and roles can be assigned to team members.

The *project status analysis view* of PROCEED has been developed for project monitoring and analysis. The development was initiated as a response to specific requirements of Comos Industry Solutions. There was a need for monitoring the huge amount of engineering and management processes in a plant engineering project. The project status analysis view comprises a *flexibly configurable pivot table* for the *multi-dimensional visualization* of different measure values. The coordinates of the pivot table show *stacked-bar charts*. The *configuration* of the pivot table is done by mapping the dimensions and measures of the data cube to the axes of the pivot table and the properties of the stacked bars. One dimension can be mapped to the color of the stack layers. The measure values are represented by the height of the stack layers.

Fig. 4 shows an example configuration of the status analysis view. The tasks dimension is mapped to the y-axis where the task-subtask relation defines the hierarchy. The plant parts dimension is mapped to the x-axis. Each cell of the pivot table holds one stacked bar for the planned and for the actual workload respectively. The roles are mapped to the colors of the stack layers. The timeframe

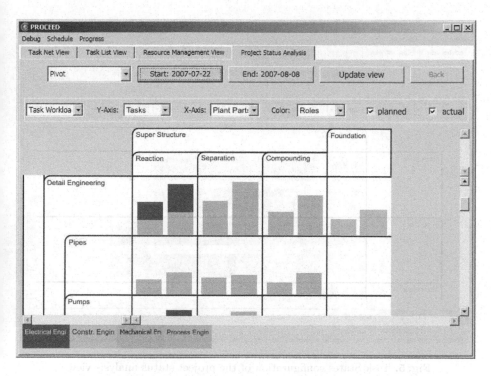

Fig. 4. Example configuration of the project status analysis view

is set from the beginning of the project to the current date. By means of this
view configuration, the project responsible can inspect, how much workload was
planned for the tasks in the project distributed over the different plant parts,
and how much effort was actually spent on the respective tasks. When this view
configuration is used after the end of the project or the end of a certain project
phase, it can reveal that the planned effort defined in the process model was
unrealistic, and that the *model has to be improved*.

The project status analysis view allows virtually any *combination* of dimensions and measures and thereby provides many *different viewpoints* on the project
data. A view configuration can be *manually assembled* by selecting the dimensions and measures from drop down menus. However, some configurations are
more useful than others for project status analysis. The most *common configurations* have been named and can be directly selected by the user. On the
one hand, common views provided by conventional project management systems (PMS) like Microsoft Project can be configured: *Gantt Chart*, *Task Usage*,
Resource Graph, and *Resource Usage*. On the other hand, there are several view
configurations, which are not provided by conventional PMS. The configuration
of Fig. 4 is called *Task Workload*. The view configuration *Technical Crews* focuses on the functional roles in the project and their planned workload in the

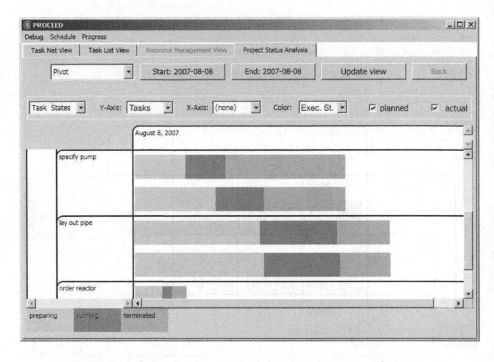

Fig. 5. Task States configuration of the project status analysis view

upcoming weeks. The view configuration *Plants Progress* provides an overview over the progress made in the main engineering tasks with respect to the different plant parts.

A different viewpoint on the tasks in the project is provided by the view configuration *Task States*, which gives insight into the *current execution states* of the tasks in the project, which may differ from the planned states. This configuration is depicted in Fig. 5. The timeframe is set to the current date. Again, the tasks dimension is mapped onto the y-axis of the pivot table. However, this time the tasks are grouped by the workflow type of which they are an instance (cf. Sec. 2). The colors of the stacked bars indicate the execution state of the tasks, i.e. workflow instances. The measure is the planned overall workload of the tasks. By means of this view configuration, the project responsible can inspect, how much work is already successfully completed (terminated), how many tasks – as measured by workload – are currently processed (running), and how much effort still remains (preparing). These values are compared with the planned values which are derived from the planned start and end dates of the tasks. This view configuration is useful for *project controlling*, to analyze the overall performance of all workflow instances of a certain type during the course of the project.

In the configuration of Fig. 5 the numbers (bar stack widths) indicate that for the workflow type *specify pump* less instances have been completed than planned, mainly because several workflows have not been started as planned. At the same time, the enactment of the workflow instances of type *lay out pipe* goes nearly as planned. The project responsible could gain even more insight into where the bottleneck is by mapping the resource dimension to the x-axis. This would reveal, if certain resources are responsible for the delay at the specification of pumps.

The information presented to the user in the *Task States* configuration is also displayed in the workflow management environment. A workflow definition is augmented by the information about all instances of this workflow type. Fig. 6 shows a cutout of the workflow definition *specify pump* as it is presented to the user. For the whole workflow type, the number of running (300), terminated (300) and created (700) workflow instances are given. For each activity, the percentage of workflow instances, which have completed the activity, is depicted. Furthermore, the average execution time of all completed activities is shown. The augmentation of workflow definitions is one aspect of the coupling between the process management system and the project status analysis view.

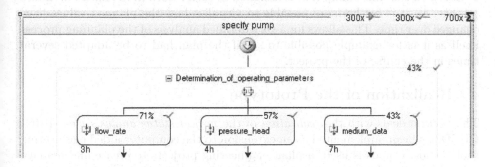

Fig. 6. Augmented workflow definition in workflow designer

The project status analysis view supports all common operations on a multi-dimensional dataset [13]: Drill-down, roll-up, pivot, slicing and aggregation. With *drill-down* and *roll-up*, a dimension is added or removed from the visualization respectively, e.g. no dimension is mapped to the x-axis or the colors of the stacked bars. Drill-down and roll-up also refer to going downwards or upwards in the hierarchy of a dimension. The *pivot* operation changes the mapping of dimensions to axes while the number of displayed dimensions stays the same. A *slicing* operation fixes the coordinate on one or more dimensions, e.g. it sets a fixed date for which the management data should be displayed. The values in the hyper cube are *aggregated* along all dimensions which are not displayed, and which were not subject to a slicing operation.

The views for project and process management are *coupled* with the project status analysis view by navigation functionality. To take immediate action based on his analysis of the running process, the project responsible can navigate from the project status analysis view to the task net or task list view. Vice versa, the project manager often needs additional information when he is replanning the project. For example, if he is looking for an additional resource for a task, he can *navigate* from a management view to the adequately configured analysis view, which shows him the utilization of the resources that can play the required role. General purpose multi-dimensional visualization tools fail to provide this tight coupling with project management views.

In general, the monitoring view can be used for two different purposes: for *process controlling* and for *process analysis* (cf. examples in Fig. 5 and Fig. 4 respectively). While the former may lead to *corrective actions* during the project, the latter can be used for *process improvement*. During the course of a development project, the different view configurations can reveal, if certain tasks exceed their time limits, or if the count of completed process instances of a certain type lies below the planned number. After the completion of an engineering project, the actual workload for activities and process instances can be compared with the required workload defined in the process definitions. The latter can be adapted if necessary.

Based on the time stamp that is assigned to each record in the data warehouse (cf. Sec. 4), it is furthermore possible to visualize how the planned values have changed over time. This allows for a very detailed analysis of the planning process itself as it is for example possible to see if the plan had to be adapted several times in the course of the project.

4   Realization of the Prototype

This section deals with the *realization* of the *project status analysis view*. PROCEED has been implemented as an extension to the computer aided engineering tool Comos. Comos is used in plant engineering projects to create and manage the engineering data, e.g. documents like technical drawings, device specifications and equipment lists.

Comos did not provide any explicit process management support until the beginning of the research project. Hence, in a first step, a *workflow management system* was implemented using the Windows Workflow Foundation [14]. The client applications of the WFMS allow for the definition and monitoring of workflows, which are enacted by the *workflow engine*. Workflow instances can be *dynamically changed at runtime*, whereby several correctness constraints apply. The developed workflow engine comprises *progress measurement* functionality. The progress of running workflow instances is automatically calculated by taking the control flow, the current execution state and experienced data for activity durations into account.

The core component of the PROCEED prototype is the *project management module*. The project management module and the WFMS are tightly integrated as described in [9]. A project plan is created in the form of a hierarchically structured *dynamic task net* [12]. The project management module checks the consistency constraints for dynamic task nets. PROCEED offers automatic *task scheduling* functionality. Furthermore, the *progress* of all tasks in the project is calculated based on different calculation methods like user estimates, document states or milestones. The measures used for project status analysis like start and end times, workload and progress are in large part calculated by PROCEED.

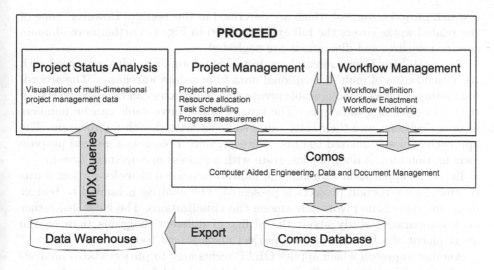

Fig. 7. General overview over the system architecture

The management data of the project management component and the WFMS is stored in the Comos database, which is accessed via the Comos API. However, for the project status analysis view of PROCEED a separate *data warehouse* was required for technical reasons. In an ETL (Extract-Transform-Load) process, the management data is extracted from the Comos database and exported to the data warehouse. The export is *incremental*: Only changed measure values are exported.

The data warehouse is realized using the Microsoft SQL Server with Microsoft Analysis Services [15]. After the hyper cube has been generated, multidimensional data records can be retrieved from the data warehouse using the query language MDX.

For each export a new *time stamp* is created. All exported measure values are associated with this timestamp. This way, the history of plan changes is stored in the data warehouse, which can be used to assess the quality of process definitions.

Dynamic changes to the project management data are *immediately reflected* in the multi-dimensional analysis view. Whenever a change to a task, task assignment, resource or the like occurs, the changed values of the affected entities are immediately exported to the data warehouse and the hyper cube is updated. This dynamic update functionality constituted a technical challenge, since the export and processing of data is time consuming even for an incremental export, but the user should not impeded in his work with the tool.

5 Related Work

The visualization of multi-dimensional data and especially the application of these techniques to project management have been tackled in several related research projects, some of which are described in this section. However, none of the related works covers the full cycle depicted in Fig. 1. Furthermore, domain specific measures and dimensions are neglected.

Polaris [16] has been a research project at Stanford University concerned with the visualization of multi-dimensional data from a data warehouse. The according prototype offers a configurable pivot table whose axes can be associated with the dimensions of a data cube. The entries of the pivot table can be numbers or even diagrams, and their color can also be associated with a dimension. The approach is closely related to ours. However, since Polaris is a general purpose visualization tool, it does not integrate with a process management system.

In [17], an application with different multi-dimensional views for project status control of construction projects is presented. The analysis is limited to budget data, and there is no pivot table among the visualizations. The focus lied rather on a comparative study about the utility of different diagrams than on the development of a UI concept for a project management tool.

Another approach which applies OLAP technology to project status analysis can be found in [18]. A multi-dimensional data model for a data warehouse is developed, which comprises five dimensions and the measures person hours, actual costs and planned costs. A pivot table is used to generate different views on the project data using MDX-queries. No information about plan changes in the monitored project is stored in the data warehouse. No graphical visualization techniques are applied to present the data in the pivot table. Only the standard functionality of the SQL-server is used. The focus of [18] lied on the evaluation of the OLAP technology for project management, but not on a suitable visualization of the data.

6   Conclusions

In this paper, a novel approach was presented for the analysis of process enactment data by means of OLAP technology and the application of visualization techniques for multi-dimensional data. The approach applies technologies from the area of business intelligence to process management. The PROCEED prototype has been developed as an extension to the CAE-tool Comos. The functionalities for project status analysis meet the requirements of the industry partner Comos Industry Solutions: There was a need for monitoring the huge amount of engineering and management processes in a plant engineering project. The prototype will be evaluated by customers of Comos Industry Solutions in the near future.

Acknowledgements

We thank Comos Industry Solutions for the valuable input and precise requirements, and the DFG for funding the project in the context of the Transfer Center 61 following the Collaborative Research Center 476 IMPROVE.

References

1. Florac, W.A., Carleton, A.D.: Measuring the Software Process: Statistical Process Control for Software Process Improvement. Addison-Wesley, Boston (1999)
2. Helmus, F.P.: Process Plant Design - Project Management from Inquiry to Acceptance. Wiley-VCH, Weinheim (2008)
3. DIN German Institute for Standardization: PAS 1059 Processing plant design – Procedural model and terminology (2006)
4. Codd, E.F., Codd, S.B., Salley, C.T.: Providing OLAP to User-Analysts: An IT Mandate (1993)
5. Keim, D.A.: Information visualization and visual data mining. IEEE Transactions on Visualization and Computer Graphics 8(1), 1–8 (2002)
6. Tufte, E.R.: The visual display of quantitative information. Graphics Press, Cheshire (1986)
7. Schleicher, A.: Management of Development Processes - An Evolutionary Approach. PhD thesis, RWTH Aachen University, Aachen (2002)
8. Comos Industry Solutions: Website (April 2009), http://www.comos.com
9. Heer, T., Briem, C., Wörzberger, R.: Workflows in Dynamic Development Processes. In: Proceedings of the 1st International Workshop on Process Management for Highly Dynamic and Pervasive Scenarios (PM4HDPS 2008) (2008)
10. Patzak, G., Rattay, G.: Projekt Management. Linde (1998)
11. Lehner, W.: Datenbanktechnologie für Data-Warehouse-Systeme: Konzepte und Methoden. dpunkt-Verlag (2003)
12. Heller, M., Jäger, D., Krapp, C.A., Nagl, M., Schleicher, A., Westfechtel, B., Wörzberger, R.: An Adaptive and Reactive Management System for Project Coordination. In: Nagl, M., Marquardt, W. (eds.) Collaborative and Distributed Chemical Engineering. LNCS, vol. 4970, pp. 300–366. Springer, Heidelberg (2008)
13. Jarke, M., Lenzerini, M., Vassiliou, Y., Vassiliadis, P.: Fundamentals of Data Warehouses. Springer, Heidelberg (2000)
14. Microsoft: Windows Workflow Foundation (2008), http://msdn.microsoft.com/en-us/netframework/aa663328.aspx
15. Microsoft Corporation: SQL Server 2008 Analysis Services (2009), http://www.microsoft.com/Sqlserver/2008/en/us/analysis-services.aspx
16. Stolte, C., Tang, D., Hanrahan, P.: Multiscale Visualization Using Data Cubes. IEEE Transactions on Visualization and Computer Graphics 9(2), 176–187 (2003)
17. Songer, A.D., Hays, B., North, N.C.: Multidimensional Visualization of Project Control Data. Journal of Computing in Civil Engineering 4, 173–190 (2004)
18. Nie, H., Sheryl Staub-French, T.F.: OLAP-Integrated Project Cost Control and Manpower Analysis. Journal of Computing in Civil Engineering 21, 164–174 (2007)

Autonomous Optimization of Business Processes

Markus Kress and Detlef Seese

Institute AIFB, Karlsruhe Institute of Technology (KIT)
University Karlsruhe (TH), 76128 Karlsruhe, Germany
{kress,seese}@aifb.uni-karlsruhe.de
http://www.aifb.uni-karlsruhe.de

Abstract. In this paper we introduce the intelligent Executable Product Model (iEPM) approach for the autonomous optimization of service industry's business processes. Instead of using a process model, we use an Executable Product Model (EPM). EPMs provide a compact representation of the set of possible execution paths of a business process by defining information dependencies instead of the order of activities. The flexibility that EPMs provide is utilized by intelligent agents managing the execution with the objective to optimize the Key Performance Indicators (KPIs) under consideration of the operating conditions. This paper demonstrates the practical application method of the iEPM approach as intelligent BPM engine where agents autonomously adapt their behavior in accordance to the current operating conditions for optimizing KPIs. The advantages of this method are discussed and statistically analyzed using a simulation based approach and the business process "new customer" found in banking.

Keywords: Business Process Modeling, Process Flexibility, Optimization, Relational Reinforcement Learning, Particle Swarm Optimization.

1 Introduction

Business process automation comprises the creation of a process model and the execution of this model during runtime by a BPM engine. The process models do not necessarily provide the required flexibility for dealing with changing operating conditions. In particular, process designs may be optimal in certain operating conditions only. If changes occur, it may be necessary to adapt the process model or process instances in order to handle the new situation accordingly.

In [1] we introduced the Executable Product Model (EPM) for modeling business processes. The EPM contains a compact representation of the set of possible execution paths of a business process by defining information relationships instead of task sequences as in process models. The different execution paths can be executed independently from each other which allows to execute the activities of different execution paths either in a sequence or in parallel. In a process model, such behavior has to be modeled explicitly. We take advantage of the flexibility provided by the EPM during runtime by using a Multi-Agent System (MAS). A MAS was chosen, as it is capable of solving complex tasks in

S. Rinderle-Ma et al. (Eds.): BPM 2009 Workshops, LNBIP 43, pp. 116–127, 2010.
© Springer-Verlag Berlin Heidelberg 2010

distributed environments and has been applied successfully in practice. In combination with self-adaptation they are a powerful tool. Self-adaptation is the ability of a software system to adapt to dynamic and changing operating conditions autonomously [2]. The MAS manages the execution of EPMs in order to optimize the KPIs. In [3,4] we introduced a learning mechanism for this task based on two combined machine learning approaches, Relational Reinforcement Learning (RRL) with Genetic Algorithm. We successfully showed how the agents can learn in a static environment.

In this paper we evaluate the advantages of the iEPM approach applied as intelligent BPM engine on the basis of a "new customer" business process. Particularly, the limitation of using regular process models in changing scenarios is shown. Several simulation based experiments are conducted in order to show how the agents are capable of optimizing the KPIs by adapting their behaviour autonomously in changing scenarios.

The paper is outlined as follows: In Sect. 2 the elements of an EPM are explained. Moreover, the requirements of the "new customer" business process and the corresponding EPM are described. The developed iEPM approach and its application are described in Sect. 3. In Sect. 4 the conducted experiments are analyzed. Related work is discussed in Sect. 5. A conclusion and an outlook to future work end the paper.

2 The Executable Product Model

In [1], the EPM was introduced which is based on the Product Data Model (PDM). PDMs were introduced as part of a process design methodology termed product-driven workflow design [5]. Both models have been developed specifically for the information-intensive service industry. Similar to the PDM, an EPM comprises all information that accrues during the execution of a business process. Information nodes and their dependencies are the main elements of an EPM.

The information nodes correspond to abstract information like application data, business objects, documents, decisions which are part of the business process. EPMs can be modeled on different levels of abstraction as an information node may be a single variable or a business object. Information nodes are visualized as circles. An EPM has exactly one root information node representing the final result of the business process (e. g. the outcome of an insurance claim or credit application). The dependencies between information nodes determine which information must be available before another information can be generated, e. g. a decision can only be made if the application form has been filled out correctly. These dependencies reflect the production or execution order of the information elements and are modeled as directed arcs. These arcs represent production rules describing which task has to be performed to create a new value stored in the information node the corresponding arc is pointing at. Thus, production rules are similar to activities in a business process. The information node(s) that the production rule depends on are called origin nodes, the created node is the destination node of the production rule. Each information node is the destination node of at least one production rule. As leaf nodes do not depend on any other node, they have special production rules that can be executed at any time - visualized as dashed arcs. Two kinds of dependencies can be specified. In an AND dependency all origin nodes of the related production rule must have been created before the production rule can become executable. By means of an OR dependency, alternative execution paths are specified which can be executed independently. As production rules are processed by resources (machines or humans), a role is assigned to each production rule. A role describes what skill or position a resource must have in order to execute the production rule. Additionally, a constraint can be attached to each production rule that determines under what circumstances this production rule can be executed (depicted as square brackets). In the following, an example of an EPM is provided based on a "new customer" business process.

The "new customer" process is implemented in a large German bank. For this paper it was simplified and made anonymously. The process is initiated when a new customer applies for one of the financial products the bank offers, e.g. a new customer intends to open a debit account. Based on the business requirements, several process designs are feasible. Due to space restrictions, only two options are considered and analyzed. In option A, the activities "Check Financial Situation", "Check Application" and "Check Customer History" are modeled in parallel (see Fig. 1). In option B these checks are modeled in a sequence as listed above. The parallel design has the advantage that it can lead to a better cycle time than the sequential design. The disadvantage of the parallel design is that certain tasks may be executed unnecessarily. This is the case, when the application is rejected due to a negative financial situation, while the customer history and the correctness of the application are still being checked. Other design options are retrieved if the order of the checks is switched.

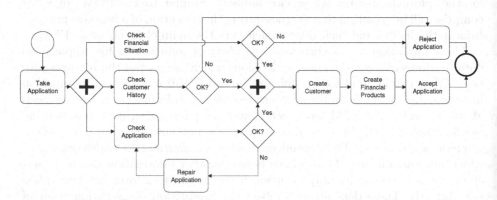

Fig. 1. The parallel design of the "New Customer" business process as BPMN model

For creating the EPM, the information elements of the business process must be identified and the dependencies between them must be specified. The resulting EPM is depicted in Fig. 2.

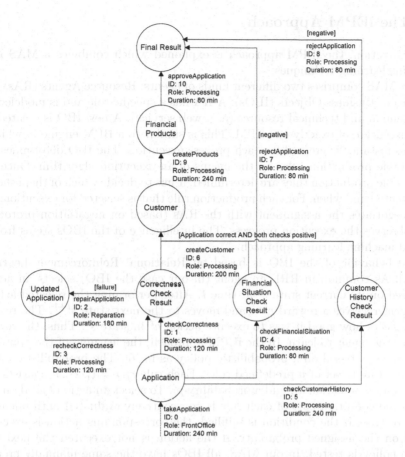

Fig. 2. Executable Product Model "New Customer". Production rule with ID 6 is an AND dependency with three origin nodes, whereas the production rules with IDs 7, 8 and 10 are an example of an OR dependency (there are three different production rules for creating root node "Final Result").

The EPM comprises different variants, among them also the execution paths corresponding to the two design options, e.g. the paths for approval without repair actions:

- Variant 1: $0 \rightarrow \{1, 4 \text{ and } 5 \text{ in parallel}\} \rightarrow 6 \rightarrow 9 \rightarrow 10$
- Variant 2: $0 \rightarrow 4 \rightarrow 1 \rightarrow 5 \rightarrow 6 \rightarrow 9 \rightarrow 10$

As one can see, the EPM comprises the execution paths of the two different aforementioned process designs. By modeling information dependencies, the EPM does not fix the actual execution order which enables the agents to choose the optimal path through the EPM for each instance. Moreover, the execution path can be changed anytime. This is an advantage that other approaches do not provide as they choose a specific variant at instantiation without having the possibility to change it afterwards.

3   The iEPM Approach

In this section, the iEPM approach is explained which combines a MAS with machine learning techniques.

The MAS comprises two different kinds of agents: Resource Agents (RAs) and Intelligent Business Objects (IBOs). A RA has a specific role and is modeled for each human and technical resource (e. g. web service). A new IBO is created for each execution of exactly one EPM. This is similar to a BPM engine in which a process instance is created for each process execution. The IBO determines the executable production rules by the means of an execution algorithm. Once the executable production rules are determined, it has to decide which of them should be executed and when. For each production rule that is selected for execution, the IBO negotiates the assignment with the RAs (based on negotiation protocols) and observes the execution progress. The intelligence of the IBOs stems from a hybrid machine learning approach.

The behavior of the IBO is based on Relational Reinforcement Learning (RRL). As common in RRL an agent (in our case the IBO) selects an action a^t based on its current state s^t at time t. After performing the selected action, the agent receives a reward r^{t+1} and moves to the next state s^{t+1}. The reward r^{t+1} reflects how good it was to execute action a^t in state s^t. Thus, the reward enables the agent to learn. In the iEPM approach, the learning of the appropriate actions is based on a probabilistic policy as in [6]. The probabilistic policy contains a finite set of n predefined rules. Each rule $r_i, i = 1, \cdots, n$ consists of a condition c_i, an action a_i, and a probability p_i. To select an action based on this policy the condition part of each rule is consecutively evaluated until one evaluates to true. If the condition is fulfilled, the corresponding action is executed based on the assigned probability. If the action is not executed the next rule in the policy is tested. In our MAS, all IBOs have the same manually created policy and use the above described policy iteration to determine their actions. Each IBO uses a PROLOG engine to represent its state. PROLOG queries are executed for determining whether a policy condition is fulfilled. The probabilities of the policy must be determined for each single scenario using an appropriate heuristic in an offline learning phase. We apply Particle Swarm Optimization (PSO) for determining the probability vector $\mathbf{P}$. PSO contains a population of particles which explores the search space by moving with particular velocities towards the optimum. The velocity of each particle is influenced by a social impact coming from the population and the individual experience of the particle (for further details see e. g. [7]). Each particle represents a solution of the optimization problem and is evaluated by a fitness function. In our optimization problem, a particle represents a probability vector and the fitness function is based on the KPIs to be optimized. In order to calculate the fitness value of a particle, a simulation is carried out. The simulation calculates KPIs such as cycle time, throughput, costs, among others. Fig. 3 illustrates the practical application method.

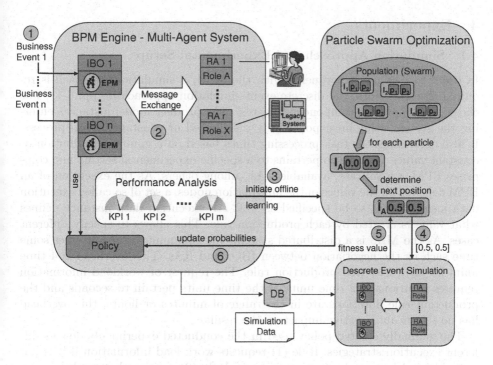

Fig. 3. The iEPM approach applied as intelligent BPM engine. (1) Business events trigger the creation of IBOs and the execution of the corresponding EPM. (2) IBOs and RAs collaborate in order to execute the EPMs. During the execution, operational data is stored in a database and the defined KPIs are calculated. (3) If necessary, the offline learning phase is triggered. PSO is illustrated on the basis of a two dimensional vector. (4) For each evaluation of a particle, a discrete event simulation is carried out. The probability vector as well as operational and simulation data are provided as input. (5) Result of this simulation is the fitness value. (6) The policy is updated with the optimal probability vector found by PSO. As one can observe, there are actually two MASs, one for the real execution and another one for the offline learning phase. The application is implemented in Java making use of the SWI-Prolog and JSwarm-PSO packages.

Our approach can be used in the BPM context as follows: The intelligent agents can act as a BPM engine and control autonomously the execution flow of business processes. The offline learning phase allows the agents to adapt their behaviour to changing situations. The learning phase can be initiated either periodically or on the basis of a defined threshold and runs in parallel to the regular execution. Once the probability vector is determined, the probabilities are updated and the agents act on the basis of the new values. The learning phase requires simulation data such as durations and arrival rates. The simulation data can be automatically calculated based on the latest production data. In our current prototype, the simulation data is provided manually. Additionally, the offline learning phase can be utilized for what-if analyses as well, e.g. to conduct business forecasts.

4   Experiments

4.1   Simulation Approach and Experimental Setup

In order to conduct experiments with the MAS, a simulation approach is required. For this work, the discrete event simulation approach [8, pp. 6-11] was chosen. A simulation component "creates" new product model instances entering the system using an exponentially distributed or constant arrival process. It also determines the task processing times based on a gamma distribution or constant values. A scenario pertains to a specific experimental setting and comprises EPM, arrival rate, available RAs, among others. As the execution of an EPM depends on the values of the information nodes, a set of so called execution data instances has to be specified as well. An execution data instance defines what value is created by each production rule. This allows to specify different cases. As the MAS is a distributed system, the communication consumes some time such as the negotiation between IBOs and RAs. This overhead is 4 time units for each executed production rule. The request of workload information requires additionally 2 time units. If the time units pertain to seconds and the production rule durations are in the range of minutes or hours, this overhead has no significant negative impact on the result.

The manually created policy used in the conducted experiments defines different execution strategies: Rule (1) requests work load information if it is not available and has not been requested yet. Rule (2) assures that work load information is kept up-to-date. Rule (3) executes all production rules that are executable. Rule (4) activates the variant with the shortest estimated execution duration if no other has been activated. If work load information is available, it is used in the calculation of the estimated duration. By activating a variant, only the executable production rules belonging to this variant are executed. Rule (5) assures that if the activated variant is still the one with the smallest estimated duration, its processing is continued. Rule (6) switches the variant if there is a shorter one than the activated.

4.2   Conducted Experiments

In this section, the conducted experiments with the "new customer" process are discussed. In the first experiment it is shown that a process model can become suboptimal if changes occur. In the second experiment it is shown how the iEPM approach is capable of handling such changes by adapting the behaviour of the intelligent agents. Let us assume that the objective is the minimization of the costs by assuring a specific service level agreement regarding the cycle time. Equation 1 defines the objective as follows:

$$\text{minimize } meanC \tag{1}$$
$$\text{subject to: } meanCT < 1200$$

where $meanC$ are the average costs and $meanCT$ the average cycle time which has to be less than a specific number of time units, here 1200. This objective can be motivated by considering a cost reduction strategy with ensuring customer satisfaction at the same time. The customer should not wait too long for the decision about his application. The costs of executing a business process are determined on the basis of the processing times, one costs unit relates to one time unit. No fixed costs are considered. Thus, the costs are calculated by summing up the processing times of each finished and unfinished task. The process is analyzed based on two scenarios. Scenario I is defined as follows:

- Constant processing times as defined in Fig. 2.
- Table 1 lists the probabilities of the different cases. A probability reflects how often a case occurs.
- Number of RAs per role: Reparation: 1, FrontOffice: 1, and Processing: 3.
- Stop criteria: 1,000 executed EPMs.
- Constant arrival rate of 1000 minutes.

Table 1. The different cases

Case	Description	Probability
1	Accept application without repair	0.6
2	Accept application with one repair action	0.2
3	Reject application due to negative financial situation	0.1
4	Reject application due to negative customer history	0.1

In scenario II, the situation is analyzed in which the completion of activity "Check Customer History" is delayed. There can be various causes for such a delay: the occurrence of unexpected quality problems that lead to rework or if new employees must be taught. Let us assume that quality problems lead to a longer processing time due to rework. The processing time of this activity is changed from 240 to 360 minutes.

The first experiment analyzes the two design options for each scenario. Each experimental run is repeated 20 times. The results of the simulations are listed in Table 2 which contains the mean cycle time as well as the 0.95 confidence interval. The experiments were conducted with our MAS, but similar results were received with the commercial BPM simulation tool iGrafx.

In scenario I, option B has lower costs than A. Thus, B is the preferable design. The situation in scenario II is different. As the cycle time of option B violates the

Table 2. Simulation results of experiment one

	Scenario I		Scenario II	
Design	Mean Costs	Mean Cycle Time	Mean Costs	Mean Cycle Time
Option A	1161.2 ± 2.3	931.0 ± 2.4	1271.7 ± 3.4	1016.1 ± 6.9
Option B	$1116,6 \pm 4.8$	1117.6 ± 4.8	1232.8 ± 6.8	1233.8 ± 6.9

constraint, option B is no longer the optimal process design. Therefore option A is preferable in scenario II as it satisfies the constraint regarding the cycle time. Thus far, it has been shown that depending on the scenario, different process designs can be optimal.

In the second experiment, the situation is analyzed, in which the processing time of activity "Check Customer History" changes as described above in the middle of the simulation run. This means, that in the first half of the simulation, the setting of scenario I is used and in the second half the setting of scenario II. Fig. 4 shows the results of this experiment.

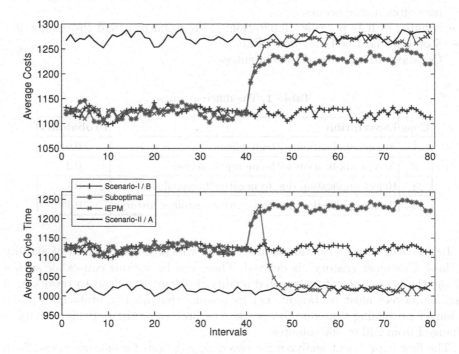

Fig. 4. Results of the different approaches. The upper figure depicts the average costs and the lower one depicts the average cycle time.

The KPIs "average cycle time" and "average costs" are calculated in fixed intervals. Run "Scenario-I / B" means that process design B is used in scenario I. Accordingly, run "Scenario-II / A" means that process design A is used in scenario II. These runs are included for comparison purposes. Run "Suboptimal" means that option B is used, but the situation changes from scenario I to scenario II in the middle of the simulation. As one can see, the cycle time increases and violates the constraint. Particularly, this shows the limitation of regular process models. Run "iEPM" shows the result of the iEPM approach. The first time that the offline learning takes place is before the simulation is started. The next time offline learning takes place is at interval 42 as the constraint regarding the mean cycle time was violated for the first time. The probabilities of the policy were updated at the beginning of the next interval. As one can see, the agents have autonomously adapted their behaviour in accordance to the changed scenario. First, they learned to execute the checks in a sequence (by applying rule (4) and (5)) and after the second learning phase to execute them in parallel (rule (3)).

Note that the iEPM approach can cope with other scenario changes. Also, other KPIs can be optimized. Let us assume that only the cycle time is optimized and a lower arrival rate is selected in such a way that waiting times occur but the RAs are still able to execute the arriving EPMs. In this case, the parallel design is optimal. But if one of the RAs with role "Processing" is not available anymore (e.g. due to illness) the parallel design can become suboptimal. This is caused by the disadvantage of the parallel design (see Sect. 2). In experiments, the advantage of the iEPM approach could be shown analogously for this scenario change.

The conducted experiments show that the flexibility of EPMs allows the autonomous optimization of KPIs in changing operating conditions. In particular, the iEPM approach overcomes the limitation of regular process models. Note, that the learning mechanism could be integrated in non-MAS environments as well, e.g. in a centralized BPM engine. But this would require an alternative scheduling approach. Moreover, alternative modeling languages could only be used if they provide the same degree of flexibility as EPMs.

5   Related Work

There exists one approach in which swarm intelligence is applied in the area of BPM [9]. But the approach has another focus as swarm intelligence is applied for dynamic task assignment in ad-hoc processes.

Several approaches exist that focus on the flexibility of business processes. The approach described in [10] makes it possible to model and manage process variants on the basis of process family engineering techniques in an efficient way. But as the actual variant is chosen on instantiation of the business process there is no possibility to change the variant during runtime. The EPM allows to switch the variant during runtime. Further approaches improve the flexibility by allowing dynamic changes on workflow instance or schema level during runtime. The approaches mainly give an overview about the different kind of changes and how they affect the instances and schemata. For an overview of these adaptive and dynamic workflow approaches see e. g. [11]. Our approach differs from these approaches as we create a fixed model, whose flexibility is utilized by intelligent agents, controlling the process flow automatically. The adaptive workflow approaches could be used to extend our approach to further improve the flexibility of our model. In [12] a set of change patterns is introduced which is the basis for an evaluation of industry and academic approaches. Regarding our approach the late binding of process fragments pattern is of interest. Process fragments can be selected during runtime. It differs from our approach as these process fragments are selected manually or based on fixed rules. In [13] a constrained-based workflow method is introduced for providing flexibility by using a declarative style of modeling. The model comprises a set of optional and mandatory constraints. This is well suited for variants handling and exception handling by giving the user more choices regarding the actual execution order of activities. An automatic optimization as in our approach is not integrated so far.

One of the core features of the case handling approach described in [14] is very similar to our approach. We also decide about the activation of activities based on the information available instead of the activities already executed. But the approach focuses more on the user by providing all case information and a flexible way of data entry.

The product-driven workflow approaches in [15,16] use life cycles of objects instead of product structures. As these life cycles are either used for compliance checks or for managing large process structures, the approaches are more related to a design methodology. The most related product-driven workflow approach is introduced in [17], which directly executes Product Data Models, but does not integrate machine learning in order to autonomously optimize the process execution. The authors state that their presented execution strategies may not necessarily lead to the best overall execution path. Furthermore, it is not mentioned how iterations are handled which are fundamental in business processes.

6   Conclusion and Future Work

In this paper the iEPM approach was introduced. It was shown how this approach can be used as intelligent BPM engine. Based on a simplified business process, the advantage of the iEPM approach was discussed. It was explained why EPMs provide more flexibility compared to regular process models. In experiments it was shown that the intelligent agents are capable of utilizing this flexibility in order to optimize autonomously the business process execution in changing scenarios. Thereby, the iEPM approach overcomes the limitation of regular process models. In our current prototype, the simulation data for the offline learning phase is provided manually. In the future this will be changed so simulation data can be automatically retrieved based on the production data of the executed EPMs, e. g. such as in [18].

References

1. Kress, M., Melcher, J., Seese, D.: Introducing executable product models for the service industry. In: Proceedings of the 40th Annual Hawaii International Conference on System Sciences, HICSS 2007, Waikoloa, Hawaii, January 3-6 (2007)
2. Weyns, D., Hovoet, T.: An architectural strategy for self-adapting systems. In: International Workshop on Software Engineering for Adaptive and Self-Managing Systems, p. 3(2007)
3. Kress, M., Seese, D.: Executable product models – the intelligent way. In: Proceedings of the International Conference on Systems, Man, and Cybernetics (SMC 2007), Montreal, Canada, October 7-10 (2007)

4. Kress, M., Seese, D.: Flexibility enhancements in bpm by applying executable product models and intelligent agents. In: Business Process and Services Computing (BPSC 2007), Leipzig, Germany, pp. 93–104 (2007)
5. van der Aalst, W.M.P., Reijers, H.A., Limam, S.: Product-driven workflow design. In: Proceedings of the 6th International Conference on Computer Supported Cooperative Work in Design, London, Ont., Canada, July 12-14, pp. 397–402 (2001)
6. Itoh, H., Nakamurra, K.: Learning to learn and plan by relational reinforcement learning. In: Proceedings Workshop on Relational Reinforcement Learning, July 8 (2004)
7. Kennedy, J., Eberhart, R.: Particle swarm optimization. In: Proceedings of IEEE International Conference on Neural Networks, Perth, Australia, vol. 4, pp. 1942–1948 (1995)
8. Law, A.M., Kelton, W.D.: Simulation Modeling and Analysis, 3rd edn. McGraw-Hill, Boston (2000)
9. Reijers, H.A., Jansen-Vullers, M.H., zur Muehlen, M., Appl, W.: Workflow Management Systems + Swarm Intelligence = Dynamic Task Assignment for Emergency Management Applications. In: Alonso, G., Dadam, P., Rosemann, M. (eds.) BPM 2007. LNCS, vol. 4714, pp. 125–140. Springer, Heidelberg (2007)
10. Schnieders, A., Puhlmann, F.: Variability mechanisms in e-business process families. In: 9th International Conference on Business Information Systems (BIS 2006), pp. 583–601 (2006)
11. Rinderle, S., Reichert, M., Dadam, P.: Correctness criteria for dynamic changes in workflow systems - a survey. Data & Knowledge Engineering 50, 9–34 (2004)
12. Weber, B., Rinderle, S., Reichert, M.: Change patterns and change support features in process-aware information systems. In: Krogstie, J., Opdahl, A.L., Sindre, G. (eds.) CAiSE 2007 and WES 2007. LNCS, vol. 4495, pp. 574–588. Springer, Heidelberg (2007)
13. Pesic, M., Schonenberg, M.H., Sidorova, N., van der Aalst, W.M.P.: Constraint-based workflow models: Change made easy. In: Meersman, R., Tari, Z. (eds.) OTM 2007, Part I. LNCS, vol. 4803, pp. 77–94. Springer, Heidelberg (2007)
14. van der Aalst, W.M.P., Weske, M., Grünbauer, D.: Case handling: a new paradigm for business process support. Data & Knowledge Engineering 53, 129–162 (2005)
15. Küster, J., Ryndina, K., Gall, H.: Generation of business process models for object life cycle compliance. In: Alonso, G., Dadam, P., Rosemann, M. (eds.) BPM 2007. LNCS, vol. 4714, pp. 165–181. Springer, Heidelberg (2007)
16. Müller, D., Reichert, M., Herbst, J.: Data-driven modeling and coordination of large process structures. In: Meersman, R., Tari, Z. (eds.) OTM 2007, Part I. LNCS, vol. 4803, pp. 131–149. Springer, Heidelberg (2007)
17. Vanderfeesten, I.T.P., Reijers, H.A., van der Aalst, W.M.P.: Product based workflow support: Dynamic workflow execution. In: Bellahsène, Z., Léonard, M. (eds.) CAiSE 2008. LNCS, vol. 5074, pp. 571–574. Springer, Heidelberg (2008)
18. Rozinat, A., Wynn, M., Aalst, W., Hofstede, A., Fidge, C.: Workflow simulation for operational decision support using design, historic and state information. In: Dumas, M., Reichert, M., Shan, M.-C. (eds.) BPM 2008. LNCS, vol. 5240, pp. 196–211. Springer, Heidelberg (2008)

Activity Mining by Global Trace Segmentation

Christian W. Günther, Anne Rozinat, and Wil M.P. van der Aalst

Information Systems Group, Eindhoven University of Technology,
P.O. Box 513, NL-5600 MB, Eindhoven, The Netherlands
{c.w.gunther,a.rozinat,w.m.p.v.d.aalst}@tue.nl

Abstract. Process Mining is a technology for extracting non-trivial and useful information from execution logs. For example, there are many process mining techniques to automatically discover a process model describing the causal dependencies between activities . Unfortunately, the quality of a discovered process model strongly depends on the quality and suitability of the input data. For example, the logs of many real-life systems do not refer to the activities an analyst would have in mind, but are on a much more detailed level of abstraction. Trace segmentation attempts to group low-level events into clusters, which represent the execution of a higher-level activity in the (available or imagined) process meta-model. As a result, the simplified log can be used to discover better process models. This paper presents a new activity mining approach based on global trace segmentation. We also present an implementation of the approach, and we validate it using a real-life event log from ASML's test process.

Keywords: Process Mining, Event Log Schema Transformation, Trace Segmentation.

1 Introduction

Process mining technology attempts to extract non-trivial and useful information about real-world processes from *event logs* recorded by IT systems that support these processes [1]. For example, there are many process mining techniques to automatically discover a process model describing the causal dependencies between activities [10,6]. Event logs are sets of traces, whereas a *trace is a sequence of events referring to one particular instance* of the process. An ideal event log for process mining analysis is well-structured and on an appropriate level of abstraction (e.g., one event in the log corresponds to the execution of one activity in the process). In many real-life situations, these requirements are, however, not fulfilled. Often, real event logs are recorded on a very low level of abstraction. Events in these logs are identifying miniscule activities within the system, which cannot be easily related to activities in the process model imagined by the analyst. It is not that these high-level activities are not represented in the event log at all, rather that their representation is scattered among many low-level events. This dissociation of activities makes it very hard for process analysts to correctly relate the observed behavior to any available, or imagined, process meta-model.

Trace segmentation is an event log schema transformation technique, which makes such low-level logs more understandable and easier to analyze. The fundamental idea of trace segmentation is illustrated in Figure 1. The starting point is a low-level trace of

S. Rinderle-Ma et al. (Eds.): BPM 2009 Workshops, LNBIP 43, pp. 128–139, 2010.

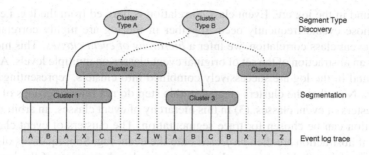

Fig. 1. Schematic description of trace segmentation

events (cf. bottom of Figure 1). Trace segmentation attempts to identify coherent *sub-sequences* of events within the trace, i.e., to "cut up" the trace into a number of event clusters. In the example in Figure 1, four clusters have been identified in the trace.

The rationale behind trace segmentation is that every cluster of low-level events is supposed to represent the execution of a higher-level activity in the (available or imagined) process meta-model. It is also important that these event clusters are properly categorized (i.e., clustered) into *types* of clusters. This allows for the discovery of corresponding activity types, which are supposed to result in a comparable sub-sequence of low-level events within and across different traces. With respect to the example in Figure 1, two cluster types A and B have been identified, each supported by two clusters. Clusters of type A consist of events from event classses A, B, or C, while clusters of type B are constituted by events of classes X, Y, Z, and W.

Trace segmentation has two main use cases. The first one is *activity mining*. In activity mining, trace segmentation is applied to elevate the log's level of abstraction, i.e., to analyze the event log from a higher-level point of view. In the example in Figure 1, the trace would have been simplified to a sequence of four events (i.e., the clusters), from two event classes (i.e., the cluster types). The second use case is *trace discovery*. In trace discovery, the discovered event sub-sequences are interpreted as traces of a hidden sub process described by their cluster type. Regarding the example, the process type represented by cluster type A would have two traces A, B, A, C and A, B, C, B.

Both activity mining and trace discovery can be implemented by trace segmentation techniques. In the following section we propose a new global approach towards trace segmentation, which is based on the correlation between event classes.

2   Global Trace Segmentation Approach

As explained earlier, trace segmentation is based on the idea that subsequences of events, which are supposed to be the product of a higher-level activity, are identified. This approach focuses on the global correlation between *event classes*, i.e. types of events. From the co-occurrence of events in the log, we derive the relative correlation between their event classes.

Our approach for global trace segmentation can be outlined as follows. (1) We use the notion of a *global event class correlation*, describing how closely related the event classes found in the log are. Event class correlation is derived from the log, i.e., event classes whose events frequently occur together in the log are highly correlated. (2) Based on event class correlation, we infer a *hierarchy of event classes*. This hierarchy represents an abstraction of the set of original event classes on multiple levels. All event classes found in the log are successively combined into clusters, representing higher-level types. Note that the clusters created in this step do not refer to groups of events, but are clusters of event classes. (3) In this hierarchy of event classes, an arbitrary level of abstraction can be chosen for trace segmentation. The clusters of event classes on that level of abstraction are then *projected* onto the event log. Subsequences of events, whose event classes belong to one cluster, are considered *segments* of the log. These segments, i.e. clusters of events, are the result of global trace segmentation.

The global approach described here works *top-down*. The association of each event to its respective higher-level cluster is not directly derived from its local, surrounding events, but rather established from the global correlation of its event class to other event classes. In the remainder of this section, we first show how the global event class correlation is determined, which is the foundation of this approach (Section 2.1). Then, we describe how, based on this correlation, our algorithm builds a global event class hierarchy (Section 2.2). Finally, we explain how this hierarchy is used to enable the actual global trace segmentation in an adaptive manner (Section 2.3).

2.1   Scanning Global Event Class Correlation

Our global approach for trace segmentation is based on the notion that there is a global relationship between event classes in the log. This relationship between event classes is then projected onto the actual event instances in the log, i.e. events inherit their mutual relationship from their respective event classes.

We can express this relationship between event classes in a correlation function.

Definition 1 (Event class correlation). *Let C be a set of event classes. The function $ecc \in C \times C \longrightarrow R_0^+$ assigns to each tuple of event classes a certain* correlation *value. The larger this value is, the more related the two respective event classes are.*

In our approach we determine the correlation function between event classes by scanning the complete log. We start with a matrix of $C \times C$, initialized with zero values before the actual scanning pass. While traversing the log, this matrix is updated for each following relation that is found. Note that this correlation matrix, as well as the correlation function itself, is symmetric, i.e. $ecc(X, Y) = ecc(Y, X)$. During the scanning pass, this symmetry needs to be maintained by the algorithm.

The scanning pass of this algorithm is illustrated in Figure 2(a). In this example, the scanning is currently inspecting an event of class A, on the bottom of the trace. We call the event currently under consideration the *reference event*. Looking at the directly preceding event of class H, the scanner can establish an observation of the co-occurrence between event classes H and A, which means that their relationship is strengthened. Correspondingly, the correlation matrix value for $ecc(A, H)$ is incremented by i, the increment value (which is usually set to 1).

In our approach, the scanning pass uses a *look-back window* for evaluating each event. This means that if the look-back window's size is six (as in the example in

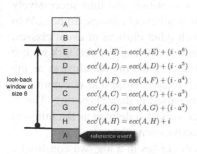

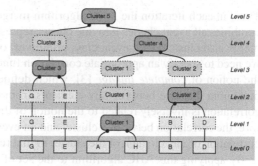

(a) Scanning event class correlation.   (b) AHC event class cluster tree.

Fig. 2. An event class cluster hierarchy is built based on an event class correlation function

Figure 2(a)) the scanner will consider the last six events which have preceded each reference event. When evaluating events in the look-back window, the scanner will attenuate its measurement exponentially, based on an attenuation factor a, where $0 < a < 1$. For any event x in the look-back window, where y is the reference event, the correlation matrix will be updated as follows: $ecc'(c(x), c(y)) = ecc(c(x), c(y)) + (i \cdot a^n)$, where n is the number of events located between x and y in the trace. This approach improves the capture of relationships within activity clusters where behavior is more unstructured, i.e., where the order of low-level events may change frequently.

After the scanning pass has evaluated all events in all traces of the log, a correlation function between event classes is established, as expressed in the aggregated correlation matrix. Our correlation function thus considers two event classes as more related, if events of these classes frequently occur closely together in traces of the log.

2.2   Building the Event Class Cluster Hierarchy

After the correlation function between event classes has been established in the scanning pass, we have a global measurement of relationship between event classes in the log. Based on this correlation function, our approach builds a hierarchy of event classes, successively combining the most related event classes into higher-level entities.

For this task, we use an adapted version of the *Agglomerative Hierarchical Clustering* (AHC) algorithm, which is a well-known data clustering technique [3]. The *primitives* to be clustered are the event classes found in the log, and we apply AHC using the correlation function established in the scanning pass. Note that the clusters created here refer to higher-level activity types, i.e., we are actually inferring *types of clusters* whose instances are event clusters in the log. The AHC algorithm can be described as follows:

1. The set of entities E initially consists of all primitives, i.e. event classes.
2. Find the two entities a and b in E which have the *largest correlation* value $ecc(a, b)$ for all tuples of entities in E.
3. Create a new event class cluster x, which contains a and b.
4. Remove a and b from E, and add x to E.
5. If E contains more than one entity, continue with the next iteration at step 2.

Thus, in each iteration the AHC algorithm merges two entities, and thus successively combines all event classes into one cluster representing all event classes. To be able to merge also clusters with event class primitives, or with other clusters of event classes, we need to specify an appropriate correlation function for clusters. For this task we use the notion of *complete linkage* [3], which defines the distance of two clusters as the maximum distance between any elements from each cluster. Note that our notion of correlation is inversely related to the notion of distance used in data clustering. Therefore, the correlation between a cluster and an event class is also defined as the minimal correlation of any element of the cluster to that respective event class.

By applying this AHC algorithm to the set of event classes in a log, we construct a hierarchical tree structure of event classes and event class clusters. Figure 2(b) shows an example of this structure. The initial set of event classes is depicted at the bottom, consisting of event classes G, E, A, H, B, and D.

During the first iteration of the AHC algorithm, event classes A and H are determined to have the maximum correlation value of all event classes. Consequently, they are combined into a new event class cluster, which is shown as $Cluster1$ in Figure 2(b). Every iteration of the algorithm creates a new *level of clustering*. For example, the first iteration creates level 1, which differs from the initial level 0 by having event classes A and H removed, and replaced by the newly created $Cluster1$.

2.3 Adaptive Global Trace Segmentation

Once the event class cluster hierarchy has been established, we can apply our global trace segmentation approach. Since this hierarchical structure successively simplifies the set of event classes in each level, we can take advantage of this and allow the analyst to adaptively simplify the event log.

After selecting the desired level of abstraction, corresponding to the different levels in the event class cluster hierarchy, every event in the log is processed as follows. Events whose event classes are still present as primitives in the desired level of abstraction are left untouched. If an event's class is contained in a cluster on the desired level of abstraction, its name is replaced by the cluster name. After rewriting the log in this way, repetitions of events which refer to the same cluster are collapsed into one event.

This procedure is illustrated in Figure 3. An original trace of the log is shown on the left, i.e. this trace is on level 0 and thus not simplified yet. For every level of abstraction

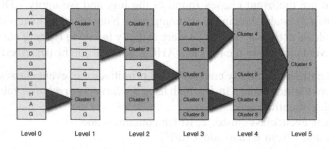

Fig. 3. Step-wise global trace segmentation

in the event class cluster hierarchy we can now apply our trace segmentation approach. In our example from Figure 2(b), event classes A and H were combined to $Cluster1$ in level 1. The example trace in Figure 3 has three events of class A and two events of class H. After rewriting these events, they can be combined into two occurrences of $Cluster1$, thus simplifying the log. As shown in Figure 3, this procedure can be applied for every level of the event class cluster hierarchy. It successively reduces the number of event classes, and the number of overall events, in the log. Note that the proposed algorithm only merges uninterrupted episodes of clustered events, which may lead to suboptimal results in the face of concurrency.

While this example shows the application of global trace segmentation for activity mining, it can be equally applied for trace discovery. With respect to level 1 in Figure 3, the algorithm has discovered two traces A, H, A and H, A, both describing the tacit subprocess denoted as $Cluster1$.

3   Implementation and Visualization

The global approach for trace segmentation has been implemented as the *Stream Scope* plugin in the *Pro*cess *M*ining (ProM) framework[1]. While the focus of this implementation is on activity mining, extending it for trace discovery purposes would be trivial. When the plugin is applied to an event log, the correlation function is scanned from the log and the event class cluster hierarchy is created. This initialization of the plugin is very fast. The stream scope visualization is based on the event class cluster hierarchy, and shows every trace in the log separately. Every event class found in the log corresponds to a vertical coordinate, while the horizontal coordinate represents the sequence of events as they occur in the trace (Note that the stream scope visualization uses an equidistant display of events, i.e. actual time is not considered for horizontal coordinates). Every event in a trace is represented by a green dot in the visualization.

In the stream scope plugin, the user can set the desired level of abstraction with a slider. This will result in a display of blue background areas in the visualization, covering the span of event classes combined in each cluster found. Note that this display of coherent cluster blocks is only possible due to the reordering of event classes from the hierarchy tree, which ensures that clusters are non-interrupted vertical subsequences.

Figure 4 shows an excerpt of a streamscope visualization for two event log traces. This excerpt is shown on three different levels of abstraction. On the left, the log is projected onto 76 event classes. 34 of these event classes are in fact clusters of event classes. The clusters of events referring to these clustered event classes have a solid blue background in the visualization. In the center of Figure 4, the log has been projected onto 18 event classes, all of which are clusters of event classes. One can see that especially events, whose classes are more located towards the top of the visualization, have been combined into larger clusters, when compared to the previous abstraction. Finally, the visualization on the right shows the log projected onto four event classes.

The plugin provides a projection of the log, which corresponds to the currently selected level of abstraction, to the framework. Thereby, this simplified log is also available for other mining and analysis techniques.

---

[1] Both software and documentation can be freely obtained from *http://prom.sourceforge.net*.

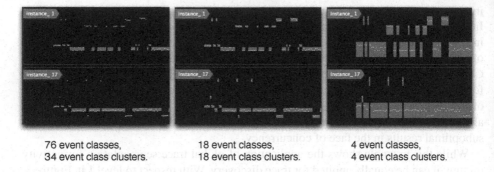

| 76 event classes, | 18 event classes, | 4 event classes, |
| 34 event class clusters. | 18 event class clusters. | 4 event class clusters. |

Fig. 4. Global trace segmentation on three levels of abstraction

4   Application to ASML's Wafer Scanner Test Log

In a previous case study [8], we have analyzed ASML's test process for wafer scanners. ASML is a leading manufacturer of wafer scanners, which are complex and expensive machines that play an integral part in the production of integrated circuits. We have analyzed ASML's test process based on event log data recorded during the wafer scanner qualification phase. The actions in this test phase can be considered on two levels of abstraction: While the actual event log data could only be obtained on a rather low level of abstraction, detailing the *single tests* which had been executed, ASML also provided us with an explicit mapping of low-level tests to so-called *job steps*. Using this mapping, a higher-level event log, describing the test process on the job step level, could be derived. These lower-level and higher-level logs were eventually used for analysis by more traditional process mining techniques.

Even for the higher-level, job step-mapped log our analysis had yielded relatively unstructured and complex spaghetti models. These models are not only cumbersome to read and hard to interpret. When compared to the reference process model provided by ASML, they indicate serious deviations in practice, i.e., the test process is in fact not executed according to specification. These deviations are due to the complexity of the testing process (e.g., failing tests may trigger the re-execution of earlier phases in the test procedure to account for changed parameters or replaced components). They are thus, in principle, expected and inherent to the test process at ASML. However, at the same time the provided grouping of low-level tests into higher-level job steps, just like the reference process itself, are created manually. Since job steps represent the *idealized* process steps, they may not reflect the actual *reality* of testing wafer steppers in practice.

Ideally, a job step, as defined by the reference process, should refer to a self-contained part of the testing process, which can be considered completed if all its tests have been successfully executed. However, if these job steps do not represent an appropriate grouping of low-level tests, this can lead to unnecessary re-executions of earlier job steps, and thus can introduce deviations to the reference process. If tests could be better grouped into job steps, the high-level process model would more accurately reflect the true process of testing wafer scanners in ASML. Furthermore, if there are strong dependencies between tests that are contained in separate job steps, this information can be used to improve the process by duplicating or re-positioning tests, so as to reveal problems earlier on, and thus shorten the completion time of the overall test procedure (by avoiding re-executions of large parts of the test process).

For investigating the suitability of the current grouping of tests into job steps, we have analyzed the original ASML log on the test code level with the global trace segmentation approach presented in this paper. If the job step compositions defined by ASML are indeed appropriate, trace segmentation should be able to rediscover the original job steps, as clusters of test codes, from the event log.

In total, 23 clusters have been derived from the event log, so as to correspond to the 23 job steps defined by ASML. We subsequently compared these 23 clusters obtained by the global trace segmentation approach to the original 23 job steps. Consider Figure 5, which visualizes the relations of the obtained clusters (clusters *1–23*) to the original job steps (the actual job step names have been anonymized to 'ae'–'zero'). We can observe relationships between clusters and job steps in two directions.

1. One can see that many clusters contain (parts of) different job steps, thus indicating a strong relation between these job steps. For example, cluster *23* completely contains the job steps 'd', 'i', 'l', and 'm', whereas cluster *1* fully covers job steps 'x', 'v', and 'u'. Another example are the job steps 'ue' and 'oe', which seem to be highly connected (cf. clusters *2*, *8*, and *7*).
2. Furthermore, many job steps are actually split-up and represented by multiple clusters. Consider, for example, job step 'j', which is in part associated to cluster *23* while another part of the same job step is associated to cluster *1*.

While relationship (1) can also be detected by analyzing clusters in hierarchical process models [6] discovered from the job step-mapped event log, especially relationship (2) generates additional insight that cannot be obtained via the more traditional process mining techniques. The reason is that for a job step that is partly associated to one group, and partly associated to another group of job steps, occurrences of tests belonging to this job step cannot be distinguished by the mining algorithm, and therefore all the job steps (of both groups) are grouped together. Here, the global trace segmentation approach yields more detailed dependencies between the job steps than can be revealed by simply analyzing the process model. As a consequence, it is easier to detect concrete opportunities to optimize the test procedure, e.g., by repositioning or replicating tests within the reference process followed by test engineers.

Since the clusters obtained by the global trace segmentation approach now offer an alternative way of grouping the low-level tests into higher-level process steps, we have used a log reflecting this new abstraction for process discovery. We have then compared the results to the model obtained from the original job step-mapped event log. First, we used the fuzzy miner [6] with exactly the same mining parameters to discover two models, one based on the original job step-mapped log, and the other based on the new mapping provided by our global trace segmentation approach. Both models showed a comparable level of complexity. However, we can judge the quality of these models using the conformance metric defined for fuzzy models. The conformance measurement indicates *to which degree the model reflects the actual behavior in the log*. The model based on the original job step-mapped log had a significantly poorer

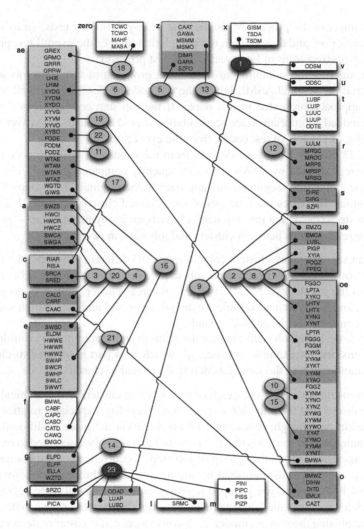

Fig. 5. Relationship between the clusters discovered by global trace segmentation (indicated by numbers), and the original job step composition (indicated by 'ae', 'zero', 'a', etc.). The background color of tests in the job steps indicate their association to the clusters discovered by global trace segmentation.

fuzzy conformance (0.28) than the model created based on our trace-segmented log (0.46). This supports the hypothesis that our trace segmentation approach creates a more realistic grouping of the low-level tests than the manual job step mapping, and thus more faithful representations of the real test process flow can be discovered. Second, we have adjusted the parameters of the fuzzy miner to discover two process models that have the same level of conformance. The model in Figure 6(a) was created using the explicit job step mapping provided by the domain experts, while the model Figure 6(b) was created using the grouping obtained from trace segmentation. The model on the left, which has

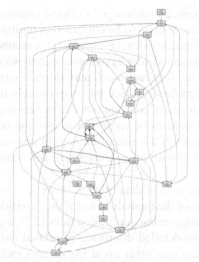 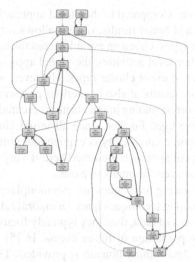

(a) Based on explicit job step map-   (b) Based on previously mined activ-
ping (more complex model).   ity clusters (less complex model).

Fig. 6. Two fuzzy models with the same conformance (≈ 0.5). The activity cluster-based model is clearly less complex, since it captures the actual steps in the process in a better way.

been mined using the original job step mapping, is clearly more complex than the model on the right, which was discovered based on the previously discovered activity clusters.

In this section, we have used our new activity mining approach to evaluate the job step abstraction provided by ASML. We have found that a more suitable abstraction can be proposed based on the actually observed behavior. This abstraction should be compared to the given job step mapping by a domain expert. Furthermore, 176 out of the total 360 test codes were not included in the given job step mapping at all. This is due to the fact that the job step mapping is manually created and maintained. To be able to compare our discovered clusters to the original job steps, we have removed these events from the log. However, using activity mining it may be possible to create an updated mapping for ASML, which also includes these currently unmapped test codes.

5   Related Work

Process mining is a field of analysis that focuses on mining behavioral aspects from log data. Since the mid-nineties several groups have been concentrating on the discovery of process models from event-based data. In [1] an overview is given of the early work in this domain. To also tackle logs from more unstructured and complex processes, flexible approaches such as Fuzzy mining [6] have been proposed recently.

While process mining has been an active research field over the last 10 years, not much attention has been paid to trace segmentation. Earlier, we had introduced a local trace segmentation approach [5], which is based on clustering event *instances*, by analyzing their proximity towards other events in their trace. In contrast, the approach presented in this paper focuses on the global correlation between *event classes*, i.e. types of events. Compared to the global approach presented in this paper, the local approach may yield better results, since it allows for one event class to be contained in multiple cluster types. Given an event log containing the same low-level event class in a number of higher-level activities, the global approach presented here cannot discover an accurate set of event cluster types. However, while the local approach may provide more accurate results, it also has serious performance problems. Since for every event in the log a corresponding initial cluster is created, the memory consumption can be very high for large logs. Further, since all initial clusters need to be compared to one another, the runtime complexity is exponential with respect to the size of the log. In contrast, the global approach presented here is very efficient with linear complexity, and is thus suitable even for interactive use.

Clustering techniques are commonplace in the area of data mining. However, most data mining techniques ignore temporal relations of the input data, and if they consider sequences of data, then they typically focus on discovering implication rules [2,7], e.g., for the prediction of future events. In [5] a more detailed discussion of related work in the data mining domain is provided. There are also other event log schema transformation approaches, which, for example, cluster traces within a log based on the assumption that the event log in fact describes a number of tacit process types [9,4]. As a consequence, similar traces within one log are grouped into more homogeneous subsets, which can subsequently be analyzed separately and yield more understandable process models than if analyzed altogether.

6   Conclusion

In this paper we have presented a new approach for trace segmentation, which can identify subsequences of events that are supposed to be the product of a higher-level activity. In contrast to earlier approaches, our solution addresses the problem in a global, top-down manner. Based on a global correlation between event classes, these classes are successively clustered into higher-level classes. By projecting these clusters onto the actual events in a log we can reduce the number of unique activities, and thus elevate the event log onto an arbitrary level of abstraction.

We have demonstrated the usefulness of trace segmentation in general, and of our global approach in particular, using the case study of ASML's test process as an example. While ASML had provided us with an explicit model for their test process, the actual testing performed in practice differed significantly, as discovered by process mining. Process discovery can show that the *control flow* of actual process execution is different from an idealized process model. In this paper, we have shown that also the *composition of activities* from lower-level process steps can be verified by using trace segmentation. The event clusters which were discovered by trace segmentation correspond much better to the actual process execution than the idealized job step mapping as envisioned by ASML. Consequently, trace segmentation provides an additional dimension for the verification of real-life processes.

Future research in the area of trace segmentation should concentrate on finding efficient methods for the recognition of repetitive event patterns, especially for situations where event classes can belong to more than one pattern. To increase the usefulness of the presented approach in practice, future extensions of the implementation should allow the user to (a) manually correct errors of the algorithm, and (b) to provide meaningful names for the found higher-level activities, before actually simplifying and further analyzing the log.

Acknowledgements. We want to thank ASML for providing us with their data, and particularly thank Ivo de Jong for his collaboration and interest in process mining.

References

1. van der Aalst, W.M.P., van Dongen, B.F., Herbst, J., Maruster, L., Schimm, G., Weijters, A.J.M.M.: Workflow Mining: A Survey of Issues and Approaches. Data and Knowledge Engineering 47(2), 237–267 (2003)
2. Bettini, C., Wang, X.S., Jajodia, S.: Mining Temporal Relationships with Multiple Granularities in Time Sequences. Data Engineering Bulletin 21(1), 32–38 (1998)
3. Duda, R.O., Hart, P.E., Stork, D.G.: Pattern Classification. Wiley-Interscience, New York (2000)
4. Greco, G., Guzzo, A., Pontieri, L., Saccá, D.: Mining Expressive Process Models by Clustering Workflow Traces. In: Dai, H., Srikant, R., Zhang, C. (eds.) PAKDD 2004. LNCS (LNAI), vol. 3056, pp. 52–62. Springer, Heidelberg (2004)
5. Günther, C.W., van der Aalst, W.M.P.: Mining Activity Clusters from Low-Level Event Logs. BETA Working Paper Series, WP 165, Eindhoven University of Technology, Eindhoven (2006)
6. Günther, C.W., van der Aalst, W.M.P.: Fuzzy Mining: Adaptive Process Simplification Based on Multi-perspective Metrics. In: Alonso, G., Dadam, P., Rosemann, M. (eds.) BPM 2007. LNCS, vol. 4714, pp. 328–343. Springer, Heidelberg (2007)
7. Mannila, H., Toivonen, H., Verkamo, A.I.: Discovery of Frequent Episodes in Event Sequences. Data Mining and Knowledge Discovery 1(3), 259–289 (1997)
8. Rozinat, A., de Jong, I.S.M., Günther, C.W., van der Aalst, W.M.P.: Process Mining Applied to the Test Process of Wafer Steppers in ASML. IEEE Transactions on Systems, Man, and Cybernetics–Part C (2009), doi:10.1109/TSMCC.2009.2014169
9. Song, M., Günther, C.W., van der Aalst, W.M.P.: Trace Clustering in Process Mining. In: Ardagna, D., et al. (eds.) BPM 2008 Workshops. LNBIP, vol. 17, pp. 109–120. Springer, Heidelberg (2009)
10. Weijters, A.J.M.M., van der Aalst, W.M.P.: Rediscovering Workflow Models from Event-Based Data using Little Thumb. Integrated Computer-Aided Engineering 10(2), 151–162 (2003)

A Formal Model for Process Context Learning

Johny Ghattas[1], Pnina Soffer[1], and Mor Peleg[1,2]

[1] Department of Management Information Systems, University of Haifa, Israel, 31905
[2] Center of Biomedical Informatics, Stanford University, Stanford, CA, 94305
GhattasJohny@gmail.com,
{morpeleg,pnina}@mis.hevra.haifa.ac.il

Abstract. Process models are considered to be a major asset in modern business organizations. They are expected to apply to all the possible business contexts in which the process may be executed, however not all of these are known a priori. Instead of identifying all contexts before the process is established, we propose to learn from runtime experience which contextual properties should be taken into account by the process model. We propose a model and an associated procedure for identifying and learning the relevant context categories of a process out of runtime experience. We postulate that the context of a process, namely, properties of the specific business case and environmental events, affects its execution and outcomes. However, when a process is launched, the exact effect and affecting variables are not necessarily known. Our approach aims at categorizing possible environmental conditions and case properties into context categories which are meaningful for the process execution. This is achieved by a context learning framework, presented in the paper.

Keywords: Business process context, Business process learning, Process goals, Soft-goals, Process model adaptation, Flexibility.

1 Introduction

Modern Organizations require their business processes (BP's) to be standardized and, at the same time, to be able to handle the variability of their environment. This variability relates to differing properties of cases handled by the process and to the unanticipated and changing requirements of the market and customers. A general term, addressing both the events and conditions in the environment and the specific properties of cases handled by the process, is the context of the process [1, 2]. Consider, for example, a customer care center, through which an organization captures its customer claims and follows up on them. Here, we consider whether the customer has a valid warranty or not to be a contextual property of the specific case. It is quite expected that the business case will be treated differently, depending on this variable.

Clearly, different contextual conditions may require different paths for the process to achieve its goals. To facilitate this, three main challenges need to be met. First, normally there is no obvious way to establish a full repository of all possible context variations that are yet to appear. Second, while it is possible to have information about an (almost) unlimited amount of case properties, we should be able to identify

S. Rinderle-Ma et al. (Eds.): BPM 2009 Workshops, LNBIP 43, pp. 140–157, 2010.

which specific properties have an effect on the process. Third, organizations need to know how to select their process paths per each one of these situations in order to achieve the best outcome.

In this paper we target the second challenge, focusing on developing a methodology for automatic learning of process context groups. Context groups cluster together process instances that have similar contexts, thereby limiting the number of context variations to be dealt with. This can be a first step towards defining process paths for each context group, such that taking that path would lead to desired process outcomes. For this purpose, we target an active process, namely, a process which has already been executed for a while, and acquired past execution data. Our basic assumption is that in these past executions, some cases were addressed "properly" according to their relevant contextual properties (although a relation between context and path selection was not necessarily formally specified). Other cases were not properly addressed, and this should be reflected in the performance achieved by the process for these cases, which should be lower when compared to the properly addressed cases. Hence, the proposed methodology is based on clustering process instance data of past executions, relating to their context, path, and outcomes. The starting point is when all this information is available, but it is not known which contextual properties are the ones that should be considered for path selection. Clustering based on the path and outcomes of process instance data finds the relevant groups of context, where each group is considered similar in terms of its process path and outcomes. Our vision is that once context groups are formed, a new process instance that has not yet been activated could be matched to an existing context group, in order to suggest a path that would yield the desired outcome.

The remainder of the paper is structured as follows. Section 2 presents our conceptual model for BP context, which is an extension of the Generic Process Model (GPM) [3, 4]. In Section 3, we provide our algorithm's architecture, illustrating each step through an example order provisioning process from the cellular service domain. Section 4 provides a review of related work and Section 5 summarizes this work and outlooks to future research.

2 The Conceptual Model for Business Process Context

We will first establish a formal definition of the generic concepts for a context learning framework. Our proposed model builds upon GPM and extends it to incorporate the relevant concepts for modeling process context.

2.1 The Generic Process Model (GPM)

GPM [3, 4] is a state-based view of a process including the concept of goals. Briefly, GPM offers a process model defined over a domain as a tuple $< L, I, G>$, as described below. Consider the state of the domain as the values of all its properties (or state variables) at a moment in time, the law L specifies possible state transitions as a mapping between subsets of states; I is a subset of unstable states, which are the initial states of the process after a triggering external event has occurred; G is a subset of stable states on which the process terminates, termed the goal of the process.

Following this, a specific path taken by a process is a sequence of states, transforming by law or as a result of external events, until a stable state is reached. If the process model is valid, this stable state is in the goal set.

The process goal as addressed by GPM is a state meeting the conditions that should be achieved by the process. GPM distinguishes process goals from soft-goals, which are defined as an order relation on goal states [4]. In other words, soft-goals relate to the desirability of possible states in the goal set (all meeting the condition that terminates the process) according to defined business objectives. For example, the goal of a process may be a state where some treatment has been given to a patient, but a state where the treatment does not incur side effects is considered as "better" than a state where side effects are observed. Finally, GPM entails criteria for assessing the validity of a process, namely, its ability to achieve its goal [3]. It enables the analysis of a process model to identify causes for invalidity.

2.2 The Conceptual Model for Context Learning

Although GPM does not provide a context model, it can be extended to support such concepts. In this section we provide a detailed description of our GPM extension for context modeling.

We postulate that a process representation depends on a context if a process instance cannot be executed correctly without having some additional inputs regarding the values of case properties (e.g., whether the customer has a valid warranty) or events arising from the external environment (e.g., the customer changes his order). We extrapolate this definition to BP context, where the context of a process or a plan would be the set of all inputs provided to the process during its enactment lifetime.

In GPM terms, the external environment provides inputs to the process through the initial triggering of the process and through external events which reach the process during runtime. We denote the set of external events reaching the process during its execution as X and the set of case state-variable values known at the initial triggering of the process as I.

Note that our interest, while trying to learn process contexts, is to group in a meaningful way all possible context instances, that is, all possible <I, X> combinations, so these groups would represent specific business cases. As an example, service providers may implement different products, price plans and processes for supporting business customers and for supporting private customers. Hence, there are two major context groups - the corporate customer context group, which includes all context instances of business customers, and the retail customer context group, which includes all context instances of private customers. Each of these groups may be further divided in sub-groups to enable more fine-grained tailoring of paths for each sub group. For example, private customers may be divided by age, by bundles of services (cellular, data, content), etc. However, we should not reach a level of granularity where we have context groups that are too specific, to avoid over fitting the context groups with the specific context instances from which the context groups were identified.

Following this intuitive discussion, we first extend GPM by formalizing the concepts of process instance and of the context of process instances. Later on we define the concepts of behavioral and context-based similarity of process instances.

Definition 1(process context): A business process context C=<I, X> is the set of all inputs provided by the external environment to the process, where I marks the state variable values at the initial state, set at process instance triggering time; X is a set of external events, which affect the process instance at runtime.

The context of a specific process instance PI_i is obtained by assigning values to I and X of PI_i:

$$C_i = < I_i, X_i > .$$

For example, considering the case of a customer ordering a cellular phone and services, I would be the set of data the customer provides at order request time (characteristics of the phone he would like – slider phone, Bluetooth capabilities, camera, etc.; the services he wants – voice calls, SMS, internet connection; customer budget limits, etc.). X would be changes the customer introduced to his order some time after the order was initiated, e.g., upgrading into a more advanced package with more features. The context model for this example would be:

$C = < I, X >$, where:

> I= {{Customer characteristics set}, {Phone charac-
> teristics set}, {Set of Services required}, {Cus-
> tomer budget}}.
> X= {{Order change during execution # 1}}.

Note that the effect of an external event over the process may be different depending on its arrival time at the process. For example, cancelling an order may affect the process differently if it it occurs before or after the handset is delivered. In the first case, the change would simply imply roll-backing the order in the system and returning the equipment to the logistical department, while in the second, the customer would be required to return the equipment before the order change.

Definition 2 (process instance): Given the context $C_i = <I_i, X_i>$, the execution of a *BP instance* would lead to the generation of a path P_i, which terminates either in a goal state $t_i \in G$, or in an exception state $t_i \in E$, where E is a set of stable states not in the goal $(E \cap G = \emptyset)$.

Based on this, we can model a process instance (PI_i) by as $PI_i = <C_i, P_i, t_i>$, where $t_i \in G$ or $t_i \in E$, and P_i is a sequence of states, following GPM's definition.

The path (P_i) and the termination state (t_i) of a process instance (PI_i) constitute its behavior. In a perfect world, process instances that have similar contexts would follow similar paths to lead to a given termination state. However, our knowledge of the process context is partial. Under partial knowledge, we may not be aware of contextual variables whose different values may differently affect the process behavior, and can be considered "different contexts". Lacking such knowledge, we may group PIs that partially share the same context but exhibit different behaviors. This would not be an effective strategy for learning the best paths that for a given context would achieve desirable outcomes. Hence, process instances can be grouped considering two types of similarities:

(1) Contextual property-based similarity.
(2) Behavioral similarity.

Clearly, these two groupings are expected to be different, since not all contextual properties necessarily affect process behavior, and some properties may have a similar effect. Our interest is to identify a third type of grouping, *context groups definition*, namely, groups of instances whose contextual property-based similarity can predict some behavioral similarity.

In the following, we first discuss behavioral similarity identification. We continue by discussing contextual property-based similarity, and then rely on these two to develop criteria for context group definition.

Behavioral Similarity of Process Instances

Our objective is to group process instances that follow similar paths and result in similar termination states (goal or exception) into homogeneous groups. In order to establish behavioral similarity of process instances, we need similarity criteria for both termination states and paths of process instances.

Definition 3 (state similarity): Let s_1 and s_2 be two states, $s_i=(x_{i1}, x_{i2},...x_{in})$, i=1, 2, where x_{ij} are state variable values. For a given similarity threshold ST, s_1 is *similar* to s_2 iff a distance measure D satisfies $D(s_1, s_2) \leq ST$. Notation: $s_1 \sim s_2$.

Note that technically, state similarity can be established by applying various clustering algorithms to state data. However, conceptually, similar states could be viewed as identical at some granularity level. For example, there may be many different states where a product has passed quality tests (with different values of test results). At a certain granularity level, all these states are identical (successfully passed). Similarity of paths and termination states of process instances is derived from Definition 3. The derivation follows since termination is a specific state, and a path, according to GPM, is a sequence of states. Note, to this end, we neglected the ordering of states in a path, taking account only of the state variable values. Also note that hereafter we assume a given similarity threshold, so the existence of similarity can be established.

Definition 4 (Process instance behavioral similarity): Consider two process instances PI_i and PI_j, $i \neq j$, where: $PI_i = <C_i, P_i, t_i>$, $PI_j = < C_j, P_j, t_j>$. These process instances are considered *behaviorally similar* if and only if their path state variable values are similar and their termination states (either in the goal or in the exception set) are similar:

$$PI_i \sim PI_j \Leftrightarrow P_i \sim P_j \text{ and } t_i \sim t_j .$$

Grouping process instances by behavioral similarity yields clusters of similar instances as defined below.

Definition 5 (process instance cluster): A *process instance cluster* (PIC_k) is the set of all process instances PI_i which are behaviorally similar to each other:

$$PIC_k = \{PI_i, PI_j \mid PI_i \sim PI_j , i \neq j\} \ \forall k .$$

Definition 5 implies that each process instance PI_i can be assigned to one specific process instance cluster PIC_k. Hence we can say that if a PI is assigned to one PIC it is not assigned to another PIC:

$$\text{Given i, k: } PI_i \in PIC_k => \forall l \neq k, PI_i \notin PIC_l .$$

We will discuss our technical approach for creating the PICs in Section 3. Basically, grouping instances into PICs as specified in Definition 5 is completely based on the behavior observed in actual process instances, that is, process path and termination data. It does not relate to the contextual properties, neither does it establish similarity of the contexts themselves, which we discuss next.

Contextual Property-Based Similarity

We now turn to discuss similarity of process instance contextual properties. Our analysis begins when we have information about the context of every process instance. However, we do not know which of these properties affect process behavior and how.

Definition 6 (contextual property): A *contextual property*, CP, is a logical predicate established over a subset of context variables, that is, state variables whose values are defined in I and X.

As an example, in the case of a service provider, the predicate "customer_type = "Business customer" is a contextual property as it establishes a logical predicate over the state variable customer_type, whose value is defined for states in the set I.

Definition 7 (contextual property-based similarity): Two process instances $PI_i = <C_i,$ $P_i,$ $t_i >$ and $PI_j = < C_j,$ $P_j,$ $t_j >$ are *contextual property-based similar* if $\exists$ contextual property CP such that $CP(C_i) = CP(C_j)$.

Note that, as opposed to behavioral similarity-based grouping, where a process instance can be included in one PIC only, here there might be a large number of groupings, each based on a different contextual property. A process instance can thus be included in more than one contextual property-based similarity group.

Context Groups

Above we showed how to identify behavioral similarity and contextual property-based similarity of PIs. Yet, we would like to find meaningful process instance groups, similar in their contextual properties, such that for each group, following a certain path would enable predicting its outcome. We term these groups *context groups*.

Definition 8 (Context group): A *Context Group* CG is a set of process instances such that: CG={$PI_i,$ PI_j | $\exists$ CP_k: $\forall i, j,$ $(CP_k(PI_i)=CP_k(PI_j) \wedge P_i \sim P_j) \Rightarrow t_i \sim t_j$}.

We assume that such context groups exist, and try to identify which contextual properties satisfy the implication relation of Definition 8. Two main difficulties need to be overcome. First, process instances in a context group may follow different paths and achieve different termination states, thus they are not necessarily behaviorally similar. Second, the possible number of contextual properties increases exponentially with the number of contextual state variables. Note that in addition to these two difficulties, in real-life situations not all the contextual information is available. There might be state variables of which partial or even no information is available, or the actual data might be "noisy". The quality of the data may be manifested as statistical errors when similarities are assessed, accounted for by the procedure presented in Section 4. However, the rest of this section addresses complete and "clean" information.

In order to identify context groups, we analyze the consequences of Definition 8. As a result, we derive two postulates characterizing behavior of instances in a context group.

Consider two process instances, PI_i and PI_j, such as: $PI_i = \langle C_i, P_i, t_i \rangle$ and $PI_j = \langle C_j, P_j, t_j \rangle$, $i \neq j$, and assume we know the actual context groups. There are eight possible combinations of whether these instances are (a) in the same context group CG_k, (b) similar at the path, and (c) similar at the termination state, as detailed in table 1. The last column of the table indicates what combinations can occur according to Definition 8; the implication of Definition 8 is false only if two PIs that are in the same context group and follow similar paths result in different termination states.

Table 1. Possible combinations of CG, path and termination state similarities (T= True, F= False)

Case #	$PI_i, PI_j \in CG_k$	$P_i \sim P_j$	$t_i \sim t_j$	Can this combination occur?
1	F	F	F	T
2	F	F	T	T
3	F	T	F	T
4	F	T	T	T
5	T	F	F	T
6	T	F	T	T
7	T	T	F	F
8	T	T	T	T

Examining Table 1, we can see that for process instances not in the same context group, all combinations of paths and termination states are possible (cases 1-4 in Table 1). In addition, for instances in the same context group that have different paths (cases 5 and 6 in Table 1), similar or different termination states are possible. If the instances are in the same context group and have similar paths, their termination states should be similar (case 8), and cannot be different (case 7). However, Table 1 relates to known context groups, while in our problem context groups are unknown. Hence, the only conclusive assertion we can make with respect to two process instances is that they are not members of the same context group if their paths are similar and their termination states are not, as formalized in Postulate 1.

Postulate 1: Let $\{PI\}$ be a set of process instances grouped by some contextual property CP_k $\{PI\}=\{PI_i, PI_j \mid \exists\, CP_k: \forall i, j, CP_k(PI_i)=CP_k(PI_j)\}$. If $\exists\, PI_i, PI_j \in \{PI\}$ such that $P_i \sim P_j$ and $\neg\,(t_i \sim t_j)$ then $\{PI\}$ is not a context group.

To illustrate this, consider an ordering process of a cellular service provider. Assume that business customers may order a specific package and be given a specific offer for a price. Also assume that some will accept this offer and some will reject it. We may conclude that "business customers" is not a context group, and some finer grained contextual property should be used in order to divide business customers further into groups where the outcome (accept or reject) can be predicted based on the path (offer given).

Postulate 1 provides a conclusive criterion for excluding a set of contextually similar process instances as a context group. However, we do not have a conclusive criterion for positively asserting a set of PIs as a context group. We cannot rely on case 8 in

Table 1 for forming such criterion because similar paths and similar termination states are also possible for two process instances which are not in the same context group (case 4 in Table 1). Nevertheless, we may assume that groups of contextually similar process instances (groups from cases 5 through 8) form a context group if they consistently (for each path from a set of different paths) achieve similar termination states given a similar path (only case 8 satisfies this condition). In the example above, consider two sets of contextual property-based similar process instances: group1 including business customers whose number of handsets is below 10 and group 2 of business customers whose number of handsets is between 10 and 20. Assume that both groups consistently accept one package and reject a second package. We may consider these two groups as one context group, since the differences in their contextual properties are not manifested in their behavior (they have the same behavior for a set of paths).

We use Figure 1 to explain the principles for proposing context groups based on consistent behavior similarity. As shown in Figure 1, PICs (columns) include PIs that follow the same path and yield the same termination state. However, a PIC can contain PIs belonging to different context groups (CGs). For example, PIC 2 contains a set of process instances that can be partitioned based on some contextual property into four subsets $\{PI\}_1$ through $\{PI\}_4$. The entire set of PIs contained in PIC2 cannot form a CG because although all PIs that are contained in PIC2 terminate in X when they follow Path B, when PIs contained in $\{PI\}_1$ and $\{PI\}_3$ follow Path A they terminate in X but when PIs contained in $\{PI\}_2$ follow Path A they terminate in Y. Therefore, PIs contained in $\{PI\}_2$ cannot belong to the same CG as PIs contained in $\{PI\}_1$ or $\{PI\}_3$. We can propose CGs based on similarity of behavior. In Figure 1, $\{PI\}_1$ and $\{PI\}_3$ have instances in exactly the same PICs, hence their behavior is consistent (they terminate in X when they follow paths A, B, or C) so they can be considered one context group. As explained above, $\{PI\}_2$ does not belong to the same context group as $\{PI\}_1$ or $\{PI\}_3$. $\{PI\}_4$ does not violate Postulate 1, but it has no instances in PIC 1 or PIC4, hence it is not consistent in its behavior with the other sets of PIs and is therefore not considered in the same context group with them. In summary, based on similarity of behavior we can see three CGs: $\{PI\}_1 \cup \{PI\}_3$; $\{PI\}_2$; and $\{PI\}_4$. The CGs are formed by splitting each PIC into subsets of instances based on context similarity and combining subsets that exhibit similar behavior across all PICs into CGs.

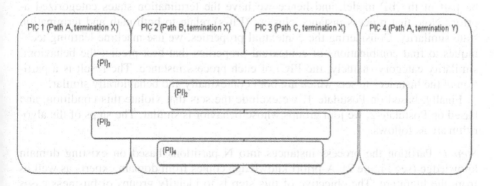

Fig. 1. PICs for a combination of path and termination states

In general, given two sets of contextual property-based similar process instances such that each one complies with Postulate 1; if they consistently exhibit similar behaviors we can relate to them as being in the same context group. This is formalized in Postulate 2.

Postulate 2: Let $\{PI\}_1$ and $\{PI\}_2$ be sets of process instances that are contextual property-based similar, such that each one complies with the criterion of Postulate 1. If $\forall PIC_k$, $\{PI\}_1 \cap PIC_k \neq \varnothing \Rightarrow \{PI\}_2 \cap PIC_k \neq \varnothing$ and $\{PI\}_2 \cap PIC_k \neq \varnothing \Rightarrow \{PI\}_1 \cap PIC_k \neq \varnothing$, then $\{PI\}_1 \cup \{PI\}_2$ is considered a context group.

Postulate 2 enables us to join small context groups into larger ones if they consistently exhibit similar behavior, thus reducing the number of context variants to be addressed.

3   An Approach for Learning Context Groups of Business Processes

Based on the model presented in Section 2, we have established a procedure which implements the context group identification in a five stage algorithm, as schematized in Figure 2.

Our starting point is a database of process instances, which includes the following data:

(1) Path data, organized as a set of states, where each state is a vector of state variable values.
(2) The termination state, which is provided as a vector of state variable values.
(3) Context data, which is composed of the initial state (I), in the form of a state variables vector, and a set of state variable vectors representing the external events received during the process execution.

The basic principles of the procedure are as follows. Behavioral similarity of process instances is identified using a clustering algorithm, where process instances are assigned to a process instance cluster ID. Termination state similarity assessment is achieved based on predefined rules, as the termination state modeling is assumed to be part of the BP model, and hence we have the termination states categorized a-priori. Note that process instance clusters (PICs) relate to both path and termination state similarity. Considering the contextual properties, we use machine learning techniques to find combinations of contextual properties that best predict the behavioral similarity category (namely, the PIC) of each process instance. The result is a partition of the instances to sets which are both contextually and behaviorally similar.

Finally, based on Postulate 1, we exclude the sets that violate this condition, and based on Postulate 2, we join groups whose behavior is similar. The steps of the algorithm are as follows:

Step 1: Partition the process instances into N partitions based on existing domain knowledge (see Figure 2). A-priori knowledge comes from domain experts as well as from the literature. The objective of this step is to identify groups of business cases that are relatively uniform in their characteristics.

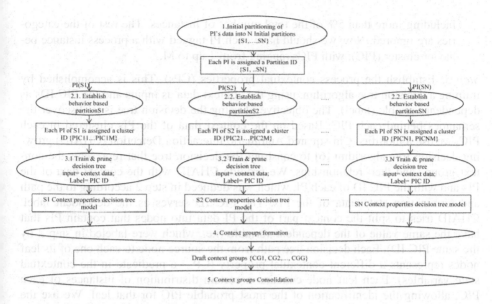

Fig. 2. Architecture of the context groups learning algorithm. PI- process instance; S- Initial partition.

For each partition (S_i), we separately apply the following three steps of the algorithm.

Step 2: Establish the behavioral similarity of the process instances PI_i (step 2 in Figure 2). This is done in three steps:

(a) Establish the process instance path (P_i) similarity using a clustering algorithm which is applied to the set of PI state vectors. The objective is to assign to each process instance a process path similarity category. This step results in the identification of p groups of instances, assumed to be similar at the process path level. The number of path similar clusters generated, p, would be selected according to goodness of fit criteria, such as Akaike Information criteria (AIC) [5]. The clustering algorithm can be applied several times, achieving a series of clustering results with an increasing number of clusters for each clustering set. Finally, the best cluster set is selected as the one that attains the first minima of the ratio of AIC changes.

(b) Establish the termination state (t_i) similarity. The termination categorization is based on a set of predefined rules stated as basic logical predicates over the termination state variables. We assume having t different categories of termination state groups.

(c) Establish behavioral similarity by selecting the process instance categories which are simultaneously similar at process instance path and termination levels. This is done by splitting up the clusters formed in part (a) into groups in which the PIs have similar termination states. Out of these categories, select only the categories which present a significant number of instances, which we consider as categories including more than 5% of the total number of instances. The rest of the categories are ignored. Now we should have each PI tagged with a process instance behavior cluster (PIC), with PICs ranging from 1 up to M.

Step 3: Establish the process contextual properties (CPs). This is accomplished by training a decision tree algorithm, using the context data as inputs and the PIC IDs as dependent variable (label). The objective of using the decision tree is to discover the semantics behind each PIC. Based on the context data of the PIs clustered in each PIC, we use a modified Chi-squared Automatic Interaction Detection (CHAID) growing decision tree algorithm [6] to construct the decision tree that represents the context groups and their relationships. We provide CHAID with the context data of the PIs and with the PIC ID of each PI, which was deduced in step 2 according to the path and termination state data of the PIs. The PIC ID serves as the dependent label. CHAID tries to split the context part of the PI data into nodes that contain PIs that have the same value of the dependent variable (i.e., which were labeled in step 2 by the same PIC ID). Each decision tree path from the source node to each one of its leaf nodes represents a different contextual property (CP – a predicate in the contextual state variables). Each leaf node contains a certain distribution of instances of each PIC, allowing the identification of the most probable PIC for that leaf. We use the Chi-Square criteria for tree growing and pruning. The tree is cross-validated using a k-fold cross-validation strategy (k=15).

Step 4: Form the context groups (CGs). Based on Postulate 1, for all tree paths, eliminate a path if it contains instances from PICs that have similar paths but different termination states[1]. We also eliminate nodes which include similar levels of different PIC's and hence have no clear output. The remaining paths are assumed to be context groups.

Step 5: Join (consolidate) context groups if their instances are included in the same PICs, based on Postulate 2.

In order to illustrate the proposed algorithm, consider a simple example of the ordering process of a cellular service provider. The process deals with ordering cellular handsets and services by both business and private customers. The context of the process consists of the customers' details (e.g. age, location, whether this is an existing customer or a new one, average expenses per month, major usage (voice, data, mobile modem connection, content services, etc.)), and the details of the services the customer requests (voice, SMS, data mobile modem, content services, mobile TV, etc.). We assume that the service provider offers service packages that include voice, data, and content services, based upon a second generation (2G) and third generation (3G) network technology. We also assume the possible offering of Blackberry handsets and services.

The first step (Step 1) would consist of identifying the initial partitions, e.g., S_1= "Business customers" and S_2 = "Private customers". This partition relies on domain

---

[1] As we need to account for a certain level of error, we consider that if a leaf node contains l_i instances of PIC_i and l_2 instances of PIC_j, with $l_1 > l_2$, where PIC_i and PIC_j are similar at path level and different at termination state level, we would eliminate the path leading to this leaf node if $l_2/l_1 > 10$ %.

knowledge, identifying these two categories as different lines of business, very different in their business goals and scenarios, and served by different organizational units.

We proceed to focus on each category separately and apply the next four steps of the algorithm to each category. Considering, for instance, S_1, we would take all PIs included in this partition and apply to their path data the clustering algorithm. Suppose that it would result in three path-similar categories: category 1 including 45 % of the instances, category 2 including 30% of the instances, and category 3 containing the remaining 25 % of the instances.

Next, we categorize the termination properties of these process instances, based on the following two rules provided by the business expert:

> Rule 1: Normal termination: Customer_feedback= "Confirmed" AND Package_status = "delivered" .
>
> Rule 2: Customer reject: Customer_feedback = "cancelled order" AND Package_status = "returned" .

Now we have three path categories and two termination categories, hence we have six potential PICs that are the different combinations of these two sets. However, assume that not all combinations exist in the process instances in the database. The PICs that represent the existing combinations are presented in Table 2.

Table 2. PICs found in the example

PIC #	Path similarity category	Termination state rule
1	1	1
2	2	1
3	3	1
4	1	2

We assume that all these combinations have more than 5 % instances out of the total sample and hence all of them would be considered as relevant PICs.

Step 3: We now proceed to the identification of the contextual properties of these four PICs.

We use the decision tree algorithm which we train with the PIC IDs and which results in the decision tree schematized in Figure 3:

The tree has seven paths, all starting with a partition over the state variable expenses, over the ranges of less than 2000 $/month, between 2000 and 4000 $/Month and more than 4000 $/month.

For the first range, the decision tree identified a sub-partition based on the service_pack variable, which divides the instances into the values of Voice and 2.5G packs. For the third range it identifies a sub-partition based on the service_pack variable, dividing the instances into the values of 2.5G, 3G and Blackberry. For the second range of expenses, the decision tree did not identify any good sub-partition of the set of PIs. For service_pack = 3G (node 8), an additional partition is proposed, using the state variable mobile_TV, resulting in nodes 10 and 11.

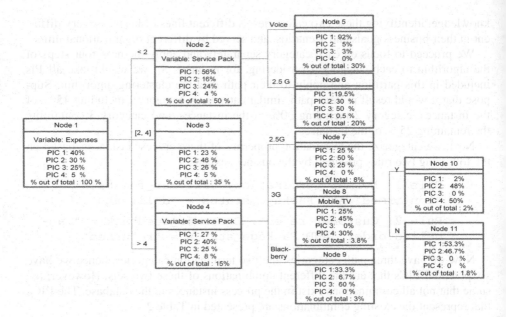

Fig. 3. Hypothetic decision tree for a service provider ordering process. The tree partitions PIs according to contextual properties that best explain the similarities in path and terminal state.

As a result, we have seven leaf nodes that stand for seven contextual properties. These should be checked for compliance with Postulate 1. According to Postulate 1, PICs whose paths are similar and termination state is not cannot be in the same context group. Examining Table 2, such PICs are PIC1 and PIC 4. Considering the decision tree results, leaf node 3 includes PIs belonging to both PIC1 and PIC4, hence, it cannot be considered as representing a context group[2]. Table 3 presents the contextual property predicates associated with each leaf node in the decision tree and an indication whether this CP stands for a context group.

As seen in Table 3, we have identified six context groups, associated with CPs 2, 3, 4, 5, 6 and 7.

Recall, our motivation for identifying context groups was the assumption that the properties defining these groups affect path selection and outcome (termination state) of process instances. Examining the details of the context groups we identified, note that the predicted PIC for group 6 (node 10 in the decision tree) is PIC4, whose termination state is defined as "customer reject" (an exception termination state). Hence, the PIs in this node are a valuable source of information about process exceptions. The indication is that 50% of the customers which fall into that context group (namely, expenses over 5000$ a month who ordered a 3G service pack and a mobile TV), when treated following path 1 have rejects concerning their orders. In contrast,

---

[2] Note that leaf nodes 6 and 10 include both PICs too but the level of PIC4 in node 6 is very low relative to PIC1 (0.5%PIC4/19.5% PIC1 = 2%, does not exceed the 5% threshold), and vice versa for node 10. Hence, we consider these as being within an acceptable margin of error.

48% of this population was treated following path 2 (PIC2), which resulted in a successful termination. The remaining 2% were treated successfully following path 1, and they are considered as not characterizing the behavior of this context group. This information can be used for establishing decision rules that relate the selected path to the context group in future executions of the process.

Table 3. Context properties based on the decision tree of Figure 3. The predicted PIC in the fourth column is calculated as the most probable PIC in each leaf node (provided in the second column).

CP#	Leaf Node	CP predicate	Predicted PIC	Other possible PICs	Is it a CG?
1	3	2< expenses < 4	2	1, 3, 4	No
2	5	expenses < 2 and service_pack= Voice	1	2, 3	Yes
3	6	expenses < 2 and service_pack= 2.5G	3	1, 2	Yes
4	7	expenses > 5 and service_pack= 2.5G	2	1, 3	Yes
5	9	expenses > 5 and service_pack= Blackberry	3	1, 2	Yes
6	10	expenses > 5 and service_pack= 3G and mobile_TV = Y	4	2	Yes
7	11	expenses > 5 and service_pack= 3G and mobile_TV = N	1	2	Yes

Next, based on Postulate 2, we see that the groups corresponding to context properties CP3 and CP5 can be joined into a single CG as they both comply with Postulate 1, include instances belonging to PICs 1, 2 and 3, and have the same predicted PIC. Note that on the basis of Postulate 2 it would also be possible to join the groups corresponding to CP2 and CP4 into the same group. However, these have a different predicted PIC. Assuming some business logic driving the path selection in the organization (although not in a conclusive manner), we would leave them as separate groups. Following postulate 2, we decide not to join CP2 and CP7 into the same CG as they do not share PIC3 in their behaviors. Hence we remain with the following final context groups shown in Table 4.

Table 4. Final context group list

CG#	Leaf Node	CP predicate corresponding to the CG	Predicted PIC	Other possible PICs
2	5	expenses < 2 and service_pack= Voice	1	2, 3
3	6+ 9	(expenses < 2 and service_pack= 2.5G) or (expenses > 5 and service_pack= Blackberry)	3	1, 2
4	7	expenses > 5 and service_pack= 2.5G	2	1, 3
6	10	expenses > 5 and service_pack= 3G and MobileTV = Y	4	2
7	11	expenses > 5 and service_pack= 3G and MobileTV = N	1	2

4 Related Work

Context awareness has just started receiving attention in the business process area. Examples include [2, 7-9], as well as our own previous work [1]. Through all these works, some agreement can be found about context as being the impact that the environment has over the process. However, to the best of our knowledge, the identification of relevant contexts for a given process has not been formally or algorithmically approached so far. Xia and Wei [9] define context as a set of business rules, each of which represents a small unit of knowledge of business management (business goal, customer requirements, business strategy, etc.). In our proposed procedure the context groups are represented through predicates, much in-line with their proposal. Yet, their definition is far from specifying how a context is formally established, leaving to the user to edit and define the context manually. Rosemann and Recker [8] propose a context-aware process design methodology in order to approach the problem of identifying contextual variables that drive the need for flexible business processes. Their definition of context remains intuitive and not formally stated as in our case. In addition, their methodology is qualitative in nature and can benefit from our formal model in order to rely less on the process designer's judgment. It can help the designer by focusing his effort on a smaller set of context groups rather than a whole set of process instances.

Context Awareness has been addressed in different domains, such as knowledge management [10] and context aware applications (e.g., mobile applications taking into account the location, the profile of the user and past usage) [11]. Additionally, context modeling and context reasoning has been largely investigated in artificial intelligence and in cognitive science. In these domains, several researchers [12-15] have pointed out that our knowledge of context is always partial; a context is primarily a subset of an individual global state, which is a partial and approximate theory of the world from some individual's perspective. As stated by Giunchiglia and Ghidini [13], context reasoning is local, that is, it is applicable only within the frame of a context and may be invalid for a different context (principle of locality). In addition, the set of facts that an individual takes into consideration in order to draw a conclusion, via deductive reasoning, is a small subset of his/her entire knowledge. This relates to our model of identifying the relevant contextual properties for each set of behaviorally similar process instances. The context property is locally-relevant only for the set of the process instances it represents.

While reasoning, people can switch between context views, depending on the relevance of the context to the next task that they are trying to accomplish. However, while doing so, compatibility of the reasoning performed in different contexts should be maintained (principle of compatibility) [13]. In our model, different ways of defining termination states with respect to goals may result in different affecting contextual properties. Still, they should all be compatible and rely on the same set of data.

Buvac et al. [15] argue that there may be multiple representations at different levels of details per any specific context. There are three dimensions in which representation of context may vary: partiality (knowledge being partial), approximation, and perspective. The level of approximation can be used to define a partial order of contexts. The appropriate level of approximation depends, among other things, on the problem to be solved. The perspective determines the content of a particular context. The authors also propose that the relationships between context definitions should be a hierarchy, described using subsumption relationships. In addition, they claim that there is a single outermost context definition. We mainly address granularity of the definition of a CG which corresponds to perspective (e.g., postulate 2 provides the criteria that we use to define the perspective under which we consider that two groups can be joined into one larger group; using a finer-granularity of context would result in smaller CGs). To some extent, we also relate to partiality (allowed statistical error in the procedure).

Our approach differs from a case-based reasoning (CBR) approach [16][17], which uses a case-base of process instances. For a given process instance awaiting execution it proposes a similar process instance from the case-base. The main differences between the approaches are: (1) CBR systems do not establish the context of the process as a main building block to compare process instances. Instead, the problem definition is left to the end user with no formal methodology to establish it; (2) CBR approaches do not establish any compatibility criteria like postulates one and 2 in our model. We consider that our approach is complementary to CBR systems and may provide them with a formal and systematic way for defining problem similarities, as well as a systematic approach for considering the process outcomes while querying for similar cases.

5 Discussion and Conclusions

While it is commonly known that the context of a process should be taken into account during execution in order to achieve the desired outcome, little has been done so far for systematically supporting this. This paper proposed an algorithmic approach for identifying context groups out of past runtime experience. Relating to context groups allows us to reduce the analysis of process behavior to a set of groups instead of addressing each one of the process instances individually. Our approach is to deduce the context groups from both the behavioral similarity of process instances and their contextual characteristics. The paper presents a formalization of these similarities, which is the basis for a context learning procedure. The procedure allows us to automatically deduce the context groups which affect the process execution and outcomes. While the example given in this paper is hypothetical, we have experimented with the proposed procedure applying it to a process taken from the health-care domain (treating urinary tract infection patients). The data included 297 patient records collected in a hospital. The state vector of a process instance included 80 state variables. Applying the procedure, we identified five context groups with an accuracy measure of 92% for 59% of the considered instances. We are currently evaluating the clinical implications of these results [18].

Our proposed procedure, as presented in Section 3, is derived from the formal model presented in Section 2. Yet, there may be other procedures that can be derived from these principles. In particular, for different domains of knowledge, different clustering and learning algorithms may be used within the framework of the proposed procedure.

Our current approach has some limitations. First, as stated earlier, we do not know for certain which contextual properties are the ones that really affect behavior. Second, there is a possibility that some context-relevant variables are unknown and hence their data was not collected. As a consequence, our results are bounded to a certain level of error, which we cannot eliminate. We face a similar situation of bounded statistical error when establishing the similarity of process instance paths;

clustering selects the set of features that best represents the data, while ignoring the rest. The similarity threshold discussed in Definition 3 is not defined using a semantic definition but is determined statistically by the clustering algorithm. The dependency between different variables within the path data may well affect the accuracy of the clustering results, although using robust feature selection algorithms prior to clustering reduces this significantly. Finally, termination states are currently roughly categorized as being within the process goal or not. In future, we intend to allow for assessing the level of soft-goal attainment as part of the terminal state similarity definition.

Our context-learning algorithm is a first step towards learning the process paths that should best be adopted for each context group and adapting the process model schema accordingly and this is our main future research direction. Future research would also include the evaluation of our algorithm though case studies from different domains. Referring to the algorithm evaluation program, While statistical measures can evaluate the significance of the predictions made by the context groups, the practical consequences of the result still need evaluation. In the long term, the identified context groups should support an improved path selection and, as a result, an improvement in business performance measures of the process under consideration. However, this result can only be evaluated over time. In the short term, the identified context groups can be evaluated by domain experts However, while expert evaluation has the advantage of relying on specific domain knowledge, it remains subjective and dependent on current domain knowledge. In contrast, the objective of our algorithm is to discover context groups that have not been known a-priori. Hence, domain experts may indicate the extent to which the proposed context groups seem logical, but the real evaluation will be in the long term.

References

1. Ghattas, J., Soffer, P., Peleg, M.: A Goal-based approach for business process learning. In: Workshop on Business Process Modeling, Development, and Support (BPMDS 2008), in conjunction with CAISE 2008, Montpellier, France (2008)
2. Ploesser, K., Peleg, M., Soffer, P., Rosemann, M., Recker, J.: Learning from Context to Improve Business Processes. BPtrends 2009(1), 1–9 (2009)
3. Soffer, P., Wand, Y.: Goal-driven Analysis of Process Model Validity. In: Persson, A., Stirna, J. (eds.) CAiSE 2004. LNCS, vol. 3084, pp. 521–535. Springer, Heidelberg (2004)
4. Soffer, P., Wand, Y.: On the Notion of Soft Goals in Business Process Modeling. Business Process Management Journal 11(6), 663–679 (2005)
5. Akaike, H.: A new look at the statistical model identification. IEEE Transactions on Automatic Control 19(6), 716–723 (1974)
6. Kass, G.V.: An Exploratory Technique for Investigating Large Quantities of Categorical Data. J. of Applied Statistics 29(2), 119–127 (1980)
7. Ludget, A.A., Heiko, M.: Exploiting User and Process Context for Knowledge Management Systems. In: Workshop on User Modeling for Context-Aware Applications at the 8th Int. Conf. on User Modeling, Sonthofen, Germany (2001)
8. Rosemann, M., Recker, J., Flender, C., Ansell, P.: Context-Awareness in Business Process Design. In: 17th Australasian Conference on Information Systems, Adelaide, Australia (2006)

9. Xia, Y., Wei, J.: Context-Driven Business Process Adaptation for Ad Hoc Changes. In: IEEE International Conference on E-Business Engineering, pp. 53–60 (2008)
10. Raghu, T.S., Vinze, A.: A business process context for Knowledge Management. Decision Support Systems 43(3), 1062–1079 (2007)
11. Mikalsen, M., Kofod-Petersen, A.: Representing and Reasoning about Context in a Mobile Environment. In: Schulz, S., Roth-Berghofer, T. (eds.) Proceedings of the First International Workshop on Modeling and Retrieval of Context, Ulm, Germany. CEUR Workshop Proceedings, pp. 25–35 (2004)
12. Giunchiglia, F.: Contextual reasoning. Epistemologia - Special Issue on I Linguaggi e le Macchine; XVI, pp. 345–364 (1993)
13. Giunchiglia, F., Ghidini, C.: Local Model Semantics, or Contextual Reasoning = Locality + Compatibility. Artificial Intelligence 127(2), 221–259 (2001)
14. Benerecetti, M., Bouquet, P., Ghidini, C.: Contextual Reasoning Distilled. Journal of Experimental and Theoretical Artificial Intelligence 12(3), 279–305 (2000)
15. Buvac, S., Buvac, V., Mason, I.A.: Metamathematics of contexts. Fundam. Inform. 23(2/3/4), 263–301 (1995)
16. Aamodt, A.: Case based reasoning: foundational issues, methodological variations and system approaches. AI Communications 7(1), 39–59 (1994)
17. Weber, B., Rinderle, S., Wild, W., Reichert, M.: CCBR-Driven Business Process Evolution. In: Muñoz-Ávila, H., Ricci, F. (eds.) ICCBR 2005. LNCS (LNAI), vol. 3620, pp. 610–624. Springer, Heidelberg (2005)
18. Ghattas, J., Peleg, M., Soffer, P.: Learning the Context of a Clinical Process. Accepted for publication. In: 3rd International Workshop on Process-oriented information systems in healthcare, BPMDS (2009)

Process Mining: Fuzzy Clustering and Performance Visualization

B.F. van Dongen and A. Adriansyah

Eindhoven University of Technology,
P.O. Box 513, NL-5600 MB, Eindhoven, The Netherlands
b.f.v.dongen@tue.nl, a.adriansyah@student.tue.nl

Abstract. The goal of performance analysis of business processes is to gain insights into operational processes, for the purpose of optimizing them. To intuitively show which parts of the process might be improved, performance analysis results can be projected onto process models. This way, bottlenecks can quickly be identified and resolved.

Unfortunately, for many operational processes, good models, describing the process accurately and intuitively are unavailable. Process mining, or more precisely, process discovery, aims at deriving such models from events logged by information systems. However many mining techniques assume that all events in an event log are logged at the same level of abstraction, which in practice is often not the case. Furthermore, many mining algorithms produce results that are hard to understand by process specialists.

In this paper, we propose a simple clustering algorithm to derive a model from an event log, such that this model only contains a limited set of nodes and edges. Each node represents a set of activities performed in the process, but many nodes can refer to many activities and vice versa.

Using the discovered model, which represents the process at a potentially high level of abstraction, we present two different ways to project performance information onto it. Using these performance projections, process owners can gain insights into the process under consideration in an intuitive way.

To validate our approach, we apply our work to a real-life case from a Dutch municipality.

1   Introduction

The goal of performance analysis of business processes is to gain insights into operational processes, for the purpose of optimizing them. Traditionally, such analysis is presented to problem owners in the form of simple pictures, such that the results are easily interpretable. Many Business Process Intelligence (BPI) tools use event logs to derive performance information. Typical performance statistics include throughput times of activities, utilization rates of departments, and so on.

Within the research domain of process mining, process discovery aims at constructing a process model as an abstract representation of an event log. The goal

S. Rinderle-Ma et al. (Eds.): BPM 2009 Workshops, LNBIP 43, pp. 158–169, 2010.
© Springer-Verlag Berlin Heidelberg 2010

is to build a model (e.g., a Petri-net, an EPC, etc.) that provides insights into the control-flow captured in the log. Both research tools like ProM and industrial tools like Protos support the construction of Petri-nets from event logs.

A recent Master project by Riemers [19] in a large Dutch hospital has shown that combining process discovery and performance analysis is far from trivial. In his work, Riemers designed a method for using a combination of process discovery and performance analysis techniques to improve processes in an healthcare setting. When applying this method to the logs of the Hospital, he identified some problems regarding the applicability of process discovery techniques.

The medical specialists from the hospital found it very hard to understand the complex process models constructed by various process discovery techniques. Instead, they thought of their treatment processes as simple, sequential processes, with very little deviation from a main path. Therefore, when presented with performance information projected onto the discovered models, they were unable to interpret them directly.

Using the experience of Riemens, as well as our own experiences in applying process mining to real-life logs taken from industry [4], we identified that the main reason for the combination of process mining and performance analysis being difficult is that process discovery algorithms are not capable of identifying events that occurred at different levels of abstraction. In the hospital for example, a large number of events were all different, but should be considered as one called "clinical chemistry".

In this paper, we present an algorithm for clustering events automatically to a desired level of abstraction. After discussing some related work in Section 2 and preliminaries in Section 3, Section 4 presents a clustering algorithm for the discovery of Simple Precedence Diagrams at a given level of abstraction. In Section 5, we show how to project performance information onto SPDs in two different ways.

In order to show that our approach is applicable to real-life situations, we used a dataset called "bezwaar WOZ" from a Dutch municipality [18,20]. The process described in this log is the process of handling objections filed against real estate taxes[1]. We conclude the paper with some conclusions and future work in Section 6.

2 Related Work

Many researchers have investigated the process discovery problem, i.e. the problem of how to discover a process model from event logs. We refer to [3,6] and the process mining website www.processmining.org for a complete overview of the whole research domain. Interestingly, most current discovery techniques derive process models from a log assuming that all events in the log refer to an activity and that these activities occur at the same level of abstraction.

---

[1] The approach presented in this paper is implemented in the pre-release version of the ProM-framework 2008, which can be obtained from www.processmining.org

The so-called fuzzy miner [15] was the first attempt to let go of the assumption that activities occur on the same level of abstraction. The graph-based models produced by the fuzzy miner have two types of nodes, namely nodes that refer to one activity and nodes that refer to more activities (clusters). Therefore, the model is able to provide a high-level view of a process by abstracting undesired details. However, the fuzzy miner still assumes that each event in the log belongs to one of these nodes, i.e. there is a one-to-many relation as each node can represent many activities, but each activity is represented by exactly one node. Our approach relaxes this restriction to a many-to-many relation.

In [5] a technique is presented the relation between nodes and activities is truly many-to-many. However, this technique first constructs a statespace from the log and then uses the theory of regions [9,10,12,13,14] to construct a Petri net from that statespace. As the theory of regions has a worst case complexity that is exponential in the size of the statespace, the second step is clearly the bottleneck and therefore this technique is less applicable on real-life logs.

Currently, very few techniques are available to projects performance related information onto discovered process models. Instead, a comparison of commercial process monitoring tools in [16] showed that (1) performance values are either measured with the requirement of having a user-defined process model directly linking events in the log to parts of the model or (2) they are measured totally independent from process model.

An exception is the work presented in [2] where performance indicator values are derived from timed workflow logs. Before the performance measures are calculated, a process model in form of colored workflow net is extracted from the logs using an extension of the α algorithm [7]. Then, the logs are replayed in the resulting net to derive performance measurements. Unfortunately, this approach relies on the discovered model to fit the log, i.e. each case in the log should be a trace in the discovered Petri net. On complex or less-structured logs, this often implies that the Petri net becomes "spaghetti-like", showing all details without distinguishing what is important and what is not [1]. Hence, it is difficult for process owners to obtain any useful insights out of these models.

For the fuzzy models mentioned earlier, animation techniques are available to visually represent the execution captured in the log in the model. Using this animation, possible deadlock activities can be identified. Even so, no performance values can be obtained from the proposed animation approach.

In the performance visualization we propose, measurements are dependent on the chosen process model and projected onto that model to provide intuitive insights into the process' performance.

3   Preliminaries

In this section, we formally introduce some concepts we use in the remainder of this paper. First, we start by defining event logs. An event log is a collection of events, such that each event occurred at a given point in time. Furthermore each event relates to an instance of an activity and occurred within the context of a specific case.

Definition 3.1 (Event Logs). An *event log* W is defined as: $W = (E, I, A, C, t, i, a, c)$, where:

E is the set of events,
I is the set of activity instances,
A is the set of activities,
C is the set of cases,
$t : E \to \mathbb{R}_0^+$ is a function assigning a timestamp to each event,
$i : E \to I$ is a function relating each event to an activity instance,
$a : I \to A$ is a function relating each activity instance to an activity, and
$c : I \to C$ is a function relating each activity instance to a case.

It is important to realize that in practical applications, event logs rarely adhere to Definition 3.1. Instead, references to activity instances are often missing, or events cannot even be related to cases directly. However, for the formalizations in this paper, we assume that logs do adhere to Definition 3.1. Furthermore, we assume that the timestamps define a total ordering on the events relating to the same case.

In this paper, we use a case study taken from a Dutch municipality [18, 20]. From the log that originally contains 1982 cases, we only kept those cases that started after the beginning of the measurement period. This resulted in a log containing 1448 cases. In total, 37,470 events were recorded, relating to 16 activities.

Another important concept for this paper is the notion of a process model. Recall from the introduction, that we later want to project performance information onto such a process model, where the process model can be a discovered model, but also a given model. The latter requirement makes that we need to define process models on a very high level. Therefore, we introduce the concept of a *Simple Precedence Diagram* (SPD).

Definition 3.2 (Simple Precedence Diagram). A *Simple Precedence Diagram* is defined as: $S = (N, L)$, where $L \subseteq N \times N$, where N is the set of nodes in the model and L a set of edges linking the nodes.

An SPD is simply a directed graph consisting of nodes and edges and should be seen as a conceptual model of a process. The nodes in an SPD identify activities in a very loose way, i.e, these nodes do not correspond one to one with activities in an event log. Furthermore, the edges define some notion of control flow, without specifying their semantics formally.

The reason for using such a conceptual model as an SPD is that in performance analysis, it is often interesting to ask the domain expert to sketch a model of the process s/he wants to analyze. The resulting model is rarely an exact copy of the process model as it is being executed. Instead, the resulting model will be a high-level view on the actual process. Nonetheless, we want to project performance characteristics onto such a model. Therefore, it is the relation between a log and an SPD which makes the SPDs useful for performance analysis. For this purpose, we define a *connected SPD* (cSPD).

Definition 3.3 (Connected Simple Precedence Diagram). Let $W = (E, I, A, C, t, i, a, c)$ be an event log and $S = (N, L)$ an SPD. We say that $S_c = (W, S, l_a, l_n)$ is a *connected SPD*, where $l_a : A \to \mathcal{P}(N) \setminus \emptyset$ and $l_n : N \to \mathcal{P}(A) \setminus \emptyset$, such that for all $a \in A$ and $n \in N$ holds that $n \in l_a(a) \equiv a \in l_n(n)$.

A cSPD is a combination of a log and an SPD, such that each activity in the log is represented by one or more nodes in the SPD and that each node in the SPD refers to one or more activities in the log. It is important to realize here that the connection between a log and an SPD is made on the level of activities, not on the level of activity instances.

Obviously, for each log, a trivial cSPD can be constructed that contains only one node and no edges. And although this model can be interesting, especially for projecting performance information onto, we typically are interested in slightly more elaborate models. Therefore, we introduce an algorithm for the discovery of SPD models.

4 Discovering SPDs

When we introduced SPDs, we noted that it is possible for an expert to sketch such a model of the process under consideration. However, we feel that it is also necessary to provide a simple algorithm to construct cSPDs from event logs. For this purpose, we use a straightforward, fuzzy clustering algorithm.

The goal of clustering algorithms is to divide observations over a number of subsets (or clusters), such that the observations in each of these clusters are similar in some sense. The idea behind the clustering algorithm we use follows this concept in a very simple way. First, we define a similarity metric on activities. Then, we choose a number of clusters and use a Fuzzy k-Medoids algorithm to divide the activities over the clusters, while maximizing the similarity of activities in each cluster.

Such a Fuzzy k-Medoid algorithm requires two metrics, namely (1) a measure for the (dis)similarity of objects (activities in our case) and (2) a measure for the probability that an object belongs to a cluster of which another object is the medoid. We define both metrics based on direct succession of events.

Definition 4.1 (Event Succession). Let $W = (E, I, A, C, t, i, a, c)$ be an event log. We define $>_W : A \times A \to \mathbb{N}$ as a function counting how often events from two activities directly succeed each other in all cases, i.e. for $a_1, a_2 \in A$, we say that $>_W (a_1, a_2) = \#_{e_1, e_2 \in E}(t(e_1) < t(e_2) \wedge a(i(e_1)) = a_1 \wedge a(i(e_2)) = a_2 \wedge c(i(e_1)) = c(i(e_2)) \wedge \nexists_{e_3 \in E}(c(i(e_3)) = c(i(e_1)) \wedge t(e_1) < t(e_3) < t(e_2)))$.

We use the notation $a_1 >_W a_2$ to denote $>_W (a_1, a_2) > 0$.

The similarity between activities is defined by looking at how often events relating to these activities follow each other directly in the log. If events relating to these activities follow each other more often, then the similarity increases. Note that if two activities a_1, a_2 are different, their similarity is never equal to 1 as $>_W (a_1, a_2) \neq >_W (a_2, a_1)$.

Definition 4.2 (Activity Similarity). Let $W = (E, I, A, C, t, i, a, c)$ be an event log. We define the similarity $\sigma : A \times A \to (0, 1)$ between two activities $a_1, a_2 \in A$, such that if $a_1 = a_2$ then $\sigma(a_1, a_2) = 1$, otherwise $\sigma(a_1, a_2) = \frac{>_W(a_1,a_2) + >_W(a_2,a_1) + 1}{1 + 2 \cdot \max_{a_3,a_4 \in A}(>_W(a_3,a_4))}$.

As stated before, we also need a measure for the probability that an activity belongs to a cluster of which another activity is the medoid. For this purpose, we use the FCM membership model from [11].

Definition 4.3 (Cluster Membership Probability)
Let $W = (E, I, A, C, t, i, a, c)$ be an event log. Furthermore, let $A^k \subseteq A$ with $|A^k| = k$ be a set of medoids, each being the medoid of a cluster. For all $a_1 \in A^k$ and $a_2 \in A$ we define the probability $u(a_1, a_2)$ to denote the probability that a_2 belongs to the cluster of which a_1 is the medoid, i.e. $u : A^k \times A \to [0, 1]$, where

$$u(a_1, a_2) = \frac{\sigma(a_1,a_2)^{\frac{1}{m-1}}}{\sum_{a_3 \in A^k} \sigma(a_3,a_2)^{\frac{1}{m-1}}}.$$

Note that $m \in [1, \infty)$ here denotes the so-called "fuzzifier", which for this paper we fixed at $m = 2$, i.e. $u(a_1, a_2) = \frac{\sigma(a_1,a_2)}{\sum_{a_3 \in A^k} \sigma(a_3,a_2)}$.

Using the cluster membership and the similarity functions, we can introduce the fuzzy k-Medoid algorithm.

Definition 4.4 (Fuzzy k-Medoid Algorithm)
Let $W = (E, I, A, C, t, i, a, c)$ be an event log. Furthermore, let $0 < k \leq |A|$ be the desired number of clusters. We search a set of medoids $A^k \subseteq A$ with $|A^k| = k$, such that this set minimizes $\sum_{a \in A} \sum a^k \in A^k (u(a^k, a)^m \sigma(a, a^k)^{-1})$.

For our implementation, we implemented the algorithm presented in [17] in ProM 2008[2]. This algorithm does not guarantee to find the global minimum. Furthermore, the result depends on an initial random selection of medoids, which could result in non-determinism. However, the algorithm is fast, which is more important for our purpose.

Finally, after the medoids have been found, we need to construct an SPD. Obviously, the found clusters correspond to the nodes in the SPD model, thereby also providing the mapping between activities in the log and nodes in the model. The edges however are again constructed using the succession relation defined earlier.

Definition 4.5 (cSPD Mining Algorithm). Let $W = (E, I, A, C, t, i, a, c)$ be an event log and let $A^k \subseteq A$ be a set of medoids. We define the mined cSPD model $M = (W, (N, L), l_a, l_n)$ such that:

- $N = A^k$, i.e. the nodes of the SPD model are identified by the cluster medoids,
- $l_a : A \to \mathcal{P}(A^k)$, such that $l_a(a) = \{a^k \in A^k \mid u(a^k, a) \approx \max_{a_1^k \in A^k}(u(a_1^k, a))\}$,

---

[2] ProM 2008 is not released yet, but available from www.processmining.org

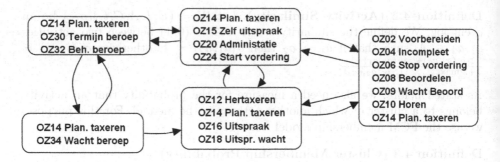

Fig. 1. cSPD with 5 clusters, clustering the 16 activities of the "WOZ bezwaar" process. Note that all clusters overlap.

- $l_n : A^k \rightarrow \mathcal{P}(A)$, such that $l_n(a^k) = \{a \in A \mid a \in l_a(a)\}$,
- $L = \{(a_1^k, a_2^k) \in A^k \times A^k \mid \exists_{a_1 \in l_n(a_1^k) \backslash l_n(a_2^k)} \exists_{a_2 \in l_n(a_2^k) \backslash l_n(a_1^k)} a_1 >_W a_2\}$.

According to Definition 4.5, an activity refers to a node (and vice versa) if the probability that the activity belongs to the cluster represented by the node is approximately the same as the maximum probability over all clusters. This implies that each medoid belongs to its own cluster. Furthermore, all other activities belong to at least one cluster, namely the one for which the function u is maximal. However, an activity can belong to multiple clusters. Note that we do not use equality of probabilities, as this would require the number of direct successions in the log to be the same for multiple pairs of activities and this is rarely the case in practice.

The edges of the connected SPD are determined using the direct succession relation. Basically, two nodes are connected if there is an activity referred to by the first node that is not referred to by the second node that is at least once directly succeeded by an activity referred to by the second node, but not by the first. It is important to realize that an SPD does not have executable semantics. Instead, one should interpret and SPD as a high-level description that a process owner would draw of his process.

Figure 1 shows an example of a cSPD. In this case, our example "bezwaar WOZ" process was used and we clustered the 16 activities into 5 clusters. Interestingly, all of these clusters overlap, as they all contain the activity "OZ14 Plan. taxeren". All the other activities appear in at most 1 cluster. In the following section, we show how to project performance information into a cSPD in two different ways.

5   Performance Analysis in cSPDs

In Section 4, we proposed SPDs which are capable of describing events at different levels of abstraction and we presented an algorithm to derive such models from event logs. The next step of our work is to project performance information

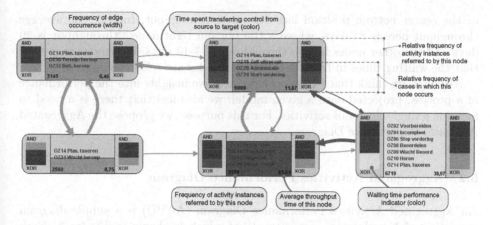

Fig. 2. Fuzzy Performance Diagram of the SPD of Figure 1

onto the SPDs. For this purpose, we propose two diagrams: the *Fuzzy Performance Diagram* and the *Aggregated Activities Performance Diagram*.

5.1 Fuzzy Performance Diagrams

A Fuzzy Performance Diagram (FPD) is a visualization of an SPD, an example of which is shown in Figure 2. It is designed to show both performance information and control flow of a process in an easily interpretable manner. In an FPD, this information is projected onto each node of the SPD (or cluster of activities from the log) and onto each edge of the SPD. The way this projection is done is highly influenced by both Fuzzy model [15] and extended Petri nets in [2, 16].

In order to obtain performance information for cSPDs, a replay algorithm is used. It is beyond the scope of this paper to introduce the replay algorithm in detail. Instead, we refer to [8] for details. However, we do mention that the replay algorithm we use is based on the replay algorithms in [2] and [15].

The size of each FPD element indicates the relative importance of the corresponding element in an overall process based on the occurrence frequency of that element. The more activities to which a node refers were executed (i.e. the more activity instances the node refers to), the bigger the node's size. The same principle is also applied to edges, i.e. the thicker an edge from a source node to a target node, the more often cases were routed from one node to another. The colors of all elements indicate whether the times spent on these elements is relatively high (red), medium (yellow) or low (green).

Already from the sizes and colors of nodes and edges, a human analyst can easily recognize important activities and paths in the process under consideration. However, we also provide insights into the types of node splits and joins, i.e. by indicating to what extend these tend to be XOR, AND or OR.

Figure 2 shows performance information of our example log projected onto the cSPD of Figure 1. From this diagram, we can immediately see that the node at the center bottom position has the worst throughput. Indeed, the average throughput here is 84 days, whereas the bottom right node's throughput is 39 days and the other nodes have a throughput of 7-12 days. Furthermore, we see that the waiting times in front of the center nodes are relatively high as well.

Although we think that FPDs provide intuitive insights into the performance of a process, projected onto a given model, we also feel that there is a need to focus on a single cluster of activities. For this purpose, we propose the Aggregated Activities Performance Diagram.

5.2   Aggregated Activities Performance Diagram

An Aggregated Activities Performance Diagram (AAPD) is a simple diagram consisting of bar elements, an example of which is shown in Figure 3. Each bar has a one-to-one relationship with a node in the FPD of Figure 2, hence, an AAPD bar indirectly refers to a cSPD node, and to one or more activity instances in the log. An AAPD is designed to show time spent between activities in a process and to show activities which often run in parallel. It is complementary to an FPD.

Every AAPD has one focus element, which determines the cases that are being considered. Only cases which contain at least one activity instance referred to by the focus element are considered in the AAPD. Besides the focus element, each AAPD contains the other relevant nodes of the FPD from which it is constructed. In our example of Figure 3, we selected the node referring to $OZ12, OZ14, OZ16$ and $OZ18$ as our focus element.

Each relevant FPD node is shown in the AAPD as a rectangle, such that the width indicates the sum of the average waiting time and the average service time for all corresponding activities in the selected cases. The height of the rectangle is determined by the percentage of cases in which any of the represented activities occurs, relative to the cases determined by the focus element. The position along the horizontal axis of all nodes is determined by the average start times of the activities represented by each node (note that the scale is non-linear, but logarithmic with the start time of the focus node being 0).

Another indicator in each element of the AAPD is a horizontal line inside the big rectangle. This indicator shows the frequency of activity instances which are represented by the element, relative to the frequency of activity instances which are represented by a focus element.

In the example of Figure 3, the height of line in element $OZ14, OZ15, OZ20$ and $OZ24$ is approximately 55%, indicating that the number of activity instances belonging to this node is about 55% of the activity instances belonging to the focus node.

Finally, using a bar below the rectangle the average time when activities of each element are performed in parallel with activities of the focus element. Note that in the example this is artificial, no activity instances belonging to two different nodes ever overlap in time. Therefore, we show this as an example in the bottom right corner of Figure 3.

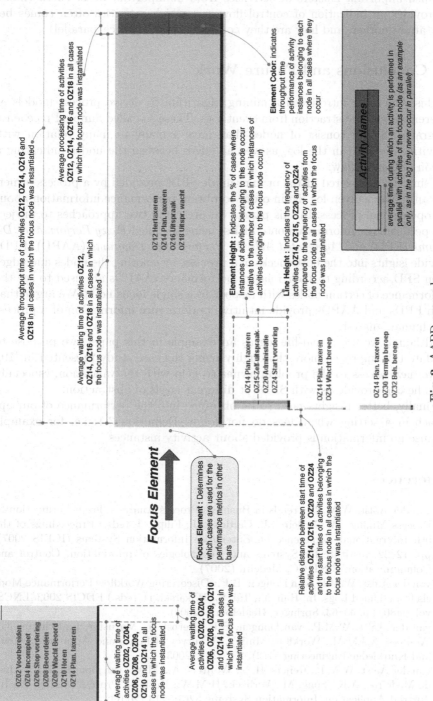

Fig. 3. AAPD example

As in an FPD node, the AAPD visualization helps a human analyst to distinguish important clusters of activities from unimportant ones. Furthermore, it provides an indication of control flow, i.e. which activities often comes before/after another, and how are they conducted (in sequence/parallel).

6   Conclusions and Future Work

In this paper, we introduced a mining algorithm to derive process models at different levels of abstraction from event logs. These so-called Simple Precedence Diagrams (SPDs) consist of nodes that have a many to many relation with activities observed in the log, as well as edges between the nodes indicating a notion of control flow.

Using the discovered SPDs, or man-made SPDs provided by a process owner, we can replay a given log file in order to obtain performance information about the operational process. In this paper, we presented two approaches to project this performance information onto SPDs, using so-called *Fuzzy Performance Diagrams* (FPD) and *Aggregated Activity Performance Diagrams* (AAPD). FPDs provide isights into the bottlenecks of a process, by coloring the nodes and edges of an SPD according to their relative performance. AAPDs are used to see the performance of certain nodes with respect to a single focus node. We argue that both FPDs and AAPDs provide intuitive performance information of a process to a human analyst.

Although we use a real-life log as an example in this paper, we propose to validate this approach more thoroughly using the case study presented in [19], as we have access to the problem owner to help with the validation, especially since he can provide us with SPDs at different levels of abstraction.

Finally, better insights need to be obtained into the performance of our approach in a setting where logs do not follow Definition 3.1, i.e. for example because no information is provided about activity instances.

References

1. van der Aalst, W.M.P.: Trends in Business Process Analysis: From Verification to Process Mining. In: Cordeiro, J., Cardoso, J., Filipe, J. (eds.) Proceedings of the 9th International Conference on Enterprise Information Systems (ICEIS 2007), pp. 12–22. Institute for Systems and Technologies of Information, Control and Communication, INSTICC, Medeira (2007)
2. van der Aalst, W.M.P., van Dongen, B.F.: Discovering Workflow Performance Models from Timed Logs. In: Han, Y., Tai, S., Wikarski, D. (eds.) EDCIS 2002. LNCS, vol. 2480, pp. 45–63. Springer, Heidelberg (2002)
3. van der Aalst, W.M.P., van Dongen, B.F., Herbst, J., Maruster, L., Schimm, G., Weijters, A.J.M.M.: Workflow Mining: A Survey of Issues and Approaches. Data and Knowledge Engineering 47(2), 237–267 (2003)
4. van der Aalst, W.M.P., Reijers, H.A., Weijters, A.J.M.M., van Dongen, B.F., Alves de Medeiros, A.K., Song, M., Verbeek, H.M.W.: Business Process Mining: An Industrial Application. Information Systems 32(5), 713 (2007)

5. van der Aalst, W.M.P., Rubin, V., Verbeek, H.M.W., van Dongen, B.F., Kindler, E., Günther, C.W.: Process mining: a two-step approach to balance between underfitting and overfitting. Software and Systems Modeling (2009)
6. van der Aalst, W.M.P., Weijters, A.J.M.M. (eds.): Process Mining. Special Issue of Computers in Industry, vol. 53(3). Elsevier Science Publishers, Amsterdam (2004)
7. van der Aalst, W.M.P., Weijters, A.J.M.M., Maruster, L.: Workflow Mining: Discovering Process Models from Event Logs. IEEE Transactions on Knowledge and Data Engineering 16(9), 1128–1142 (2004)
8. Adriansyah, A.: Performance Analysis of Business Processes from Event Logs and Given Process Models. Master's thesis, Eindhoven University of Technology, Eindhoven (2009)
9. Badouel, E., Bernardinello, L., Darondeau, P.: The Synthesis Problem for Elementary Net Systems is NP-complete. Theoretical Computer Science 186(1-2), 107–134 (1997)
10. Badouel, E., Darondeau, P.: Theory of regions. In: Reisig, W., Rozenberg, G. (eds.) APN 1998. LNCS, vol. 1491, pp. 529–586. Springer, Heidelberg (1998)
11. Bezdek, J.C.: Pattern Recognition with Fuzzy Objective Function Algorithms. Kluwer Academic Publishers, Norwell (1981)
12. Cortadella, J., Kishinevsky, M., Lavagno, L., Yakovlev, A.: Synthesizing Petri Nets from State-Based Models. In: Proceedings of the 1995 IEEE/ACM International Conference on Computer-Aided Design (ICCAD 1995), pp. 164–171. IEEE Computer Society, Los Alamitos (1995)
13. Cortadella, J., Kishinevsky, M., Lavagno, L., Yakovlev, A.: Deriving Petri Nets from Finite Transition Systems. IEEE Transactions on Computers 47(8), 859–882 (1998)
14. Ehrenfeucht, A., Rozenberg, G.: Partial (Set) 2-Structures - Part 1 and Part 2. Acta Informatica 27(4), 315–368 (1989)
15. Gunther, C.W., van der Aalst, W.M.P.: Fuzzy Mining: Adaptive Process Simplification Based on Multi-perspective Metrics. In: Alonso, G., Dadam, P., Rosemann, M. (eds.) BPM 2007. LNCS, vol. 4714, pp. 328–343. Springer, Heidelberg (2007)
16. Hornix, P.T.G.: Performance Analysis of Business Processes through Process Mining. Master's thesis, Eindhoven University of Technology, Eindhoven (2007)
17. Krishnapuram, R., Joshi, A., Yi, L.: A fuzzy relative of the k-medoids algorithm with application to web document and snippet clustering. In: Proc. IEEE Intl. Conf. Fuzzy Systems - FUZZIEEE 1999, Snippet Clustering, Korea (1999)
18. de Medeiros, A.K.A.: Genetic Process Mining. PhD thesis, Eindhoven University of Technology, Eindhoven (2006)
19. Riemers, P.: Process Improvement in Healthcare: a Data-Based Method Using a Combination of Process Mining and Visual Analytics. Master's thesis, Eindhoven University of Technology, Eindhoven (2009)
20. van der Aalst, W.M.P., Dumas, M., Ouyang, C., Rozinat, A., Verbeek, E.: Conformance checking of service behavior. ACM Trans. Interet Technol. 8(3), 1–30 (2008)

Trace Clustering Based on Conserved Patterns: Towards Achieving Better Process Models

R.P. Jagadeesh Chandra Bose[1,2] and Wil M.P. van der Aalst[1]

[1] Department of Mathematics and Computer Science, University of Technology, Eindhoven, The Netherlands
j.c.b.rantham.prabhakara@tue.nl, w.m.p.v.d.aalst@tue.nl
[2] Philips Healthcare, Veenpluis 5-6, Best, The Netherlands

Abstract. Process mining refers to the extraction of process models from event logs. Real-life processes tend to be less structured and more flexible. Traditional process mining algorithms have problems dealing with such unstructured processes and generate "spaghetti-like" process models that are hard to comprehend. An approach to overcome this is to cluster process instances such that each of the resulting clusters correspond to coherent sets of process instances that can each be adequately represented by a process model. In this paper, we present multiple feature sets based on conserved patterns and show that the proposed feature sets have a better performance than contemporary approaches. We evaluate the goodness of the formed clusters using established fitness and comprehensibility metrics defined in the context of process mining. The proposed approach is able to generate clusters such that the process models mined from the clustered traces show a high degree of fitness and comprehensibility. Further, the proposed feature sets can be easily discovered in linear time making it amenable to real-time analysis of large data sets.

Keywords: Clustering, fitness, process mining, process discovery, case similarity.

1 Introduction

Process mining refers to the extraction of process models from event logs [1]. An event log corresponds to a set of process instances following a particular business process. A process instance is manifested as a trace (a trace is defined as an ordered list of activities invoked by a process instance from the beginning of its execution to the end). Process mining techniques can deliver valuable, factual insights into how processes are being executed in real life. These insights are obtained by analyzing event logs. Real-life processes tend to be less structured than what the stakeholders typically expect. Healthcare, product development, customer support etc. are some of the examples of such flexible environments. In such environments, discovering the actual process which is being executed/followed is of significant importance. These insights help organizations to improve the understanding of current situation, and is a prerequisite

S. Rinderle-Ma et al. (Eds.): BPM 2009 Workshops, LNBIP 43, pp. 170–181, 2010.

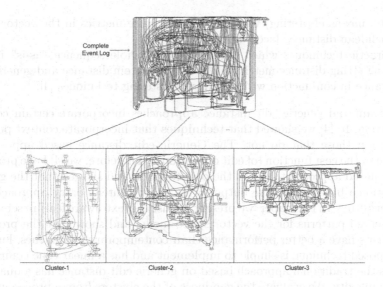

Complete
Event Log

Cluster-1   Cluster-2   Cluster-3

Fig. 1. Significance of trace clustering in Process Mining

for any process improvement or quality control effort. However, traditional process mining algorithms have problems dealing with such unstructured processes and generate "spaghetti-like" process models that are hard to comprehend. This is caused by the inherent complexity of processes; all possible behaviors are shown in a single diagram. Considering the set of traces in the event log all at once might lead to ambiguities for the mining algorithms which often result in spaghetti-like models. An approach to overcome this is to *cluster the traces such that each of the resulting clusters correspond to coherent sets of cases that can each be adequately represented by a process model.*

The application of process mining techniques to traces from such clusters should generate models that have a (i) high degree of fitness and (ii) low degree of structural complexity (less "spaghetti like"). Fitness quantifies how much of the observed behavior is captured in the model. Figure 1 illustrates the significance of trace clustering in process mining. The process model on the top of Figure 1 is a process model mined from the entire event log (of a real-life case study described as in Section 4). The model is quite complex to comprehend. The bottom rectangle of Figure 1 depicts the process models mined from clustered traces. It is evident that clustering enables the comprehension of process models by reducing the spaghetti-ness.

Traditional approaches (to trace clustering) in the literature can be classified into two categories:

1. Techniques where the traces are transformed into a vector space model whose features are defined by the activities (bag-of-activities), transitions and k-grams (subsequence of k-activities) [2], [3], [4]. Clustering can then be done using a variety of techniques (such as Agglomerative hierarchical clustering

and k-means clustering) with different distance metrics in the vector space (Euclidean distance, Jaccard distance etc).

2. Syntactic techniques which operate on the whole sequence "as-is" by applying string distance metrics such as Levenshtein distance and generic edit distance in conjunction with standard clustering techniques [4].

The k-gram and generic edit distance approaches incorporate certain context information. In [4] we showed that techniques that incorporate context perform better than those that do not. The Generic edit distance based approach is sensitive to the cost function (of edit operations). Therefore, we [4] have proposed an automated approach to derive the cost function and showed that the generic edit distance based technique outperforms other contemporary approaches to trace clustering. In this paper, we present robust context-aware feature sets based on conserved patterns for the vector space model and show that the proposed feature sets have a better performance than contemporary approaches. Further, the proposed technique is simple to implement and has a linear time complexity whereas the traditional approach based on generic edit distance has a quadratic time complexity. We evaluate the goodness of the clusters from a process mining perspective as mentioned above on a real-life log of Philips Healthcare.

The remainder of the paper is organized as follows. In Section 2, we define the feature sets based on conserved patterns, and explain the means to discover the feature sets. Section 3 presents the clustering approach and introduces the metrics used to evaluate the goodness of clusters. In Section 4, we present and discuss the experimental results. Related work is presented in Section 5. Finally, Section 6 concludes with remarks on future directions.

2   Context-Aware Feature Sets Based on Conserved Patterns

In this section, we propose new feature sets that are context-aware for the vector-space model. The basic idea is to consider sub-sequences of activities that are conserved across multiple traces. Unlike the k-gram approach where we consider sub-sequences of k-activities (for a fixed k), these feature sets are based on sub-sequences of different lengths. Finding similar regions (sequence of activities) common within a trace and/or across a set of traces in an event log signifies some set of common functionality accessed by the process. In other words, a region of high similarity shared within a process instance or between two or more process instances might be evidence of common functionality (often abstracted as a sub-process). Using these conserved sub-sequences as features will enable the clustering of traces in such a way that two traces having a lot of conserved regions common between them are put in the same cluster. We now formally describe the definition of these sub-sequences and the feature sets.

- *Maximal Pair:* A maximal pair in a sequence, T, is a pair of identical sub-sequences α and β such that the symbol to the immediate left (right) of α is different from the symbol to the immediate left (right) of β. In other words, extending α and β on either side would destroy the equality of the two strings. A maximal pair is denoted by the triple $\langle i, j, \alpha \rangle$ where i and j corresponds to the starting position of α and β respectively in T with $i \neq j$.

- *Maximal Repeat:* A maximal repeat in a sequence, T, is defined as a subsequence α that occurs in a maximal pair in T.
- *Super Maximal Repeat:* A super maximal repeat in a sequence is defined as a maximal repeat that never occurs as a substring of any other maximal repeat.
- *Near Super Maximal Repeat:* A maximal repeat α is said to be a near super maximal repeat if and only if there exist at least one instance of α at some location in the sequence where it is not contained in another maximal repeat.

Consider the event log, $\mathcal{L} = \{$aabcdbbcda, dabcdabcbb, bbbcdbbbccaa, aaadabb ccc, aaacdcdcbedbccbadbdebdc$\}$ over the alphabet $\mathcal{A} = \{$a, b, c, d, e$\}$. Table 1 depicts the maximal, super maximal and near super maximal repeats present in each trace of the event log. For trace T_1, the set of maximal repeats is $\{$a, b, bcd$\}$. Since maximal repeat b is subsumed in maximal repeat bcd, b does not qualify to be a super maximal repeat. The occurrence of maximal repeat b at position 6 in T_1 does not overlap with any other maximal repeat. Hence b qualifies to be a near super maximal repeat. In trace T_3 all occurrences of maximal repeats b and bb coincide with the maximal repeat bbbc. Hence both b and bb does not qualify to be near super maximal repeat. The occurrence of maximal repeat c at position 10 in T_3 does not coincide with any other maximal repeat. Hence, c qualifies to be a near super maximal repeat.

Table 1. Maximal, Super Maximal and Near Super Maximal Repeats in each trace in the Event Log $\mathcal{L}$

Id	Trace	Maximal Repeat Set	Super Maximal Repeat Set	Near Super Maximal Repeat Set
T_1	aabcdbbcda	$\{$a, b, bcd$\}$	$\{$a, bcd$\}$	$\{$a, b, bcd$\}$
T_2	dabcdabcbb	$\{$b, dabc$\}$	$\{$dabc$\}$	$\{$b, dabc$\}$
T_3	bbbcdbbbccaa	$\{$a, b, c, bb, bbbc$\}$	$\{$a, bbbc$\}$	$\{$a, c, bbbc$\}$
T_4	aaadabbccc	$\{$a, b, c, aa, cc$\}$	$\{$b, aa, cc$\}$	$\{$a, b, aa, cc$\}$
T_5	aaacdcdcbedbcc- badbdebdc	$\{$a, b, c,d, e, aa, bd, cb, db, dc, cdc$\}$	$\{$e, aa, bd, cb, db, cdc$\}$	$\{$a, c, e, aa, bd, cb, db, dc, cdc$\}$

Let us denote the set of maximal repeats, super maximal repeats and near super maximal repeats by M, SM and NSM respectively. The following relation holds between the three.

$$SM \subseteq NSM \subseteq M$$

Near super maximal repeats are a hybrid between maximal repeats and super maximal repeats in that it contains all super maximal repeats and those maximal repeats that can occur in isolation in the sequence without being part of any other maximal repeat. Near super maximal repeats can assist in identifying *choice constructs* in the process model. The set $NSM \setminus SM$ (the set difference) depicts all maximal repeats that occur both in isolation and are also subsumed in some other maximal repeat. For any repeat $r \in NSM \setminus SM$, a super maximal repeat r^s which contains (subsumes) r can be either of the form αr or $r\beta$ or $\alpha r \beta$ (where α and β are subsequences of activities). This indicates that r can be a common functionality which might occur in conjunction with α and/or β. In other words, it indicates that α and β can potentially be optional (sequence of) activities in the context of r.

In order to find the commonalities across the traces in the entire event log, we first construct a single sequence which is obtained by the concatenation of traces in the event log with a distinct delimiter between the traces and apply the repeat definitions on the concatenated sequence. Table 2 depicts the maximal/super maximal/near super maximal repeats present in the entire event log, $\mathcal{L}$. These are the repeats in the sequence obtained by concatenation of all traces in the event log.

Table 2. Maximal, Super Maximal and Near Super Maximal Repeats in the Event Log $\mathcal{L}$

M	{a, b, c, d, e, aa, ab, ad, bb, bc, bd, cb, cc, cd, da, db, dc, aaa, abc, bbc, bcc, bcd, cdc, dab, abcd, bbbc, bbcc, bbcd, bcda, dabc, bcdbb}
SM	{e, ad, bd, cb, aaa, cdc, abcd, bbbc, bbcc, bbcd, bcda, dabc, bcdbb}
NSM	{e, aa, ad, bb, bd, cb, cc, db, dc, aaa, bcc, cdc, dab, abcd, bbbc, bbcc, bbcd, bcda, dabc, bcdbb}

We consider a *maximal repeat, super maximal repeat* or *near super maximal repeat* as a *repeat* henceforth (and distinguish between them where necessary). Repeats signify some common functionality (sub-process) present across traces. For a repeat, r, let repeat alphabet $\Gamma(r)$, denote the set of symbols/activities that appear in the repeat. For example, for the repeats abba, abdgh, and adgbh, the repeat alphabets correspond to $\{a, b\}$, $\{a, b, d, g, h\}$, and $\{a, b, d, g, h\}$ respectively.

2.1 Equivalence Class of Repeats under a Repeat Alphabet

Different repeats can share a common repeat alphabet. In the above example, the repeats abdgh and adgbh share the same repeat alphabet $\{a, b, d, g, h\}$. We can define equivalence classes on repeat alphabet.

$$[X] = \{r \mid r \text{ is a repeat and } \Gamma(r) = X\}$$

For the above example, $[\{a, b, d, g, h\}] = \{abdgh, adgbh\}$. Furthermore, the equivalence class under repeat alphabet will capture any variations in the manifestation of a process execution due to *parallelism*.

2.2 Feature Sets

Based on the above definitions of maximal repeat, super maximal repeat, near super maximal repeat and repeat alphabet, we define multiple feature sets.

1. *Maximal Repeat Feature Set* (**MR**): In this feature set, the features are based on the maximal repeats in the entire log. This can be discovered by concatenating all the traces in the event log (with a distinguishing delimiter between the traces) and identifying the maximal repeats in this concatenated sequence. From these maximal repeats, we filter those repeats that are activities themselves. The presence of repeats that are activities generates the scenario of the bag-of-activities approach and its pitfalls are discussed in [4]. In other words,

$$\mathbf{MR} = \{r \mid r \text{ is a maximal repeat } \wedge |r| > 1\}$$

2. *Super Maximal Repeat Feature Set* (**SMR**): In this feature set, the features are based on the super maximal repeats present in the concatenated sequence of all traces in the event log. Similar to **MR**, super maximal repeats that are activities themselves are filtered out.

$$\mathbf{SMR} = \{r \mid r \text{ is a super maximal repeat } \wedge |r| > 1\}$$

3. *Near Super Maximal Repeat Feature Set* (**NSMR**): In this feature set, the features are based on the near super maximal repeats present in the concatenated sequence of all traces in the event log. Similar to **MR**, near super maximal repeats that are activities themselves are filtered out.

$$\mathbf{NSMR} = \{r \mid r \text{ is a near super maximal repeat } \wedge |r| > 1\}$$

4. *Maximal Repeat Alphabet Feature Set* (**MRA**): This is a feature set derived from **MR**. The features of this set correspond to the repeat alphabets of the event log where the repeats are the filtered maximal repeats in the entire event log (as in **MR**).

$$\mathbf{MRA} = \{\Gamma(r) \mid r \in \mathbf{MR}\}$$

5. *Super Maximal Repeat Alphabet Feature Set* (**SMRA**): This is a feature set derived from **SMR**. The features correspond to the repeat alphabets of the event log where the repeats are the filtered super maximal repeats in the entire event log (as in **SMR**).

$$\mathbf{SMRA} = \{\Gamma(r) \mid r \in \mathbf{SMR}\}$$

6. *Near Super Maximal Repeat Alphabet Feature Set* (**NSMRA**): This is a feature set derived from **NSMR**. The features correspond to the repeat alphabets of the event log where the repeats are the filtered near super maximal repeats in the entire event log (as in **NSMR**).

$$\mathbf{NSMRA} = \{\Gamma(r) \mid r \in \mathbf{NSMR}\}$$

For feature sets **MR, SMR, NSMR**, each trace is transformed into a vector whose values correspond to the number of occurrences of each feature in that trace. For feature sets **MRA, SMRA, NSMRA**, each trace is transformed into a vector whose values correspond to the sum of occurrences of all repeats that are under the equivalence class of the repeat alphabet.

2.3   Reducing the Number of Features

Large data sets and data sets with a large alphabet might contain many repeats. But not all of them might be significant. For example, there might be repeats which occurs only in a small fraction of traces. One way to tackle this is to filter the repeats. One can retain only those repeats that are contained in a large fraction of traces in the event log, i.e., repeats that have a high support in the event log.

2.4   Approaches for Discovering the Feature Sets

Maximal, super maximal and near super maximal repeats can be efficiently discovered in linear time using suffix trees for strings [5], [6]. Repeats that exist across the traces in the event log can be determined by applying the repeat identification algorithms on the sequence obtained by concatenating the traces in the event log with a delimiter not present in the alphabet $\mathcal{A}$. Such a concatenation of traces might yield a very long sequence. One can adopt efficient suffix-tree construction techniques such as [7] to handle very long sequences. We have adopted Ukkonen's algorithm [8] for the construction of suffix-trees in linear-time.

3   Evaluating the Significance of Clusters: A Process Mining Perspective

Statistical metrics such as the average cluster density, silhouette width etc., have been proposed in the literature to evaluate the goodness of the clusters [9]. The underlying motive for all these metrics is to prefer clusters that are compact. Compact clusters have a lot of significance in pattern classification where the objective is to enable the discovery of decision boundaries. The objective for clustering event logs is to ease the discovery of process models by grouping together traces that conform to similar execution patterns/behavior. To evaluate the significance of the clusters formed, one can compare the process models that are discovered from the traces within each cluster. In this paper, we propose two hypotheses to evaluate the goodness of clusters from a process mining point of view. A good cluster tends to cluster traces such that:

1. the discovered process model has a high fitness
2. the process model mined is less complex

The rationale behind these evaluation criteria is that if the clusters formed are meaningful (all traces belonging to related cases are in the same cluster and traces that are unrelated are not), then the process model resulting from the traces in a particular cluster should be less complex (more comprehensible and less spaghetti like). Algorithm 1 depicts the evaluation approach. Algorithm 1 is run over various clustering criteria/techniques and choice of cluster size.

Algorithm 1. Evaluating the significance of clusters

Require: Given an event log $\mathcal{L}$ consisting of M traces, and a clustering algorithm $\mathcal{C}$
Ensure: Partition the M traces into N-clusters (for some $N \geq 2$) using $\mathcal{C}$
1: Discover the process model P_i for each cluster, C_i, $1 \leq i \leq N$
2: Evaluate the fitness of the process models P_i
3: Evaluate the complexity of the process models. The number of control-flows, and/xor joins/splits and the size of the model defined in terms of the nodes, transitions and arcs signify the complexity of a process model.

For the experiments in this paper, we have generated the process models with the Heuristics miner [10] plug-in in ProM[1] and used the following metrics for comparison:

- *The average number of event classes per cluster:* The intuition is that clustering should enable the partitioning of traces based on functionality and that the resulting clusters should have event classes pertaining only to those events that constitute the functionality. Good clusters tend to form clusters such that the number of event classes is minimal per cluster.
- *Weighted Average Improved Continuous Semantics:* Improved continuous semantics metric (ICS) is a measure of fitness and is proposed in [10]. Let ics_k denote the ICS of the process model mined from traces in cluster k and let n_k denote the number of traces in cluster k. Then, weighted average improved continuous semantics metric can be defined as $wics_{avg} = \sum_{k=1}^{N}(n_k * ics_k)/\sum_{k=1}^{N} n_k$ where N is the number of clusters.
- *Average Number of Arcs:* This metric is a measure of spaghetti-ness of the process model and measures the average number of arcs per cluster.
- *Average Number of Arcs Per Node:* This metric is a measure of spaghetti-ness of the process model and is defined as the average of the number of arcs per node over all the clusters. In other words, $apn_{avg} = \sum_{k=1}^{N} apn_k/N$ where apn_k is the number of arcs per node in cluster k.

We evaluated different clustering strategies. We applied the Euclidean distance metric on the following feature sets in the vector space model: bag-of-activities (BOA), MR, SMR, NSMR, MRA, SMRA and NSMRA. In the syntactic domain, we studied the Levenshtein distance (LED) and generic edit distance (GED). In all the above strategies, we have used the Agglomerative Hierarchical Clustering technique with minimum variance criteria [11] as the clustering algorithm.

---

[1] ProM is an extensible framework that provides a comprehensive set of tools/plugins for the discovery and analysis of process models from event logs. See www.processmining.org for more information and to download ProM.

4   Experimental Results and Discussion

Description of the Data Set: We used a real-life case study of Philips Health-care logs. Philips Healthcare collates logs from their medical systems across the globe. These logs contain information about user actions, system events etc. Medical systems are huge machines with thousands of (sub-)parts and with many things happening in parallel. This compounded by the fact that the logging of events from these parts is distributed in nature makes the logs very complex for analysis. The specific log that we analyzed contains the commands (pertaining to beam limitation, fluroscopy/exposure procedures, table movement, image processing, etc.) that were executed on the system during an examination. The sequence of commands that were executed on an X-ray system during a patient examination on a particular day constitute a trace. We randomly picked 331 traces for our analysis. The traces vary between 100 and 200 in length and there were a total of 46716 events and 155 event classes ($|\mathcal{A}| = 155$) in the log. It is important to note that the log is rather complex and that there is a large activity set. Let us call this log as the *original* log. As the log contains information about commands that were executed on an X-ray system, there are instances where a functionality is repeatedly invoked (signifying loop constructs). We have considered a variant of the original log wherein we have replaced all loop manifestations with just a single iteration over the loop. Let us call this log as *filtered* log. For example, consider the trace abcdbcdbcde; there exists three iterations of the loop over bcd in the trace. This trace would be replaced as abcde in the filtered log. In the filtered log, there were a total of 26865 events and 155 event classes. For the results reported in this section, we have partitioned the logs into four clusters.

The goodness of the process models mined from Heuristics miner plugin is dependent on a few parameters (such as the number of positive observations, dependency threshold, relative to best threshold etc). Choosing an ideal set of parameter values is non-trivial and should depend on the characteristics of the dataset. A constant or a default value does not always work. Further when the event log is clustered, the resulting clusters can have different characteristics (the number of traces/events in each cluster can be different). We have experimented with both default/constant parameter settings as well as with parameter settings that are based on the characteristics of the dataset. This particular dataset is quite complex in that there are a few commands or a sequence of commands that can be repeatedly invoked and that there is less strict ordering on the commands pertaining to an abstract functionality. As a heuristic, we have used the following settings: number of positive observations equal to 3*number of process instances, relative-to-best threshold = 0.05, dependency threshold = 0.9, length-one/length-two loop threshold = 0.9 and long-distance threshold = 0.9.

Figure 2(a) depicts the weighted average improved continuous semantics value of the mined process models over different cluster strategies on the original log. It can be seen that the proposed feature sets perform better than the others. The value for the super maximal repeats is low because as per the definition, super maximal repeats capture only the maximum functionality. This log has a lot of

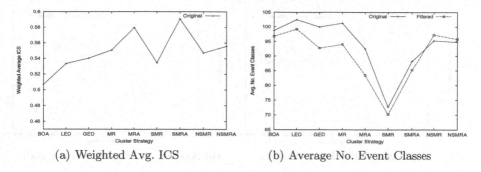

(a) Weighted Avg. ICS   (b) Average No. Event Classes

Fig. 2. Weighted average improved continuous semantics and average number of event classes of the process models mined from the clustered traces

loop constructs and the super maximal repeat will capture only the loop manifestation with maximum iterations as a feature ignoring other manifestations of the loop. For example, if there is a loop over ab and if there are ababab and abab as two manifestations of the loop in the log and if ababab occurs in more than one trace, then only the sequence ababab is considered as a feature. Figure 2(b) depicts the average number of event classes per cluster for both the original and filtered log. It can be seen that the pattern based features perform better than the other approaches. Even within the pattern based features, the super maximal repeat based feature sets perform better because they capture the maximal functionalities and traces sharing the maximal functionality are put in the same cluster. Figure 3(a) depicts the average number of arcs per cluster for the different cluster strategies while Figure 3(b) depicts the average number of arcs per node. Again it can be noted that the the pattern based feature sets are able to cluster traces such that the overall spaghetti-ness of the process models is less compared to BOA, GED and LED approaches. The peak in Figure 3(b) for the SMR feature set can be attributed to the relatively low number of event classes per cluster for this cluster strategy. To summarize, the pattern-based feature sets are able to partition the traces better such that the process models mined from the clustered traces show a high degree of fitness at a relatively less structural complexity thereby enhancing the comprehensibility of process models. Figure 1 depicts the process models mined on the entire original log and from traces in three of the clusters of the original log.

5   Related Work

Data clustering is one of the most important fields of data mining and a lot of techniques exist in the literature [12]. There is a growing interest in process mining and many case studies have been performed to show the applicability of process mining e.g., [13]. The significance of trace clustering to process mining has been discussed in [14], [15]. Greco et al. [14] used trace clustering to partition the event log and this way discovered more simple process models. They used the vector space model over the activities and their transitions to make clusters.

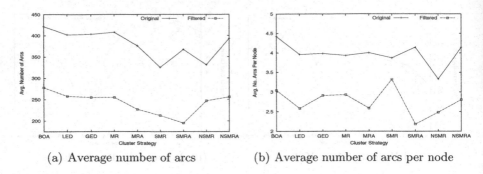

(a) Average number of arcs   (b) Average number of arcs per node

Fig. 3. Average number of arcs and average number of arcs per node of the process models mined from the clustered traces

More specifically, Greco et al. [14] considered significant k-grams (subsequences of activities whose frequency is above a threshold) of different lengths for clustering. Transitions can be considered as a specific case of the k-gram model where the value of k is 2. On similar lines, Song et al. [2] have proposed the idea of clustering traces by considering a combination of different perspectives of the traces (such as activities, transitions, data, performance etc.) as the feature vector. For the activities and transition perspectives, this approach can be thought of as a combination of the bag-of-activities and the k-gram approach (with $k = 2$). Though this combined approach might yield better results than either of the approaches in isolation, it still suffers from the pitfalls highlighted as in [4]. We have proposed a generic edit distance based approach to trace clustering in [4]. Distances on other perspectives (such as data, performance etc) can be seamlessly combined with the feature sets proposed in this paper just like in [2]. This helps in further boosting the results of process mining algorithms by leveraging the superior performance of the pattern-based features. A comprehensive list of metrics that influence the comprehensibility of process models was reported in [16].

6   Conclusions

In this paper, we have proposed multiple feature sets for trace clustering. The goal of clustering is to be able to generate several simpler models each explaining a coherent group of process instances. This way one can avoid spaghetti-like processes that mix very difference instances. The feature sets used are all based on conserved patterns. The proposed feature sets show good promise in identifying coherent cases. It was shown over a real-life log that the proposed clustering approach outperforms contemporary approaches to trace clustering in process mining. We have used the heuristics miner algorithm to evaluate the goodness of clusters. However, there is a bias associated with a mining algorithm over the class of process models that it can generate and thereby the evaluation metrics. Further, the parameters on which a mining algorithm depends on influence the end result. So far, little research has been done in this area. As future work, we would like to investigate the influence (bias) of a mining algorithm on the evaluation criteria.

Acknowledgments. The authors are grateful to Philips Healthcare for funding the research in process mining.

References

1. van der Aalst, W.M.P., Weijters, A.J.M.M., Maruster, L.: Workflow Mining: Discovering Process Models from Event Logs. IEEE Trans. Knowl. Data Eng. 16(9), 1128–1142 (2004)
2. Song, M., Günther, C.W., van der Aalst, W.M.P.: Trace Clustering in Process Mining. In: Ardagna, D., et al. (eds.) BPM 2008 Workshops. LNBIP, vol. 17, pp. 109–120. Springer, Heidelberg (2009)
3. Song, M., Gunther, C.W., van der Aalst, W.M.P.: Improving Process Mining with Trace Clustering. J. Korean Inst of Industrial Engineers 34(4), 460–469 (2008)
4. Jagadeesh Chandra Bose, R.P., van der Aalst, W.M.P.: Context Aware Trace Clustering: Towards Improving Process Mining Results. In: Proceedings of the SIAM International Conference on Data Mining, SDM, pp. 401–412 (2009)
5. Gusfield, D.: Algorithms on Strings, Trees, and Sequences: Computer Science and Computational Biology (1997)
6. Kolpakov, Kucherov: Finding Maximal Repetitions in a Word in Linear Time. In: FOCS: IEEE Symposium on Foundations of Computer Science, FOCS (1999)
7. Cheung, C.F., Yu, J.X., Lu, H.: Constructing Suffix Tree for Gigabyte Sequences with Megabyte Memory. IEEE Trans. Knowl. Data Eng. 17(1), 90–105 (2005)
8. Ukkonen, E.: On-Line Construction of Suffix Trees. Algorithmica 14(3), 249–260 (1995)
9. Rao, S., Rodriguez, A., Benson, G.: Evaluating distance functions for clustering tandem repeats. Genome Informatics 16(1), 3–12 (2005)
10. Weijters, A.J.M.M., van der Aalst, W.M.P.: Rediscovering workflow models from event-based data using Little Thumb. Integrated Computer-Aided Engineering 10(2), 151–162 (2003)
11. Ward, J.H.: Hierarchical Grouping to Optimize an Objective Function. J. Amer. Stat. Assoc. 58, 236–244 (1963)
12. Jain, A.K., Dubes, R.C.: Algorithms for Clustering Data. Prentice-Hall Inc., Englewood Cliffs (1988)
13. van der Aalst, W.M.P., Reijers, H.A., Weijters, A.J.M.M., van Dongen, B.F., de Medeiros, A.K.A., Song, M., Verbeek, H.M.W.: Business Process Mining: An Industrial Application. Info. Sys. 32(5), 713–732 (2007)
14. Greco, G., Guzzo, A., Pontieri, L., Sacca, D.: Discovering Expressive Process Models by Clustering Log Traces. IEEE Trans. Knowl. Data Eng., 1010–1027 (2006)
15. de Medeiros, A.K.A., Guzzo, A., Greco, G., van der Aalst, W.M.P., Weijters, A.J.M.M., van Dongen, B.F., Sacca, D.: Process Mining Based on Clustering: A Quest for Precision. In: BPM Workshops, pp. 17–29 (2007)
16. Mendling, J., Strembeck, M.: Influence Factors of Understanding Business Process Models. BIS, 142–153 (2008)
17. Mendling, J., Neumann, G., van der Aalst, W.M.P.: Understanding the occurrence of errors in process models based on metrics. In: Meersman, R., Tari, Z. (eds.) OTM 2007, Part I. LNCS, vol. 4803, pp. 113–130. Springer, Heidelberg (2007)

Visualization of Compliance Violation in Business Process Models

Ahmed Awad and Mathias Weske

Business Process Technology Group
Hasso Plattner Institute at the University of Potsdam
D-14482 Potsdam, Germany
{ahmed.awad,mathias.weske}@hpi.uni-potsdam.de

Abstract. Checking for compliance is of major importance in nowadays business. Several approaches have been proposed to address different aspects of compliance checking. One of the important aspects of compliance checking is to ensure that business activities will be executed in a certain order. In a previous work, we have presented a formal approach for efficient compliance checking based on model checking technology. A limitation of that approach and of similar approaches is the lack of explanation about how violations could occur. In this paper we resolve this limitation by exploiting the notion of patterns/anti patterns. Execution ordering compliance rules are expressed as BPMN-Q queries. For each query a set of anti pattern queries is automatically derived and checked against process models as well. When a violation (an anti pattern) finds a match, the violating part of the process is shown to the user.

1 Introduction

Enterprises are using business process models to run their services smoothly. These artifacts define how the enterprise works and they are a good means of checking control requirements. To be in line with their business goals, but also with legal regulations, companies need to make sure that their operations satisfy a set of policies and rules. i.e. they need to design compliance rules and implement compliance checking mechanisms.

Aspects of compliance are divergent. They also are changing by time. Some of them have the force of law e.g. the Sarbanes-Oxley Act of 2002 [1]. Keeping processes compliant is an expensive operation [11]. Automated approaches emerged to address compliance issue from different points of view. On one hand, some approaches favor deriving process models by compliance rules [13,8]. On the other hand delaying the checking of the compliance rules to a post design step is discussed in [15,3]. With respect to compliance rules regarding execution ordering of activities, deriving the business process model by compliance rules guarantees a compliant by design business process. However, there is still a need to recheck for compliance each time rules change or new rules are added. A limitation of the second approach is its binary nature of answer, i.e., it reports either compliant or non compliant. Both approaches are missing a mechanism that helps modelers focus on parts of models that violate the rules.

Explaining violation of compliance rules is necessary to help modelers take corrective actions. Formal approaches such as model checking have the capability of providing counter examples when the rule to be checked is not satisfied by the process

S. Rinderle-Ma et al. (Eds.): BPM 2009 Workshops, LNBIP 43, pp. 182–193, 2010.
© Springer-Verlag Berlin Heidelberg 2010

model [3,15]. Unfortunately, these counter examples are given in terms of internal state transitions rather than in terms of process models that are too technical to be understood by a non-technical user. To benefit from these counter examples, the output of the model checker must be translated to the notation the user can understand. These translations are usually dependent on both the model checker software and the visual notation the user understands. Also, these translations form a cost in the tool chain added to the cost of first mapping the system to be checked into the input language of a model checker.

In [3] we used BPMN-Q queries to express compliance rules regarding execution ordering of activities. A Query was used in a twofold way. As a query, it was used to find the set of process models that are subject to compliance checking in a repository of process models. Therefore, saving the effort of manually identifying such models. Later on, a temporal logic formula was derived from the query that is checked against the process model. To check the temporal formula against the process model, we used BPMN semantics in [4] to derive the behavioral model of a BPMN process.

In this paper, we build upon our work in [3] by showing how BPMN-Q [2] queries can be used to show violation to compliance rules regarding ordering of activities execution. Our contribution comes in Section 2 where we extend the set of execution ordering compliance rules that can be expressed in BPMN-Q. Also, we show how BPMN-Q is used to visualize possible violation scenarios. Section 3 discusses a case where rules about ordering of execution of activities needs to be validated. Related work is discussed in Section 4. Paper is concluded in Section 5 with a discussion.

2   Patterns and Anti Patterns

In the next subsection we briefly introduce BPMN-Q and how it was used to was used to express compliance rules. In subsequent subsections we discuss how BPMN-Q queries can be used to express more compliance rules (patterns) and violation scenarios (anti patterns) respectively.

2.1   BPMN-Q

Based on BPMN, BPMN-Q [2] is a visual language that is designed to query business process models by matching a process to a query structurally. In addition to the sequence flow edges of BPMN, BPMN-Q introduces the concept of path edges as illustrated in Fig. 1(b). Such a path might match a sub-graph of a BPMN process — the highlighted part of Fig. 1(a) is the matching part to the path edge of Fig. 1(b).

While such a path considers only the structure of a process, execution semantics have to be considered in the query if BPMN-Q is used for compliance checking. In this case, we type paths between two activities as being either *precedes* (cf. Fig. 1(d)) or *leads to* (cf. Fig. 1(c)) paths [3]. The former requires that before activity B is about to execute, activity A has already been executed. The latter, in turn, states that an execution of the first activity is *eventually* followed by an execution of the second activity. Considering the process in Fig. 1(a), it is obvious that A *precedes* D is satisfied, while A *leads to* D is not. A BPMN-Q query with path edges typed as *leads to* and/or *precedes* is a behavioral query. Otherwise, it is a structural query.

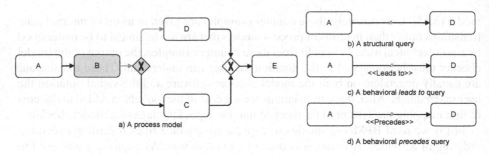

Fig. 1. BPMN-Q Path Edges

The path edge has one more property called the *exclude* property. Imagine a structural query with a path from activity A to activity E where *exclude* is set to D. Matching this query to the process in Fig. 1(a) yields the whole model except activity *D*.

Moreover, behavioral BPMN-Q queries are wrappers for past linear time temporal logic PLTL [21] expressions, PLTL provides more temporal operators that allows reasoning about the past states of a system. That is, `leads to` paths are transformed into an implication with the *eventually* quantifier, whereas `precedes` paths map to an implication with the *once* operator, see Table 1 for the mapping. Setting the *exclude* property for behavioral paths affects the PLTL formula.

Matching a behavioral BPMN-Q query to a process model is a two-step approach. Firstly, the implied structural query is matched to the process model. Secondly, depending on the result the behavior of the matching part is checked against the PLTL formula of the behavioral query. Matching a structural query is in turn a two-step approach. Firstly, *all* activities mentioned in the query have to be present in the process model. Secondly, *all* path edges in the query have to evaluate to a non empty subgraph of the process model.

2.2 Patterns for Execution Ordering Compliance Rules

Based on [5], we can describe the presence, absence, and/or the ordering of activities within a scope. A scope is either global, i.e., the whole process model, before some other activity, after some other activity, or between two activities.

With regard to a single activity, it might be required execute it in all process instances, e.g., in a shipment process the received packets must be inspected in every case. Thus, we call such pattern a global presence as shown in Fig. 2(a). On the other hand, it might be the case that certain activity must not execute at all i.e. such an activity is absent from the process model. This case is called the global absence as shown in Fig. 2(b). For a *before* scope, an activity A might be required to be absent before the execution of another activity B as shown in Fig. 2(c), e.g., it is not allowed to send goods to the customer before receiving payment. Similarly is the after scope as shown in Fig. 2(d). Response pattern [5] is the typical case of leads to compliance rule that was presented in [3]. It is shown in Fig. 2(e). This pattern also is the case of *after* scope presence. The case of absence of an activity in a scope *between* two other activities is shown in Fig. 2(f). Also, the precedence pattern, which is similar to the precedes compliance rule in [3] is shown in Fig. 2(g). This pattern can be used also to express *before* scope

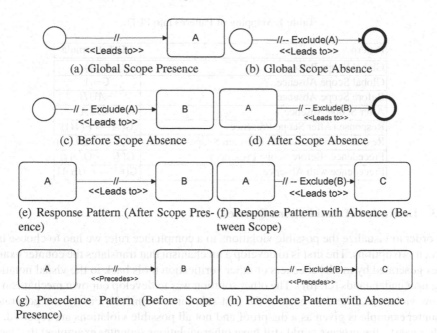

(a) Global Scope Presence   (b) Global Scope Absence

(c) Before Scope Absence   (d) After Scope Absence

(e) Response Pattern (After Scope Presence)   (f) Response Pattern with Absence (Between Scope)

(g) Precedence Pattern (Before Scope Presence)   (h) Precedence Pattern with Absence

Fig. 2. Patterns for Execution Ordering Compliance Rules

presence. A different way to represent the *absence* in *between* scope is as shown in Fig. 2(h). This is a core set of patterns from which one can build more complex ones. For instance, a *before* scope only *presence* pattern of Activity A and B i.e. activity A must execute before activity B but no after it. This rule is shown in Fig. 3.

Each of these patterns (Compliance Rule) is mapped into a PLTL formula. The mapping is shown in Table 1. In PLTL, classical logical operators are extended with new ones that allow to evaluate the truth value of predicates in past states of a system, process models in this case. The temporal opera-

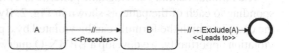

Fig. 3. A Before Only Presence Pattern

tors used by this paper are **G** the global operator where its argument has to hold in *all future* states.The eventually operator **F** describes that its argument must hold in *some* future state. **O** is its past counter part. The binary operator **U** is called the until operator where pUq describes that p has to hold *until* the point in time q holds. The past operator since **S** is it counter part.

According to Table 1, each compliance query (pattern) has a mapping into PLTL. Thus, each of these queries can be verified against a process model using model checking as we described earlier. Since our objective in this paper is beyond model checking, i.e., we need to know *how* the rule was violated. We describe in the next subsection the derivation of so-called anti pattern queries. For each pattern query, there is a set of anti pattern queries. Each anti pattern declaratively describes a violation scenario.

Table 1. Mapping of Patterns into PLTL

Pattern	PLTL Formula
Global Scope Presence	$F(A)$
Global Scope Absence	$G\neg A$
Before Scope Absence	$\neg AUB$
After Scope Absence	$\neg BSA$
Response (After Scope Presence)	$G(A \rightarrow F(B))$
Response with Absence (Between Scope Absence)	$G(A \rightarrow \neg BUC)$
Precedence (Before Scope Presence)	$G(B \rightarrow O(A))$
Precedence with Absence	$G(C \rightarrow \neg BSA)$

2.3 Derivation of Anti Pattern Queries

In order to visualize the possible violations to a compliance rule, we had to choose between two options. The first is to develop a mechanism that translates the counter examples generated by model checkers or other verification tools back to the visual notation the user understands (cf. [6]). The other solution was to develop our own mechanism to show violations. The drawback of the first solution is manifold. Firstly, the generated counter example is given as a dis-proof and not all possible violations are reported. In other words, the process could still have other violations (counter examples) that were not reported by the model checker. Secondly, the generated counter example depends on the input state transition system of the process model. In case the transition system is generated after using reducing the original process model (cf. [3,16], the resulting counter example would not be usable on the original process model. Finally, the usability of such approach depends on the output format of the specific model checker used. Each time model checking software is changed, a re-implementation of the translation software is required (cf. [6]).

The rational behind deriving anti-patterns is 1) to analyse the PLTL formula corresponding to each of the patterns shown in Fig. 2. By analysis, we study and enumerate the cases in which the formula can be violated by a process model. 2) For each possible violation opportunity, we develop a BPMN-Q query that captures execution scenario(s) in which violation occurs.

Global Scope Anti Patterns. The global scope *presence* requires that certain activity must be executed in *all* instances of a process. This is also similar to the response pattern. Within process models, the violation of such requirement occurs when there are execution paths that lack the required activity. This is captured by the anti pattern query in Fig. 4(a). The opposite case of global *absence* is violated when there is at least one execution path in which activity A is executed. This is represented in Fig. 4(b).

Before Scope Anti Patterns. The *presence* case requires that an Activity A is always executed before another activity B. So, the violation occurs when there is in the business process a chance to execute activity B without executing A at all before. This violation is expressed as the BPMN-Q query in Fig. 4(e) where there is an execution path from the start of the process to activity B without doing A at all. The other case of absence necessitates that A must *never* execute before B and B must always execute. The interpretation of this anti pattern is a bit complicated. The rule is violated in one of two

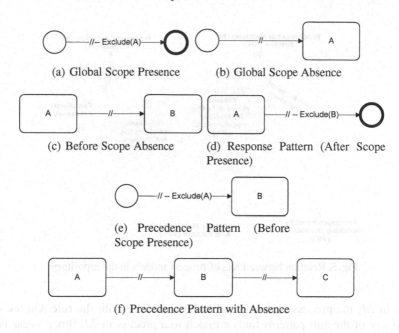

(a) Global Scope Presence   (b) Global Scope Absence

(c) Before Scope Absence   (d) Response Pattern (After Scope Presence)

(e) Precedence Pattern (Before Scope Presence)

(f) Precedence Pattern with Absence

Fig. 4. Anti Patterns for Execution Ordering Compliance Rules

cases. Either the activity A occurs and then B occurs thereafter. This case is shown in Fig. 4(c). The other possibility of violation is that activity B in some instances is not executed at all. This violation can be captured by the query in Fig. 4(b) for activity B.

After Scope Anti Patterns. In a similar way, the *presence* case is similar to the response pattern where after activity A is executed; activity B must be executed in some point in the future. The violation for this pattern is that in some instance A executed but never B after that. This meaning is captured by the query in Fig. 4(d). The absence pattern is on the other hand violated when after A executes B also executes. So the query in Fig. 4(c) would also capture this case of violation.

Between Scope Anti Patterns. Finally the between scope with presence could be interpreted similarly to the before scope. The only difference that we replace the start event of a process with an activity that determines the beginning of the scope. The absence case violation is captured in Fig. 4(f).

2.4   The Validation Process

The validation process starts by a pattern expressed by the user. A set of anti patterns are generated automatically as discussed in Section 2.3. When the pattern query is processed by BPMN-Q, the set of process models in the repository can be divided into two disjoint sets. The set of matching process models M, and the set of non matching process models NM. If the pattern query finds a match in a process model, we need to check for a match for any of the anti patterns. If none of the anti patterns finds a match

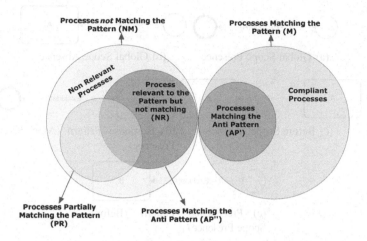

Fig. 5. Relation between sets of process models in the repository

process in M, the process is guaranteed to be *compliant* with the rule. On the other hand, if any of the anti patterns finds a match to a process in M, this process is *non compliant* and its subgraph matching the anti pattern query is the scenario that violates the rule.

With respect to the pattern query, the set NM can be further subdivided into the set relevant but not matching processes NR, the set of partially relevant processes PR, and the set of non relevant processes NP. The set NR holds process models containing violations where activities mentioned in the pattern exist in the process but (some) path edges in the query are not satisfied. The set PR contains violating process models where a proper subset of the pattern activities exist in a process model.

Fig. 5 represents the relationship between these sets on one hand, and the set $AP = AP' \cup AP''$ represents process models matching anti pattern queries on the other hand. From Fig. 5, we can see that AP intersects with sets M, NR, PR. All elements contained in AP represent a way to violate the compliance rule (pattern). The three possible intersections correspond to the three possible cases of violation mentioned in Section 2.

- ○ NR is the set of process models containing activities mentioned in the rule but without execution paths at all.
- ○ $AP \cap M$ is the set of process models that contain all activities in the rule but the order can be violated in some execution scenarios.
- ○ $AP \cap PR$ contains process models where some of the activities in the rule exist.

This approach to detect and visualize violation is fully implemented in an extension of BPMN-Q query processor. Once the pattern query is received, the query processor generates anti pattern queries for each `leads to` or `precedes` edge in the query. If any matches to any of the anti pattern queries is found, the matching part of the process to the anti pattern query is highlighted and returned to the user.

3   Compliance Example

In this section, we apply our approach on a business process from the banking sector. Consider the process model in Fig. 6 (expressed in BPMN notation) for opening a correspondent bank account.

The process starts with "Receive correspondent Account open request" to open an account. Bank Identity is determined in order to go on with the procedure of opening the account. If this is the first time such respondent bank requests to open an account, some checks must take place. The bank to open the account needs to conduct a study about the respondent bank due diligence "Conduct due diligence study", it also needs to assess the risk of opening an account for that respondent bank "Assess Respondent Bank risk", and to check respondent bank certificate in order to proceed with opening the account. On the other hand, if such respondent bank has a record with the bank, these checks are skipped. In any of the cases, the bank has to obtain a report about the performance of the respondent bank "Obtain Respondent Bank Annual Report". This report is analyzed by the bank "Analyze Respondent Bank annual report", and the respondent bank rate is reviewed "Review Respondent Bank rating". If the respondent bank passes the checks, an account is opened "Open Correspondent Account".

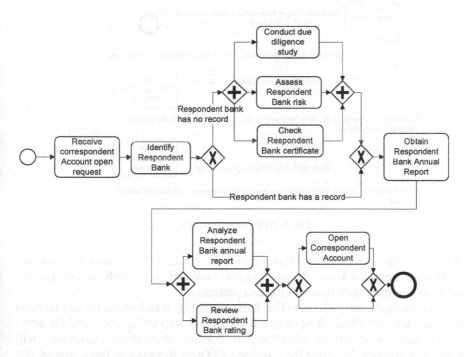

Fig. 6. Opening a correspondent account business process

New rules to prevent money laundering have been developed be a central bank. The compliance officer of the bank wants to check the compliance of the process in Fig. 6 with the following rule.

Before opening a correspondent account, a due diligence study must be conducted. Respondent annual report is analyzed when it is obtained before opening the correspondent account.

Based on the above rule, the officer formulated a compliance rule (pattern) as the BPMN-Q query shown in Fig. 7. By starting to process this query, anti pattern queries are generated automatically for each type of path edge in the compliance rule. The generated anti pattern queries are shown in Fig. 8.

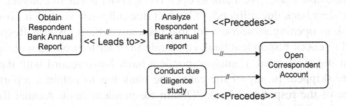

Fig. 7. A BPMN-Q query capturing the compliance rule

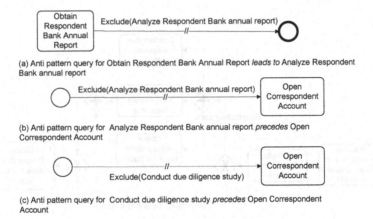

(a) Anti pattern query for Obtain Respondent Bank Annual Report *leads to* Analyze Respondent Bank annual report

(b) Anti pattern query for Analyze Respondent Bank annual report *precedes* Open Correspondent Account

(c) Anti pattern query for Conduct due diligence study *precedes* Open Correspondent Account

Fig. 8. Anti pattern queries

The pattern query found a match in the process of Fig. 6. This means that there are execution scenarios that satisfy the rule. In order to declare full compliance, the process must be free from a match to any of the anti patterns.

By examining the anti patterns in Fig. 8,the one in Fig. 8(a), looking for an execution path where activity "Obtain Respondent Bank Annual Report" executes and the activity "Analyze Respondent Bank Annual Report" does not till the process terminates, will not find any matches. Note that the sequence <Obtain Respondent Bank Annual Report, AND Split, Review Respondent Bank rating, AND Join, ..., end event > cannot be considered as a match, because AND Split node after "Obtain Respondent Bank Annual Report" activity will activate both activities "Review Respondent Bank rating" and "Analyze Respondent Bank Annual report". This is a feature of BPMN-Q query processor, whenever a node is excluded, all parallel nodes to it are excluded as well in

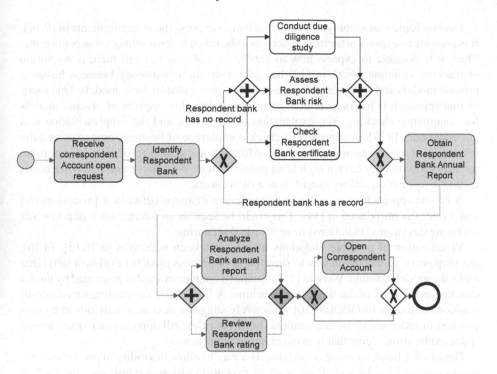

Fig. 9. A violation to the compliance rule

order to guarantee correct results. Similarly, anti pattern query in Fig. 8(b) will not find a match.

Anti pattern in Fig. 8(c) finds a match. The match is shown in Fig. 9 where there is an execution scenario that starts from the beginning of the process and selects the lower choice branch (`Respondent bank has a record`). It is clear that this scenario represents the way the compliance rule can be violated, and this case needs correction by experts.

4 Related Work

Compliance Checking approaches can be categorized as either (a) Compliance by Design, where compliance rules are taken as input in the design process of *new* process models. The other approach depends on checking for compliance in a post design step. Thus, separating the modeling phase of a process model from the checking phase [19]. Our approach belongs to the second category.

Work in [13,8,17] deal with the enforcement of compliance requirements in the design process of new business process models. By definition, there is no chance for violations to occur. However, once a new compliance requirement is introduced or the process model is modified, the checking for compliance is needed.

On the other hand, approaches like [20,15] employ model checking to verify that process models satisfy the compliance rules. Comparing to our work, the notion of explaining violations in an intuitive way to the user was not addressed in that work.

Deontic logic was employed as a formalism to express these requirements in [9,19]. It is possible to express *alternative* actions to be taken when a primary one is not done. Thus, it is possible to express how to handle *exceptions* but still there is no notion of tracking violation. Work in [12] has addressed the consistency between business process models and lifecycle of business objects processed in these models. One merit of that approach is to consider both control and data flow aspects of process models for compliance checking. Yet, explanation of deviations and their representation was not addressed. In [7] an approach to check compliance of business processes and the resolution of violations was introduced. Although automated resolution is important, the paper discussed it from a high level point of view. We believe that this point needs further investigation and we remark it as a future work.

A recent approach to measure the compliance distance between a process model and a rule was introduced in [14]. This could be seen as an intermediary step towards capturing deviations (violations) from the ideal scenarios.

Visualization of possible violations to rules has been addressed in [6,15]. In [6], the purpose of visualization was to show parts of process models (workflow nets) that make the model unsound. Work in [15] visualized counter examples generated by model checker on the level of the finite state machine. A framework for guiding service compositions based on PROPOLS [10] proactively suggests next step activities in a composition in order not to violate temporal business rules. All approaches require a state space exploration, a cost that is avoided in our approach.

Declarative business process modeling is a way to allow flexibility in processes. Processes are modeled by specifying a set of execution ordering constraints on a set of activities [18]. In this way, compliance rules discussed in this paper could be expressed to guide the execution of process instances. Thus, there is no chance for violation. Comparing to our approach, we are concerned with detecting and visualizing possible violations on *imperative* process models.

5 Discussion

In this paper we discussed an approach to visualize violation of control flow ordering compliance rules. This step provides useful feedback to the user in order to correct violations. The compliance rules are expressed as behavioral BPMN-Q queries and are called patterns. The anti pattern queries are derived automatically as structural BPMN-Q queries.

The merits of the approach are 1) Expressing rules visually in BPMN-Q in a way similar to modeling 2) The querying nature of BPMN-Q allows to discover the process models in a repository that are subject for compliance checking 3) Automatic generation of anti pattern queries.

A limitation of the approach is the assumption that activity names are aligned to a common ontology respected by all business modelers. The presented patterns/anti patterns are core ones. However, extensibility to express more complex situations is possible as was shown in Section 2.2.

In future, we investigate the inclusion of data aspects for both verification and visualization of violation. However, the challenge is to find/develop appropriate formalism that helps explain violations.

References

1. Sarbanes-Oxley Act of 2002. Public Law 107-204 (116 Statute 745), United States Senate and House of Representatives in Congress (2002)
2. Awad, A.: BPMN-Q: A Language to Query Business Processes. In: EMISA. LNI, vol. P-119, pp. 115–128. GI (2007)
3. Awad, A., Decker, G., Weske, M.: Efficient compliance checking using bpmn-q and temporal logic. In: Dumas, M., Reichert, M., Shan, M.-C. (eds.) BPM 2008. LNCS, vol. 5240, pp. 326–341. Springer, Heidelberg (2008)
4. Dijkman, R.M., Dumas, M., Ouyang, C.: Semantics and analysis of business process models in BPMN. Inf. Softw. Technol. 50(12), 1281–1294 (2008)
5. Dwyer, M.B., Avrunin, G.S., Corbett, J.C.: Patterns in property specifications for finite-state verification. In: ICSE, pp. 411–420. ACM, New York (1999)
6. Flender, C., Freytag, T.: Visualizing the soundness of workflow nets. In: AWPN 2006, Department Informatics Report 267, University of Hamburg, Germany (2006)
7. Ghose, A., Koliadis, G.: Auditing business process compliance. In: Krämer, B.J., Lin, K.-J., Narasimhan, P. (eds.) ICSOC 2007. LNCS, vol. 4749, pp. 169–180. Springer, Heidelberg (2007)
8. Goedertier, S., Vanthienen, J.: Designing Compliant Business Processes from Obligations and Permissions. In: Eder, J., Dustdar, S. (eds.) BPM Workshops 2006. LNCS, vol. 4103, pp. 5–14. Springer, Heidelberg (2006)
9. Governatori, G., Milosevic, Z., Sadiq, S.: Compliance checking between business processes and business contracts. In: EDOC, pp. 221–232. IEEE Computer Society, Los Alamitos (2006)
10. Han, J., Jin, Y., Li, Z., Phan, T., Yu, J.: Guiding the service composition process with temporal business rules. In: ICWS, pp. 735–742. IEEE Computer Society, Los Alamitos (2007)
11. Hartman, T.E.: The Cost of Being Public in the Era of Sarbanes-Oxley. Foley & Lardner, Chicago (2006)
12. Küster, J.M., Ryndina, K., Gall, H.: Generation of Business Process Models for Object Life Cycle Compliance. In: Alonso, G., Dadam, P., Rosemann, M. (eds.) BPM 2007. LNCS, vol. 4714, pp. 165–181. Springer, Heidelberg (2007)
13. Lu, R., Sadiq, S., Governatori, G.: Compliance aware business process design. In: ter Hofstede, A.H.M., Benatallah, B., Paik, H.-Y. (eds.) BPM Workshops 2007. LNCS, vol. 4928, pp. 120–131. Springer, Heidelberg (2008)
14. Lu, R., Sadiq, S., Governatori, G.: Measurement of Compliance Distance in Business Processes. Inf. Sys. Manag. 25(4), 344–355 (2008)
15. Lui, Y., Müller, S., Xu, K.: A static compliance-checking framework for business process models. IBM Systems Journal 46(2), 335–362 (2007)
16. Mendling, J.: Detection and Prediction of Errors in EPC Business Process Models. PhD thesis, Institute of Information Systems and New Media Vienna University of Economics and Business Administration (WU Wien) Austria (May 2007)
17. Milosevic, Z., Sadiq, S.W., Orlowska, M.E.: Translating business contract into compliant business processes. In: EDOC, pp. 211–220. IEEE Computer Society, Los Alamitos (2006)
18. Pesic, M., Schonenberg, H., van der Aalst, W.M.P.: DECLARE: Full Support for Loosely-Structured Processes. In: EDOC, pp. 287–300. IEEE Computer Society, Los Alamitos (2007)
19. Sadiq, S.W., Governatori, G., Namiri, K.: Modeling control objectives for business process compliance. In: Alonso, G., Dadam, P., Rosemann, M. (eds.) BPM 2007. LNCS, vol. 4714, pp. 149–164. Springer, Heidelberg (2007)
20. Yu, J., Manh, T.P., Han, J., Jin, Y., Han, Y., Wang, J.: Pattern based property specification and verification for service composition. In: Aberer, K., Peng, Z., Rundensteiner, E.A., Zhang, Y., Li, X. (eds.) WISE 2006. LNCS, vol. 4255, pp. 156–168. Springer, Heidelberg (2006)
21. Zuck, L.: Past Temporal Logic. PhD thesis, Weizmann Institute, Rehovot, Israel (August 1986)

BPMS2 Workshop

Introduction

Selmin Nurcan[1] and Rainer Schmidt[2]

[1] University Paris 1 Panthéon Sorbonne, France
[2] HTW-Aalen, 73430 Aalen, Germany

Social software is a new paradigm that is spreading quickly in society, organizations and economics. It supports social interaction and social production. Social interaction is the interaction of non-predetermined individuals. Social production is the creation of artifacts, by combining the input from independent contributors without predetermining the way to do this [1]. Users are supported in creating new contacts, presenting themselves and collaborating with other users. As a result, content, knowledge and software is not created by a hierarchy of experts, but by combining a multitude of contributions of independent authors/actors. Examples for such a social production are wikis, blogs, social bookmarking and tagging, etc.

Social software follows a more egalitarian and meritocratic approach compared to traditional approaches where the role of the software user is determined by the enterprise senior management and its representatives. Thus, trust and reputation play a crucial role in the use of social software instead of authority granted by the top management.

The paradigm of social software and social production has created a multitude of success stories such as wikipedia.org and the development of the Linux operating system. Therefore, more and more enterprises see social software and social production as a means for further improvement of their business processes and business models. For example, they integrate their customers into product development by using blogs to capture ideas for new products and features. Thus, business processes have to be adapted to new communication patterns between customers and the enterprise: for example, the communication with the customer is increasingly a bi-directional communication with the customer and among the customers. Social software also offers new possibilities to enhance business processes by improving the exchange of knowledge and information, to speed up decisions, etc.

Up to now, the interaction of social software and the underlying paradigm of social production with business processes have not been investigated in depth. Therefore, the objective of the workshop is to explore how social software and social production interact with business process management, how business process management has to change to comply with social production, and how business processes may profit from social techniques.

The workshop discussed three topics:

1. New opportunities provided by social software for BPM
2. Engineering next generation of business processes: BPM 2.0 ?
3. Business process implementation support by social software

S. Rinderle-Ma et al. (Eds.): BPM 2009 Workshops, LNBIP 43, pp. 197–199, 2010.
© Springer-Verlag Berlin Heidelberg 2010

The workshop started with an introduction given by Selmin Nurcan and Rainer Schmidt. The paper "Enabling Community Participation for Workflows Through Extensibility and Sharing" shows how business processes and workflows can be designed collaboratively using a workflow-management system using a software-as-a-service oriented architecture. The extension of process modeling and execution systems by social software features is proposed in the paper "AGILIPO: Embedding Social Software Features into Business Process Tools". Based on a study about Wikipedia, suggestions for the design of socially enriched workflow technology are made in the paper "Workflow Management Social Systems: a new socio-psychological perspective on process management". The documentation of social processes needs formal means on their own according to the paper "Requirements Elicitation as a Case of Social Process: an Approach to its Description".A Semantic Media Wiki is used as platform for the elicitation of requirements in the paper "Co-Creation of Value in IT Service Processes using Semantic MediaWiki". The use of social tagging for the integration of process models into knowledge management is proposed in the paper "Models, Social Tagging and Knowledge Management – A fruitful Combination for Process Improvement". The use of gestural analysis of human agents is the basis for a new approach to support for human agent-based processes presented in the paper "Micro Workflow Gestural Analysis: Representation in Social Business Processes"

We wish to thank all authors for having shared their work with us, as well as the members of the BPMS2'09 Program committee and the workshop organizers of BPM'09 for their help with the organization of the workshop.

Workshop Program Committee

Ilia Bider - IbisSoft, Sweden

Jan Bosch - Intuit, Mountain View, California, USA

Dragan Gasevic - School of Computing and Information Systems, Athabasca University, Canada

Werner Geyer - IBM T.J. Watson Research, Collaborative User Experience Group, Cambridge, USA

Tad Hogg - HP Information Dynamics Laboratory, Palo Alto, USA

Ralf Klamma - Informatik 5, RWTH Aachen, Germany

Sai Peck Lee - University of Malaya, Kuala Lumpur, Malaysia

Gustaf Neumann - Vienna University of Economics and Business Administration, Vienna, Austria

Selmin Nurcan - University Paris 1 Pantheon Sorbonne, France

Anne Persson - School of Humanities and Informatics, University of Skövde, Sweden

Gil Regev - Ecole Polytechnique Fédérale de Lausanne, Itecor, Switzerland

Michael Rosemann - Faculty of Information Technology Queensland University of Technology, Australia

Nick Russell - Eindhoven University of Technology, The Netherlands
Rainer Schmidt - University of Applied Sciences, Aalen, Germany
Miguel-Ángel Sicilia - University of Alcalá, Madrid, Spain
Pnina Soffer - Department of Management Information Systems, University of Haifa, Israel

Reference

[1] Schmidt, R., Nurcan, S.: BPM and Social Software. In: Ardagna, D., et al. (eds.) BPM 2008 Workshops. LNBIP, vol. 17, pp. 623–624. Springer, Heidelberg (2009)

Augmenting BPM with Social Software

Rainer Schmidt[1] and Selmin Nurcan[2]

[1] Department of Computer Science, University of Applied Sciences,
Beethovenstraße 1, 73430 Aalen, Germany
+49 178 180 4116
Rainer.Schmidt@htw-aalen.de
[2] University Paris 1 Panthéon Sorbonne –CRI & Sorbonne
Graduate Business School, France
+33 - 1 53 55 27 13
nurcan@univ-paris1.fr

Abstract. The relationship of social software and business processes can be twofold. On one hand, business processes may use social software. On the other hand, business processes maybe the object of social software. That means social software is used to act upon the business processes and augment classic BPM approaches. In particular, the benefits from coupling BPM and social software are based on the integration of four principles within social software and their application to business process management (BPM): weak ties, social production, egalitarianism and Service-Dominant Logic. Weak ties are spontaneously created connections between non-predetermined individuals. Social production is the creation of artifacts, by combining the input from independent contributors. The merging of the role of contributor creates the egalitarianism of social software and the consumer of the artifacts created. Thus social software implies, a mutual provisioning of services instead of a unidirectional one.

1 Introduction

The success of social software is based on the integration of four principles: weak ties, social production, egalitarianism and Service-Dominant Logic. Weak ties [1] are spontaneously created contacts between non-predetermined individuals. Social production e.g. Benkler [2], Tapscott [3] is the creation of artifacts, by combining the input from independent contributors without predetermining the way to do this. Egalitarianism is realized in social software by merging the roles of contributors and consumers and introducing a culture of trust instead of formal access procedures. Social software is based on mutual service provisioning [4]. As there is no clear separation between the contributor and the consumer of the artifacts created, both render services mutually. By combining these services, a cooperatively created service is rendered. For example, using social software more and more enterprises integrate their customers into product development by using blogs to capture ideas for new products and features. Thus, also the customers render services that flow into the total service provided.

S. Rinderle-Ma et al. (Eds.): BPM 2009 Workshops, LNBIP 43, pp. 201–206, 2010.

This paper will investigate the relationship between BPM and social software especially with respect to the support of BPM by social software and proceed as follows. First, the principles of social software are illuminated to show, that the success of social software is not by accident but in accord with important principles identified in research. Based on this foundation, the relationship of BPM and social software is analyzed. Finally, a summary and conclusion is made.

2   Principles Implemented in Social Software

The success of social software can be explained by the integration of four principles. Some of these principles have been already identified a long time ago, but not properly implemented.

2.1   Weak Ties

Social software supports the creation of weak ties, spontaneously created connections between non-predetermined individuals. Weak ties enable individuals to collect information etc. out side their established team environment. Weak ties have been identified by Granovetter [1] already in the 1970s but they have been constrained to the physical world. However ubiquitous and Internet access created the base for applying the concept of weak ties to the digital world. Weak ties drastically improve the knowledge exchange within organizations. Enterprises can improve their agility and innovative capabilities.

2.2   Egalitarianism

Egalitarianism is the assignment of equal rights to all members of a society and tightly connected to democratic principles. It is implemented in social software by merging the roles of contributors and consumers. Thus, it supports the ideas, which Surowiecki collected under the title "wisdom of the crowds". Empirical data shows, that for many decision and planning problems combining as many inputs as possible delivers statically better results than relying on experts, which creates the insolvable problem of expert selection[5]. (In fact, to adequately select an expert you must be an expert at the same level of expertise as the expert you are selecting.

This egalitarian view can be seen in the blogs used by many enterprises to interact with customers and partners. They allow the users to contribute to the further development of products.

2.3   Social Production

Social production is an alternative organization of production introduced by several authors e.g. Benkler [2], Tapscott [3]. They consider the free flow of information and knowledge as a precondition for a sustainable development of economy and single enterprise. Thus, you must open your company to capture new ideas from outside and you have to cooperate with many different people. In this way, you are able to combine the best thoughts and create competitive product.

To support the idea of social production, social software enables the community of users to organize information and knowledge. All users develop the structures interactively. Thus, no predefined taxonomies or structures organized by a specialist are used. Instead, trust and reputation play a crucial role in the use of social software. They replace access-rights based solutions found in standard approaches. The individuals strive for not damaging their reputation by false or even malicious contributions. This "optimistic" access policy allows a continuous fusioning and aggregation of information and knowledge, which becomes immediately visible and effective. Thus all users may continuously assess the artifacts created and a quickly rotating improvement cycle can be initiated.

2.4 Service-Dominant Logic

Service-Dominant Logic [6] is a highly successful approach in marketing which says, that the traditional, goods-oriented approach for marketing has to be replaced by a service-oriented. Service-Dominant logic postulates, that the customer does not want a product but the service rendered by the product [6]. Furthermore, it is necessary to interact with the customer to render the service. Thus, there is a mutual rendering of services and not a uni-directional one. Therefore, customer is not a consumer of value but a co-creator of value.

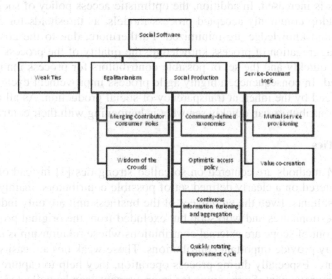

Fig. 1. Principles implemented in Social Software

3   The Relationship of Social-Software and Business Process Management

The relationship of social software and business processes can be twofold. On one hand business processes may use social software e.g. to improve the interaction with the customer. It offers new possibilities to enhance business processes by improving the exchange of knowledge and information, to speed up decisions, etc. It facilitates new communication patterns between customers and the enterprise: for example, the communication with the customer is increasingly a bi-directional communication with the customer and among the customers.

On the other hand, business processes may be the object of social software. That means social software is used to act upon the business process. Thus, social software augments BPM by supporting the design, modeling, etc. of business processes. This is of particular importance, because on workshops and conferences such as BPMDS, BPM, there is a growing concern about the divide between abstract process models and the executed processes, procedures etc. This model - reality divide [7] means, that although BPM models and structures are well designed, they are not used in practice but end up in the filing cabinet. Therefore, based on the description of principles implemented in social software, possible contributions to overcome the model-reality divide shall be identified.

3.1 Social Production

Social Production is able to deliver important contributions to overcome the model-reality divide. The definition of business processes and their underlying taxonomy can be done on a true peer-to-peer basis instead of simply imposing centrally defined processes and terms on the employees. Thus, the identification of the employees with the processes is increased. In addition, the optimistic access policy of social software helps to develop commonly accepted process models, as thresholds for contributing information and knowledge are minimized. Furthermore, due to the continuous fusioning and aggregation of process knowledge, the quality of the process models can be improved quickly and the set of possible contributors for process innovations can be maximized. In consequence, a highly agile process improvement cycle is realized. This is enforced by the inherent transparency of social production. As all changes are visible, the contributors can quickly see what is happening with their contributions.

3.2 Weak Ties

Present BPM methods are centered on so-called strong ties [1] instead of weak ties. They are centered on a clearly defined set of possible contributors, mainly internal or external consultants. Even the employees of the business unit are only indirectly integrated by questionnaires and workshop but excluded from the original process definition. Totally out of scope are external contributions whose relationship is not obvious, but which may provide important contributions. These weak ties are easily created by social software. Especially during process operation, they help to capture knowledge for process improvement. Suggestions for improvements can be collected more easily and can be instantly evaluated by all stakeholders.

3.3 Egalitarianism

One important reason for the model-reality divide is the strict separation between modelers and model users inherent in classical BPM. Social software allows to reducing this separation by merging the modeler role with model user role. By this means, the set of contributors is increased and thus the quality of the solution –potentially- improved. Using the egalitarian approach of social software, constraints for implementation and deployment are captured in finer detail. Especially during process deployment, the broad collection of relevant issues and distribution of planning data is of high importance for project success.

3.4 Service-Dominant Logic

The model-reality divide can also be reduced by applying thoughts of Service Dominant Logic implemented in social software. Following Service Dominant Logic, the creation of a process model is no longer understood as an unidirectional activity delivering a process model to the business unit but as a bidirectional process consisting of mutual service provisioning. The services contributed by the business unit are highly important to align the business process to the specific needs and increase the acceptance of the final business process model.

4 Summary and Conclusion

The integrative implementation of four principles: weak ties, social production, egalitarianism and Service-Dominant Logic are the key to success of social software. Weak ties are spontaneously created connections between non-predetermined individuals. Egalitarianism is realized in social software by the assignment of equal rights to all members and by merging the roles of contributors and consumers. Social production enables the community of users to organize information and knowledge. An "optimistic" access policy allows a continuous fusioning and aggregation of information and knowledge, minimizing the thresholds to contribute. Service Dominant Logic provides the mutual rendering of services and enables the former consumer to be a co-creator of value.

Based on this principle, social software is able to augment BPM and to overcome deficiencies of classic BPM approaches, such as the model - reality divide. Social Production is able to deliver important contributions to overcome the model-reality divide. The definition of business processes and their underlying taxonomy can be done on a true peer-to-peer basis instead of simply imposing centrally defined processes and terms on the employees. Social software better integrates the needs of all stakeholders in a more complete way and constraints for implementation and deployment are captured in finer detail. Weak ties are easily created by social software and allow capturing knowledge for process improvement. Social software also allows to highly reducing this separation by merging the modeler role with model user role. The model-reality divide can also be reduced by applying thoughts of Service Dominant Logic: the creation of a process model becomes a bidirectional process consisting of mutual service provisioning.

References

[1] Granovetter, M.S.: The Strength of Weak Ties. American Journal of Sociology 78, 1360 (1973)
[2] Benkler, Y.: The Wealth of Networks: How Social Production Transforms Markets and Freedom. Yale University Press (2006)

[3] Tapscott, D., Williams, A.D.: Wikinomics: How Mass Collaboration Changes Everything, Portfolio (2006)

[4] Vargo, S., Lusch, R.: "Why "service"?". Journal of the Academy of Marketing Science 36, 25–38 (2008)

[5] Surowiecki, J.: The Wisdom of Crowds: Why the Many Are Smarter Than the Few and How Collective Wisdom Shapes Business, Economies, Societies and Nations, Doubleday (2004)

[6] Vargo, S., Lusch, R.: Service-dominant logic: continuing the evolution. Journal of the Academy of Marketing Science 36, 1–10 (2008)

[7] Schmidt, R., Nurcan, S.: BPM and Social Software. In: Ardagna, D., et al. (eds.) BPM 2008 Workshops. LNBIP, vol. 17, pp. 649–658. Springer, Heidelberg (2009)

Enabling Community Participation for Workflows through Extensibility and Sharing

Rania Khalaf, Revathi Subramanian, Thomas Mikalsen, Matthew Duftler,
Judah Diament, and Ignacio Silva-Lepe

IBM T.J. Watson Research Center, 19 Skyline Dr., Hawthorne NY 10532, USA
{rkhalaf,revathi,tommi,duftler,djudah,isilval}@us.ibm.com

Abstract. This paper describes how community participation may be
enabled and fostered in a hosted BPM system. We envision an open,
collaborative system, wherein users across organizational boundaries can
work together to develop and share design-time and run-time artifacts;
namely extension activities, workflow models and workflow instances.
The system described in this paper enables this collaboration and also
allows the community to provide feedback on the shared artifacts via
tags, comments and ratings.

Keywords: Social Software, BPM, Collaboration, Extensions, SOA.

1 Introduction

Workflow languages and systems are steadily making the transition to a more
open and collaborative space as the idea of offering business process management systems as hosted services gains momentum. One step in this evolution
is the emergence of Service Oriented Architecture, where services from different providers can be integrated using the Web services stack of XML standards [24]. WS-BPEL is the workflow language in the stack, providing a rich
flow-based model for aggregating interactions with several Web based services,
and in which the workflow is itself exposed as a set of such services. The next
step is the move to simpler Web services created using the REpresentational
State Transfer (REST) [7] architectural style. REST services are offered with a
uniform interface over HTTP and have facilitated the current movement towards
Mashups: new services created quickly and easily by aggregating several existing
Web based services and visual components. Mashups come in different flavors:
User Interface mashups like putting one's running route on a Google map, data
mashups like a new RSS feed that combines existing news feeds using Yahoo!
Pipes or the IBM Mashup Center, and more recently service mashups [3]. The
Bite workflow language [5] is a result of this transition, created to enable fast and
easy authoring of workflows that aggregate interactions with RESTful services,
humans via forms, e-mails, collaboration software, and back-end services. Bite
is by design ready for community participation capabilities, due to its extensible
nature and REST based interaction model. The current state in the evolution

S. Rinderle-Ma et al. (Eds.): BPM 2009 Workshops, LNBIP 43, pp. 207–218, 2010.
© Springer-Verlag Berlin Heidelberg 2010

has been the realization of the software as a service vision, enabled by the move to Cloud Computing [1]. Hence, we now see commercial offerings of hosted BPM systems with pay-per-use models.

The combination of a hosted, multi-tenant enabled BPM system with a lightweight, Web-friendly language like Bite offers organizations and users the ability to design, execute and monitor workflows directly from the Web browser. In this paper, we show how this combination can effectively enable workflow systems to take advantage of the social software paradigm. We focus on enabling social production [2,18] for two specific aspects in a hosted workflow system: (a) extension activities and (b) the workflows themselves. An 'extension activity' is a new kind of activity that is not present in the definition of the workflow language itself. In particular, we enable independent IT developers to easily create and publish extension activities which can be shared with and used by workflow designers and other developers. The community, consisting of both IT developers and workflow designers, can provide feedback on these extensions by using the tagging, commenting, and rating features of a shared catalog. Workflow designers can then create new workflows by selecting from a default palette of basic Bite activities, as well as from a catalog of extensions provided by the community. In addition to this collaboration between workflow designers and developers, collaboration is also fostered between developers by sharing the source code of their extensions and between workflow designers by sharing flow models and/or instances.

Providing this functionality in an open cross-enterprise environment necessitates solving problems in two complementary but distinct areas: (1) Designing a method for social production of worfklows and extension activities and supporting it in the underlying system and (2) providing mechanisms and contracts to cover general software as a service concerns including malicious code, billing, IP issues resulting from reuse, etc. In this paper, we focus on the first area.

The following scenario illustrates a true community experience around authoring and sharing workflows and extensions. In it, we make use of LotusLive (http://www.lotuslive.com), a software as a service offering from IBM providing cross-enterprise collaboration services.

Carol, a LotusLive developer, writes an extension that zips up files in the LotusLive 'Files' file sharing service that are shared with a user within a specified date range. She contributes this extension to the shared catalog, where it gets high ratings.

Brainshare Inc. is attending a career fair hosted by McGrath University where it hopes to attract the brightest student attendees. Ted, Brainshare's event coordinator, invites the Dean of the University to participate in developing the workflow model for the event. The Dean suggests engaging students via a design contest, with the winning design featured in some of the company brochures. Brainshare's existing recruiting workflow model is modified to include additional activities for the contest and to feed the contest results into the brochure design activity. For example, Ted adds to the workflow Bite extension activities for the LotusLive 'Activities' collaboration service [17]. The Dean also informs Ted that all student resumes are available via the LotusLive Files service, but are typically private. On the day of the career fair, interested students will share their resumes with Ted using the Files service. Ted looks at the catalog of extensions and finds Carol's extension. It is just what he needs. He wires that to an email activity so that he can email himself and his HR department a zip file containing the students' resumes.

2 Related Work

We first address related work for social software around shared artifacts on the Web and then focus specifically on workflow. A large array of sites already exists for sharing artifacts via tagging, ranking and commenting such as for photos(Flickr), videos(YouTube) and goods(Amazon.com). More recently, structured content types such as reusable lists [9] are gaining traction as socially shared artifacts types.

A common type of application sharing, specifically among developers, is sharing source code. While this is not new [20], some popular code sharing sites [10] and tools [14] either already include or are working to include social aspects of development. These aspects include public vs. private repositories, project activity graphs, collaborative development tools, etc. While our work is not designed for collaborative development of source code per se, it is leveraged in the context of developing extension activities for process-based applications, as described in sections 4 and 7.

Another popular, but perhaps more minimalist, mode of sharing applications on the web is to index application code [4] or web service APIs [16] available elsewhere on the web and provide community features, such as forums, How-Tos, blogs, etc., around the index. Our service catalog, described in section 7, indexes applications and artifacts that are under the control of the BPM system.

Enabling social software for Web based services is explored in [15] and [21]. In [15], a Wiki-based approach for describing services uses a UDDI [24] registry complemented by a wiki-based semantic annotation subsystem. A service published to the registry contains keywords from the ontology, enabling the resulting wiki page to contain those keywords as well as semantic links obtained by automatic reasoning from the ontology. In [21], service communities are introduced as the combination of social and business communities with the purpose of exchanging services. A dynamic Service Communities platform [6] enables services of interest to be contributed, grouped, consumed, and managed. Drawing a parallel, our work extends that concept to workflows: as users form 'BPM communities' to share workflow applications, they enrich the BPM community platform by adding and refining processes, extension activities, and tags.

The concepts of social software in relation to workflow are described in [18], where social production [2] enabling community contributions in the context of workflow is encouraged. A wiki-based workflow system is described in [8], based on state machine based flows driven by forms. In [12], social networks are created either via a recommender system or a process model repository. This could be layered on our system to enrich the design process by encouraging the reuse of models and model snippets and extended to handle a repository of extension activities.

Examples of commercial BPM as a service systems include Lombardi Blueprint, Serena Business Mashups, RunMyProcess, and IBM's recently announced BPM BlueWorks. Lombardi Blueprint enables modeling and sharing process models with collaborative editing but not execution, while Serena and RunMyProcess also offer execution. RunMyProcess provides a set of pre-configured connectors that seem similar to extension activities. It is not clear from the available description how one can extend this set with new connectors, but seems possible. Note that while WS-BPEL [24] is extensible, the standard does not (by design) cover how extensions can be created or shared. While IBM's BPM BlueWorks enables a host of collaboration capabilities around BPM, it is focused on a higher level of abstraction and therefore does not include direct deployment, hosted Bite flow execution or dynamic addition of extension activities. Its workflow editor and workflow model sharing modules are based on the system in this paper which itself is part of [13].

Our work enables the creation, immediate sharing, and dynamic deployment of extension activities into a BPM as a service design and runtime environment, as well as community participation between users across organizational boundaries via sharing, contributing, and collaborating around extension activities, workflow models and workflow instances.

3   The BPM as a Service System

A 'BPM as a service system' is one in which workflow design and management capabilities are offered as a hosted service accessible via the Internet [13]. In this section, we provide an overview of our system and how users work with it.

Figure 1 shows the modules and roles of the system. The modules are: (1) an Extension Development module for the development and sharing of extension activities; (2) a Workflow Editor module for editing and sharing Bite workflows, deploying workflows into the Workflow Runtime, and monitoring running instances; (3) a Workflow Runtime module that provides a Bite workflow engine

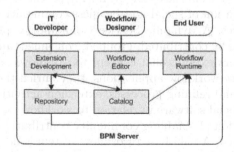

Fig. 1. BPM as a service system and its user roles

with APIs for monitoring and deployment; (4) a Catalog of extension activities; (5) a Repository of extension activity implementations. These modules run in a Web server environment where extension activities and workflow instances are added dynamically to the running system. The roles are: (1) an IT Developer who develops workflow extension activities; (2) a Workflow Designer who designs workflows; (3) an End User who runs and interacts with workflow instances. Interactions with the system occur via REST HTTP calls, so a user requires no installed software beyond a Web browser.

The system can be deployed within an enterprise for internal use, or hosted externally for use by multiple companies. The former allows integration with a company's private user registries, databases, and other internal systems; the latter allows for a larger community of users within which to share workflows and extensions. Additionally, if the system is deployed as part of an external, multi-tenant environment like LotusLive, a user's or company's network of contacts can be used in determining share lists and in searching for other workflows and extensions. This enables cross-company collaboration, such as allowing Ted to use Carol's extension and share the flow with the Dean. The Workflow Editor contains a palette populated with various activities, organized by categories, available for use in composing workflows. The activities consist of both native Bite activities, like 'receiveGET' and 'sendMail', as well as extension activities that have been added to the palette, for example, to perform database operations or consume calendaring services. The set of activities depends on the services the current designer is authorized to consume. Designers develop workflows by dragging activities from the palette to a canvas, wiring them together, and providing each with additional details. For example, the 'GET' activity requires a URL; the 'sendMail' activity requires an email address and subject. The additional details, presented as collections of fields in a properties pane, are populated by typing in values directly, selecting values from pull-down lists, or using expression builders. One property that is common to several types of activities is the list of users/groups/roles that can interact with an entry-point.

Once a workflow model is saved, it can be shared. When a workflow is ready to be run, it is deployed via a menu option. Once deployed, the workflow can be used by end users specified by the workflow designer.

Next, we describe creating and sharing extension activities for such a system.

4   Creating and Sharing Extension Activities

The mechanisms for adding workflow extension activities depend on the flow language and environment in use. In Bite, the developer need only provide an extension activity implementation that will be called by the engine at runtime when the extension activity is reached in the flow. The implementation may be written in either Java or any of a set of scripting languages like JavaScript and python. Workflow extension activities may be developed using various tools, either locally or hosted. The choice of development tool will depend on the complexity of the extension; a simple text editor or Web page form is sufficient for many script-based extensions, while tools like the Eclipse [23] Java Development Tools and AppBuilder [11] will be more appropriate for Java-based extensions. When development tools support features such as collaborative editing (real time or more along the lines of revision control systems), creating an extension activity can become a truly collaborative experience.

IT developers share their work by publishing extension activities to the catalog. For each extension activity, the catalog maintains basic bookkeeping information (e.g., name, owner), implementation details (e.g., schemas and executable code), visibility (e.g., public or private), and informal semantic descriptions (e.g., tags and comments); for complex extension activities (e.g., those implemented in Java) extension implementation modules are stored in the repository. Once in the catalog, extension activities can be discovered by other users. For example, Ted finds Carol's zipUpSharedFiles in the catalog.

In addition to traditional search capabilities, the catalog supports tag-clouds and bookmarking, allowing users to easily discover new extension activities and to organize those that they have previously encountered. Further, bookmarks can include tags and comments, allowing the community to contribute to the description of an extension activity.

The catalog and repository are integrated, via REST-based APIs, directly into the extension activity development tool and workflow editor. This deep integration allows IT developers to publish extension activities directly from their development environment; developers can also import existing extension activities, which can serve as templates or examples for new extension activities. The integration also allows workflow designers to discover available extension activities directly from the workflow editor tool.

In the following section we describe how workflow designers can use extension activities in workflows and deploy the workflows into the environment.

5 Using Extension Activities in Workflows

We will use our scenario to illustrate how a designer uses extension activities. The experience is somewhat similar to selecting an iPhone application from the iTunes AppStore. Once Ted agrees to the Dean's suggestion to pull the students' resumes from LotusLive Files, Ted opens the workflow model and looks in his palette for an activity that can retrieve the resumes from the Files service. Not finding such an activity, he searches the catalog for extension activities that he can pull into his palette to do this work. He finds Carol's highly-ranked extension and clicks to import it into his palette, where it becomes available for use like any of the pre-existing activities with the appropriate property sheets. When the Dean opens the shared workflow with the new extension activity, he has the option to add this extension to his palette as well.

In the case that Ted does not find a suitable extension, he can request one to be created by his company's IT department. Alternatively, he could post a request to an online developer marketplace such as Guru.com or GetACoder.com. One could also extend the catalog site to include such a service geared specifically to workflow extensions.

The workflow runtime is integrated into the workflow editor (via REST APIs) allowing designers to deploy workflows directly into the BPM server environment. When a workflow containing any extension activities is deployed, both the extension implementations and workflow are bundled into a Bite workflow application. To do so, meta-data for the extension activities used in the workflow is located using the catalog and used to add appropriate configuration details into the application. For extensions implemented in Java, the implementation modules are retrieved from the repository and, along with any other dependencies, injected into the application. The generated Bite application is then deployed to the BPM server environment, where it can serve requests from end users.

6 Creating and Sharing Workflows

The ability to share workflows is a key enabler for social participation as well as for improving efficiency within an organization or across the cloud. Sharing a workflow consists of sharing the workflow model and/or any of its (running) instances between users within and across enterprise boundaries.

Workflow Models. A workflow model may need to be shared for collaboration, for soliciting comments, for circulating information or for promoting reuse. A workflow model can be shared with all the users in the cloud (public), a group of users (restricted) or nobody (private). Shared models appear in the list of workflows a user may view/edit. There are two types of privileges for each model - Read Privilege dictates who can view or download it and Write Privilege controls who can make changes to it. Figure 2 shows the UI for inviting additional authors via email. In the case of a restricted read or write privilege, a user group needs to be defined. This group can be your company directory, a subset of the company directory, your contact list (which might be cross-company), and so on.

Workflow Instances. Sharing workflow instances is enabled by leveraging the Bite language's addressability model for the workflow definitions, instances, and individual points of interaction (entry points) within a particular instance. This model allows each of the above items to be identified by a unique URI. A workflow definition has a base URI, and each addressable entry-point (i.e. each receive activity) has a path segment that is composed with the base URI to create unique, fully-resolved, URIs. When a particular receive activity is a starter node, an HTTP GET or POST request directed at its associated URI results in the creation of a new workflow instance. The address of this newly-created instance is defined to be the base URI of the workflow definition, with a generated, unique, instance id appended as a URI path segment. This instance-specific URI is returned to the caller in an HTTP 'Location' header (similar to the way the Atom Publishing Protocol works). Any system designed to allow many users to collaborate and share resources must also enable specifying and enforcing security policies. In our system, each entry-point of a workflow can be secured for use only by particular users, groups of users, or users serving particular roles.

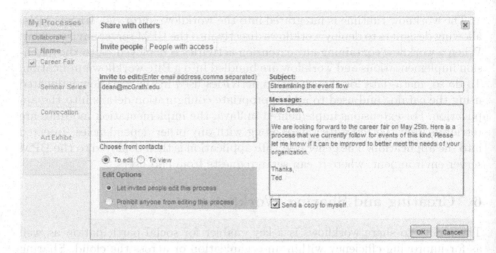

Fig. 2. Inviting users to collaborate on workflow models

The use of a REST-based workflow language makes it very easy to give a community the ability to share and execute the flows. Sharing a flow simply means sharing a link for one or more starter nodes for that flow. Likewise, in order to share a running instance, just provide links to the entry points for the running instance (recall that this URI will include a path segment that uniquely identifies the running instance).

This URI-based mechanism for addressing workflow definitions and instances also makes it straightforward to leverage existing services (e.g. del.icio.us) and/or create a UI specifically for workflows in order to discover and interact with them.

7   Implementation

We have implemented a prototype of the BPM system described above that builds on the BPM as a service platform in [13] and specifically the SOAlive [19] platform and Bite runtime [5] subcomponents to provide an integrated, hosted environment for developing and sharing extension activities, and for modeling, deploying, and sharing workflows that may use such activities.

Figure 3 illustrates the major system components relevant to this paper. All server-side components are built on WebSphere sMash [11]. sMash is an agile Web application development platform, providing a new programming model and runtime that promotes REST-centric application architectures.

Catalog. The catalog maintains extension activity meta-data, including zero or more usage specifications describing how the extension activity is to be used. Such specifications can include human readable documents (e.g., HTML) as well as machine readable schemas (e.g., XML Schema.) The meta-data also speci-fies the extension activity's implementation. For simple script-based extension

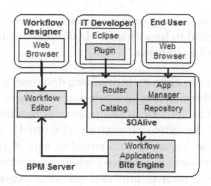

Fig. 3. BPM System Implementation

activities, the implementation script is included in the meta-data. For complex extension activities, the meta-data includes a reference to an implementation module stored in the repository.

The metadata shown below is for Carol's extension activity, which creates a zip archive of all files shared with a given user within a certain date range.

```
{ "name" : "zipUpSharedFiles"
"display_name" : "Zip Shared Files",
"description" : "Create a zip of all files ...",
"uri" : "http://extensions.bite.lotuslive/zipUpSharedFiles",
"module_id":"lotuslive:lotuslive.bite.extensions:1.0"
"visibility" : 1, "tags" : [ "Zip", "Files"],
"schema" : [{"type" :"apiDesc", "value":
    "{'attributes':,{'name':'startDate','display':'start date'}
    ,{'name':'endDate','display':'end date'}]}"} ...] ...
```

Repository. The repository is an implementation of an Ivy [22] HTTP server providing a REST-based interface for manipulating repository artifacts. Java-based extension activities are packaged as sMash [11] modules and stored as artifacts in the repository. A sMash module can include extension activity implementations (e.g., Java classes,) extension activity meta-data, and dependencies on other modules. Dependencies are described using Ivy meta-data.

Eclipse Plugin. The SOAlive Eclipse plugin extends the sMash Eclipse plugin to integrate intracting with the catalog and repository into the Eclipse IDE. The plugin supports building and publishing extension activities as sMash modules, where a single sMash module may provide the Java implementation of multiple extension activities. The developer declares the names of the extensions and their implementation classes in the file 'config/extensions.config', and creates a JSON meta-data file (in the 'extensions' directory) for each extension. When ready, the developer uses the plugin to publish the sMash module, and its extension meta-data, to SOAlive: the plugin uploads the implementation module to the repository and publishes the extension meta-data to the catalog.

To import, customize, and republish existing extensions, the developer uses the plugin's import wizard to import the sMash implementation from the repository, makes changes, and publishes.

Workflow Editor. The workflow editor allows designers to easily include extension activities in their flows. When an extension activity is used in the workflow, the property sheet of the activity in the palette is modified based on the configurable meta-data of the extension activity (Figure 4). This enables the flow designer to configure the extension and suitably wire it to the tasks that precede/follow it. The meta-data is also used when generating the Bite flow XML.

Currently, one palette item is provided for all extension activities. It gets bound to a chosen extension once it is dragged to the canvas. To support different palette items for each as described in section 5, we are adding an icon image and a category to the meta-data and adding an 'import' option to the palette.

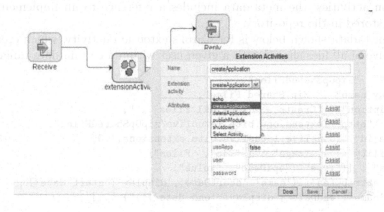

Fig. 4. Workflow with open property sheet of the zipUpSharedFiles extension

Application Manager. The Application Manager is responsible for deploying and managing workflow applications. For a given workflow, the application manager creates a sMash-based Bite application that includes the Bite workflow (XML file), the extensions it uses, and the minimal set of modules needed to execute it. The application manager locates, in the catalog, the meta-data for each extension used in the workflow. Simple script-based extensions are added to the application's 'extensions' directory; Java-based extensions have their implementation modules added as dependencies in the application's ivy.xml file.

Each workflow application executes in a separate JVM process, providing security and fault isolation between running workflows and other system components. Such isolation is critical in hosted, multi-tenant systems, in particular when user-provided code (e.g., a Java extension activity) is allowed to execute. Further, it allows us to easily deploy (and re-deploy) workflow applications into the running system. The sMash runtime model efficiently manages these processes, activating and de-activating JVMs as needed to service user requests. By tailoring each sMash application for a given workflow, we minimize the resources consumed by the workflow when it is active in a JVM.

Bite Workflow Engine. The Bite workflow engine and monitoring module are among the set of modules bundled in the sMash application of a deployed workflow. The engine creates and executes flow instances; the monitoring module forwards flow events (e.g., 'new instance') to the editor. An extension activity is registered with the engine by providing the extension's implementation module and a mapping between it and the activity's name. No meta-data is required. Once an extension activity is reached by the engine's navigator logic, control is handed to the corresponding implemenation module. The module gets access to the activity definition, with any expressions already resolved. Once the module completes its work, it hands control and any output data back to the navigator. The navigator places the data in the activity's output variable, marks the activity complete, and continues. The workflow instance itself is a REST-based resource.

Router. The router enables a cloud computing environment for running workflows, where each workflow application is installed on one of several available nodes in the cloud. Acting as a reverse proxy, the router manages HTTP connections between end users and workflow applications. Each deployed workflow is assigned an external URL prefix that uniquely identifies the workflow application; the router is responsible for maintaining the mapping between these external URLs and the locations of installed workflow applications, and for forwarding requests from end users to workflow applications. Our prototype supports a pluggable cloud architecture where different cloud environments can be supported: we currently support a simple 'embedded' cloud that scales horizontally across a limited number of nodes and are experimenting with large-scale clustered environments that support load-balancing and fail-over.

8 Conclusion and Future Work

We have presented a method for enabling social participation around extension activities, workflow models and instances and an implementation supporting it in an underlying BPM as a service system. Our method and prototype offer a browser-based workflow editor, IDE support for extension activity publishing and reuse, a shared catalog of extension activities that supports community features, and a lightweight flow language and engine that support dynamic extensions, direct deployment, and browser-based interaction. Using this as a base, one could provide more advanced social software for hosted workflows such as community-based process improvement and a marketplace for extensions and workflows. We are currently working to address the equally important 'soft' issues (security, trust, IP in reuse, pricing, etc) in providing BPM as a service in the presence of the presented dynamic extensibility.

Acknowledgements. This work is part of a larger effort. A list of contributors is at http://bit.ly/v1nqC.

References

1. Armbrust, M., Fox, A., et al.: Above the clouds: A berkeley view of cloud computing. Technical Report UCB/EECS-2009-28, University of California, Berkeley (2009)
2. Benkler, Y.: The Wealth of Networks: How Social Production Transforms Markets and Freedom. Yale University Press (2006)
3. Benslimane, D., Dustdar, S., Sheth, A. (eds.): IEEE Internet Computing, special issue on Services Mashups, vol. 12. IEEE, Los Alamitos (2009)
4. Black Duck Software. Koders, http://www.koders.com/
5. Curbera, F., Duftler, M.J., Khalaf, R., Lovell, D.: Bite: Workflow composition for the web. In: Krämer, B.J., Lin, K.-J., Narasimhan, P. (eds.) ICSOC 2007. LNCS, vol. 4749, pp. 94–106. Springer, Heidelberg (2007)
6. Desai, N., Mazzoleni, P., Tai, S.: Service Communities: A Structuring Mechanism for Service-Oriented Business Ecosystems. In: Digital EcoSystems and Technologies Conference (DEST 2007) (2007)
7. Fielding, R.T.: Architectural Styles and the Design of Network-based Software Architectures. PhD thesis, University of California, Irvine, CA (2000)
8. Erol, S., Neumann, G.: From a social wiki to a social workflow system. In: BPM 2008 Workshops. LNBIB. Springer, Heidelberg (2008)
9. Geyer, W., Dugan, C., DiMicco, J., Millen, D.R., Brownholtz, B., Muller, M.: Use and reuse of shared lists as a social content type. In: CHI 2008, Florence, Italy. ACM, New York (2008)
10. GitHub.com. GitHub - Social Coding, http://github.com/
11. IBM. WebSphere sMash, http://www.ibm.com/software/webservers/smash/
12. Koschmider, A., Song, M., Reijers, H.A.: Social software for modeling business processes. In: BPM 2008 Workshops. LNBIB. Springer, Heidelberg (2008)
13. Lau, C.: BPM 2.0-a REST based architecture for next generation workflow management. In: Devoxx Conference, Antwerp, Belgium (2008), http://www.devoxx.com/download/attachments/1705921/D8_C_11_07_04.pdf
14. Mozilla Foundation. Bespin - Code in the Cloud, https://bespin.mozilla.com/
15. Paoli, H., Schmidt, A., Lockemann, P.C.: User-driven semantic wiki-based business service description. In: Int'l Conference on Semantic Technologies (I-Semantics 2007), Graz (2007)
16. ProgrammableWeb.com. Programmable Web, http://www.programmableweb.com
17. Rosenberg, F., Curbera, F., Duftler, M.J., Khalaf, R.: Composing RESTful services and collaborative workflows: A lightweight approach. IEEE Internet Computing 12(5) (2008)
18. Schmidt, R., Nurcan, S.: BPM and social software. In: Ardagna, D., et al. (eds.) BPM 2008. LNBIP, vol. 17, pp. 649–658. Springer, Heidelberg (2009)
19. Silva-Lepe, I., Subramanian, R., Rouvellou, I., Mikalsen, T., Diament, J., Iyengar, A.: SOAlive Service Catalog: A Simplified Approach to Describing, Discovering and Composing Situational Enterprise Services. In: Bouguettaya, A., Krueger, I., Margaria, T. (eds.) ICSOC 2008. LNCS, vol. 5364, pp. 422–437. Springer, Heidelberg (2008)
20. SourceForge, Inc. SourceForge.net, http://www.sourceforge.net/
21. Tai, S., Desai, N., Mazzoleni, P.: Service communities: Applications and middleware. In: Proc. of the Int'l Workshop on Software Engineering and Middleware (SEM 2006). ACM, New York (2006)
22. The Apache Ant Project. Ivy, http://ant.apache.org/ivy/
23. The Eclipse Foundation. Eclipse, http://www.eclipse.org/
24. Weerawarana, S., Curbera, F., Leymann, F., Ferguson, D.: Web Services Platform Architecture. Pearson Education, London (2005)

AGILIPO: Embedding Social Software Features into Business Process Tools

António Rito Silva[1,2,3], Rachid Meziani[4], Rodrigo Magalhães[1,3],
David Martinho[1,3], Ademar Aguiar[5], and Nuno Flores[5]

[1] Center for Organizational Design and Engineering - INOV, Rua Alves Redol 9,
Lisbon, Portugal
{rito.silva,rodrigo.magalhaes,david.martinho}@inov.pt
[2] INESC-ID, Rua Alves Redol 9, Lisbon, Portugal
[3] IST/Technical Institute of Lisbon, Av. Rovisco Pais, 1049-001, Lisbon, Portugal
[4] Laboratoire Paragraphe Université de Paris 8, Saint-Denis Cedex 02, France
rmeziani@gmail.com
[5] INESC Porto, Faculdade de Engenharia da Universidade do Porto, Rua Dr.
Roberto Frias, Porto, Portugal
{ademar.aguiar,nuno.flores}@fe.up.pt

Abstract. In today's changing environments, organizational design must
take into account the fact that business processes are incomplete by nature
and that they should be managed in such a way that they do not restrain
human intervention. In this paper we propose the embedding of social software features, such as collaboration and wiki-like features, in the modeling
and execution tools of business processes. These features will foster people empowerment in the bottom-up design and execution of business processes. We conclude this paper by identifying some research issues about
the implementation of the tool and its methodological impact on Business
Process Management.

Keywords: Business Process Modeling and Execution, Social Software,
Bottom-up Business Process Management.

1 Introduction

In today's dynamic market environments, the only certainty is permanent change.
The way that organizations have found to cope with such changes is to keep their
business models flexible. Business models are made up of business processes and
these are crucial in supporting a culture of innovation. However, if business
processes are left unattended and not consciously adapted to the changing environment, they become impediments to innovation [11]. Since the organizations'
products, which are released to the market, are generated by business processes,
having them flexible is important for coping with market changes in an effective
manner [17].

Current Business Process Management (BPM) approaches still work on the
AS-IS/TO-BE paradigm, inherited from the Business Process Reengineering

S. Rinderle-Ma et al. (Eds.): BPM 2009 Workshops, LNBIP 43, pp. 219–230, 2010.

(BPR) era, which was widely used during the nineties. BPR is a top-down, holistic, and cross-cutting approach that takes months of analysis and impact assessment to achieve. [10; 2]. The problems identified with the AS-IS/TO-BE approaches to business process management are related to the temporal gap between the modeling and implementation phases as well as the lack of involvement of the users. These problems have created a gap between business and Information Technologies (IT), where the business has always believed that IT does not understand the semantics of business processes, while IT believes that the business has no conception on what it takes for automated business processes to execute successfully.

In this paper we focus on the human-intensive aspects of business processes, where human participation is required for activities operation, even if these activities are automated. We present here a new approach to BPM, more human-centered, following the principles of agile software development [1], properly supported by a collaborative environment, and we apply them to organizational design [8]. This research aims to define an Agile Business Process Methodology and a set of associated Tools that foster the collaborative and incremental design and implementation of work processes. This is achieved by modeling the most critical business activities first, activity by activity, and undertaking modeling and implementing business processes in a continuous cycle that receives feedback from the real use of the last implemented processes.

2   The Problem

In today's business environment, characterized by non-stop and fast occurring change, it is very hard to follow an AS-IS/TO-BE approach to Business Process Management. AS-IS/TO-BE approaches assume a complete approach to the design of business processes, meaning that it requires to completely describe business processes both AS-IS and TO-BE, before any intervention can begin (either technological or managerial). This gives rise to lengthy modeling activities aiming at capturing a complete model of both the existing business processes (AS-IS) and the new business processes (TO-BE). There are several reasons why AS-IS/TO-BE approaches do not work as well as they should:

- Different people have different perspectives on processes: top managers have a high-level perspective while users have more detailed perspectives. IT consultants, on the other hand, have a systems-slanted view of the same processes. As a result, it is difficult to get all the players to agree on what the process definitions are.
- Top-down process design is driven by the organization's institutional strategies, policies and procedures and does not take into account the tacit knowledge users deploy in operating the real organization. Type-based approaches are used in top-down process design to model abstractions that represent the common structure and behavior of several process instances. Using type-based approaches to process design disregards the representation of tacit

knowledge that is mostly gathered on a case-by-case approach. These approaches intend to capture abstractions too soon and do not capture tacit knowledge.

- The organization and its rules and structures are constantly emerging and changing. This requires intervals of (very) short duration between design, implementation and automation.
- TO-BE approaches follow mechanistic models of planned change which, as a whole, restrict collaboration and reduce the empowerment of people, disengaging them from organizational responsibilities and delegating intelligence to the Information Systems (IS).
- A business process contains many exceptions that take time to model and increase dramatically the complexity of the model (i.e. the ensemble of the business processes). Furthermore, most of these exceptions only occur in a few business process instances [13; 7].
- A technology-free process design is a naïve approach because it ignores that there is an entangling between coordination of people and the technology used by people in the execution of the business processes. The business process design, in the absence of a technological perspective, results in processes that do not fit with organizations real praxis.

3   Requirements

Within dynamic organizations, Business Process Management should follow a new agile approach characterized by short feedback cycles [1]. In their proposals about Organizational Design and Engineering, [8] suggest that organizational development projects (i.e. projects involving design and engineering activities) should be planned and executed through a series of small activities of short duration, such that after each intervention a new observation is carried out to identify how the organization was changed by the last intervention. The organizational routines contained in the computer-based artefacts provide the required stability for observation points to be created. Instead of strategic alignment of IS/IT, those authors propose organizational steering. Steering emphasizes continuous analyses through observation of the organization's evolution, making small adjustments between interventions, in moving the organization towards the goals defined by the strategy. The engineering activities should be of short duration followed by the artefacts integration in the organization, where design is a continuous activity and not only a starting point but an ever changing destination.

The agile business process proposal should be characterized by:

Incompleteness

- The process does not need to be completely understood. Trying to completely understand a process is time expensive, reducing the number of feedback cycles and increasing the chances that automated processes does not conform to organizational needs.

- The process does not need to be completely specified in the sense that it is allowed that activities not pre-specified occur in some of its instances. This allows the instantaneous adaptation of process instances to the emergence of new organizational needs.
- Incompletely defined processes should be executable and its execution integrates planned and unplanned activities such that incompletely specified processes will not limit the normal operation of the organization.

Empower people

- Processes should promote collaboration, creativity and intelligence instead of restricting them.
- The system should allow people to perform unplanned activities and integrate them with planned activities.

Business process design integrated with technological usage

- To avoid a situation of paralysis by analysis due to different perspectives on processes, a modeling approach based on the operation of the business should be enforced. This way, the different perspectives on process modeling will be focused on bottom-up leveraging of the actual operation of the business.
- Integrate the execution and modeling of the process, such that the process executor is also one of its modelers, thus avoiding the shortcomings of top-down modeling of processes.

Design at the instance level

- It should be possible to describe processes on a case-by-case approach instead of trying to model all the possible situations in the process specification. This will allow a reduction of the complexity of business process models and it will provide two views of the process: the type view, containing the expected behavior common to all instances, and the instance view, containing exceptions to the expected behavior present on the type view of the process.
- It should be possible to promote unplanned exceptions, described at the instance level, to become part of the planned behavior of the business process, described at the type level. This approach promotes the bottom-up definition of processes.

4   The Proposal

Considering the set of requirements identified above, we propose an agile business process approach for bottom-up modeling and implementation of incomplete business processes. AGILIPO follows the principles of agile software development [1] and of organizational design and engineering [8]. AGILIPO is supported by collaborative modeling and execution tools that embed social software-like functionalities. The distinctive feature of AGILIPO tools is the integration of modeling with execution activities blurring the differences between definition and operation of business processes. While executing a particular instance of an incomplete business process, users are empowered to execute, on a case-by-case basis, activities that are not specified.

An incomplete process definition is specified by a set of activities that describe part, but not all, of the process instances behavior. A process instance contains activity instances which can be either specified or non-specified, where non-specified activities are called generic. An activity definition can either be automated, when it includes the interaction with external applications, even requiring the user participation, or non-automated. Automated activities contain hardcoded functionality and require programming activities to implement them.

Figure 1 shows business process management stakeholders interacting through a modeling and execution environment. The stakeholders can play three different roles: executor, modeler and developer. The executor is able to conduct business process execution either by making use of specified activities or create generic activity instances whenever the specified ones cannot fulfill the current execution situation. The modeler is capable of changing the business process model, specifying new non-automated activities. The developer may rely on these non-automated activities and automate them by coding the interaction with external systems. Note that executors, modelers and developers are roles that can be played by the same person.

When executors create generic activity instances they are contributing to the business process model following a case-by-case approach. The generic activity instances capture business process exceptions, allowing the process instance adaptation without requiring all possible situations to be specified in the process model. Moreover, process instance adaptation occurs in the context of process execution, where generic activity instances are integrated with instances of specified activities. Afterwards, executors can tag generic activities and participate in the creation of ontologies for the business process. Following a folksonomy

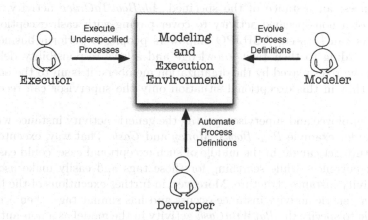

Fig. 1. Modeling and Execution Environment

approach, executors tag activities, share their tags, and search for activities based on these tags.[9; 16; 18]

Modelers analyze the set of generic activity instances with its associated folksonomy, and generalize the exceptions over the existing business process model, synthesizing a new version of the model. Once integrated in the model, modeler's suggestions enrich the set of specified activities although in a non-automated form. Afterwards, developers rely on such suggestions to automate the non-automated activities. Developers' decision on which non-automated activities to implement is driven by cost-effectiveness. Cost-effectiveness can be determined by the frequency of activity occurrence in process instances or by the time consumption in activity execution.

Model evolution is a concern of AGILIPO tools. Suggestions are synthesized by modelers following a wiki-like approach[3], where new suggestions leverage on previous ones, thus creating new revisions of the model. In this way, AGILIPO intends to foster a knowledge creation process, organically and incrementally (Wikipedia-like)[12], where contributors are motivated to participate in the modeling of an incomplete process by reading contributions of others and continuously adding their own knowledge[6].

As an example, consider an online bookstore and the *Selling* process which has three specified activities: *AddBookToOrder* followed by either *PayWithCheck* or *PayWithCreditCard*. However, as a client goes directly to the physical store and wishes to pay with cash, there is no activity that will cover such situation. The employee may then create an instance of a generic activity and associate it to the current instance of the *Selling* process. Afterwards, the employee needs to assign this generic activity instance to a supervisor because she does not have enough authority to receive the money herself. Therefore, the employee, instead of executing this generic activity instance, addresses it to its supervisor. The supervisor is then able to execute the generic activity instance created by the employee and finish the *Selling* process. The specified *Selling* process instance is terminated having two different types of activity instances: an instance of the specified *AddBookToOrder* activity, and an instance of a non-specified activity to cover paying with cash exceptional situation. As can be seen, AGILIPO empowers people to perform business processes according to their tacit knowledge and allows responsibility delegation based on the roles played by the organization members: it is up to the employee to know that in this exceptional situation only the supervisor can receive the money.

Both, employee and supervisor can tag the generic activity instance with keywords like for example *Pay*, *Books*, *Money* and *Cash*. That way, executors that in the future get caught in the middle of such exceptional case, could easily find similar occurrences while searching for those tags and easily make use of the same activity instance structure. Moreover, in further executions of the business process, a generic activity instance occurs and has similar tags, then a modeler can decide to specify the *PayWithCash* activity in the model as a non-automated activity. This would create a model evolution such that the employee does not need to search for similar exceptions: the exceptional behavior becomes a suggestion. Finally, the non-automated suggested activity *PayWithCash* could be hardcoded into the application model by a developer automating for example the delegation procedure.

In synthesis, AGILIPO tools support the modeling and execution of business processes, integrate automated and non-automated parts of the process, support both execution and modeling of exceptional behavior, and enforce a continuous knowledge creation process around incompletely defined and understood processes.

5   Social Software Features

AGILIPO strategy for business process modeling is similar to wikipedia's strategy for knowledge gathering [14], blurring the distinction between consumers and producers of information. It emphasizes the synthesis of the different suggestions to the business process model through collaborative participation.

To foster collaboration among executors, modelers and developers, social-software features are used to promote communication:

- **Tagging** - Create folksonomies around generic instances in order to add semantic value to their content and foster business process model evolution.
- **Versioning** - The AGILIPO model is presented in versioned wiki-like pages, keeping track of all suggestions made by modelers and enforcing suggestion synthesis.
- **Comments** - Comments can be used to allow discussion when modelers do not agree on business process model evolution and also to justify execution of generic behavior.
- **Ratings** - Ratings can be used to gather executor's quantitative data about the suitability of the business process model for the particular business process instance she is executing.

AGILIPO business process tools use two sorts of human interaction interfaces: type interfaces and instance interfaces. A type interface provides features to manipulate the business process model while execution is done at an instance interface. For instance, we can have an interface that allows us to make suggestions on the *Selling* process specification and another that allows us to execute a particular selling case, *sell : Selling*.

These interfaces include social software features to foster the bottom-up design of business processes. Figure 2 shows an example of a process type interface for the *Selling* business process presented in Section 4.

The *Selling* business process is on its third version and the last suggestion was created by John. A new version is created whenever a modeler changes the process's name or description, or when he deletes, updates or creates an activity type. This will result in a new version of the business process, being possible to navigate between versions. Jack wrote a comment about the lack of the possibility to pay with cash.

The type interface contains accounting information about the business process instances. In this case it is shown the number of instances and exception cases as well as the conformance and suitability rates. The conformance rate is automatically calculated matching the business process definition with the structure of its executed instances. This calculation is based on data mining techniques. The suitability rate represents users satisfaction with the business process definition when they are executing its instances.

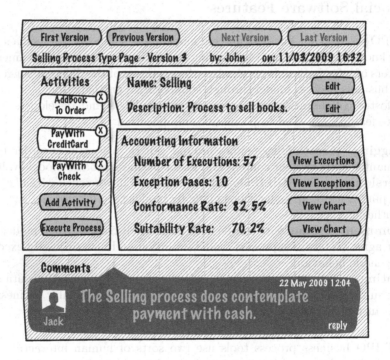

Fig. 2. Process Type Interface Example

Figure 3 shows the execution interface of a *Selling* process instance, which is associated with version 3 of the *Selling* process type. The interface shows the log of executed activities and their executors. It also prompts the executor with the possible next actions. In the shown case, the executor had just created a generic activity instance for payment with cash and tagged it with keywords *Cash*, *Pay*, *Book* and *Money*. The user is empowered to decide whether she receives the payment (Execute) or delegates it to her supervisor (Send to another User). On the top right corner of the interface the executor can rate her satisfaction with the execution of the process instance.

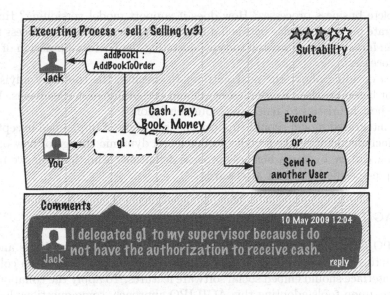

Fig. 3. Process Instance Page Example

6   Research Issues

The AGILE BPM approach is rooted in AGILIPO tools, which embed social software features within business processes modeling and execution functionalities. There are several open research problems, related with the design and implementation of the business tool and with the methodological impact of its use that should be addressed:

- What should be the AGILE BPM tool implementation model?
- How should be the wiki-like interface of the AGILE BPM tool?
- What should be the methodology of AGILE BPM?

6.1   AGILIPO Model

AGILIPO Model is based on business process models whose incompleteness is tackled by simultaneously allowing new model suggestions and their respective execution. Such suggestion making reflects flexibility requirements around the implementation model while using social software features to smoothly synthesize the suggestions. AGILIPO tools should be built on a kernel containing an integrated model for both automated business processes and suggestions. This model should uniformly support several degrees of incompleteness and model evolution. Several questions arise.

How does the combined model integrates specific business activities with generic activities? How should we define such generic activities (pre-conditions and execution procedures)? How does it enable the modeling and execution of incomplete business processes? How does it support model versioning? How do we migrate process instance between different versions of the same process type? How can instances be promoted to types fostering the bottom-up design of business processes?

When deciding about the next activity to execute, the tool may advise the executor based on the execution context and on similar past executions. What are the best heuristics to generate recommendations?

The integrated model should support the execution of unplanned exceptions, which include facilities like activity rollback and dynamic change of flow of control. How can we bypass a business process definition? And, how can we return to the pre-specified behavior afterwards?

6.2   AGILIPO Collaborative Interface

AGILIPO Collaborative Interface should empower executors, modelers and developers to simultaneously model and execute business processes. Such collaborative interface should embed social software features. To apply the collaborative interface, upon tools adopting this AGILIPO approach, some questions have to be considered.

Should the suggestion interface be a context sensitive user interface? For instance, when in the context of a particular process instance it shows which generic activities occurred in similar processes, fostering reuse and classification of generic activity instantiations.

How do we seamlessly present automated and non-automated parts of the business process and, at the same time, make them distinguishable in the interface? How do we present suggestions on the automated part of a business process but that do not override the implementation? How do we integrate execution and modeling interfaces?

An important concept to support would be the sense of "neighbourhood", that is, who are the other users that also have a "proximity" relationship with the context one is visualizing or editing. Who are the most frequent readers? Who are the most frequent editors? Who gives the most comments? What other models do these "neighbours" keep close?

6.3   AGILIPO Methodology

AGILIPO Methodology should foster the collaborative and incremental design and implementation of business processes. To achieve this, we need to address many research questions.

We all know the success of Wikipedia, a collaboratively created encyclopedia, owned by no one and authored by tens of thousands of enthusiasts [15]. Can we downscale the Wikipedia approach to the context of AGILIPO, which is targeted for organizations, and where the number of contributors is very limited? Can some Wikipedia policies, such as consensus, administration, and dispute be used for AGILIPO? Do we need privileges within the AGILIPO approach to moderate dispute? Will these privileges create a distinction among executors, modelers and developers?

Bottom-up and top-down approaches are two different schools of thoughts within the BPM field [4]. Each one presents its advantages and disadvantages. The research question which is raised here, is on whether the AGILIPO methodology will enforce the bottom-up business process approach, which is naturally embedded within its concept, or whether there is a need to come up with a hybrid approach, that combines the best practices of both bottom-up and top down approaches, without actually loosing the reality of the working with operations processes?

Process incompleteness is a fundamental aspect of the AGILIPO concept, but this raises a question about the degree of process completeness. When can we decide that the incomplete process is ready for execution? Is the degree of completeness the same for all types of processes? What type of organization design can this fit?

7   Conclusions

Agility is being recognized as a crucial new quality for future BPM approaches [5]. In this paper we propose a novel approach for agile BPM based on the embedding of social software features into the business process modeling and execution tools. The distinctive feature of these tools promotes process modeling as a continuous activity that is intertwined with process execution activities, fostering a knowledge creation process that blurs the separation between users and designers of business processes.

The use of AGILIPO tools will impact in the AS-IS/TO-BE paradigm: the AS-IS model is given by the executing business activities while the TO-BE model is given by the incremental changes proposed to the AS-IS model. As soon as incremental changes are implemented, it is not possible to distinguish the TO-BE model from the AS-IS. So, the steps of the AS-IS/TO-BE cycle are unified in a single short duration step where the business processes are perceived AS-Executing and become as incrementally TO-Extend.

To accomplish the AGILIPO vision we identified the need to have an implementation model that smoothly integrates business process features with social software features and a user interface that preserves the wiki-like usability for business process modeling. Moreover, it is necessary to investigate whether the analogy with Wikipedia for knowledge creation downscales in the context of smaller organizations.

References

[1] Beck, K., Beedle, M., van Bennekum, A., Cockburn, A., Cunningham, W., Fowler, M., Grenning, J., Highsmith, J., Hunt, A., Jeffries, R., Kern, J., Marick, B., Martin, R.C., Mellor, S., Schwaber, K., Sutherland, J., Thomas, D.: Agilemanifesto (2001), http://www.agilemanifesto.org (accessed June 1, 2009)

[2] Cumberlidge, M.: Business Process Management with Jboss Jbpm. Packt Publishing, City (2007)

[3] Cunningham, W.: "what is a wiki". wikiwikiweb (2002),
http://www.wiki.org/wiki.cgi?WhatIsWiki (accessed June 1, 2009)

[4] Dean, D.L., Orwig, R.E., Vogel, D.R.: Facilitation methods for collaborative modeling tools. Group Decision and Negotiation (2000)

[5] Dreiling, A.: Business process management and semantic interoperability - challenges ahead. In: Handbook on Business Process Management. Springer, Heidelberg (2009)

[6] Garud, R., Jain, S., Tuertscher, P.: Incomplete by design and designing for incompleteness. Organization Studies 29(03), 351–371 (2008)

[7] Golani, M., Gal, A., Toch, E.: Modeling alternatives in exception executions. In: Business Process Management Workshops (2007)

[8] Magalhaes, R., Rito-Silva, A.: Organizational design and engineering. Technical report, Center for Organizational Design and Engineering (2009)

[9] Marlow, C., Naaman, M., Boyd, D., Davis, M.: Ht06, tagging paper, taxonomy, flickr, academic article, to read. In: HYPERTEXT 2006: Proceedings of the seventeenth conference on Hypertext and hypermedia, pp. 31–40 (2006)

[10] Morgan, T.: Business Rules and Information Systems: Aligning It with Business Goals. Addison-Wesley Longman Publishing Co., Inc., Boston (2002)

[11] Prahalad, C.K., Krishnan, M.S.: The new age of innovation: Driving cocreated value through global networks. McGraw-Hill, New York (2008)

[12] Riehle, D.: How and why wikipedia works: An interview with Angela Beesley, Elisabeth Bauer, and Kizu Naoko. In: Workshop Wikisym 2008 (2008)

[13] Russell, N., van der Aalst, W.M.P., ter Hofstede, A.H.: Exception handling patterns in process-aware information systems. BPM Center Report BPM-06-04 (2006)

[14] Spek, S., Postma, E.O., van den Herik, H.J.: Wikipedia: organisation from a bottom-up approach (2006)

[15] Tapscott, D., Williams, A.D.: Wikinomics: How Mass Collaboration Changes Everything. Portfolio Hardcover (December 2006)

[16] Wal, T.V.: Folksonomy (2007), http://vanderwal.net/folksonomy.html (accessed June 1, 2009)

[17] Weske, M.: Business Process Management: Concepts, Languages, Architectures, 1st edn. Springer, Heidelberg (2007)

[18] Wu, H., Zubair, M., Maly, K.: Harvesting social knowledge from folksonomies. In: HYPERTEXT 2006: Proceedings of the seventeenth conference on Hypertext and hypermedia, pp. 111–114 (2006)

Workflow Management Social Systems: A New Socio-psychological Perspective on Process Management

Marcello Sarini, Federica Durante, and Alessandro Gabbiadini

University of Milano-Bicocca. Department of Psychology. Milan, Italy
{marcello.sarini,federica.durante,alessandro.gabbiadini}@unimib.it

Abstract. The paper presents a study about one of the most successful cases of social software: Wikipedia. In particular we focused on the investigation of some socio-psychological aspects related to the use of the Italian Wikipedia. In our study, we considered Wikipedia active users classified into three different roles: registered users, administrators, and bureaucrats in order to discuss our findings with respect to these different groups of users. Workflow Management Systems are applications designed to support the definition and execution of business processes. Since we consider that social aspects are relevant in the accomplishment and coordination of activities managed by such technologies, we advocate for a new class of Workflow Management Systems, i.e., *Workflow Management Social Systems*. These systems should emphasize the social nature of workflow management. For this reason, we propose to consider some of the relevant psychological aspects we identified in our study, interpreted in the light of some relevant socio-psychological theories, for the design of this socially enriched workflow technology.

Keywords: Workflow Management Systems, Social Software, Social Psychology, Wikipedia.

1 Background and Motivations

There is a growing interest for what is called *Social Software*. However, there is no clear definition of the concept, but rather different ones each of them focusing on different aspects: in [24] the emphasis is on both social interaction and social production of knowledge. In both cases the authors consider as pivotal the concept of *non pre-determination*; in the first case, it refers to interactions among individuals; in the second case, non-predetermination refers to the way people collaborate to create an artifact. Another definition of social software [29] emphasizes the *bottom-up nature of the interactions* among community members, (i.e., collaboration for the achievement of goals; organization of the related contents). This is a complementary view to top-down interactions occurring when the actors are assigned to rigidly predetermined roles and their actions are almost predetermined to fulfill the organization's goals. According to Stowe Boyd [5],

S. Rinderle-Ma et al. (Eds.): BPM 2009 Workshops, LNBIP 43, pp. 231–242, 2010.

the social software is a software built around one or more of these premises, that is, providing support to: i) conversational interaction between individuals or groups; ii) social feedbacks to rate others' contributions; iii) creation and management of social networks to handle people's personal relationships.

According to these definitions, Wikipedia is clearly a social software. In fact, in this collaborative encyclopedia, each individual is given the possibility to both create a new page and edit an existing one. In this way, through a collective interaction, knowledge is created and maintained by means of bottom-up not pre-determined interactions among Wikipedia's users. In particular, Wikipedia is an application of a Wiki [30], a software emphasizing social interactions among people on the basis of two concepts: *edit*, and *save*. Edit allows people to create and edit a content; Save allows people to publish it on the Web and to share it with others.

Workflow Management Systems (WfMSs) provide the infrastructure to design, execute, and manage business processes spread over a network of people and resources [2]. From this point of view, the workflow technology can be hardly considered a social software. However, considering a social software as an IT-based object aiming at helping its users to constructing and reproducing their social relations [4], WfMSs can be seen as a specific kind of social software: a social software to facilitate people at managing social relations occurring during the accomplishment of their work activities. As a consequence, we should focus on the role that this technology could play in facilitating individuals in the coordination of their work activities, rather than in the accomplishment of the activities per se. If WfMSs are seen as mere tools to improve the execution of business processes, designed not considering their social nature, some problems may arise. The work that those systems support is structured overlooking the fact that it is often accomplished in a local and bottom up fashion, and that rarely it can be completely predetermined without taking into account the current situation [26]. Moreover, in usual WfMSs no support is provided to exploit the "internal life of a process" –i.e., how people make sense of what they do– and no consideration is given to the fact that sense-making is often achieved by sharing experiences with the others [6]. Generally, issues related to the workflow technology use have been discussed considering the sociological and anthropological point of views (see e.g., [21]). To our knowledge, very little attention has been devoted to the psychological aspects involved in the workflow technology use. We believe it is important to also consider these aspects with reference, in particular, to the findings of Social Psychology. Differently from pure sociological and anthropological approaches, which both aim at identifying and describing a phenomenon, Social Psychology tries to identify the underlying causes that explain a specific behavior, feeling or attitude. In fact, Social Psychology is the scientific study of how people's thoughts, feelings, and behaviors are influenced by the actual, imagined, or implicit presence of others [3]. Here, it is important to stress that people's behaviors (including their work related activities) can be influenced by the environment, both because of the people involved in the accomplishment of the same goal, and because of the social influence emerging from the shared use of artifacts, such as the process representations provided by WfMSs.

In the present study we identify some socio-psychological aspects related to the use of a social software, i.e. the Italian version of Wikipedia. Given the fact that also WfMSs should be considered as a social software, we highlight some of our findings in order to be considered when designing social software. More specifically, we suggest how to move from Workflow Management Systems (WfMSs) to *Workflow Management Social Systems (WfMSSs)*. The paper is organized as follows: first, material and method of our study are presented; then, results are illustrated. Finally, interpreting our results according to some pertinent socio-psychological constructs, we discuss how to include such relevant psychological aspects into the workflow technology in order to move towards a conceptualization of Workflow Management Social Systems.

2   The Study

In order to investigate the socio-psychological aspects involved in the use of Wikipedia, registered users of Wikipedia Italia were interviewed.

2.1   The Study Method

Participants. Using the tools available in Wikipedia (i.e., personal pages, forums, mailing-lists), 246 users were contacted and invited to join the study. Among those, only 28 people (8 administrators, 3 bureaucrats and 17 registered users) agreed to participate.

Material. A structured interview was used. The interview schedule included questions addressing the following issues: the hierarchy, if there is one, in Wikipedia Italia (16 questions); the conflict management (10 questions); the sense of belonging to such a community and its consequences (12 questions); the use of a pseudonym and its implications (9 questions); the Wikipedia content's creation and reliability (5 questions). Finally, participants were asked to use a metaphor to describe their idea of the organization underlying the Wikipedia community. Questions related to gender, age and professions were also included in the interview.

Procedure. Participants's recruitment. After registering to Wikipedia Italia, one of the author of the present research created a personal page where he presented himself as a researcher, posted the main goal of the study and invited registered users to participate. Afterwards, he posted the same request on other users' pages, in the section dedicated to their discussions. In total, 50 requests were posted. Among those who accepted to collaborate (N=28), 10 participants were interviewed face-to-face; the remaining 18 were interviewed by chatting through instant messaging applications. Before starting the interview, participants were invited to fill up a Consent Form. Participants that were interviewed by chat received the form via e-mail and sent it back filled up.

Interviews' analysis. The interviews were content analyzed according to the participants' role in Wikipedia (either administrator, bureaucrat or registered user) in order to identify whether the aspects we investigated were perceived differently if different was the participant role. Hence, we first assessed whether only one single group of users did exist among our participants –i.e., the Wikipedia active users irrespective of their role– or three different ones –i.e., depending on the role. This was done because, although all active users shared the same interest, they had different duties and responsibilities according to their role: while registered users are people who registered to the service providing an identity and an Internet address, and have the possibility to both add and edit Wikipedia contents, administrators are Wikipedia editors who have been entrusted by the community with the access to restricted technical features ("tools") for the system maintenance. For example, administrators can protect and delete pages, block other editors, as well as undo these actions [31]. In the Italian version [28], this role is considered as serving the community, without additional privileges, but with additional duties and responsibilities; only for this reason, administrators are provided with additional tools. Bureaucrats, instead, are usually a small group of Wikipedia administrators associated to the Wikimedia Foundation; they can promote other users to the role of administrator and bureaucrat; grant or revoke an account's bot status; rename user accounts. They are expected to be capable to facilitate the reachment of a consensus, and to explain the reasons behind their actions (if requested) [32]. Therefore, we were interested to investigate whether these different skills, duties and responsibilities could affect the way Wikipedia is perceived, even though all users collaborate on a voluntary base, and Wikipedia rests on a collaborative bottom-up organization of contents.

2.2   Results

As expected, the status of our interviewees affected their perceptions on relevant issues. In particular, their views on conflict management, hierarchy and the use of a pseudonym differed. In fact, administrators' and bureaucrats' answers were often similar and usually in contrast with what registered users reported. In examining the participants' answers concerning hierarchy and the use of power, it emerged that for the administrators the power is not held by a single person, rather it is within the community. Registered users, instead, hold a more heterogeneous vision: users acknowledged that the administrators' power is a consequence of both the role they play and the trust they receive from the community; however, they also mentioned the influence that the administrators have on others due to their experience, notoriety, and visibility. It seems that in Wikipedia two contradictory visions coexist. This contradiction was also identified by [22] and [7]: on the one hand, the perception of Wikipedia as a self-organized system reported by administrators and bureaucrats who exercise a form of power and control; on the other hand, Wikipedia as a hierarchical organization as perceived (and often advocated) by registered users. A different perception also emerged when interviewees were asked to describe the Wikipedia organization using a metaphor: the majority of both bureaucrats and users described the system as an anthill. This choice can be associated with the idea of an organization that grows up relying on the collaboration among peers. Differently, administrators mainly referred to beehives and flocks, which instead reflect organizations where concepts like hierarchy, task assignment, and leadership are strongly evaluated. Interestingly, this seems in contrast with what administrators answered when directly asked about power relationships in Wikipedia.

Given the collaborative nature of creating and editing Wikipedia pages, sometimes conflicts arise among users, especially for pages related to topical, political and religious subjects. However, we acknowledged in accordance also to what showed in [15], that conflicts generally revolve around topics concerning the way contents are managed in Wikipedia, as also reported by an administrator: "most edited pages in this year refer to disclaimers and to topics concerning the community". In Wikipedia, guidelines and rules have been established to manage conflicts, e.g., the *three-revert rule* (often referred to as 3RR) which prevents contributors in performing more than three reverts on a single page within a 24-hour period [33]. When asked about conflict management strategies, participants pointed to two main strategies: attacking other people and escaping the conflict. Most of the administrators stated to use both strategies depending on the situation, while the majority of users preferred to escape the conflict. This was also confirmed by the fact that administrators and bureaucrats tended to consider their behaviors in Wikipedia as similar to those performed in a real life working situation, while users reported a more sharp distinction between Wikipedia and their everyday life. The latter attitude is linked to the use of a pseudonym: while some users considered the use of a pseudonym as a personal signature, others considered it as a way to keep real life and Wikipedia clearly separated. Administrators and bureaucrats always sign their contributes with a pseudonym (which sometimes corresponds to the real name), and this makes them feel responsible for what they wrote as in real life. However, for the remaining participants, signing with a pseudonym do not affect their sense of responsibility for the contents they contributed to create. Finally, the attitude of all our interviewees toward the non-registered users (identified only by means of their IP addresses) is really strict: they are not considered as a part of the community, and often administrators take stronger positions and apply sanctions to the behaviors of non-registered users.

2.3   Discussion

The present study tried to investigate the psychological aspects underlying the use of Wikipedia among its users. First of all, we wanted to identify whether the users' status within Wikipedia played a role in shaping users' perceptions, attitudes, and beliefs. Results are in line with our expectations. Administrators and bureaucrats seemed to hold a similar view in terms of hierarchy, power, and conflict management. Registered users, instead, held a different perception especially in terms of hierarchy. All our participants acknowledged that Wikipedia Italia is a hierarchically-organized system, and that hierarchy is democratically established as a result of a bottom-up process. However, registered users also acknowledged the presence of a top-down process of control and influence exerted by administrators and bureaucrats. In our opinion, this indicates how, as in real life, the position an individual occupies in Wikipedia can affect his/her perceptions of the system (see also the results concerning the use of a metaphor in describing Wikipedia). Recently, Social Psychology investigated the role that anonymity plays in Internet. According to Social Psychology, a state of deindividuation lead people to classic mob behavior: in other words, the inner restrains against counternormative behavior fall away (see [19] for a meta-analysis of the construct). Deindividuation occurs under certain conditions, such as anonymity and low individual responsibility. Interactions in Internet are often characterized by anonymity (even when using a pseudonym) and, therefore, by a sense of low individual responsibility (see [13]). This seems to be partially supported by our study. In fact, while registered users, that signed their contributions with a pseudonym, stated that this help them in keeping a separation between their real life and Wikipedia, administrators and bureaucrats reported to feel responsible of what they write and decide regardless of the use of pseudonym. Again, it seems that the status plays a role in the users' perceptions of responsibility. In our opinion, though, the differences among participants with different status are not enough to consider their relationship as a typical intergroup situation. In fact, when they have to deal with non-registered users, they share the same attitude: non-registered users are not considered as part of the community, therefore, they are not perceived as members of the same group [27]. In other words, they are the outgroup. For this reason, they are subjected to more severe sanctions compared to registered users, which seem to share common social identity, fate and goals.

It is worth noting that these are just preliminary evidence of the psychological mechanisms at work in a social software. In fact, the number of participants is too small to allow any generalizations of our results to other social software. Further studies should try to recruit a larger number of participants with a representative number of people for each category (i.e., administrators, bureaucrats and registered users). Moreover, the present study was carried out on Wikipedia Italia. Carrying out similar studies on other Wikipedia systems would help scholars to better assess the inner organization of such a kind of social software in terms of hierarchy, power and conflict management. Finally, this is just an explorative study that collected qualitative data. In fact, we aimed at increasing our knowledge concerning the way social relations work within a social software, in order to include such relevant aspects into the workflow technology design towards a conceptualization of Workflow Management Social Systems. Future studies should employ a more quantitative approach to allow generalization.

3   Towards the Design of Workflow Management Social Systems

The literature is rich of contributions about Workflow Management Systems and social software. The point here is to identify contributions boosting a fruitful integration of these two technologies. In this respect, literature presents some proposals to combine functionalities of social software, such as flexibility and integrated revision management of Wikis, with Workflow Management Systems. In [18], for instance, the principles underlying workflow management (like the modeling of processes and their execution) have been implemented in terms of a Wiki system. In addition, the peculiarities of a Wiki make possible to add functionalities, aiming at increasing the awareness of others' presence to facilitate collaboration. In fact, on the basis of revision history, this enriched Wiki system displays two kinds of graphs: activity graph and personal collaboration graph, which make salient to all members the relationships among people and the performed activities. In a similar vein, [11] focused on integrating wiki-based communities with process-oriented knowledge structures. Most of the other proposals instead focuses on collaborative process descriptions: to this aim in [10] it is proposed an extension of the Semantic Media Wiki. Related to this topic, some approaches emphasize how social networks can be used as means promoting recommendations in the collaborative design of business processes (e.g., [20] and [16]).

Instead of implementing Workflow Management Systems with social software applications (e.g. Wikis), so to benefit of functionalities promoting sociality, we propose an alternative approach: first, integrating traditional Workflow Management Systems with social software to allow the impact of social behavior, promoted by the system, on the use of Workflow Management Systems, and to facilitate users' acceptance; second, setting a research agenda for the enhancement of Workflow Management Systems with social features to improve both their flexibility and the users' acceptance. This approach takes into account, both what observed in our study, and what discussed in the domain of *Social Usability* [12], a set of methods and socio-psychological theories that allow to design not only human-computer interactions in isolation, but also human to human interactions mediated by a technology.

We also suggest two complementary strategies towards the design of socially-enhanced Workflow Management Systems: i) facilitating users in forming a positive attitude towards Workflow Management Systems emphasizing the sense of belonging to the organization; ii) relaxing the constraints posed by current Workflow Management Systems towards the definition of informal modes of control. The former strategy relies on traditional Workflow Management systems; the latter requires a flexible process management system so to allow users not to necessarily comply with what proposed by the system (e.g., [9]). These two strategies can be more or less pertinent depending on the considered domain and the related requirements. The first strategy seems to be more pertinent for those domains where production workflow can be applied, i.e. where processes are more repetitive and precisely set (e.g., in a bank or in an insurance company). The second strategy seems to better suit the domains where the processes concern procedural knowledge [8], as in the clinical domain where clinicians, in order to cure a common pathology, often refers to what is called clinical pathway. Possibly, the two strategies can also be combined according to the specific situation.

Forming a positive attitude towards WfMSs. With the first strategy, WfMSs would provide the users with a process representation, that is, a set of formal rules they have mandatorily to comply with. It is in the nature of the technology that users cannot escape from the order embedded in the process representation. In this way, rules embedded in the process would allow controllers (e.g., managers of the organization) to exert control: i.e., they ensure that individuals act consistently with the organizational goals and objectives [14]. Since this form of control can influence the controllees' behaviors, socio-psychological theories seem pertinent to be used: a conflict may arise among controllers and controllees especially when the rules proposed by controllers change controllees' consolidated work practices; this might happen as a consequence of internal company re-organizations, when process are reengineered to improve efficiency and quality, and to reduce costs. In this case, a Workflow Management System represents a tool for exerting a formal mode of control [14]. We suggest to design a Workflow Management Social System aiming at promoting reconciliation between controllers and controllees. In our study on Wikipedia we identified some strategies our participants used to manage the conflict; in particular, these strategies seem to be either attacking the individual who causes the conflict, or escaping the conflict. In our opinion, these are not winning strategies regardless of the social system we consider. In particular, not only managing a conflict in this way would result on either the exclusion or the isolation of a potential contributor, but additionally it would not favor the generation of a freely accessible knowledge, which is the goal of Wikipedia. According to the Realistic Conflict Theory [25], an intergroup conflict may be reduced introducing a super-ordinate goal, that is, a task related to desire, challenge, predicament or peril that both parties in conflict need to get solved, and that neither party can solve alone. This seems, indeed, the case of Wikipedia: generating freely accessible knowledge, a goal that can be reached only if each of the users contributes to this effort. When conflicts arise, it seems that our participants forget the main goal of the community in which they are involved. Instead, this should always be salient for all the users. It is worth noting, however, that what RCT suggests could be insufficient when dealing with structured, and hierarchical organizations. As also emerged from our study, when there is a hierarchical organization, individuals perceive the system according to their status. Therefore, a super-ordinate goal could be not enough. Beside the perception of a super-ordinate goal, we argue that the perception of a common identity would help people in forming a positive attitude towards the workflow system: both controllers and controllees should perceive to be part of the same group, sharing objectives, beliefs, intentions, fate. This is harder for controllees who may perceive to be forced to behave accordingly to what the system and the high-status people want them to behave. In order to facilitate both controllers and controllees in the creation and maintenance of a common group identity, controllees should be allowed to express their opinion concerning the way the workflow system regutates their work activities: this would help them to perceive that their contribution is fundamental for the achievement of the organization goals, increasing their motivation and their commitment to it. Therefore, a Workflow Management System should be augmented with a social component, firstly aiming at both making and keeping explicit to all users super-ordinate goals, stressing how much each user is important to achieve such goals. Secondly, this social component should allow members to leave comments, suggestions, claims related to the way the workflow system regulates work activities, implementing a sort of *workflow suggestion box*: i.e., a device usually implemented within organizations to garner employees' inputs but specifically customised to consider comments about how work activities are regulated by the WfMS. It could be crucial for the organization to decide whether to make this suggestion box anonymous or not. On the one hand, unsigned comments could be easier to do, but they could tend to sacrify accountability making this system prone to abuse; on the other hand, signed comments could be considered as a way to control the freedom of expression. Therefore, we propose to implement this workflow suggestion box using an unmoderated Forum allowing both signed and unsigned contributions. To improve the sense of being listened, the organization should also consider to define a new institutional role, the community manager, aiming at gathering and organizaning the different people's contributions (e.g., by creating a monthly report visible to all and discussing it in regularly scheduled meetings). However, in order to prevent the possible misuses of the system due to anonymous contributions, some internal policies should be set, such as considering only signed contributions for the montly report. In order to facilitate users in posting pertinent comments, the workflow system should be integrated with the aforementioned forum application; in this way, the users' contributions could be more easily managed since they would be contextualized according to the process activities regulated by the workflow system.

Supporting informal modes of control. The second strategy instead can be applied to those cases where both the formal mode of control and the rigidity of the workflow technology used are not justified. In other words, these are the cases where a process representation has to be considered in terms of a map: an artifact giving guidance rather than just a script (an artifact exerting behavioral control [23] as discussed above for the first strategy). An example is traceable in the clinical domain, where all the physicians working in the same ward are members of a group in which knowledge, beliefs, and goals are largely shared. In this context, it often happens that to guarantee effectiveness and efficacy of the care process, clinicians' interventions for common (e.g., gastroenteritis) or rare but critical (e.g., meningitis) problems/diseases have been codified in the form of clinical pathways. A clinical pathway is a schematic representation of an action plan to follow (from the beginning to the end of each episode of care) for the management of a homogeneous population of patients associated with a specific diagnosis [1]. In this case, a technology implementing such a clinical process should not perform like usual Workflow Management Systems; instead, it should only suggest to a clinician which is the most pertinent care activity to be undertaken according to the clinical pathway and the current patient conditions, but not enforcing the physician to strictly follow the system. This technology should implement what has been called informal modes of control: mechanisms to ensure proper behaviors according to social and people strategies [14]. In particular, in our analysis on Wikipedia, we identified that informal modes of control have been applied since registered users perceive them as members of a group sharing a set of common goals and they feel almost responsible for their actions. In fact, we noticed that behaviors are regulated, and non-normative behaviors are avoided in order not to be exiled by the community. In socio-psychological terms, people usually tend to behave in order to enhance their reputation, and to avoid exclusion by their community or group; this also implies that people's behaviors generally conform to the community norms they belong to, and tend not to deviate from them. Acting in a non-normative way would lead to the so-called "black sheep effect" [17]: the tendency of ingroup members to treat or evaluate a deviant member of their own group more harshly than an outgroup member for a similar behavior. Going back to our clinical scenario, clinicians generally tend to conform to clinical pathways probably also to avoid black sheep effect. However, there might be situations in which the patient's conditions need a different action plan. In our opinion, the system should put the physician in the condition to justify the "deviant" behavior. This could be done by letting the physician to put an annotation related to the variation and by making this annotation visible to all. In this way, other colleagues could exert a form of control, judging the reasons behind the deviation. This way of implementing informal control could improve self-monitoring and reducing the unjustified variability of behaviors, though letting the clinicians free to behave as they consider appropriate.

Final remarks. The conceptualization of Workflow Management Social Systems requires to frame the aforementioned strategies in an overall conceptual WfMSS architecture; this encompasses three main components (see Fig. 1): a

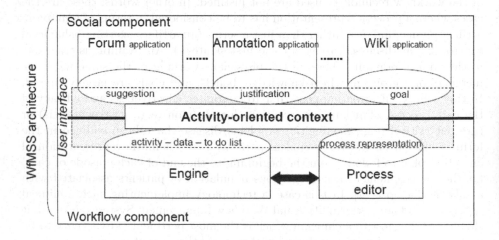

Fig. 1. An overview of the WfMSS architecture

Workflow component, a *Social component* and a *User Interface*. The Workflow component refers to the usual functionalities provided by a WfMS (like process representation and execution). The Social component, instead, refers to a pool of different applications aiming at supporting users' social interactions. Finally, this architecture stresses the role of the user interface which aims at organizing the information from both the Workflow and the Social components, in order to emphasize the social nature of a workflow. On the one hand, the interface provides the user with usual information related to workflow management. On the other hand, it provides the user with information related to the different social software applications embedded in the Social component to enrich the social interactions related to the workflow management. For the proposed strategies, we consider the following social software applications: i) an unmoderated Forum application implementing the workflow suggestion box; ii) a Social annotation application allowing users to justify their "deviant" behavior; iii) a Wiki application to give users the opportunity to discuss and collaboratively define from the bottom some super-ordinate goals. Since we aim at supporting users in both defining and accessing information related to social interactions contextualized according to the different workflow activities, the Workflow and the Social components have been tightly integrated through the definition of an *Activity-oriented context*: contextual information concerning current activities by a specific user. In this way people should be facilitated in managing their social interactions, relating them to the work context provided by the Workflow component; consequently, the system should support its users in the formation of a positive attitude towards the WfMS, and it should facilitate the application of informal modes of control.

References

1. Ulster community and hospitals trust, policy commitee - policies, precdures, standards, protocols and care pathways – definitions (2005)
2. Abbott, K.R., Sarin, S.K.: Experiences with Workflow Management: Issues for the next generation, pp. 113–120. ACM Press, New York (1994)
3. Allport, G.W.: The historical background of social psychology. In: The handbook of social psychology. McGraw Hill, New York (1985)
4. Bouman, W., Hoogenboom, T.: A league on its own: Towards a new ontology for social software. In: OLKC 2009 Proceedings (2009)
5. Boyd, S.: Are you ready for social software? (2006)
6. Brown, J.S., Duguid, P.: The Social Life of Information. Harward Business School Press, Boston (2000)
7. Butler, B., Joyce, E., Pike, J.: Don't look now, but we've created a bureaucracy: the nature and roles of policies and rules in wikipedia. In: CHI 2008 Proceedings, pp. 1101–1110. ACM, New York (2008)
8. Cabitza, F., Sarini, M., Simone, C.: Knowledge Artifacts as Bridges between Theory and Practice: The Clinical Pathway Case. In: Knowledge Management In Action, IFIP 20th World Computer Congress, Conference on Knowledge Management in Action, pp. 37–50. Springer, Heidelberg (2008)
9. Cabitza, F., Simone, C., Zorzato, G.: ProDoc: an electronic patient record to foster process-oriented practices. In: ECSCW 2009 Proceedings. Springer, London (2009)

10. Dengler, F., Lamparter, S., Hefke, M., Abecker, A.: Collaborative process development using semantic mediawiki. In: Wissensmanagement, pp. 97–107 (2009)
11. Fuchs-Kittowski, F., Köhler, A.: Wiki communities in the context of work processes. In: WikiSym 2005 Proceedings, pp. 33–39. ACM, New York (2005)
12. Giacoma, G., Casali, D.: Design motivazionale. usabilità sociale e group centered design. Creative Commons by-sa 2.5, ita (2008)
13. Joinson, A., McKenna, K., Postmes, T., Reips, U.-D.: Oxford Handbook of Internet Psychology. Oxford University Press, Inc., New York (2007)
14. Kirsch, L.S.: Portfolios of Control Modes and IS Project Management. Information Systems Research 8(3), 215–239 (1997)
15. Kittur, A., Suh, B., Pendleton, B.A., Chi, E.H.: He says, she says: conflict and coordination in wikipedia. In: CHI 2007 Proceedings, pp. 453–462. ACM, New York (2007)
16. Koschmider, A., Song, M., Reijers, H.A.: Social software for modeling business processes. In: Ardagna, D., et al. (eds.) BPM 2008 Workshops. LNBIP, vol. 17, pp. 666–677. Springer, Heidelberg (2009)
17. Marques, J.M., Paez, D.: The "black sheep effect": Social categorization, rejection of ingroup deviates, and perception of group variability. European Review of Social Psychology 5, 37–68 (1994)
18. Neumann, G., Erol, S.: From a social wiki to a social workflow system. In: Ardagna, D., et al. (eds.) BPM 2008 Workshops. LNBIP, vol. 17, pp. 698–708. Springer, Heidelberg (2009)
19. Postmes, T., Spears, R.: Deindividuation and anti-normative behavior: A meta-analysis. Psychological Bulletin 123, 238–259 (1998)
20. Qu, H., Sun, J., Jamjoom, H.: Scoop: Automated social recommendation in enterprise process management. In: SCC 2008 Proceedings, pp. 101–108. IEEE Press, Los Alamitos (2008)
21. Randall, D., Rouncefield, M., Hughes, J.A.: Chalk and cheese: Bpr and ethnomethodologically informed ethnography in cscw. In: ECSCW 1995 Proceedings, pp. 325–340 (1995)
22. Reagle Jr., J.M.: Do as i do: authorial leadership in wikipedia. In: WikiSym 2007 Proceedings, pp. 143–156. ACM, New York (2007)
23. Schmidt, K.: Of maps and scripts: the status of formal constructs in cooperative work. In: GROUP 1997 Proceedings, pp. 138–147. ACM Press, New York (1997)
24. Schmidt, R., Nurcan, S.: BPM and social software. In: Ardagna, D., et al. (eds.) BPM 2008 Workshops. LNBIP, vol. 17, pp. 649–658. Springer, Heidelberg (2009)
25. Sherif, M., Harvey, O.J., White, B.J., Hood, W.R., Sherif, C.: Intergroup conflict and cooperation: the Robbers Cave experiment. Norman (1954)
26. Suchman, L.A.: Plans and situated actions: The problem of human-machine communication. Cambridge University Press, Cambridge (1987)
27. Tajfel, H.: Human Groups and Social Categories. Cambridge University Press, Cambridge (1981)
28. Wikipedia contributors. Wikipedia:wikipediani/wikipediano, (accessed 30–04–09)
29. Wikipedia contributors. Software sociale (accessed 27–04–09)
30. Wikipedia contributors. Wikiwikiweb (accessed 27–04–09)
31. Wikipedia contributors. Wikipedia: administrators (accessed 30–04–09)
32. Wikipedia contributors. Wikipedia: bureaucrats (accessed 30–04–09)
33. Wikipedia contributors. Wikipedia:three-revert rule (accessed 30–04–09)

Requirements Elicitation as a Case of Social Process: An Approach to Its Description

Giorgio Bruno

Dip. di Automatica e Informatica, Politecnico di Torino, Torino, Italy
giorgio.bruno@polito.it

Abstract. The point of view of this paper is that social software and business software need different kinds of processes, referred to as social processes and business processes, respectively. Business processes are mainly thought of as orchestrators of external activities to be carried out by users or by services; they embody a centralized perspective in which users are meant to interact with processes and not with each other. Social processes rely on a different paradigm, centered on the participants acting in a social space. The social space keeps track of the past actions so that each participant knows what has been done by the other participants; by acting on the social space, the participants can influence each other. This paper intends to investigate the features of social processes and to bring them to an explicit level of representation by means of an original language, called SPL (Social Processes Language). To this end, this paper analyzes a case of software production, in particular the requirements elicitation phase inspired by the CoREA method, and presents an SPL description of it.

Keywords: Social software, social processes, requirements elicitation.

1 Introduction

Business processes and social software are terms denoting cooperative approaches based on different viewpoints; nevertheless increasing attention is being devoted to initiatives (such as [1]) trying to bridge the gap between these two disciplines.

Current notations and languages for business processes, such as BPMN [2] and BPEL [3], provide an orchestration-oriented perspective, since they organize the work into a flow of steps (or tasks) assigned to the participants in a centralized way; a business process is like a master distributing the work among the subordinates. Users are presented with to-do lists showing the tasks that have been assigned to them by the processes; by clicking on the items of their todo lists, they can perform the corresponding activities.

Because of the centralized perspective, users are meant to interact with processes and not with each other. As a matter of fact, a collaboration that logically takes place between two users, say, A and B, such as A asking B for the approval of a certain request, is mediated by a process and therefore it results in two collaborations, one between A and the process and the other between the process and B.

S. Rinderle-Ma et al. (Eds.): BPM 2009 Workshops, LNBIP 43, pp. 243–254, 2010.

More flexible approaches have been proposed so as to emphasize the involvement of the users. In the RAD (Role Activity Diagramming) approach [4], the process is decomposed into several role components. Each component is structured as a process including the tasks pertaining to the role; components interact with each other by means of send/receive operations.

What is missing from the orchestration-oriented perspective is that, in most cases, human work is cooperative and therefore human activities are not performed in isolation but in structured frameworks referred to as conversations. The term "conversation for action" was introduced in [5] to indicate the kind of conversations aimed at producing an effect on the real world through the cooperation of two parties.

Conversations are the basis of the language/action perspective [6], or LAP, which was proposed for the design of information systems and business processes. Several modeling approaches based on LAP have been presented, among which stand out Action Workflow [7], DEMO [8] and BAT [9].

Another direction of improvement is concerned with the integration between control flow issues and data flow ones. Traditional approaches to process modeling emphasize the tasks to be carried out and their ordering constraints at the expense of the artifacts dealt with by the tasks. Recent approaches try to give equal emphasis to both aspects (tasks and artifacts) [10] or consider "case handling" [11] to be the major purpose of a business process.

On the other side, social software is based on web technologies, such as blogs and wikis, which promote informal interactions among the participants as well as the cooperative production of documents and software ([12], [13]).

The major difference between social software and business processes is not the absence of processes from the former but the presence of a different kind of processes, referred to as social processes. Social processes "can be viewed as processes in which group members perform sequence of actions in a shared space of actions, such that the actions of one group member can affect the space of actions of the others" [14].

This paper intends to investigate the features of social processes and to bring them to an explicit level of representation; this is the first step towards the integration between social processes and business processes.

To this end, this paper presents an original language, called SPL (Social Processes Language), aimed at defining social processes and applies it to a case of software production. The case study addresses the requirements elicitation phase and has been inspired by the CoREA method [15].

In SPL, a social process describes a collective action. As a collective action develops over time, the roles involved may change as well as the actions to be carried out: therefore social processes can be divided into a number of phases. Phases are characterized by the roles involved and the actions to be carried out.

Social processes cannot be orchestrated like business ones, but require a different paradigm. As a matter of fact, a social process is carried out by participants acting transparently in a social space made up of social entities. Social entities include the participants themselves (as a participant can see the state of the others), their actions (as the participants operate transparently) and the artifacts produced (as they are produced cooperatively). SPL defines the behavior of each role (separately from the others) in terms of a behavioral clause including the expected actions; actions can be subjected to preconditions on the state of the social space. The structure of a social process is then given by a number of phases together with their ordering constraints and each phase describes the behavior of the roles involved in terms of behavioral clauses.

This paper is structured as follows. Section 2 illustrates the case study, section 3 gives an introduction to SPL, section 4 presents an SPL process addressing the requirements elicitation phase, section 5 makes a comparison between social processes and business processes on the basis of a portion of the process described in section 4, and section 6 presents the conclusion.

2   The Case Study

The case study has been inspired by the CoREA method [15] for the collaborative elicitation and analysis of requirements. In particular, it addresses the first phase, i.e. requirements elicitation. The CoREA method iterates over a number of steps which, for the sake of simplicity, have been reduced to three, in this case study. On the other hand, two initial phases concerned with the organization of the working team have been added. Moreover, the purpose of the cooperative environment has been made more precise in the sense that it is meant to enable a software company, called swCompany, to assist its customers (which are organizations) to produce effective documents of requirements definition for their intended systems.

The social process defining requirements elicitation is led by two major actors, one coming from swCompany and the other from the customer organization which commissioned the work. The first actor plays the coordinator role and the other the supervisor one.

At the beginning, these actors build the team involved in the process. The supervisor appoints a number of members of their company as stakeholders and the coordinator appoints a member of swCompany as analyst. Then, the stakeholders elect the members of the board (of stakeholders), who are in charge of defining the categories of requirements.

At that time, the core of the work can take place: it consists in developing a hierarchical document in a collaborative way through a wiki system. The supervisor is responsible for the vision document (i.e. the root of the tree) to which the board members may contribute; the vision document points to a number of categories grouping the corresponding requirements. The requirements are introduced and handled by the stakeholders; the categories are authored by the board members while the stakeholders may contribute. The coordinator is the moderator of the whole document. A glossary of terms is also built: it is in charge of the analyst and moderated by the coordinator.

When the documents are completed, the coordinator measures the consensus of the participants through a voting activity after which they may decide to end the process or to go back to the development phase. Additional details are given in section 4.

3 An Introduction to SPL

A social process defines a collective action to be carried out by several participants subdivided into a number of roles. The term role is used in a collective sense so as to denote a group of participants entitled to perform specific actions.

The participants in a social process share a space of actions "such that the actions of one group member can affect the space of actions of the others" [14]. In SPL, this common space is referred to as social space and is made up of a number of entities, referred to as social entities, which are visible to all the participants: by acting on the social entities, they can influence each other. Social entities include the participants themselves (as a participant can see the state of the others), their actions (as the participants operate transparently) and the artifacts produced (as they are produced cooperatively).

The actions carried out by participants are like speech acts [16], which are utterances affecting the real world. Although in practice an action consists of several implementation steps, from the process viewpoint, it is an event added to the social space and affecting the subsequent actions.

There are three major kinds of actions, i.e. generative actions, labeling actions and relational ones. They are illustrated in the example that follows.

The higher-level construct in SPL is the social environment, which encompasses a community of users operating on shared social entities on the basis of certain social processes.

An example of social environment is shown in Fig. 1. A social environment can grow as new definitions are added; the requirements elicitation process described in the next section is built on this basic environment.

There are three major sections in the definition shown in Fig. 1, i.e. the entity model, the initial action and the social processes (one in the example).

The entity model is a kind of class-relationship model and includes the definitions of classes, relationships and labels.

The classes introduced in Fig. 1 represent users and organizations (i.e. user entities and organization entities) and their attributes are written between parentheses (String is the default type). Users are enrolled in organizations by means of the member relationship. The default multiplicity of relationships is (1:*).

Labels are a kind of optional attributes (possibly multi-valued) that may be attached to the social entities; the default multiplicity is (1). The roles played by the users are determined by the role labels attached to them. The participant label is illustrated in the next section.

At the beginning, the social environment is empty and the initial action has the purpose of introducing the initial entities. The initial action in Fig. 1 is a compound action consisting of a sequence of four simple actions (the comma is the sequencing operator).

```
social environment {
entity model {
enum roleName: admin, supervisor, coordinator, stakeholder, analyst,
boardMember.
classes: organization (name), user (login, password).
relationships: member (organization, user).
labels: role (user) (roleName r),
participant (user) (roleName r) (*) <local>.
}
initial action {
organization ("swCompany") org, user ("admin", "admin") u,
member (org, u), role (u) (admin).
}
process manageUsers startedBy admin {
action enrollUser: user u, member (organization, u), [role (u)].
admin: {organization} || {enrollUser}.
}
}
```

Fig. 1. Definition of social environment in SPL

The first simple action generates a social entity of type organization with the name swCompany: this is the organization hosting the social environment. The entity generated is referred to as org and this identifier has a local scope restricted to the subsequent part of the initial action. Next, the first user is generated, who will then be made a member of swCompany and will finally be given the admin role.

Role admin is a kind of master role in that the users playing this role can generate organization entities and enroll users in them. In order to exert such capabilities, administrators need to instantiate process manageUsers shown in Fig. 1. The heading of a process definition indicates the role(s) entitled to generate its instances. A more complex example of social process is illustrated in the next section.

A process definition includes a number of role behaviors (or behavioral clauses), where a role behavior has the syntax "role: behavioral expression". A behavioral expression consists of actions and ordering operators: repetition ({}), optional ([]), parallel composition (| |) and alternative (|).

Role admin can perform the organization simple action or the enrollUser compound action, whenever they want to. The first is a generative action; the actual values of the action parameters (e.g. the organization name) are decided by the subject. The term subject denotes the user performing the action being considered.

Compound actions are defined outside the role behaviors and imply a transactional nature. By performing enrollUser, the subject introduces a new user entity (along with its attributes), associates it with an organization entity and possibly labels it with a role. Action member(organization, u) is a relational action and implies a search of the intended organization among the existing ones. The details of the search as well as the validation of the values given to the attributes are left to the implementation phase of the actions, because the processes are only concerned with the resulting events. Action role(u) is a labeling action; the actual role name is decided by the subject among the possible ones.

4   Representation of the Case Study

This section illustrates a social process handling requirements elicitation on the basis of the guidelines introduced in section 2.

New social processes can be added to an existing social environment so as to increase its capabilities; therefore the definition shown in Fig. 2 draws on the one shown in Fig. 1.

A social process represents a collective action that may be repeated (or instantiated) several times, when needed. The occurrences are called process instances.

The heading of process requirementsElicitation shows that it can be instantiated by role coordinator (assumed to denote a member of swCompany) and the coordinator is to involve a supervisor (assumed to belong to the customer organization commissioning the work). These two users form the initial team of participants in the new process instance.

The participants in a given process instance are referred to as the team of the instance (or simply the team). The team is implicitly formed by the users who are labeled as participants during the execution of the instance. The participant label has a local scope, i.e. a scope restricted to the instance in which it is generated. On the contrary, the role labels have a global scope and they are visible in all the process instances.

At the beginning of the process instance, the coordinator and the supervisor are implicitly labeled as participants; they are the first two members of the team and keep their external roles as their participant roles.

The roles appearing in behavioral clauses are matched against the participant roles: this is how SPL enables selected parts of the whole community to take part in the process instances.

A collective action is an ordered course of actions leading to a certain goal. In most cases, as the collective action develops over time, the roles involved may change as well as the actions to be carried out: therefore social processes can be divided into a number of phases. Phases are characterized by the roles involved and the actions to be carried out.

The structure of a social process is then given by a number of phases together with their ordering constraints and each phase is made up of the appropriate behavioral clauses. Process requirementsElicitation is divided in a number of sequential phases, the first of which is teamBuilding. This phase is concerned with the setting of the team. Members of the customer organization are added to the team with the stakeholder role by the supervisor and a member of swCompany is added to the team with the analyst role by the coordinator.

The term colleague is a short cut for indicating a search space made up of the members of the organization the subject belongs to. In the definition of

```
process requirementsElicitation startedBy coordinator
involves supervisor {
// implicit: participant (coordinator) (coordinator).
// implicit: participant (supervisor) (supervisor).

labels: nominate (stakeholder) (*).
let colleague = ^member/member (!= subject).

phase teamBuilding {
supervisor: {participant (colleague) (stakeholder)}.
coordinator: participant (colleague) (analyst).
}

phase boardElection startedBy coordinator ends after 2 days {
stakeholder: {nominate(stakeholder)}2 ||
[N(nominate)>=3| accept, participant (subject) (boardMember) <auto>]
}.
supervisor: {participant (stakeholder) (boardMember)}.

let reqDoc = wikiTree("vision/category+/requirement+",
"vision (supervisor, boardMember),
category (boardMember, stakeholder),
requirement (stakeholder, stakeholder)", coordinator).
let reqGlossary = glossary(analyst, coordinator, analyst).

phase writingRequirements startedBy coordinator endedBy coordinator {
auto: editing (reqDoc), editing (reqGlossary).
supervisor: {participant (colleague) (stakeholder)} ||
{participant (stakeholder) (boardMember)}.
}

phase votingRequirements startedBy coordinator endedBy coordinator {
auto: voting (reqDoc).
}

coordinator: end || continue(writingRequirements).
}
```

Fig. 2. SPL definition of process requirementsElicitation

colleague, the expression ^member/member (!= subject) is a path expression
showing how to reach the target entities: starting from the subject of the action,
the subject's organization is reached by traversing the member relationship in the
reverse direction (from the second entity, user, to the first one, organization),
and then the organization members are returned except for the subject. The
reverse direction is indicated by operator ^.

A phase can be initiated and ended in several ways. It may begin automatically
when the previous phase has ended (the default way), or at a specific instant,

or it may be started by a member of the team, referred to as its initiator. The initiator is denoted by their participant role. Phase teamBuilding is initiated automatically at the beginning of the process instance.

A phase can be terminated by its initiator, or when the allotted time ends or when all the members involved have finished (the default way). Phase team-Building ends when the supervisor and the coordinator have finished.

A team may be a self-organizing group in which new responsibilities are assigned on the basis of an election. This is the case of the team being considered, in which the board of stakeholders is established by means of a simple mechanism based on nominations taking place in the second phase, the boardElection phase.

The second phase is started by the coordinator and ends automatically after two days. During this phase, the stakeholders may nominate other stakeholders (up to two of them): this is expressed by the behavioral term "nominate(stakeholder)2". When a participant role, such as stakeholder, appears in an action, it defines a search space including all the members of the team playing that role (subject excluded). Therefore action "nominate(stakeholder)" means that the subject first will select a stakeholder and then will nominate them.

The nominate action attaches a nominate label to another stakeholder. The nominate label is multi-valued because stakeholders may receive several nominations. As a matter of fact, if a stakeholder has received three nominations, they may accept, although the acceptance is not mandatory; if they do so, then they automatically get members of the board. This course of action is optional and then it is enclosed with []. In addition, action accept is guarded: it can be performed only if and when the preceding condition is true. Separator | divides the precondition from the action. The term N(nominate) returns the number of nominate labels attached to the subject. The relational action, which assigns the participant role boardMember to the subject, takes place automatically, as shown by the auto qualifier that follows it.

At the end of the boardElection phase, the supervisor is given the possibility of co-opting new members onto the board, if needed. This takes place through an in-line phase made up of a single behavioral clause.

The phases analyzed so far were aimed at shaping the team. The next phase, writingRequirements, is concerned with the core of the work, i.e. the writing of the first draft of the requirements definition document. It is a collaborative effort for developing a shared document and as such it can take advantage of the approaches and services provided by wiki systems, such as version management, searching and linking.

Wiki systems may be seen as social environments (whose definition has been given in section 3), because they enable a number of users with different roles to work out shared artifacts. What is more, they are amenable to being considered as general-purpose building blocks which can be used in different higher-level processes, provided that they are equipped with suitable parameters.

Process requirementsElicitation postulates the usage of a customizable tree-like wiki system (referred to as wikiTree) and of a glossary.

The customized entities are called reqDoc and reqGlossary, respectively.

The customization of a wikiTree addresses the tree structure and the allowed participants. Although at the heart of a wiki system there is a collection of inter-related web pages (acting as the sub-documents), it is necessary to be able to define a hierarchical structure in terms of the intended meaning of the sub-documents and consequently of the participants entitled to work on them. The structure imposed on reqDoc is given by the first parameter, which is the expression vision/category+/requirement+: the root of the tree is a document called vision, which includes a number of categories pointing to the related requirements. Vision, category and requirements are a kind of document types for which two groups of participants need to be defined, i.e. the authors and the contributors. Such groups are given in the second parameter as participant roles. The third parameter provides the moderators in terms of a participant role.

Since a wiki system is a kind of social environment, a usage paradigm should be provided in terms of phases: two of them could be the editing phase in which the overall document is worked out, and the voting phase in which the working group can give their appraisal. When the editing of reqDoc is enabled, the vision document will be under the responsibility of the supervisor, while the board members may contribute; the categories will be authored by the board members and any stakeholder may contribute, and the requirements will be handled by the stakeholders. The general moderator will be the coordinator.

A glossary system, instead, has a predefined structure made up homogeneous documents; they are authored by the analyst while the coordinator may contribute. There is only one phase, the editing phase.

When phase writingRequirements is started by the coordinator, the editing phase of the wiki document and the glossary are automatically started, as shown by the behavioral expression attributed to role auto: then the participants are enabled to operate according to their roles. In the meantime, the supervisor is able to co-opt additional colleagues into the team and/or new stakeholders into the board, if needed. This increases the flexibility of the process, as the team can grow or shrink (not considered in Fig.2) depending on the circumstances. When the phase is ended (by the coordinator), the editing phases of the two above-mentioned documents are automatically ended.

Voting takes place in the subsequent phase after which the results are available to the team and the coordinator can end the process instance or go back to phase writingRequirements, if they think there is no broad consensus in the team on the documents produced.

5   Differences between Social Processes and Business Processes

In the orchestration-oriented perspective, users are meant to interact with processes and not with each other. From a logical point of view, the run-time interpretation of a task results in a request/response interaction with the intended performer. The request, such as "provide a review for paper xyz", is meant to

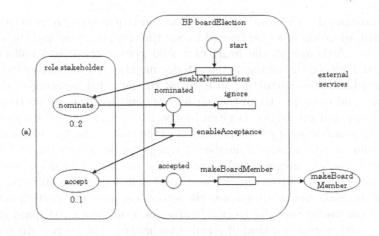

(a)

(b)   phase boardElection startedBy coordinator ends after 2 days {
       stakeholder: {nominate(stakeholder)}2 | |
       [Σnominate >= 3 | accept, participant (subject) (boardMember) <auto>]
       }.

Fig. 3. Phase board election as a business process (a) and in SPL (b)

make a particular user perform a certain activity on a specific information entity, and the response returns the outcome of the activity. The request conveys the information on the intended performer(s): the assignment of activities to users can be made in several ways as illustrated in the workflow resource patterns [17]. In addition to mandatory tasks, there are optional tasks and user-driven ones, as well. The former are enabled by the processes through output events, while the latter send input events to the processes and are often used to instantiate them.

Social processes, as discussed in the previous sections, rely on a different paradigm, centered on the participants acting in a social space. The social space keeps track of the past actions so that each participant knows what has been done by the other participants.

The comparison between two representations of the boardElection phase (illustrated in the previous section) is shown in Fig. 3; one representation is based on a business process notation (Fig. 3a) and the other is based on SPL (Fig. 3b).

The two user activities (nominate and accept) are shown as annotated use cases: they are both optional. The business process is shown with a Petri-net like notation; at the beginning, it enables the nominations by sending output events to the stakeholders. When a stakeholder has performed a nominate action, the process collects the event produced in input place nominated; then it ignores the event, if the nominee has not yet received three nominations, otherwise it enables the accept action for the nominee. When the process receives an accepted event, it has the sender appointed as a board member by calling an external service.

In order to fully understand the process logic, the description of the data flow should be added. A complementary information model is then needed along with a navigational language (such as OCL [18]): in that case, the above mentioned conditions and actions could be expressed in a formal way.

The SPL representation is simpler because the actions represent the corresponding user activities and the events produced; since they are stored, they represent the underlying information system as well.

6   Conclusion

The viewpoint of the research reported in this paper is that social initiatives, including the social production of software, cannot be orchestrated like business ones, but require a different paradigm. As a matter of fact, a social initiative is carried out by participants acting transparently in a social space made up of social entities. A proof-of-concept language, i.e. SPL, addressing social processes has been illustrated and special emphasis has been placed on the collaborative production of documents based on wiki technologies.

Further work will be devoted to two lines of development. The first line is concerned with the definition of a suitable personal workspace in which each participant can perform their actions and can observe the results of the actions of the other participants. A prototype is being developed based on the seam platform (http://seamframework.org/).

The second line of development is about the introduction of conversational features into SPL so as to enable pairs of participants to interact directly (and privately) on the basis of predefined protocols, while the shared space, in general, promotes indirect (and public) interactions.

References

1. Neumann, G., Erol, S.: From a social wiki to a social workflow system. In: Ardagna, D., et al. (eds.) BPM 2008 Workshops. LNBIP, vol. 17, pp. 623–624. Springer, Heidelberg (2009)
2. Business Process Modeling Notation, V.1.1, http://www.bpmn.org
3. Web Services Business Process Execution Language, V.2.0, http://docs.oasis-open.org/wsbpel/2.0/OS/wsbpel-v2.0-OS.html
4. Ould, M.: Business process management: a rigorous approach. The British Computer Society (2005)
5. Winograd, T., Flores, F.: Understanding computers and cognition. Ablex Publishing Corporation, Norwood (1986)
6. Weigand, H.: Two decades of the Language-Action Perspective: introduction. Communications of the ACM 49, 44–46 (2006)
7. Medina-Mora, R., Winograd, T., Flores, R., Flores, F.: The Action Workflow approach to workflow management technology. In: Turner, J., Kraut, R. (eds.) 4th Conference on Computer Supported Cooperative Work. ACM, New York (1992)
8. Dietz, J.L.G.: The deep structure of business processes. Communications of the ACM 49(5), 59–64 (2006)

9. Goldkuhl, G., Lind, M.: The generics of business interaction - emphasizing dynamic features through the BAT model. In: Aakhus, M., Lind, M. (eds.) 9th Conference on the Language-Action Perspective on Communication Modelling (2004)
10. Liu, R., Bhattacharya, K., Wu, F.Y.: Modeling business contexture and behavior using business artifacts. In: Krogstie, J., Opdahl, A.L., Sindre, G. (eds.) CAiSE 2007 and WES 2007. LNCS, vol. 4495, pp. 324–339. Springer, Heidelberg (2007)
11. van der Aalst, W.M.P., Weske, M., Grunbauer, D.: Case handling: a new paradigm for business process support. Data and Knowledge Engineering 53, 129–162 (2005)
12. Koschmider, A., Song, M., Reijers, H.A.: Advanced social features in a recommendation system for process modeling. In: Abramowicz, W. (ed.) BIS 2009. LNBIP, vol. 21, pp. 109–120. Springer, Heidelberg (2009)
13. Hildenbrand, T., Rothlauf, F., Geisser, M., Heinzl, A., Kude, T.: Approaches to collaborative software development. In: International Conference on Complex, Intelligent and Software Intensive Systems, pp. 523–528. IEEE Computer Society, Los Alamitos (2008)
14. Simon, S.M., Carroll, A.M., MacGregor, K.J.: Supporting collaborative processes with ConversationBuilder. Computer Communications 15, 489–501 (1992)
15. Geisser, M., Hildenbrand, T.: A method for collaborative requirements elicitation and decision-supported requirements analysis. IFIP, vol. 219, pp. 108–122 (2006)
16. Austin, J.L.: How to do things with words. Harvard University Press, Cambridge (1962)
17. Russell, N., van der Aalst, W.M.P., ter Hofstede, A.H.M., Edmond, D.: Workflow resource patterns: identification, representation and tool support. In: Pastor, Ó., Falcão e Cunha, J. (eds.) CAiSE 2005. LNCS, vol. 3520, pp. 216–232. Springer, Heidelberg (2005)
18. UML 2.0 OCL Specification, http://www.omg.org/docs/ptc/03-10-14.pdf

Co-creation of Value in IT Service Processes Using Semantic MediaWiki

Rainer Schmidt[1], Frank Dengler[2], and Axel Kieninger[3]

[1] HTW-Aalen, now on sabbatical at Karlsruhe Service Research Institute
Rainer.Schmidt@htw-aalen.de
[2] Institute AIFB, Universität Karlsruhe, TH
Frank.Dengler@kit.edu
[3] Karlsruhe Service Research Institute, Universität Karlsruhe, TH
Axel.Kieninger@ksri.uni-karlsruhe.de

Abstract. Enterprises are substituting their own IT-Systems by services provided by external providers. This provisioning of services may be done in an industrialized way, separating the service provider from the consumer. However, using industrialized services diminishes the capability to differentiate from competitors. To counter this, collaborative service processes based on the co-creation of value between service providers and prosumers are of huge importance. The approach presented shows how the co-creation of value in IT-service processes can profit from social software, using the example of the Semantic MediaWiki.

Keywords: Service, Process, SD-Logic, Co-Creation, Semantic MediaWiki.

1 Introduction

Offering and using IT-services is becoming more and more important for many enterprises. Customers substitute owning IT-systems by service [1] [2]. They request IT-services instead of IT-systems and IT-enterprises have to change their offer to fulfil this changing demand. Using service helps customer enterprises to facilitate outsourcing and thus allows them to concentrate on their core competencies. The innovative potential of IT-services has been an important topic of discussion and lead to the term service science [3][4]. Some see IT as a commodity [5]. Using commoditized, industrialized IT-services may create cost benefits. However, an enterprise using commoditized IT-services diminishes its capability to differentiate from competitors. By contrast, individualized services are necessary to differentiate from competitors. Therefore, enterprises should use a mixture of industrialized commodity services for cost-cutting and individualized services for differentiation [6]. The ratio between these two has to be selected according to enterprises' strategies.

In Service Dominant Logic (SD-Logic) [7], developed by Vargo and Lusch, a "service is defined as the application of specialized competences (knowledge and skills) for the benefit of another entity, rather than the production of units of output"

S. Rinderle-Ma et al. (Eds.): BPM 2009 Workshops, LNBIP 43, pp. 255–265, 2010.

[7][1]. The co-creation of value and not the output of production should be in the centre of interest (The term value will be regarded in more detail within the next paragraph). Thus service is regarded as a process of interaction with the customer and not as an interface to the customer. Value is co-created in a service process by a service provider and his customer as shown in Fig. 1, instead of producing a good and delivering it to the customer. Therefore it is better to name the role of the customer as prosumer [8][9].

Service

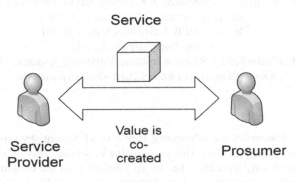

Service   Value is   Prosumer
Provider   co-
                 created

Fig. 1. SD-Logic

Service-Dominant Logic is not an isolated theory, but is related to a number of emerging ideas, from which several showed their applicability. Thus, SD-Logic is embedded in a stream of ideas and thoughts that emphasize the collaboration of independent individuals to co-create value. The co-creation of value is described in its general form, that means also for material goods, in [10] and [11]. The integration of the customer into value creation is based on the conviction that putting together the contributions of many different stakeholders, a better result can be achieved than by expert decisions. Therefore, the wisdom of the crowds [12] is an important foundation for co-creation of value. The most prominent approach is the collaborative creation of software following an open source approach, following Linus' law instead of Brook's law [13]. Behind these ideas, there is the possibility to create a new kind of economy, as discussed by Benkler in [14]. Co-creation of value also influences the discussion about intellectual property [15].

The contribution of this paper is to show how the co-creation of value in IT-service processes can profit from social software, using the example of a Semantic MediaWiki [16]. The paper proceeds as follows: first, the notion of value created in service processes and its implications are discussed in more detail. Then, service processes and their elements are introduced. In the next sections, the co-creation of value is introduced and the obstacles to achieve it are analysed. Afterwards a concept for the co-creation of service specifications using a Semantic MediaWiki is developed. An application

---

[1] The services discussed here are not services, which are part of so-called service-oriented architectures [33]. A service in the context of SOA is a special kind of interface for an encapsulated unit of software and thus something completely different than the services discussed here. However, the services considered in this article may be part of a Service Oriented Enterprise Architecture (SOEA) [34].

scenario shows the use of the concept developed in practice. Finally, the results are discussed and a summery is given.

2 Value of Services

Before we discuss the co-creation of value, we give a definition of the term value. For a long time, only the final effects of service have been of interest and influenced the notion of value of service (e.g. that a good has been transported from A to B). More and more also the way how service has been provided became important (for example, if the good arrived in time). Therefore also non-functional properties have been incorporated into the notion of value. However, functional and non-functional properties do not capture a number of features of service, which are important for the customer, but are on a higher abstraction level. This third dimension is created by management interactions between the service provider and the prosumer. A basic example of a management interaction is the complaint about an inadequate service. Further examples are changes to functional and non-functional properties of the service. Based on these considerations, the value created by services can be interpreted as the product of three dimensions: Functional-properties, non-functional-properties and management interactions, as shown in Fig. 2.

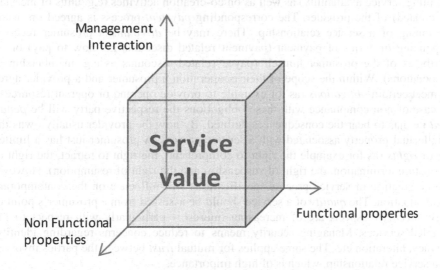

Fig. 2. Value created by service

3 Service Processes

Service is a process "consisting of a series of activities where a number of different types of resources are used in direct interaction with a customer, so that a solution is found to a customer's problem" [17]. Active and passive resources are involved in service. Active resources act on passive resources to create service. In SD-Logic, active resources are called operant resources; passive resources are called operand resources [18]. Service processes have many properties in common with ordinary business processes. However, there are also a number of crucial differences [19]. There are interactions with the customer to co-create value: So-called critical incidents are specific encounters resulting in satisfaction or dissatisfaction of the customer [1]. It is necessary to know, that there may be obligations of the customer that are critical for success or failure of the service process. For example, it may be necessary that the customer provides some information required for the further proceeding of the process.

During the recent years non-functional properties of services have been widely discussed in literature as for example in the field of Software Engineering (see e.g. [20], [21], [22]). In [23] O'Sullivan examines these properties of services in general, abstracting from a particular (computer) science field's perspective. According to his work non-functional properties of services are constraints associated to services' functionality and may be divided into nine different classes. In the following these groups – namely availability, price, payment, discounts and penalties, obligations, rights, quality, security and trust – are briefly introduced.The *availability* of a service defines the time (when) or the location (where) a prosumer is able to accept a provider's proposition to co-create value. Regarding the *price* of a service there are different charging techniques a provider may select to specify the value of his work. The amount of money a prosumer is charged can depend on proposition activities (e.g. enabling service availability) as well as on co-creation activities (e.g. units of measure co-created) of the provider. The corresponding *payment* process is agreed on in the beginning of a service relationship. There may be *discounts* a prosumer receives depending on terms of payment (payment related discounts i.e. how to pay) or on attributes of the prosumer himself (payee related discounts as e.g. membership to associations). Within the scope of their cooperation a prosumer and a provider agree to meet certain *obligations* (as for example to provide operand or operant resources). In case of non-compliance with these obligations the respective party will be *penalized* i.e. has to bear the consequences defined. By now the provider usually owns the intellectual property associated with a service process. A prosumer just has a limited set of *rights* (as for example the right to comprehend, the right to retract, the right of premature termination, the right of suspension and the right of resumption). However the co-creation of service process specifications will influence on the contemporary legal situation. The *quality* of a service should be assessed from a prosumer's point of view. *Security* aspects are of increasing interest – particularly with respect to IT-enabled services. Managing security means to reduce concerns regarding identity, privacy, alteration etc. The same applies for mutual *trust* between the parties involved in a service relationship, which is of high importance.

4   Co-creation of Value

Co-creation of value requires changing the locus of interaction [10]. To co-create value, the interaction between service provider and customer has to come about along the whole value chain. In industrialized production the interaction takes place at the end of the value chain.

Unfortunately, there are a number of obstacles for the co-creation of value in service processes. The most important one are thresholds for the passing-on of information between stakeholders and the lack of information fusioning (Fig. 3).

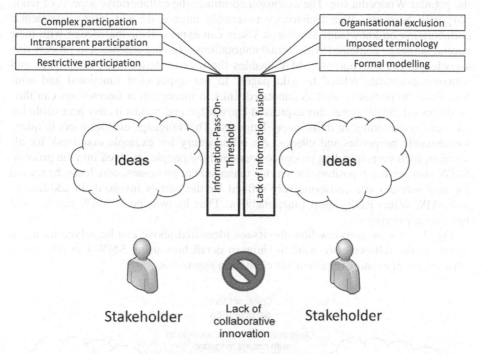

Fig. 3. Obstacles for the co-creation of value

Information pass-on threshold: Ideas for improvement are not exchanged between stakeholders because this creates too much effort ("Why shall I write a memo or a letter"). The further processing is not transparent to the stakeholders ("What will happen to my suggestion...") or the success is considered as improbable ("Will not succeed anyway ..."). The information pass-on-threshold may also be increased if the entering of information is strongly regulated; the process to submit changes is too restrictive or simply takes too long due to approval steps. This causes that stakeholders cannot bring in easily their ideas. Important and valuable information is lost and improvements remain undone.

Lack of information fusion: The other important obstacle for value co-creation is the lack of information fusion. Even if the organizational environment allows the stakeholders to contribute they are partially excluded because the terms used to describe services are defined without their participation or simply imposed on them. Often, stakeholders are excluded due to the project organisation or because they have not been taught to use formal modelling methods. Thus stakeholders are only "consumers" of the terms created and are forced to accept those. Therefore, they tend to retain contributions.

5   Using Semantic MediaWiki to Support Value Co-creation

In order to address the issues mentioned in the previous sections we propose the use of a Semantic MediaWiki (SMW). SMW extends the MediaWiki software that runs the popular Wikipedia site. The extension combines the collaborative aspects of wikis [24] with Semantic Web technology to enable large-scale and inter-departmental collaboration on knowledge structures. Users can express their knowledge with their natural language combined with formal annotations allowing machines to process this knowledge. For this purpose SMW enables the user to define class hierarchies and semantic properties related to wiki pages. In our application functional and non-functional properties as well as annotated links to management interactions can thus be discussed. SMW stores this expressed knowledge and makes it easy accessible for all users by providing an inline query language. This language enables users to query for semantic properties and classes. An inline query for example could ask for all services, their corresponding process owners and the people involved into the process. SMW also act as a repository for service management processes, which can be reused for new services and collaboratively refined by the parties involved. In addition to that SMW offers RDF export functionalities. Thus knowledge in SMW can be used by other applications.

Fig. 4 gives an overview how the issues identified above can be solved by using SMW. In the following we want to show in detail how using SMW can reduce the deficiencies of existing requirements elicitation approaches.

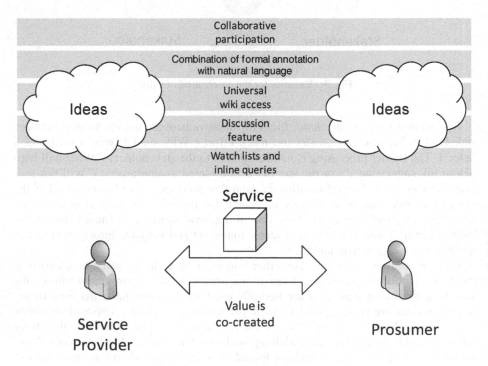

Fig. 4. Issues addressed

Reduction of the information pass-on threshold: Service providers and prosumers can participate in the process by expressing collaboratively their ideas in SMW. The responsible persons can also access the SMW. Thus the ideas are forwarded directly to the responsible stakeholder. SMW features like watch list and inline queries can be used to support this information flow. Each SMW user can register wiki pages in his watch list. When someone updates the watched wiki page, the user gets a notification by email. Inline queries can be used to show relevant information on wiki pages dynamically. For instance, all relevant information in SMW about one process can be displayed on a dynamic created summary page [25]. The effort for each user is also lower, because the ideas can be developed collaboratively. A user can pick up an idea of another user and broaden it. The versioning capability of SMW allows tracing the changes of each user. Different versions can also be compared with each other. Important information is stored within the SMW and ideas as well as improvements can directly be represented in the process definition. The process to submit changes is not restrictive anymore. In addition to that the users can see in SMW what has happened with their suggestion by using for example the watch list or inline queries as stated above for the responsible persons. Now, the further processing is more transparent to them.

Lack of information fusion: Information fusion can be promoted by using SMW. All stakeholders and thus the users can access the SMW and thus participate in service process modelling. No one is excluded by organisational means. Existing service management processes can easily be linked to emerging services and refined if necessary. Thus existing information is reused and it is less time-consuming for the parties involved as starting from scratch. The users are able to use their natural language in combination with formal annotations. Thus the user describes the process with his own language and adds classes and semantic properties in his text. This fact lowers the participation barrier that exists through the use of a formalised modelling tool. Users in companies are familiar with the wiki syntax, because it is easy to apply and many of them have used it before. The effort the user has to invest to learn modelling processes is low. Users are not only "consumers" anymore who are forced to accept the processes created for them (e.g. by externals), but active participants. In addition to that all users can contribute to the definition of terms in a collaborative way. That can be realized by additional wiki pages, like a glossary, or by using the discussion functionality provided by SMW. Thus users can discuss and evolve the meaning of terms.

As a conclusion SMW can support requirement elicitation by addressing most of the deficiencies of existing approaches. Other advantages of using SMW are the template functionality of MediaWiki[2] and existing extensions for SMW like Semantic Forms[3], which provide more user-friendly forms to enter semantic annotations into SMW.

6 Application Scenario

The concepts introduced above have been used to support the IT-service processes of a gardening tool manufacturer [26]. The IT department of this manufacturer looked for a tool to improve the cooperation with business units.

---

[2] http://www.mediawiki.org/wiki/Help:Templates
[3] http://www.mediawiki.org/wiki/Extension:Semantic_Forms

Before, the business units did not contribute much and there has been little transparency regarding the services to be offered and their properties. Furthermore, the design of new services has been a very painful process. Customers' requirements could not be identified in full extent, because there had been information pass-on thresholds and a lack of information fusion. The business units did not use the tools offered by the IT department and used other terms to describe services. Therefore, the IT department often designed IT-services and respective Service Level Agreements (SLAs) without proper contribution of the business units. However, after service implementation, the business units often complained about lacks of alignment with their requirements.

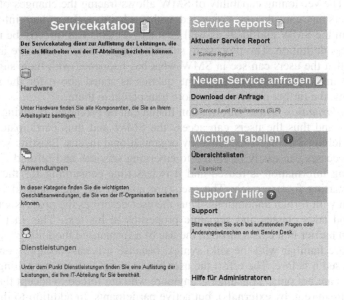

Fig. 5. Screenshot of user interface [26]

To adress these issues, a Semantic MediaWiki based solution has been created. It contains a catalogue with the services already implemented including the associated Service Level Agreements. Reports of the service performance are also available. The most important features are service proposals. By this means, business units are able to easily enter their suggestions for new services or improvements of services. The information flow has been improved, because suggestions are visible to all stakeholders. Business units can use natural language to describe their requirements, which then are annotated by the IT department. Inline queries are used to summarize all relevant information concerning a service proposal. By using a watch list, all users get informed about changes relevant to them. Using the collaborative features of Semantic MediaWiki, the effort of the business units to create suggestions is much lower, because they can profit from already made contributions.

By the application of Semantic MediaWiki a much more homogenous use of terms has been achieved. Participation barriers that existed before – especially for the business units – have been abolished. A screen shot of the user interface is shown in

Fig. 5. The information is structured in a better way and every individual information demand can be addressed by providing a customized view generated with inline queries.

7 Related Work

A fundamental analysis of value and value co-creation in services is done in [27]. A conceptual analysis of co-creation of value is made in [28]. Especially the debate of value-in-use vs. value-in-exchange is considered in a very detailed manner. Especially the importance to interact with the customer and to use small steps for innovation is emphasized. Differences between goods and service innovation are analysed in [29]. The importance to collaborate and to co-create value in services to achieve a strategic advantage is examined in [30]. The importance to interact with the customer in general is shown in [10]. The nature of value co-creation in services is analyzed in [31]. In [32] the role of the customer in new service development is discussed.

8 Discussion

The integration of the customer as prosumer does not only provide advantages but also a couple of issues [10], which also appeared when using the Semantic MediaWiki application described above. First, using a social software solution is a drastic change for many employees who are used to hierarchic structures. Often, employees do not dare to contribute because they are not familiar with egalitarian approaches. Instead they wait for a management approval or initiative. On the other side, managers fear to lose control of their processes. They are accustomed to exactly defined change procedures, enabling perfect control over the entire process. Often, they just learn slowly, that social control can be much more effective than a tight governance structure.

When content is created collaboratively, the effort is higher. Furthermore, the time used for content creation cannot be easily associated with a person. Thus it is difficult to calculate the costs and to respect the time consumed in the task planning of the associated persons. This lack of resource control is of particular importance in the case of disputes. Then it is nearly impossible to quantify the effort caused by discussions etc. Another point is the distribution of responsibility. Due to the multiple contributors, the responsibility for the process design can no longer be associated with a distinct person. However, the process put into production needs a unique responsible process owner. To fulfil his responsibilities, the process owner also has to create a formal model of the collaboratively created model.

9 Summary and Conclusion

Enterprise substitute owning IT-systems more and more by using IT-services. The value created by an IT-service can be increased by supporting the co-creation of value by the service provider and the prosumer, by providing knowledge as an active resource, and by tight cooperation during the execution of the respective service process. However, there are some obstacles for value co-creation such as information pass-on thresholds and a lack of information fusion. By using a Semantic MediaWiki it is possible to overcome most of these deficiencies. As also shown by the presented application scenario, the information and knowledge exchange between all stakeholders has been improved. Customers are no longer excluded from contributing ideas for improving service due to organizational or technical barriers and become true prosumers. Furthermore, the homogenisation of terms is facilitated and thus the fusion of information is improved.

Acknowledgements

Research reported in this paper was partially funded by the European Commission through the IST project ACTIVE (ICT-FP7-215040). We would like to thank our colleagues at KSRI and AIFB for the many fruitful discussions. Special thanks go to H. Reiner for conceptualizing and implementing the Semantic MediaWiki application.

References

[1] Lovelock, C.H., Wirtz, J.: Services marketing. Prentice Hall, Upper Saddle River (2001)
[2] Lacity, M.C., Willcocks, L.P., Feeny, D.F.: The value of selective IT sourcing. Sloan Management Review 37, 13–25 (1996)
[3] Spohrer, J., Maglio, P.P., Bailey, J., Gruhl, D.: Steps Toward a Science of Service Systems. Computer, 71–77 (2007)
[4] Spohrer, J.: Steps Toward a Science of Service Systems (January 2007)
[5] Carr, N.G.: IT Doesn't Matter. IEEE Engineering Management Review 32, 24–32 (2004)
[6] McAfee, A.: Enterprise 2.0: the dawn of emergent collaboration. IEEE Engineering Management Review 34, 38 (2006)
[7] Vargo, S.L., Lusch, R.F.: Evolving to a new dominant logic for marketing. Journal of Marketing 68, 1–17 (2004)
[8] Toffler, A., Longul, W., Forbes, H.: The third wave. Bantam Books, New York (1981)
[9] Tapscott, D., Williams, A.D.: Wikinomics: How Mass Collaboration Changes Everything, Portfolio (2006)
[10] Prahalad, C.K., Ramaswamy, V.: Co-creating unique value with customers. Strategy & Leadership 32, 4–9 (2004)
[11] von Hippel, E.: Democratizing Innovation. MIT Press, Cambridge (2005)
[12] Surowiecki, J.: The Wisdom of Crowds: Why the Many Are Smarter Than the Few and How Collective Wisdom Shapes Business, Economies, Societies and Nations, Doubleday (2004)
[13] Neus, A., Scherf, P.: Opening minds: Cultural change with the introduction of opensource collaboration methods. IBM Systems Journal 44, 215–225 (2005)
[14] Benkler, Y.: The Wealth of Networks: How Social Production Transforms Markets and Freedom. Yale University Press (2006)
[15] Lessig, L.: Remix: Making art and commerce thrive in the hybrid economy. Penguin Press (2008)

[16] Krötzsch, M., Vrandecic, D., Völkel, M., Haller, H., Studer, R.: Semantic Wikipedia. In: Web Semantics: Science, Services and Agents on the World Wide Web, December 2007, vol. 5, pp. 251–261 (2007)

[17] Grönroos, C.: Service Management and Marketing: A Customer Relationship Management Approach. Wiley, Chichester (2000)

[18] Vargo, S.L., Lusch, R.F.: Evolving to a new dominant logic for marketing. Journal of Marketing 68, 1–17 (2004)

[19] Schmidt, R.: Sercomp: A Component Oriented Method for Flexible Design and Support of Interorganizational Service. Software Process: Improvement and Practice 12, 7–20 (2007)

[20] Glinz, M.: On non-functional requirements. Proc. RE 7, 21–26 (2007)

[21] Chung, L.: Representation and utilization of non-functional requirements for information system design. In: Andersen, R., Solvberg, A., Bubenko Jr., J.A. (eds.) CAiSE 1991. LNCS, vol. 498, pp. 13–15. Springer, Heidelberg (1991)

[22] Sommerville, I.: Software Engineering. Addison Wesley, Reading (2004)

[23] O'Sullivan, J.J.: Towards a precise understanding of service properties (2006)

[24] Leuf, B., Cunningham, W.: The Wiki way: quick collaboration on the Web. Addison-Wesley Longman Publishing Co., Inc., Boston (2001)

[25] Dengler, F., Lamparter, S., Hefke, M., Abecker, A.: Collaborative Process Development using Semantic MediaWiki. In: Proceedings of the 5th Conference of Professional Knowledge Management, Solothurn, Switzerland (2009)

[26] Reiner, H.: Aufbau des Service Level Managements mithilfe eines Semantic MediaWiki+, Diploma Thesis, HTW Aalen (2009)

[27] Vargo, S.L., Maglio, P.P., Akaka, M.A.: On value and value co-creation: a service systems and service logic perspective. European Management Journal 26, 145–152 (2008)

[28] Kambil, A., Friesen, G.B., Sundaram, A.: Co-creation: A new source of value. Outlook Magazine 3, 23–29 (1999)

[29] Tether, B.: Do Services Innovate (Differently)? Insights from the European Innobarometer Survey. Industry and Innovation 12, 153–184 (2005)

[30] Lusch, R.F., Vargo, S.L., Brien, M.: Competing through service: Insights from service-dominant logic. Journal of Retailing 83, 5–18

[31] Payne, A., Storbacka, K., Frow, P.: Managing the co-creation of value. Journal of the Academy of Marketing Science 36, 83–96 (2008)

[32] van der Wind, B.S.F.: The Use of Customers in the New Service Development Process. Writer 4, 9–2007

[33] Papazoglou, M.P., Heuvel, W.: Service oriented architectures: approaches, technologies and research issues. The VLDB Journal 16, 389–415 (2007)

[34] Steen, M.W.A., Strating, P., Lankhorst, M.M., ter Doest, H., Iacob, M.E.: Service-Oriented Enterprise Architecture. In: Service-oriented Software System Engineering: Challenges and Practices (2005)

Models, Social Tagging and Knowledge Management – A fruitful Combination for Process Improvement

Michael Prilla

Information and Technology Management
Institute for Applied Work Science, Ruhr University of Bochum
Universitaetsstr. 150, 44780 Bochum, Germany
michael.prilla@rub.de

Abstract. Process Models are the tools of choice for capturing business processes and communicating them among staff. In this paper, an approach focusing support in creation and usage as well as the dissemination of process models in organization is described, intending to improve business processes. To accomplish this, the approach makes use of social tagging as an approach to integrate process models into knowledge management (KM). In the paper, the empirical foundation of the approach is described and a corresponding prototype implementing a tagging mechanism for process models is discussed.

Topics: New possibilities for the design of business processes by social software (1), phases of the BPM lifecycle affected by social software (2), use of social software to support business processes and new kinds of business knowledge representation by social production (3).

1 Introduction: Processes, Models and Knowledge Management

Process models are well-established tools in business. They capture business processes as well as related knowledge and are used for a multitude of purposes [6]. However, the active usage of process models in organizations is usually limited to a small group of people and models are usually not well known as resources in organizations [22]. This paper argues that the dissemination of models and their active use by more users can help to get input from those both interested and competent enough to improve processes: people involved in the conduction of processes [24].

The value of models aside from being expert tools for the documentation, creation and maintenance of processes in organizations is widely neglected. It can be found in models capturing knowledge related to processes, mediating its acquisition [15] and helping to solve related problems [17]. Nevertheless, because of poor findability and acceptance of models [20], they are scarcely used. Additionally, modelling as a knowledge intensive task [22] can obviously benefit from KM providing relevant information and a context for understanding [17].

Therefore, *research questions* concerned with the work presented here are which needs are imposed by the current situation of neglected process models, how these needs can be diminished and how the support needed can be implemented.

S. Rinderle-Ma et al. (Eds.): BPM 2009 Workshops, LNBIP 43, pp. 266–277, 2010.
© Springer-Verlag Berlin Heidelberg 2010

Overcoming scarce usage and supporting model creation mean shifting attention towards models and intertwining them with other content. In this paper I argue that this can be done by semantic integration of process models into KM. In a previous analysis, *formalized semantics* were identified to not suit the needs of this purpose [22]. Therefore, I use *social tagging* for models and other content in order to abstract from content types and focus on relevance instead in KM.

To reach the goals described above, models as the best way to capture processes [4], [10] have to be considered an important factor in process improvement. This is an observation backed up by earlier findings on the role models play in business process improvement [12]. I argue that the approach presented here provides a step towards in making models artefacts of everyday use and therefore helps to improve business processes. The approach contributes to the improvement of business processes in multiple ways. First, social tagging provides access to processes for all stakeholders and thus disseminates models in organizations. Second, by making people aware of models, it increases the chance that those formerly excluded will give valuable feedback to business processes. Third, it supports the creation of models by providing relevant information and therefore improves the quality of models and processes.

The *concept* of the approach has been described in [20] and *basic requirements* of it have been presented in [22]. This paper focuses on an *empirical study* to analyze tasks and respective *requirements*. As an outcome of that, the paper presents a *prototype* of process model tagging, which is tailored to the needs found in the study. In what follows, section 2 gives an overview of the approach's background. In section 3, the empirical study is described and the resulting fields of support are analyzed for requirements. Section 4 then describes the prototype. The paper concludes with a discussion of *related work* (section 5) and an outlook to further work.

2 Social Tagging for the Integration of Process Models into KM

Knowledge Management aims at "capture, validation, and subsequent technology-mediated dissemination of valuable knowledge from experts"[3]. This aim makes no difference between content types. Thus, if knowledge is supposed to be shared, we should not rely on separate systems for different content, and we should not favour one content type over the other, be it text or models. The current situation of KM favouring textual content while neglecting process models and the existence and usage of specialized management tools for models counteracts this demand. Thus, we should aim for an integrative solution capitalizing on the potential of models in KM.

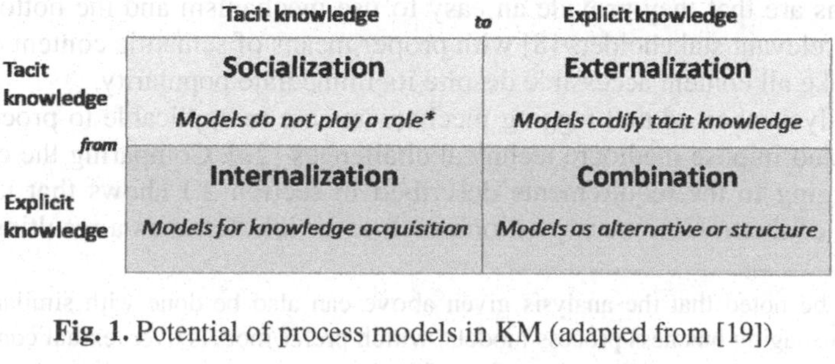

	Tacit knowledge	to	Explicit knowledge
Tacit knowledge *from*	**Socialization** *Models do not play a role**		**Externalization** *Models codify tacit knowledge*
Explicit knowledge	**Internalization** *Models for knowledge acquisition*		**Combination** *Models as alternative or structure*

Fig. 1. Potential of process models in KM (adapted from [19])

The potential benefits of process models being visible and accessible in KM applications is grounded in the distinction of *tacit and explicit knowledge* [18]. Tacit knowledge is in the head of people and not codified anywhere, whereas explicit knowledge is formalized by e.g. writing it down. In Fig. 1, this distinction and the transitions between knowledge being tacit or explicit are shown with respect to the potential benefits of models in KM. First, as shown in the upper right corner, models capture tacit knowledge related to processes. Therefore, neglecting them means leaving out relevant knowledge. Second (lower left), models should be usable to acquire process related knowledge. Third, models should be available for users in order to combine different content types (Fig. 1, lower right), which, as Nonaka [19] states, is what "can lead to new knowledge". Neglecting existing model content hinders this process[1]. Therefore, the integration of models into KM bears potential for publicity and improvement of processes in organizations (see also [12]).

2.1 Basic Requirements for the Integration of Process Models into KM

Currently, to my knowledge there is no KM system properly supporting process models as its content. In a prior analysis [22], I found some basic requirements for the integration of models into KM: First, *semantic content description* to overcome the "complexity gap" [22] by providing homogeneous access to different content types such textual content and process models. Second, semantic content description must not be implemented at the expense of user effort. Such a mechanism has to provide a *low usage burden* while maintaining *a high ceiling* to provide a sufficient surplus in content handling. This makes formalized semantics such as Ontologies less applicable for this task. Third, *all stakeholders of processes have to be integrated*, bringing together their perspectives of how process can be improved [24]. Fourth, such functionality has to be *integrated into daily work tasks*, meaning that these tasks must be tightly integrated into existing tools and give users a benefit for their sharing behaviour [9]. In [22], these requirements are analyzed and as the result of that, social tagging is proposed as a mechanism fulfilling all requirements.

2.2 Social Tagging for Process Models

The approach to integrate process models into KM proposed here is based on the mechanism of social tagging. *Tagging* means assigning unrestricted keywords to all kinds of content. It becomes *social* when tags are shared among users and different users are allowed to tag the same content unit. The key learnings from social tagging applications are that they provide an easy to use mechanism and the bottom-up integration of relevant stakeholders [8] with proper means of semantic content description [7] and make all content accessible despite its immediate popularity.

Our analysis showed that tagging mechanisms are in applicable to process modelling tools and impose mediocre technical challenges [20]. Comparing the characteristics of tagging to the requirements described in section 2.1 shows that tagging can fulfil each of them. However, questions such as which demands a resulting approach

---

[1] It should be noted that the analysis given above can also be done with similar results for systems managing business process models, which prefer models over textual content and are usually used by only a small number of people.

has to cover and how tagging can be applied to process models remain unanswered. The remaining paper will be focused on this question.

3   Model Knowledge Usage in Practice: An Empirical View

To analyze the daily practices and KM needs of people using models, a series of six interviews with practitioners was conducted[2]. The participants worked in different business such as call centre organization, public energy supply and software development. All participants had a graduate degree and their age varied from 36 to 53. With the exception of one interviewee, they had more than ten years of experience in using models, making them viable candidates for the interviews.

The interviews covered the entire lifecycle of models, including their creation, the integration of knowledge into models, their exchange, their understanding by users and their reuse. Afterwards, the interviews were transcribed and a catalogue of codes was developed out of the resulting material. The interviews were then analyzed according to patterns of support needed in the work with models and seven fields of support were identified. In this section, these fields are described and analyzed.

3.1   Observations from Practice: Seven Fields of Support

In the interviews with practitioners, a detailed set of requirements complementing the basic ones described in section 2.1 could be identified. In this set, the abovementioned problems of lacking support in model creation and usage, neglected content and inadequate support for the acquisition of knowledge are present as cross cutting concerns. The set consists of seven fields of support: *creating models, ensuring understanding and quality of models, using models together, using models for communication with others, finding and contextualizing models, connecting models with other content* and *facilitating and extending model usage*. In what follows, these fields are described including sub-tasks, observations and resulting requirements[3].

Table 1. Support field „Creating Models"

Task	Observation	Requirement
Information research and integration	Hard to find matching content and competent partners needed during the modelling process.	Provide a means to match available content in KM, the current model and expertise.
Model reuse	Hard to find similar models for reuse.	Provide a means to find models by content similarity.

The first field identified is model *creation* (Table 1). In the interviews, respondents mostly reported on *information research and its integration* into models for the preparation of modelling as well as *model reuse* during the modelling process. For the first task, interviewees described the process of modelling as preceded by collecting

---

[2] To ensure anonymity, I will refer to the interviewees as I1 to I6 in this section.
[3] Please note that for the sake of brevity, the description of the analysis can only cover a choice of observations and requirements here.

information on the respective processes and that their sources for this are people working in processes and documents describing the process. They stated that it was often hard to find the right people or content for the preparation and model reuse: "(...) for a co-worker in a subsidiary, there is no occasion in which he becomes aware of models, (...) diagrams drown in the depths of IT"[4] (I2). From a *requirements* perspective, model creation and reuse need to be supported by mechanisms to find relevant content and people. This results in the need to match content available in KM systems, models and a description of users' expertise. Integrating this into everyday work means coupling such mechanisms with modelling tools.

Table 2. Support field „Ensuring Understanding and Quality of Models"

Task	Observation	Requirement
Ensuring Understanding	Hard to find relevant information when encountering problems in understanding.	Provide a means to retrieve information relevant for understanding.
Assuring Quality	Relevant people for approval hard to reach.	Provide a means to distribute models for expert approval according to their content.

In the interviews, participants put an emphasis on means to *ensure both understanding and quality of models* for their later use (Table 2). For better understanding and higher quality of models, they combined models with additional textual descriptions, named model elements carefully and tried to get their models approved by stakeholders: "(...) the quality of a model is closely related to the amount of people that have talked about the model" (I3). However, they felt badly supported by existing tools in this task: "It would be nice if we could find additional content for models" (I5). They reported that they had a hard time to reach acceptance and find people to approve models. These observations result in two *requirements*. First, the understanding of models should be fostered by providing relevant content to users encountering these problems. Second, for approval a mechanism to reach people both competent and willing to give feedback on a model should be available.

Table 3. Support field „Using Models together"

Task	Observation	Requirement
Model exchange	Task-specific distribution hinders availability.	Provide a central repository for models with task-specific notifications.
	Hard to share and sustain descriptions of models.	Provide a means for context descriptions sticking to models.

Interviewees reported several means they use for the *exchange of models* (Table 3) with others such as email, shared folders and content repositories, which worked reasonably well but had some shortcomings: "(...) and then it is present somewhere,

---

[4] The statements of interviewees have been translated from German to English by the author.

because you sent it by email and it is bound to a certain sent-folder" (I1). They stated that it was difficult to properly describe models to make others aware of their relevance and that additional text in emails was not sufficient as it is bound to the email and provides no help if the model is used in practice. Most interviewees reported that the result of this situation is a lack of transparency concerning which models are available and thus sharing is difficult. From a *requirements* point of view, model sharing should be supported by a centrally accessible repository supporting users willing to share content to point people to models relevant for specific tasks. Additionally, the description of model content has to be attached directly to models.

Table 4. Support field „Using Models for Communication with others"

Task	Observation	Requirement
Using Models as communication artefacts	Lacking awareness of models as information sources	Make models as findable in repositories as textual content is.
	Notion of models as technical artefacts.	Provide a content description of models in order to demonstrate their relevance.

Most interviewees regarded *models as a means for communication* (Table 4). They reported different variants for this, including models as guidance in discussions and models as a specification for work processes. They also reported that models were not as frequently used by people as they intended them to be because people were not aware of models as relevant information or do not accepted them: "(…) they are mostly regarded as my artefact" (I2). There are two *requirements* stemming from this. First, to make people aware of models, they have to be able to find them as easy as they can find textual content. Second, in order to show that models contain valuable content the content of a model has to be made explicit to users.

Table 5. Support field „Finding and Contextualizing Models"

Task	Observation	Requirement
Searching and Finding	Search engines cannot use the content of a model.	Provide a means to make a model's content description accessible to search engines.
Naming and structuring	Model names are not sufficient for describing models.	Provide a means to give content descriptions extending model names.

Interviewees reported that *finding and contextualizing models* (Table 5) was hard to accomplish due to the lacking fit of existing retrieval methods. Rather than searching models for a long time, they would usually redo a model: "if I can't find it quickly, I stop searching" (I3). Even for corporate naming conventions, they stated that they were of no help: "these conventions should be adapted continuously, but this is not done properly, making them hard to use" (I4). The basic *requirement* stemming from these observations is that if models are to be found, a retrieval engine has to include a description of their content, which must not rely on proper naming, as 'proper' is dependent on both search intention and context. On the contrary, there has to be a means to provide context information to a model *besides* its name.

Table 6. Support field „Connecting Models with other Content"

Task	Observation	Requirement
Connecting models with other content	Manual linkage of content is costly and erroneous.	Provide a mechanism handling models and other content equally, identifying possible relationships and proposing them to a user.

Interviewees reported that for the usage of models by others, they need to *relate models and other content* to e.g. create the documentation of their work and make it accessible to others (Table 6). They also reported that this was poorly supported in their companies and took a lot of time: "I wish there was a more lightweight way of linking content to models" (I2). This observation raises the *requirement* of easing the linkage of models and other content. For this, a mechanism handling models and other content equally and identifying possible relationships by their content and proposes these to a user should be provided.

Table 7. Support field „Facilitating and Extending Model Usage"

Task	Observation	Requirement
Extending the user group	Scarce usage of models in organizations.	Provide a mechanism pointing out models as relevant sources of information.
Supporting target groups	Specific models versions needed for each target group.	Provide a mechanism to generate views from existing models.

Concerning the *facilitation and extension of models use* (Table 7), the interviewees stated that models are usually bound to a small group made up by e.g. analysts and developers. They explained this by the poor acceptance of models and stated that they needed users to see the relevance of models. Additionally, they reported that they needed adequate models for different target groups such as clients, developers and users, but had no tool support for this task: "I don't see any need to discuss design details with a client" (I3). Two *requirements* result from these observations. First, for promoting model usage in organizations, people should be supported in perceiving the relevance of models. Second, it should be possible to generate versions of models for target groups and provide these versions to them in a KM application.

3.2 Discussion

As can be seen from the analysis above, topics like knowledge acquisition, preventing the loss of knowledge and supporting the creation and active use of process models are present in nearly all fields of support. Moreover, the analysis shows the potential the approach bears for the improvement of business processes. As an example, for *creating models*, it is obvious that if a modeller is provided with relevant information in preparation and modelling, the quality of the model and the corresponding process will increase. Other fields of support such as *using models for communication* or *finding and contextualizing models* underpin this – if people in organizations have a better chance to find models and learn about processes from them, the quality of processes captured in these models is likely to benefit from their input.

4 Applying Social Tagging in a Modelling Tool

From a technical perspective tagging mechanisms are not hard to integrate into existing applications due to manageable complexity and their straightforward mode of operation. After I integrated it in conformance to the requirements [22], it had to be tailored to the needs of the fields of support described in section 3. To face this challenge, a series of participatory design workshops was conducted, including potential users and experts in the field. In the workshops, we iterated through the fields of support described in section 3. The resulting prototype consists of the modelling tool SeeMe [13] and the KM application Kolumbus 2 [21]. In what follows, some features of the resulting prototypes will be demonstrated and related to the fields of support described above. These features represent a choice of the overall design and are restricted to the work on the process modelling tool. It should be noted, however, that tagged process models are analyzed in the KM application, which possesses a tagging mechanism and corresponding functionality to search and structure content by tags (see [20] for more details).

4.1 Prototypical Implementation: A Tagging Mechanism for Process Models

The integration of a tagging mechanism into a process modelling tool has to start with *enabling the assignment of tags* to process models. Considering the structure of process models, this has to be done on three levels: elements, groups of elements or subprocedures and models. Fig. 2 shows an example for basic tagging support in process models. In the figure, the element "Action 3.1" is tagged as a single element and the elements "Action 3.2" and "Action 3.3" are tagged as a group of elements (indicated by a box around them). While the former is important for the reception of information from the KM application, the latter provides a means to mark up groups and share them with others.

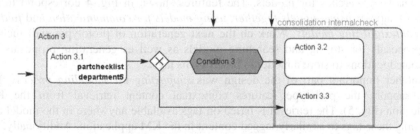

Fig. 2. Tagging in Process Models

Considering the basic requirements described in section 2.1, a tagging mechanism has to be *smoothly integrated* into a process modelling tool. Therefore, tagging was not implemented as an isolated feature to be reached from an extra menu but integrated into existing dialogues used for e.g. naming elements (Fig. 3).

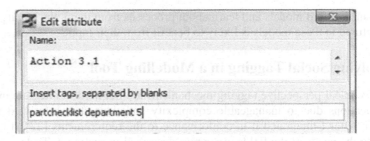

Fig. 3. Smooth integration of tagging into the modeling tool

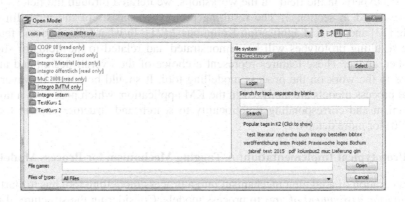

Fig. 4. Tag-based support for searching and opening models in a KM tool

An important part of the design was focused to the *connection of the modeling tool to the KM application*. The resulting prototype currently supports adding tags to models and using these tags for storing the models in the KM application (Fig. 4, left side). The other way round, models and other content can be explored with tag-based navigation from the application (Fig. 4, right side). This e.g. enables a user to perform contexualized searches for models. The features shown in Fig. 4 correspond to the fields of support *using models together*, *using models for communication* and *finding and contextualizing models*. Work on the next generation of prototypes will include tag proposals for storing and searching models as well as generating proposals for adequate locations to store a model to based on its tags.

Another important part of the design was *supporting the modeling process*. For such support, the prototype features contextual content retrieval from the KM application (Fig. 5). The retrieval is based on tags available anywhere in the model and matching these tags to similarly tagged content in the KM application. Additionally, the names of elements are parsed and used as tags for the search. Figure 4 shows this function in the prototype. In the figure, similar content to the tags assigned to „Activity 3.1" is displayed and offered to the user. This feature corresponds to the field of *creating models*, enabling modelers to find and intergrate existing knoweldge on processes in a model. It also applies to the field of *ensuring understanding of models* as well as *connecting models with other content* by interrelating similar content found by tags with the model currently viewn.

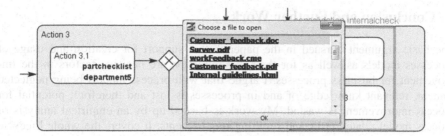

Fig. 5. Tag-based contextual content retrieval from the KM tool

Besides the integration of tagging into a process modeling tool, the mechanism is intended to combine the tool with a KM application in order to foster the findability of models and contextually share models with others. Corresponding fields of support such as *facilitating model usage* and aspects of these fields not covered in the description above such as *ensuring the quality of models* are covered by functionality implemented in the KM application Kolumbus 2. This system, as described in [20], [22], also has a tagging mechanism and is able to handle content on this basis.

5 Related Work

There are several research areas related to and influencing the approach presented in this paper. In the following, some of these areas are briefly sketched. A more detailed discussion and a comparison to the approach presented here can be found in [22].

Familiar research areas can be found in approaches aiming at the *management of process models* by either creating model catalogues [6] or building applications for maintaining and editing models [25]. Another familiar area can be seen in *(semantic) business process management*, which is focused to managing process execution and monitoring [11], [23]. Additionally, in KM there is an area of research on *process oriented KM*, which uses process models for navigational and structural purposes [16]. As shown in [22], all of these approaches are valuable for the problems they work on, but these problems differ from the one tackled here and therefore, these approaches do not provide a solution to the problems described above.

Recently, approaches using social software in combination with model management have appeared. In [14], the authors describe an approach using *social networks to support the work with process models* by providing recommendations for processes to people and supporting the collaboration among people and processes. The approach described in [5] puts forward the idea of *tagging process models* for their management, but while the authors provide a solid ground for this idea, they do not show a system implementing it. What can be learned from both approaches is that social software can provide benefits in the management of process models and therefore improve business processes in organizations. The second approach also shows that tagging process model is worthwhile. It corresponds with an early description [20] of the approach presented in this paper.

6 Conclusion and Further Work

The basic argument pursued in the paper is that support for creation and usage of processes models as well as for their dissemination are decisive factors in the improvement for business processes. I argue that with process models being neglected content, relevant knowledge of and in processes is lost and therefore, potential for process improvement is wasted. My work is backed up by an empirical analysis of process model related tasks and resulting requirements. It covers the whole lifecycle of process models in organizations and therefore identifies needs and problems in various aspects.

This paper presents tagging as a lightweight mechanism for semantic description and shows it that can accomplish the task of integrating process models into KM and therefore improve work with process. The resulting prototype shows how such potential benefits can be implemented in prototype aiming to tackle the problem of business process improvement and the involvement of stakeholders from a different side than existing approaches do.

The approach presented here represents a concept of integrating process models into KM and should not be seen as the only way for that. Rather than that, there is potential for synergies with existing solutions, including combining it with business process management systems and other modelling and KM tools. Including such potential in future generations of the prototypes provides a both a challenge and huge potential for generalizing the approach and making it applicable in organizations.

Right now, we are developing the next generation of the prototypes and experiments to explore its impact on process model usage and process handling in organizations. This generation will use tags as guidance for storing and finding processes models as well as mechanisms to match people, content and information needs in the modelling process. Additionally, the prototype will be tailored to all needs found in the empirical work. In general, we are confident to make the approach a successful step towards the dissemination of process models in organizations and therefore to business process improvement. Concerning its benefits, the approach will have to prove whether it eases process knowledge acquisition, supports the acceptance of models and improves the quality of models created with its support.

References

1. Aurnhammer, M., Hanappe, P., Steels, L.: Integrating Collaborative Tagging and Emergent Semantics for Image Retrieval. In: Collaborative Web Tagging Workshop at WWW 2006, Edinburgh (2006)
2. Brooks, C., Montanez, N.: Improved annotation of the blogosphere via autotagging and hierarchical clustering. In: Proceedings of the 15th international conference on World Wide Web, pp. 625–632 (2006)
3. Dalkir, K.: Knowledge Management in Theory and Practice. Elsevier Butterworth Heinemann, Burlington (2005)
4. Dori, D.: Words from pictures for dual-channel processing. CACM 51, 47–52 (2008)
5. Fengel, J., Rebstock, M., Nüttgens, M.: Modell-Tagging zur semantischen Verlinkung heterogener Modelle. In: Proceedings of EMISA 2008. Auswirkungen des Web 2.0 auf Dienste und Prozesse. EMISA Fachgruppentreffen (2008)

6. Fettke, P., Loos, P., Zwicker, J.: Business process reference models: Survey and classification. In: Bussler, C.J., Haller, A. (eds.) BPM 2005. LNCS, vol. 3812, pp. 469–483. Springer, Heidelberg (2006)

7. Golder, S., Huberman, B.: The structure of collaborative tagging systems. Journal of Information Science, 198–208 (2006)

8. Grudin, J.: Enterprise Knowledge Management and Emerging Technologies. In: Proceedings of HICSS 2006 (2006)

9. Grudin, J.: Why CSCW Applications fail: Problems in the Design and Evaluation of organizational Interfaces. In: Proceedings of CSCW 1988, pp. 85–93 (1988)

10. Harel, D., Rumpe, B.: Meaningful Modelling: What's the Semantics of "Semantics"? Computer 37, 64–72 (2004)

11. Hepp, M., Roman, D.: An Ontology Framework for Semantic Business Process Management. In: Proceedings of Wirtschaftsinformatik (2007)

12. Herrmann, T., Hoffmann, M.: The Metamorphoses of Workflow Projects in their Early Stages. Computer Supported Cooperative Work 14, 399–432 (2005)

13. Herrmann, T., Hoffmann, M., Kunau, G., Loser, K.: A modelling method for the development of groupware applications as socio-technical systems. Behaviour & Information Technology 23, 119–135 (2004)

14. Koschmider, A., Song, M., Reijers, H.A.: Social Software for Modelling Business Processes. In: First Workshop on Business Process Management and Social Software (2008)

15. Larkin, J., Simon, H.: Why a Diagram is (Sometimes) Worth Ten Thousand Words. Cognitive Science 11, 65–100 (1987)

16. Maier, R., Remus, U.: Towards a framework for knowledge management strategies: process orientation as strategic starting point. In: Proceedings of HICSS 2001 (2001)

17. Neuwirth, C., Kaufer, D.: The role of external representations in the writing process: Implications for the design of hypertext-based writing tools. In: Proceedings of the second annual ACM conference on Hypertext, pp. 319–341 (1989)

18. Nonaka, I., Takeuchi, H.: The Knowledge Creating Company. Harvard Business Review 69, 96–104 (1991)

19. Nonaka, I.: A dynamic theory of organizational knowledge creation. Organization Science, 14–37 (1994)

20. Prilla, M., Herrmann, T.: Semantically Integrating Heterogeneous Content: Applying Social Tagging as a Knowledge Management Tool for Process Model Development and Usage. In: Proceedings of IKNOW 2007 (2007)

21. Prilla, M., Ritterskamp, C.: Finding Synergies: Web 2.0 and Collaboration Support Systems. In: Proceedings of COOP 2008 (2008)

22. Prilla, M.: Semantic Integration of Process Models into Knowledge Management: A Social Tagging Approach. In: Proceedings of BIS 2008 (2008)

23. Smith, H., Fingar, P.: Business Process Management: The Third Wave. Meghan-Kiffer Press (2003)

24. Suchman, L.: Office Procedure as Practical Action: Models of Work and System Design. ACM Transactions on Office Information Systems 1, 320–328 (1983)

25. Thomas, O., Scheer, A.: Tool Support for the Collaborative Design of Reference Models - A Business Engineering Perspective. In: System Sciences, HICSS 2006 (2006)

Micro Workflow Gestural Analysis:
Representation in Social Business Processes

Ben Jennings and Anthony Finkelstein

University College London
London, UK
b.jennings@cs.ucl.ac.uk, a.finkelstein@cs.ucl.ac.uk

Abstract. Enterprises are finding limitations with current modelling and hierarchical methodologies which have human agents as a key component. By requiring a priori knowledge of both workflow and human agents, when an unanticipated deviation occurs, the rigidity of such models and hierarchies reveals itself. This paper puts forward the position of an inversion of current approaches, in a real time context, by analysing the specific lightweight ad hoc processes, or flexible micro workflows, which occur in expert driven domains. Using gestural analysis of human agents within such flexible micro workflows in combination with social analysis techniques, new flexibility in business processes can be found. These techniques can be applied in differing expert driven problem domains and the resultant data from such analysis of gestural meta data can help to build a reputational representation of human agents within specific business processes, which will assist in finding the most appropriate human agent for a given task.

Keywords: Workflow, Reputation, Identity, Representation, RMR, WFMS.

1 Introduction

Business processes in many domains require human agent expertise. With the growth of Service Orientated Architecture (SOA) in the enterprise, integrating human agents into business processes is a focus of much work, based on hierarchical business structures and models built upon a priori data. The necessity to integrate human agents is often predicated upon the requirements of a process to react to uncertainty. The dichotomy of this methodology creates a schism between the desire to prescribe specific models and the stipulation for flexibility. Such rigidity in processes has led to the exploration in other areas, specifically that of open and social based software.

This paper puts forward the position that in some domains, specifically those that are expertise driven, applying a ridged hierarchical model may not result in the most advantageous results. By leveraging social software analysis, a different approach is possible, revealing a more subtle manner of lightweight ad hoc processes, or flexible micro workflow. Rather than presenting a specific architecture, this paper presents a grounding conceptual framework. From this foundation layer, a bifurcated analysis of human agent interaction with both data and other such agents can reveal new reputational data. This reputational data about human agents will reveal a basis from which to perform gestural analysis of human agent social intercommunication.

S. Rinderle-Ma et al. (Eds.): BPM 2009 Workshops, LNBIP 43, pp. 278–290, 2010.

The rest of this paper is structured in five main sections. In the first section, business practices in relation to processes and social systems are examined. The second section looks at current business approaches with respect to human agents and classification. Sections three and four present a different social mechanism from which to gain new insight into both the discovery and analysis of human agent reputation in the context of social interaction. The concluding section provides a final framing of the new social concepts presented in this paper and how they can provide the basis for a novel mechanism from which to create new social business processes.

2 Business Practices and Social Systems

Flexible workflow and related computer systems have been an area of research for over thirty years. As computer technology has advanced and massively networked systems have become readily available, the concept of what a computer system can provide, in the context of business processes, has shifted. This section of the paper will outline general trends in business processes, specifically as they related to human agents. The subsequent subsection will address the attention that is being captured by the possible application of social software techniques to business processes.

A fundamental concept, which emerges when looking at the work carried out in business processes, is that of creating abstractions to increase flexibility in the execution of work. In the early periods of the 70s and 80s, there was the shift towards design time execution via an abstracted modelling process. When computing resources became less constrained in the 90s and moving forward, there has been the shift towards run time execution of work via Service Oriented Architecture (SOA) and composition of services. A key component of this work has been human agents. Earlier work in this area looked at workflow support tools and SOA seeks to address human agents via a services metaphor such as a Worklist (see section 3).

Approaches in the space of the utilisation of human agents within business practices have, in the main, taken the position of complete domain and process knowledge. Working from the basis of full a priori knowledge an abstraction in the form of a workflow model or hierarchy of abstracted human agents would be created. Whilst in fixed criteria processes, where there is little ambiguity or unanticipated deviation, this approach is highly appropriate. In expert driven domains involving human agents, such a priori approaches lead to fragility of process. Business processes which are either poorly defined or are inherently not precise, such as in exploratory domains, perform sub-optimally when using these constrictive methodologies.

Nuanced human agent behaviour, whose nature is typical when working within an expert domain, can be seen to be problematic when using contemporary approaches to business processes, as has now been framed. A logical source of alternatives from which enterprises are seeking to draw would be that of the open social software domain. The next subsection will outline some of the potential in this area.

2.1 Enterprise Getting Social

Social software has many forms, such as wikis, blogging and micro messaging services. There are also strong social similarities within standardised software development tools, for example: mailing lists and ticketing systems. These similarities may be seen in the low barriers to entry: from commenting on a blog to signing up for a mailing list; and human agent to human agent communication working on a communal goal: collaboratively editing content on a wiki to produce a document to a discussions on a ticketing system as to the most effective solution for a bug.

There are two main facets of interest within the enterprise in relation to engagement with social software: direct interaction with customers and encouraging independence of human agents within a business process. The first of these, direction interaction, may be seen as the call for "markets as conversations" [21] and serves to increase the potential value to both the customer and the provider, the provider in this instance being the process stake holders within the enterprise. This increased value may come from such interactions as eliciting feedback on products [7] or support for fellow customers [20]. This manner of interaction is not the main focus of this paper. The social software methodology which is the primary focus of this paper is that brought about by encouraging independence.

Much attention has been created by the success of such social productions from Wikipedia and the Linux project. In addition to the independence of process that these projects share, an additional feature is that of still having a supporting hierarchy. The *Linus doesn't scale* event [29] led to the creation of a supporting infrastructure hierarchy of *trusted lieutenants*. There is a similar notion within Wikipedia of the Wikipedians [3], a trusted subset of the contributors to the project with an addition of a maintenance role to ensure quality and reduce vandalism. Adopting social software practices does not inherently mean having an entirely flat hierarchical structure or process. Lowering the cost of entry by ad hoc flexible micro workflows encourages the bounded ecosystem to contribute but business processes can still maintain an underpinning process mechanism. There is now a sense of the problem space which flexible micro workflows looks to address. In the next section, contemporary approaches to the integration of human agents within business processes will be outlined. This will then form the basis for the requirement for a more flexible approach presented in section 4.

3   Top Down Thinking

A priori thinking has been touched upon in the previous section of this paper. This top down thinking is an evident pattern found when analysing business practices and has seen great success in many business domains. This section of the paper will present some of the strengths and weakness of this approach. The nature of human agents within business processes will be discussed, then the differential between processes, and where flexibility presents an issue. The last topic raised in this section will discuss the classification strategies commonly used in modelling and hierarchical approaches and how this leads to fragility in flexible business processes. This will put in context the lack of social interaction of the human agents within such a process.

A workflow is a formal, or implementation specific, representation of a business process. A business process has been defined as: "... any activity or group of activities that takes an input, adds value to it, and provides an output to an internal or external customer. Processes use an organization's resources to provide definitive results" [14].

This definition gives the notion of adding value to an input. Optimising processes for human agents, as mentioned above, is the focus of this paper. With the above definition, those human agents are those likely to be adding value to such a process, thus previous approaches to the integration of human agents will frame the discussion presented in sections 4 and 5.

3.1 Previous Human Integration

In the period of the 1970s to 1980s, when computer systems were first being applied to the problem of flexible workflows, there were initial hard constraints of the expense of computational power. This led to centralised decision support systems and interoffice communication (groupware) being the first flexible workflow problem, in relation to human agent integration, to be tackled [19]. These first steps in integrating computer based systems to increase flexibility in workflow had issues such as brittle implementation, lack of interoperability and requiring too much upfront work by the users [11].

A wide variety of approaches to groupware solutions have been explored and it is beyond the scope of this paper to review them. Two brief examples show some significance of the issues from this period, those of computational expense: The Information Lens [22] was a tool that, via proprietary extensions to a mail server and email clients, allowed the users of the system to add meta data to email. Meta data could then be processed by rules on the client systems to automate some actions. This approach highlights the problem of computational power constraint, depending on human agents to do all of the processing. Increased upfront learning time for users will decrease the likelihood of adoption. This low adoption is due to the dependancy on custom client and server replacement software and the upfront user cost. There was also no sense of aggregation from this human annotation of data, or of mining social information from such data.

The second example from this period was a tool which was studied for potential deployment by Pacific Bell [4] called The Coordinator. This product was intended to combine group email, calendaring and word processing to improve focus on related conversations. The system highlights some of the problems outlined in this time period: difficulty learning the system due to limited interface, proprietary implementation leading to lack of interoperability and rigidity. With such a system one of the users reported frustration with the system "worse than a lobotomized file clerk". These two brief examples highlight a problem with the integration of human agents, that of prescriptive behavioural constraints. Rather than providing a low barrier to entry ad hoc approach, the systems enforce interaction mechanisms in a predetermined ridged manner.

3.2 Models and Abstracted Humans

From as early as 1977, putting abstractions in place to facilitate modelling of processes have been worked on in such examples as Business Decision Language (BDL)[12] and in Zisman's PhD work on office procedures [41]. Significant further work on this problem space has been carried out furthering the abilities and scope in the modelling of business processes [27,30]. A more complete look at some of the evolution of the modelling abstraction in relation to flexible workflow is outside the scope of this paper but other work has been done in this area [18]. As business has shifted more of its core process components online, the ability to interconnect those parts became of more importance. The emergence of Service Oriented Architecture (SOA) enabled some of these requirements. By putting in place a clean, defined interface to logical units of work, interconnection of services was possible. The modelling concepts were extended by an industry driven modelling language called BPEL. With this extended modelling abstraction in place, a conceptual shift occurred within the actual steps of the business process. The abstractions free the workflow from specific interdependencies [13] in the parts of the workflow and allow interchangeable steps themselves.

Whilst the abstraction of steps within a business process model adapts well to computer service driven areas, human agent integration presents a more challenging issue. The most common approach to solving this problem is the integration of a so called Work List Web Service [6]. The general notion behind this concept is to present the services stack with a human agent abstraction as a Web Service, providing a generalised interface with which to interact. Other mechanisms have been used in order to capture human generated interactions [8], but the Work List metaphor, or variant thereof is the most prevalent. Extensions to BPEL specifically targeting the modelling of human agents have been proposed, BPEL4People and WS-HumanTask [33], but are only at the initial OASIS procedural stages and look to model abstractions in a service context.

The SOA approach to human agent integration has a significant issue as it has no notion of finding the most appropriate human agent to perform a specific workflow instance. By abstracting away differing human agent abilities, other than in broad sub groupings of hierarchal structure, the very nature of expertise and social interaction is hidden. The last subsection in Top Down Thinking looks at the fundamental tenant of both modelling and hierarchical abstraction, classification.

3.3 Aristotelian Classification

Both previous subsections have essentially been focused on classification; in the case of subsection 3.1, the classification was focused on finding an abstracted sense of groups of human agents within a process and in subsection 3.2, a mechanism for classifying human agents into roles to be addressed as a generic service. Such generalisations can be seen as a top down approach to finding the fundamental nature of either the business process, or the human agent within such a process. Top down classification, or nesting, can be traced from the Aristotelian concepts [1] of categories as definitions in a tree structure. Rather than looking for individual traits of a specific instance of either an ad hoc process or a human agent, such nesting seeks to find an abstraction that can be fitting to many instances, so any agent or workflow found to fit into such a classification may serve equally well. This approach fits well with standardised computer modelling which tends to search for the general case.

The hierarchal modelling paradigm, while useful for deterministic production style business processes [23], captures neither specialisation nor enables unique or short lived ad hoc processes. Therefore a new paradigm needs to be included in current methodologies to facilitate more complex styles of interactions, particularly where interaction of expert human agents is required. In order to find the most appropriate human agent to carry out a specific task within a complex workflow, rather than creating broad generalisations in grouping of abilities, this paper proposes a bottom up ad hoc approach to classification via a flexible micro workflows metaphor in the context of meta data, or gestures, created by human agent experts in the execution of their work and by social interaction with fellow agents in larger business processes. The next section of this paper will present such a social conceptual space.

4   Flexible Micro Workflows

In the previous section of this paper (3), the normative approach to human agent analysis was put forward and some of the inherent limitations examined. In the next two sections of this paper, an alternative, multi-layered approach to social business processes will be presented. The first, flexible micro workflows, will examine a new method for the analysis of inter-agent activities. The subsequent section, Gestural Analysis, will present a bifurcated approach to the analysis of social interactions.

There is an asymmetry in the relation between the top down approach (see section 3) and the human agents engaged in the prescribed business process. The former provides modelling tools, process mining and hierarchies whereas the human agents performing specifically assigned ad hoc steps within a workflow are viewed in the manner of black boxes. The next subsection will describe the qualities of business domains which are suited to the flexible micro workflow approach. From this domain foundation, hidden social productions will show an inverted view of black box opaque sub process. In the last subsection, an architectural approach and representational paradigm will be discussed, putting the application of flexible micro workflows in context.

4.1   Adhocracies

The traditional Service Oriented Architecture concept of ad hoc workflows tend to have a fixed concept space [5]. The architecture is based around the idea of an agent being able to either pick or create a sub workflow, or to delegate an assigned task. Other possible examples of such ad hoc workflows would be start, stop or defer for example [15]. Other non-SOA approaches can increase flexibility [2] but only via significant upfront disruptive costs via data training periods. Such flexibility would be entirely dependant on implementation and, with the state of current vendor technology, little or no interoperability would be possible.

The flexible micro workflows concept is based on two principles: no a priori knowledge and the assistance of domain experts in the execution of their work. As such, a flexible micro workflow may be defined as an expansion of a hitherto opaque node, within an exploratory domain complex workflow, whereby lightweight non-deterministic sub-process human agent interaction occurs, such as to facilitate the successful completion of said node. In the main, the standard business practices methodology comes from modelling, process mining or hierarchical creation, as mentioned in section 3. With design time abstractions, time would be taken by the workflow expert to ascertain the generalised, abstracted workflow model and, from that knowledge of the business process, to create the model or hierarchy. This is an entirely appropriate approach for many problem domains. The issue occurs when there is no perfect abstraction to reach, such as an exploratory model rather than that of a waterfall [35].

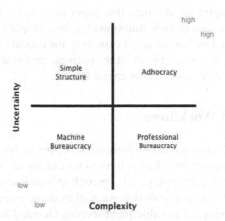

Fig. 1. Picture of high complexity and high uncertainty, based on work from [28]

Expert Driven Domains and Flexibility. In expert driven domains, or subsets of a larger workflow, where elements of expertise are required, rather than treating solely a step or node in a pre-modelled workflow as an atomic unit, flexible micro workflows suggest that there are many exploratory interactions which occur but are ignored by standard approaches, as they require a priori knowledge.

As can be seen in diagram (figure 1), in an environment where there is high complexity and high uncertainty, an adhocracy [39] is the highly probable outcome. In an adhocracy, there is inherently the lack of a priori knowledge and therefore the need for a different approach to business processes, via the concept of flexible micro workflows. By creating a mechanism that will support such lightweight, ad hoc, quick fire human to human interactions, a different kind of flexible workflow can be revealed.

4.2 Prototype Theory

There is now a sense of the inverted approach of flexible micro workflows, in the context of human agents, and in which genre of business processes the approach would be suitable. Section 3 of this paper described the standard approach of analysing business processes from an a priori position in order to construct models and hierarchies. Those procedures are, in essence, looking to create a classification ontology on a given process. In this subsection, prototype theory[32] will be discussed in conjunction with a social extension, creating a different solution space for the flexible integration of human agents. Predetermined hierarchical structures in business processes have been discussed in section 3.3. Flexible micro workflows, rather than relying on an a priori analysis, put forward the position of building an ad hoc lightweight dynamic categorisation based on the analysis of human agents carrying out their work.

Prototype theory puts forward the position of looking at base-level categories rather than classical hierarchies as "Most, if not all, categories do not have clear-cut boundaries" [40]. This position strikes clear resonance with current bottom up folksonomical strategies [24]. Flexible micro workflows looks to extend this with the application of social analysis, moving it into a multidimensional space [10]. Rather than finding a specific archetype of a business process or deriving an abstracted classification of a workflow with engaged human agents as an ancillary concept, flexible micro workflow looks to extend the prototype theory notion further. In expertise driven problem domains, building information around specific human agents enacting a given process, in the form of a layer of reputational meta data, will enable more flexible solutions when finding the most appropriate human agent for any given process. Reputation in the context of flexible micro workflows and Passive/Active Gesture Analysis (see section 5), refers to a body of data which can be acquired, analysed and represented programatically via a web service called Reputation-based Message Routing. The details of such a service fall outside the scope of this paper but are described in further detail elsewhere [17].

Many to Many Social Construct. The support to the execution of ad hoc business processes poses two fundamental classification questions: what is the nature of the task? and who is the most appropriate human agent to execute such a task? Flexible micro workflows' proposed paradigm, in the context of human agents in an expert driven domain, effectively creates a many to many mapping. This concept moves the question from that of a predetermined hierarchy created by a small group of people, through the thought process of many possible types of a class, to the social state of an ecosystem of opinions on the nature of such a class.

Just as tagging via folksonomies gives a greater degree of flexibility to providing meta data over that of formal ontologies [26], the flexible micro workflows paradigm suggests a similar many to many relationship. Formal ontological work endeavours to find the one *best* classification for a specific object by an individual, or group, of experts. Folksonomies suggest that many classifications by many people provide greater flexibility and insight into the objects and process. The classic representation of this idea comes from finding the specific Dewey classification for a new book in a formal ontology rather that of a digital representation of the same book being able to have many differing classifications. By removing the gating factor of physical limitations, new mechanisms are possible. Likewise in flexible micro workflows, rather than relying on a formal, hierarchical structuring of what is the one *best* workflow pattern, flexible micro workflows suggests a many to many, free flowing style of interaction provided by the human agents carrying out the work. The inverted concept behind the flexible micro workflows addresses the business requirements for increased flexibility in ad hoc processes and the desire to leverage social knowledge in a wisdom of crowds manner [38]. The next section will address where such social data can be mined and a bifurcated approach to the analysis of such data.

5   Passive/Active Gesture Analysis

Passive/Active Gesture Analysis, or PAGA, is an inversion of the normative behaviour when looking at human agents and flexible business processes. In the previous section, the concepts of flexible micro workflows were introduced. From this basis, Passive/Active Gesture Analysis and the inherent human and socially focused approach will be discussed and potential usage examined. The next subsection will present a bottom up approach to the analysis of human generated data in the context of flexible micro workflows which were presented in the previous section. From this basis the subsequent subsections will identify the notions and differentiation between passive and active gestures rather than a single source style aggregation of a distributed voting system [31]. In the final subsection, the notion of a representation of such gestures in the domain of a RESTful architecture will be outlined in relation to potential WFMS integration.

5.1 Hidden Social Production

Social production, in the context of business processes, may be viewed as the product of an assertion made by a human agent in the execution of an assigned task. There is another facet of human agent activity which, when used in aggregate, help to reveal a broader context from which to infer reputational data about specific human agents. It is important to note that in any such work where a system, or group thereof, is addressing specific human agents within a complex set of systems and workflows, identity must be a primary factor. Such a digital identity resource approach is outside the scope of this paper but has been examined in details with a practicable approach in another work [16]. This subsection will now look specifically at differentiating active and passive gestures.

Active Gestures. Typical data artefacts which may be present in a business process interested in adopting social software might be: a wiki, blogs, group ticking systems, cvs, mailing lists and micro messaging services such as Twitter or the open source clone, Laconica. Three simple examples of an active gesture, within the context of social production, could be: the addition of content to a wiki system within a business process, the annotation of a data object via a tagging mechanism and the process of RT (re-tweeting) a micro message of a co-agent to promote the content of the message.

Passive Gestures. Passive gestures can help bring a broader context to those of active gestures. Whereas active gestures focus on specific assertions made by an individual within the execution of a step within a business process, passive gestures may be seen as the consequence of the execution of work. Looking at the examples of social software listed above, three examples of passive gestures might be: analysing who emailed whom within mailing lists, analysing which blog posts are interacted with via a commenting mechanism and the process of reassigning a specific ticket to another human agent. This form of gesture may also be viewed as a form of ambient analysis as it looks for the patterns of human agent data generated in passing.

Passive/Active Gesture Analysis looks to combine the analysis of both of these forms of data. This approach has two benefits: the first is a broader context of data relating to a specific human agent or group thereof, the second is that by combining assertions and observed behaviour the analysis will ameliorate reciprocal behaviour. Such unchecked reciprocity could lead to human agents gaming any reputational metrics within a system for mutual benefit.

5.2 Densely Connected Microcosm

There is now a clear sense of the differentiated sources of data provided by the Passive/Active Gesture Analysis approach and where such data might be obtained within a human agent centric business process. The next two subsections will look first at the interconnectedness of such data and secondly how such data can be represented within a WFMS.

Hierarchical methods as mentioned in section 3, lead to a *vertically* orientated pattern of information flow, from the designer down to the bottom of the pyramid to the human agents executing the actual business processes. This can lead to situations, particularly in expert driven exploratory domains, of the model mismatch problem. Utilising the inverted approach suggested by Passive/Active Gesture Analysis, the method only concerns itself with the person to person communication in a densely connected *horizontal* manner. By enabling expert human agents to interact in a quick fire, ad hoc manner to form transitory workflows, a new kind of flexibility is revealed. The dense horizontal connectivity applies to that of relationships between human agents and to the data with which they interact.

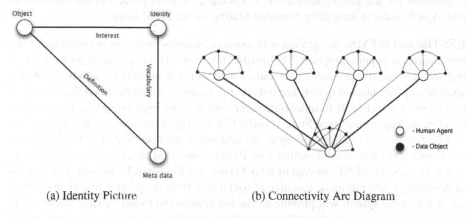

(a) Identity Picture   (b) Connectivity Arc Diagram

Fig. 2. Nodal Relationship

In the tripartite graph (figure 2a), it is possible to see the relationship between the gestures of a human agent and the data object with which they interact. The meta data can be obtained either by a passive or active gesture analysis of that agent, through a tagging mechanism or by observational data. When this dense connectivity is applied to all data objects and all human agents within the ecosystem, a deeper level of connectivity may be observed. The definition informs not only the individual and aggregate view of what the data object is but also, from that same definition, it is possible to infer the very nature of the human agents interacting with the system.

In the connectivity arc (figure 2b), the deep relationship between the creators of the data and the data itself may be seen. A deep level of nodal connection density is only revealed via an analysis of flexible micro workflows. Such a concept takes the ability of being able to execute further a workflow based on a loosely or partially specified model [34]. By utilising an inverted paradigm, rather than a traditional hierarchical abstraction, the flexible micro workflows concept optimises for direct, quick fire, human to human interaction [37] and subsequently utilises this gestural data as a basis for reputation calculations.

5.3 Representation of Social Resources via Reputation

With the structure of flexible micro workflows in place and the bifurcated data analysis suggested by Passive/Active Gesture Analysis, the open question of how such information can be represented and integrated within the context of existing WFMS remains. Whilst giving specific technical architectural details are outside the scope of this paper, this subsection will give a brief overview of the suggested approach.

There are a variety of metrics that gestural data could use to build reputation profiles dependant on the quality of domain. Such analyses could look at: *freshness*, *popularity*, *velocity* or *clustering* via a *friend of a friend (FOAF)* view. To expand upon *velocity*, in the example given in section 5.1, an analysis could look at the rate of RT (re-tweet) on a specific topic within a business process and which agents were interacting with such a RT in a given unit of time. From this basis, a system could infer related areas of reputation and which human agents within a given flexible micro workflows were responsible for the propagation thereof. Taking a broad approach to the methods of PAGA, will assist in mitigating potential Matthew Effect [25] issues.

RESTful and WFMS. Integration with existing business processes is essential for any new approach to gain adoption. The flexible micro workflow approach looks at existing and new socially produced data and as such works in adjunct to such tools. Whilst specific implementation details are outside the scope of the conceptual framework of this paper, the technical foundational layer will now be highlighted. In the work by Fielding on Representational State Transfer (REST) [9], there is notion of a lightweight architecture describing how resources are addressed and specified. The flexible micro workflows approach, in conjunction with Reputation-based Message Routing (see section 4.2), uses the REST concept of a URI (Uniform Resource Identifier). The process of providing a programmatic resource of social data from the perspective of any human agent within the system will provide a valuable component to any flexible micro workflow. Using and extending the URI makes interoperability with any legacy system trivial as all that is required is a simple HTTP call, rather than any WS-* SOA middleware.

By creating pockets of flexibility within a larger business process, the flexible micro workflow concept, in conjunction with Reputation-based Message Routing, highlights a new type of lightweight, ad hoc, human to human communication. The inversion in the hierarchy of experts provided by such an approach helps capture the nuance of human communication style in flexible processes and builds on the wisdom of the individuals executing a business process in a flexible domain: "When it really comes down to the details of responding to the currents and handling a canoe, you effectively abandon the plan and fall back on whatever skills are available to you"[36].

6 Conclusions and Future Work

This paper has identified the need for a new paradigm when looking at lightweight business processes in the context of expert driven domains. This form of lightweight ad hoc business process, or flexible micro workflow, presents a rich ground from which to create new business value by increasing flexibility and building on the expertise of individuals.

Leveraging social assets such as blogs, wikis, micro messaging and traditional development interactions, provides a rich ground from which to perform social and human agent centric analysis. These passive and active gestures (PAGA) when used in combination and aggregate, can form the basis for novel styles of analysis in the context of flexible business practices, such as velocity or FOAF. From such information, a rich reputational layer of meta data can be created and presented as a programmatic resource representation of both workflow instance and specific human agent.

The extension to this work is to create a full system, supporting such lightweight interactions. Such a system would create the notion of a reputation metric around *all* human agents within the ecosystem of interacting business processes and would provide an architecture to enable rapid intercommunication between human agents. Reputation would, in part, be derived from PAGA which would, in turn, be based upon data mined from flexible micro workflows. A reputational system would both support and help in the execution of more social and human centric bottom up business processes.

References

1. Aristotle. The metaphysics, p. 322 (January 1991)
2. Bernstein, A.: How can cooperative work tools support dynamic group process? bridging the specificity frontier. In: 2000 ACM conference on Computer supported cooperative work (January 2000)
3. Bryant, S., Forte, A., Bruckman, A.: Becoming wikipedian: transformation of participation in a collaborative online encyclopedia (2009), portal.acm.org
4. Carasik, R., Grantham, C.: A case study of cscw in a dispersed organization. In: Proceedings of the SIGCHI conference on Human factors in computing systems, pp. 61–66 (1988)
5. Chappell, D.: Understanding bpm servers (2004)
6. Clugage, K., Shaffer, D., Nainani, B.: Workflow services in oracle bpel pm 10.1.3 (2006)
7. Dellarocas, C.: The digitization of word of mouth: Promise and challenges of online feedback mechanisms. Management Science (January 2003)
8. Faustmann, G.: Configuration for adaptation–a human-centered approach to flexible workflow enactment. In: Computer Supported Cooperative Work (CSCW) (January 2000)
9. Fielding, R.: Architectural Styles and the Design of Network-based Software Architectures. PhD thesis (2000)
10. Gärdenfors, P.: Conceptual spaces: The geometry of thought (January 2000), books.google.com
11. Grudin, J.: Why cscw applications fail: problems in the design and evaluation of organizational interfaces. In: Proceedings of the 1988 ACM conference on Computer-supported ... (January 1988)
12. Hammer, M., Howe, W., Kruskal, V., Wladawsky, I.: A very high level programming language for data processing applications. Communications of the ACM (January 1977)
13. Han, Y., Sheth, A., Bussler, C.: A taxonomy of adaptive workflow management. In: Workshop of the 1998 ACM Conference on Computer Supported ... (January 1998)
14. Harrington, H.: ... process improvement: The breakthrough strategy for total quality, productivity, and competitiveness (January 1991), books.google.com
15. Iyengar, A., Jessani, V., Chilanti, M., Books, S.: Websphere business integration primer process server, bpel, sca, and soa, January 2008. IBM Press (2008)
16. Jennings, B., Finkelstein, A.: Digital identity and reputation in the context of a bounded social ecosystem. In: Proceedings of BPMS2, July 2008, p. 11 (2008)

17. Jennings, B., Finkelstein, A.: Flexible workflows: Reputation-based message routing. In: CAiSE, BPMDS, April 2008, p. 10 (2008)
18. Jennings, B., Finkelstein, A.: Service chain management: Flexible workflows. Springer, Heidelberg (2008)
19. Keen, P.: Decision support systems: the next decade. Decision Support Systems (January 1987)
20. Kling, R.: Social relationships in electronic forums: Hangouts, salons, workplaces and communities. Computerization and controversy: Value conflicts and social ... (January 1996)
21. Levine, R.: The cluetrain manifesto: The end of business as usual. Da Capo Press (January 2001)
22. Malone, T., Grant, K., Lai, K., Rao, R., Rosenblitt, D.: The information lens: An intelligent system for information sharing and coordination. Technological support for work group collaboration (January 1989)
23. Mangan, P., Sadiq, S.: On building workflow models for flexible processes. In: Proceedings of the 13th Australasian database conference- ... (January 2002)
24. Mathes, A.: Folksonomies-cooperative classification and communication through shared metadata. Computer Mediated Communication (January 2004)
25. Merton, R.: The matthew effect in science the reward and communication systems of science are considered. Science 159, 56–63 (1968)
26. Millen, D., Feinberg, J., Kerr, B.: Dogear: Social bookmarking in the enterprise. In: Proceedings of the SIGCHI conference on Human Factors in ... (January 2006)
27. Milner, R., Parrow, J., Walker, D.: A calculus of mobile processes-part i. topps.diku.dk (January 1990)
28. Mintzberg, H.: Structure in fives. Prentice-Hall, Englewood Cliffs (1983)
29. Moody, G.: Rebel code: the inside story of linux and the open source revolution, p. 344 (January 2002)
30. Petri, C.: Communication with automata (January 1966), stinet.dtic.mil
31. Resnick, P., Kuwabara, K., Zeckhauser, R.: Reputation systems (January 2000), portal.acm.org
32. Rosch, E.: Cognitive representations of semantic categories. Journal of Experimental Psychology, General (January 1975)
33. Russell, N., van der Aalst, W.M.P.: Work distribution and resource management in bPEL4People: Capabilities and opportunities. In: Bellahsène, Z., Léonard, M. (eds.) CAiSE 2008. LNCS, vol. 5074, pp. 94–108. Springer, Heidelberg (2008)
34. Sadiq, S.K., Sadiq, W., Orlowska, M.E.: Pockets of flexibility in workflow specification. In: Kunii, H.S., Jajodia, S., Sølvberg, A. (eds.) ER 2001. LNCS, vol. 2224, pp. 513–526. Springer, Heidelberg (2001)
35. Sommerville, I.: Software Engineering (2006)
36. Suchman, L.: Response to vera and simons situated action: A symbolic interpretation. Cognitive Science: A Multidisciplinary Journal (January 1993)
37. Suchman, L.: Plans and situated actions: The problem of human-machine communication (January 1994), books.google.com
38. Surowiecki, J.: The wisdom of crowds: why the many are smarter than the few and how collective wisdom shapes business, economies, societies, and nations (2004)
39. Toffler, A.: Future Shock (1970)
40. Weinberger, D.: Everything is miscellaneous: the power of the new digital disorder, p. 277 (January 2007)
41. Zisman, M.: Representation, specification and automation of office procedures. University of Pennsylvania (January 1977)

CBP Workshop

Introduction to the Third International Workshop on Collaborative Business Processes (CBP 2009)

Business Process Management (BPM) is a well researched scientific area and also established in practice. It is founded on the insight to overcome a department-isolated view of the enterprise and it fosters an enterprise-spanning understanding of the relationship between tasks and its synchronization. Thus, BPM mainly focuses on intra-corporate business processes. However, business processes have changed over the past few years. More and more enterprises work in close co-operations with other companies. Collaborative, work-sharing ways of production are constantly becoming more important.[1] Outsourcing (of business processes) is one of the hot topics in the last years.

Accordingly, the classic BPM does not cover such scenarios. Here, the approach is more to overcome the limited view of one enterprise towards an integrated understanding of the whole, cross-enterprise-spanning process of generating a product. Thus, it is important to examine BPM in a collaborative context and to extend the conventional understanding towards cross-company scenarios.

In such scenarios, business processes are no longer carried out by a single company but by a multitude of different business partners and therefore split into several independent processes. Therefore we understand a Collaborative Business Process (CBP) as a set of mutually co-ordinated business activities of coequal, autonomous organisations that aims to generate an added value in division of labour for an external customer.[2] The concept reflects the actual trend for highly flexible structures in long-term business relations. This provokes an extended demand for *flexibility*, *decentralisation* and *interoperability*. Special focus lies on interactions with all market participants – customers, suppliers, business associates, as well as competitors. Especially here, a rethinking has started from an ad-hoc, short-term technology-based implementation of data-exchange-driven co-working towards a systematic management of cross-enterprise business processes. This collaborative business process management incorporates a holistic, integrated view and covers all phases of the lifecycle of a CBP - from the strategic level to the technical blueprint, from the implementation to its controlling.[3] Within this lifecycle, we can examine how collaborative scenarios pose new challenges to BPM.

In the phase **Business Process Strategy** the current environment is analysed. Needs are identified and requirements defined. Collaborative business processes have to be identified by the business associates. The nomination of process responsible persons is no longer unique and the inclusion of independent external partners is far more complex than those of dependant departments within one company. Finally, the

---

[1] Camarinha-Matos, L. (2002): Collaborative Business Ecosystems and Virtual Enterprises. Kluwer, Boston.

[2] Werth, D. (2007): About the Nature of Collaborative Business Processes. In: Proceedings of the conference on e-Learning, e-Business, Enterprise IS. and e-Government. CSREA, Las Vegas. P. 252.

[3] Walter, P, Werth, D., Loos, P. (2007): Managing the Lifecycle of Cross-organizational Collaborative Business Processes. In: Enterprise Interoperability. Springer, Berlin. P. 397.

S. Rinderle-Ma et al. (Eds.): BPM 2009 Workshops, LNBIP 43, pp. 293–294, 2010.
© Springer-Verlag Berlin Heidelberg 2010

agreement of a common objective is subject to negotiations and demands mechanisms to align, balance and compensate.

The **Business Process Design** phase transfers this strategic concept into a process blueprint. Here, business processes are designed and modelled. However, facing collaborative structures, this design process is more a construction and engineering task than a design task. Here, the different organizations act as process part suppliers. Consequently, we need mechanisms to align, merge, integrate and consolidate partial process descriptions (usually models).

Having a specification of the intended business process, the next phase is the deployment and implementation. In contrast to a singe-enterprise environment, here the implementation spans over multiple IT-systems where each of them is in charge of only a part of the CBP. So, the overall **Business Process Execution** is distributed over several technical environments. This raises the need to propagate process state and context information over the organisational and system borders and it requires the technical overall system interoperability.

During the **Business Process Controlling** phase the monitoring of the execution and its analysis takes place. Due to the distributed execution, the need is to agree on viewable information that is distributed around the participating parties. Having given these information, they have to be composed and correlated in order to calculate meaningful figures and reports.

In all these phases, the existence of various organisational interfaces increases the complexity to co-ordinate the CBP lifecycle between companies. Therefore methodologically, the process of managing the CBP lifecycle is a CBP itself. Beyond the methodological and conceptual research challenges, in practise collaborating enterprises encounter a tooling problem. In the worst case, each partner uses its own modelling tool to describe their processes and uses its own (perhaps legacy) IT system for execution. This makes it even more difficult to manage, control and analyse real CBPs.

In this workshop, we focus on the subject collaborative business process and address the above mentioned challenges. Conceptual and technological approaches to solve those collaborative problems are presented and discussed.

October, 2009

Co-organisers
Chengfei Liu (Swinburne University of Technology, Australia)
Dirk Werth (DFKI, Germany)
Marek Kowalkiewicz (SAP Research, Australia)
Xiaohui Zhao (Swinburne University of Technology, Australia)

HLA/RTI-Based BPM Middleware for Collaborative Business Process Management

Byoung Kyu Choi, Duckwoong Lee, and Dong Hun Kang

VMS Lab., Department of Industrial & Systems Engineering, KAIST
335 Gwahak-ro, Yuseong-gu, Daejeon 305-701, Republic of Korea
{bkchoi,ldw721,donghun.kang}@vmslab.kaist.ac.kr

Abstract. Business processes in global economy need closer collaboration with partner enterprises and there is a growing need for BPM systems to support collaborative business processes. Previous researches on collaborative BPM have some shortcomings and there remains a gap between the demand and supply for collaborative BPM. This paper presents a mediator-based collaborative BPM (CBPM) framework together with a CBPM middleware implementing the CBPM framework. The CBPM middleware is built around the HLA/RTI (high level architecture/run time infrastructure) which is the de facto standard in modeling & simulation. Distinctive features of the proposed CBPM middleware include (1) it covers all workflow interoperability models specified by Workflow Management Coalition (WfMC), (2) it has a hub architecture allowing scalability and generality, (3) all interoperation messages are handled by a set of standard APIs of WfMC and of HLA/RTI so that anyone who is familiar with those APIs can easily implement the middleware.

Keywords: Workflow interoperability, collaborative BPM middleware, HLA/RTI, collaborative object model.

1 Introduction

A *workflow management system* (WfMS) defines and automatically executes workflows in order to manage the actual flow of work so that the right work is done at the right time with the right information by the right person in the organization [1]. Recently, a WfMS used for business process management (BPM) is often called a *BPM system*, with an emphasis on orchestrating operational business processes that are driven by explicit process designs. As BPM systems have expanded its coverage to the corporate level and then to the extended enterprise level, the need for workflow interoperability (or collaborative BPM) was recognized by many organizations [2, 3] and researchers [4, 5, 6, 7, 8, 9, 10]. The two terms "workflow interoperability" and "collaborative BPM" may be used interchangeably. For example, business processes often need to interact with each other, in order to synchronize the execution of their activities, to exchange process data, to request execution of services, or to notify progress in process execution [7].

S. Rinderle-Ma et al. (Eds.): BPM 2009 Workshops, LNBIP 43, pp. 295–304, 2010.

Standard workflow interoperability models were proposed by Workflow Management Coalition (WfMC) more than 10 years ago [1, 2]. Recently, a couple of frameworks for collaborative BPM were proposed [9, 10] aiming to realize the workflow interoperability models. However, [9] does not cover the parallel synchronized model and its communication structure is P2P (peer-to-peer), which may hamper its general applicability. Also, [10] has a serverless decentralized (or P2P) architecture and it is an agent-based abstract framework that has yet to be materialized. Therefore, these frameworks have these shortcomings and there remains a gap between the demand and supply for collaborative BPM. This paper aims to fill the gap by presenting a collaborative BPM middleware that is scalable and easy to implement and covers all three workflow interoperability models specified by WfMC.

The paper is organized as follows. Section 2 presents our collaborative BPM framework having hub architecture. Key elements of the propose framework are Collaboration Mediator, Collaboration Planner, Collaboration Manager and COM (collaboration object model). Section 3 presents a HLA/RTI-based collaborative BPM middleware realizing the proposed framework, followed by an illustrative implementation in the next section. Conclusions and discussions are provided in the last section.

2   Collaborative BPM Framework

2.1   Workflow Interoperability Standard

Workflow Management Coalition (WfMC) provides a workflow interoperability standard (Interface 4) for interoperation among different workflow engines [1, 2], in which three types of possible collaboration models (i.e., chained, nested sub-process, parallel synchronized) are specified. Interface 4 provides abstract specifications regarding the level of interoperability and WfXML-based message format [2, 3, 9]. The three workflow interoperability models are shown in Fig. 1.

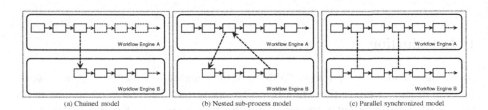

(a) Chained model   (b) Nested sub-process model   (c) Parallel synchronized model

Fig. 1. Three models of workflow interoperability [1, 2]

In the chained model of Fig. 1-(a), an activity of Workflow Engine A simply invokes the creation of a process instance in Workflow Engine B. In the nested sub-process model of Fig. 1-(b), an activity of Workflow Engine A invokes the creation of a process instance of Workflow Engine B and waits until the invoked process instance is completed. Finally, in the parallel synchronized model of Fig. 1-(c), a pair of activities (one in Workflow Engine A and the other in Workflow Engine B) is synchronized such that one activity can be completed only when its partner activity is completed as well.

2.2 A Collaborative BPM Scenario

Depicted in Fig. 2 is a BPM scenario covering the three workflow interoperability models proposed by WfMC (Fig. 1). A nested sub-process interoperation is defined between Workflow Engines 1 and 3, and chained and parallel-synchronized interoperations are defined between Workflow Engines 1 and 2. In this scenario, *request/response*-type [10] interoperation messages are used for the nested sub-process case, while *send/receive*-type [10] messages are used for the chained and parallel synchronized cases.

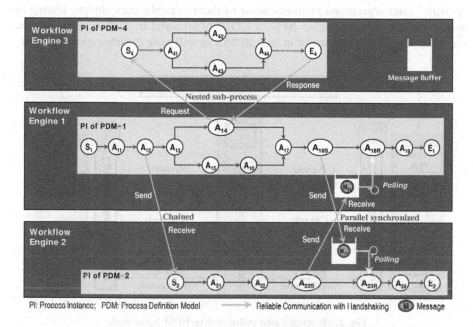

Fig. 2. A collaborative BPM scenario

In the **Nested sub-process scenario** of Fig. 2, Workflow Engine 1 (at activity A_{14}) requests Workflow Engine 3 to execute a Process Instance of PDM-4 and waits for a response message from Workflow Engine 3 notifying the completion of the execution. In the **Chained scenario**, Workflow Engine 1 (at activity A_{12}) sends a message to Workflow Engine 2 asking to execute a Process Instance of PDM-2 (and proceeds to the next activity without waiting for a response message). Workflow Engine 2 starts executing a Process Instance of PDM-2 upon receiving the message from Workflow Engine 1.

In the **Parallel synchronized scenario**, the two activities A_{18} (in Workflow Engine 1) and A_{23} (in Workflow Engine 2) are synchronized. Workflow Engine 1 (at the completion of A18S) sends a message to Workflow Engine 2 notifying the completion of A_{18S}, and Workflow Engine 2 (at the completion of A_{23S}) sends a message to Workflow Engine 1. In both workflow engines, the received messages are stored in a message buffer [11]. At each workflow engine, a polling mechanism is employed to detect the arrival of the message from other workflow engine.

2.3 Collaborative BPM Framework

Shown in Fig. 3 is our collaborative BPM framework covering all the three workflow interoperability models depicted in Fig. 1. The proposed framework employs three collaboration modules: Collaboration Mediator, Collaboration Planner and Collaboration Manager. Our collaborative BPM framework has a hub architecture based on the concept of Mediator [12]. Also employed in the framework is the concept of *COM (collaborative object model)* in which all the *public data objects* (i.e., PDMs and Activities needed for collaboration) are stored. Each workflow engine has its own *"private" data objects* and publishes some of them as public data objects. During the *build-time* [1] of collaborative BPM, a COM is prepared by Collaboration Planner and a copy of the COM is stored in each BPMS as well as in Collaboration Manager.

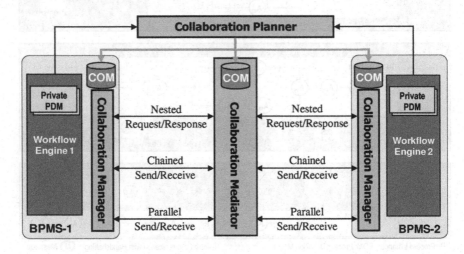

Fig. 3. Mediator-based collaborative BPM framework

During the *run-time* [1] of collaborative BPM, Collaboration Manager residing in each BPMS uses the data objects in the COM for interoperation and Collaboration Mediator handles communication traffic control. In the proposed collaboration framework, three types of *interoperation mechanisms* (one type for each workflow interoperability model of Fig. 1) are employed: (1) Nested request/response interoperation, (2) Chained send/receive interoperation and (3) Parallel send/receive interoperation. An interoperation message carries a COM data object together with its publisher (producer) and subscriber (consumer). Throughout the paper we will use the HLA/RTI terms *publisher and subscriber* [13, 14].

Shown in Fig. 4 are basic operations performed inside the Collaboration Planner: (1) loading of *public data objects* from the participating workflow engines and (2) defining publish-subscribe relations of the public data objects. For the collaborative BPM scenario of Fig. 2, all the three process definition models (PDM-1, PDM-2 and PDM-4) are public data objects. Also Activities A12, A14 and A18 (of PDM-1) as well Activity A23 (of PDM-2) are public data objects. The publisher of a public data object is the workflow engine from which the data object has come. A *public data object* is not fully "public" in that only the subscriber of a public data object is allowed to access it. All the public data objects together with their publisher and subscribers are stored as a COM (collaboration object model).

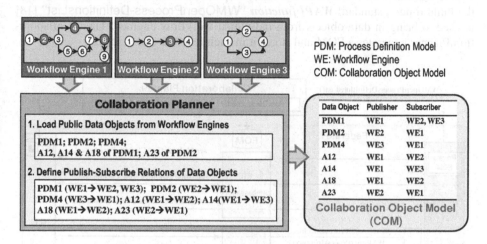

Fig. 4. Construction of COM by Collaboration Planner

3 Collaborative BPM Middleware

Now we present the architecture of a collaborative BPM middleware which is an implementation of the collaborative BPM framework. The mediator-based interoperability framework (Fig. 3) could have been implemented from the scratch [15], but HLA/RTI [13, 14] turned out to be suitable for implementing the proposed framework. HLA/RTI was created in 1990s by the initiative of the Defense Modeling and Simulation Office of the U.S. Department of Defense [14] and it became a widely accepted standard in the simulation community [13]. HLA (High Level Architecture) is a common distributed simulation infrastructure to support interoperability for defense modeling and simulation and reuse of defense simulations [16], and RTI (Run Time Infrastructure) is a software system supporting HLA. There are available a number of commercial RTI software systems [17].

3.1 Architecture of HLA/RTI-Based Collaborative BPM Middleware

Fig. 5 shows a detailed architecture of the HLA/RTI-based middleware for the collaborative BPM framework in Fig. 3. In HLA/RTI, the entire collaborative system is called a *federation*, each participating module (simulator) is called a *federate*, the interface between a federate and RTI is called *ambassador*, and a pre-define structure for the collaborative data objects is called *FOM* (federation object model). Thus, each

BPMS in the collaborative BPM framework becomes a federate and the COM (collaboration object model) becomes a FOM. Further, the Collaboration Mediator is implemented by RTI, and Collaboration Manager is implemented by *WAPI*, *RTI Ambassador* and *Federate Ambassador*. A salient feature of the proposed middleware is that all interoperation messages are handled by a set of standard APIs so that anyone who is familiar with those APIs can easily implement the middleware. At the start of the build-time, a standard ***WAPI function*** "WMOpenProcess-DefinitionsList" [18] is used to bring in data objects from individual workflow engines. Then, Collaboration Planner generates a FOM and stores it in each federate and in RTI.

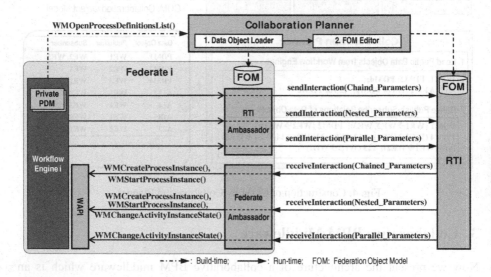

Fig. 5. Architecture of HLA/RTI-based collaborative BPM middleware

In the run-time phase, a workflow engine sends out an interoperation message (Parameters) by invoking the ***HLA API function*** "sendInteraction" [13]. More details about the "Parameters" will be given in the next sub-section. A RTI module handling the outbound messages is referred to as ***RTI Ambassador***. Inbound messages are handled by the HLA API function "receiveInteraction" and the WAPI functions for creating a PI (process instance), starting a PI, and changing an activity of a PI. A RTI module handling the inbound messages is called ***Federate Ambassador***.

3.2 Parameters of HLA API Functions

The parameters of the HLA API functions "sendInteraction" and "receiveInteraction" are the actual value of an interoperation message from a publishing federate (i.e., BPMS) to its subscribing federates. Summarized in Table 1 are parameters of the API functions for the three types of workflow interoperability defined earlier in Fig. 1.

Table 1. Parameters of HLA API functions

Type	Parameters
Chained	<Source WE, Source PI, Source A>, <Target WE, Target PDM>, Data
Nested	<Source WE, Source PI, Source A>, <Target WE, Target PDM>, Data
Parallel	<Source WE, Source PI, Source A>, <Target WE, Target PI, Target A>, Data

WE: Workflow Engine Id; PDM: Process Definition Model Id; PI: Process Instance Id; A: Activity Id.

Reproduced in Fig. 6 is the Nested interoperability model of Fig. 1 with ID numbers of the process instances. Also shown in the figure is a sequence of API calls for interoperation of the Nested model. Federate-1 Requests Federate-3 to execute an instance of PDM-4. Federate-3 creates and executes a process instance (PI#6 of PDM-4) and then sends a Response message back to Federate-1. The "Request" part of the Nested interoperation is executed as follows (See Fig. 6):

(1) RTI Ambassador of Federate-1 invokes the function sendInteraction (<1, 1-8, 4>, <3, 4>)

(2) RTI invokes the call-back function receiveInteraction (<1, 1-8, 4>, <3, 4>). Federate-3's Federate Ambassador catches this call since "Target WE" is 3

(3) Federate-3's Federate Ambassador executes receiveInteraction(), which in turn invokes the WAPI functions WMCreateProcessInstance() and WMStartProcessInstance()

The "Response" part of the Nested interoperation is executed similarly. The "Data" field of the parameters is omitted in the figure for brevity.

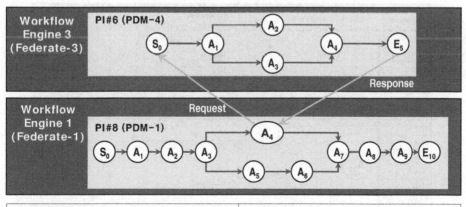

<REQUEST>
1) RTI Ambassador of Federate-1 → RTI:
   sendInteraction(<1, 1-8, 4>, <3, 4>)
2) RTI → Federate Ambassador of Federate-3:
   receiveInteraction(<1, 1-8, 4>, <3, 4>)
3) Federate Ambassador → Federate-3 WAPI:
   WMCreateProcessInstance();
   WMStartProcessInstance()

<RESPONSE>
4) RTI Ambassador of Federate-3 → RTI:
   sendInteraction(<1, 1-8, 4>, <3, 4>)
5) RTI → Federate Ambassador of Federate-3:
   receiveInteraction(<1, 1-8, 4>, <3, 4>)
6) Federate Ambassador → Federate-3 WAPI:
   WMChangeActivityInstanceState();

Fig. 6. Execution flow for the Nested interoperability model

4   Illustrative Implementation

The collaborative BPM middleware (Fig. 3) was realized using a workflow engine [available at: http://bpm.kaist.ac.kr] and a HLA/RTI [17]. All the APIs of the workflow engine are standards APIs from WfMC [1]. As an illustrative implementation of the collaborative BPM scenario of Fig. 2, three workflow engines were installed on separate computers. On each of the three computers, a federate was formed with a workflow engine (equipped with a process designer), WAPI and FOM (RTI was installed in one of the three computers). Execution of workflows at each workflow engine was carried out with a Participant Emulator [19].

Shown in Fig. 7 are Gantt charts showing the results of an execution of the collaborative BPM scenario (Fig. 2) involving three workflow engines. Shown in the left-side column of each GUI are participants of the corresponding BPMS. The Gantt charts shown that the collaborative BPM scenario is executed correctly: (1) Activity A12 of Workflow Engine 1 triggers the execution of the process instance of Workflow Engine 2 (Chained interoperability case); (2) Activity A14 of Workflow Engine 1 starts the process instance of Workflow Engine 3 and waits until the process instance is completed (Nested sub-process case); (3) Activity A18 of Workflow Engine 1 and Activity 23 of Workflow Engine 2 are completed "at the same time" (Parallel synchronized case). However, one may have noticed that the dashed arrows in Fig. 7 are not vertical. In theory they have to be vertical because the "head" and "tail" of each dashed arrow represent the same time. In practice, however, there exist some time delays due to the network communication latency (and times required to create the process instances).

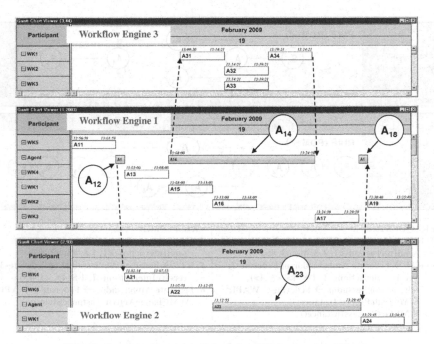

Fig. 7. Gantt char for the collaborative BPM scenario of Fig. 2

5 Conclusions and Discussions

A mediator-based collaborative BPM framework and the architecture of a HLA/RTI-based collaborative BPM middleware implementing the framework are proposed in the paper. Distinctive features of the proposed collaborative BPM middleware include (1) it covers all three models of workflow interoperability specified by WfMC, (2) it has a hub (as opposed to P2P) architecture allowing scalability and generality, (3) all interoperation messages are handled by a set of standard APIs (of WfMC and HLA/RTI) so that anyone who is familiar with those APIs can easily implement the middleware.

Workability of the proposed collaborative BPM middleware was demonstrated by implementing it with a WfMC-compliant workflow engine and a commercial RTI software system, and then testing it with a collaborative BPM scenario involving the three workflow interoperability models. As mention above, the proposed middleware is scalable in that a large number of BPMSs can be incorporated (because the RTI system can support a large number of federates). As an academic research, the proposed middleware may be regarded as an effective solution to the collaborative BPM problem. However, to be used as a practical tool, the proposed middleware may need some rigorous testing and refinement under a real-life environment. Other issues to be addressed (and deserve further investigation) include network security, handling of exceptions (such as network failures and latency), and managerial issues in collaboration. Another, but not the least, research issue is simulation of collaborative BPM process.

Acknowledgments. This work was supported by the Korea Science and Engineering Foundation (KOSEF): No.R01-2006¬000-11118-0.

References

1. WfMC-TC-00-1003, The workflow reference model, Workflow Management Coalition (1995), http://www.wfmc.org
2. WfMC-TC-1012, Interoperability abstract specification, Workflow Management Coalition (1999), http://www.wfmc.org
3. WfMC-TC-1023, Interoperability Wf-XML binding, Workflow Management Coalition (2001), http://www.wfmc.org
4. Meng, J., Su, S., Lam, H., Helal, A.: Achieving dynamic inter-organizational workflow management by integrating business processes, events, and rules. In: Proceedings of the 35th Annual Hawaii International Conference on System Sciences (2002)
5. Muehlen, M., Klien, F.: AFRICA: workflow interoperability based on XML-messages. In: Proceedings of the CAISE 2000 Workshop on Infrastructure for Dynamic Business-to-Business Service Outsourcing (2000)
6. Liu, D.R., Shen, M.: Business-to-business workflow interoperation based on process-views. Decision Support Systems 38, 399–419 (2004)
7. Casati, F., Discenza, A.: Modeling and managing interactions among business processes. Journal of System Integration 10(2), 145–168 (2001)

8. Li, H.X., Fan, Y.S., Dunne, C., Pedrazzoli, P.: Integration of business processes in web-based collaborative product development. International Journal of Computer Integration Manufacturing 18(6), 452–462 (2005)
9. Yan, S.B., Wang, F.J.: A cooperative framework for inter-organizational workflow system. In: Proceedings of the 27th Annual International Computer Software and Applications Conference, pp. 64–71 (2003)
10. Biegus, L., Branki, C.: InDiA: a framework for workflow interoperability support by means of multi-agent systems. Engineering Applications of Artificial Intelligence 17, 825–839 (2004)
11. Chen, Q., Hsu, M.: Inter-enterprise collaborative business process management. In: Proceedings 17th International Conference on Data Engineering, pp. 253–260 (2001)
12. Gamma, E., Helm, R., Johnson, R., Vlissides, J.: Design Patterns. Addison-Wesley, Reading (1995)
13. IEEE Std 1516-2000, IEEE standard for modeling and simulation (M&S) high level architecture (HLA)-framework and rules, IEEE Computer Society (2000)
14. Frederick, K., Richard, W., Judith, D.: Creating computer simulation systems. Prentice Hall, Englewood Cliffs (1999)
15. Lee, D.W., Shin, H.Y., Choi, B.K.: Mediator approach to direct workflow simulation. Simulation Modeling Practice and Theory (2008) (submitted)
16. Fujimoto, R.M.: Parallel and distributed simulation systems. John Wiley & Sons, Chichester (2000)
17. RTI NG Pro®, Virtual Technology Corporation, http://www.virtc.com
18. WfMC-TC-1009, Workflow management application programming interface specification, Workflow Management Coalition (1998), http://www.wfmc.org
19. Choi, B.K., Lee, D.W., Kang, D.H.: DEVS modeling of run-time workflow simulation and its application. In: Proceedings of the 22nd European Conference on Modeling and Simulation (2008)

Collaborative Specification of Semantically Annotated Business Processes

Marco Rospocher, Chiara Di Francescomarino, Chiara Ghidini,
Luciano Serafini, and Paolo Tonella

FBK–irst, Via Sommarive 18 Povo, I-38100, Trento, Italy
{rospocher,dfmchiara,ghidini,serafini,tonella}@fbk.eu

Abstract. Semantic annotations are a way to provide a precise meaning to business process elements, which supports reasoning on properties and constraints. The specification and annotation of business processes is a complex activity involving different analysts possibly working on the same business process.

In this paper we present a framework which aims at supporting business analysts in the collaborative specification and annotation of business processes. A shared workspace, theoretically grounded in a formal representation, allows to collaboratively manipulate processes, ontologies as well as constraints, while a dedicated tool enables to hide the complexity of the underlying formal representation to the users.

1 Introduction

Semantic annotation of business processes allows analysts to give a precise meaning to the process elements they are modelling and enables automated reasoning on the process and its properties. However, semantic annotation involves skills and competences that go beyond the typical background of a business analyst, such as ontology construction and extension, formulation of queries and constraints in descriptive logics. Moreover, the semantics of a business process is almost never unique. Different view points on the process elements and properties bring in different concepts and constraints. For example, for a security expert relevant concepts are *sensible data* or *authentication*, while for a warehouse expert important notions are *product supplier* or *order*.

Integrating and reconciling different views of the same process is not an easy task, and available tools for process construction (e.g., Hyperwave, InterPROM) provide functionalities for collaborative process definition. The problem becomes even harder when the process elements are given a precise semantics by means of an ontology. In fact, incremental ontology creation and extension is expected to be carried out in parallel with the incremental definition of the process. Available tools do not provide any explicit support to the complex activity of collaborative ontology creation/extension, neither they support the related activities of collaborative semantic annotation of process elements and constraint specification.

In this paper, we present a framework for the collaborative specification of semantically annotated business processes. The framework takes advantage of a shared workspace to store the main artefacts that are manipulated collaboratively, i.e., (1)

S. Rinderle-Ma et al. (Eds.): BPM 2009 Workshops, LNBIP 43, pp. 305–317, 2010.

process; (2) ontology; and, (3) constraints. Analysts work on these artefacts concurrently, without any notion of ownership (so they can modify artefacts initially created by others). Conflicts are managed through mutually exclusive lock, and disputes causing instabilities are resolved through discussion forums. To hide the complexity of the underlying formal ontology and descriptive logics formulas the framework includes a dedicated tool.

We have conducted a case study in which four analysts with different competences have collaboratively defined an on-line shopping process. The case study is described as a sequence of snapshots, which highlight the interactions among the work performed by different analysts on different parts of the process.

The paper is organized as follows: Section 2 describes the proposed framework and Section 3 presents the case study. Finally Related Works and Conclusions are presented.

2 Framework

We propose a framework for the collaborative specification of semantically annotated business processes based on the notion of shared workspace illustrated in Figure 1. This workspace makes the artefacts necessary for this activity visible to all actors who are contributing to the definition of the annotated process. These artefacts are then collaboratively developed by the actors, according to their role. Typical actors working concurrently on the business process specification are the analysts who are expert of different aspects of the business. For instance, an organization may ask a customer relationship expert, a logistic and warehouse expert, a payment expert, and a security expert to collaboratively define an on-line shopping process. These different analysts may specify different parts of the process. They can also modify the parts defined by others, so as to make them consistent with their own modifications. The usage of a collaborative workspace aims at supporting the integration of different perspectives.

The artefacts manipulated in the collaborative workspace are the process itself, a domain ontology used to annotate the process elements, and a set of constraints which makes use of both the business process and the domain ontology. The collaborative workspace includes also a "read only" part composed of a BPMN ontology and some BPMN axioms, which are used by the collaborative framework to give a precise semantics to the process elements.

Analysts working collaboratively on a given business process carry out four main activities: (1) incremental process construction; (2) ontology definition or extension; (3) constraint specification; and (4) addition of semantic annotations. These four activities are illustrated in detail in the final part of this section. What is important to note here is that there is no precedence relationship or prescribed workflow in the execution of these four activities. They can be executed concurrently, in any order, and the collaborative workspace must support multiple analysts working on different artefacts and carrying out multiple activities at the same time. To realize such a concurrent working environment we need to address two main problems: (i) concurrent modification of the same artefact; and (ii) instabilities deriving from incompatible modifications that are repeatedly done and undone. For the first problem, we adopt a solution, widely used to address concurrent database accesses, which is based on the acquisition of a *lock*

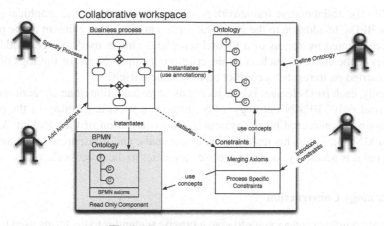

Fig. 1. The collaborative workspace

(i.e., a mutually exclusive access). When an analyst starts working on an artefact, she acquires the lock on it and the workspace provides such an artefact to the other analysts in "read only" mode. When the editing is finished, the analyst commits the changes. This produces an update of the workspace, which triggers an automated verification of the constraints on the new version of the workspace. It also results in the release of the lock on the changed artefact, which becomes available to the other analysts. Incompatible changes are instead managed by resorting to solutions widely used in collaborative content management systems (e.g., Wikipedia). Once a problem on some artefact modification is detected (with the help of automated change monitoring and analysis tools), the first attempt to solve the conflicts consists of initiating a discussion forum, which involves the contributors who made the conflicting changes, as well as experts about the object of the dispute. The project or team leader is in charge of starting such a forum. If no consensus is achieved by the discussants participating in the forum, the solutions used in collaborative content editing involve voting (with different voters having different weights) and/or authoritative decisions by an expert or by the project leader.

Another key characteristic of the collaborative workspace is that the four components illustrated in Figure 1 together with their inter-connections are theoretically grounded in a formal representation of semantically annotated business processes illustrated in [1]. In that work, we have defined and implemented these components as parts of a modular Business Processes Knowledge Base (BPKB), expressed using the semantic web language OWL, based on Description Logics [2]. The illustration of this formal representation is out of the scope of this paper. Nevertheless it is important to note here that an alignment between the informal representation provided in the workspace and their underlying formal representation is maintained by the tool implementing the workspace, as described in Section 2.5.

2.1   Process Construction

The main purpose of the collaborative workspace is to obtain annotated Business Process Diagrams (BPDs) specified using the Business Process Modeling Notation

(BPMN)[1]. The collaborative framework provides instruments for the graphical specification of BPDs. In addition to the graphical representation, each element of the process is also represented by means of a textual template. This is used to record additional properties of the element, such as its description, its annotations, or the logs of a discussion carried on to resolve a conflict on the element itself.

Formally, each BPD element is considered as an instantiation of an element specified in the "read only" BPMN ontology[2]. For instance a specific gateway in the process being drawn is considered by the system as an instantiation of the element Gateway in the BPMN ontology. This instantiation is automatic and transparent to the analysts' activity, but it is necessary to give a precise semantics to the process elements.

2.2 Ontology Construction

The domain ontology is necessary to give a precise semantics to the terms used to annotate business processes. This ontology is typically constructed together with the process and the collaborative workspace supports incremental process and ontology construction. In fact, even if existing domain ontologies can be used to annotate processes, they often need to be adapted to the specific needs of the process being designed. Ontology construction is also a collaborative activity. For instance the security expert may specify a portion of the process concerning her expertise and at the same time she may introduce the concepts needed for the security aspects of the business process. Other analysts may refine or extend the ontology later, with more concepts, as soon as the process grows. In addition, top level (upper) ontologies can be used as the starting point, to be refined later during process definition or to specify constraints as we describe in Section 2.3.

The domain ontology is formally represented in OWL, but analysts interact with this artefact by using graphical and natural language templates which do not expose the formal ontology structure explicitly.

2.3 Constraints Definition

The collaborative workspace makes use of constraints to ensure that important semantic properties of process elements are satisfied. To support the analysts in this activity, it is possible to define a set of predefined templates in which (constrained) natural language is used to express the constraints. These templates are then formally translated to DL axioms. We distinguish among two different kinds of constraints: merging axioms and process specific constraints.

Merging axioms. These constraints are expressions used to state the correspondence between BPMN elements and elements of the domain ontology. Intuitively they define criteria for correct / incorrect semantic annotations. Examples of these criteria are:

---

[1] OMG - BPMN v1.1 - http://www.omg.org/spec/BPMN/1.1/PDF

[2] We assume availability of a BPMN ontology such as the one described in our previous work [1] and available online at: http://dkm.fbk.eu/index.php/BPMN_Ontology.

A BPMN data-object *can be annotated only* with objects of the domain ontology (1)

A BPMN activity *can be annotated only* with activities of the domain ontology (2)

A BPMN sub-process *cannot be annotated* with atomic activities of the domain ontology (3)

The action "to_manage" *can be used only to annotate* BPMN sub-processes (4)

Expressions (1)–(3) describe "domain independent" criteria as they relate elements of BPMN, such as data-objects, activities or sub-processes to elements of a top-level ontology, such as DOLCE [3]. These kinds of constraints can be thought of as "default" criteria for correct / incorrect semantic annotations. In this case DOLCE is provided as a "default" component of the ontology in the collaborative workspace. Note that these "default" criteria could still be modified by the analysts to reflect the actual annotation criteria for the specific domain at hand, although these changes should be agreed upon and justified carefully before the start of the annotation process. Other expressions, such as (4), are instead domain specific as they constrain the usage of a specific term, the action "to_manage", to annotate certain BPMN elements. Another characteristic of the expressions above is that they can describe positive constraints (see (1), (2) and (4)) or negative constraints (see (3)) for annotations. Finally these expressions can constrain a BPMN element to a domain specific element, as in (1)–(3), or vice-versa as in (4). To allow the business analysts to specify these kinds of positive and negative annotation criteria, in [1] we have introduced four different constructs:

- *annotatable only by.* The merging axiom $x \xrightarrow{AB} y$ expresses that a BPMN element of type x can be annotated only with a domain specific concept equivalent or more specific than y;
- *not annotatable by.* The merging axiom $x \xrightarrow{nAB} y$ expresses that a BPMN element of type x cannot be annotated with a domain specific concept equivalent or more specific than y;
- *annotates only.* The merging axiom $y \xrightarrow{A} x$ expresses that any domain specific concept equivalent or more specific than y can be used to denote BPMN elements of type x;
- *cannot annotate.* The merging axiom $y \xrightarrow{nA} x$ expresses that any domain specific concept equivalent or more specific than y cannot be used to denote BPMN elements of type x.

For instance, expression (1) can be represented with the merging axiom data_object $\xrightarrow{AB}$ object which in turn is formally represented with the DL statement BPMNO:data_object $\sqsubseteq$ BDO:object, where BPMNO and BDO are labels used to indicate the BPMN ontology and the domain ontology respectively.

The formal representation of the merging axioms allows reasoning to: (i) check whether the annotations satisfy or violate the annotation criteria expressed by the merging axioms, and (ii) identify the list of admissible annotations that can be suggested to the analysts in the collaborative framework. If a violation of a constraint occurs, explanation techniques similar to the ones described in [4] can be used to provide an indication of what went wrong and can be used by the analysts to repair the annotation or to trigger a revision of the merging axiom(s).

Process specific constraints. These constraints are expressions used to state specific properties that apply to the process under construction. Differently from merging axioms these expressions can have many different forms to match a variety of different properties of the process. In this paper we focus on two types of process specific constraints: (i) precedence relationship constraints, and (ii) BPMN constraints.

Precedence relationship constraints express restrictions over the sequence of activities contained in a process. For instance, in an on-line shopping process, the security expert may wish to introduce properties related to privacy, so that before providing any kind of sensible data, the customer has to read the company's privacy policy related with personal data management. This can be done by imposing that all activities annotated with the concept to_provide_sensible_data are always preceded by an activity annotated with the concept to_read_policy as follows:

$$\text{to\_provide\_sensible\_data } always\_preceded\_by \text{ to\_read\_policy} \qquad (5)$$

A similar constraint, holding for messages, is: *preceded_by_message_from*. Constraint (5) can be formalized in DL by means of two statements

$$\text{BDO:to\_provide\_sensible\_data} \sqsubseteq \forall \text{BPMNO:connect}^-.\text{BDO:to\_read\_p}^*$$
$$\text{BDO:to\_read\_p}^* \equiv \neg\text{BPMNO:se} \sqcap (\text{BDO:to\_read\_policy} \sqcup \forall\text{BPMNO:connect}^- \text{BDO:to\_read\_p}^*)$$

where BPMNO:connect is the transitive closure of the connections provided by the connecting elements contained in the BPMN ontology (see [1]) and BPMNO:se denotes the start event element.

BPMN constraints are expressions which are used to impose additional restrictions over the semantics of BPMN. In other words, these are constraints used to impose limitations on the usage of certain BPMN elements. Examples are:

$$\text{Inclusive\_gateway cannot be used in the business domain} \qquad (6)$$

$$\text{Each gateway must have at most 2 outgoing gates} \qquad (7)$$

Differently from the precedence relationship constraints, these expressions do not depend upon the domain ontology or the annotations of the different BPMN elements. Nevertheless they also depend upon the specific business domain to be modelled and not from the specification of BPMN. For instance the constraint (7) could be specified by the customer relationship expert to keep the structure of an on-line shopping process simple and to limit alternative choices available to the customer. Constraints (6) and (7) can be formally expressed by means of the DL statements BPMNO:inclusive_gateway $\sqsubseteq$ $\bot$ and BPMNO:gateway $\sqsubseteq$ (≤ 2)BPMNO:has_gateway_gate.

2.4   Process Semantic Annotation

Analysts are required to annotate process elements with concepts taken from the domain ontology. The collaborative framework allows the analysts to associate elements of the domain ontology with the BPMN elements that are supposed to refer to that particular concept. This is done in the natural language based template which describes the element to be annotated. To simplify the task, the collaborative framework provides also suggestions, and presents the analysts with a list of admissible annotations, based on the constraints specified upon it.

Formally, an annotated process element is also an instance of the domain ontology concept it is annotated with. Thus if a certain activity is annotated with the concept to_provide_sensible_data, then that activity is an instance of Activity concept in the BPMN ontology but also of to_provide_sensible_data concept in the domain ontology.

2.5 Tool

To support the collaborative specification of semantically annotated business processes we are currently developing BP-MoKi, a collaborative tool based on Semantic MediaWiki (SMW)[3]. Inspired by the work presented in [5], BP-MoKi extends SMW offering specific support to edit and semantically annotate business processes, and it allows to build an OWL implementation of the BPKB.

The main idea behind BP-MoKi is that the ontologies and the process are represented as a collection of interrelated wiki pages connected by typed links. A wiki page is associated to each concept of the BPMN and Business Domain ontologies, and to each element of the Business Process. A typical page contains: (1) an informal description of the element in natural language (images or drawings can be used as well), whose purpose is to document and clarify the models to users not familiar with their formal representation; (2) a structured part, where the element is described by means of triplets of the form *(subject, relation, object)*, to represent the intra/inter-connection between the elements of the models (e.g., the subclass relation between elements of ontologies). This part is used to automatically create the formal representation in the BPKB.

To support creation and editing of a business process in BPMN, BP-MoKi integrates Oryx[4], a state of the art collaborative web-based tool for the graphical modelling of business processes. To each element of the process corresponds a page in BP-MoKi where a semantic annotation of the element can be added, and additional information/documentation about that element can be inserted.

To support creation and editing of the Business Domain ontology, BP-MoKi provides ontology modelling functionalities similar to the ones described in [5]: among them, we have *import functionalities*, which allow to set up BP-MoKi with available business domain knowledge, *editing functionalities*, which provide the basic support for creating, editing and deleting ontology elements, and *visualization functionalities*, which allow to produce different types of graphical overviews of the ontology.

Currently, BP-MoKi allows to specify the merging axioms (via a form included in the pages associated to the concepts of the BPMN and the Business Domain ontology), and we are working to extend the support to the other constraints described in the paper.

3 Use Case

In this section, we describe the definition and the semantic annotation of an on-line shopping process. Four domain experts are involved in its collaborative creation: (1)

---

[3] See http://semantic-mediawiki.org
[4] See http://bpt.hpi.uni-potsdam.de/Oryx

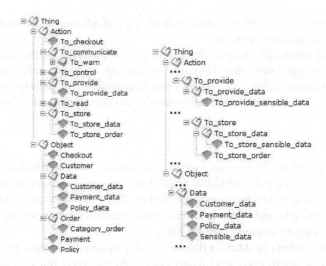

Fig. 2. Ontology evolution

a *customer* relationship *expert*, responsible for the product presentation and selection; (2) a logistic and *warehouse expert*, responsible for the warehouse management (e.g. availability checks and order preparation); (3) a *payment expert*, responsible for the checkout process; and (4) a *security expert*, responsible for privacy and security aspects.

In the following we comment snapshots, captured at different times, of the artefacts in the workspace, providing an example of how collaborative process construction may work in practice.

Snapshot 1: security constraint specification. Initially, the security expert introduces some constraints related to privacy. Before providing any kind of sensible data, the customer has to read the company's privacy policy related with personal data management. Symmetrically, before storing any sensible data, the on-line shop application must show the company's privacy policy to the customer. We assume that an initial domain ontology (left in Figure 2) was previously imported into BP-MoKi. However, the initial ontology does not contain the concept sensible_data so that the security expert needs first of all to modify the ontology, by introducing the new concepts: sensible_data, to_store_sensible_data and to_provide_sensible_data (right in Figure 2). Once the lacking concepts are available, the following three constraints (*C1*, *C2* and *C3*) can be added to the process specific constraint set:

(*C1*) to_provide_sensible_data *always_preceded_by* to_read_policy;

(*C2*) to_store_sensible_data *always_preceded_by* to_provide_policy;

(*C3*) to_read_policy *preceded_by_message_from* to_provide_policy.

Snapshot 2: modelling presentation and selection. The customer expert starts drawing the process in BP-MoKi, by modelling the optional authentication activity as well as the information exchange between the customer and the on-line shop (i.e. product presentation, browsing and selection). Using the ontology artefact edited by the security expert, the customer expert can semantically annotate his process elements. He

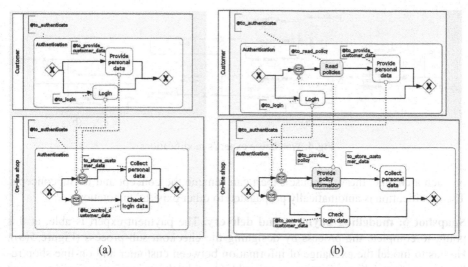

(a)   (b)

Fig. 3. Authentication sub-processes before and after inconsistency fixing

extends the ontology with specific concepts as, for example, to_provide_customer_data and to_store_customer_data. The customer expert's authentication sub-process is shown in Figure 3(a). Semantic annotations are visualized as standard BPMN textual annotations preceded by the symbol "@".

Snapshot 3: managing sensible data. At this point, in our scenario, the security expert realizes that customer_data and payment_data are actually sensible_data, and therefore she modifies the ontology in BP-MoKi by introducing an is_a relationship between them. As soon as she commits the change, the automatic constraint check will detect an inconsistency in the workspace, due to the violation of the constraints C1 and C2. The customer expert will fix the problem, by introducing the activities annotated with to_read_policy and to_provide_policy_data in customer and on-line shop pools, respectively (as shown in Figure 3(b)).

Snapshot 4: modelling warehouse management. When the warehouse expert is called to design her part of the process, besides modelling the sub-process related to ordering missing or scarce products, she may notice that no check about the actual product availability in the warehouse is performed. Therefore she modifies the customer expert's process, by introducing in the control flow new activities realizing this kind of control. The new activities and decision points are depicted with a dark background in the process fragment in Figure 4(a).

Snapshot 5: discussion forum to rename a concept. The warehouse expert needs also to extend the ontology with specific concepts (e.g. to_store_category_order). However, when annotating the activity for checking the product availability in the warehouse, she notices that the to_control concept is already in the ontology. In order to avoid to introduce too many synonym concepts in the ontology and with the assumption that the verb "to_check" would be more suitable for the annotation of her activities, she starts a discussion forum about renaming to_control into to_check. Since all other analysts agree

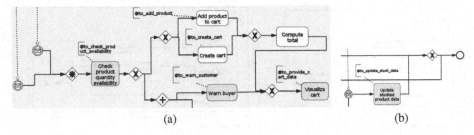

Fig. 4. Warehouse expert's modifications

on such a change, the warehouse expert can rename the concept and its subconcepts. The modification is automatically propagated to other experts' annotations.

Snapshot 6: modelling payment and delivery. The payment expert is able, at this point, to complete the process by designing the checkout sub-process (Figure 5(a)). He has to model the exchange of information between customer and on-line shop related to product delivery (i.e. customer's address and delivery preference) and payment (i.e. credit card data). The checkout process strictly requires authentication, already introduced as an optional activity by the customer expert. However, since the needed authentication sub-processes (customer and on-line shop sides) are exactly the same as those modeled by the customer expert, the payment expert decides to reuse them.

When committing his modifications, the payment expert has to deal with new inconsistencies detected by BP-MoKi. In fact, (1) the constraints C1 and C2 have been violated, due to the is_a relationship between payment_data and sensible_data; (2) the "default" merging axiom restricting the semantic annotations of activities to subconcepts of Action has been violated too, due to the sub-process annotation checkout, a subconcept of Object. The payment expert fixes these problems (as shown in Figure 5(b)), by replacing the concept checkout with the concept to_checkout (subconcept of Action) and introducing the tasks in charge of providing (shop side) and reading (customer side) the policies. While annotating the activity labelled with "Read policies", the payment expert decides to modify the ontology by introducing a new is_a relationship between the concepts to_communicate and to_read. Since this ontology modification is just a refinement that does not impact the other analysts' work, there is no need to start a discussion to reach an agreement.

Snapshot 7: modelling the warehouse update. Finally, after the purchase is confirmed, stock quantities in the warehouse need to be updated. The warehouse expert will therefore complete the process by inserting the missing activities in the payment expert's flow (Figure 4(b)).

4   Related Works

The problem of adding formal semantics to business processes has been extensively investigated in the literature [6,7,8,9,10,11].

Thomas and Fellmann [10] consider the problem of augmenting EPC process models with semantic annotations. They propose a framework which joins process model and

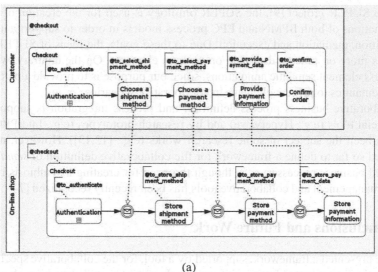

(a)

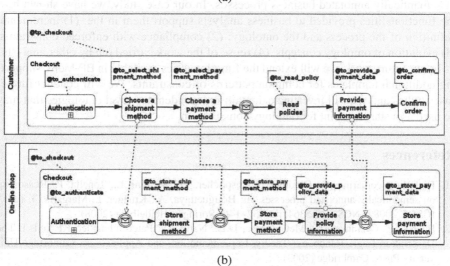

(b)

Fig. 5. Checkout sub-processes before and after inconsistency fixing

ontology by means of properties (such as the "semantic type" of a process element). Using is-a relations between the classes of the two ontologies being integrated (BPMN and domain ontology), instead of associating annotation properties to the process instances [10], allows us to simplify consistency verification.

De Nicola *et al.* [11] propose an abstract language (BPAL) that bridges the gap between high-level process description (e.g. in BPMN) and executable specification (e.g. in BPEL). The formal semantics offered by BPAL refers to notions such as activity, decision, etc., while the problem of integrating process model and *domain* ontology (e.g., by semantically annotating the process) is not their focus.

In the SUPER project [9], the SUPER ontology is used for the creation of semantic annotations of both BPMN and EPC process models in order to support automated composition, mediation and execution. Due to these goals, the focus of SUPER annotations is more on process data than on process elements. On the contrary, we focus on process element semantic annotations, since our purpose is to provide a precise and shared semantics to process elements in collaborative scenarios.

Collaborative business process definition and process integration is supported by commercial tools (e.g., Hyperwave) and by research prototypes (e.g., InterPROM). It has also been the subject of some research works (e.g., [12,13]). However, no work attempted so far to define a framework for the collaborative definition of *semantically* annotated business processes, even though the need for creating a symbiosis between project management and collaborative tools has been recently recognized [14].

5   Conclusions and Future Work

We have presented a framework, supported by a tool, for the collaborative specification of semantically annotated business processes. In our case study, we have shown how the functionalities provided to business analysts support them in the: (1) incremental definition of the process and the ontology; (2) compliance with enforced constraints; (3) evolution of ontology concepts; (4) reuse of the work carried out by other analysts.

In our future work, we will extend the functionalities available in BP-MoKi, supporting additional templates for common patterns of constraints. We will conduct further case studies and we will investigate domain independent top level ontologies that may be used as a starting point for ontology construction.

References

1. Di Francescomarino, C., Ghidini, C., Rospocher, M., Serafini, L., Tonella, P.: Reasoning on semantically annotated processes. In: Bouguettaya, A., Krueger, I., Margaria, T. (eds.) ICSOC 2008. LNCS, vol. 5364, pp. 132–146. Springer, Heidelberg (2008)
2. Baader, F., Calvanese, D., McGuinness, D.L., Nardi, D., Patel-Schneider, P.F. (eds.): The Description Logic Handbook: Theory, Implementation, and Applications. Cambridge University Press, Cambridge (2003)
3. Gangemi, A., Guarino, N., Masolo, C., Oltramari, A., Schneider, L.: Sweetening Ontologies with DOLCE. In: Gómez-Pérez, A., Benjamins, V.R. (eds.) EKAW 2002. LNCS (LNAI), vol. 2473, pp. 166–181. Springer, Heidelberg (2002)
4. Horridge, M., Parsia, B., Sattler, U.: Explanation of owl entailments in protege 4. In: Bizer, C., Joshi, A. (eds.) Proc. of ISWC 2008. CEUR-WS, vol. 401 (2008)
5. Ghidini, C., Kump, B., Lindstaedt, S., Mahbub, N., Pammer, V., Rospocher, M., Serafini, L.: MoKi: The Enterprise Modelling Wiki. In: Aroyo, L., et al. (eds.) ESWC 2009. LNCS, vol. 5554, pp. 831–835. Springer, Heidelberg (2009)
6. Dijkman, R.M., Dumas, M., Ouyang, C.: Formal semantics and automated analysis of bpmn process models (2007), http://eprints.qut.edu.au/archive/00005969/
7. Wong, P., Gibbons, J.: A Relative Timed Semantics for BPMN. (2008) (submitted), http://web.comlab.ox.ac.uk/oucl/work/peter.wong/pub/bpmntime.pdf
8. Beeri, C., Eyal, A., Kamenkovich, S., Milo, T.: Querying business processes. In: VLDB 2006, pp. 343–354 (2006)

9. Dimitrov, M., Simov, A., Stein, S., Konstantinov, M.: A bpmo based semantic business process modelling environment. In: Proc. of ESWC 2007. CEUR-WS, vol. 251 (2007)
10. Thomas, O., Fellmann, M.: Semantic epc: Enhancing process modeling using ontology languages. In: Proc. of SBPM 2007, June 2007, pp. 64–75 (2007)
11. Nicola, A.D., Lezoche, M., Missikoff, M.: An ontological approach to business process modeling. In: Proc. of IICAI 2007, December 2007, pp. 1794–1813 (2007)
12. Leser, F., Alt, R., Osterle, H.: Implementing collaborative process management: the case of net-tech. International Journal of Cases on Electronic Commerce 1(4), 1–18 (2005)
13. Chen, Q., Hsu, M.: Inter-enterprise collaborative business process management. In: Proceedings of 17th International Conference on Data Engineering, pp. 253–260 (2001)
14. Donker, H., Blumberg, M.: Collaborative process management and virtual teams. In: Proc. of CHASE 2008, pp. 41–43. ACM, New York (2008)

A Modeling Approach for Collaborative Business Processes Based on the UP-ColBPIP Language

Pablo David Villarreal[1], Ivanna Lazarte[1], Jorge Roa[1], and Omar Chiotti[1,2]

[1] CIDISI, Universidad Tecnológica Nacional - Facultad Regional Santa Fe, Lavaisse 610,
S3004EWB, Santa Fe, Argentina
{pvillarr,ilazarte,jroa}@frsf.utn.edu.ar
[2] INGAR-CONICET, Avellaneda 3657, S3002GJC, Santa Fe, Argentina
{chiotti}@santafe-conicet.gov.ar

Abstract. The modeling of collaborative business processes is an important issue in order to allow enterprises to implement B2B collaborations with their business partners. We have proposed an MDA-based methodology for the modeling, verification and implementation of collaborative processes. Since collaborative process models are the main artifacts in this MDA-based methodology, a suitable modeling approach is required to design collaborative processes. In this work we describe a modeling approach for collaborative processes based on the UP-ColBPIP language, which is oriented to support the model-driven development of collaborative processes and B2B information systems. The behavior of collaborative processes is modeled through interaction protocols. Enhances to the control flow constructors of interaction protocols are introduced. In addition, we describe an Eclipse-based tool that supports this language.

Keywords: Collaborative Business Process, Business-to-Business, Model-Driven Development, UML Profile, Interaction Protocol.

1 Introduction

The modeling of collaborative business processes is an important issue in order to allow enterprises to implement B2B collaborations. *Business-to-Business collaborations* entail a process-oriented integration among heterogeneous and autonomous enterprises at a business level and a technological level. At the business level, enterprises focus on the design of collaborative processes to define and agree on the behavior of the inter-enterprise collaboration. A *collaborative business process* defines the global view of the interactions between enterprises to achieve common business goals [20]. Through these processes, partners agree to jointly carry out decisions, coordinate their actions, and exchange information through B2B systems.

At the technological level, enterprises focus on the implementation, integration and interoperability of their B2B information systems to execute collaborative processes. This implies the generation of B2B specifications, i.e. interfaces of the partners' systems and business process specifications based on a B2B standard, required by each enterprise to execute the role performed in a collaborative process and implement it in a *business process management system (BPMS)*.

S. Rinderle-Ma et al. (Eds.): BPM 2009 Workshops, LNBIP 43, pp. 318–329, 2010.
© Springer-Verlag Berlin Heidelberg 2010

In previous works, a methodology for the modeling, verification and implementation of collaborative processes was proposed [16, 17, 20]. This methodology uses techniques, languages and methods that exploit the principles of the model-driven architecture (MDA) [13] to guarantee the alignment between the business solution and the technological solution of a B2B collaboration. This MDA-based methodology enables both the design of collaborative processes independent of the idiosyncrasies of particular B2B standards, and the automatic generation of B2B specifications based on a B2B standard from conceptual collaborative process models. The main benefits of this methodology are: (1) the increase of the abstraction level because the main development artifacts are the technology-independent collaborative process models; (2) the reduction of development time and costs along with the guarantee of alignment of the business solution with the technological solution, since process specifications are generated automatically from collaborative process models; and (3) the independence of collaborative process models from B2B standards.

Since collaborative process models are the main artifacts in this MDA-based methodology, a suitable modeling approach is required for collaborative processes. A collaborative process model should be independent of the implementation technology, understandable and easy to read by business analysts and system developers. Besides, the modeling approach should fulfill the capabilities required by B2B interactions [20, 22]: global choreography of B2B interactions, enterprise autonomy, decentralized management, peer-to-peer interactions and representation of complex negotiations.

In this work we describe a modeling approach for collaborative business processes based on the UP-ColBPIP language (UML Profile for Collaborative Business Processes based on Interaction Protocols). This is oriented to support the model-driven development of collaborative processes and B2B information systems and fulfill the requirements mentioned above. The behavior of collaborative processes is modeled through interaction protocols, which are focused on the representation of the communicative aspects of B2B interactions. Enhances to this language are introduced to provide a complete set of control flow constructors to model collaborative processes. In addition, a case tool that supports the UP-ColBPIP language is presented, which is built on the Eclipse open development platform [3].

This paper is organized as follows. Section 2 describes the MDA-based methodology for collaborative processes. Section 3 describes the modeling approach for collaborative processes based on the UP-ColBPIP language. Section 4 presents the Eclipse-based tool that supports this language. Section 5 discusses related work and Section 6 presents conclusions and future work.

2 MDA-Based Methodology for Collaborative Business Processes

The model-driven architecture (MDA) [13] was identified as a key enabler to support the development of collaborative processes [17]. An MDA-based approach was proposed to support the modeling of collaborative processes and the automatic generation of process specifications and partners' system interfaces based on a B2B standard [20]. Also, an MDA-based approach was proposed to generate formal specifications of collaborative processes and verify if they are well-formed [21]. Both approaches make up the MDA-based methodology for collaborative processes [17], which consists of three phases: *analysis and design of collaborative processes, verification of collaborative processes and generation of B2B specifications.*

The analysis and design of collaborative processes is about the modeling of these processes from a business perspective, i.e. using concepts that are less bound to the implementation technology and are closer to the B2B collaboration domain. To support this phase, the UP-ColBPIP language [16, 20] is used in order to enable the modeling of technology-independent collaborative processes.

The second phase consists of verifying the correctness of collaborative processes defined in a UP-ColBPIP model. The purpose is to support the verification of these processes at an early stage of the development, when most of the fundamental decisions of a B2B collaboration are carried out, i.e. previous to the generation of the technological solution. The verification is essential to allow partners to make sure the behavior of collaborative processes is well-defined. To support this, the MDA-based approach for generating Petri Net specifications from a UP-ColBPIP model is applied [21] (see Figure 1.a). Interaction protocols are formalized, transformed and mapped into Colored Petri Net [7] specifications, which are then verified with CPN Tools [2].

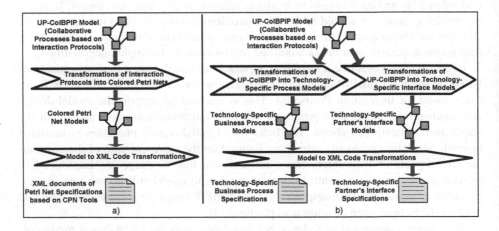

Fig. 1. MDA-based approaches for Collaborative Business Processes

Finally, the third phase consists of selecting the target implementation technology (i.e. the B2B standards) and generating the B2B specifications (i.e. the business process specifications and interfaces of the partners' systems) that fulfill the collaborative processes defined in the first phase. Figure 1.b shows the MDA-based approach that supports this phase. The input is a UP-ColBPIP model that contains collaborative processes based on interaction protocols and partners' business interfaces. From this model, technology-specific business process models and technology-specific partners' interface models are made. Then, B2B specifications are generated. In previous work we described the application of this MDA approach to generate technological solutions based on the widely used B2B standards: ebXML [20], WS-BPEL [18] and WS-CDL [19]. We showed how UP-ColBPIP models can be used to generate technological solutions with these standards.

3 Modeling Collaborative Processes with the UPColBPIP Language

The UP-ColBPIP language extends the UML2 semantics to model technology-independent collaborative processes [16, 20]. The language was defined as a UML Profile in order to provide well-known graphical notations for modeling collaborative processes that were easy to understand by business analysts and system designers. This language encourages a top-down approach to model collaborative processes and provides the conceptual elements to support the modeling of five views:

- The *B2B Collaboration View* defines the participants (partners and their roles) of a B2B collaboration with their communication relationships. UP-ColBPIP extends the semantics of UML2 collaborations to represent B2B Collaborations. This view also describes the hierarchy of common business goals that partners agree on. To represent it, UP-ColBPIP extends the semantics of UML classes and objects.
- The *Collaborative Business Process View* is concerned with the identification of collaborative processes required to achieve the agreed business goals. Current management principles suggest a business process should achieve a business goal. Key performance indicators can be associated with business goals to allow the evaluation of collaborative processes for their redesign or improvement. UP-ColBPIP extends the semantics of use cases to define collaborative processes as informal specifications of a set of actions performed by partners to achieve a goal.
- The *Interaction Protocol View* defines the behavior of collaborative processes through the definition of interaction protocols. This view is described below.
- The *Business Document View* focuses on representing business documents to be exchanged in collaborative processes. Business documents and their types are represented in class diagrams, and they are referenced in collaborative processes and interaction protocols. UP-ColBPIP does not provide any particular concepts to define the syntactic and semantics structure of business documents. To do that, other suitable languages can be used, such as the approach proposed in [1].
- The *Business Interface View* describes the interfaces of each role performed by partners. A business interface (service) contains business operations that support the asynchronous message exchange of interaction protocols. To represent it, UP-ColBPIP extends the semantics of the UML2 composite structures and interfaces.

Due to space limitations, in this work we only describe the *Interaction Protocol View* in order to present the modeling approach we propose to model the behavior of collaborative processes. More details about this language can be found in [20].

3.1 Interaction Protocol View

One of the main purposes of this language is to fulfill the requirements for the conceptual modeling of collaborative processes and B2B collaborations [20, 22]: global view of the interactions between partners, enterprise autonomy, decentralized management, peer-to-peer interactions and representation of complex negotiations. To fulfill these requirements, the UP-ColBPIP language incorporates the interaction protocol concept to define the behavior of collaborative processes. An *interaction protocol* describes a high-level communication pattern through a choreography of business messages between partners who play different roles.

Modeling interaction protocols focus on representing the global view of the inter-actions between partners. The message choreography describes the global control flow of peer-to-peer interactions between partners as well as the responsibilities of the roles they fulfill. This also enables the representation of the decentralized manage-ment of the interactions between partners.

Interaction protocols focus on the exchange of business messages representing in-teractions between partners, preserving the enterprise autonomy. Internal activities of the partners cannot be defined in protocols and hence, they are hidden to partners.

In addition, B2B interactions should not only represent the information exchange but also the communication of actions between partners. Coordination and communi-cation aspects of B2B interactions are represented in interaction protocols through the use of *speech acts*. In an interaction protocol, a business message has an associated speech act, which represents the intention the sender has with respect to the business document exchanged in the message. Thus, decisions and commitments between partners can be known from the speech acts. This enables the definition of complex negotiations and avoids the ambiguity in the semantics and understanding of the busi-ness messages of collaborative processes.

UP-ColBPIP extends the semantics of UML2 Interactions to model interaction pro-tocols. Hence, they are defined using UML2 Sequence Diagrams. Following we de-scribe the main conceptual elements used to define interaction protocols.

Partners and the *Role* they fulfill are represented through lifelines. The basic build-ing blocks of an interaction protocol are the business messages. A *business message* defines a one-way asynchronous interaction between two roles, a sender and a re-ceiver. It contains a *business document* (the exchanged information) and its semantics is defined by the associated *speech act*. In this way, a business message expresses that the sender has done an action that generates the communication of a speech act repre-senting the sender's intention with respect to the exchanged business document. Also, the message indicates the sender's expectation is that the receiver acts according to the semantics of the speech act.

A *Protocol Reference* represents a sub-protocol or nested protocol. When the sub-protocol is called, the protocol waits until the sub-protocol ends. Protocols have an implicit termination. A *Termination* represents an explicit end event of a protocol. Termination events are: *success*, which implies the successful termination; and *fail-ure*, which implies the protocol business logic ends in an unexpected way.

A *Time Constraint* denotes a deadline associated with messages, control flow seg-ments or protocols; i.e. the available time limit for the execution of such elements. A time constraint can be defined using relative or absolute date and time.

A *Control Flow Segment (CFS)* represents complex message sequences. It contains a control flow operator and one or more interaction paths. An interaction path con-tains a ordered sequence of protocol elements: messages, termination events, protocol references and nested control flow segments. The semantics of a CFS depends on the operator used. Some control flow operators of exception handling were adapted and other advanced synchronization and multiple instance operators were introduced in order to provide a complete set of control flow constructors to model collaborative processes. The aim is to fulfill the main workflow patterns [14] for the modeling of collaborative processes. The control flow operators of the UP-ColBPIP language are:

- The *And* operator (Table 1.a) represents the parallel execution of paths. The thread of control is passed to the next protocol element when all paths are completed.
- The *Xor* operator represents that only one path can be executed from a set of alternative paths. A *data-based Xor* contains conditions on the paths to be evaluated to select the execution path (see Table 1.b). An *event-based Xor* is based on the occurrence of the sending event of the first message of each path to select the execution path. Paths have no associated conditions. A timer can also be defined on a path to represent the execution of the path when a time event occurs.
- The *Or* operator represents two or more alternative paths that can be executed. Path conditions must be evaluated to allow the execution of each path. Four types of path synchronization can be defined, which are denoted by the corresponding label at the top-left of the CFS (see Table 1.c). (1) *Synchronizing Merge* (<<Sync-Merge>>): the thread of control is passed to the next protocol element when each enabled path is completed. (2) *Discriminator* (<<Disc>>): the thread of control is passed to the next protocol element when the first interaction path is completed. (3) *N out of M* (<<N out of M>>) represents the convergence of two or more paths (say M) into a single subsequent path. The synchronization event must be enabled once N paths are completed. The remaining paths (M-N) are ignored. (4) *Multi-merge* (<<Multi-Merge>>): for each completed path there is a thread of control which is passed to the next protocol element.
- The *Loop* operator represents a path that is executed several times while its condition is satisfied. An "Until" loop has the condition "(1, n)" so that the path is executed at least once; a "While" loop has the condition "(0, n)" and it means that the execution of the path is performed zero or more times (see Table 1.d).
- The *Exception* defines the path to be followed after an exception takes place, which is identified at design time. A CFS with the *Exception* operator consists of one path that encloses the scope of the exceptions (for all protocol element involved in the path) and other exception handler paths, one for each exception to be caught and managed. An exception handler path has an exception condition to determine when the exception is raised. After an exception handler path is completed, the protocol continues with its normal execution. Two types of exception can be managed: time and logical. (see Table 1.e).
- The *Cancel* operator defines the path to be followed after an exception takes place. The difference between Cancel and Exception operators is that the former finalizes the execution of the protocol when the path that handles the exception is completed. A control flow segment with a Cancel operator is used to finalize a protocol in a coherent and consistent way after an exception.
- The *Multiple Instances* operator is used to represents multiple instances of an interaction path. Four types of synchronization of multiple instances can be defined, which are denoted by a label at the top-left of the CFS (see Table 1.f). The number of instances can be defined: (1) at design-time (<<DT>>); (2) at run-time (<<RT>>), where the variable that contains the number of instances is indicated; (3) without a priori run-time knowledge (<<WRTK>>), where the expression condition that enables the creation of new instances is indicated. Multiple instances without synchronization are denoted by the <<WS>> label.
- The *If* operator represents a path which is enabled when its condition is evaluated to *True*. Else, a path with the *Else* condition is executed if it is defined.

Table 1. Graphical notations of the control flow segments of an interaction protocol

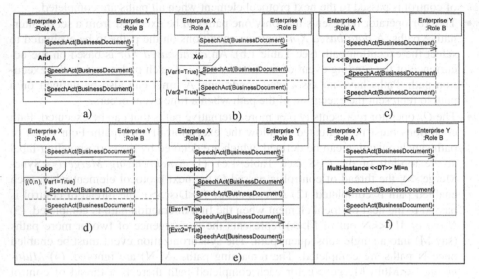

As an example, Figure 2 shows a sequence diagram of the *Collaborative Demand Forecast* protocol, which describes a collaborative process to be carried out as part of a *Collaborative Planning, Forecasting and Replenishment (CPFR)* business model [15]. This protocol defines a simple negotiation process between a customer and a supplier to collaborate and agree on a demand forecast of products to be exchanged.

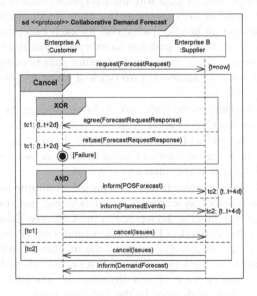

Fig. 2. Collaborative Demand Forecast protocol

The process begins with the customer who requests for a demand forecast. The *request message* conveys the data to be considered in the forecasting (e.g.: products, forecast time-frame). The supplier handles the request and should respond by accepting or rejecting it. If it is accepted, the supplier undertakes to realize the required forecast, as it is indicated by the *agree* speech act; otherwise, the process finishes with a failure. If the supplier accepts the request, the customer informs in parallel a sales forecast of its points of sales (POS) and its planned sale policies. With this information, the supplier then generates a demand forecast, informs it to the customer and the process ends.

The response messages that the supplier sends and the information messages the customer sends have defined time constraints with relative times that represent the deadline for the sending and reception of these messages. As an example, the deadlines of the *agree* and *refuse* messages indicate these messages have to be sent two days in advance, after the occurrence of the first message. In order to handle time exceptions on these messages, the control flow segment cancel is added. It contains an interaction path that spans the messages with time constraints, and it also contains two other exception paths that handle the time exceptions defined in the above messages. In both paths, the exception handling consists of the sending of a cancel message.

4 Eclipse-Based Tool for Modeling Collaborative Processes

In order to provide a development environment for the MDA-based methodology for collaborative business processes and support the modeling approach based on the UP-ColBPIP language, we have developed a tool that supports this language and the model transformations proposed in this methodology. Several requirements were considered in the development of the tool: implementation of visual editors to support the UP-ColBPIP language, implementation of the metamodel of this language to manipulate and validate the constraints of UP-ColBPIP models, extension mechanisms to allow the addition of new editors and model transformation machines, management of B2B collaboration projects, and separation of UP-ColBPIP model and diagram files to facilitate model-to-model and model-to-code transformations.

The developed tool is based on the Eclipse open development platform [3]. There are several tools for modeling business processes that are based on this platform. Thus, we take advantage of a well-known development environment and we can also make a reuse and integration of other Eclipse-based tools with our tool.

The Architecture of the Eclipse-based Tool for Modeling Collaborative Processes consists of the following components (Figure 3):

- A set of Eclipse-based plug-ins, which are graphical editors that support the definition of UP-ColBPIP diagrams and models. They were built with the Graphical Modeling Framework (GMF) [5], which provides an infrastructure for developing visual editors based on the Eclipse Modeling Framework (EMF) [4]
- A Transformation Machine for Petri Net specifications, which was built using the Eclipse Java Emitter Templates (JET) [9] to carry out model-to-code transformations. This machine takes a UP-ColBPIP model as input and produces a Petri Net specification for each interaction protocol defined in the input model.

- A Transformation Machine for BPEL specifications that is built using the ATL [10]. It takes a UP-ColBPIP model as input, and by means of model transformations [18] it produces BPEL specifications of partner roles for each protocol of the input model, as well as a WSDL specification for each partner.

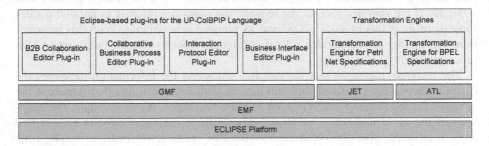

Fig. 3. Architecture of the Eclipse-based Tool for Collaborative Processes

The Eclipse plug-ins for the UP-ColBPIP language were developed by means of GMF and support the UP-ColBPIP language. The UP-ColBPIP metamodel was implemented by means of EMF. In order to define a B2B Collaboration and its collaborative processes it is necessary to create a new UP-ColBPIP project. A UP-ColBPIP model is created when a new B2B Collaboration diagram is generated with the *B2B Collaboration Editor* plug-in. Then, collaborative processes and interaction protocol diagrams can be created by using the *Collaborative Business Process Editor* and the *Interaction Protocol Editor*. An interaction protocol diagram is created when a new collaborative process is defined. Each diagram is stored in a file separated from the file containing the UP-ColBPIP model. Thus the model is clearly separated from its graphical representation.

Figure 4 shows the Eclipse-based tool with the example described in section 3.1. The organization of the UP-ColBPIP project is shown in the Project Explorer view. It consists of a folder for the UP-ColBPIP model and a folder for each view of the UP-ColBPIP model with their corresponding diagrams. The main edition area shows tabs that contain the editors. In particular, the Interaction Protocol editor with the interaction protocol *Collaborative Demand Forecast* is shown. In the right side of Figure 4 is the tool palette with the elements to model an interaction protocol. A protocol can be defined and modified through the drag and drop of the palette's elements into the diagram. On the bottom side, the property view is used to set attributes of the model elements defined in the diagrams.

5 Related Work

Several modeling languages allow the representation of B2B business processes. However, it is necessary to highlight what kind of B2B processes they support. Modeling interaction protocols focus on representing the global control flow of interactions between partners, required to model collaborative processes. Instead, activity-oriented business process languages such as UML2 Activity Diagrams or the Business Process Modeling Notation (BPMN) [12] are more suitable to model interface or private processes from the viewpoint of a partner. Although BPMN allows the definition of B2B processes by representing the message exchange among interface processes of the partners (BPMN *pools*), it does not provide the semantics to describe the dependencies of the global control flow of the message exchange.

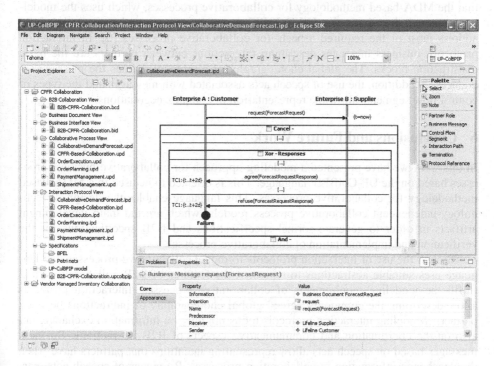

Fig. 4. A B2B Collaboration project created with the Eclipse plug-ins for UP-ColBPIP

The UN/CEFACT modeling methodology (UMM) [8] is a UML modeling approach for global choreographies of B2B scenarios. It is a top-down approach that makes use of worksheets to capture domain requirements. UMM encourages the definition of the global choreography of a collaborative process in a hierarchy of views. A business collaboration view represents a collaborative process described by a choreography of business transactions, which are its basic construction blocks. The partner actions and exchanged business documents are described in each business transaction view, according to a business transaction pattern. This hierarchical approach makes it difficult to model and understand the interactions between partners in a high abstraction level along with the global choreography of a collaborative process. Thus, to identify these interactions into a business collaboration, the knowledge of each business transaction, which is modeled in a separate way of the choreography of the business collaboration, is required. This also results in a higher complexity to model negotiations in collaborative processes.

In [11], a UML2 modeling approach that supports platform independent modeling of Web Service collaboration protocols was proposed. This approach uses a hierarchy of views similar to the approach proposed by UMM to model collaborative processes.

Another modeling approach to describe global choreographies is Let's Dance [23]. This is an independent-technology language, although it focuses on the modeling of Web Services choreographies that support service interaction patterns.

A survey of business process modeling methodologies based on UML has shown that the MDA-based methodology for collaborative processes, which uses the modeling approach based on the UP-ColBPIP language, is comprehensive enough to address most of the required aspects for collaborative processes [6]. In interaction protocols, business messages describing interactions between partners are the basic construction blocks. The global choreography of a protocol defines the message sequences. In addition, the use of speech acts associated with messages and the types of control flow segments allow the representation of complex negotiations.

6 Conclusions and Future Work

In this work we have presented a modeling approach for collaborative business processes based on the UP-ColBPIP language. This is oriented to be used in a MDA-based methodology for collaborative processes. This language enables the design of technology-independent collaborative process models, which are the main development artifacts in order to generate formal specifications and B2B specifications for the verification and implementation of collaborative processes.

Through the use of interaction protocols to model collaborative processes, the language uses suitable abstractions to represent the features of B2B collaborations and fulfill the modeling requirements of collaborative processes. Interaction protocols allow describing the commonly agreed global choreography of interactions between partners. Modeling interaction protocols focus not only on information exchange, but also on the coordination and communicative aspects of B2B interactions. Business messages based on speech acts allow representing intentions that partners have when they exchange information in collaborative processes. By means of speech acts, parties can create, modify, cancel or fulfill commitments. This enables the definition of complex negotiations as well as provides a suitable semantics without ambiguity to achieve a common understanding of the meaning of each message.

In this work we have provided a complete set of control flow operators to model the message choreography of interaction protocols, based on the workflow patterns, in order to model complex control flow structures in collaborative processes.

Through the use of this UML Profile, business analysts and system developers can apply well-known notations for modeling collaborative processes and can also use existing UML2 case tools to model these processes. However, in order to provide a tool that can enforce the metamodel of the UP-ColBPIP language and enable the automatic generation of formal specifications and B2B specifications, we have introduced a case tool based on the Eclipse platform. This tool consists of visual editors implemented as Eclipse plug-ins that support the UP-ColBPIP language.

Future work is aimed at providing a verification and validation methodology for collaborative processes. To enhance the support for verification, the new control flow constructors of interaction protocols will be formalized by using Colored Petri Nets and the model transformations that generate CPNs will be updated. The validation will be done through an ontology-based semantics analysis of the speech acts used in the messages of a protocol.

References

1. Caliusco, M.L., Galli, M.R., Chiotti, O.: Technologies for Data Semantic Modeling. International Journal of Metadata Semantics and Ontology 1(4), 320–331 (2006)
2. CPN tools, http://www.daimi.au.dk/CPNtools/
3. Eclipse Org. Eclipse Platform, http://www.eclipse.org
4. Eclipse Org. Eclipse Modeling Framework, http://www.eclipse.org/emf/
5. Eclipse Org. Graphical Modeling Framework, http://www.eclipse.org/modeling/gmf/
6. Folmer, E., Bastiaans, J.: Methods for Design of Semantic Message-Based B2B Interactions Standards. In: Enterprise Interoperability III, pp. 183–194. Springer, London (2008)
7. Girault, C., Valk, R.: Petri Nets for System Engineering: A Guide to Modeling, Verification, and Applications. Springer-Verlag New York, Inc. (2001)
8. Huemer, C., Liegl, P., Motal, T., Schuster, R., Zapletal, M.: The Development Process of the UN/CEFACT Modeling Methodology. In: Int. Conf. on Electronic Commerce 2008 (2008)
9. Java Emitter Templates, http://www.eclipse.org/modeling/m2t/?project=jet
10. Jouault, F., Kurtev, I.: Transforming Models with ATL. In: Bruel, J.-M. (ed.) MoDELS 2005. LNCS, vol. 3844, pp. 128–138. Springer, Heidelberg (2006)
11. Kramler, K., Kapsammer, E.: Towards Using UML 2 for Modelling Web Service Collaboration Protocols. In: First International Conference on Interoperability of Enterprise Software and Applications (2005)
12. OMG. BPMN V1.1 (January 2008), http://www.omg.org/spec/BPMN/1.1/PDF
13. OMG. MDA Guide V1.0.1 (2003), http://www.omg.org/mda
14. van der Aalst, W.M.P., ter Hofstede, A.H.M., Kiepuszewski, B., Barros, A.P.: Workflow Patterns. J. Distributed and Parallel Databases 14(3), 5–51 (2003)
15. VICS. An Overview of Collaborative Planning, Forecasting and Replenishment (CPFR), http://www.vics.org/docs/committees/cpfr/
16. Villarreal, P.: Method for the Modeling and Specification of Collaborative Business Processes. PhD Thesis. National Technological University, Santa Fe, Argentina (2005)
17. Villarreal, P., Salomone, E., Chiotti, O.: A MDA based Development Process for Collaborative Business Processes. In: European Workshop on Milestone, Models and Mappings for Model-Driven Architecture (3M4MDA), Bilbao, España (2006)
18. Villarreal, Salomone, Chiotti: MDA Approach for Collaborative Business Processes: Generating Technological Solutions based on Web Services Composition. In: 9th Ibero-American Workshop of Requirements Engineering and Software Environments (2006)
19. Villarreal, P., Salomone, H.E., Chiotti, O.: Transforming Collaborative Business Process Models into Web Services Choreography Specifications. In: Lee, J., Shim, J., Lee, S.-g., Bussler, C.J., Shim, S. (eds.) DEECS 2006. LNCS, vol. 4055, pp. 50–65. Springer, Heidelberg (2006)
20. Villarreal, P., Salomone, H.E., Chiotti, O.: Modeling and Specifications of Collaborative Business Processes using a MDA Approach and a UML Profile. In: Rittgen, P. (ed.) Enterprise Modeling and Computing with UML. Idea Group Inc. (2007)
21. Villarreal, P., Roa, J., Salomone, H.E., Chiotti, O.: Verification of Models in a MDA Approach for Collaborative Business Processes. In: 10th Ibero-American Workshop of Requirements Engineering and Software Environments, Venezuela (2007)
22. Weske, M.: Business Process Management: Concepts, Languages, Architectures. Springer Press, Heidelberg (2007)
23. Zaha, J.M., Barros, A., Dumas, M., ter Hofstede, A.H.M.: Let's Dance: A Language for Service Behavior Modeling. In: 14th Int. Con. on Cooperative Information Systems, France (2006)

Process Design Selection Using Proximity Score Measurement

Bernardo N. Yahya[1], Hyerim Bae[1], and Joonsoo Bae[2]

[1] Industrial Engineering Dpt., Pusan National University, Busan, Korea
{bernardo,hrbae}@pusan.ac.kr
[2] Industrial and Information Systems Engineering Dpt., Chonbuk National University,
Jeonju, Korea
jsbae@chonbuk.ac.kr

Abstract. Recently, business environments have become exceedingly dynamic and competitive. In this situation, many enterprises strive to attract customers by constructing multiple business process (BP) variants. Variances within a single process model are created by a process designer to comply with customers' needs. However, customers are rarely involved in the design phase. In the near future, a customer-centric system will request more flexibility in design customization. The advantages from the establishment of a user analysis tool will be necessary to any organization. This paper presents an analysis technique for measuring the proximity among processes. The proposed proximity score follows the concept of workflow mining in observing the closeness of the relationships among all activities within process variants. The method enables a process modeler to generate a proximity score directly once a user starts to design. A higher proximity score for a new process design emphasizes a closer relationship with the existing activities among process variants. A simple case study is presented to demonstrate the idea of proximity score in the BP design environment.

Keywords: Workflow mining, proximity score, process design, process variant.

1 Introduction

The existence of many potential service providers forces customers to compare and to choose based on criteria such as hours, proximity, service scope, and prices [Frei, 2008]. In service industries, a service provider attempts to customize processes by somehow creating new process variants in respect of customers' needs. Obviously, then, user involvement could yield a better quality of process design.

It is certain that customers will respect a truly "personal touch," either in process or product design. Design *with* the customer, which entails the customer's involvement, instead of design *for* the customer, which excludes the customer from any such involvement, is necessary in the service design phase [Magidson, 2001]. That is to say, customization, in imparting the individual preferences of customers to process design, needs to involve customers' participation if the utmost in service excellence is to be achieved. The *design with customer* concept helps any enterprise to maximize profit.

S. Rinderle-Ma et al. (Eds.): BPM 2009 Workshops, LNBIP 43, pp. 330–341, 2010.
© Springer-Verlag Berlin Heidelberg 2010

However, the danger is that customers' involvement can wreak havoc with costs [Frei, 2008].

The difficulty is that fully understanding customers' needs is often a costly and inexact process. This motivated [Magidson et. Al (2001)] and [Thomke et al (2002)] to propose an idea akin to design *by* customer, which represented a shift from the "expert mode" to the "wish mode". A company that utilizes the "wish mode" strategy asks customers to dream up their ideal product or service in order to create for themselves a more compelling experience.

Still, customers need guidance in designing a totally customized process model. The present study attempted to develop a method by which companies and customers could more easily and effectively implement and use the "wish mode" strategy. The activity condition, the input values and output values are some of the significant attributes to be considered in the user design environment. However, these features, in the case of the present study, were held over for further research. Rather, proximity score, considered as a guideline indicating the closeness of the relationship between two activities, is used to analyze the business process as designed by customers. The proximity score for a new process design emphasizes how close is the pair-activity relationship to any existing activity among process variants. The operative principle is that the proximity of a new process design to the previous process design means better service in the view of cost and time. Additionally, statistical analysis results provide a recommendation to the user as to whether to use his "wished" new strategy or the existing process variants.

This paper is organized as follows. Section 2 casts light on the previous, related studies. Section 3 details the methodology to enumerate the proximity score. Section 4 presents a simple case study in which the formula was implemented. Finally, Section 5 includes a discussion and provides conclusions.

2 Literature Review

The world's enterprises have become aware of the value to product- or process design of the "personal touch," as measured in customer satisfaction. IKEA, one of the top furniture retailers in the USA, proposed a strategy that involved asking customers to dream up their ideal product or service. To develop a process or product tailored to customers' desires is to transform the role of the customer from "listener only" (the traditional role) to innovator. [Magidson, 2001].

[Soffer, P. 2005] stated that the impact of a change in a business process can extend beyond the specific aspect that has been changed, to affect, for example, preconditions, inputs or outputs requirement for other activities. Therefore, customers' new requirements will necessitate further efforts to meet the requisite quality of service. The approach to process design selection pursued in the present study did not address attribute changes, leaving that issue to further research. Nonetheless, Soffer's notion significantly influenced the ideas that were pursued.

[Al-Salim (2007)] employed a mass customization strategy in order to design travel packages to minimize the operation and processing costs to the service provider and to maximize customer satisfaction. Hidden relations discovered using data mining tools were used to identify the rules of association with this mechanism.

[Moon et al. (2008)] introduced a product-family-design-related knowledge discovery methodology for use with data mining techniques. The product in this research was categorized into components and attributes in functional hierarchies. The authors used fuzzy clustering and a module categorization technique in employing data mining to partition product functions into subsets in order, respectively, to identify the similarity level of components and to support association rule mining for knowledge discovery related to platform design.

A workflow clustering method based on process similarity (WCM-PS) proposed by [Jung et al. (2006)] is a two-phase approach to classifying domains and analyzing patterns in a process model. Domain classification executes an activity similarity measure, whereas pattern analysis runs a transition similarity measure. An implementation using cosine measures for the similarity of either activity or transition is claimed to support process repository analysis and new process design. This approach affords distance information between two processes rather than homogeneity among all stored processes in a database.

Another approach, called Business Process Similarity Analysis Tools (BPSAT), proposed by [Bae et al. (2007a)], measures similarity using a process dependency graph that is converted into a normalization matrix. The distance measure used in this approach is considered as a quantitative and qualitative tool in process mining. Moreover, the important aim of this approach is to reduce or minimize the costs involved in the design phase. The process dependency graph represents the relationship among activities within a process. However, there is no exact value to express the split and merge activities.

[Weitjers et al. (2001)] proposed a technique for process mining using WF-Nets. This technique can be used to validate workflow processes by uncovering and measuring the discrepancies between a build-time model and a run-time execution process. This paper provided an insight into the construction of the dependency and frequency of activities in a process instance. [van der Aalst et al. (2004)] presented an algorithm to extract a process model from such a log and to represent it in terms of a Petri net. This research tried to demonstrate that it is not possible to discover any arbitrary workflow process.

Process Variants Mining (PVM) proposed by [Li et al. 2008] was designed to satisfy the need for deriving a process model that is easily configurable. The authors claimed that their approach could create a generic process model allowing for easy and optimized configuration for process variants.

The basic idea of measuring all processes and activity comes from [Henikoff et al. 1992] and [Dayhoff et al. 1978]. Both of them proposed a similarity measurement approach that matches the sequence alignment of protein. Their respective proposed methods, Point Access Matrix (PAM) and Block Substitution Matrix (BLOSUM), are the most popular methodological approaches to sequence alignment in the domain of biology. The idea of generating a proximity score, presented in the present paper, was inspired by the mechanism by which PAM and BLOSUM scoring matrices are generated.

3 Methodology

3.1 Process Model

In this study, we used the business process model defined in [Bae, 2007b], which is defined in Definition 1.

Definition 1. (Process Model)
We define a process p as a tuple of $<A, L,>$ and labeling function f, each element of which are defined below.

- $A = \{ a_i \mid i=1,...,I \}$ is the set of activities, where a_i is the i-th activity of p and I is the total number of activities in p
- $L \subseteq \{ l_{ij} = (a_i, a_j) \mid a_i, a_j \in A \}$ is the set of links, where l_{ij} is the link between two activities a_i and a_j. The element (a_i, a_j) represents the fact that a_i immediately precedes a_j
- a_{i+} is the activity following a_i and a_{i-} is the activity preceding a_i
- For a split activity a_i, such that $|SA_i| > 1$, where $SA_i = \{ a_{j+} \mid (a_i, a_{i+}) \in L \}$, $f(a_i) = $ 'AND' if all a_{i+}'s should be executed; otherwise, $f(a_{i+}) = $ 'OR'
- For a merge activity a_i, such that $|MA_i| > 1$, where $MA_i = \{ a_{j-} \mid (a_i, a_{i-}) \in L \}$, $f(a_{i-}) = $ 'AND' if all a_{i-}'s should be executed; otherwise, $f(a_{i-}) = $ 'OR'

Figure 1 is a typical example of a business process. We used a string label on an activity name for ease of identification in the calculation. The split from activity A to B and D is identified as the AND-split using the symbol ")". The other split, from activity E to F and G, represents the OR-split.

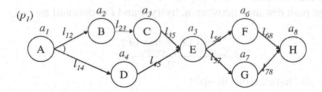

Fig. 1. Typical example of BP

3.2 Proximity Score Measurement (PSM)

This study aimed to derive a proximity score among activities in a process variant. Before we obtained the score, we calculated the distance between activities as is denoted in Definition 2.

Definition 2. (Path, distance, reachability)
We define a set of paths PA_{ij} from an activity a_i to another activity a_j. Since there might be multiple paths between the two activities, an element of the set pa_s is defined as the s-th path.

$$PA_{ij} = \{ pa_s \mid s = 1, 2, 3, ..., S \}$$

- $pa_s = \{a_i, a_k, a_{k+1}, \ldots, a_{k+m}, \ldots, a_{k+M}, a_j\}$, $(a_i, a_k) \in L$, $(a_{k+M}, a_j) \in L$, and for all m, $(a_{k+m}, a_{k+m+1}) \in L$
- S is the number of paths from a_i to a_j,

If there is a path from a_i to a_j , we say that a_i is reachable to a_j, and to present the reachability, we use a '$\rightarrow$' notation.

- $a_i \rightarrow a_j$: a_j is reachable from a_i
- $a_i \parallel a_j$: a_i is not reachable to a_j

When there is a path pa_s ($\in PA_{ij}$) from a_i to a_j, the distance between the two activities is

$$d_s = |pa_s| - 1 = M + 1.$$ (1)

When we consider the path between two activities, there can in fact be multiple paths owing to split structures between the two. For this reason, we introduce the concept of the average distance between two activities that are reachable.

Multiple paths exist where there are split and merge activities. Those activities are considered as a single block structure. [Bae, 2007b] explains more about the block structure as it pertains to parallel activities such as the AND- and OR-splits. However, in the present study, we limited the problem by not considering the loop activity.

Definition 3. (Average Path Distance)
With regard to a split-merge block, we introduce the Average Path Distance, which is the average distance, among several existent paths, from a split activity a_s to a merge activity a_m.
• Average Path Distance of AND-split
The average path distance between activity k and l is denoted as

$$\overline{d}_{kl} = \frac{\max_{pa_s \in PA_{kl}} (d_s) + \min_{pa_s \in PA_{kl}} (d_s)}{2}.$$ (2)

•Average Path Distance of OR-split
The average path distance between activity k and l is denoted as

$$\overline{d}_{kl} = \sum_{pa_s \in PA_{ij}} pr_s . d_s,$$ (3)

where pr_s is the probability of executing the s-th path between the k-th activity and the l-th activity and $\sum_s pr_s = 1$. The initialization value of pr_s is usually determined by experts or any previous experiences. The pr_s is equal to 1 if the relationship of activity a_i and a_j is direct sequential order.

Example (obtained from Figure 1): $\overline{d}_{AE} = \frac{\max(d_{AE}) + \min(d_{AE})}{2} = \frac{3+2}{2} = 2.5$

Definition 4. (Activity Proximity Score: APS)

We define Q_{ij} as the existence probability of path pa_s ($\in PA_{ij}$) from a_i to a_j in all existing processes, which probability is called the Activity Proximity Score (APS). To compute Q_{ij}, we have to obtain the activity proximity value in each process. The value, which is noted by q_{ij} is presented in the following.

$$q_{ij} = \frac{h_s}{\overline{d}_{ij}}. \tag{4}$$

where

$$h_s = \begin{cases} 1, \text{ if } a_i \rightarrow a_j \\ 0, \text{ otherwise} \end{cases}$$

$\overline{d}_{ij}$ is the distance between activity a_i and a_j in $pa_s \in PA_{ij}$,

Each process has a single value of q_{ij}^k, $k=\{1,2,3,...,K\}$, where q_{ij}^k is the activity proximity value of the k-th process index, and K is the total number of processes. If there is no relationship between activity a_i and a_j in k-th process, or denoted as $a_i \parallel a_j$, then $q_{ij}^k = 0$.

To gain the average proximity score of activity a_i and a_j among K process variants, we should sum all q_{ij}^k and divide it by K. The average proximity score, equal as existence probability of activity a_i and a_j among K process variants (APS), is measured by the following equation:

$$Q_{ij} = \frac{\sum_{k=1}^{K} q_{ij}^k}{K}. \tag{5}$$

If activities a_i and a_j are adjacent at all process variants, then q_{ij} is equal to 1 for all K. Thus, Q_{ij} is definitely equal to 1. We could say that the relationship between a_i and a_j are pair-wise activity.

Definition 5 (Total Proximity Score)

We denote ρ to measure the total proximity score (TPS) of new process. TPS is determined by the summation value of all existing Q_{ij} over the distance $\overline{d}_{ij}$ and divide it by the total combination of pair activity that can occur in the new process. Parallel activity is inconsequential to the scoring. Thus, the combination of all of the pair activities is subtracted by the number of parallel activities, either the AND- or the OR-split. The TPS is represented as follow:

$$\rho = \frac{\sum_{i=1}^{m} \sum_{j=1,i\neq j}^{m} \frac{Q_{ij}}{\overline{d}_{ij}}}{{}_mC_2 - \sum_{i,j} |a_i \parallel a_j|}, \tag{6}$$

where, $\overline{d}_{ij}$ is the distance between activities a_i and a_j in $pa_s \in PA_{ij}$

m is the total number of activities at process i, $\sum|a_i||a_j|$ is the number of cases in which the j-th activity is not reachable from the j-th activity as defined in Definition 2, and $_mC_2$ is a combination of m activities in pair-wise relationship.

3.3 Computing PSM in Process DB

To demonstrate the formulation, we conducted a simple case study that can represent the real process variant. There are 6 activities listed by which users can design a new process model. Here, we simply established 6 process variants as the basis.

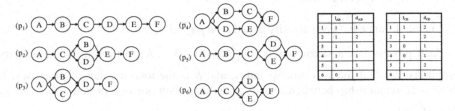

Fig. 2. Example of activity proximity score calculation

The system follows the procedure illustrated in Figure 2. First, an activity proximity score is generated. Then, the system can show the total proximity score in real time when a user creates the new process model. A user who intends to design a new process can select the appropriate activity in the list. The system reckons the proximity score between each of the connected activities, either directly or indirectly connected. The proximity score is obtained from the relationship shown in Figure 3 and is represented in Table 1.

The APS calculation of PA_{AB} and PA_{CE} is as follows:

$$Q_{AB} = \frac{\frac{1}{1}+\frac{1}{2}+\frac{1}{1}+\frac{1}{1}+\frac{1}{1}+0}{6} = \frac{9}{12} \qquad Q_{CE} = \frac{\frac{1}{2}+\frac{1}{2}+0+0+\frac{1}{2}+\frac{1}{1}}{6} = \frac{5}{12}$$

Table 1. Activity proximity score table

	A	B	C	D	E	F
A	-	0.75	0.75	0.5	0.208	0.283
B	0	-	0.5	0.292	0.264	0.347
C	0	0.167	-	0.75	0.417	0.528
D	0	0	0	-	0.5	0.667
E	0	0	0	0	-	0.75
F	0	0	0	0	0	-

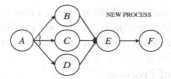

Fig. 3. New process variant designed by user and including total proximity score

The total proximity score of the new process is enumerated as follows:

$$\rho = \frac{0.75 + 0.75 + 0.5 + ... + \dfrac{0.283}{3}}{15 - 3} = \frac{4.92}{12} = 0.408$$

4 Applications of Business Process – Proximity Score Measurement (BP-PSM)

4.1 Convenient Process Modeling Using BP-PSM

Our BP-PSM can be applied to the BP design phase. To design a process, a user commonly uses a graphical tool like the one illustrated in Figure 4. To facilitate the design work, commercial BPMSs provide convenient aids such as templates, versioning, and patterns. All these approaches originated from the idea of utilizing past experience. In this paper, we report a new method of convenient process design using PSM.

For customer convenience, a process modeler should provide a homogeneity tool instead of similarity measurement. The process-homogeneity concept addresses the issue of customer process design being the same as prior processes, whereas similarity measurement aims to enumerate the distance between the two processes and provide information on which process is the most similar according to the similarity value. Most of the previous research has treated similarity measurement rather than homogeneity.

Some applications that can implement this approach are the process revision and versioning systems. Homogeneity analysis helps the process designer to determine whether a new process is homogenous within a particular cluster or requires a new process model. The idea of homogeneity, as discussed in section 4.2 below, can be applied to address the issues of process revision and versioning as well. When the result statistically proves that the null hypothesis is rejected, the system may automatically generate a new version instead of a revision. This surely facilitates a process designer's delimitation of the scope of a process versioning system when it is the same as the common process modeling system.

Figure 4 represents a typical scenario of a purchasing process at any supply chain. Suppose that all activities have included all required rule management system. The user at a retailer can design arbitrarily with respect to stock replenishment at a distribution center. There are 6 basic activities that should be included in the initialization of an activities list. They are OrderEntry, Ord_Review, Fin_Chk, Stock_Chk, Mngr_Review, and Decision. These process variants are designed exactly the same as the examples discussed in section 3.4. Moreover, a new user constructs a new process model based on his wish. Our approach, as already explained, assesses the variance of the pair-wise activity relationship using the proximity score.

4.2 Homogeneity of Set of Processes

From the time of the introduction of the BPMS, maintaining a business process repository has become more of a necessity. In a process repository, the homogeneity of the set of processes should be evaluated for various reasons. For example, in process versioning [Bae, 2007b], a process designer might want to check the degree to which process versions of a process model are homogeneous. [Hallerbach et al. 2008] define a business process variant as an adjustment of a particular process to specific requirements in building the process context. The business process variants have to be adapted separately to meet the new requirements. This paper presents a scenario of process variant homogeneity by means of our approach. It was expected that BP-PSM could assist the process designer and user in their evaluation of the new process design according to the homogeneousness of the existing process variants.

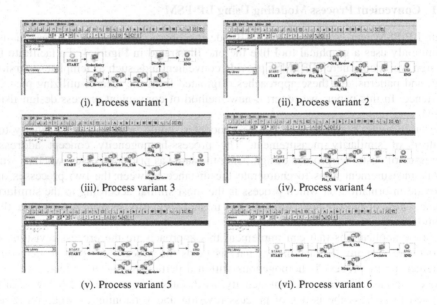

(i). Process variant 1   (ii). Process variant 2

(iii). Process variant 3   (iv). Process variant 4

(v). Process variant 5   (vi). Process variant 6

Fig. 4. Process variant model and new process model

The proximity score measurement of all of the existing process variants (Table 2) was assumed to be a normal distribution. Using a t-test statistical analysis hypothesis, we obtained the T- (= -1.03) and associated p-values (= 0.348). This p-value indicates that there is a 34.8% probability that we would have obtained our sample if the *mu* was actually 0.408333. It is certain that the new created process was statistically consistent among the existing process variants, since the p-value was greater than the α-level (α=0.05). The rest of the analysis information is presented in Figure 5.

Table 2. Scores and p-values of t-test of two samples between new processes with any of existing process variants

Process	# Activity	$_mC_2 - |a_i||a_j|$	Total Proximity Score
1.	6	15	0.329241
2.	6	14	0.345503
3.	5	9	0.443364
4.	6	11	0.418939
5.	6	14	0.258862
6.	5	9	0.449537

One-Sample T: New Process

Test of mu = 0.408333 vs not = 0.408333

Variable	N	Mean	StDev	SE Mean	95% CI	T	P
C1	6	0.376771	0.074737	0.030511	(0.298339, 0.455203)	-1.03	0.348

Fig. 5. Result of one-sample t analysis using Minitab

The prototype of the process design in the modeler is shown in Figure 6. Eventually, the system shows a proximity score between the chosen activities in real time. The proximity score will not show any compliance result if the process has not reached the 'end' activity. Once the 'end' activity is selected by the user, the system directly generates a homogeneity analysis among other existing process variants, according to the p-value and consistency results.

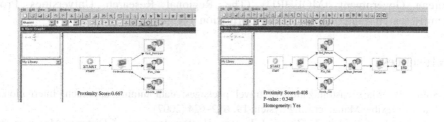

Fig. 6. Simple example of process design with proximity score calculation

5 Conclusions

The proximity score offers a better indication of the closeness of two activities in a process modeling stage than the similarity concept. Pair-wise activity information from among various existing processes is compiled into one single score. An inexperienced user in process modeling can obtain such feedback information after connecting any activity in the specific required process. The feedback information, called the proximity score, is surely important for representing the closeness of the design to any other process variant in real time.

A high proximity score can be interpreted in several possible ways, as follows:

- Many pair-wise activities exist in the process repository
- The service provider has more experience executing the pair-wise activities, due to customer requirements.
- Most customers prefer to have those pair-wise activities. The service quality is p redicted to be high, and both cost and time are predicted to be reduced compared with a lower proximity score process.

However, the present study attempted to observe the homogeneity of new process design among existing processes. Compared with the similarity process, the homogeneity concept can be utilized as a process modeling tool in regard to process versioning, a process awareness information system, and process revision. Our approach gives a comprehensive result based on the proximity score among all existing processes. Still, more complicated process models and experiments are necessary in order to prove the effectiveness in more detail.

There are still many research questions left open. Further investigation into cost and time is a promising and contributory approach in the BPM research domain. Each relationship score can connect to any cost or time value to generate the effectiveness function of this approach. Another research avenue is the homogeneity of attributes of activities. This aspect surely could support process versioning and revision in the configuration not only of the process structure but also of the activity attribute property.

Acknowledgements

This work was supported by a Korea Research Foundation Grant funded by the Korean Government (MOEHRD) (The Regional Research Universities Program/Research Center for Logistics Information Technology).

References

Al-Salim, B.: Mass customization of travel packages: data mining approach. International Journal Flexible Manufacturing System 19, 612–624 (2007)

Bae, J., Liu, L., Caverlee, J., Zhang, L.J., Bae, H.: Development of Distance Measures for Process Mining, Discovery and Integration. International Journal of Web Services Research 4(4) (2007a)

Bae, H.: Business Process Management. Lecture Notes in Pusan National University (2007b)

Dayhoff, M.O., Schwartz, R.M., Orcutt, B.: A model of evolutionary change in proteins. Atlas of Protein Sequence and Structure 5(suppl.), 345–352 (1978); National Biomedical Research Foundation, Silver Spring, MD

Frei, F.X.: The Four Things a Service Business Must Get Right. Harvard Business Review, 70–80 (April 2008)

Hallerbach, A., Bauer, T., Reichert, M.: Context-based Configuration of Process Variants. In: 3rd International Workshop on Technologies for Context-Aware Business Process Management (TCoB 2008), Barcelona, Spain (June 2008)

Henikoff, S., Henikoff, J.G.: Amino acid substitution matrices from protein blocks. Proc. Natl. Acad. Sci. U.S.A 89, 10915–10919 (1992)

Jung, J.Y., Bae, J.: Workflow Clustering Method based on Process Similarity. In: Gavrilova, M.L., Gervasi, O., Kumar, V., Tan, C.J.K., Taniar, D., Laganá, A., Mun, Y., Choo, H. (eds.) ICCSA 2006. LNCS, vol. 3981, pp. 379–389. Springer, Heidelberg (2006)

Li, C., Reichert, M.U., Wombacher, A.: Issues in Process Variants Mining. Technical Report TR-CTIT-08-10, Centre for Telematics and Information Technology, University of Twente, Enschede (2008)

Magidson, J., Brandyberry, G.: Putting Customers in the 'Wish Mode. Harvard Business Review (September 2001)

Moon, S.K., Simpson, T.W., Kumara, S.R.T.: A methodology for knowledge discovery to support product family design. Annals of Operation Research (2008)

Soffer, P.: Scope Analysis: Identifying the Impact of Changes in Business Process Models. Softw. Process Improve. Pract. 10, 393–402 (2005)

Thomke, S., Hippel, E.v.: Customers as Innovators: A New Way to Create Value. Harvard Business Review (April 2002)

Van der Aalst, W.M.P., Weijters, T., Maruster, L.: Workflow Mining: Discovering Process Models from Event Logs. IEEE Transactions on Knowledge and Data Engineering 16(9) (September 2004)

Weijters, A.J.M.M., van der Aalst, W.M.P.: Process Mining Discovering Workflow Models from Event-Based Data. In: Proc. 13th Belgium-Netherlands Conference Artificial Intelligence, BNAIC 2001 (2001)

Yu, Y.W.: Improvement Plan of the Processes Similarity Comparison Criterion for Process Search. Master Thesis (2007) (in Korean)

edBPM Workshop

Introduction to the Second International Workshop on Event-Driven Business Process Management (edBPM09)

Rainer von Ammon, Opher Etzion, Heiko Ludwig, Adrian Paschke,
and Nenad Stojanovic

The recently coined term «Event-Driven Business Process Management» (EDBPM) is nowadays an enhancement of BPM by new concepts of Service Oriented Architecture, Event Driven Architecture, Software as a Service, Business Activity Monitoring and Complex Event Processing (CEP). In this context BPM means a software platform which provides companies the ability to model, manage, and optimize these processes for significant gain. As an independent system, CEP is a parallel running platform that analyses and processes events. The BPM- and the CEP-platform correspond via events which are produced by the BPM-workflow engine and by the – if distributed - IT services which are associated with the business process steps. Also events coming from different event sources in different forms can trigger a business process or influence the execution of a process or a service, which can result in another event. Even more, the correlation of these events in a particular context can be treated as a complex, business level event, relevant for the execution of other business processes or services. A business process – arbitrarily fine or coarse grained – can be seen as a service again and can be "choreographed" with other business processes or services, even between different enterprises and organizations.

Loosely coupled event-driven architecture for BPM provides significant benefits:

- Responsiveness. Events can occur at any time from any source and processes respond to them immediately, whenever they happen and wherever they happen.
- Agility. New processes can be modeled, implemented, deployed, and optimized more quickly in response to changing business requirements.
- Flexibility. Processes can span heterogeneous platforms and programming languages. Participating applications can be upgraded or changed without breaking the process model.

The importance of the topic is emerging due to the need of the future service systems (part of the so called Internet of Services) for the context-awareness and reactivity, that can be achieved by introducing event-driven awareness.

The main goal of the workshop was to create awareness about the role of the event processing for the BPM, define the challenges and start establishing a research community around these two areas.

S. Rinderle-Ma et al. (Eds.): BPM 2009 Workshops, LNBIP 43, pp. 345–346, 2010.
© Springer-Verlag Berlin Heidelberg 2010

The technical program of the workshop showed a carefully selected presentation of current research and developments in 7 workshop papers, and one keynote about "Events, Rules and Processes: why you need all 3" by Paul Vincent (CTO for Business Rules and CEP at TIBCO).

The main outcome of the workshop is the very clear need for the further research in this area. Among others, especially challenging are questions related to the representation of the events and event-driven adaptivity, as well as methodologies for maintaining knowledge about event patterns.

Feasibility of EPC to BPEL Model Transformations Based on Ontology and Patterns

Lucas O. Meertens, Maria-Eugenia Iacob, and Silja M. Eckartz

University of Twente,
Drienerlolaan 5, 7522 NB, Enschede, The Netherlands
{l.o.meertens,m.e.iacob,s.m.eckartz}@utwente.nl

Abstract. Model-Driven Engineering holds the promise of transforming business models into code automatically. This requires the concept of model transformation. In this paper, we assess the feasibility of model transformations from Event-driven Process Chain models to Business Process Execution Language specifications. To this purpose, we use a framework based on ontological analysis and workflow patterns in order to predict the possibilities/limitations of such a model transformation. The framework is validated by evaluating the transformation of several models, including a real-life case.

The framework indicates several limitations for transformation. Eleven guidelines and an approach to apply them provide methodological support to improve the feasibility of model transformation from EPC to BPEL.

Keywords: Model transformation, EPC, BPEL, Guidelines.

1 Introduction

In most traditional software application development practices, the ultimate product of the design process is the "realization", deployed on available realization platforms. In several model-driven approaches, however, intermediate models are reusable and are also considered final products of the design process. These models are carefully defined so that they abstract from details in platform technologies, and are therefore called computation-independent models (CIMs) and platform-independent models (PIMs), in line with OMG's MDA [1][2]. MDA (Model-Driven Architecture) has emerged as a new approach for the design and realization of software, and has eventually evolved into a collection of standards that raise the level of abstraction at which software solutions are specified. Thus, MDA fosters a design process and tools, which support the specification of software in modelling languages such as UML, rather than in programming languages such as Java.

The central idea of MDA is that design models at different levels of abstraction are derived from each other through model transformations. More specifically,

S. Rinderle-Ma et al. (Eds.): BPM 2009 Workshops, LNBIP 43, pp. 347–358, 2010.

different platform-specific models (PSMs) can be derived (semi-) automatically from the same PIM, making use of information contained by a platform model. Thus, MDA eventually advocates the principle that models can automatically be made directly executable, instead of being delivered to programmers, only as a source for inspiration or requirements, in order for them to create the real software [3]. The complete route from business model to executable code requires model transformations that function as a bridge between business process modelers and the IT department, and actually bring us one step closer to real and (partially) automated business-IT alignment. In this paper, we focus on a specific model transformation, namely the transformation from EPC (Event-driven Process Chains) [4] to BPEL (Business Process Execution Language version 1.1) [5]. The business uses EPCs to model its processes. BPEL serves as the executable code used by IT, in order to manage the control flow, for example to invoke web services.

The contribution of this research is threefold. First, we propose an approach to evaluate to what extent model transformation between two process modeling languages are possible. Secondly, we apply the proposed framework to the specific case of EPC to BPEL transformations. Furthermore, we evaluate the accuracy of these transformations as implemented in the Oracle BPA Suite, and uncover some of the limitations one may expect when using the above-mentioned implementation in practice. Finally, we propose several practical modeling guidelines and an algorithmic approach, which allow modelers to improve the feasibility of EPC to BPEL transformations.

The paper has the following organization. Section 2 briefly explains the research method that we use in this paper for analyzing and evaluating model transformations. Section 3 is devoted to the presentation of the theoretical framework and its application to the case of EPC and BPEL. Transformation of several diagrams in Section 4 puts the framework to the test and reveals several practical issues. In Section 5, we propose our guidelines and approach to improve the feasibility of EPC to BPEL model transformation. Section 6 discusses the results and relates our findings to previous research. Finally, in Section 7, we present our conclusions and pointers to future research.

2   Methodology

In order to analyze to what extent transformation from EPC to BPEL is possible, a theoretical framework is developed first. Then, in order to validate the framework, several models are transformed from EPC to BPEL using the Oracle BPA Suite, and the practical results are compared to the expectations (as resulted from the application of the framework). Finally, guidelines are devised to provide methodological support to improve the feasibility of EPC to BPEL transformation.

The theoretical framework consists of two components that combined form an approach for the analysis of model transformations between process modeling languages in general. The first component is represented by the Bunge-Wand-Weber (BWW) representational model [6]. The BWW model defines the concepts that modeling languages should be able to represent. Evaluating the languages according to this model indicates their completeness and clarity. The second component entails the workflow control patterns (WFCP), proposed by Van Aalst et al. [7]. These represent the patterns that commonly occur in business processes. Both EPC and BPEL have been evaluated separately already with respect to the BWW model and WFCPs [8][9][10]. In this research, we compare the evaluations of the two languages with each other in order to discover the theoretical limitations of transformation.

The models used during the evaluation cover the patterns and concepts that EPC is able to represent according to the framework. We compared the resulting BPEL specifications to the code fragments documented by Mulyar [11], who analyzed the capability of Oracle-BPEL to represent patterns. Furthermore, we transformed a composite model from a real-life case to discover additional, practical limitations.

Based on the uncovered limitations, we devised guidelines. More precisely, they resulted from workarounds to the limitations and ways to avoid the limitations altogether. We validate the guidelines by applying them to the composite case. As both EPC and BPEL focus on the static flow of control, this research only deals with the control flow aspects of both languages. Other aspects, such as data and resources, fall outside our scope.

3   A Framework to Evaluate Model Transformation

This section presents the framework, which provides a method for evaluating model transformation. Language evaluation using ontological analysis (using the BWW model) and workflow patterns form its basis, and comparison based on those two components completes the framework. We argue that it is possible to use this framework to evaluate the model transformation from any business process modeling language to another. As explained in the sequel, when applying this framework to EPC and BPEL we conclude that it is possible to map most patterns and constructs from EPC to BPEL. However, our research shows that one pattern is impossible to transform, and several constructs cause ambiguities.

3.1   Ontology

As part of this research, ontology provides a theoretical foundation, as it studies the way the world, business processes in this case, is viewed, and especially modeled. The BWW representational model [6] is one of the two components that we selected for the framework.

An ontological analysis of a modeling language consists of checking which concepts in the BWW model, the language is able to represent through its constructs, and how. Any deficiency (no language constructs exist to represent a certain BWW concept) found during such an evaluation renders the representation less complete. Three other types of "defect" affect the clarity of the representation: redundancy (more than one language construct for a BWW concept), overload (more than one BWW concept for a language construct), and excess (a language construct that has no related BWW concept).

Not all cases of lack of clarity and completeness in a modeling language lead to problems for model transformation. It mainly depends on whether the source or the target language contains the issue. For example, in the case of a deficiency in the source language, a certain BWW concept is impossible to model in that language. Therefore, it will never be necessary to transform that particular concept (since it does not exist in the source) and, consequently, no issue arises. Similarly, if both languages have some excess construct with the same meaning, but no related concept in the BWW model, it is still possible to map the constructs to each other.

The BWW model was used to evaluate both EPC and BPEL separately already [8]. However, it was not yet used to compare the two languages to each other, which is done in the remainder of this section.

Table 1 shows how many of the EPC and BPEL constructs have been found to represent the concepts in the BWW model. We left out the concepts that EPC is unable to represent, as it will never be necessary to transform them. Noticeably, EPC has no redundant constructs; all concepts are represented in EPC by a single construct. BPEL, on the other hand, has redundant constructs for several concepts. Especially the availability of eleven constructs for Transformation stands out. Besides redundancy, BPEL also lacks constructs for several concepts that EPC is able to represents, such as State Law.

Table 1. Ontological completeness and redundancy

BWW Concept	EPC	BPEL 1.1
State	1	1
State Law	1	
Stable State	1	
Event	1	4
External Event	1	1
Internal Event	1	3
Well-Defined Event	1	1
Transformation	1	11
Lawful Transformation	1	3
Level Structure	1	

Table 2. Ontological excess and overload

Excess		Overloaded	
EPC	BPEL	EPC	BPEL
AND-connector	Empty	Function	Partners
OR-connector	Message property	Event	
XOR-connector	Message definition		
	Sequence		
	Flow		
	Scope		

Table 2 shows the overloaded and excess constructs in each of the languages. For EPC all three connector types are considered excess, as they are not strictly needed to model a process. However, with the exception of the OR-connector, they directly match to BPEL constructs. Both other EPC constructs are overloaded. The small number of constructs in the language explains both this, and the lack of redundancy.

3.2   Patterns

A second approach to evaluate and compare modeling languages, as well as their mappings to other languages, is to identify their support for patterns. For this research, the applicable patterns appear in workflow literature, specifically the patterns by Van Aalst et al. [7]. Only the twenty standard static workflow control patterns (WFCP) are the patterns considered as a component for this research, as opposed to data, resource, and advanced patterns. Patterns were used to evaluate both EPC [9] and BPEL [10] separately already. However, a comparison of the two languages, EPC and BPEL, in order to detect which patterns may cause problems in case of a transformation, was not done before.

Similar to EPC completeness with respect to the BWW model, only those patterns that the source language is able to represent are of interest. Table 3 lists those patterns for EPC. Problems only arise when the target language is not able to represent one of those patterns. For the case of EPC to BPEL transformation, the only problematic pattern is WFCP 10, Arbitrary Cycles.

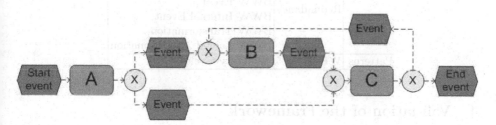

Fig. 1. Workflow control pattern 10: an arbitrary cycle

Table 3. Capability of representing patterns

Patterns		EPC	BPEL
WFCP 1	Sequence	+	+
WFCP 2	Parallel Split	+	+
WFCP 3	Synchronization	+	+
WFCP 4	Exclusive Choice	+	+
WFCP 5	Simple Merge	+	+
WFCP 6	Multi Choice	+	+
WFCP 7	Synchronizing Merge	+	+
WFCP 10	Arbitrary Cycles	+	-
WFCP 11	Implicit Termination	+	+

Fig. 1 shows a variant of this pattern with a loop that has two entry points. It is just one of the many possible variants of this pattern. Thanks to its graph-structure, EPC is able to represent this pattern inherently. On the other hand, BPEL has a block-structure, which does not allow most variants of this pattern.

3.3   Issues and Solutions

Table 4 shows all issues for transformation from EPC to BPEL based on the framework. For each of these issues, a solution must be proposed when trying to implement a (partially) automated transformation. Two of the most straightforward solutions in nearly any situation are to forbid the use of the problematic construct or pattern, or to leave that part of the transformation to a human developer. A third solution is to disregard the part altogether. The best solution depends on the situation.

Table 4. Theoretical issues for transformation

Criteria		Issues
Ontology	Deficiency	State Law
		Stable State
		Level Structure
	Excess	OR-connector
	Overload	EPC Event
		EPC Function
	Redundancy	BWW Event
		BWW Internal Event
		BWW Transformation
		BWW Lawful Transformation
Patterns	WFCP 10	Arbitrary Cycles

4   Validation of the Framework

The Oracle Business Process Analysis (BPA) Suite contains an implementation for model transformation from EPC to BPEL. In order to both validate the theoretical framework and to assess the ability of this tool to perform the transformation correctly, we used the Oracle BPA Suite to transform a set of small models and a larger composite real-life case from EPC to BPEL. The component of the suite used for modeling and transformation is the Business Process Architect. The version of the tool used in this research is 10.1.3.4. We found no tools that provide EPC to BPEL transformation, other than the Oracle BPA Suite, and IDS Scheer's SOA Architect, which is its basis.

4.1   Pattern Transformation

The set of small models consists of relatively small EPC models based on the patterns that EPC is able to represent, as listed in table 3. Besides the patterns themselves, these models also contain all the concepts and issues that we found in the ontological analysis. We compared the resulting BPEL code of the pattern fragments to the BPEL code documented by Mulyar [11]. For several patterns, he proposes two possible mappings, one with link-constructs, and one without. Use of the link-construct allows for a transformation, which is applicable for more cases. This is good for automatic transformation. However, it has several drawbacks. Especially for understandability, the mapping may be unacceptable.

Patterns 1 to 5 and 11 transform successfully, and preserve their semantics. Two things stand out in the resulting BPEL code. Firstly, the models transform to the proposed variant without the use of link-constructs. Secondly, the transformation of the function-construct of EPC, which represents the BWW concept of transformation, catches the eye. As table 1 shows, BPEL overloads this concept with eleven constructs. In the tool, the choice is made to transform the concept to an invoke activity within a sequence within a scope.

The tool fails to transform 'multi choice' and 'synchronizing merge' patterns. It provides the error message that this version (10.1.3.4) of the tool does not support the OR-connector. While Mulyar [11] provides a mapping to BPEL code for these patterns, the OR-connector is indeed a possible issue according to the framework.

The tool succeeds in transforming only certain variants of the 'arbitrary cycle' pattern. More specifically, we refer to those variants that are possible to model with a while-loop. Other variants of the pattern are impossible to transform, for example loops with multiple entry and exit points. By using the framework, we predicted that this pattern cannot be transformed. For the general case, this holds true.

4.2   Composite Case Transformation

To further validate the framework and investigate the feasibility of the model transformation in practice, we also transformed an existing EPC model from a real-life case. The case was the monthly "Accounting Close"-process in order to bill customers, as modeled for a large, Dutch insurance organization. It involves several departments and many information systems but, as this research focuses on the control flow, these resource and organizational entities are not present in the diagrams. Originally, the process was modeled as a composition of several smaller business processes. The main process consists of six sub-processes, which differ in size and complexity.

Fig. 2 shows the full composite case diagram. It shows all the sub-process combined. Together, the sub-processes cover all patterns and BWW concepts, which EPC is able to represent.

Before attempting to transform the full composite process, we transformed the sub-processes one by one. Some of the diagrams transform successfully without changes, while others need modification first. They require modification, either because part of the transformation is theoretically impossible, or because the Oracle BPA Suite does not (yet) support the structure or construct.

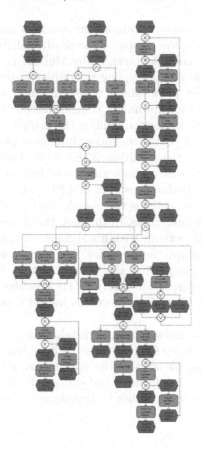

Fig. 2. Full composite case

Successful transformation, according to the Oracle BPA Suite, does not always indicate that the control flow in BPEL is the same as in EPC. Multiple start-events occasionally results in exclusion of a branch of the EPC diagram. While the transformation happened successfully, this is clearly not correct. Therefore, *successful* indicates that the Oracle BPA Suite performs the transformation, and *correct* indicates that the resulting BPEL retains the meaning of the input EPC diagram. While successfulness is apparent from the message given by the tool, we checked correctness by manually evaluating the resulting BPEL.

As opposed to the transformation of the patterns, the case from practice shows more limitations than theory predicted, as well as confirming those acquired from theory. Several things that should be possible, according to theory, are not possible for the transformation in the Oracle BPA Suite. This mainly includes diagrams with while-loops. These loops are possible, but often cause unexpected, incorrect results in practice, especially when contained by parallel branches. Multiple start-events may lead to similar issues. They are possible but, under certain circumstances, branches are missing. We encountered further limitations with multiple end-events and unstructured ("spaghetti") structures. Of all these limitations, we consider unstructured structures and certain cases of multiple end-events related to "unstructuredness" as issues for transformation from EPC to BPEL in general. The other limitations we consider as issues for the particular implementation of the Oracle BPA Suite.

5   Guidelines

Based on the issues encountered during the application of the framework and during transformation in practice, we devised a set of guidelines. Together with a sequencing, specifying the order in which the guidelines should be applied, they provide methodological support to improve the feasibility of EPC to BPEL transformation. Table 5 shows the guidelines. The priority indicates the necessity to apply them for model transformation. We determined this by assessing whether it is possible to transform the model without the modification. For example, the tool does not transform the model at all if it contains an OR-connector, however using descriptive labels only improves communication.

Table 5. List of Guidelines

Nr.	Priority	Guideline
1	Must	Do not use the OR-connector.
2	Could	Avoid loops.
3	Must	If loops are necessary, then use only while-loops with a single exit.
4	Should	Avoid multiple start events.
5	Should	Converge multiple end events.
6	Could	Minimize the amount of arcs attached to a construct.
7	Must	Create structured models.
8	Should	Decompose processes containing problematic structures.
9	Should	Always follow XOR-splits with events.
10	Could	Alternate functions and events.
11	Would	Use clear, descriptive labels.

The guidelines are best to be applied in the order in which they are listed in the table. In this order, the first six guidelines handle issues for transformation that are relatively simple to solve. These issues are the OR-connector, loops, multiple start- and end-events, and constructs with a too high degree of incoming or outgoing arcs. Solving these issues also makes the next steps easier. The next two steps (guidelines 7 and 8) solve harder issues for transformation, such as unstructured models. These two guidelines should be used iteratively, if complex issues remain after a first iteration. The final three guidelines are mainly for communication. These steps require that the other steps completed already.

The above steps can be viewed as a normalization algorithm. It is a model transformation on its own, as it transforms one EPC model, which cannot transform correctly, to another EPC model, which can. Further details and (partial) automation of the algorithm remain an issue for future research.

By applying them to the composite case, we validated the guidelines. This resulted in a modified model, which the Oracle BPA Suite was then able to transform successfully. We checked the resulting BPEL specifications manually, and found them to be transformed correctly too.

6   Discussion and Related Work

Rigorous prior research provides the foundation for the framework. Both the BWW model and the workflow patterns proved their use individually. Combined, they provide us with a more powerful instrument. Not only does it allow us to establish correspondences between the constructs and relationships of the two languages, but it also facilitates the mapping of complex structures, and the assessment of whether the two languages are comparable in terms of expressive power. The predictions we made by using the framework show its correctness for the case of EPC to BPEL transformation. As these predictions resulting from theory match the results obtained during the empirical validation, the framework appears to be valid and lead to accurate results. As both parts of the framework, ontology and patterns, were used individually for other languages, literature confirms with high probability that the approach can be applied to assess transformation between any other process modeling languages too [8][12].

While the combination of workflow patterns and the BWW model provides a complete framework, the two components also overlap on some points. Some of the concepts of the BWW model inherently cover parts of the workflow patterns. In the case of control flow, these include the law concepts, which overlap with the splitting and joining patterns. If data patterns would be included, the overlap is even clearer, as data by nature are the thing and property concepts. Removing the overlap improves (the clarity of) the framework. This is necessary to use the framework as an evaluation tool to judge the quality of model transformations.

The choice for the BWW model to evaluate a single business process modeling language is debatable [13], as it has excess on several parts, and is incomplete on some others [14]. For evaluating the capabilities of transformation, this is less of an issue. The combination with workflow patterns solves the incompleteness, and the workflow patterns fill the gaps. Evaluation of both languages solves the excess, as only the comparison is important for the transformation.

While no other tool was found for direct EPC to BPEL transformation, transformation from EPC to BPEL is also indirectly possible in two steps; It is possible to go from EPC to another language, and then from that other language to BPEL. Theory development shows promise in this area, especially if using EPML (EPC Markup Language) or AML (ARIS Markup Language) as intermediary language [15]. Tools are available to do these individual steps.

To enable model transformation, a conceptual mapping from one language to the other is necessary. A conceptual mapping is also a way to deal with the lack of clarity revealed by the framework. A prerequisite for a conceptual mapping is the formalization of the languages. Van der Aalst [16] has done this for EPC by mapping it to Petri nets. Formal semantics are not yet complete for BPEL [17]. However, one of the concepts that received adequate attention in the literature is the formalization of the control flow [18]. As this research focuses on the transformation of the control flow, it suffices that the control flow semantics are formalized. For the case of EPC to BPEL transformations, Ziemann and Mendling [19] propose a conceptual mapping. Several assumptions limit this mapping. These assumptions resemble the issues we encountered when applying the framework and carrying out the validation.

7 Conclusion and Future Research

This research has proved that automated transformation from EPC models to BPEL specifications is possible to a large extent. Conceptual mappings from EPC to BPEL exist. They indicate which concepts, constructs, and patterns can transform from EPC to BPEL. We encountered several problems that impose limitations on the structure of the models that can be transformed, according to the presented framework. The problems most difficult to solve have to do with the graph-structure of EPC versus the block-structure of BPEL. It makes transformation of arbitrary cycles and some other structures hard or even impossible. Besides this, several ambiguities exist when defining a mapping from EPC to BPEL. Lack of clarity is the cause of them. Therefore, it is hard to define a normative mapping.

Following the presented guidelines results in EPC models, which the Oracle BPA Suite can transform to BPEL specifications automatically. While some of the guidelines can be applied in general, several of the guidelines are specific for EPC modeling and models, which are meant for transformation to BPEL. This provides methodological support to improve the feasibility of EPC to BPEL transformation.

Much research on transformation from BPMN to BPEL also exists. A comparison of the two transformations based on the presented framework is now a possibility. The comparison may lead to a more founded choice for the use of BPMN or EPC over the other. It may also shed light on general issues of BPEL, which need improvement.

The main limitation for applying this research in practice is that the Oracle BPA Suite does not deliver executable code. In order to arrive at executable code, the modeler has to provide more than just the modeled control flow. For example a data model, and interaction with partners. Therefore, a question for future research is "What does transformation to executable code require from the input model?"

We based the framework on the basic workflow control patterns. Further research can also handle the other patterns in the same manner. This includes the advanced control flow patterns, as well as the data and resource patterns.

Acknowledgement. This work is part of the IOP GenCom U-Care project which is sponsored by the Dutch Ministry of Economic Affairs under contract IGC0816.

References

1. Miller, J., Mukerji, J.: MDA guide version 1.0.1. Technical Report doc. no. omg/2003-06-01, Object Management Group (2003)
2. Soley, R.: The OMG Staff Strategy Group: Model driven architecture. OMG white paper, Object Management Group (2000)
3. Bézivin, J.: In search of a basic principle for model driven engineering. Novatica Journal, Special Issue (March-April 2004)
4. Scheer, A.W., Schneider, K.: ARIS (Architecture of integrated Information Systems). Springer, Heidelberg (1992)
5. Andrews, T., Curbera, F., Dholakia, H., Goland, Y., Klein, J., Leymann, F., Liu, K., Roller, D., Smith, D., Thatte, S.: Business process execution language for web services, version 1.1. Standards proposal by BEA Systems, IBM Corporation, and Microsoft Corporation (2003)
6. Wand, Y., Weber, R.: An ontological model of an information system. IEEE Trans. Softw. Eng. 16(11), 1282–1292 (1990)
7. van der Aalst, W.M.P., ter Hofstede, A.H.M., Kiepuszewski, B., Barros, A.P.: Workflow patterns. Distributed and Parallel Databases 14(1), 5–51 (2003)
8. Rosemann, M., Recker, J., Indulska, M., Green, P.: A study of the evolution of the representational capabilities of process modeling grammars. In: Dubois, E., Pohl, K. (eds.) CAiSE 2006. LNCS, vol. 4001, pp. 447–461. Springer, Heidelberg (2006)
9. Mendling, J., Neumann, G., Nuttgens, M.: Towards workflow pattern support of Event-Driven process chains (EPC). In: Proc. of the 2nd Workshop XML4BPM, pp. 23–38 (2005)
10. Wohed, P., van der Aalst, W.M.P., Dumas, M., Hofstede, A.H.M.: Analysis of web services composition languages: The case of BPEL4WS. In: Song, I.-Y., Liddle, S.W., Ling, T.-W., Scheuermann, P. (eds.) ER 2003. LNCS, vol. 2813, pp. 200–215. Springer, Heidelberg (2003)
11. Mulyar, N.A.: Pattern-based evaluation of Oracle-BPEL (v.10.1.2). Technical report BPM-05-24, BPMcenter.org (2005)
12. Wohed, P., van der Aalst, W.M.P., Dumas, M., Hofstede, A.H.M., Russell, N.: Pattern-Based analysis of the Control-Flow perspective of UML activity diagrams. In: Delcambre, L.M.L., Kop, C., Mayr, H.C., Mylopoulos, J., Pastor, Ó. (eds.) ER 2005. LNCS, vol. 3716, pp. 63–78. Springer, Heidelberg (2005)
13. Wyssusek, B.: On ontological foundations of conceptual modelling. Scandinavian J. Inf. Syst. 18(1), 63 (2006)
14. Gehlert, A., Esswein, W.: Toward a formal research framework for ontological analyses. Adv. Eng. Inform. 21(2), 119–131 (2007)
15. Mendling, J., Nuttgens, M.: Transformation of ARIS markup language to EPML. In: Proc. of the 3rd GI Workshop on EPCs, Luxembourg, pp. 27–38 (2004)
16. van der Aalst, W.M.P.: Formalization and verification of event-driven process chains. Information and Software Technology 41(10), 639–650 (1999)
17. Reichert, M.U., Rinderle, S.B.: On design principles for realizing adaptive service flows with BPEL (2006)
18. Ouyang, C., Verbeek, E., van der Aalst, W.M., Breutel, S., Dumas, M., ter Hofstede, A.H.: Formal semantics and analysis of control flow in WS-BPEL. Sci. Comput. Program. 67(2-3), 162–198 (2007)
19. Ziemann, J., Mendling, J.: EPC-Based modelling of BPEL processes: a pragmatic transformation approach. In: Proc. of MITIP 2005, Italy (2005)

New Event-Processing Design Patterns Using CEP

Alexandre de Castro Alves

Oracle Corporation, Redwood Shores, CA, USA
alex.alves@oracle.com

Abstract. Complex Event Processing (CEP) is a powerful technology for supporting advanced event-processing scenarios at a higher level of abstraction. Because of its expressiveness, CEP allows prompt creation and classification of new event-processing design patterns, some of which have been implemented in the past in a non-reusable form. This paper documents a set of new patterns for event processing, describing their problem domain and providing a solution template implemented using CEP, which is both succinct and highly re-usable.

Keywords: CEP, stream management, stream processing, SQL, CQL, design pattern.

1 Introduction

CEP [1] is an emerging technology that allows the implementation of advanced event-processing scenarios. One of the main advantages of CEP is the usage of a domain-specific declarative language to perform the event processing, which is commonly referenced to as the event processing language (EPL) [6].

Because of the expressiveness of EPLs, scenarios that were in the past laboriously implemented over large extend of time can be now supported with a few lines of code, thus allowing us to largely re-use the solutions as design patterns [2] for event-processing. This easiness of implementation also allow us to rapidly create and document new patterns, hence contributing to the library of techniques that can be used to solve event-processing scenarios. Before describing the event-processing design patterns we have worked on we provide some basic background on the building blocks of CEP. This is needed so that the reader can better understand the solution template provided for each pattern.

In this paper we will describe four event-processing design patterns. We will start by describing event filtering, which is arguably the most common and simple event-processing pattern. We choose this pattern as a way to familiarize the reader with the building blocks and concepts used by CEP. Following, we will describe three patterns that, although some users may know them in one way or the other, have not been documented using CEP in a manner that they can be re-used as design patterns for solving event-processing problems. These are the new event detection pattern, the old event detection pattern, and the missing event detection pattern.

S. Rinderle-Ma et al. (Eds.): BPM 2009 Workshops, LNBIP 43, pp. 359–368, 2010.

The patterns are described by first stating their problem domain, that is, by describing the problem that the event-processing application is trying to solve. Next, we provide a semi-formal structure of the problem. The intent of the structure is to help users understand the family of problems that can be solved by applying the pattern. Finally, a solution template using our EPL language of choice, called CQL, is provided. We conclude the paper with observations of the results we have seen so far by systematically employing these patterns and describing on-going work on the matter.

2   Preliminaries

The work in this paper is based upon the Stanford STREAMS project [3] and in particular uses the Continuous Query Language (CQL) [7], an extension to SQL, as the event processing language of choice. Granted that any work on design patterns should be demonstrated using more than a single programming language, otherwise there is a chance that the pattern is a reflection of a programming idiom rather than the solution of a real use-case. Nevertheless, the author feels that CQL is generic enough that the problem is avoided. In particular, the CQL extensions to SQL are presented in isolation and details, facilitating porting to other languages. Furthermore, future work on this subject should include examples on other language, such as a logic programming language.

Before we begin, one high level clarification is needed. In this paper we opt for the term CEP, even though there exists other terms in the industry and academia, such as stream processing and business event processing, that are also attributed to event-processing technologies. As this paper is driven from use-cases, the author hopes that details around the implementation technology is immaterial and that the solution is generic enough to be applicable in different event-processing technologies.

3   Building Blocks

The author strongly encourages the reader to go through the cited references; nevertheless in this section we revise a few important concepts that are extensively used through out the rest of this paper.

An event is a tuple of event properties defined by a schema. The event schema is also commonly referenced as the event type. For example, a stock event type may define three event properties: symbol of type string, lastBid of type float, and lastAsk of type float. An example of an event of the stock event type is:

```
{symbol: AAA, lastBid: 10.0, lastAsk: 12.0}
```

Streams and relations are two types of collections of events. Streams are time-ordered sequence of events. Streams support only the append operation, that is, one can append an event to the end of the stream, but events cannot be deleted from the stream. Streams are unbounded by nature, that is, have (conceptually) no fixed limiting size. An example of a stream of stock events is:

```
{{1t, AAA, 10.0, 12.0}, {2t, BBB, 11.0, 12.5},
{3t, AAA, 10.5, 11.5}, ...}
```

Relations are also collections or events, or more precisely, a bag of events. However, relations (also known as instantaneous relations) are bounded and are always tied to some instantaneous time t. Relations support insert, delete, and update operations. Lets consider relation R that also contains stock events.

```
At time t = 0, R = {{AAA, 10.0, 12.0}, {BBB, 11.0, 12.5}}
```

```
At time t = 1, R = {{BBB, 11.0, 12.5}, {CCC, 5.0, 5.5}}
```

That is, initially relation R contained stock price for symbols AAA and BBB. Next, stock AAA is deleted and stock CCC is inserted.

Event processing agents (EPA) are entities whose input and output are streams and relations and whose role is to process events by executing rules (or queries) specified using some EPL. The execution of a rule can be potentially divided into the execution of separate operators, which may convert streams into relations and vice-versa. One of the goals of CEP is to leverage operators from existing technologies, such as from database systems.

4   Event-Processing Design Patterns

4.1   Event Filtering

Problem Description. The simplest and most common design pattern for event processing is the idea of event filtering. In this case, the problem an application is trying to solve is to discard events that do not meet some criteria.

Some examples of applications performing event filtering are:

- A financial application receiving stock events from the market exchange is looking for a set of stock symbols (e.g. AAA, BBB) and discarding the rest (e.g. CCC, DDD).
- A medical application receiving health status from medical devices is interested when some threshold is crossed (e.g. high blood pressure) and discarding the statuses otherwise.

Problem Structure. Before describing the solution, we must model the problem in terms of event processing concepts [2]. Event filtering consist of an event-processing agent (EPA) whose input is a stream S1 and output is a stream S2, where S2 contains a subset of events of S1:

$$S2 \subseteq S1 \tag{1}$$

Lets consider the scenario of a stock filtering application. This application is receiving events from a stream called stockstream, which is defined by the Stock-Tick event type:

- symbol: string
- lastBid: float
- lastAsk: float

The stock filtering application is looking for events whose symbol is equal to AAA. The following table provides an example of event filtering for three input events coming from a stream where time is progressing in 1t units. The first two events meet the criteria and are not filtered out. The last event does not meet the criteria and is discarded.

Table 1. Example of input and output events for event filtering

Time	Input Stream	Output Stream
1	{AAA, 10.0, 10.5}	{AAA, 10.0, 10.5}
2	{AAA, 10.0, 10.5}	{AAA, 10.0, 10.5}
3	{BBB, 10.0, 10.5}	-

Solution Template. Using the event processing language CQL, a solution to the problem consists of the following query:

```
SELECT * FROM stockstream [NOW] WHERE symbol = AAA
```

To understand this query, lets break into a set of steps or operations. Firstly, we specify the event source, this is done by means of a FROM clause. In this case, the source is a stream named stockstream. Secondly, we must convert the stream into a relation. This is needed because the filter operator, which is used afterwards, works off a relation and not a stream. The reason why the filter operator uses relations instead of streams is that the filter operator is leveraged from the well-known relational model of database systems. To convert the stream stockstream into a relation we make use of the window operator NOW. This stream-to-relation operator outputs a relation containing the event as of the current time from its input. With a relation, we are now able to apply the filter operator described by the predicate symbol = AAA in the WHERE clause.

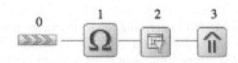

Fig. 1. Query plan for event filtering query

Finally, the output of the filter operator is projected out as the overall output of the query. In summary, a total of four operators are applied, as depictured in Figure 1.

4.2   New Event Detection

Problem Description. In this case, an application is interested on detecting if an event is new in some defined context. Generally the context is specified by some predicate. Examples of applications performing new event detection are:

- A financial application receiving stock events from the market exchange is interested on detecting if a particular stock has its price changed, but otherwise if the price has not changed then the application discards the event. It is important to observe that the market exchange, as it is the generally the case of any stream, outputs events constantly even when these events are not changing. This is so because consumers of the events in the stream may join and leave at any time.
- A medical application receiving health status from medical devices is interested on detecting if some health metric has changed (e.g. blood pressure has gone up or down). The context in this case maybe a particular patient, that is, the medical application is only interested on health status changes for a patient.

Problem Structure. The problem of detecting new events can be modeled as an EPA whose input is a stream S1 and output is a stream S2, where the event e is only present in S2 if the event e is also present in S1 at time t, but is not present in S1 at time t - 1; or more precisely, at time t - delta, where t - delta is the time of the last event at S1 that shares the same context as event e.

$$S2 = \{e \in S1 \mid e \in S1(t) \wedge e \notin S1(t - delta)\} \tag{2}$$

Lets continue with the stock application we used in the previous section. The following table illustrates the input and output to the stock application when it detects if the last bid or the last asking price changed for a particular stock symbol:

The event at time 1, being the first one, is outputted normally. However, the same event at time 2 is not outputted, as it is similar to the previous event. This pattern repeats itself for events 3 and 4. Event at time 5 is not outputted, however it is not outputted because it is similar to the event at time 2, which

Table 2. Example of input and output events for new event detection

Time	Input Stream	Output Stream
1	{AAA, 10.0, 10.5}	{AAA, 10.0, 10.5}
2	{AAA, 10.0, 10.5}	-
3	{BBB, 10.0, 10.5}	{BBB, 10.0, 10.5}
4	{BBB, 10.0, 10.5}	-
5	{AAA, 10.0, 10.5}	-
6	{BBB, 10.1, 10.6}	{BBB, 10.1, 10.6}

also shares the same stock symbol of AAA. If we were to compare event 5 to event 4, we would have outputted event 5, as it is different than event 4. Finally, event 6 is outputted because the prices differ from event 4.

Solution Template. The new event detection pattern for the stock application scenario can be solved with the following CQL query: query:

```
ISTREAM(SELECT * FROM stockstream [PARTITION BY symbol ROWS 1])
```

This query receives events from the stream stockstream, and converts the stream into a relation by using the window operator [PARTITION BY symbol ROWS 1]. The clause PARTITION BY symbol partitions the stream into separate relations where the event in the relation has the same value for the event property symbol. The clause ROWS 1 keeps the last event per partition. Finally, the ISTREAM (i.e. INSERT STREAM) operator is a relation-to-stream operator that only outputs an event if the event exists in the relation at time t and does not exist at time $t - 1$, that is, the event is new in the relation.

4.3   Old Event Detection

Problem Description. This is the opposite case of the new event detection pattern, where the application is interested on detecting if an event is no longer valid, that is, the event has become stale. Examples of application performing old event detection are:

- A financial application receiving stock events from the market exchange is interested on detecting if the price for a particular stock is no longer valid.
- A medical application receiving health status from medical devices is interested on detecting if some condition (e.g. high blood pressure) is no longer holding.

Problem Structure. The problem of detecting old events can be modeled as an EPA whose input is a stream S1 and output is a stream S2, where the event e is only present in S2 if the event e is also present in S1 at time $t - 1$, or more precisely, at time t - delta, where t - delta is the time of the last event at S1 that shares the same context as event e, but is not present in S1 at time t.

$$S2 = \{e \in S1 \mid \notin S1(t) \land e \in S1(t - delta)\} \tag{3}$$

The following table illustrates the input and output to our stock application as it detects if the last bid or the last asking price is no longer valid for a particular stock symbol:

In this case, no event is outputted until the application receives event 5, which replaces event 2. Note that at this time, event 2 and not event 5 is outputted. Likewise, when the application receives event 6, it outputs event 4.

Table 3. Example of input and output events for old event detection

Time	Input Stream	Output Stream
1	{AAA, 10.0, 10.5}	-
2	{AAA, 10.0, 10.5}	-
3	{BBB, 10.0, 10.5}	-
4	{BBB, 10.0, 10.5}	-
5	{AAA, 10.0, 10.6}	{AAA, 10.0, 10.5}
6	{BBB, 10.1, 10.6}	{BBB, 10.1, 10.6}

Solution Template. Very similarly to the new event detection pattern, the old event detection pattern for the stock application scenario can be solved with the following CQL query:

```
DSTREAM(SELECT * FROM stockstream [PARTITION BY symbol ROWS 1])
```

The main difference is the usage of the relation-to-stream operator DSTREAM (i.e. delete stream). DSTREAM only outputs an event if the event exists in the relation at time t - 1 and does not exist at time t, that is, the event is no longer in the latest relation.

4.4 Missing Event Detection

Problem Description. In the missing event detection pattern, an application is interested on being alerted if some expected event is not received within some amount of time.

Examples of this pattern being employed are:

- A retail application handling order requests needs to verify if shipment of the goods is executed within some time of the request of the order.
- A service monitoring application needs to verify if every service request issued by a client receives a response within some maximum amount of time.

Problem Structure. The problem of detecting missing event can be modeled as an EPA whose input is a stream S1, and output is a stream S2, where the event $e1$ is only present in S2 if the event $e2$ is not present in S1 after t time.

$$S2 = \{e \in S1 \mid e2 \notin S1(t) \Rightarrow t_s < t < t_e\} \tag{4}$$

For this pattern, lets consider a stream salesstream, whose events are of the event type SalesRequest:

- requestId: string
- type: order, shipment, or delayed

A sales request can be an order request or a shipment request. An order request for a requestId must be followed by a shipment request within 10 minutes; otherwise a delay event must be outputted by the application. In the context of this

Table 4. Example of input and output events for missing event detection pattern

Time	Input Stream	Output Stream
1m	{1, order}	-
5m	{2, order}	-
10m3	{1, shipment}	-
15m	{3, order}	-
15m+t	-	{2, delayed}
20m	{3, shipment}	-

scenario, the table 4 illustrates the missing event detection pattern for a set of input samples:

The first order request is received at time 1 minute, and its shipment happens at time 10 minutes, that is, within our service agreement of 10 minutes. The second order is received at time 5 minutes, but by the time 15 minutes + 1t, where t is the smallest accountable time increment for the application, no shipment has been processed yet, hence a delayed event is outputted.

Solution Template. The missing event detection scenario can be solved by the following query:

```
SELECT request.requestId, "DELAYED" as type,
FROM salesstream MATCH_RECOGNIZE (
        PARTITION BY requestId
        MEASURES Order.requestId AS requestId
        PATTERN (Order NotTheShipment*) DURATION 10 MINUTES
        DEFINE
                Order AS (type = ORDER),
                NotTheShipment AS ((NOT (type = SHIPMENT)))
) AS request
```

As usual, the query receives events from a stream, in this case the salesstream. However, differently than all previous cases, we dont need to convert the stream into a relation because MATCH RECOGNIZE is a stream-to-stream operator.

Lets investigate MATCH RECOGNIZE, which is a very useful tool for performing complex pattern matching. Firstly, we define the objects we are interesting in matching. This is done with the DEFINE clause, where we specify an order object and a not-a-shipment object. The not-a-shipment object is defined as being any event that is not of type SHIPMENT. Secondly, we define the actual pattern to match with respect to those objects defined in the previous step. In this case, the pattern is defined as an order object followed by zero or more numbers of not-a-shipment objects. The pattern is open-ended; hence we specify duration of 10 minutes to close the pattern. Finally, if the pattern is matched, the MEASURE clause defines the event being outputted to the final projection (i.e. SELECT clause) operator.

4.5   Discussions and Related Work

In [12], Tsimelzon documents ten design patterns for CEP, including a filtering design pattern. In his work, there is a mixture of concerns around the selected design patterns. The filtering design pattern, similar to the patterns aforementioned in this paper, is centered on the semantic of the events. However other scenarios, such as database lookup and dynamic queries, are centered on the processing agent, that is, they can be seen as engine capabilities. Furthermore, the paper does an excellent job of explaining the scenarios and applicability, but does not provide a framework for describing the problem, nor details the underpinnings of the solution. In this paper, we have tried to identify the abstractions for the problem domain, such as events, streams, and relations; as well as provide implementation tools for the solution, for example, by explaining relation-to-stream, stream-to-relation, and stream-to-stream operators.

In Paschke [11] and Ammon, et al [12], a pattern language is presented for CEP. A pattern language is a template for the definition of instances of concrete design patterns. Paschke also documents several categories for the CEP design patterns, including the categories workflow patterns and coordination patterns, which seem the most applicable to the patterns provided in this paper. The pattern language is a useful one, and we should attempt to adhere to its template in future works.

4.6   Conclusion and Future Work

Developers are used to working with events and tables, however the concept of streams and (instantaneous) relations and the high expressiveness of EPLs may overwhelm new adopters of CEP. The documentation of event-processing design patterns implemented using CEP is able to lower the entry barrier and bring users up-to-speed with CEP. Furthermore, it has allowed us to identify new event-processing design patterns, some which have being known in the past, but were never documented as a design pattern thus facilitating their re-use. In the future, we hope to continue to increase the library of event-processing design patterns, by including other patterns, such as event batching, and the W pattern detection, and also documenting commonly known patterns, such as event enrichment, event aggregation, and event correlation.

Acknowledgements. The author would like to thank the members of the Oracle CEP group Anand Srinivasan, Andy Piper, Eric Shiao, Parul Jain, Manju James, Mohit Thattle, Seth White, Shailendra Mishra and others for their invaluable work in implementing the software that supports these CEP design patterns.

References

1. Luckham, D.: The Power of Events, An Introduction to Complex Event Processing in Distributed Enterprise Systems (2002)
2. Gamma, E., Helm, R., Johnson, R., Vlissides, J.: Design Patterns: Elements of Reusable Object-Oriented Software (1995)

3. Arasu, A., Babcock, B., Babu, S., Cieslewicz, J., Datar, M., Ito, K., Motwani, R., Srivastava, U., Widom, J.: STREAM: The Stanford Data Stream Management System (2004)
4. Schulte, R., Bradely, A.: A Gartner Reference Architecture for Event Processing Networks, ID G00162454 (2009)
5. Etzion, O.: EDA Conceptual Model (work in progress) IBM. In: 3rd EPTS Event Processing Symposium, Orlando (September 2007)
6. Luckham, D., Schulte, R.: Event Processing Glossary Version 1.1 (2008)
7. Arasu, A., Babu, S., Widom, J.: The CQL Continuous Query Language: Semantic Foundations and Query Execution. Technical report, Stanford University (October 2003), http://dbpubs.stanford.edu/pub/2003-67
8. Srivastava, U., Widom, J.: Flexible time management in data stream systems. In: Proc. of the 23rd ACM SIGACT-SIGMOD-SIGART Symposium on Principles of Database Systems (June 2004)
9. White, S., Alves, A., Rorke, D.: WebLogic event server: a lightweight, modular application server for event processing. In: Proceedings of the second international conference on Distributed event-based systems (2008)
10. Jain, N., Mishra, S., Srinivasan, A., Gehrke, J., Balakrishnan, H., Cetintemel, U., Cherniack, M., Tibbetts, R., Zdonik, S.: Towards a streaming SQL standard. In: Proceedings of the VLDB Endowment (2008)
11. Paschke, A.: Design Patterns for Complex Event Processing. In: Proceedings from Distributed Event-Based Systems Symposium (2008)
12. Tsimelzon, M.: Coral8 Design Patterns (2006), http://www.coral8.com/blogs/blog-entry/cep-design-patterns
13. Ammon, R., Silberbauer, C., Wolff, C.: Domain Specific Reference Models for Event Patterns (2007)
14. Paschke, A.: EuroPLop 2008 Focus Group on CEP Patterns and Rule Patterns, http://www.biotec.tu-dresden.de/ãdrianp/europlop08_cep/EuroPLoP_CEP_Focus.pdf
15. Anonymous, Pattern matching in sequence of rows (2007), http://asktom.oracle.com/tkyte/row-pattern-recogniton-11-public.pdf

Towards an Executable Semantics for Activities Using Discrete Event Simulation

Oana Nicolae, Gerd Wagner, and Jens Werner

Department of Internet Technology
Institute of Informatics
Brandenburg Technical University at Cottbus, Germany
{nicolae,G.Wagner,wernejen}@tu-cottbus.de

Abstract. The paper aims at answering to the challenge of defining an executable semantics for the *activity* concept, in the context of Business Process Modeling and Simulation. The main purpose for introducing an activity concept on top of the basic Discrete Event Simulation concepts of objects and events is to define an activity as consisting of a start event and an end event. This idea is well-known from the business process modeling literature, e.g. from BPDM. We also expect the adoption of this concept view for the BPMN activity in the future BPMN 2.0 Specification. A case study is used throughout the paper to illustrate the concepts and to present our results.

Keywords: Discrete Event Simulation, Business Process Modeling and Simulation, AORSL, BPMN, BPDM, Activity Semantics.

1 Introduction

Each existing simulation methodology focuses on some particular aspects of the system under consideration, by highlighting its specific aspects. Business Process Simulations (i.e. BPS) or Simulation Modelling usually deal with coordinating business processes made up of a workflow queue of activities undertaken by the human and/or computer resources of an organisation ([7], [8]). The construct that is specific here is the activity seen as an executable step in the business process enactment.

In order to use a Discrete Event Simulation (i.e. DES) approach (e.g. the open source Agent-Object-Relationship (i.e. AOR) Simulation Language) for simulating business processes it is necessary to relate the elements of a business system to the entities and events used in a DES system. To achieve this, the workflow steps should be conceptualised as a series of tasks and events that occur through time. Tasks occur in response to events and are performed by the actors operating in the system, or by the system itself. Notice that our discussion envision the representation of the simulation as a graphical diagram, where we make use of the concepts specific to business processes modeling such as tasks and events.

S. Rinderle-Ma et al. (Eds.): BPM 2009 Workshops, LNBIP 43, pp. 369–380, 2010.

Therefore, one important aspect when developing business simulations models is the ability of designing them using an interactive, graphical interface. Business Process Modeling (i.e. BPM) offers this possibility by using expressive and complex artifacts, joined in a graphical notation language accepted by both industry and academia e.g. BPMN [2] (now at version 1.2). However, unlike a BPS language, OMG[1]'s BPMN is still not executable, but expected to be in the future 2.0 version.

We plead for open-source and standardises technologies that enable interoperability. On the actual business market the majority of the vendors are offering open source products that concern only business processes modeling and enactment (e.g. using BPEL). On the other side, proprietary BPS tools and languages offers expensive solutions that make them to be seldom used in the research. Usually, their model simulations are based on assigned parameters of tasks, performers, gateways, and events. Standardization of those parameters was omitted from BPMN 1.x, and is expected to be included in the 2.0 version.

With this in mind, we envision BPMN as a standardised graphical notation for simulation modeling. We made use of BPMN as a graphical notation in order to represent our case study simulation scenarios. Our ongoing research work is double focused: studying BPMN with the purpose of enriching AORSL by adding appropriate business concepts that allow it to be a business process simulation language and, in the same time, the conceptualization of different simulation scenarios in AORSL (i.e. use-cases) will obtain a useful feedback for the BPMN essential structure of its metamodel. In doing so, it will be examined how discrete-event simulation systems specific constructs elements can be represented in BPMN and in which way BPMN has to be extended for this purpose.

In this paper we present a solution for modeling activities, and business processes, on top of the basic discrete event simulation (i.e. DES) concepts of objects (or entities) and events. Our solution is obtained as an extension of the AOR simulation framework, which is an ontologically well-founded agent-based DES framework with a high-level rule-based simulation language and an abstract simulator architecture and execution model available from http://www.AOR-Simulation.org.

The paper is structured as follows: Section 1 motivates our topic and provides an overview of the AORS concepts, Section 2 presents a show case example and discusses its BPMN graphical representation and the AORSL implementation. Section 3 focuses on the activity concept introduced as an extension of AORSL and also its conceptual relation with the BPMN /BPDM task concept. We also discuss the show case enriched with the activity concept. In Section 4 we discuss the related works in domain. We conclude with Section 5.

1.1   Introduction to AOR Simulation

The AOR Simulation framework was proposed in [12]. It supports both basic discrete event simulations without agents and complex agent-based simulations

---

[1] OMG - http://www.omg.org

with (possibly distorted) perceptions and (possibly false) beliefs. A simulation scenario is expressed with the help of the XML-based AOR Simulation Language (AORSL).

The scenario is then translated to Java source code, compiled to Java byte code and finally executed. A simulation scenario consists of a simulation model, an initial state definition and zero or more view definitions.

A simulation model consists of: (1) an optional space model (needed for physical objects/agents); (2) a set of entity type definitions, including different categories of event, message, object and agent types; and (3) a set of environment rules, which define causality laws governing the environmental state changes.

An entity type is defined by means of a set of properties and a set of functions. There are two kinds of properties: attributes and reference properties. Attributes are properties whose range is a data type; reference properties are properties whose range is another entity type.

The upper level ontological categories of AOR Simulation are objects (including agents, physical objects and physical agents), messages and events. Notice that according to this upper-level ontology of AOR Simulation, agents are special objects. For simplicity it is common, though, to say just *object* instead of using the unambiguous but clumsy term *non-agentive object*. Both the behavior of the environment (i.e. its causality laws) and the behavior of agents are modeled with the help of rules, which support high-level declarative behavior modeling.

1.2   Basic Discrete Event Simulation with AORSL

In basic DES, we deal with two basic categories of entities: objects and events see Figure 1. A simulation model defines a number of object types and event types, each of them with one or more properties and zero or more functions (to be used for all kinds of computations such as for computing pseudo-random numbers following an empirical distribution). Among the event types, we distinguish those that define *exogenous events* (typically with some random periodicity) and those that define *caused events* that follow from the occurrence of other events.

The state of the environment (i.e. the system state) is given by the combination of the states of all objects. Environment rules define how the state of objects is changed by the occurrence of events. An environment rule is a 5-tuple ⟨ *EvtT, Var, Cond, UpdExpr, ResEvtExpr* ⟩ where: (1) *EvtT* denotes the type of event that triggers the rule; (2) *Var* is a set of variable declarations, such that each variable is bound either to a specific object or to a set of objects; (3) *Cond* is a logical formula allowing for variables; ex-pressing a state condition, (4) *UpdExpr* specifies an update of the environment state; and (5) *ResEvtExpr* specifies a list of resulting events, which will be created when the rule is fired.

In each simulation step, all those rules are fired whose triggering event types are matched by one of the current events and whose conditions hold. The firing of rules may lead to updates of the states of certain objects and it may create new future events to be added to the future events list. After this, the simulation time is incremented to the occurrence time of the next future event, and the evaluation and application of rules starts over.

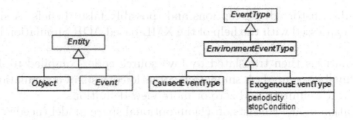

Fig. 1. a) AORSL Entities and b) The ontology of event types as required for modeling discrete-event simulation

2   Simulating a Double Queue System Using DES

In this section we show how to model and simulate a double queue system purely with events, without using activities. We use the BPMN-like graphical notation to describe our simple simulation scenario i.e. the general case - a double queue system where the entities are waiting in line for some resources with restricted capacity to be available. The purpose of the simulation is to estimate the load and scale resource utilization statistics (i.e. the percentage of time they are busy in the system).

2.1   Simulation Showcase

Our particular case is the Dump-Truck problem: trucks are arriving periodically at the Loading Service consisting of two loaders. If there is already a waiting line and the Loading Service is busy, the truck gets in line and waits for its turn. As soon as a serviced truck departs from the Loading Service, the next truck is started to be loaded and a new departure (i.e. end of service) event for this truck is scheduled. If there are no more trucks in line, the Loading Service becomes available. After being loaded, trucks immediately move to the Scale Service (a resource with capacity equal to 1) to be weighed as soon as possible. The Scale Service also has a FIFO waiting line for the trucks. The travel time from the Loading Service to the Scale Service is considered negligible. After being weighed, the truck begins a travel (during which it unloads) and then returns to the Loading Service queue.

We abstract away from the individual truck objects and also from the composition of the queues, since for calculating the resource utilization statistics we do not need any information about them.

2.2   Using BPMN for Simulation Modeling

We decided to build a BPMN representation of our simulation model that is different from the classical view of BPMN diagrams with which business people and academia members are used to.

Our motivation involves the impossibility of classical BPMN diagrams to represent some basic simulation models components such as: the queues. In simulation languages we define and use queues where entities wait for available resources or messages. BPMN has no explicit, corresponding equivalent to this concept of queues of entities, as the entire workflow is viewed from the perspective of that entity. This matter of facts does not exclude the existence of some *transparent queueing process for tokens* that, for example, arises in routing patterns of splitting and joining token flow through gateways and also in the synchronization of the message flow between tokens. Figure 2 provides a BPMN diagram that describes the dynamics of the Double Queue System. In our BPMN representation we can actually model the queues that form in front of the resources i.e. when an entity departs from a service, the following step is a decision logic where if there still are entities in the queue, the next entity will move forward and benefit from the resource and therefore an *EndService* event will be scheduled.

We use the BPMN *task* concept to represent the logic steps that update the state of the system involving the manipulation of state variables such as `loadersQL/freeLoaders/scaleBusy` and to schedule appropriate events. The state of the system is also affected by decision logic (i.e. BPMN exclusive data-based gateway) e.g. the decision to get in line, waiting for the Loading Service

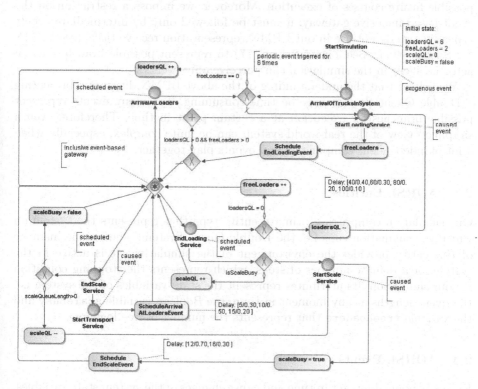

Fig. 2. Modeling a Double Queue System without activities

to be available, otherwise begin to use the Loading Service if the state variable (freeLoaders > 0).

In order to differentiate between different logic steps types in the graphical representation of our simulation, we used different task to reflect the AORSL structure of rules. For example, we used the task freeLoaders -- to denote the updating procedure of the variable freeLoaders and the task ScheduleEnd LoadingEvent to schedule the occurrence of an event in the system with a particular delay. With other words, we want to represent some logic step in the simulation where some resource is busy for a definite period of time. The time while the resource is busy varies in minutes with associated probabilities (see Figure 2).

We use in our BPMN representation the *event-based gateway* as a central coordinator of the entire system. We also used the following text annotation: *inclusive event-based gateway*. This means that our gateway does not comply with the deferred choice pattern behavior that provides the ability to defer the moment of choice in a process, i.e. the moment as to which only one of several possible courses of action should be chosen is delayed to the last possible time and is based on factors external to the process instance. An *inclusive event-based gateway* has an OR-semantics, meaning that the interaction with the environment may cause one or more branches (i.e. events to be triggered) to represent possible future courses of execution. Moreover, we impose a restriction on the event-based inclusive gateway: it must be followed only by intermediate events types (i.e. we do not use in our BPMN representation receive tasks (see BPMN 1.2 Specification - Section 9.5.2.4 pp. 77) to represent possible branches, as an actor i.e agent in the simulation can perceive only events).

We believe that the understanding of the above BPMN diagram representing a Double Queue System may be time-consuming. Too many events represent possible branches for execution at a certain point in time. Therefore, even a simplified view of the real-world system can be quite complex, especially when a lot of independent components and events play together.

2.3   AORSL Entities

Our simulation comprises a primary entity type that represents the system on which the simulation runs i.e. the Double Queue System. The unique instance of this entity provides the environment of the simulation. It is active in the system for a definite number of steps, which represents the stopping condition for our simulation. Its attributes represent the state variables of the system i.e. the queue lengths at any moment in time, the Boolean variable scaleBusy and the variable freeLoaders that represents the number of free loaders.

2.4   AORSL Events

Events happen at a point in time and cause changes of the system state variables. They represent the pivot point in all DES-based simulation systems as the entire simulation model comprises a sequence of scheduled discrete events which are triggered when some logic steps are completed.

The real computation time does not influence the time of the simulation. The modeled scenarios imagine situations that must be simulated much faster that their occurrences in the real life. The time of the simulation skip among events that are scheduled to occur at different moments in time, facilitating this way the simulation of complex systems. We exemplify the use of the event-based inclusive gateway in our diagram when, more than one event can occur: a truck is finished to be loaded (i.e. an `EndLoadingService` event), a truck starts to be weighted (i.e. an `StartScaleService` event) or a truck arrives at loaders resource (i.e. an `ArrivalAtLoaders` event).

When reading the text annotation of the events we can observe the distinction between *caused event* and *scheduled event*. The scheduled event is also a caused event, but a scheduled event always ends a service after some definite delay of time.

3   Extending AORSL by Adding an Activity Concept

The Activity concept is introduced into the AORSL meta-model by making activities a special case of complex events having a start event and an end event components. In our simulation language the entities have types, therefore, an Activity has an `ActivityType` represented by an abstract class that refines the top-level class `EntityType` with optional start and end event correlation properties (i.e. `UML::Property`). The values of these correlation properties act just like identifiers for the start event and end event types that belong to an activity, placed in some flow of activities.

It is a way to define the semantic of the next step in a chain of activities that follow each other in time, and to correlate the activity end event with the triggering (i.e. start event) of the next activity in sequence. This behavior is closely related with the BPDM way to define sequence of activities. We agree with their perspective and simply consider AORSL activities as steps in the simulation process that can be ordered in time. As we already mentioned, BPDM ([1]) uses the concept of *successions* to express time ordering of the end event of the *predecessor activity* and the start event of the *successor activity*. In this view, events enable the time ordering of triggered events in order to identify exactly which attached event they are referring to, at each end (see BPMN 2.0 Proposal pp.205).

BPMN adds its notation to the above explained semantic i.e. the BPMN Sequence Flow. For simplification, BPMN uses the same notation to denote: (1) an activity that immediately succeeds another activity, (2) an activity that succeeds another activity in a flow of a process, but have other intermediate activities in between, (3) an activity that succeeds a sub-process, (4) an activity that succeeds an event, and (5) an activity that succeeds a gateway. Using the same notation, the different semantics that a succession may have collapse in the unique, classical notation of BPMN sequence flow.

An AORSL `ActivityType` has a mandatory `StartEventType` that triggers the activity instance, and one or more `EndEventTypes` (i.e. specialization subclasses of `EnvironmentEventType`) that express different possible completion horizons of the activity (see Figure 3). As the `Activity` class extends the `Event` class, we can also specify the duration of the work performed by using the optional `duration` attribute. In this case, the activity is triggered by the mandatory `StartEvent` and has a random established duration. When the time expires, we do not have to specify the `EndEvent`, as it is automatically generated in a form of a default `ActivityEndEvent`. An activity may have associated an actor that deals with the activity enactment. The same concept, but under different terminology we can find it in BPDM ([3]) and BPMN ([4]) Specifications (i.e. the *Performer* concept).

In our simulation model, when an activity is performed by an actor, it is usually triggered by an `ActionEventType`, therefore the activity's `StartEvent` should be explicitly defined. The association of an actor with an activity may be done dynamically by the activity triggering event. This is the case when the actor of the triggering event becomes also the actor for the activity.

But, there are situations when the activity is not performed by an actor of the environment i.e. an agent type in the simulation system, but by the environment itself. In this case, we consider that the activity has no defined actor. A consequence is that the activity will be triggered by a default `ActivityStartEvent`. Our simulation model also allows us the possibility not to mention the actor for an activity in certain cases i.e. the case of our example where the unique entity in the simulation model is the Double Queue System agent itself, therefore all activities and environment events have it as a default actor.

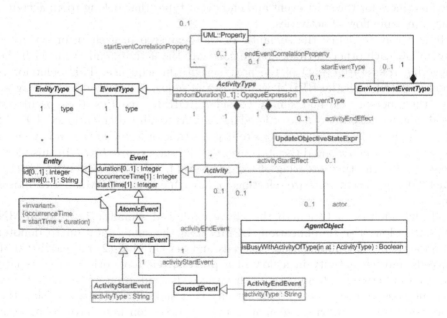

Fig. 3. AORS Activity - Metamodel

Real situations in life show us that the start and the end of an activity usually have some consequences or event effects. The start event of the `PerformScale` activity will cause the service to became busy in the system i.e. (`scaleBusy == true`), and the end event effect of the same activity is to update the same state variable i.e. (`scaleBusy == false`).

3.1 Simulating a Double Queue System Using Activities

Further on, we show how to model and simulate the Double Queue System by using the activity concept introduced in the previous Section. This example includes three activities: (1) *Loading at the Loading Service*, (2) *Weighing at the Scale Service* and (3) the *Transportation Service*. In our scenario there are described the entity types used in our simulation. We considered the Double Queue System entity as an agent enriched with attributes that allow us to manipulate the characteristics of the two queues: the length and the state when they are busy or not in the system. The Double Queue System plays the role of the environment of our simulation model and its attributes are state variables.

For each activity from the system we have to define the `ActivityType`. The activity is triggered by an implicitly activity start event, therefore we do not have to explicitly mention it in code. The activity have a duration calculated using

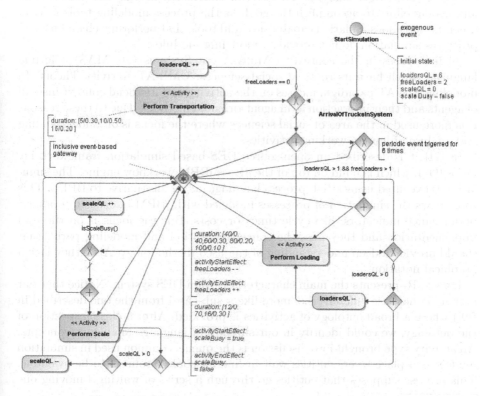

Fig. 4. Modeling a Double Queue System with Activities

the `randomScaleTime()` inner function implementation and expressed using the `Duration` child element.

One should notice that the Figure 4 includes the inclusive event-based gateway, whose semantics is not yet included into the BPMN set of core elements, but scheduled to be included in the future version[2]. Moreover, the inclusive event-gateway can be succeeded by an activity, as it triggers the activity start event. We consider in our example only activities that have delays i.e. a duration in time, implicitly expressed by a scheduled activity end event, or explicitly mentioned by the activity duration.

We can easily remark that the diagram becomes more readable in what regards the quantitative measurement of used symbols and also their semantics. Activity symbols, represented using BPMN task notation with added stereotypes `Activity` simplifies the diagram semantic by make it easier to be followed by an inexperienced user.

4   Related Works

In ([10]) is presented a study on the suitability of the available tools for BPS, by evaluating their capabilities for modeling /simulation /execution and the quality of statistical analysis. The overall conclusion reveals the existence of an ongoing effort to accomplish the goal, as the process modeling tools lack on different percents simulation capabilities, and tools that perform well on business processes simulation do not provide a modeling module.

[6] introduces in the context of Multi-Agent Systems (i.e. MAS) a formal language which have its roots in social sciences: UML-AT Activity Theory. In modeling, the AT paradigm focuses on the activity and its social context instead of agents and their interaction as in agent-oriented methods. Due to these reasons it is more used in the area of social sciences where the focus is on understanding and analyse of human-working activities.

In [11] it is described an open-source DES-based simulation framework i.e. DESMO-J, which is build on top of the JBoss jBPM workflow engine. The simulation is executed using jPDL process language, as an alternative to BPEL. This tool allows the simulation of processes modeled with jBPM in order to evaluate performance indicators, like cycle times or costs. But the focus is on the tool implementation and they miss the conceptualisation and modeling parts, that should provide a deep understanding of the used methodology. Also, they lack a graphical notation.

Ingalls, R. presents the main characteristics of a DES system. Notice that our activity concept is different (i.e. more like a sub-case) from the one described in ([9]) where a broad ontology of activities is provided. After a close inspection of the ontology, we could identify in our simulation language analogous concepts. An activity type brought into discussion is the queue: common used in simulation models as a place where entities wait in line for some resources to be available. This process supposes that entities go through a series of waiting - moving one

---

[2] http://www.omg.org/issues/bpmn-ftf.html#Issue10096

step further - steps and also involves entities state changes. Our example comprises two queues that form when waiting for loaders and scale resources to be available. The queue is more like a complex activity type i.e. the sub-process concept.

Greasley et al. envision in [7] a DES approach for simulation of a workflow system. The workflow steps are conceptualised as a series of tasks and events that occur through time. Tasks occur in response to events and are performed by actors. But, the concept of activity, mentioned in their terminology as task, is unnecessary too complicated and comprises: an event type, which can be a seed event (T0) or a completion event (T3), a start event type (T1), an end event type (T2), the lead time before task needs to start (T1- T0 or T1- T3), the task duration (T2 - T1), and next event relation and identifier.

In the actual BPMN/BPDM 2.0 Specification Proposal ([5]) that aims at joining both BPDM ([3]) and (BEA, IBM, Oracle, SAP) team ([4]) working results, the concept of activity is envisioned as a construct that involves two events i.e. *start-event* and *end-event* and/or the *time in between*.

The activities are described *steps in a process* that can be ordered in time by *successions* (i.e. BPMN Sequence Flow), and are based on start event, end event, or other events of the activities. Successions express the time ordering of the end of their predecessor activity and the start of their successor activity, unless other events are specified (see BPMN 2.0 Specification Proposal pp.204).

5   Conclusions and Future Works

Our work involves aspects from modeling, management and simulation of DESs. We presented an ongoing work that extends the AORSL meta-model with the *activity* concept, a special case of complex events having a start event and an end event components. We showed that our approach is closely related with BPDM/BPMN (i.e. BPMN 2.0 Specification proposals) perspective of modeling activities. With this in mind, the purpose of future works is to identify an extension of the core BPMN for capturing important simulation concepts such that the extended BPMN can be used as a simulation modeling language. To clarify this, the applicability of BPMN for modeling agent-based simulations has to be investigated. Future work directions also envision a BPMN graphical notation for AORSL business process simulation.

References

1. Bock, C.: Tutorial: Introduction to the Business Process Definition Metamodel (2008), http://www.omg.org/cgi-bin/doc?omg/08-06-32
2. (OMG) Business Process Modeling Notation 1.2, (BPMN 1.2) (2009), http://www.omg.org/docs/formal/09-01-03.pdf
3. (BPDM Team) Adaptive, Axway Software, EDS, Lombardi Software, MEGA International, Troux Technologies, Unisys, BPMN 2.0 Specification Proposal (2008), http://www.omg.org/cgi-bin/doc?bmi/08-02-03

4. (BEA, IBM, Oracle, SAP), BPMN 2.0 Specification Proposal (2008), http://www. omg.org/cgi-bin/doc?bmi/08-02-06
5. BPMN/BPDM 2.0 Specification Proposal (2008), http://www.omg.org/docs/bmi/ 08-09-07.pdf
6. Fuentes-Fernandez, R., Gomez-Sanz, J.J., Pavon, J.: Model Integration in agent-oriented development. Int. Journal of Agent-Oriented Software Engineering 1(1), 2–28 (2007)
7. Greasley, A., Chaffey, D.: A Simulation of an Estate Agency Workflow System. In: Proceedings of the 2000 Summer Computer Simulation Conference, Society for Computer Simulation, San Diego, USA (2000)
8. Greasley, A.: The book: Simulation Modeling for Business. Ashgate Publisher, England (2004)
9. Ingalls, R.G.: Introduction to Simulation. In: Mason, S.J., Hill, R.R., Mönch, L., Rose, O., Jefferson, T., Fowler, J.W. (eds.) Proceedings of the 40th Conference on Winter Simulation, pp. 17–26 (2008)
10. Jansen-Vullers, M.H., Netjes, M.: Business Process Simulation - A Tool Survey. In: Jensen, K. (ed.) The Seventh Workshop on the Practical Use of Coloured Petri Nets and CPN Tools. DAIMI PB, vol. 579, pp. 77–96. University of Aarhus, Aarhus (2006)
11. Ruecker, B.: Master Thesis: Building an open source Business Process Simulation tool with JBoss jBPM (2008), http://www.camunda.com/content/ publikationen/bernd-ruecker-business-process-simulation-with-jbpm.pdf
12. Wagner, G.: AOR Modeling and Simulation - Towards a General Architecture for Agent-Based Discrete Event Simulation. In: Giorgini, P., Henderson-Sellers, B., Winikoff, M. (eds.) AOIS 2003. LNCS (LNAI), vol. 3030, pp. 174–188. Springer, Heidelberg (2004)

External and Internal Events in EPCs: e²EPCs

Oliver Kopp, Matthias Wieland, and Frank Leymann

Institute of Architecture of Application Systems, University of Stuttgart, Germany
lastname@iaas.uni-stuttgart.de

Abstract. The notion of event-driven process chains (EPC) is widely used to model processes. It is an ongoing discussion of how to reach executable workflows from EPCs. While the transformation of the general structure and the functions is well-understood, the transformation of events is an open issue. This paper discusses different possible events types and their semantics. Furthermore, it presents a transformation of the introduced event types to workflow constructs respecting the semantics of each event.

1 Introduction

Companies have a strong interest in Business Process Management (BPM) technology to align and support their business processes with IT infrastructure. A business process is a collection of related, structured activities and tasks that produce a specific service or product for customers. Business processes can be executed on an IT infrastructure using workflows. Business processes are expressed using specialized visual process modeling languages such as the Business Process Modeling Notation (BPMN, [1]) or Event-Driven Process Chains (EPC, [2,3]). BPMN and EPCs are mostly concerned with the modeling aspect of business processes, and therefore put an emphasis on being easy to use by providing a standardized set of visualization elements, whereas not defining exact execution semantics. They are designed for the use by non-technical thinking people who want to concentrate on modeling the high-level business process.

In contrast, the Web Service Business Process Execution Language [4] (WS-BPEL or BPEL for short), facilitates business process execution by providing and standardizing execution semantics for orchestrating business activities as workflows. It defines the way in which basic services (business activities in the form of Web Services) are used to build new, coarser grained services. For example, a loan approval workflow orchestrates the basic services "RiskAssessment", "CreditCheck" and "IncomeReview". Since Web Services are an implementation of the SOA architectural style, process systems using BPEL as orchestration language are naturally embedded into an existing service oriented architecture implemented by Web Services.

The BPM lifecycle (Phases: Modeling, Execution, Analysis and Optimization) has the aim to continuously improve the process. This is known as business process reengineering. Thus, a process definition is never stable and is permanently adapted. As a consequence, the workflow implementing the changed business

S. Rinderle-Ma et al. (Eds.): BPM 2009 Workshops, LNBIP 43, pp. 381–392, 2010.

process also has to be remodeled all the time. This is the main motivation for automatic transformation of business processes to workflows without ignoring parts of the business process that have to be inserted again in the workflow. In this paper we show how EPC processes can be transformed to workflows not only based on the functions but also transforming the events of the EPC. In the following, we assume that the modeled processes are intended to serve as basis for an automatic execution by a workflow engine.

Event-driven Process Chains (EPCs, [3, 2]) are an event-centric business process modeling language that treats events as "first class citizens", i.e. the occurrence of events are fundamental elements of the business process. EPCs are part of the ARIS framework [5], a "holistic modeling approach" to design and document architectures of integrated information systems from a business' perspective. In ARIS, EPCs are used in the "control view" to describe business processes, allowing for integration and reuse of elements from other views of a model. EPCs consist of four main elements: (i) events (depicted as hexagons), (ii) functions (depicted as rounded boxes), (iii) connectors (depicted as circles) and (iv) control flow arcs. Events in EPCs are *passive*, i.e. they represent a state change in the system, but do not cause it (e.g. they do not provide decisions, but represent decisions taken). Events trigger functions, which are *active* elements that represent the actual work and again raise events upon completion. Connectors are used to *join and split* control flow, represented by arcs in the EPC graph. An EPC starts and ends with one or more events, process control flow itself strictly follows an *alternating sequence of functions and events*, possibly with connectors specifying the kind of control flow join and split in between. The extended event driven process chain (eEPC) extends the EPC by associations to functions. For example, a function may be associated with the organizational unit performing the function or the data needed and produced by the function. Common accepted associations may be found in the EPC Markup Language (EPML, [6]).

eEPCs are in strong contrast to other established process languages such as the Web Services Business Process Execution Language (WS-BPEL or BPEL for short, [4]) or the Business Process Modeling Notation (BPMN, [1]). BPEL and BPMN are rather *service centric* and do not enforce to use events as an integral part already at the modeling level. BPMN distinguishes a wide range of events including timer and message events. Mapping of events to BPEL is not an issue here, since there exists a corresponding BPEL construct for each event. BPMN exists in parallel to EPCs. Since EPCs currently do not offer an explicit distinction between internal and external events, we use eEPCs as basis for integration of process logic with the environment.

In current eEPC models, only functions may be annotated with additional information. In the case of events, the semantics is given by their label only. The number of events is three times the number of functions in the SAP reference model containing about 10.000 models [7]. Thus, events are an important information container. While [2] states that "events may reference information objects of the data model", this possibility is not used in products and not regarded in research.

Figure 1 presents an example eEPC. It models an excerpt of the business process "order processing" and is taken from [3]. The excerpt shows the function "Manufacture Item" and its context: after the supplier processed the order (event "(Supplier) Order Processed") the manufac-

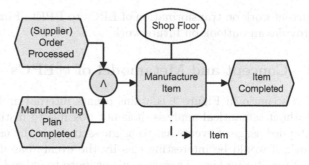

Fig. 1. Example scenario, taken from [3]

turing plan is completed (event "Manufacturing Plan Completed"), the function "Manufacture Item" can start. The conjunction of the two events is modeled by the and connector. The function itself is executed at the shop floor (association with the organizational unit "Shop Floor"), which produces an item. The IT relevant data of the item is represented in the data object "Item". After "Manufacture Item" completes, the event "Item Completed" occurs.

Events in eEPCs may be internal or external. *Internal* denotes that the event occurs as a direct result of a function. *External* denotes that the event occurs because of a state change in the environment. The EPC metamodel does not foresee explicit distinctions between internal and external events. Therefore it is not stated whether the event "Item Completed" is an internal or an external event. In case the function "Manufacture Item" denotes that a new manufacture request is sent to the shop floor without waiting for completion, the "Item Completed" events gets an external event, since the shop floor has to notice the process of completion. The other possibility is that the "Manufacture Item" function models the manufacturing of the item and finishes as soon as the item is finished. In this case, the event "Item Completed" is an internal event and the data produced by the function can be used to decide whether this event occurs.

In workflows, internal events are transition conditions between activities and external events are notifications by a message. Current transformation approaches either ignore events, treat them all as external events or treat them all as internal events. In this paper, we propose a modeling extension for eEPCs to allow the business modeler to distinguish internal and external events. This distinction allows generating a fine-grained BPEL workflow model out of the input eEPC. In addition, we use the additional information to generate a participant topology capturing the relation between the process and its environment. This artifact can then be used to wire existing services with the generated process.

Consequently, this paper is organized as follows: The concept and metamodel of our extension to extended event-driven process chains, e²EPCs, is presented in Sec. 2. Section 3 shows how the introduced distinction between internal and external events in e²EPCs can be transformed to BPEL and a participant topology which forms a choreography description. Section 4 provides an overview on current work on transformation of EPCs to BPEL. Finally, Sec. 5 concludes and provides an outlook on future work.

2   Concept and Metamodel of e²EPCs

The scenario in Figure 1 contains events internal and external to the process. Without semantical analysis, it is not possible to distinguish them because the intended usage of events has to be guessed out of the used IT systems. As future work, it would be interesting classify the events based on the analysis of audit and monitoring logs. Therefore, we propose to extend the eEPC metamodel by adding associations between events and outputs of functions or organizational units to enable the explicit modeling of internal and external events.

This results in a new version of the scenario as shown in Fig. 2. In this figure, the new associations are marked and can be used to distinguish between internal and external events. The two start events (Order processed, Manufacturing plan completed) are connected to organizational units. This means, they receive messages from these systems. Start events always are external events and have to be connected to a organizational unit. In contrast, the "Item completed" event is an internal event recognized by the association to the output "Item" of the function "Manufacture Item". Thus, the event can be evaluated based on that data only and does not need further information. In summary, an event is an internal event if it is associated with output data. An event is an external event, if it is associated with an organizational unit. It is not possible to associate an event with both an organizational unit and output data. e²EPCs allow an event to be unassociated with any organizational unit or output data. In this case, the event cannot be transformed to BPEL, since it is not clear whether it is an internal or external event. Other possibilities to model internal and external events include the usage of swim lanes. The drawback of that approach is that the layout of existing EPCs has to be changed, since for each organizational unit and data item, a separate lane has to be introduced.

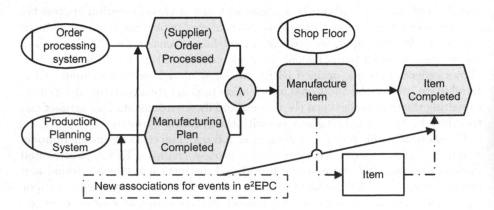

Fig. 2. Example Scenario modeled using e²EPC

In Fig. 3 all types of associations added to the eEPC metamodel [3] are shown. They are used to distinguish the two different event types. In e²EPCs, the symbol for an organizational unit is used as superclass for any kind of executor such as an IT system (computer hardware, machine, application software as listed in [3]), a Web Service and a human user. The different types of organizational units shown in Fig. 3 are used to illustrate the different possi-

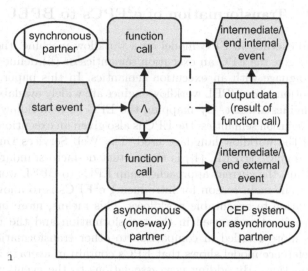

Fig. 3. Elements of e²EPCs

ble types of organizational units used in the transformation. For the modeler, these organizational units do not visually differ. The different types have to be stored in the repository of the used modeling tool and the type information of each organizational unit has to be handed over to the transformation. In that way, the business user has not to be aware of the different types, but the IT expert responsible for the addition of existing IT service operations as organizational units to the repository.

Start events are at the beginning of a process and have no incoming arcs. These events are always triggered by messages and start the process execution. An association between a start event and the organizational unit producing the message is the only possible association allowed in the meta model.

Intermediate events have an incoming and an outgoing arc. An *external intermediate event* is triggered by a message from an organizational unit which makes it similar to a start event. No additional information, such as output data, may be needed to check whether the event happens. Otherwise, the event is not an external intermediate event anymore. An *internal intermediate event* is always connected with an output of an preceding function. The data contained in the output has to be sufficient to determine whether the event happens. If more information was needed, the event would have to receive an message or would have to use an information system for evaluation. In this case, it is not intermediate event anymore and possibly an external intermediate event or even a function with a subsequent event.

End events are at the end of a process and have no outgoing arcs. The distinction between internal end events and external end events is the same as in the case of intermediate events.

3   Transformation of e²EPCs to BPEL

To execute an EPC model on a workflow machine, there are two general ways:
(i) give the EPC an execution semantics or (ii) define a mapping to a workflow
language with an execution semantics. In this paper, we focus on the second
option, since BPEL workflow engines are widely available, whereas EPC workflow
engines are not. By mapping the EPC to a workflow language with a defined
execution semantics, the EPC is also given an execution semantics: the semantics
of the workflow language used. The Web Services Business Process Execution
Language (BPEL, [4]) is the current de-facto standard for workflow execution.
Thus, the current approaches map EPCs to BPEL workflows.

The main reason for introducing e²EPCs is to allow a higher value transformation to executable workflows. This means, more information of the process
specification is used in the transformation and the resulting workflow model
is more detailed in comparison to other transformation approaches. The SAP
reference model shows that EPCs contain in average 3 times more events than
functions. By adding new associations to the events we enable to inclusion of
them in the generated workflows. Without that association the events usually
are simply ignored. In the following, we present a transformation which makes
use of the events and transforms them to elements in the generated abstract
workflow.

A BPEL workflow does not need to be executable by itself. The BPEL specification offers to model abstract workflows, which may hide operational details.
So called opaque activities can be used to model left-out behavior. Abstract
workflows may be refined by IT experts to executable workflows enabling the
execution on a workflow engine. It is widely acknowledged that a transformation
cannot generate an executable workflow, since necessary execution details, such
as the concrete message formats and format transformation is missing.

Figure 4 provides an
overview on the transformation. The list of participants
is essential for the choreography the abstract workflow is embedded in. The
participants can be derived
from the associations to the
functions, start events, intermediate external events and
end external events. Each organizational unit becomes a
participant in the choreography. A choreography captures the interplay between
different workflows [8].

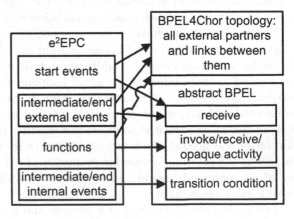

Fig. 4. Transformation

The BPEL workflow itself is transformed out of the EPC process. Each output
data element is transformed to a variable declaration in the process. Then, the

structure of the process is determined as described in [9], which applies the techniques presented in [10,11] to EPCs. In general, the graph-structure is preserved and thus this transformation follows the Element-Minimization strategy presented in [12] with the addition that pick and while structures are transformed to the respective structure in BPEL. A BPEL workflow defines an orchestration of Web services and consists of structured and basic activities. The actual business functions are not implemented by BPEL itself, but by Web services, where the business data is sent to and received from using messages (events are represented as messages, too). Hence, the most important basic activities are invoke and receive. An invoke activity is used to send a message to a Web service. A receive activity is used to receive a message. The structured activity pick realizes a one-out-of-n choice of messages to receive: the first arrived message wins and the other messages are ignored at that activity. Control flow itself is either modeled block-structured using if and sequence activities or using graph-based constructs realized by the flow activity. In a flow activity, activities are connected using links. The issue of non-local join semantics is solved by applying Dead-path Elimination (DPE) which in turn uses negative control tokens. DPE itself is formally defined in [13], specified for BPEL in [4] and explained in detail in [14].

An EPC function is mapped to an invoke, receive or and opaque activity based on the associated organizational unit. In case the organizational unit models an IT service operation, which is already specified, the interaction is known. In the case of current common IT service operations, the interaction patterns are (from the view of the service) in, in/out and out. The view of the business process is dual, therefore in and in/out are transformed to invoke and out to a receive. In case the organizational unit does not model an IT service operation, an opaque activity is generated. If the association from the external event to the organizational unit was directed, the interaction pattern could be derived. We did not introduce directed associations in e²EPCs, since it is unlikely that a business user is aware of the interaction paradigm of a special IT system.

The work of [15] shows that start events in EPCs can be interpreted as message events and also as condition filters. To instantiate a process, BPEL supports message events only. Due to the design of BPEL, we will also treat EPC start events as message events. Similar to [16,9], start events joined by a XOR connector are transformed to a pick activity. Start events joined by an AND connector are transformed to receive activities. End events are treated as intermediate events targeting a special function. This special function is transformed to an empty activity used as target for the link.

Intermediate external events are transformed dependent on the preceding connector. In the case of a XOR connector, the each external event is transformed to a receive activity. In the case of an AND connector, the external event is transformed to a branch of a pick activity. OR predecessors are not supported. This part of the transformation is described in detail in [9].

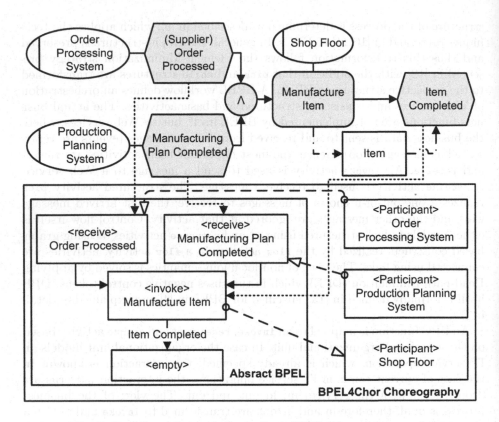

Fig. 5. Transformation and the result as BPEL4Chor choreography

Intermediate internal events are transformed to transitions conditions on a control link. The link connects the transformation of the element preceding the event to the transformation of the element succeeding the event. The label of the event is put as condition on the control link. This part of the transformation follows the algorithm described in [17].

Currently, BPEL4Chor is the only language based on BPEL which is capable to capture the links between multiple process models [18]. BPEL4Chor's participant topology lists the participants of the choreography and the message links between them. For each generated communication activity, a message link in the BPEL4Chor topology is generated. For example, the message link for the "(Supplier) Order Processed" event is as follows:

```
<messageLink sender="OrderProcessingSystem" receiver="OrderProcess"
receiveActtivity="OrderProcessed">
```
. Note that the activity gets the camel case version of the label of the respective EPC function or event as name.

After the abstract BPEL workflow and the topology information has been generated, the abstract workflow has to be manually refined to an executable workflow model which can be enacted by a workflow engine. For wiring the generated workflow with the other participants in the choreography, a BPEL4Chor participant grounding has to be defined, where each message link is assigned to a Web Service operation. Using that information, the workflow can be deployed. If the other participants do not exist, their behavior can be derived by generating a view on the generated abstract BPEL workflow containing only the interaction with the missing participant as outlined in [19]. Note that a participant in a choreography does not necessarily need to be implemented as a BPEL workflow. It may also implemented as plain Web Service, since the participant behavior description in a choreography only specifies the public visible behavior and not the actual implementation.

Figure 5 presents the transformation idea and a graphical representation of the transformation result. An implementation is not available, but is possible by extending the ProM tool or by extending other EPC to BPEL transformations. There exists a formal syntax of EPCs [20] and BPEL [21]. Thus, a formal transformation can be defined but is not part of this paper.

Since the BPM lifecycle has the aim to continuously improve the process model, a process definition is never stable and is permanently adapted. Thus, the EPC process has to be changed all the time and consequently the BPEL workflow will change accordingly. The abstract BPEL workflow $BPEL_g$ is manually refined to an executable workflow $BPEL_e$. In order to keep the added technical details, the BPEL workflow cannot simply be regenerated, but rather needs to be updated in a smart way. Therefore we take the original generated model $BPEL_g$ and the model generated within the second lifecycle round $BPEL_g'$ to compute the difference $\Delta(BPEL_g, BPEL_g')$. Now, it is possible to apply this difference Δ to the original executable workflow $BPEL_e$ in order to get a starting point for the executable workflow $BPEL_e'$ that contains both, the new semantics of the process model and the refinements made in the previous lifecycle round. It may be possible that not all differences can be applied to the new model in case the model has significantly changed. Nevertheless, the derived executable workflow $BPEL_e'$ contains more information than the generated abstract workflow $BPEL_g'$. A detailed discussion of advantages and drawbacks in the case of applying differences to models is presented in [22].

Events concerning the lifecycle of events are out of scope of the paper. These kinds of events are neither treated in the EPC process nor the BPEL workflow itself, but by the workflow engine.

4   Related Work

This section provides an overview on current approaches to transform EPCs to BPEL and to choreographies.

A general overview of all available transformations from EPCs to BPEL is provided in [23, 24]. Figure 6 summarizes the different possibilities to transform events into a workflow: (i) An event can be ignored. (ii) An event can be transformed to a message receipt. (iii) Finally, an event can be transformed to a transition condition. The transformation approach presented in this paper distinguishes between internal and external events and transforms start events,

intermediate events as well as end
events. Our approach also distinguishes between external and internal events. Current related work
either does not handle all events or
does not distinguish between external
and internal events. Table 1 shows how
each related work deals with events.
[17] deals with a variant of EPCs and
translates them to a graph-structure.
[12] presents different transformation
strategies from EPC to BPEL. The
transformation strategies are divided

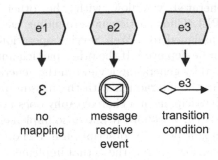

Fig. 6. Different possibilities to transform events into a workflow

into two categories: Preserving the
graph-structure or translating as much structures as possible into the corresponding BPEL structures. [25] shows possible annotations to EPCs to enable Web
Service specific details in BPEL workflows. [26] identifies workflow patterns [27]
in the EPC and translates each pattern to the respective BPEL construct. [16]
presents on overview on the transformation using in the ARIS toolset. [9] argues that all events in EPCs should be treated as external events and show how
complex event processing can be used to transform EPCs to BPEL. Finally, [28]
shows how EPCs can be used to model all details of BPEL processes such as
concrete associations to services and variable modifications.

In [29] the authors translate Petri nets into "readable" BPEL code. The algorithm follows the Structure-Maximization strategy presented in [12]. Since
Petri-nets are used as input, the translation is not aware of events. Using the
event distinction presented in this paper, the translation of [29] may be adopted
to use e^2EPCs as input language.

Table 1. Current EPC-to-BPEL transformation approaches and their treatment of events

Reference	Distinction	Start Event	Intermediate Event	End Event
[17] Kopp et al. 2007	n	–	transition condition	–
[12] Mendling et al. 2008	n	pick/empty	–	terminate
[25] Schmelzle 2007	n	receive	transition condition	reply
[26] Specht et al. 2005	n	–	transition condition	–
[16] Stein et al. 2007	n	receive	–	invoke
[9] Wieland et al. 2009	n	pick/receive	pick/receive	pick/receive
[28] Ziemann et al. 2005	y	–	pick/receive	–
This paper	y	pick/receive	transition condition/ pick/receive	transition condition/ pick/receive

Currently, there is no work on transforming EPCs to a choreography definition. Besides choreographies, business landscape [30] also provide an overview on the interplay of services. The work presented in [31] shows how a business landscape can be generated out of EPCs and lists other work generating system overviews out of EPCs.

5 Conclusion and Outlook

This paper presented an extension to eEPCs to enable an unambiguous distinction between internal and external events. We showed how this distinction can be used to improve the mappings from eEPCs to BPEL by generating transition conditions out of an internal event and generating a receiving activity in case of an external event.

Future work is to provide suitable tool support for the presented method. Future area of research includes the evaluation of combined intermediate events. These combined events may be associated with both, an organizational unit and output data. These associations denote that a received message and the evaluation of process internal data is needed to determine whether the event happens.

Acknowledgments. This work has been supported by the BMBF funded project Tools4BPEL (01ISE08B) and the DFG project Nexus (SFB627). We thank Wil van der Aalst for the fruitful discussions at BIS 2009.

References

1. Object Management Group: Business Process Modeling Notation, V1.2. (2009)
2. Keller, G., Nüttgens, N., Scheer, A.W.: Semantische Prozessmodellierung auf der Grundlage Ereignisgesteuerter Prozessketten (EPK). Technical Report Heft 89, Universität des Saarlandes (1992)
3. Scheer, A.W., Thomas, O., Adam, O.: Process Modeling Using Event-Driven Process Chains. In: Process-Aware Information Systems: Bridging People and Software Through Process Technology, pp. 119–146. Wiley & Sons, Chichester (2005)
4. OASIS: Web Services Business Process Execution Language Version 2.0 (2007)
5. Scheer, A.W.: ARIS-Modellierungs-Methoden, Metamodelle, Anwendungen. Springer, Heidelberg (2003)
6. Mendling, J., Nüttgens, M.: EPC markup language (EPML): an XML-based interchange format for event-driven process chains (EPC). ISeB 4(3) (2006)
7. Mendling, J.: Errors in the SAP Reference Model. BPTrends (June 2006)
8. Decker, G., Kopp, O., Barros, A.: An Introduction to Service Choreographies. Information Technology 50(2), 122–127 (2008)
9. Wieland, M., Martin, D., Kopp, O., Leymann, F.: SOEDA: A Methodology for Specification and Implementation of Applications on a Service-Oriented Event-Driven Architecture. In: Abramowicz, W. (ed.) BIS 2009. LNBIP, vol. 21, pp. 193–204. Springer, Heidelberg (2009)
10. Vanhatalo, J., Völzer, H., Koehler, J.: The Refined Process Structure Tree. In: Dumas, M., Reichert, M., Shan, M.-C. (eds.) BPM 2008. LNCS, vol. 5240, pp. 100–115. Springer, Heidelberg (2008)

11. García-Bañuelos, L.: Pattern Identification and Classification in the Translation from BPMN to BPEL. In: Meersman, R., Tari, Z. (eds.) OTM 2008, Part I. LNCS, vol. 5331, pp. 436–444. Springer, Heidelberg (2008)
12. Mendling, J., Lassen, K.B., Zdun, U.: On the Transformation of Control Flow between Block-Oriented and Graph-Oriented ProcessModeling Languages. IJBPIM 3(2), 96–108 (2008)
13. Leymann, F., Roller, D.: Production Workflow: Concepts and Techniques. Prentice Hall PTR, Englewood Cliffs (2000)
14. Curbera, F., Khalaf, R., Leymann, F., Weerawarana, S.: Exception Handling in the BPEL4WS Language. In: van der Aalst, W.M.P., ter Hofstede, A.H.M., Weske, M. (eds.) BPM 2003. LNCS, vol. 2678, pp. 276–290. Springer, Heidelberg (2003)
15. Decker, G., Mendling, J.: Process Instantiation. Data & Knowledge Engineering 68, 777–792 (2009)
16. Stein, S., Ivanov, K.: EPK nach BPEL Transformation als Voraussetzung für praktische Umsetzung einer SOA. In: Software Engineering 2007. GI (2007)
17. Kopp, O., Unger, T., Leymann, F.: Nautilus Event-driven Process Chains: Syntax, Semantics, and their mapping to BPEL. In: EPK 2006 (2006)
18. Decker, G., Kopp, O., Leymann, F., Weske, M.: Interacting Services: From Specification to Execution. Data & Knowledge Engineering (April 2009)
19. Lohmann, N., Kopp, O., Leymann, F., Reisig, W.: Analyzing BPEL4Chor: Verification and Participant Synthesis. In: Dumas, M., Heckel, R. (eds.) WS-FM 2007. LNCS, vol. 4937, pp. 46–60. Springer, Heidelberg (2008)
20. Kindler, E.: On the Semantics of EPCs: A Framework for Resolving the Vicious Circle. Data Knowl. Eng. 56(1), 23–40 (2006)
21. Kopp, O., Mietzner, R., Leymann, F.: Abstract Syntax of WS-BPEL 2.0. Technical report, University of Stuttgart, IAAS, Germany (2008)
22. Kindler, E., Könemann, P., Unland, L.: Difference-based model synchronization in an industrial MDD process. In: MDTPI 2009 (2009)
23. Stein, S., Kühne, S., Ivanov, K.: Business to IT Transformations Revisited. In: Ardagna, D., et al. (eds.) BPM 2008 Workshops. LNBIP, vol. 17, pp. 176–187. Springer, Heidelberg (2009)
24. Wieland, M., et al.: Events Make Workflows Really Useful. Technical report, University of Stuttgart, IAAS, Germany (2008)
25. Schmelzle, O.: Transformation von annotierten Geschäftsprozessen nach BPEL. Master's thesis, Gottfried Wilhelm Leibniz Universität Hannover (2007)
26. Specht, T., et al.: Modeling cooperative business processes and transformation to a service oriented architecture. In: CEC 2005, July 2005, pp. 249–256 (2005)
27. van der Aalst, W.M.P., ter Hofstede, A.H.M., Kiepuszewski, B., Barros, A.P.: Workflow Patterns. Distributed and Parallel Databases 14(1), 5–51 (2003)
28. Ziemann, J., Mendling., J.: EPC-Based Modelling of BPEL Processes: a Pragmatic Transformation Approach. In: MITIP (2005)
29. van der Aalst, W.M.P., Bisgaard Lassen, K.: Translating unstructured workflow processes to readable bpel: Theory and implementation. InfSof 50(3) (2008)
30. Keller, F., Wendt, S.: FMC: An approach towards architecture-centric system development. In: ECBS 2003 (2003)
31. Kopp, O., Eberle, H., Leymann, F., Unger, T.: From Process Models to Business Landscapes. In: EPK 2007 (2007)

An Event-Driven Modeling Approach for Dynamic Human-Intensive Business Processes

Nancy Alexopoulou[1], Mara Nikolaidou[2], Dimosthenis Anagnostopoulos[2],
and Drakoulis Martakos[1]

[1] Department of Informatics & Telecommunications, University of Athens,
Athens, Greece
[2] Department of Informatics & Telematics, Harokopio University of Athens,
Athens, Greece

Abstract. One of the most challenging business process categories in terms of
agility are those exhibiting dynamic behaviour and involving intense human decision. Any effort to automate such processes may constrain their agility, which
constitutes an intrinsic requirement for this process category. Therefore, these
two factors, i.e. intense human involvement and dynamic behaviour, pose a
challenge regarding the role of a BPMS for such processes. In this paper, we
explore the role of BPMS for dynamic, human-intensive processes and propose
an event-driven modeling approach that efficiently supports modeling requirements of such processes. To validate our approach we provided a case study
from the medical arena concerning medical treatment, which is a typical example of dynamic, human-intensive processes. While the focus of this paper is to
introduce the modeling concepts, enactment aspects of the proposed approach
are also discussed.

Keywords: Dynamic business processes, human-intensive business processes,
event-driven model.

1 Introduction

Nowadays, business process automation is usually accomplished through the utilization of process-aware information systems [1] based on BPMS (Business Process
Management System) technology and explicit process models that follow a strict
action sequence. Such a sequence dictated by the most traditional approaches [2], [3]
is suitable for well structured processes whose objective is to impose this sequence to
the involved actors. However, there are processes in which activities performed are
strongly based upon human decision influenced by the circumstances as well as un-
predicted contingencies. Such processes are characterized by dynamic behaviour and
intense human involvement and cannot be described through a specific order of actions, since such a description would hinder significantly the agility required by the
nature of these processes. Therefore an approach is required permeated by a different
logic from that governing traditional action-driven approaches.

To this end, we adopted the event-driven paradigm for the development of a business process modeling approach eligible for the design of dynamic, human-intensive
processes. Though the event-driven paradigm is well-established for the execution of

S. Rinderle-Ma et al. (Eds.): BPM 2009 Workshops, LNBIP 43, pp. 393–404, 2010.

business processes (e.g. ECA model [4]), the potential of applying events as a core concept (as opposed to the complementary fashion appearing in modeling approaches such as Aris [3]) for the design of business processes has not been explored. We show in this paper that events can be effectively used to promote agility in the design of dynamic, human-intensive processes.

An event represents something that happens that is meaningful for the enterprise. As such, it can express in a more abstract manner the conditions under which an action should be initiated. Such conditions may arise from data modifications, human decisions, timing states or anything that could lead to a situation that should be handled, which can even be of an unknown source. An event of unknown source may be defined in a model in case it is meaningful for the organization, which means that its occurrence should be handled somehow, e.g. the sudden fall of the stock market may initiate a number of actions despite the fact that what caused the fall may be unknown. The event-driven paradigm inherently supports the description of processes that are affected by unexpected contingencies, since contingencies may be regarded unexpected events. The proposed event-driven modeling approach is called 'Notify and Register' (N&R).

The objective of this paper is to introduce the N&R approach and delineate how dynamic human-intensive processes can be efficiently modeled using this approach. For this purpose, a case study from the medical arena is provided. While the focus of this paper is to introduce the N&R modeling concepts, enactment aspects of N&R models are also discussed in the paper. This paper is organized as follows. The role of automation in dynamic, human-intensive business processes is discussed in section 2. In section 3, the 'Notify & Register' approach is analytically presented. A case study from the medical arena is provided in Section 4 in order to demonstrate the proposed modeling approach. Section 5 includes a discussion concerning enactment issues and implementation aspects of the approach. Conclusions and future work lie in section 6.

2   The Role of BPMS in Dynamic, Human-Intensive Business Processes

In most cases, when considering business process automation through a Business Process Management System (BPMS), what comes to one's mind is the automated coordination of specific actions that must be accomplished in a predetermined order. Indeed, business process automation has been mainly associated with action-driven processes [2], [3]. In such processes, actors perform specific tasks according to the order imposed by the BPMS. In this respect, the role of BPMS is to appropriately distribute work and ensure that process execution is realized according to a predefined flow.

However, there are processes for which task sequence cannot be prescribed, since what will be executed and when is strongly based upon human decision. In such human-intensive processes [5], execution is efficient if actors are free to decide what to do and when, depending on the specific case and unexpected events that may occur. Patient treatment and crisis management are typical examples of such processes. In such processes, what would be the role of a BPMS? Let us consider the example of patient treatment. While treating a patient, all data concerning, for example, diagnoses, examinations scheduled, medication provided, results of clinical and paraclinical examinations, etc., are registered in the patient record created when a patient is admitted to the hospital. Thus, information included in the patient record is formed by activities carried out by actors, such as physicians and nurses. Essentially, this information depicts how each patient case was handled. The way a patient's case is handled can be affected by special characteristics exhibited by the specific patient (e.g. a patient may be allergic to a specified medication) or unexpected conditions that may arise (e.g. a patient may suffer a heart attack). The information is included in patient record and used by the doctors that collaboratively treat the patient, nurses and the rest personnel involved in the treatment process. Involvement in treatment occurs after notification either in a regular or in an ad hoc manner. For example, microbiologists in the laboratory department are daily notified to perform blood examinations for each patient. Radiologists, on the other hand, are notified less regularly, i.e. whenever an imaging examination is required. Ad hoc notifications may also take place, for example, to a physician to examine a patient who suddenly complained for an intense chest pain or to doctors of the Intensive Care Unit, if a patient that has suffered a heart attack needs to be immediately transferred there.

Obviously, employing a typical BPMS to automate the treatment process and impose a specific sequence of actions would not only be inappropriate, but in addition would hinder agility. In alignment with the actual process, what would be required is a BPMS that would "sense" the events occurring in the real world and in response to them perform the required notifications as well as the registrations in patients' records. Likewise, in crisis management, when meaningful events occur, the BPMS should register information associated with these events and notify the relevant parties that something should be done to deal with the crisis encountered. In this respect, the BPMS responds to events, which are proactively generated by actors. The latter is in contrast to the traditional BPMS approach, where actors adopt a rather reactive attitude, since they wait for the tasks indicated by the BPMS in their task list. In summary, we state that *for dynamic, human-intensive business processes, the role of a BPMS should be to handle events, which are proactively generated by actors, by registering information related to these events and/or performing the required notifications to the actors that need to be involved in the process.*

It follows that for a BPMS to function in such a way, an appropriate executable model is needed. To this end, we propose in the following a modeling approach which produces executable models that serve event handling through registrations and notifications, being thus eligible for the description of dynamic human-intensive business processes.

3 Introducing the 'Notify and Register' Modeling Approach

The objective of the proposed modeling approach, called 'Notify & Register' (N&R), is to depict the events that occur in the real world specifying thus when registration and notification actions should be performed. Thus, the central concept of N&R approach is that of event. More specifically, business events of instantaneous and permanent occurrence are used in N&R approach to represent traces of real world activities performed by humans that are of significance to the business process model. In dynamic human-intensive processes, activities do not take place in a strict predetermined order. While there may be cases of activities carried out in a regular fashion, most often, they are performed whenever required, following human decision. Clinical examinations, for example, are performed every morning as well as whenever an unexpected symptom occurs. Therefore, N&R does not focus on the order of activities performed by humans, instead depicts, using events, 'stamps' of activities that have been accomplished, which signify the need for registering relevant information and/or notifying specific actors that need to be involved in the process. How an activity will be carried out is left to the actor and thus does not fall within the scope of a N&R model. This makes sense in human-intensive processes, as in these processes most tasks cannot be automated. Consequently, *stamp events*, as they are named, imply activities performed by humans either regularly or in an ad hoc manner. The latter case indicates that dynamic behavior is inherently accommodated in a N&R model.

A stamp event is generated by the actor category responsible to indicate that the corresponding non-automated activity has been accomplished. Usually, the generator of a stamp event coincides with the performer of the corresponding activity. However, this is not always necessary. As such, a stamp event in a N&R model, is always associated with a role that denotes the actor category responsible for its generation.

A stamp event, as described above, denotes that an activity has been accomplished. However, apart from confirmation, a stamp event may imply a request or a reply. The former case holds when an activity accomplishment causes the need for someone else to do something. The latter gives notice that the requested activity has been performed through a reply stamp event.

Apart from stamp events, N&R supports also time events. Time events can serve the need for sending reminders to the relative actors, in case they have not performed an activity that was meant to be performed. However, even in this case, the actors may not perform the activity, if they do not find it necessary. In general, through time events, N&R may support the description of routine activities that are performed in a regular basis and not because of human decision. Obviously, time evens are automatically generated and thus they are not related to roles.

The generation of a stamp event leads to registrations and/or notifications. As already mentioned, these activities should be automated by a BPMS. The rest, i.e. the human-intensive activities, are made known to the BMPS through the respective stamp events. Apparently, if a stamp event is a request or a reply, it definitely causes a notification action, while it may also cause a registration.

Every N&R model comprises a data folder composed of a unit hierarchy. Atomic units, i.e. units at the lowest level of the hierarchy, comprise data fields that specify the actual data. The data for each atomic unit are provided by the role that generates the stamp event and are registered to this unit by the BPMS. Registration is always associated with a specific atomic unit. Access policies may be defined, specifying the data fields that each role can alter. Alteration of an atomic unit can take place only if a stamp event occurs signifying that an activity was performed. The outcome of this activity is depicted through the data inserted in the corresponding data unit. As such, the N&R approach concerns only insertion of additional information. Updates or deletions of existing data are regarded as exceptional situations required as a result of human error.

Notification is related to roles indicating that respective actors playing these roles should be involved in the process when the corresponding event occurs. Notification informs the notified actors that a specific event has and indicates him/her the data folder in concern.

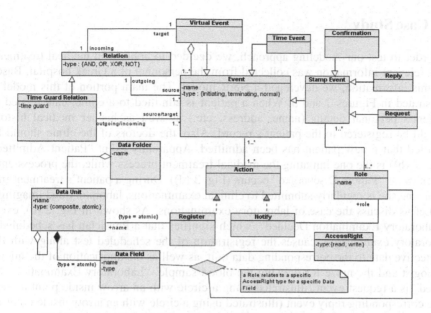

Fig. 1. The metamodel of the N&R business process modeling approach

Registration and notification can be triggered by a combination of events. For modeling efficiency, instead of directly connecting the combined events with the registration or notification actions, a virtual event can be defined aggregating the combined real events (stamp and/or time events) [6]. Then, the defined virtual event may be related with the corresponding registration or notification. Through virtual events, complexity is hidden within events. Registration or notification actions do not need to be aware of complicated event combinations that cause their execution. They only sense the produced conceptual event. A virtual event may also be defined through a simple causality relation, "aggregating" only one event if this serves the modeling purposes.

Stamp events can also be interrelated through timing guard relations. The latter impose that the occurrence of an event will follow the occurrence of another event within a specific time interval. A typical use of timing guards is to denote a temporal constraint between a request and a reply event, although timing guards may also be defined between two confirmation events.

It should be noted that every event defined in a N&R model is either directly or indirectly (through a virtual event) associated with registration or notification. If for example events A and B cause the event C, all of them are stamps of actions (i.e. no virtual) and only event C leads to registration or notification then the causality relation (A and B) → C is not defined in a N&R model, as events A and B are meaningless for the model. Meaningful events are only those causing registrations and/or notifications.

Lastly, it should be also noted that according to the N&R approach, a process is triggered by an event defined as initiating and ends because of the occurrence of an event defined as terminating. All the concepts described in the previous section are included in the metamodel of N&R approach depicted in Fig. 1.

4 Case Study

In order to test our modeling approach, we decided to apply it in medical treatment. The relevant information was collected from the personnel of a Greek hospital. Based on this information, we developed a N&R model. The main portion of this model is illustrated in Figures 2 and 3. When a patient is admitted to a clinic, data related to patient's personal details (name, address, etc.) as well as his/her medical history should be registered to the patient's record. Also, the doctors of the clinic should be notified that a new patient has been admitted. Apparently event "Patient Admitted" (Fig. 2 (b)) is the one initiating the medical treatment process while, the process ends when event "Patient Discharged" occurs (Fig. 3 (d)). During a patient's treatment in a clinic, he/she is regularly submitted to clinical examinations, laboratory and imaging.

Let us discuss the case of laboratory examinations. As shown in Fig. 2 (c), event "Laboratory Examination Decided", which signifies that a Physician has scheduled a laboratory examination, causes the registration of the scheduled test along with the respective date to the corresponding data unit, as well as the notification of the microbiologist and the nurse for drawing the blood sample. "Laboratory Examination Decided" is a request event (illustrated using a circle with an arrow inside pointing up). The corresponding reply event (illustrated using a circle with an arrow inside pointing down) is shown in Fig. 2 (d). According to Fig. 2 (d), when the examinations are ready, the microbiologist will generate the respective reply event which will lead to the registration of the results in the data unit "Laboratory Findings" as well as to the notification of the Physician that the results are ready.

As already mentioned, a registration or a notification can be initiated by more than one events. As presented in Fig. 3 (c), the registration of data related to the medication provided is initiated when the medication is specified or whenever the medication is adjusted (e.g. in case a patient manifests an allergy to the current medication) or even when ad hoc medication is provided. The latter concerns the case a nurse gives, for example, an analgesic pill to a patient suffering from a headache. Even this slight intervention is important to be registered in the patient's record, as the provided pill may counteract with the medication provided and produce adverse reactions. In Fig. 3 (c), a virtual event could have been alternatively defined aggregating through an OR relationship events "Medication Specified" and "Medication Updated". Then the virtual event would have been related to Medication unit and Nurse. However, as this was a simple OR relationship, the definition of a virtual event was not deemed necessary. Events of Fig. 3 (c) are confirmation events and are depicted using a double-lined circle.

Fig. 2 (f) and 3 (g) show causality relations with a time guard. Fig. 2 (f), for example, denotes that events "Laboratory Examinations Decided" and "Laboratory Findings Ready" are request and reply events respectively that must occur within a time interval. Time guard has been defined in the model in a parametric manner so that it can be instantiated with a specific value during run time.

Fig. 3 (b) presents a time event called "Time is 8 a.m.", using a circle with the clock hands inside it, which causes the virtual event "Clinical Examination Decided" This event is virtual in the sense that it is not a stamp event of a human activity, i.e. the clinical examination has not been decided in reality. The event is created to express the case of the routine clinical examination that takes place every morning.

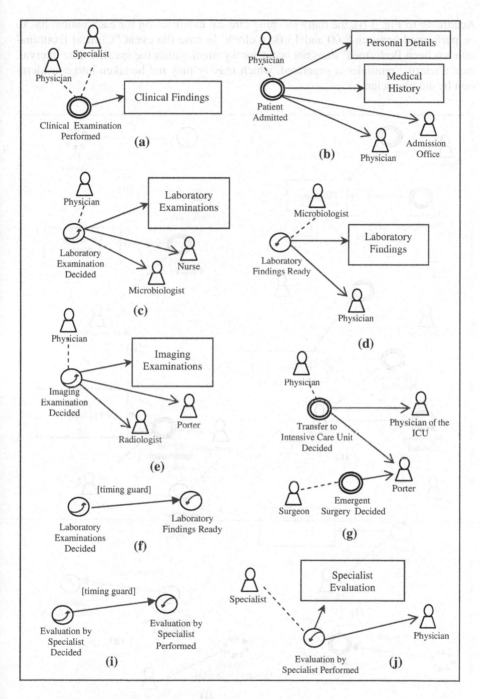

Fig. 2. Modeling the medical treatment process using the 'Notify & Register" approach

According to Fig. 3 (i), the daily morning clinical examination for each patient has to be performed between 8:00 and 13:00 o'clock. In case the event "Clinical Examination has been Performed" does not occur for a patient within the specific time interval, then a relative reminder is generated, which may or may not be taken into consideration by the physician.

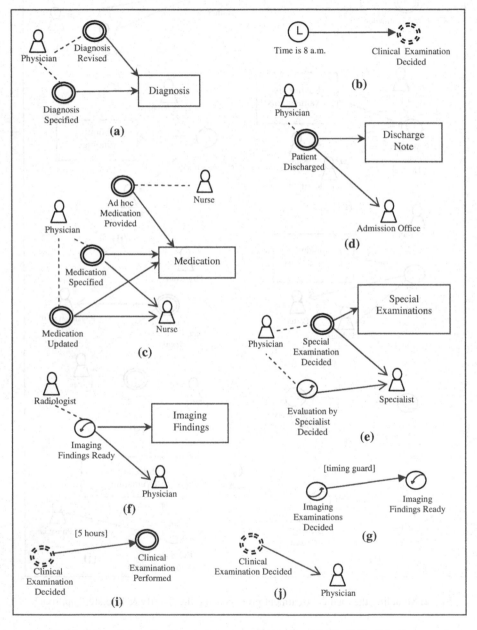

Fig. 3. Modeling the medical treatment process using the 'Notify & Register" approach

In the medical example, patient record represents the data folder that is managed during the process execution. Its structure is presented in Fig. 4. Patient record, as deduced from Fig. 2 and 3, comprises the following units: Personal Details, Medical History, Diagnosis, Discharge Note, Medication, Specialist Evaluation, Examinations and Examination Findings. As opposed to the rest, the last two units are not atomic. Examinations is further decomposed to the atomic units Imaging Examinations, Laboratory Examinations and Special Examinations, while Examination Findings include the atomic units Clinical Findings, Imaging Findings and Laboratory Findings. Each of the atomic units comprises specific data fields.

As revealed by the medical case study, there is no process flow defined. Instead, for each event identified, the actors that should be notified and/or the data that need to be registered are defined through a notify or register action respectively. This is done for each event independently. In addition, as confirmed by the treatment process, stamp events denoting both regular (e.g. event "Laboratory Examination Decided" in Fig. 2 (c)) as well as ad hoc activities (e.g. event "Emergent Surgery Decided" in Fig. 2 (g)) are modeled in a unified fashion. Event "Evaluation by Specialist Decided" may be generated by a physician that needs consultation in the interpretation of a symptom, while another physician capable of interpreting the symptom on his own may not need a specialist's consultation. It depends, thus, on human decision whether event "Evaluation by Specialist Decided" will be generated or not. It follows that N&R offers a simple, yet efficient way to model functionality of dynamic, human-intensive processes. Apart from agility, N&R offers another advantage. It enables a consistent evolution of the data folder aiding in the production of high quality data. Such data can be explored using data mining technologies and lead to the extraction of valuable information. In case of medical treatment, patient data produced can be used in short or long term studies for the extraction of valuable information that may contribute in the formation of international medical guidelines [7].

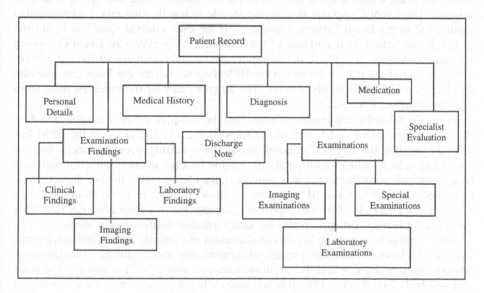

Fig. 4. The structure of Patient Record

5 Enactment of "Notify and Register" Business Process Models

Enactment of event-driven models requires a BPMS that is based on an event-driven BPM engine. Two indicative event-driven BPM engines proposed in the literature are Yeast [8] and Eve [9]. Eve is based on the ECA model [4]. An ECA rule dictates that when an event occurs, a condition is evaluated. If the condition is satisfied, the respective action is executed. Yeast, on the other hand, uses EA (Event-Action) model also proposed in [10]. EA model is based on only two entity types (event-actions). A condition in EA model is expressed through two opposite events corresponding to the condition's true and false outcomes.

Fig. 5 presents a proposed conceptual architecture for the implementation of N&R approach. The N&R models are developed using the *N&R Specification Environment* presented at the upper part of Fig. 5. The developed models are stored into the *N&R Models* repository. Obviously these models have to be translated into executable event patterns and EA rules in order to be readable by the BPM engine. The EA rules, for example, for Fig. 3 (e) could be as follows:

EVENT Special_Examination_Decided(Patient_Record, Physician)
ACTION Register (Patient_Record, Special_Examinations) AND Notify (Specialist);

EVENT Evaluation_by_Specialist_Decided (Patient_Record, Physician)
ACTION Notify (Specialist);

Actors generate event instances through an appropriate *User Interface*. When an event instance is generated, it is received by the *Event Composer*, which is responsible for combining events to composite ones based on the information stored in the *Event Patterns* repository. The Event Composer examines whether the received event participates in any event combination using the event pattern definitions stored in the repository. If it does not, the Event Composer directly forwards it to the *BPM Engine*, while if it does, it also keeps it in a record until instances of the rest events related to it occur. The Event Composer is also responsible to handle time guard relations also maintained in the Event Patterns repository. If the time interval specified by a time guard elapses before the occurrence of the respective reply event, the Event Composer forwards a message along with the required information (i.e. name of the reply event and identifier of the patient folder) to the BPM Engine, so that the latter can generate an alert message to the involved roles. The Engine can find the involved roles from the corresponding EA rule.

When the related event instances occur and the complex event is created based on the information stored on Event Patterns Repository, it is forwarded to the BPM Engine. In parallel, the Event Composer stores the occurring event instances into an *Event Log*, which includes additional information for each event occurrence such as a timestamp indicating the time it was generated, the identification data of the actor that generated it, etc. When the BPM engine receives an event instance from the Event Composer, it checks the *EA rules* repository and executes the respective EA rule. This means that it invokes the appropriate registration and/or notification services.

N&R approach ensures agility in the execution of dynamic human-intensive processes as it allows the business process to dynamically evolve during execution time based on human decision and the circumstances that may arise. The order of the steps that will be followed is not known in advance. When a process ends, its structure can be traced by viewing the event log.

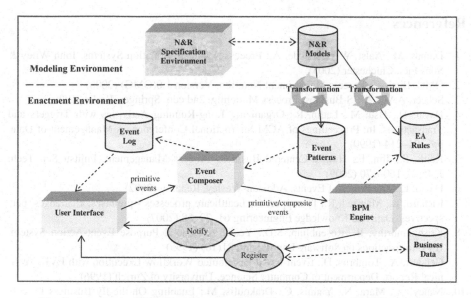

Fig. 5. A conceptual BPMS architecture for the implementation of N&R approach

6 Conclusions – Future Work

In this paper, we presented an event-driven business process modeling approach called "Notify & Register". The objective of this approach is not to describe how tasks are carried out, as in traditional action-driven logic, but to depict the events that occur in the real world specifying thus when registrations and notifications should be performed. The event-driven paradigm guided our minds away from the conventional way of designing processes for automated execution and made us think in a totally different way for the development of an approach that does not hinder but promotes agility required by the dynamic, human-intensive processes. For the demonstration of the N&R approach we provided a case study from the medical arena that concerned medical treatment, which is a typical example of dynamic, human-intensive processes. Our future work involves applying the N&R approach in the design of other dynamic, human-intensive processes, as well as developing a prototype based on the proposed conceptual architecture, in order to test the enactment of N&R models. Currently, in an effort to formalize our modeling approach, we are exploring the UML extension mechanisms taking into considerations the concepts introduced in UML profiles for business process modeling, as BPMN[2].

Acknowledgments. This paper is part of the 03ED470 research project, implemented within the framework of the "Reinforcement Programme of Human Research Manpower" (PENED) and co-financed by National and Community Funds (25% from the Greek Ministry of Development-General Secretariat of Research and Technology and 75% from E.U.-European Social Fund.

References

1. Dumas, M., Aalst, W., Hofstede, A.: Process-Aware Information Systems. John Wiley & Sons Inc., Chichester (2005)
2. OMG, Business Process Management Notation. Version 1.0(OMG) (2006)
3. Scheer, A.W.: ARIS-Business Process Modeling, 2nd edn. Springer, Berlin (1999)
4. Dayal, U., Hsu, M., Ladin, R.: Organizing Long-Running Activities with Triggers and Transactions. In: Proceedings of ACM International Conference on Management of Data, pp. 204–214 (1990)
5. Keith, S., Jim, F.: Human-Centered Business Process Management. Fujitsu Sci. Tech. J. 45(2), 160–170 (2009)
6. David, L.: The Power of Events. Addison-Wesley, Reading (2002)
7. Richard, L., Manfred, R.: IT support for healthcare processes - premises, challenges, perspectives. Data and Knowledge Engineering 61, 39–58 (2007)
8. Krishnamurthy, B., Rosenblum, S.D.: Yeast: A General Purpose Event-Action System. IEEE transactions on Software Engineering 21(10) (1995)
9. Geppert, A., Tombros, D.: Event-based Distributed Workflow Execution with EVE, Technical Report, Department of Computer Science, University of Zurich (1996)
10. Nancy, A., Mara, N., Yannis, C., Drakoulis, M.: Enabling On-the-fly Business Process Composition through an Event-based Approach. In: HICSS 2008 (2008)

Healthcare Process Mining with RFID

Wei Zhou[1] and Selwyn Piramuthu[2]

[1] Information Systems and Technologies
ESCP Europe, 75543 Paris cedex 11, France
[2] Information Systems and Operations Management
University of Florida, Gainesville, FL 32611, USA

Abstract. The working environment in health care organizations is characterized by its demand for highly dynamic human resource management in which (a) medical personnel are generally associated with several disparate types of tasks, (b) service location and service personnel change frequently, (c) emergency issues could arise at any time, and (d) the stakes are high since invaluable human lives are involved. There is an urgent need from both researchers and health care organizations to develop mechanisms for maintaining a good balance between efficient management and superior medical service quality. We discuss the potential for real-time health care coordination and effective medical human resource management enabled by event-driven RFID item-level tracking/tracing identification technology. We explore the uniqueness of instance-level process mining and its application in health care environment. We propose an adaptive learning framework that supports real-time health care coordination.

Keywords: RFID, healthcare, process mining.

Introduction

The number of preventable patient safety incidents and/or medical errors such as wrong drug item and/or quantity, transfusion using the wrong blood bag, mislabeled blood sample is on the rise as budget cuts in health care institutions and pharmaceutical industry translate to related adverse effects. RFID tags are touted to be primary contenders among the technologies used to address this issue. IDTech (2008) predicts the market for RFID tags and associated systems and services in health care to rise from \$120.9 million in 2008 to \$2.03 billion in 2018.

RFID tag use in health care and pharmaceutical industries has seen phenomenal growth in recent years spurred primarily through developments in tagging of drugs, real time location and instance-level information (for items such as medical equipment, patients and medical staff), and automated error prevention. Developments in tagging of drugs is driven by the need for improved anti-counterfeiting measures, theft deterrence, and improved stock control and recalls. Real-time instance-level information, generated through RFID-tagged entities, enable effective use of constrained resources while reducing errors due to inadvertent mismatches (e.g., mother-baby, patient-blood bag mismatch). RFID tag use in automating processes (e.g., appropriate medical record delivery) can reduce possible errors due to human input. Unlike their use in other applications (e.g., toll-payment systems), RFID use in health care and pharmaceutical

S. Rinderle-Ma et al. (Eds.): BPM 2009 Workshops, LNBIP 43, pp. 405–411, 2010.

industries carries with it unquantifiable benefits such as safety and security and higher tolerance for longer payback periods.

While patient privacy is a concern when using RFID tags that broadcast information without knowledge of the tagged entity, means to address such issues through cryptography has been under way for the past several years (e.g., Piramuthu, 2008). The existence of multiple privacy frameworks including the Health Insurance Portability and Accountability Act (HIPAA), the Electronic Privacy Information Center (EPIC)'s RFID guidelines, the principles of Fair Information Practices (FIP), and the general concerns associated with the generation and use of any personally identifiable information guide the extent to which personally identifiable information can be gathered, stored, and used.

Togt, et al. (2008) demonstrated that, under certain worst-case conditions when maximum power settings were used, electromagnetic interference (EMI) from RFID readers can interfere with medical devices used in critical care. Seidman et al. (2007) considered the Electromagnetic Compatibility (EMC) between RFID readers and several pacemakers and Implantable Cardiac Defibrillators (ICD) and report that reactions ranged from "non-clinically significant events to the potentially harmful inappropriate tachyarrhythmia detection and delivery of therapy or complete inhibition of cardiac pacing." Standards for RF emissions such as those from the Federal Communications Commission (FCC) and European telecommunications Standards Institute (ETSI) alert medical device manufacturers of possible interference from RFID and other RF sources.

RFID tags have been successfully incorporated at various levels in a health care setting. The recently introduced *Daily RFID* Silica Gel RFID wristband tag stores medical record information in a chip rather than paper. This reusable (after high-temperature sterilization) waterproof and heat-resistant wristband helps identify and match the correct patient and medical staff as well as providing privacy to patients through electronic records. Siemens' use of RFID tags for marking sponges used during operations and in identification tags for the operating team itself to eliminate missing sponges that are unintentionally left inside the operated person by tracing them from storage to disposal or reduce errors due to unintended mismatches in personnel.

The health care environment is highly dynamic in its demand for real time human resource management where (a) medical personnel are generally associated with several disparate types of tasks, (b) service location and service personnel change frequently, (c) emergency issues could arise at any time, and (d) the stakes are extremely high since invaluable human lives are involved. There is an urgent need from both researchers and health care organizations to develop mechanisms for maintaining a good balance between efficient management and superior medical service quality within such a high stress working environment.

RFID tag applications, despite its popularity in heath care industry and its unique applications, have not been extensively studied in this area. Their benefits including both tangible and intangible pay-offs and possible application mechanisms are generally not completely known in many business sectors, including health care. We consider the uniqueness of RFID, such as their ability to provide instantaneous item-level information (Zhou, 2009) in health care environments and propose an adaptive learning framework to utilize this technology to facilitate human resource management decisions

While existing research addresses some of the issues discussed above, there is a paucity of published research on improving process mining in health care environments using information generated through RFID tags. Although various applications of process mining have been studied in the field of health care, we find that a majority of existing research in this field are focused at the process optimization stage. We extend this to investigate health care optimization problem from a human resource management perspective to dynamically determine and update medical personnel assignments based on an RFID instance-level tracing/tracking system. Our proposed mechanism provides a fresh look at medical human resource management utilizing advanced instance-level identification data to improve health care provider/patients efficiency/satisfaction.

1 Motivating Example

Consider a small clinic in which the medical staff include two doctors, three nurses and two supporting staff. Our objective is to optimize the health care resource management such that certain efficiency and service quality can be maintained. An initial task and resource allocation is determined by a group meeting and adjustment will be made after the clinic is run for a certain period.

Let's assume that necessary jobs in this clinic includes 10 repetitive tasks and an uncertain number of non-repetitive tasks. Each repetitive tasks follows a pre-designed routine with an initial learning cost and only a marginal service cost thereafter. Non-repetitive tasks may involve emergency situations and other unexpected events in a health care environment with both learning cost and service cost. Without considering the non-repetitive tasks, the assignment of workload forms a 7 by 10 matrix, $[\Omega]_{7\times 10}$. Conceptually, knowing the ability of each employee $[\Psi]_{7\times 10}$ enables the decision maker to identify task assignments such that a required efficiency and service quality can be obtained and maintained. $E_{ij} = \Omega_{ij}/\Psi_{ij}$ indicates the efficiency of a specific task performed by a chosen medical staff.

A simplified version of this problem is solvable for maximum efficiency for an example when $\Omega \sim \{\Omega \in \{0, 1\}\}$. Practically, it is more complicated because the service location changes over time and some tasks are shared by multiple medical personnel such that $\Omega \sim \{\Omega \in [0, 1]\}$. In a hospital that involves large service area even within the same department and with the demand for non-repetitive tasks that could arise any time any where, it is rather difficult to determine and operationalize an optimal staff allocation. With adaptive learning ability that is based on instantaneously acquired instance-level information in a constrained hospital area, we claim that our suggested framework is able to provide better efficiency and improved medical care personnel and patient satisfaction.

1.1 Health Care Human Resource Management

Health care process optimization has been studied extensively through various disciplines. The unique problem of human resource management in the health care scenario, however, has not been extensively studied. The problem of allocating the resource including medical personnel is very different from other human resource management because, in a health care environment employees are more prone to be simultaneously involved in multiple tasks, to handle emergency issues, and to work with different sets of colleagues even within the span of a single day. The working environment at a health care organization is much more dynamic and more tense than most other organizations simply because human lives are more at stake.

2 Health Care Process Optimization with RFID

Figure 1 illustrates a medical human resource allocation scenario where each medical personnel is assigned multiple tasks based on their skill-set and skill requirements at this organization based on average estimates. We consider a repetitive task as one that is pre-assigned to each medical personnel and follows certain procedure and a set of standard protocol. For example, pre-surgery preparation as a repetitive task may include sanitizing, preparing surgical equipment, arranging service room, etc. Non-repetitive tasks, represented by dot lines, on the other hand do not occur on a frequent basis from the perspective of each individual medical personnel and is therefore not pre-assigned. Medical personnel may need to be trained in order to take on certain health care tasks and it is resource intensive for the health care organization.

Traditionally health care job assignments are under a predesigned form that is periodically evaluated and updated. Once the assignments are determined, they are held static until the next reevaluation period. Computational and coordination expense are

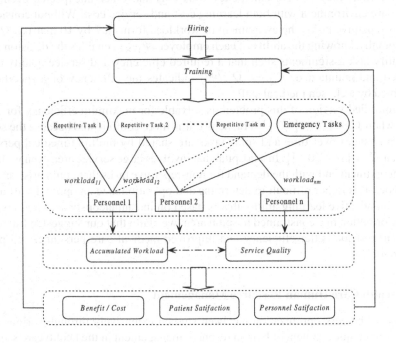

Fig. 1. Personnel resource management in health care

minimized at the expense of less flexibility. In our proposed framework, efficiency and service quality are constantly evaluated on a real time basis so that improved flexibility can be achieved. Efficiency can be measured by accumulated workload on each medical personnel. Full service quality is evaluated after the procedure and partial service quality can be obtained during the procedure. While the appropriate hiring of more personnel generally results in increase in overall service quality by reducing average workload and stress on each medical personnel, efficiency (workload) and service quality are negatively correlated. Measured workload and evaluated service quality are further analyzed to balance the economic issues, patient satisfaction level of both the medical personnel and patients. Based on these analysis, further decisions are made on hiring new personnel and training existing personnel.

Figure 2 illustrates a framework for optimal health care design with RFID instance-level identification information on medical equipment, staff and patients. Equipped with an RFID tracking/tracing technology, all physical entities in a hospital are instantaneously traced and monitored via a centralized computer system. Information about the movement of tagged item/person and of any property updates is further analyzed through process mining to discover useful and actionable patterns and to form a knowledge base for future decision making.

Next, we present a simplified procedure of the proposed dynamic real-time health care job allocation mechanism. The proposed framework operates by first observing the profiles of current patients and events. The system extracts knowledge of these constraints as well as event-driven information from instance-level RFID tags that are embedded in identification tags of medical personnel as well as critical equipments and other resources. The decision variables include the temporal and spatial allocation of resources including equipment and medical staff based on the task structure for the

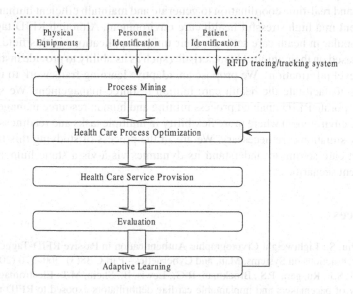

Fig. 2. Adaptive learning scheme of item level health care process optimization

set of current events, patients and available staff. The output is performance efficiency and service quality considered at both instant (short-term) and accumulated (long-term) levels. The general steps that are involved in this process can be summarized as follows:

1. Set length of time between evaluations at the top administrative level (T)
2. Set initial job arrangements in all units
3. repeat steps 4-11 until time T
4. $HRM_i(Input(Patients, Events)) \Rightarrow i^{th}$ unit-level task arrangement strategy
5. Service begins. Specify local time threshold (τ). Set local-time=0.
6. If performance(patients,staffs,events)$\ll$S, goto step 8.
7. If local-time $< \tau$, go to step 6
8. Calculate Ξ_i. Learn arrangement/performance knowledge
9. If $E\{\sum_{i=1}^{n} \Xi_i(\Delta(arrangementstrategy_i))\} <$ pre-determined threshold, goto 11
10. Else, goto step 4
11. Calculate $\sum_{i=1}^{n} \Xi_i(\Delta(arrangementstrategy_i))$. Learn global knowledge and suggest improved global HRM strategy
12. Goto step 1

3   Discussion

Health care human resource management problems have unique characteristics given that they occur under highly dynamic medical environments. The primary characteristic that differentiates this scenario is the fact that human lives are at stake with every patient who walks in and every decision that is made in these work environments. Although we have traditional static human resource management has its advantages and is meritable, we develop an innovative mechanism based on instantaneous item-level information and real-time coordination to generate and maintain efficient human resource management in a high stressful health care environment. Although RFID tags are becoming popular in heath care settings, their unique applications in this field beg to be explored based on their unique characteristic (such as its ability to provide instantaneous instance-level information). We propose an adaptive learning framework to utilize this technology to facilitate the health care human resource management. We simultaneously incorporate RFID-enabled process mining and human resource management in a health care environment where more flexibility in multiple tasks and readiness to handle emergency situations are necessary. We are in the process of studying this framework in a health care setting to understand its dynamics vis-à-vis a static human resource management scenario.

References

1. Piramuthu, S.: Lightweight Cryptographic Authentication in Passive RFID-Tagged Systems. IEEE Transactions on Systems, Man, and Cybernetics - Part C 38(3), 360–376 (2008)
2. Seidman, S.J., Ruggera, P.S., Brockman, R.G., Lewis, B., Shein, M.J.: Electromagnetic compatibility of pacemakers and implantable cardiac defibrillators exposed to RFID readers. International Journal of Radio Frequency Identification Technology and Applications 1(3), 237–246 (2007)

3. van der Togt, R., van Lieshout, E.J., Hensbroek, R., Beinat, E., Binnekade, J.M., Bakker, P.J.M.: Electromagnetic Interference From Radio Frequency Identification Inducing Potentially Hazardous Incidents in Critical Care Medical Equipment. The Journal of the American Medical Association 299(24), 2884–2890 (2008)
4. Zhou, W.: RFID and Item-Level Visibility. European Journal of Operational Research 198(1), 252–258 (2009)

SLA Contract for Cross-Layer Monitoring and Adaptation

Mariagrazia Fugini and Hossein Siadat

Dipartimento di Elettronica e Informazione, Politecnico di Milano
Piazza Leonardo da Vinci 32, 20133 Milano, Italy
{fugini,siadat}@elet.polimi.it

Abstract. This paper discusses a framework for Service Level Agreement (SLA) contracts for Service Based Applications (SBA) with respect to customers' goals seen as an important part of such contracts. Within standard SLA contracts concepts, as mutual agreements between service providers and users, we introduce *Key Goal Indicators* (KGIs). These are parameters that state how well service-based processes achieve the customers' goals. The SLA contract includes parameters of KPI, KGI and IT infrastructure type. Possible violations of each type are checked in the monitoring phase and an action is taken to adapt the violated condition through an adaptation mechanism. We describe the phases of a methodology for creating, monitoring, and adapting an SLA contract, in particular, leveraging aspects of Quality of Service (QoS) violations.

Keywords: Service Level Agreement, Key Goal Indicator, Contract, Business Process Execution, Monitoring, Adaptation.

1 Introduction

Propagation of service systems have influenced the implementation of business processes in organizations. Organizations expect their service systems to be aligned with the execution of their business processes and with their business strategies. The former issue refers to the degree of performance of the business, while the latter issue refers to the degree of success in the achievement of customers' goals. Therefore, service designer need to understand the business processes of the organization and their influencing factors in order to implement service systems that achieve the business goals of the organization. Besides, the need to consider customer parameters when evaluating business services has become increasingly noticeable [9].

Considering adaptation, requirements of service systems change so fast that the research community is studying how to build systems that are able to monitor and adapt on the fly to (some of) these changes. When this happens, the system does not need to undergo a new development cycle, thus increasing its availability and, to a certain extent, its robustness. However, the presence of parameters pertaining to the business, the service, and the user levels have dramatically increased the complexity of cross-layer monitoring and adaptation in SBAs. So far, research in the area of monitoring

S. Rinderle-Ma et al. (Eds.): BPM 2009 Workshops, LNBIP 43, pp. 412–423, 2010.
© Springer-Verlag Berlin Heidelberg 2010

and adaptation has been focusing on the definition of the mechanisms for supporting monitoring and adaptation [12, 13]. What is currently missing is a structured cross-layer framework associated to these mechanisms. In particular, [14] demonstrates a quality framework for service monitoring and adaptation. In this paper, we discuss the SLA contract as a possible candidate for cross-layer model to be applied in monitoring and adaptation of service based applications.

Service Oriented Architecture (SOA) promises a better realization of composite services modeled as business processes. In order to achieve this aim, business processes need to be aligned with the SOA. To keep the promises of SOA, the ability to deliver composite services to end-users according to pre-defined agreements is increasingly becoming an essential. These agreements are defined in Service Level Agreement. We believe that the value of a service is not only influenced by composite services parameters but also highly influenced by parameters of business processes, customers who are going to use the services, and IT infrastructures. Therefore, business service parameters and Key Performance Indicators (KPI) are not always appropriate to express the users' satisfaction. In doing so, we emphasize the importance of the customers perspective and their parameters as a complimentary measurement for parameters defined from the business service perspective. We introduce Key Goal Indicators which are parameters that state how well services or processes achieve the customers' goals. It is worth it to state that IT infrastructure factors have to be considered since they have properties that influence the parameters of users and services.

In order to have a comprehensive SLA contract suitable for the cross-layer model, it is increasingly important to consider the three aforementioned factors together, namely KPI, KGI and IT infrastructure, as long as they have a close inter-relation. As a result, parameters of an SLA contract should be a merge of KPI, KGI and IT infrastructure type. The SLA contract is a fundamental part for monitoring and adaptation of service based applications. In fact, this contract will be checked in the monitoring phase to see if there is any deviation or violation from the predefined contract occurring at the run time. Besides, the SLA contract is continuously checked for the purpose of optimization. Such a violation could be due to the defiance of IT infrastructure, business service and user parameters. Taking advantage of the comprehensive SLA contract, we propose a contract based framework for monitoring and adaptation of service based applications. Our approach consists of five major phases: (1) Identifying KPI, KGI and IT infrastructure parameters (2) Mapping of parameters into a contract (creation of an SLA contract and contract set up through negotiation) (3) Evaluation and monitoring (4) Adaptation (5) Updating of the contract.

The remainder of the paper is organized as follows. Section 2 introduces Key Goal Indicators. In section 3, we propose our framework for cross-layer monitoring and adaptation. Finally, section 4 discusses related work and some concluding remarks.

2 Key Goal Indicators

A Service Level Agreement is a contract introduced in the business level to set up common understanding of parameters regarding the relationship between a business service provider and a service consumer (client). The value of a service is highly influenced by the business of the organization, the customers who are going to use the service, and the IT infrastructure. Therefore, we distinguish between the *formulation* and *evaluation of the business service performance* and the *formulation* and *evaluation of the customers' goals*. From the business level, the output of a service provider is evaluated by Key Performance Indicators (KPIs) that show the degree of performance of a business service. On the other hand, from the users' perspective, the evaluation is done through *Key Goal Indicators* (KGIs) which show how well the services are successful in the achievement of the customers' goals. In this sense, the *Output* of the service provider is differentiated from the *Outcome* obtained by the service users, as stated in [6]. Typical examples of business service indicators are response time, process duration, process cost and service availability while some parameters related to KGIs could be financial return, satisfaction, reputation and trust. There are parameters in common between service, business and user such as time and cost; however, they are observed from different perspectives. Furthermore, there are also domain-dependent business process parameters and users parameters.

In order to have a comprehensive SLA contract, it is increasingly important to consider the mixture of the three aforementioned factors, namely KPI, KGI and IT infrastructure, as long as they have a close inter-relation. Such an SLA contract is extremely practical in the process of cross-layer monitoring and adaptation.

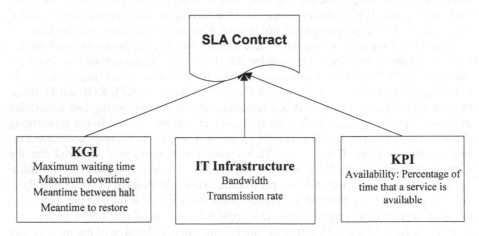

Fig. 1. An example for KGI and related KPI and IT Infrastructure parameters

Here we give an example to show that common service parameters are not sufficient to evaluate the user satisfaction, unless they are formulated in a more user-related way. Availability, generally defined as the percentage of the time that a service is available for use, from the user's perspective, expresses that customers only care if the service is available when they want to use it, for example in their work hours or in their free time. Suppose that there are two service types. One service is working for a month and then stops for one whole day. The other service works for about 8 hours and then has a 15 minutes downtime. Although the overall availability of both services is equivalent, users may not have the same level of satisfaction for both services, depending on the time of the day the user is accessing the service. Some of the most appropriate parameters related to customer's perspective include: Is the service up if the customer wants to use it; the actual time spent by the customer activating the service, the maximum waiting time, the maximum downtime, the meantime between halt and the meantime to restore.

As evident from the example, service parameters alone are not enough to express user satisfaction, which is typically related to KGI issues, and they do not consider the perspective of customers. Therefore, parameters of an SLA contract should be a mix of KPI, KGI and IT infrastructure. Fig. 1 illustrates an example of an SLA contract taking into account user parameters (KGI), IT infrastructure parameters and KPIs.

3   SLA Contract for SBA

Monitoring and adaptation of service based application is a complex issue due to the heterogeneity and dynamicity of composite services. Research works in the area of monitoring and adaptation has been focusing on the definition of the techniques and mechanisms for supporting monitoring and adaptation at both run time and design time [12, 13]. The problem is these works are rather fragmented and only deal with the technical service level aspects. Therefore, there is a need for a structured cross-layer model associated to those mechanisms which deals with different perspectives of business services, users and infrastructures. Particularly, in this work, we argue that user perspective should be taken into account together with the business service aspects. SLA contract is a possible candidate for cross-layer model to be applied for cross-layer monitoring and adaptation of service based applications.

We propose a comprehensive SLA contract between business service provider and users considering KPI, KGI and IT infrastructure factors. The SLA contract is a fundamental part for monitoring and adaptation of SBAs. In fact, the SLA contract will be checked at run time in the monitoring phase to detect any deviations or violations from predefined parameters in the contract. Furthermore, it will be continuously checked for optimization (it is not discussed in this paper). A violation could be due to the defiance of any of the IT structure, service, business or user parameters. Service Level Agreement have a certain life cycle. We propose a framework and a step-wise approach towards contract-based monitoring and adaptation of SBAs. Our approach consist of five major phases:

(1) Identifying KPI, KGI and IT infrastructure parameters;
(2) SLA Contract creation;
(3) Evaluation and monitoring;
(4) Adaptation;
(5) Contract Update.

Fig. 2 demonstrates our proposed framework which is an SLA contract-based approach for monitoring and adaptation of service based applications. In the first phase, the corresponding parameters related to KPI, KGI and IT infrastructure are specified. This should be done through a requirement engineering phase with an early participation of users in order to understand their actual needs. The second phase is the SLA contract creation which includes the aggregation of parameters defined in the first phase through a mapping phase. The final parameters in the contract are specified by parameters from the service provider with respect to the customer's parameters and the limitations that IT infrastructure parameters impose. Therefore, the contract has parameters resulted from a mapping process combining parameters from composite business services, IT infrastructures, and users and finally setting up them through a negotiation.

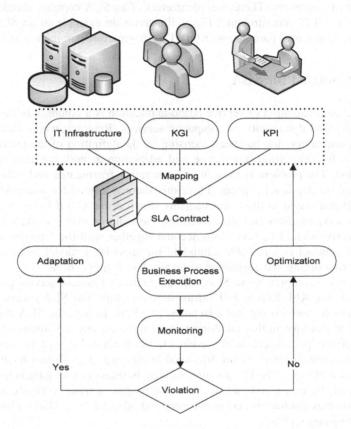

Fig. 2. Framework for SLA contract-based monitoring and adaptation

Once the contract is created, it is considered as a token which is applied in the business process execution and then will be passed to the Monitoring phase. The SLA contract is evaluated in the monitoring phase and checked for possible violations from the predefined values of any type of parameters, the rules and constraint set up in the contract. According to the source of violation event, detected via a diagnosis, an appropriate action is taken to adapt the violated condition to the new values, through an adaptation mechanism. Therefore, if SLA contract is not respected, an adaptation strategy should be taken (e.g., penalties are applied and/or the service provider is substituted) and new requirement-driven values are set up. The last phase of the framework is the contract update which is the reformulation of the contract (or parts thereof) driven by the new conditions and requirements.

3.1 SLA Contract Creation

Creating an SLA contract is a major step in our framework. In the following, we discuss about various issues with respect to parameters identification, mapping and contract creation. The true goal of SLA is to guarantee a valuable service to users. Hence, it is desirable to identify service parameters that are highly related to user satisfaction. A poor choice of SLA parameters in contract will result major wrong behavior in service execution and affect user satisfaction. Currently, there is almost no general consensus in selecting the appropriate metrics for SLA between practitioners. [17] proposes a general categorization of SLA content and metrics. Metrics are categorized according to service object, namely: Hardware, Software, Network, Storage and Help Desk. It is possible for composite metrics to be broken down into the smaller metrics and assigned to one of these basic objects types. [1] and [5] list some of different parameters that can be considered in the SLA contract, in particular, leveraging aspects of Quality of Service (QoS). Considering IT infrastructure elements such as server, database, hardware, or network connections, the characteristics of these elements have influence and sometimes pose limitation on the specification of other parameters. Therefore, these parameters should be taken into account in the SLA contract by linking them reciprocally in linking rules. A sample rule can state that if the "connection speed" parameter decreases during service provisioning, then the "cost" parameter related to that service should also decrease to compensate the lower QoS. Such rule must be specified within the contract and checked at run time.

Service providers and Customers need to work together early on determining parameters – meaningful and technically measurable – and their reciprocal links, in order to have a comprehensive SLA contract. In order to express the user requirements and parameters, which we called here KGI, we leverage the concept of QoS contract, which typically considers non functional parameters of service provisioning, such as time, cost, response time, or data quality parameters. Also, the concept of Rules will be defined to determine whether a QoS violation event takes place and possibly how to react to the event. Such reaction can spam from retrying a service, checking if in the re-invocation the service responds with suitable parameters (and hence had a temporary fault), to substituting a service with a compatible one (a service that provides the same functionality), in a way that is transparent for the client. The rules are used to allow the contract owner to define his set of feasible values with respect to a fixed value stored in the contract. According to the definitions of QoS contract given in [1], if the contract is not respected, a QoS violation event arises, and has to be managed, e.g., by raising a QoS fault. Moreover, the notion of QoS recovery mechanisms is introduced that can be employed to repair the fault, each with a given cost. The QoS parameters is composed of a set of parameters customizable by means of contract between a client (service consumer) and service provider. These contracts define the level of QoS acceptable for the interaction between the given client and service provider.

The contract should also take into account parameters related both to the business Services and the associated objects delivered through such services [2]. Such consideration involves both the quality of the conveyor of the service, of the external services connected to the conveyor, and of the associated object. For example, when purchasing a product, say a book, through an on line process, the user evaluates both the response time of the selling service and the quality of the book product (if the ordered book is correct, if it is delivered on time by the external delivery service, and if the book is in good shape). An understanding is required concerning both the quality aspects definition and how quality parameters are combined by users [2,7]. A modeling framework, for the definition of contracts between the user and service provider, should be outlined and discussed within the preparatory steps which enable a set of variables for contract publication.

This way, the user's goals should be described with respect to the quality in using the process (e.g., how quick the interaction is or how secure the purchase is), in the phases which are carried out by external partners (e.g., the delivery of the receipt letter, which is the responsibility of a courier), and the user's perceived quality of the product (e.g., the price of the purchased products). We do not consider the object level in our contract, as discussed in [2], since our focus here is on the user level. To this aim, we introduce a user level in the contract, which has parameters from the users point of view, namely related to KGIs. An example of an SLA contract for an Internet Book Purchasing Process is given in Table 1.

The contract instance of Table 1 is composed of three contract elements. CE0 is a contract element in the process level and represents the book purchasing process. CE1 predicates at the Service Level on the availability, response time, and downtime of the business process. CE2 reports at the User Level about the downtime and the availability of the Process, as perceived by users, namely the KGIs. The first linking rule LR1 defines that the two contract elements CE1 and CE2 are not exclusive. The second linking rule LR2 states that if the Availability of the Service decreases below 90%, then at the User Level this is evaluated as a Low value of Availability, which is out of the specified values (High and Medium are the acceptable values in the Contract), possibly giving a contract violation event. The third rule LR3 indicates that if service availability is lower than 95% and higher than 90%, it is perceived as Medium availability from user side. Finally, the fourth rule LR4 states that if the process behaves beyond the expectations (the Reputation parameter is more than the value defined in CE0), than the user is satisfied and is ready to pay (ideally) any cost. This last rule poses the basis for an evolution of the contract itself, in that in a future delivery of the Process, previous behaviors (in this case, positive) of one provider can be taken into account. The Integrity Constraint guarantees that the downtime of the purchased object deliveries be no higher than the downtime of the whole business process. It has to be noticed that this last constraint is not actually shown to customers, but rather is used by the provider to check the integrity of a generated contract.

As shown, in specifying Linking Rules in the contract, we combine contract elements. About this, we argue that for instance the Availability parameters, such as response time and downtime, described from the service provider, are not sufficient to evaluate the user satisfaction. In our contract model, a linking rule is defined to consider both parameters from the service and user levels so relating composed services into a process and its related customer satisfaction. An *integrity constraint* could be applied to guarantee that the downtime of the online service shouldn't be higher than the maximum acceptable downtime that the user specified in the contract.

Table 1. Example of an SLA contract

Contract Elem. CE0	*Process Level*	Book Purchasing Process
	Price	100€
	Reputation	High
Contract Elem. CE1	*Service Level*	Online Purchase Service
	Availability	95%
	Response time	5 Min
	Downtime	15 Min
Contract Elem. CE2	*User Level (KGIs)*	Online Purchase Process
	Acceptable downtime	20 Min
	Availability	High, Medium
	Cost	100$
	Reputation	High
	Process Completeness	Very High
Linking Rule LR1		CE1^ CE2
Linking Rule LR2		If CE1.Availability <=90% then CE2.Availability= Low
Linking Rule LR3		If 90%<=CE1.Availability <=95% then CE2.Availability= Medium
Linking Rule LR4		If CE0.Reputation = Very High then CE2.Cost:Any
Integrity Constraint		Downtime(CE1)< Downtime(CE2)

3.2 Monitoring and Adaptation

After the SLA contract is created, the business service will be executed by a business process engine which takes into account the contract. Then, the contract is evaluated in the monitoring phase to check for the possible deviations or violations. Several approaches have been proposed for the SLA monitoring [15, 16]. However, they only take into account technical service parameters and do not consider user parameters. In particular, [1] proposes an approach to evaluate the SLA contract with respect to QoS violation through monitoring. Various mechanisms for monitoring QoS and reacting to possible QoS violation through adaptation have been discussed as factors enabling the achievement of performance targets as pre-defined in service level agreements. They present an approach and consider a QoS fault detection module (called Controller in the approach) and a recovery manager module to face QoS mismatches. The former is devoted to catch a fault, while the second works to choose the proper set of recovery action to be performed to recover from the QoS violation. In choreography monitoring, a tracking system can be used to check if the execution of the composite services is based on the predefined global choreography description. Therefore, the monitoring phase is able to detect any mismatches between the order of exchanging massages taking place during service execution.

In our approach, we evaluate the contract from both service and user level. We particularly monitor the contract from any deviation of the KGI parameters, namely from the users point of view. First of all, KGI parameters should be identified properly in the first phase. Second, these parameters should be mapped into the contract considering other service, business and IT infrastructure parameters. We take advantage of linking rules and integrity constraint to identify if the contract is not respected. For example in Table 1, considering service availability, downtime of the online service shouldn't be higher than the maximum acceptable downtime that user has specified in the contract.

We also suggest the idea of having *user profiles* in the contract. A User Profile includes *preferences* which are rules to express interests on data and parameters as numerical scores or explicit ordering relation. They are used for ensuring common units of measure in evaluating compliance to stated service levels. Violations could then be categorized according to the user profile indicating which one should be considered a major violation and which one a minor violation. Based on such a violation which will be recognized in the monitoring phase, an appropriate adaptation strategy is decided and new requirements will be driven. A first sample of categorization of SLA violations with some details about adaptation strategies is reported in Table 2.

Table 2. Sample adaptation strategies against various SLA violations

SLA Violation	*Adaptation*	*Example*
KGI violation		
High	Change Provider	Downtime>20min
Low	Discount, Redo	Downtime>15min
KPI violation		
High	Substitute Service	Response Time>100ms
Low	Re-Invoke Service	Response Time>10ms
IT Level Violation		
High	Change Router	Wrong Packet Switches
Low	Split on Cloned Server	Network Packet Transfer>10μsec

For example, if Downtime is greater than 15min, this is considered a violation, since the Downtime parameter was specified in Table 1 as 15min for service provider. According to the given KGI, the maximum acceptable Downtime from the user side is 20min. Therefore the downtime between 15 to 20 min could be considered as a "low" violation, while more than 20min is considered as a "high violation" for the end user.

A violation can involve KGIs and other parameters. Focusing on KGIs, a violation to a user requirement can be categorized as High, requiring radical recovery and heavy penalties, or Low, requiring adjustments and contract renegotiation of some parameters or compensating actions. Under a High violation, recovery actions can be undertaken, such as changing the service provider, while under a Low violation, a bonus can be negotiated to compensate the problem and a redo of the service is simply performed. Adaptation can be designed via fault handlers encoded in the process, or can be executed at run time by the execution engine by performing self-healing repair actions, decided by the engine on the basis of a set of predefined repair actions to be executed depending on the severity of the violation.

Adaptation strategies convey a contract re-negotiation and a consequent update of the contract, which depend on the part of the contract which was violated. For example, if a Rule has been violated, the adaptation has to consider the insertion of a further rule in the new contract or of a new constraint. Moreover, the User Profile has to be considered when KGIs are violated, in order to update the contract coherently with the user's goals.

4 Related Work and Concluding Remarks

Monitoring and adaptation of service based application are increasingly becoming more and more complex due to the rapid change in the parameters and requirements of users, business and services. In this paper, we have proposed an SLA contract including parameters from user, business service and IT infrastructure as an alternative approach for the cross-layer monitoring and adaptation of SBAs. Given the proposed contract, we created a framework for such a monitoring and adaptation. Several issues have been discussed in this paper but still there are challenges that need to be addressed. In the following we address open challenges corresponding to the phases in our framework.

The first phase is identifying parameters from different perspectives. Identifying and mapping between service and KPI parameters have been studied in recent literatures [3]. [4,8,10,11] represent some qualitative and quantitative approaches. We argued what is missing here is that the business and service parameters are not sufficient in terms of user satisfaction and they should take into account parameters considering users perspective. Therefore, in this study we emphasized the user parameters as part of SLA and introduced the concept of Key Goal Indicators. Extracting users' parameters and formulate and mapping them to the technical business service parameters are interesting issues for future work. In particular, [9] distinguishes between quality of service, quality of experience and quality of business.

The second phase is creating the contract. Issues such as violations, penalties, linking rules and constraints are introduced and discussed in this paper. The contract should identify and describe the violations condition, more specifically what is considered a violation and what is not. Moreover, penalties should take into account in the contract. Penalties should be described in order to have a clear relationship between customers and providers. Number of violations in a time period could be applied to identify penalties. Contracts are evaluated in the monitoring phase, and if the contract is not respected, penalties will be applied and appropriate adaptation strategy will be taken. The last phase is contract update. How to update and when to update a contract are challenges that need to be studied. Possible update strategies could be based on a timely approach, according to the number of violation or a hybrid approach.

Acknowledgements

The research leading to these results has received funding from the European Community's 7th Framework Programme under the Network of Excellence S-Cube – Grant Agreement no. 215483.

References

1. Buccafurri, F., De Meo, P., Fugini, M., Furnari, R., Goy, A., Lax, G., Lops, P., Modafferi, S., Pernici, B., Redavid, D., Semeraro, G., Ursino, D.: Analysis of QoS in Cooperative Services for Real Time Applications. Data & Knowledge Engineering 67, 463–484 (2008)
2. Comuzzi, M., Fugini, M.G., Modafferi, S.: Quality Contracts for Cooperative Services and Associated Resources. In: Collaborative Business Processes (CBP) Workshop – 6th International Conference on Business Process Management (BPM 2008), vol. 17, pp. 561–572. Springer, Heidelberg (2009)
3. Wetzstein, B., Karastoyanova, D., Leymann, F.: Towards Management of SLA-Aware Business Processes Based on Key Performance Indicators. In: 9th Workshop on Business Process Modeling, Development, and Support (BPMDS 2008), Montpellier, France (2008)
4. Bitsaki, M., Danylevych, O., van den Heuvel, W., Koutras, G., Leymann, F., Mancioppi, M., Nikolaou, C., Papazoglou, M.: An architecture for managing the lifecycle of business goals for partners in a service network. In: Mähönen, P., Pohl, K., Priol, T. (eds.) ServiceWave 2008. LNCS, vol. 5377, pp. 196–207. Springer, Heidelberg (2008)
5. Ardagna, D., Pernici, B.: Adaptive Service Composition in Flexible Processes. IEEE Trans. on Software Engineering 33, 369–384 (2007)
6. Akatsu, M.: Identifying the Value for Service Management. In: The 9th IEEE International Conference on E-Commerce Technology and The 4th IEEE International Conference on Enterprise Computing, E-Commerce and E-Services (CEC-EEE 2007), pp. 491–492 (2007)
7. Pouyllau, H., Haar, S.: Distributed end to end qos contract negotiation. In: Bandara, A.K., Burgess, M. (eds.) AIMS 2007. LNCS, vol. 4543, pp. 180–183. Springer, Heidelberg (2007)
8. Caswell, N.S., Nikolaou, C., Sairamesh, J., Bitsaki, M.: Estimating value in service systems: a case study of a repair service system. IBM System Journal 47(1), 87–100 (2008)
9. Van Moorsel, A.: Metrics for the Internet Age: Quality of Experience and Quality of Business. HP Labs Technical Report HPL-2001-179 (2001),
   http://www.hpl.hp.com/techreports
10. van der Raadt, B., Gordijn, J., Yu, E.: Exploring Web Services Ideas from a Business Value Perspective. In: Atlee, J., Roland, C. (eds.) Proceedings of the 13th IEEE International Conference on Requirements Engineering (RE 2005), Los Alamitos, CA, pp. 53–62 (2005)
11. Gordijn, J., Akkermans, H.: Design and Evaluating E-business Models. IEEE Intelligent Systems 16, 11–17 (2001)
12. Hielscher, J., Metzger, A., Kazhamiakin, R.: Taxonomy of Adaptation Principles and Mechanisms. S-Cube project deliverable: CD-JRA-1.2.2 (2009),
   http://www.s-cube-network.eu/achievements-results/
   s-cube-deliverables
13. S-cube knowledge model (2009),
   http://www.s-cube-network.eu/knowledge-model

14. Cappiello, C., Kritikos, K., Metzger, A., Parkin, M., Pernici, B., Plebani, P., Treiber, M.: A quality model for service monitoring and adaptation. In: Workshop on Monitoring, Adaptation and Beyond (MONA+) at the ServiceWave 2008 Conference (2008)
15. Sahai, A., Machiraju, V., Sayal, M., van Moorsel, A., Casati, F.: Automated SLA Monitoring for Web Services. In: Feridun, M., Kropf, P.G., Babin, G. (eds.) DSOM 2002. LNCS, vol. 2506, pp. 28–41. Springer, Heidelberg (2002)
16. Keller, A., Ludwig, H.: The WSLA Framework: Specifying and Monitoring Service Level Agreements for Web Services. Technical report, IBM (2002)
17. Paschke, A., Schnappinger-Gerull, E.: A Categorization Scheme for SLA Metrics. In: Proceedings of Multi-Conference Information Systems (MKWI 2006), Passau, Germany (2006)

ER-BPM Workshop

Introduction to the First International Workshop on Empirical Research in Business Process Management (ER-BPM 2009)

Providing effective IT support for business processes has become crucial for enterprises to stay competitive. In response to this need numerous process support paradigms (e.g., workflow management, service flow management, case handling), process specification standards (e.g., WS-BPEL, BPML, BPMN), process tools (e.g., ARIS Toolset, Tibco Staffware, FLOWer), and supporting methods have emerged in recent years. Summarized under the term "Business Process Management" (BPM), these paradigms, standards, tools, and methods have become a success-critical instrument for improving process performance.

Research in the area of BPM has traditionally focused on the development and extension of associated tools, methods, standards and technologies. However, when evaluating the suitability of existing BPM technology for a particular project, it is important for practitioners and academics alike to have an informed opinion about their qualities and deficiencies. In particular, the demand for insights or evaluations of BPM technology based on empirical research has largely been neglected so far. This is surprising as the benefits of empirical research have been demonstrated in areas like software engineering (e.g., in the context of software development processes or code reviews), information systems, or, indeed, business for a long time. In fact, from the introduction of empirical research methods such as experimental or case study methods into BPM (as well as into the development of process-aware information systems), we expect more valid, quantitative or qualitative data on the various aspects and effects of BPM technology. This becomes important, not only for IT professionals, but also for researchers dealing with analytical, theoretical or technical challenges in the field of BPM.

The ER-BPM'09 workshop picks up this demand and seeks to stimulate empirical research that, in turn, can contribute to a better understanding of the problems, challenges and existing solutions in the BPM field. In particular, the workshop provides an interdisciplinary forum for both researchers and practitioners to improve the understanding of BPM-specific requirements, methods and theories, tools and techniques. Therefore, the ERBPM'09 workshop deals with different facets of applying and using BPM methods and technologies; and it will give new insights into the challenges, applications, and perspectives emerging for BPM technology.

We accepted 8 papers (out of 15 submissions) for presentation at ER-BPM '09 that provide examples for how empirical research in BPM can be conducted, and what insights such research can uncover. In her paper, Stephanie Meerkamm empirically analyzes the BPM approach in praxis. By means of interviews at companies located in Franconia, her work allows to gain insights into the way process management is actually realized in praxis (elaborating discrepancies between theory and praxis without focusing explicitly on the elaboration of the reasons). The paper by Koster et. al, in turn, defines a framework for evaluating BPM products, and discusses how this framework has been applied in the development of an open and objective evaluation method for respective products. The paper by Ricken and Petit presents the results of

S. Rinderle-Ma et al. (Eds.): BPM 2009 Workshops, LNBIP 43, pp. 427–428, 2010.
© Springer-Verlag Berlin Heidelberg 2010

an empirical study in which critical success factors are derived for the application of SOA technologies. The paper by Melcher et. al proposes concepts to meaningfully argue about a person's understanding of process models (for the sake of improving future measurement instruments). Their findings from an experiment, involving 178 students from three different universities, underline the importance of this topic. The paper of Grosskopf et. al intends to improve process elicitation and strengthen the role of the domain expert. The paper by Fahland et. al deals with the rise of interest in declarative languages for process modeling and both justifies and demands empirical investigations into their presumed advantages over more traditional, imperative alternatives. The paper by Gruhn and Laue presents the results from a comparative study that analyzed differences between the semantics of a large collection of EPCs using different tools. Finally, the paper by Melcher and Seese presents an experimental system for empirically analyzing error probability in process models. Results of a conducted experiment with 165 students using this experimental system are reported as well.

Besides these research papers, two short papers have been included in the proceedings. Both illustrate current developments towards community enablement in BPM. The first paper by Grosskopf et. al presents the new "BPMN community" platform. The second paper by Dadam et. al introduces the new AristaFlow community.

September 2009

Bela Mutschler, Jan Recker & Roel Wieringa (ER-BPM co-chairs)

PC Members

Markus Aleksy, Germany
Ralph Bobrik, Switzerland
Islay Davies, Australia
Maya Daneva, The Netherlands
Peter Fettke, Germany
Jaap Gordijn, The Netherlands
Wolfram Höpken, Germany
Marta Indulska, Australia
Jan Mendling, Germany
Michael zur Muehlen, USA
Bela Mutschler, Germany (Co-chair)
Markus Nüttgens, Germany
Jan Recker, Australia (Co-chair)
Manfred Reichert, Germany
Hajo Reijers, The Netherlands
Ralf Schimkat, Germany
Reiner Siebert, Germany

Ramin Tavakoli, Sweden
Roel Wieringa, The Netherlands (Co-chair)
Barbara Weber, Austria
Norbert Weber, Germany

The Concept of Process Management in Theory and Practice – A Qualitative Analysis

Stephanie Meerkamm

University of Bayreuth, Chair of Applied Computer Science IV, Universitätsstr. 30,
95447 Bayreuth, Germany
stephanie.meerkamm@uni-bayreuth.de

Abstract. Today, process management is a well established management tool both in theory and in practice. Its objective is the increase of the efficiency and it is thus regarded as a fundament to both the economic development of the companies and of the economy as a whole. Examination of the literature reveals many theoretical concepts which in some aspects may differ considerably - even to the point of mutual contradiction. How does practice looks like? To answer this question, we wanted to carry out an empirically analysis of management practice focusing on general conditions, process modeling and execution, the IT and the employees. This will be compared with an examination of the theoretical concepts and we will try to elaborate the main concepts used in practice, which are finally presented in this full paper.

Keywords: Process management in theory, process management in practice, quantitative analysis.

1 Introduction

Process management is a frequent topic of discussion both in theory and in practice due to its recognition as an essential facet of economic growth both at company and at national level. Economic success is largely dependent upon the control of processes, and lack of control gives rise to inefficiencies and hence to a reduction in effectiveness [9].

There is an abundance of literature on process management (e.g. [1][4][7][12][13]), but many of these approaches differ considerably or may be mutually contradictory (e.g. [15][16]). It is this lack of consensus within the literature the prompts us to the empirical analysis of management practice. We shall do this by means of interview at a number of companies located in Franconia to establish the actual methods by which process management is achieved within these companies. In doing so, we hope to elaborate the discrepancies between theory and practice, without necessarily examining the reasons for these discrepancies.

We first introduce into the concept of process management in Section 2 and shortly discuss other studies. Section 3 provides an overview about the methodology used in the analysis. Section 4 presents the results and we shall discuss these in Section 5.

S. Rinderle-Ma et al. (Eds.): BPM 2009 Workshops, LNBIP 43, pp. 429–440, 2010.

2 Process Management

Process management is an integral management concept to guide, organize and manage a company. It aims at a target-orientated management of time, quality and costs to achieve both strategic and operative goals. The entire process is illustrated in the (so called) "process life cycle". The process life cycle in Fig. 1 was adapted from [1][4][7][12][13] and generally includes the following phases:

Strategy: Firstly, the company's strategy for the achievement of its goals must be defined as this provides the framework for all of its business activities. It should be pointed out, that the strategy need not be re-defined for every process cycle. This is illustrated by the dotted line in Fig. 1.

Modeling: In this phase the processes and their relevant aspects have to be identified. A process model is constructed by means of an appropriate modeling tool and the resulting model is validated by, for example, workshops or simulation.

Implementation and Execution: At this stage the model has to be installed in the company. The method of doing this will depend on the type of business and may range from the publication of the process in manuals to the importation to a fully automated workflow system.

Monitoring and Controlling: For quality management reasons the processes must be monitored during execution. Actual data (i.e. execution or cycle time) has to be compared with planned data outcomes so that, in case of serious deviation from the plan, corrective measures can be applied. Experience gained from completed processes should be applied to improve subsequent ones. This results in a flow of continuous improvement as the process life cycle repeats.

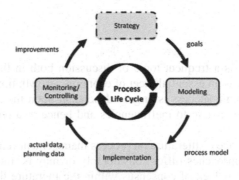

Fig. 1. Process life cycle according to [1][4][7][12][13]

This is a theoretical concept which cannot be translated directly into practice which has already been validated by some studies (see for example [3][10]). The studies revealed that in many cases there is a lack of support from management with absence of the methodology required for implementation. It is therefore perhaps not surprising that many companies continue to think in a function orientated way. Quite often, the

IT is not sufficiently aligned with the processes - even where this is regarded as an important factor for success. Other studies (see, for example, [5]) discovered that process orientation results in an increase in both the quality of the output and the overall productivity. We would like to gain further insight into this phenomenon as there are few published studies in this field.

3 Research Design

This Section gives an overview of the research design and is concerned with data collection and analytical methodology. Subsection 3.1 describes the type of interview, subsection 3.2 shortly presents the interviewees and subsection 3.3 provides an explanation of the analytical method used.

3.1 Guided Interview

We considered that we could best achieve our research goal by means of qualitative methodology [6][8], in form of the guided interview [6][8][14].

The *qualitative methodology* utilizes open questions to collect data and is mostly carried out by interview using only a small sample of interviewees. The subjects to be discussed are defined prior to the interviews but without the formulation of any hypotheses. The order in which the subjects are to be arranged and how much relevance is attached to them will crystallize in each interview situation.

The *guided interview*, as the name implies, seeks to impose structure on both the interview and the collected data. To achieve this, the interviewer follows a (printed) guideline to ensure that all essential points are raised during the interview. That said, guided interview still permits spontaneous questions.

The design of the guideline for the interview is as follows:

1. **Importance of process management in general:** To establish the situation within the company we need to identify the means of process management in use as well the degree to which the interviewee is familiar with it.
2. **General conditions:** In the second step, we try to identify the general strategic and operative conditions of the companies e.g. the operational and the organizational structure.
3. **Process identification and execution:** Here we continue the interview by asking how the processes are identified, how they are illustrated and how the processes are finally implemented.
4. **Information technology:** At this stage we analyze the information technology used for process identification, modeling and execution.
5. **Employees:** Finally, we must take into account the role the employees and their qualifications in respect of the implementation of the process management.

After the initial contact (see 3.2) by telephone the interviews were carried out on the company's premises. Interviews were recorded electronically with the use of supplementary notes; the data gathered was later transcribed. The researchers attempt to derive rules. The detailed analysis method is presented in 3.2.

3.2 Contacts

We found interviewees based on industrial contacts of the chair and/or the university. In the end we could interview nine companies. Table 1 gives a statistical overview.

Table 1. Contacts

no.	description of the organization	role of the interviewee	number of employees	profit in €/ year
1	medical technology	manager	40.000	n/a
2	IT services	chief executive officer	13	n/a
3	trade	manager	170	n/a
4	tool making	chief executive officer	380	44 Mio €/ year
5	electrical engineering	manager	170	n/a
6	automobile	manager	330.000	108.897 €/ year
7	plant engineering	chief executive officer	40	>10 Mio €/ year
8	IT services	manager	100	n/a
9	shipping	controller	1.300	150 Mio €/ year

Table 1 show that the companies were active in the manufacturing and the service sector of the economy. The number of employees in each firm varied considerably, from 13 employees at the lower end to more than 10.000 in the two largest firms.

3.3 Pragmatic Analysis Method

The goal of interpreting qualitative data is the formulation of general rules and new theories [6][8]. There are many different methods of interpretation. It is not our intention to explain all of them, see [6][8] for more information.

Our final decision was to use the *pragmatic analysis method according to Mühlfeld* [6][8]. This method does not attempt as wide as an interpretation of the data possible, but rather seeks to identify the problematic and critical aspects. As such, it is a very efficient analysis method well suited to our specific context and research goal.

The procedure is as follows:

1. Highlighting those answers which correspond to respective question of the guideline in the transcripted interviews
2. Classifying the paragraphs of the interview data according to the predefined subjects
3. Developing an "internal logic" based on the single pieces of information
4. Displaying the "internal logic" textual form
5. Writing a text including extracts of the interviews
6. Writing a report based on the analysis

In the following Section, we shall present our report. The extracts of the interviews (which are tagged with the number of the company concerned) are translated into English.

4   Results

In this Section we shall present our results. The structure of the Section follows the interview guideline in 3.1.

4.1   Importance of Process Management in General

According to the interviewees, process management is widely accepted as a *management tool* at both the strategic and the operative management level. Only one company dissented but this company has a more critical view of process management. Process landscapes or process houses illustrate the strategic concept of the companies. In only two cases was this abstract definition not transposed to the operative level in concrete terms.

More than three quarter of the companies justified the introduction of process management *for certification use, especially the ISO-certification 9000 and 9001.* Since ISO certification is an integral part of *quality management,* process management integrates with or completes quality management. This correlation is also discussed in the literature (see for example [2][16]). In addition to ISO, other norms and standards (for example VDI-guidelines, ITIL) are also mentioned by four out of nine companies. But their importance, however, appears to be marginal to process management.

Furthermore, the companies introduce the process management tool in order to completely *reorganize* their business. In two cases, process management served as a 'sheet anchor' for the company's survival (no.4) leading to a dramatically improvement of their business. In the other companies, where the situation was/is much less critical, use of this management tool was aimed at continuous process improvement mainly directed at the improvement of the internal communication and the interface design.

4.2   General Conditions

A. Strategic general conditions: Where process management is implemented successfully, the companies have a *flat organization structure,* usually combined with *project organization* structuring the day to day business. This corresponds with the common idea of the organization type best suited to the concept of process management as found in the literature (see for example [2][4]). In contrast, companies that are unhappy with the adaption of this management tool and with its consequences are those with a multi layered management hierarchy and which have no interest beyond their own specific area of business.

Except for two companies, all the companies in our sample are *certificated to ISO 9000 and 9001.* As illustrated in 4.1 process management correlates with quality management and, in particular, with ISO. Of the two companies not using process management in combination with ISO it must be said that the first is a very small service provider for which the cost-benefit ratio does not justify the implementation of process management. The other is active in a highly specialized area in which special regulations prevail over the ISO standard.

The idea of processes is used *for planning and guiding the strategic business activities*. Primarily process models in form of process landscapes or process houses are defined for illustrating the main process. They also include the definition of milestones which mark the completion of a phase or a work package. The aim of all this is to fix the goals of the companies and to illustrate the correlation between different business areas. In most cases the *strategic definition* is followed by an *operative concretization of the processes*. The situation where operative processes alone are defined does not exist. It follows, therefore, that the implementation of process management must begin at management level. If established here it can be introduced at the operative level. In only one case processes are not used for planning or guiding but this was a very small company with only 13 employees and for this reason, management did not consider process management an appropriate tool.

B. Operative general conditions: *Projects* structure the everyday business. This confirms which was set out in 4.2.A. *Models describing phases* are used as well. In contrast, procedure models are not very common and rather unknown with only one third of the companies in the sample using them. Obviously they do not meet company requirements. There is thus a discrepancy between the idea of procedure models and their implementation. Special methodologies for the implementation of process management are not mentioned with exception of no.1. They use for example CRM (customer relationship management) and SCM (= supply chain management).

In addition, all companies pointed out that it is not enough to document the processes either on paper or electronically - they must *"be carried also in the minds"* (no.1) of the employees. A procedure cannot be imposed upon the business and the staff. Employees must first have a *general idea of the process*; given the freedom of action they use their experience to structure the process. *Overall co-ordination* should be carried out by *the project leader,* who must take into account the goals of the company and the final outcome of the project.

Almost all companies agree, regarding the *scope of executing the processes* that the process models do not have to be translated exactly but should serve as a framework. In only two companies was a strict implementation required but this was for special reasons. In the first case, the process definition is quite general and the emphasis rests more on the output of a process than on its functional aspect. Thus compliance with the process model does not limit the freedom of action and, for this reason it cannot be compared with the concept of workflow management where the focus is on the automation of process by a system. In the other case we are faced with a production plant in which compliance with production rules (the process model) is an essential precondition for high quality output. This implementation concept here corresponds with the concept of workflow management (see also paragraph 4.3.B).

4.3   Process Identification and Process Execution

A. Process identification and modeling: According to the interviewees, identification and modeling of processes is carried out in *all areas* of the companies. This demonstrates that process management is a tool that is integrated throughout the companies although, however, there are *differences in terms of the level of detail* between the companies. The level of detail depends mainly upon the area of application or the actual processes themselves. An administrative process can be modeled in greater detail than a product development process - a fact as well known in theory as it is in practice.

Normally, *project leaders, representatives for process management or quality management, (who are senior employees), are charged with* the identification and the modeling of processes. This illustrates the importance the companies attach to this area. Process management (as mentioned in paragraph 4.2.A) must be installed from the management level downwards. In addition, the companies take particular care to *reconcile the modeled processes at special meetings* in which also processes which already running are discussed to ensure continuous process improvements.

With respect to the content of process models, the most important elements are *tasks which are broken down into sub-tasks.* These are arranged in order of occurrence by the so called *control flow.* With the exception of one small company, where the number of employees is less than 100, the focus is on the *objects of the processes* in terms of the process in-, or output (for example a document, template or a physical product). Furthermore, the definition of *roles,* describing which kind of person has to execute the process, forms an integral part of the process models. Only in small enterprises is this inessential (if they model processes at all). As already mentioned in paragraph 4.2.A, *milestones* are defined in most cases. They are used to define spaces of time and deadlines, but not to fix an exact time table.

All of these aspects are mentioned in the literature, too; see for example [2][4] and [13]. It seems that for small companies the content of the process model does not have to be as detailed as for the larger ones. The scale and complexity of the business could be an explanation for this. *Costs* are rarely used to specify the content of process models, although process management is always linked to the three factors: time, quality and cost. We were unable to find a reason for this. The specification of *tools or systems,* which are necessary to execute a process e.g. Word or a CAD-system, does not appear to be of any greater relevance either.

All in all, it appears that modeling in practice focuses mainly on the *function orientated aspect and more detailed information is necessary.* This is surprising bearing in mind what is said in the literature. A data- and knowledge orientated perspective plays an important part, for example in [1][2] and [13], to illustrate which information is necessary for a process. Even if the content of the process models does not have to be very detailed (see above), the two large companies favor a *perspective orientated view* on the process in order, for example, to reduce complexity. There is apparently no need for this in smaller companies. In addition, the compactness of the process models is appreciated as this means, for example, that one sheet of paper may be enough to draw up a process. In summary, the process models should give an overview of the business and its main activities so that everyone has an understanding what has to be done and how it is to be done.

There are several requirements of the kind of *documentation of the processes.* The companies, without exception, demand textual and/ or graphical documentation. Where they are ISO-certified (only two companies are not certified), the documentation has to meet ISO requirements. What these requirements are about was not specified.

The companies also did not specify a *modeling tool;* only two companies used specialized modeling software. Unfortunately were unable to discover the reason, but the literature indicates that it is difficult to adapt a modeling tool to a special context. It seems, therefore, that the inflexibility of a specialized modeling tool account for a company's failure to use it.

In the end, all the companies aim at *improving their business activities* by means of identifying and modeling their processes. Process documentation reveals ineffective and insufficient processes. Such analysis is not restricted to the first stage of identification and modeling, but must continue throughout the execution of the process. This idea is also discussed in the literature and the result is the process life cycle presented in Section 2.

B. Process execution: It is not sufficient, however, to have the processes identified and modeled. For a company to be successful in terms of process management, the processes also have to be implemented. In this regard, the companies agree that the *"processes have to be in the minds of the employees"* (no.1). They have to think in a process orientated way and be familiar with company specific procedures. Combined with experience and freedom of action the employees work independently and without following the exact process definition (as mentioned in 4.2.B). It should be pointed out that this is not explicitly focused on in the literature. The process models offer the basic structure for the organization of the business activities but have to be specified and adapted to the actual context. They are used as a guideline for a *"target and value orientated way of working"*, whereas "the structure of the tasks results from the goals of the company" (no.7). This also results in an increased *transparency and awareness of interfaces*. Besides, an integration of the employees and their knowledge into a team is possible; the employees develop a much broader view of the task they themselves and their colleagues are doing. Furthermore the interviewees noted an increased *quality of their procedures and results*; the process definition "helps to execute processes properly" (no.5) of the processes. The companies agree that the reason for this is the explicit display of the processes, which makes it easier to work in a structured way and to find misconceptions in the business activities.

As it was already stated in 4.2.B, the workflow management concept, which aims at the automation of the process by a system, is only applied once by a production plant. All of the other companies prefer the holistic management approach of process management.

The process models serve to *control the procedure and business activities*. This is very useful both within the single company and in a company with several locations. With the help of process models it can be more easily guaranteed that the procedure used in one location is the same as that in another one. Within the context of process controlling, the interviewees pointed out that the process analysis is a never ending task. After the identification and modeling phase, when they begin the execution, they *continuously try to improve their processes*. The processes are analyzed again and again in case where the goals of the company cannot be achieved in order to identify the reasons for the failure and to identify solutions. This concept is also used in the literature (see for example [12]) and finally results in the process life cycle presented in Section 2, without referring explicitly to monitoring and controlling.

In addition to this, process models are mostly a *precondition for audits or certification*. For certification, process management is also a means of implementation. Furthermore the process models are *used for training*; thus the employee should get enough information to be able to execute the process autonomously. This is completed with the experience and the general knowledge of the employees.

4.4 Information Technology

A. Implementation structure: *Small enterprises* (i.e. those with fewer than 100 employees) operate a *global system* of information technology. This is allowed by both the size of the company and the size of its business. Only one of the *large companies* operates a global system, while the other companies have *different applications, which are not necessarily integrated into one single system*. The reasons for this are understandable: on the one hand, the IT has grown up with the company. Over the years new applications were added according additional requirements; on the other hand, however, large companies always work with diverse suppliers and customers, produce different products and provide different services so that different applications become necessary to fulfill these diverse requirements.

All of the *large companies agree, however, that it is necessary to integrate the different applications* into one single system using, for example, a central repository or an ERP system. This demonstrates that the actual IT structure is not the optimum one and that the theoretical concepts which focus sharply on the integration of different applications (see for example [2]), have not yet been realized.

B. Functionality: Although the companies are engaged in different types of business activity, some of the applications that they use similar.

The *Microsoft office package* is in general use (one company uses Excel as its main application). *Administrative applications* are widespread (seven of the nine companies). *Product data or project management systems* can be found in five of the seven manufacturing companies. No relationship between this and the number of employees was discovered. In addition to this, most of the companies have special applications corresponding to their business activities. An example of this is a special hall layout system (no.6).

Although almost all of the companies approved practicing process management, it was *surprising to find that only two of them are working with a real process management system*. It seems that, at the moment, the optimal process management system does not exist (see as well [1][2]). This result is comparable with that regarding the procedure models in paragraph 4.2.B. A reason for not using real process management systems was that they were not suitable for the requirements of the companies concerned.

In addition to this, the companies pointed out that the use of IT has to be combined with human interaction among the employees. *Project leaders* have to ensure that the employees receive the necessary information; the *communication between the employees themselves* is also of crucial importance in this regard. IT, thus, serves more as a data repository used by the employees alongside their own implicit knowledge.

Even in case where the employees execute the process using the IT the linkage between the IT and the process is not very apparent. Consequently there are many aspects of the IT that have to be improved if real process orientation is to be achieved.

C. Implementation: A mere existence of a system alone does not improve the success or profitability of a company; to achieve this it must be used by the employees.

For this to happen, technical access is not enough - the system must be both comprehensive and user-friendly. This is well known to the companies and they make every effort to implement *self-explanatory applications* and to run *training schemes* for special systems. Moreover, as was mentioned in paragraph 4.4.B, the *communication between the employees,* with experienced employees handing down their knowledge to less experienced colleagues, is an important factor.

The final observation of all of the companies that the implementation is suboptimal is a logical consequence of points made in paragraphs 4.4.A and 4.4.B. Again, *integration of the applications must take place* alongside detailed discussion of the overall processes and of the development of user-friendly interfaces.

4.5 Employees

A. Everyday work life: Most companies offer *training* programs for new employees to familiarize them with internal company procedures. On a day to day basis they are assigned a *mentor* to assist their assimilation into the company. It appears that *on the job training* (learning by doing) is one of the most important and frequently used ways to introduce staff to the business. This is also reflected in the statement on the implementation of the process models in paragraph 4.3.B. It is not vital to have the detailed definitions of the process. This final definition has to be found on the job where hand-on experience concretizes the process framework according to the actual context.

The overall integration of the employee into the business is done by means of the *project organization* which is typical of process management (see for example [4]). Corresponding to this *team working* is implemented by seven of the nine companies. This demonstrates that process management is much more than a theoretical concept.

On the issue of the need for optimization in respect of the daily work flow, the companies' responses were fairly diverse and, for this reason, are not specifically here. There is, nevertheless, agreement about the need for discussion about the interfaces and that there should be a less function orientated way of thinking. It can, therefore, be seen that companies appreciate the implications of process management - even if the reality is a sub-optimal result.

B. Qualification/ further education: To gain employment *no specific knowledge of process management* is necessary. Instead, the workers have to have an understanding of the workings of the particular company. This corresponds with the idea of on the job training mentioned earlier in this paragraph and that the processes have to be in the mind of the workers (see paragraph 4.2.B). *Human beings with both their abilities and the deployment of common sense* (no.8), as oppose to robots or computers, are important in day to day business. The interviewees pointed out that this is necessary because of the discrepancy between theory and practice to be found mainly in large companies. Despite this, *professional qualification* is also an important factor.

Many large companies operate training programs but this is much less common in smaller companies for cost-benefit reasons. To enable independent access to this field, most companies publish the process documentation on the intranet or in the form of quality manuals.

5 Discussion, Limitations and Future Work

This paper provides an overview of the actual concept of process management in practice as opposed to theoretical aspects discussed in the literature.

In summary, it may be confidently asserted that process management is more than a theoretical concept found in the relevant literature - it is widely accepted in practice as both a *strategic and operative management tool*. The companies in our sample agree that it makes significant improvements to their business activities, and that this is particularly the case where it has been the basis for a complete reorganization. All this findings confirm the initial premise that the management and control of the business processes is an important factor of economic success.

It seems that the focus of process management rests on the internal domain of the companies themselves i.e. there is no integration of customers or suppliers. Concepts such as SCM or CRM which are to be found in the literature (see [12]) were mentioned only once. It is clear that a more *holistic approach* to process management, in which external partners are integrated with the concept of quality management [16], would bring further improvements.

The detailed modeling of the processes seems to be less critical and focuses mainly on the functional aspect (see also [1][2][13]). Consequently, the exact transformation of the defined process models is not required. Next to the *process definition on a conceptual level, the experience of the employees enjoying freedom of action to deploy their experience and common sense appears to be the most important factor for the implementation of the processes*. It follows, therefore, that it would be useful to develop practical methodologies that help workers to execute the processes so that the companies will achieve their goals. This will further reinforce companies' in working in a process oriented way.

According to our results technical systems are not the main vehicle for the implementation of process management. At this time high quality, or at least satisfactory, process management systems do not seem to be available and this is particular true of the availability of adequate modeling tools. This points are confirmed in the literature (see [1][2]). This may explain why, in practice, IT is not central to the concept of process management although the architecture and functionality are discussed at some length in the quoted literature (see for example [1][2][12][13]). In reality, IT is used simply to store data and it is clear that the link between the processes and IT needs to be strengthened.

In conclusion, we may summarize as follows: *process management is seen as an important management tool* for the efficient and effective direction of an enterprise. Even in case where process management is not implemented, in practice, in strict accordance with all of its theoretical aspects, most of the companies in our sample do use process management at a level appropriate to their requirements.

There are many issues which have to be addressed in order to allow the approach to become more holistic and to provide more practical guidance to the users. We expect the findings of our study to be of benefit to both process management research and as a guide to practitioners. The study is, of necessity, limited by the small number of companies that participated in our research. As a result, the formulation of generalization from the results is not possible but we intend to carry out further interviews to this end.

References

1. Abdecker, A., Hinkelmann, K., Maus, H., Müller, H.J.: Geschäftsprozessorientiertes Wissensmanagement – Effektive Wissensnutzung bei der Planung und Umsetzung von Geschäftsprozessen. Springer, Heidelberg (2002)
2. Allweyer, T.: Geschäftsprozessmanagement – Strategie, Entwurf, Implementierung. Controlling. W3L-Verlag, Herdecke (2005)
3. Bandara, W., Indulska, M., Chong, S., Sadiq, S.: Major Issues in Business Process Management: An Expert Perspektive. In: Proceedings ECIS 2007 – The 15th European Conference on Information Systems, St.Gallen, Switzerland, pp. 1240–1251 (2007)
4. Becker, J., Kugler, M., Rosemann, M.: Processmanagement. Springer, Heidelberg (2003)
5. Kueng, P.: The effects of Workflow Systems in Organisations: A Qualitative Study. In: van der Aalst, W.M.P., Desel, J., Oberweis, A. (eds.) Business Process Management. LNCS, vol. 1806, pp. 301–315. Springer, Heidelberg (2000)
6. Lamnek, S.: Qualitative Sozialforschung. Band 1 Methodologie. Beltz-Verlag, Weinheim (1995)
7. Lee, R.G., Dale, B.G.: Business Process Management: a review and evaluation. Business Process Management Journal 4(3), 214–225 (1998)
8. Mayer, H.: Interview und schriftliche Befragung. Oldenburg Wissenschaftsverlag, München (2002)
9. Meerkamm, H.: Prozesse: eine aktuelle Herausforderung in der Produktentwicklung. In: Birkhofer, H., Feldhusen, J., Lindemann, U. (eds.) Konstruktion, vol. 9, p. 1 (2007)
10. Rosemann, M., de Bruin, T.: Application of a Holistic Model for Determing BPM Maturity. BPTrends (2005)
11. Scheer, A.-W., Boczanski, M., Muth, M., Schmitz, W.-G., Segelbacher, U.: Bausteine und Prozesse im PLM. In: Scheer, A.-W., Boczanski, M., Muth, M., Schmitz, W.-G., Segelbacher, U. (eds.) Prozessorientiertes Product Lifecycle Management. Springer, Heidelberg (2006)
12. Schmelzer, H., Sesselmann, W.: Geschäftsprozessmanagement in der Praxis. Hanser Verlag, München (2008)
13. Weske, T.: Business Process Management – Concepts, Languages, Architectures. Springer, Heidelberg (2007)
14. Witzel, A.: Das problemzentrierte Interview. Forum: Qualitative Social Research (Online-Journal) 1(1) (2000), http://qualitative-research.net/fqs
15. Van der Aalst, W., ter Hofstede, A., Weske, M.: Business Process Management: A Survey. In: van der Aalst, W.M.P., ter Hofstede, A.H.M., Weske, M. (eds.) BPM 2003. LNCS, vol. 2678, pp. 1–12. Springer, Heidelberg (2003)
16. Zairi, M., Sinclari, D.: Business process re-engineering and process management. A survey of current practice and future trends in integrated management. Business Process Reengineering & Management Journal 1(1) (1995)

An Evaluation Framework for
Business Process Management Products

Stefan R. Koster, Maria-Eugenia Iacob, and Luís Ferreira Pires

University of Twente,
P.O. Box 217, 7500AE, Enschede, The Netherlands
s.r.koster@alumnus.utwente.nl, l.ferreirapires@ewi.utwente.nl,
m.b.iacob@mb.utwente.nl

Abstract. The number of BPM products available has increased substantially in the last years, so that choosing among these products became a difficult task for potential BPM users. This paper defines a framework for evaluating BPM products, and discusses how this framework has been applied in the development of an open and objective evaluation method for these products. Our framework has been developed based on the BPM lifecycle we developed as a result of a thorough literature survey. Our method consists of a set of criteria, a test case and a rating schema. The paper also discusses how we evaluated our method (and indirectly our framework) by applying it to three BPM tool suites. We show that our method allows the rigorous comparison of these products according to different criteria, so that the choice of BPM product can be tuned to the specific goals of the users of these products.

Keywords: Business Process Management, BPM evaluation framework, BPM lifecycle, KPI, business process monitoring.

1 Introduction

Many different vendors have recently released products that support Business Process Management (BPM). Some vendors of BPM products, like Cordys, Pegasystems and Savvion, have always targeted BPM as their main activity area, while others, like IBM, Oracle and TIBCO Software, are in the BPM market for some time but started their businesses in other areas. The number of BPM products available in the market has increased substantially, so that choosing between these products became a difficult task for potential BPM users. Some advice can be gathered from companies like Gartner and Forrester, but their research methods are not open and their results are difficult to verify. This has motivated us to develop an open and objective evaluation method for BPM products grounded on scientific principles. To the best of our knowledge such a method is still not available nowadays.

This paper defines a framework for evaluating BPM products, and discusses how this framework has been applied in the development of an open and objective evaluation method. The foundation for our framework is the BPM lifecycle that we developed as a result of a thorough literature survey. Our method consists of a set of criteria, a test case and a rating schema. The paper also discusses the evaluation of our

S. Rinderle-Ma et al. (Eds.): BPM 2009 Workshops, LNBIP 43, pp. 441–452, 2010.
© Springer-Verlag Berlin Heidelberg 2010

method (and indirectly our framework). Our method was evaluated by applying it to three available BPM tools, namely Cordys BPMS, Oracle BPM Suite and IBM Web-Sphere BPM. We show that our method allows a rigorous comparison of these products according to different criteria, so that for a potential user of a BPM product (or some consultant on behalf of this user) the choice of product can be tuned to the specific goals of this user, by focusing on the criteria related to these goals.

This paper is organised as follows: Section 2 presents our research approach, Section 3 concentrates on one criterion of our evaluation method and discusses the application of our evaluation method to three BPM suites with respect to this criterion, Section 4 discusses the results of the evaluation of the three BPM suites with respect to all the criteria considered in our method, Section 5 discusses the suitability of our evaluation method, gives our conclusions and identifies topics for future work.

2   Research Approach

In order to define our evaluation method, we have first developed a framework based on the BPM lifecycle. This framework identifies tasks, their relationships and responsible actors, which have formed the basis for the criteria and the steps that should be considered when defining an evaluation method. In the method we defined, we still selected a couple of steps based on their relevance and taking into consideration our practical limitations. Our method was finally tested by applying it to three popular BPM products.

2.1   Evaluation Framework

We defined our framework in terms of the phases of the BPM lifecycle. We performed a thorough survey to identify relevant literature related to these phases [1-21]. By studying this literature, we identified tasks that have to be performed in each phase.

Fig. 1 depicts schematically the BPM lifecycle considered in our framework. In our BPM lifecycle, we start with the assumption that implicit business processes in an organisation have to be made explicit, i.e., the business processes have to be discovered. Implicit business processes are normally embedded in the working patterns of employees and in the application logic of software applications. An implicit *business process* is represented schematically in Fig. 1. Once a business process is made explicit, a model of this process can be produced, making the business process more precise. Alternatively an inexistent business process can be devised to support some business objectives, in which case it has to be defined and properly modelled.

The business process model should be analysed and improved if found necessary. This business process can be then implemented with or without IT support, or it can be even outsourced. When implementing a business process without IT support, new policies and work patterns may be created with which the employees have to comply. In case IT support is available, the business process model is made executable and a business process execution environment is normally designed to support this process. This business process execution environment consists, among others, of a business process execution engine, which is able to execute the executable business process models, interaction means for the users to interact with the executable business process models, and some management functionality. An executable business process model can be translated into code and executed by a business process execution engine. Employees can interact with running process instances and managers can monitor and control them. Running and finished process instances can be analysed and improved accordingly.

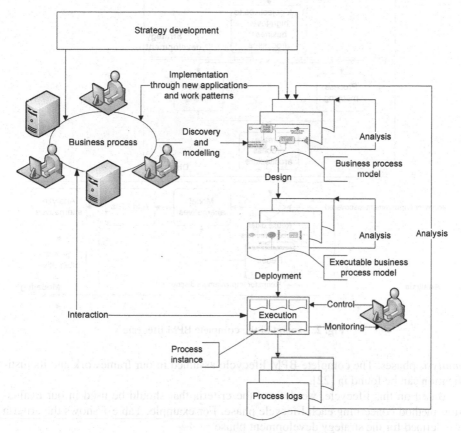

Fig. 1. Simplified representation of the BPM lifecycle assumed in our framework

Strategy development is expected to be performed on top of these activities. This is the process in which the organisation's management defines the strategic objectives of the organisation.

Our initial assumptions on the activities of the BPM lifecycle have been further refined based on a literature survey. For example, according to [1,2], the first phase of the BPM lifecycle (strategy development) contains three steps: (i) capturing the organization's objectives, (ii) creating an overview of the organization's business processes and (iii) linking the objectives to the business processes. Fig. 2 shows an excerpt of our BPM lifecycle, which shows the strategy development, discovery and modelling phases. This complete lifecycle consists of the *strategy development, discovery, modelling, design, deployment, execution, monitoring & control, interaction* and

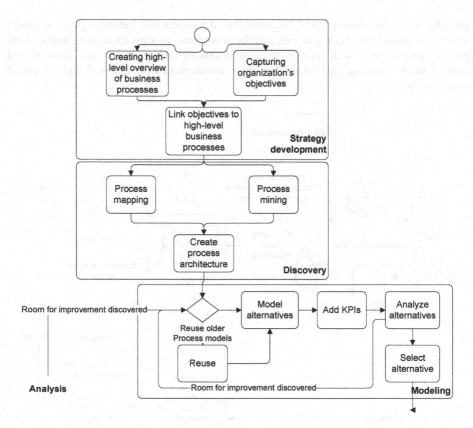

Fig. 2. Excerpt of the complete BPM lifecycle

analysis phases. The complete BPM lifecycle assumed in our framework and its justification can be found in [22].

Based on this lifecycle, we defined the criteria that should be used in our evaluation method concerning each lifecycle phase. For example, Table 1 shows the criteria we defined for the strategy development phase.

Table 1. Strategy development criteria

#	Strategy development criteria
1	Support for capturing the organization's objectives (for example, using a Balanced scorecard).
2	Support for creating a high-level overview of the business processes (for example, using a value-added chain diagram).
3	Support for linking the organization's objectives with the high-level business processes.

Summarising, our BPM framework consists of a detailed description for the BPM lifecycle phases and their corresponding evaluation criteria. These criteria have been the input for the development of our evaluation method.

2.2 Evaluation Method

Our evaluation method consists of set of criteria, a test case and a rating schema. Due to the time constraints imposed by the project (the duration of the Master graduation project reported in [22]), the criteria supported by our method are a subset of the criteria defined in our framework. We have selected only criteria from the modelling, design, interaction and monitoring & control phases and we have ignored criteria from these phases that would be difficult to evaluate in the time-frame of our project. For example, complex criteria that would require extensive training or that required specialised execution environments were ignored. In total we selected ten criteria in our method; some of these criteria are structured in terms of sub-criteria, so that even with the scope limitation our method is far from trivial. Appendix A gives the criteria supported by our method.

In order to make our method operational, we defined a test case based on the selected criteria. Our method prescribes that this test case should be implemented using the BPM product under evaluation. This test case consists of a business process in which a client applies for a mobile phone subscription, and it has been described both informally and an event-driven process chain diagram produced with IDS Scheer's ARIS Business Architect [23] (figure omitted here due to space limitations). This test case has been defined as follow:

A customer applies for a mobile phone subscription through an application form. In this form he enters his name (first and family name), address (street, number, city and postal code), date of birth (day, month and year) and the type of mobile phone subscription he wants (price per month and length of subscription). Based on the information the customer enters in his application form, and the risk is determined automatically by a risk service. This service classifies the application either as low risk or as high risk. If an application is classified as high risk, the customer is checked for any debts, and based on the result of this check, a supervisor decides to approve the application or not. If the application is of low risk it is approved automatically. Approved applications are verified by an employee. If the data in the application form is correct, the application is verified. The customer is informed by e-mail of the acceptance or rejection of his application. The contents of this e-mail message are determined by the acceptance or rejection of his application. When an application is rejected the reason for this rejection is given in an e-mail message (for example, no person with the given name lives at the provided address or he has too much debt).

This test case was chosen because of its average complexity: it is not so complex, so that the evaluator can concentrate on the evaluation task and is not distracted by too many details, but it is not so simple that it can be trivially implemented.

For each of the selected criteria, the method prescribes how to use the criterion in the test case and how to rate the criterion for the BPM product being evaluated. The rating schema applied in our method is meant to quantify the criteria and to allow comparison of evaluation results. Our current rating scheme features a distribution of points based on our own judgment and does not assign weights to different criteria.

2.3 Testing the Method

In order to test the suitability of our evaluation method, we have applied it on three BPM suites. We have selected BPM suites from different quadrants out of the latest

Gartner's Magic Quadrant for BPM suites [3]. We have selected IBM WebSphere BPM from the leaders' quadrant, Cordys BPMS from the visionaries' quadrant and Oracle BPM Suite from the challengers' quadrant. For each of the BPM suites, we have worked through our test case and applied the selected criteria. We have done this after we have made ourselves familiar with each BPM suite by using all the (online) documentation and product expertise that was available at the consultancy company where this project took place. At the end we obtained an evaluation of these three BPM suites. Each evaluation consists of a description of the evaluated suite and a radar chart showing the rating for each criterion.

3 Method Illustration

Since it is not feasible to discuss all the criteria considered in our method in detail here due to space limitations, we only illustrate our method by discussing the 'Support for KPIs' criterion in detail. This criterion was chosen because it is representative for the criteria supported by our method. In the sequel we describe this criterion and the way it has been tested and rated for the three evaluated BPM suites.

3.1 Support for KPIs

In our BPM framework we consider that Key Performance Indicators (KPIs) normally have to be defined in order to monitor the performance of the running business processes. By assessing KPIs while business processes are being executed, business analysts can check whether these processes currently fulfil their objectives or they can estimate whether these objectives will ever be fulfilled.

A BPM product needs to offer support to business analysts for defining KPIs for a business process. We have identified two dimensions of this support that should be evaluated for a certain BPM product [4,5]:

- *Flexibility.* This dimension determines the types of KPIs that can be defined using the KPI model supported by the BPM product.
- *Ease of use.* This dimension determines if the definition of KPIs is facilitated by the BPM product. The definition of KPIs can be facilitated if templates are available, possibly to be applied in combination with (structured) natural language. In contrast, the BPM product may force the user to write implementation code of some sort, with negative consequences for the ease of use.

In order to evaluate the BPM products according to this criterion, we defined the following two KPIs for the test case in our method:

- Number of accepted applications from the total number of applications.
- Number of high risk applications from the total number of applications.

Flexibility has been evaluated by checking whether these KPIs can be completely defined using the BPM product being evaluated. Five points are granted for each of these KPIs in case they can be defined using the product. Ease of use has been evaluated by checking how the definition of KPIs is supported by the product. Natural language support yields seven points, graphical notation five points and code three points. In case templates for defining KPIs are available, three additional points are assigned to this tool for this dimension. A total of twenty points can be rewarded for the 'Support for KPIs' criterion, equally distributed over the two dimensions. We rated this criterion by dividing the total number of points by two.

3.2 Cordys BPMS

The Cordys Business Process Management Suite C3 version 4.2 [24] was evaluated by the first author of this paper in [22]. This product is developed by Cordys, which is a Dutch vendor specialised in BPM. Cordys BPMS supports the definition of KPIs with the KPIComposer. In order to calculate KPIs, the required information has to be stored in a database and retrieved from this database by using user-defined methods. These methods are called in the KPIComposer and the KPIs are built based on the information that these methods retrieve. The definition of KPIs in Cordys is therefore not really user-friendly, since the user is forced to write these methods.

For our test case, an application information entity had to be stored in the database, and a method had to be written to retrieve this information from the database. We were able to write a method that retrieved all applications from the database, but with KPIComposer it was not possible to define the required KPIs since KPIComposer only allows the user to define KPIs based on some predefined elements (mainly based on arithmetic operations). We concluded that the definition of KPIs in Cordys is inflexible and assigned zero points to this dimension. However, Cordys offers templates to generate code, so that we assigned six points for ease of use. The total of number points for the 'Support for KPIs' criterion is six points for Cordys BPMS, which corresponds to a three on our one to ten scale.

3.3 Oracle BPM Suite

The Oracle BPM Suite version 10gR3 [25] was evaluated by the first author of this paper in [22]. This product is developed by Oracle, which is originally a databases developer. However, Oracle also entered the BPM market after the acquisition of BEA. The Oracle BPM Suite supports the definition of KPIs with the Oracle BPM Studio, which allows the use of widgets to define graphs on activity workload, activity performance and process performance. These widgets can be considered as templates with limited options and underlying code. They can be used on a BAM dashboard that can be shown in the Oracle BPM Workspace.

We have been able to define our KPIs using Oracle BPM Studio, but we had to modify their definitions slightly. We were not able to compare the number of high risk applications with the total number of applications. Instead, we had to define a KPI that compares the number of high risk applications with the number of low risk applications. Similarly, we had to define a KPI that compares the number of accepted applications with the number of applications that were not accepted.

Because we could define KPIs with the supported KPI model, but not exactly the ones we wanted, we awarded six points for this dimension instead of the total ten points. KPIs can be defined using templates with underlying code, so that for the ease of use we awarded six points. The total of number points for the 'Support for KPIs' criterion is twelve points for Oracle BPM Suite, which corresponds to a six on our one to ten scale.

3.4 IBM WebSphere BPM

The IBM WebSphere BPM suite version 6.2 [26] was evaluated by the first author of this paper in [22]. This product is developed by IBM, which is originally a computer manufacturer with a long tradition in the servers market. IBM WebSphere BPM supports the definition of KPIs with the Integration Developer. This tool allows its user to define a monitor model in which a certain event, for example, the start or end of an activity, fires a trigger, which updates some metrics. These metrics are updated at process instance level, so that KPIs can be calculated based on the metrics of multiple process instances.

KPIs can be defined with the Integration Developer by using templates. Information like an aggregation function between two KPIs or a trigger condition can be defined by writing code, but many options are provided, so that KPIs can be defined by selecting the right elements in the right order.

Both our KPIs could be modelled using the KPI model offered by this tool without modification. Therefore, we awarded ten points to the flexibility dimension. Since the KPIs are defined using templates with underlying code, we awarded six points to the ease of use dimension. The total of number points for the 'Support for KPIs' criterion is sixteen points for IBM WebSphere BPM, which corresponds to an eight on our one to ten scale.

4 Global Results

We tested the suitability of our method by comparing the evaluation results of the three BPM suites. These evaluations allowed us to discriminate between the BPM products, indicating that the criteria supported by our method are not too general or too specific, and the method is useful, i.e., it is suitable for our evaluation task.

We have compared the evaluations by comparing the outcome of the ratings for all criteria. In this way we established the suitability of the method, but we also identified the criteria for which all products scored maximum points. These appear to be too general (supported by any BPM product) and could be excluded from the evaluation method. For example, there were two criteria which evaluated the support for business rules: the support for implicit business rules and the support for explicit business rules. All three BPM suites support business rule implicitly in a business process model by allowing a business rule to be modelled as a decision point. Furthermore, all three BPM suites support the business rules explicitly by including a reference to the business rule in the business process model, and by allowing a business rule to be managed by a business rules management application. Support for business rules either implicitly or explicitly appears to be a common feature for BPM suites, and therefore all three evaluated BPM suites scored the maximum points for these features. In our evaluations, these two criteria were found to be too general and not useful for distinguishing between BPM suites. If the evaluation of other products confirms these observations, these criteria can be removed from our method in future.

Fig. 3 shows the combined results of our evaluations plotted on a single radar chart, so that these results can be compared.

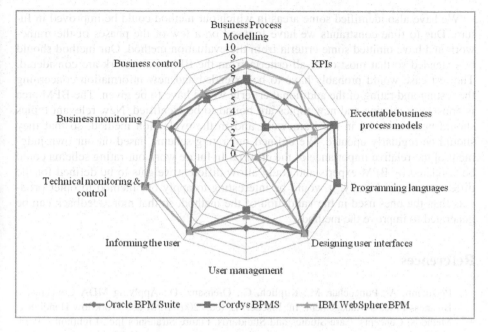

Fig. 3. Combined radar chart with the evaluation results of the three BPM suites

5 Conclusions

Although our method has shown to be suitable for the evaluation task at hand, comparing products using this method may require a lot of time, depending on the evaluator's experience with these products. For example, for each BPM suite, about two to three weeks were needed to master the product and to perform the evaluation, with no prior experience with these products. Therefore, we suggest using our method in a setting where each different vendor is asked to evaluate its own product. A representative of each vendor could then walk through our method, while a neutral observer applies our rating schema to rate the product. This should result in an objective evaluation of all the relevant criteria.

The results of this work have been delivered to a consultancy company. Consultants from this company found these results interesting and useful, but they have been reluctant to apply these results in their advising tasks. This is possibly due to their personal preferences or to the bonds they maintain with certain BPM vendors, which may prevent them from giving a truly objective advice.

We tested the suitability of our evaluation method by applying it to BPM suites, which consist of tools sets. This gives a good impression of these BPM suites' capabilities, but the results from this evaluation become depend of the specific tool packaging chosen by the vendor. Some vendors may keep some relevant functionality in tools that are shipped separately from the BPM suite, so that to get a better evaluation of the BPM capabilities of a vendor we should also include other relevant products of this vendor in the evaluation, in addition to the vendor's BPM suite.

We have also identified some areas in which our method could be improved in future. Due to time constraints we have focused on a few of the phases of the framework and have omitted some criteria from the evaluation method. Our method should be extended so that most of or all criteria from the BPM framework are considered. The test case would probably have to be extended and new information concerning the testing and rating of the additional criteria would have to be given. The BPM area is constantly moving and new topics are bound to be identified. New relevant topics should be considered in the framework and in the evaluation method, so that they should be regularly updated. We defined our rating schema based on our own judgment of the relative importance of the criteria. In future work our rating schema could be validated by BPM experts and could allow different weights to be defined for the different criteria. Finally, it would be interesting to apply our method to other products than the ones used in the validation of the method, so that more feedback can be generated to improve the method.

References

1. Petzmann, A., Puncochar, M., Kuplich, C., Orensanz, D.: Applying MDA Concepts to Business Process Management. In: Fischer, L. (ed.) 2007 BPM and Workflow Handbook: Methods, Concepts, Case Studies and Standards. Future Strategies Inc., Lighthouse Point (2007)
2. Ricken, J.: Top-Down Modeling Methodology for Model-Driven SOA Construction. In: Meersman, R., Tari, Z., Herrero, P. (eds.) OTM-WS 2007, Part I. LNCS, vol. 4805, pp. 323–332. Springer, Heidelberg (2007)
3. Hill, J.B., Cantara, M., Kerremans, M., Plummer, D.C.: Magic Quadrant for Business Process Management Suites. In: Gartner's Magic Quadrant for Business Process Management Suites. Gartner Inc. (2009)
4. Castellanos, M., Casati, F., Shan, M.C., Dayal, U.: iBOM: a Platform for Intelligent Business Operation Management. In: 21st International Conference on Data Engineering, pp. 1084–1095. IEEE Computer Society, Washington (2005)
5. Grigori, D., Casati, F., Castellanos, M., Dayal, U., Sayal, M., Shan, M.-C.: Business Process Intelligence. Computers in Industry 53(3), 321–343 (2004)
6. Gruhn, V., Laue, R.: Complexity Metrics for Business Process Models. In: 9th International Conference on Business Information Systems, pp. 1–12. Springer, Heidelberg (2006)
7. List, B., Korherr, B.: An Evaluation of Conceptual Business Process Modelling Languages. In: 2006 ACM Symposium on Applied Computing, pp. 1532–1539. ACM, New York (2006)
8. Nuno Melão, M.P.: A Conceptual Framework for Understanding Business Processes and Business Process Modelling. Information Systems Journal 10(2), 105–129 (2000)
9. Ross, R.G.: Principles of the Business Rule Approach. Addison-Wesley Professional, Boston (2003)
10. Smith, H., Fingar, P.: Business Process Management (BPM): The Third Wave. Meghan-Kiffer Press, Tampa (2003)
11. van der Aalst, W.M.P., Leymann, F., Reisig, W.: The Role of Business Processes in Service Oriented Architectures. International Journal of Business Process Integration and Management 2, 75–80 (2007)

12. van der Aalst, W.M.P., van Dongen, B.F., Herbst, J., Maruster, L., Schimm, G., Weijters, A.J.M.M.: Workflow Mining: A Survey of Issues and Approaches. Data & Knowledge Engineering 47(2), 237–267 (2003)
13. Ouyang, C., Dumas, M., ter Hofstede, A.H.M., Van der Aalst, W.M.P.: Pattern-Based Translation of BPMN Process Models to BPEL Web Services. International Journal of Web Services Research (JWSR) 5(1), 42–62 (2007)
14. Recker, J.C., Mendling, J.: On the Translation between BPMN and BPEL: Conceptual Mismatch between Process Modeling Languages. In: 18th International Conference on Advanced Information Systems Engineering, pp. 521–532. Namur University Press, Namur (2006)
15. Leymann, F.: Web Services: Distributed Applications Without Limits – An Outline. In: Database Systems for Business, Technology and Web. Springer, Heidelberg (2003)
16. Chiu, D.K.W., Li, Q., Karlapalem, K.: A Meta Modeling Approach to Workflow Management Systems Supporting Exception Handling. Information Systems 24(2), 159–184 (1999)
17. Brambilla, M., Ceri, S., Comai, S., Tziviskou, C.: Exception Handling in Workflow-driven Web Applications. In: 14th International Conference on World Wide Web, pp. 170–179. ACM, New York (2005)
18. zur Muehlen, M.: Process-driven Management Information Systems - Combining Data Warehouses and Workflow Technology. In: 4th International Conference on Electronic Commerce Research, pp. 550–566 (2001)
19. Golfarelli, M., Rizzi, S., Cella, I.: Beyond Data Warehousing: What's Next in Business Intelligence? In: 7th ACM International Workshop on Data Warehousing and OLAP, pp. 1–6. ACM, New York (2004)
20. Leymann, F., Roller, D., Schmidt, M.T.: Web Services and Business Process Management. IBM Systems Journal 41(2), 198–211 (2002)
21. zur Muehlen, M., Rosemann, M.: Workflow-based Process Monitoring and Controlling - Technical and Organizational Issues. In: 33rd Hawaii International Conference on System Sciences, pp. 1–10. IEEE Computer Society, Los Alamitos (2000)
22. Koster, S.R.: An evaluation method for Business Process Management products. Master Thesis. University of Twente (2009)
23. ARIS Business Architect,
    http://www.ids-scheer.com/en/ARIS/ARIS_Software/
    ARIS_Business_Architect/3731.html
24. Cordys BPMS,
    http://www.cordys.com/cordyscms_com/cordys_bpms.php
25. Oracle Business Process Management Suite,
    http://www.oracle.com/technologies/bpm/bpm-suite.html
26. IBM Business Process Management,
    http://www-01.ibm.com/software/websphere/products/businessint/

Appendix A: Selected Criteria

#	Criteria
1	Business Process Modelling [6-12], includes support for:
	I. Different business process modelling languages.
	II. Interoperability between different business process modelling languages.
	III. Interoperability between simple process modelling methods and business process modelling languages.
	IV. Different views when modelling a business process.
	V. Different perspectives of a business process.
	VI. Modelling with implicit business rules.
	VII. Modelling with explicit business rules.
	VIII. Modelling business processes using explicit business rules.
	IX. Facilitating the definition of explicit business rules.
2	Support for key performance indicators [4,5].
3	Development of executable business process models [7,11,13,14], includes support for:
	I. Business process execution languages.
	II. Manual translation between business process modelling languages and business process execution languages.
	III. Automatic translation between business process modelling languages and business process execution languages.
	IV. Linking the business process execution model the business process model.
4	Supported programming languages for implementing services/applications.
5	Designing input [10,15], includes support for:
	I. Separate applications for data entry.
	II. Portal technology.
	III. Activity list.
6	User management [16], includes support for:
	I. Describing roles (by names/description or by capabilities).
	II. Determining user capabilities based on organizational role.
	III. Importing organizational structure from other systems.
	IV. Determining user capabilities based on tokens (capabilities to execute certain functions, procedures or activities).
	V. Manually assigning a user to a role.
	VI. Automatically assigning a user to a role, based on his capabilities.
	VII. Activity permissions based on roles.
7	User information [16,17], includes support for:
	I. Active information.
	II. Passive information.
8	Support for technical monitoring and control [18].
9	Business-related monitoring [5,18-21], includes support for:
	I. Active monitoring.
	II. Passive monitoring.
	III. Various level of detail.
	IV. Different views of monitoring information.
10	Business-related control [16,18], includes support for:
	I. Process instance evolution.
	II. Changing business rules.
	III. Changing activities.
	IV. Changing the workload balance between users.

Requirements for BPM-SOA Methodologies: Results from an Empirical Study of Industrial Practice

Jan Ricken and Michaël Petit

University of Namur, Computer Science Department
Rue Grandgagnage, 21, B-5000 Namur, Belgium
+32 81-725259
{Jan.ricken,Michael.petit}@fundp.ac.be

Abstract. The Service Oriented Architecture (SOA) approach has been developed to enhance the integration of various systems functionalities to allow organizations to be more flexible in case of business changes. This paper will explain what aspects (hereafter called "*components*") need to be included into a SOA methodology. These components are defined in a model developed from an analysis of the state of the art in SOA and related areas. The components are classified into five groups (hereafter called "*domains*"). From August 2008 to January 2009, an empirical study has been performed on a world-wide basis to test the SOA domain model with the identified critical success factors. The results of this questionnaire give first answers to questions and assumptions discussed in academia about process-driven SOA implementation methodologies.

Keywords: Empirical study, service-oriented architectures, BPM, process modeling languages, notations and methods, management issues, SOA methodology.

1 Introduction

1.1 Motivation

Recently, the trend in software development has shifted from developing software systems to developing service-oriented systems. In service-oriented systems, software is built by composing services. This new architectural style enables the re-usability and quicker adoption of new business requirements. Evolving business requirements are the consequence of changes in the market environment or customer demand and are translated in changing business processes. These constant changes define the requirements for the supporting IT Systems. Depending on the degree of changes necessary, the underlying IT architecture might be impacted. The dynamic process of ensuring that the organization's IT system is best supporting the business strategy and goals is often referred to as Business-IT alignment. According to [1], alignment can be considered from various perspectives. In our research, though not excluding other perspectives, we favor a top-down implementation strategy as changing to SOA must be motivated and supported from the IT strategy. The bottom-up strategy is coming from the web-service inventory and neglecting the business motivation for SOA. The

S. Rinderle-Ma et al. (Eds.): BPM 2009 Workshops, LNBIP 43, pp. 453–464, 2010.

assessed SOA implementations showed a clear tendency towards successful implementation if top-down strategy was selected [2]. In order to support the flexibility required in the business processes, service oriented architectures represent a promising way to implement IT needs [3]. The SOA paradigm is defined as "an architectural concept in which all functions, or services, are defined using a description language and have invokable, platform-independent interfaces that are called to perform business processes" [4].

This paper presents preliminary empirical results of a survey performed during a PhD research with the objective to define a process-oriented and model-driven SOA implementation methodology. The lack of methodology for SOA construction, identified by [5] as the main challenge for SOA, is a key driver for our work. The basic idea of our research is to combine principles of Business Process Management (BPM) and SOA, including business strategy aspects in order to propose a top-down model-based methodology for SOA engineering. The expectations on such a methodology and then the concrete application will depend of the enterprise context (financial situation, enterprise culture, IT maturity and competencies, etc.) A research group is analyzing the organizational factors in detail [6].

In this research, we developed a SOA Domain Model as main outcome of a state-of-the-art analysis. This model has been defined and presented in detail through a former publication [7]. In that paper, we argue and underline the need for the development of such a model as a usefull model for for future work by researchers and practitioners.

Zdun and Dustdar [8] identify the integration of the different kinds of models and abstractions as one of the central challenges for the modelling of process-driven SOAs. So far there is no formal and precise modelling approach for integrating all kinds of models. The missing integration of process-driven SOA models for different modelling domains needs to be further analysed. Methodologies to manage and implement strategies into processes such as Balanced Scorecard [9] or Value Chain [10] exist but the question how to derive an effective service-oriented IT architecture from business processes is so far not resolved. The research issues in this context, based on Service –Oriented Modelling and Architecture (SOMA) [11] are currently focussed on resolving mainly technical questions regarding service identification, service specification, composition of services and service realisation. Traditional software engineering methodologies are simply not adapted any more to the changed requirements related to modern SOA implementations [12]. Novel techniques must be developed to support the refinement from the early phases of requirement analysis to the final steps of implementation and deployment. Similarly, novel techniques must be devised to construct compositions of Web services that at run-time can provide feedback and significant information to business analysis and stakeholders, who can use this information to devise new business strategies or take strategic decisions at design time [5].

1.2 Objectives

The main objective of the first round of the survey presented in this paper was to test and validate the proposed SOA Domain Model and the related critical success factors for the implementation of SOA methodologies. In the sequel, we summarize the information provided by 54 respondents who took part in the survey from August 2008 until January 2009. As the questionnaire was covering a wide area of the complete SOA domain model with 36 detailed questions, we will in this paper present only some detailed findings related to the *Modelling* and *BPM* domains. First, the survey should provide an indication if the SOA Domain Model provides a complete view of issues to be addressed during a model-driven and process oriented SOA implementation. Second, questions were asked to estimate the awareness and effective application of academic SOA implementation approaches by practitioners. Third questions were related to the identification of promising candidate modeling languages and notations and of important issues related to Modelling and BPM domain.

1.3 Structure

The complete study detailing all identified issues within the SOA domain model is available in a technical report [13]. The paper is structured as follows. In Section 2, we will briefly introduce the SOA Domain Model and explain the five domains it contains. This model has been constructed based on a comprehensive state-of-the-art analysis of available SOA methodologies in academia and practice [7]. Section 3 will describe very briefly how the study has been conducted, who answered and the limitations of the survey research design. Section 4 will summarize the questions with the findings from the survey. Section 5 will then present related work on process-oriented SOA methodologies and section 6 will conclude with the contributions of the paper and give an outlook to remaining issues, challenges and future work.

2 Model for SOA Methodology Analysis

2.1 Introduction to SOA Domain Model

According to Kruchten [14], the definition of a SOA methodology consists in phasing and grouping activities in a plan, using modelling to abstract from the very complex reality related to a specific chosen viewpoint and recognizing the necessity of tools to work efficiently and to cope with complexity. He introduced the notions of "conception" and "domains". In his terminology, "conception" corresponds to the SOA methodology and the "domains" correspond to any coherent subsets of issues related to this conception. In our work [7], the domains have been gathered through the analysis of the state-of-the-art in the area of SOA, SOA methodologies, BPM and SOA Management. The initial number of 14 SOA methodologies has been reduced to 7 through a preliminary analysis. After the detailed analysis of methodologies, some parts needed to be taken out, as they were not fitting within the proposed definition of methodology stated by Vernadat [15]: "It needs to be a set of methods, models and tools to be used in a structured way to solve a problem." Therefore, only the following methods from the analysed list meet the requirements:

- ARIS Value Engineering for SOA (AVE for SOA) [16]
- Enterprise SOA [17]
- Model-Driven Integration of Process driven SOA Models [8], [18]
- Platform-independent model for service-oriented architecture (PIM4SOA) [19]

- Service-oriented Design and Development Methodology (SoDD) [20]
- Service oriented Modelling & Architecture (SoMA) [11]
- SOA Practitioners Guide [21]

Table 1 summarises all the domains and components relative to the proposed conception "SOA methodology" (our *model of SOA methodologies*). The state of the art analysis allowed us to identify all relevant aspects, issues and tools relevant in SOA methodologies. These aspects were then grouped into coherent domains.

Table 1. SOA Domain Model for process & model-driven SOA implementation

Conception	Domains	Issues
SOA Methodology	Modelling	Model Languages (UML, BPMN, BPEL, EPC,...etc.) Meta Model Languages (MOF), Notations (WSDL, WPDL, XPDL, XML,...etc.) Data Management (Master Data Management)
		Interoperability, Modelinterfaces, Modeling strategy (Top-Down, Meet-in-the-Middle, Bottom-Up)
		Enterprise Architecture, Enterprise Hierarchy (Enterprise Components, Systems, Portal/Presentation) Views (e.g. Process, Data, Organisation, Physical, development)
		Model Driven Architecture, Mapping of Abstraction Layers
	BPM	BPM Knowledge (BPM Usage Szenarios, Decomposition of Processes, Common Language, Process Conventions)
		Business BPM (Process Strategy, Process Definition, Event Specification, Rule Mgt Definition, Business BPM Tools)
		Technical BPM (Process Implementation, Event & Rules Implementation, Technical BPM Tools, Process Monitoring & Performance)
	Project	SOA Maturity Models (Stages of Maturity to asses As-Is Situation and define To-Be Situation)
		SOA Governance (SOA Roles & Responsibilities, SOA Skills, SOA Rules, SOA Principles)
		SOA Phases (SOA Strategy, SOA Planning, SOA Education, SOA Execution, SOA Implementation & Development, SOA Control, SOA Change Mgt.)
		SOA Objectives (SOA IT Objectives, SOA Business Objectives), SOA KPI's, SOA Funding Model, SOA Drivers, SOA Critical Success Factors
	Tool	SOA BPM Design Time for web-service design (incl. Business Rules & Event Mgt)
		SOA BPM Run-Time for operating web-services (incl. Business Rules & Event Mgt)
		SOA Project Management for Planning & Change Management
		SOA Process and Web-Service Simulation and Performance Management
	Web Service	SOA Heartbeat (Service Provider, Service Consumer, Registry, Messaging)
		SOA Security (Authentication, Authorization and Identity Mgt)
		SOA Decomposition of Web-Services (Granularity, Orchestration)
		Quality of Web-Services
		Service Level Agreements (Web-Service Measurement, Web-Service Cost & Pricing)

Due to space restrictions, we can only focus on two domains (Modelling and BPM) and the related questions as presented in the first chapter. The SOA Domain Model is explained in detail in former work [7]. For a better understanding, we briefly describe the two domains by listing the issues they include.

2.2 SOA Domain Modelling

The description of business content through **different model types** depending on viewpoints and concerns is specifically important for SOA construction, as modelling experts need to choose specific viewpoints related to specific concerns. Needed viewpoints include the logical view with *Business Processes* (e.g. UML Activity and Sequence diagrams, EPC, BPML, IDEF, Value Chain, ...etc), *Data* (e.g. UML Class Diagrams, ERM Models...etc.), *Organisation* (e.g. Organizational Chart, Knowledge

Competency Chart...etc.), *physical* (e.g. Software & Hardware maps...etc.), *development notations (e.g. Application System Type Diagrams, WSDL, WPDL, XPDL, XML ,etc...)*. The reason for using a specific model-type should be justified. The issue of **interfacing and interoperability** between models and modelling levels is raised. **MDA** may be a relevant approach in this context. An overall perception of **Enterprise Architecture** and their composing blocks should be addressed. The choice of an implementation strategy **"top-down", "meet in the middle" or "bottom-up"** approach needs to be part of the modelling discussion. **Conceptual, applicative and technical** views of an enterprise need to be addressed.

2.3 SOA Domain BPM

A sound basis of **BPM knowledge** is considered as critical. BPM knowledge implies knowing who is doing what, with what data, supported by which system and with what objective. Different business needs addressed by BPM usage scenarios (e.g. Documentation, Reengineering, Compliance, Cost Improvement, Certification, System Development, Enterprise Architecture) can be satisfied. Without this knowledge of processes, activities, structure and decomposition of processes and activities, it is hardly imaginable to identify all relevant activities that might be candidates for becoming services. The concept of re-utilization within SOA is hardly feasible without clear understanding of the context in which services are consumed. Therefore well documented business processes are critical to avoid questions and waste of time. Furthermore, the issue of communication between functional and technical teams is also a key. Therefore, a distinction can be made in **Business BPM** (Process Conventions, Process Definition, Event Specification, Rules Management) and **Technical BPM** (Process Implementation, Event & Rules Implementation, Real-time Process Performance Measurement). Once processes are executed, the measurement of their performance is analysed and is used as input for the BPM strategy phase.

3 Survey Design and Limitations

3.1 Survey Design

A comprehensive literature review was conducted at the first stage of this study; (a) to identify a list of existing SOA implementation methodologies matching to the definition proposed by Vernadat and, (b) to identify a list of issues extracted from the methodologies and, (c) to regroup the issues into domains and, (d) derive an a-priori model to be tested and validated through, (e) a survey approach and, (f) a multiple case-study. Hence, as [22] and [23] argue, research methods should be combined meaning to gather quantitative and qualitative data. In the specific context of the present research, this might provide a research design to allow a more holistic study and validation of the research questions. Furthermore, they argue that experiments may not fit within the proposed research design as experiments need to take place in a controlled environment. The presented research question is structured around a range of issues simply too broad e.g. the domains BPM, Modelling, Project Management, Tools and Web Services. The quantitative study should bring the advantage of a data condensing technique to allow the big picture across various data collection points. It is a promising way to validate patterns of behavior related to SOA adoption. Since it allows measuring of concepts and establishing causability across variables [24], quantitative analysis seems to be the best attempt to validate on a world-wide basis the implementation challenges on available SOA methodologies.

After completion of the quantitative survey with a second round to follow to the first, it is planned to validate the SOA Domain Model by multiple case studies from Luxembourg. A validation by questionnaire combined with case study approach has been chosen as Benbasat et al [25] argue that case study research may be used successfully in validating state-of-the art. Following to this the testing of hypotheses is a legitimate vehicle to add knowledge to the IS world of research. The chosen approach can help to analyze technology implementations despite the identified risk of generalizability. Other potential weaknesses will be identified and addressed in the case study design.

3.2 Limitations to Survey Design

The paper reports from the findings derived from the first round of the survey which took place from August 2008 to January 2009. The survey was accessible by following a web-link, available 24h/7 and all answers were recorded in a database. The chosen channels for the announcement of the survey were professional communities related to SOA including qualified profiles of managing IT members[1]. With the chosen approach, it was unfortunately not possible to calculate a ratio of participation. A first attempt getting access to worldwide IT specialists in companies was to ask IT market research providers to participate e.g. Gartner, Forrester, AMR Research. Unfortunately, this initiative failed as the questionnaire was rated too academic and too time consuming to fill. Out of the total number of answers (79) we selected 54 relevant ones by eliminating responses not being serious or complete (less than 80% of answered questions). The top five countries to respond were Luxembourg (17,1%), USA (17,1%), Germany (14,3%), Belgium (11,4%), Australia and Brazil (8,6%). The respondents' countries are obviously correlated with the distribution over countries of the members of the community of the three BPM/SOA websites.

72,1% of respondents are Managers, Directors, CIO/CPOs or CEOs. The profiles show clearly that those who responded have a good overview of the subject. Obviously most of the respondents are also profiles who will decide about implementing SOA and how this will be done. This is on the one hand a strength because we have collected the viewpoint of deciders, but on the other hand this might represent also a weakness as SOA analysts and programmers are underweighted. On the other hand, the responsible managers have filled the technical questions together with their analysts and architects. Unfortunately, the research design was not able to provide a validation that respondents have well understood the questions and eventually have referred to analysts being more competent to answer the questions. However to reduce

---

[1] BPtrends: http://www.bptrends.com, IT Nation: http://www.itnation.eu, SOA Know-How: http://www.soa-know-how.de

this risk, it was proposed in the survey introduction to ask questions by email to get clarification if necessary. Despite the fact that the respondents left their contact details with an underlying matching of name and email address (they were promised to get the survey results by e-mail), we will need to improve the survey design in order to get a more reliable validation of response correctness. In total, the number of 54 respondents is not sufficient to deduct highly statistically significant final conclusions. Therefore, we plan to re-use the questionnaire to collect more answers and achieve better statistical significance. Furthermore, the sample of respondents can be considered as interested and experienced in BPM and SOA. Those, who have no interest or belief in SOA, also had no interest in responding to the questionnaire as this was a time consuming commitment.

4 Survey Results

4.1 Main Question: "Is the Presented SOA Domain Model Reflecting All Domains to Consider for a Process-Oriented and Model-Driven SOA Methodology?"

Regarding the validation and completeness of our SOA domain model, 90,66% of respondents are responding that the presented model is reflecting all domains to consider for an exhaustive SOA implementation methodology based on a process-oriented approach. Within the 9,44% not agreeing, respondents were pointing to change management or top management support as lacks. However, the mentioned issues are already addressed in our model as a part of the SOA project management domain. Some other respondents were pointing to related approaches e.g. Web-Oriented Architecture (WOA) or Representational State Transfer (REST) approach. WOA, like SOA, is an architectural approach to system design, though WOA is resource-oriented rather than service-oriented. While the core SOA design unit is a re-usable service that fulfils a distinct business function, resource-oriented services are more limited and data-focused. SOA and WOA work at different layers of abstraction. SOA is a system-level architectural style that tries to implement new business capabilities so that they can be consumed by many applications. WOA is an interface-level architectural style that focuses on the means by which these service capabilities are exposed to consumers [26]. Therefore, WOA and REST are approaches standing for their own. They could certainly add value for specific questions.

4.2 Sub Question: " For SOA Methodologies Specifically, Please Rate the Following SOA Methodologies in Alphabetical Order"

The next question to address is about the knowledge and usage of both academic and industrial SOA implementation methodologies. The respondents were asked to evaluate a list of SOA methodologies resulting from the state-of-the-art analysis of all current/available SOA methodologies in the academic and practice worlds, as shown on Figure 1:

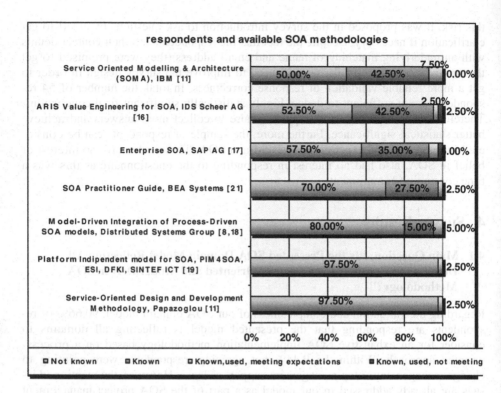

Fig. 1. Respondents and available SOA methodologies

In general, most of respondents are not aware of the wide range of existing methodologies. The most known methodologies are industrial ones e.g. IBM (known by 42,50%), IDS Scheer (42,50%), SAP (35,00%) and BEA (27,50%). The academic proposals are even less known than the industrial SOA methodologies. Unfortunately, the number of reported successful application of such methodologies is too low to deduct reliable findings. IBM was the first IT company to invest in SOA run-time engines and SOA methodology (SoMA) [16]. Therefore, their solutions and methodologies are more known than these of the competitors. IBM is well known world-wide where academic proposals dissemination towards industry is bound to regional or country spread. For SODD [28], only 2.50% of respondents are aware of this methodology beside the fact that the methodology is based on SoMA [16] and has decreased the detected shortcomings. A reason for this might be that the researchers are located in the Netherlands and no respondents filled the questionnaire from the Netherlands. However, the evaluation of the question identifies the low degree of spread academic SOA methodologies have.

4.3 Sub Question 2: "Are Modelling and BPM Domains Considered as Critical Success Factors for SOA Implementation? "

Business Process Management Knowledge is considered as critical success factor and enabler. Therefore, 84,4% manage completely (46,7%) or partly (37,8%) their processes in a real BPM programme including strategy, design, implementation & controlling. Within their BPM, various usage scenarios are covered.

Most of respondents have already documented processes (84,78%) and use BPM also for other objectives e.g. certification (36,96%), risk management (32,61%), cost control (50%), process driven application management (52,17%) and process-driven web-service construction (39,13%). In the context of SOA, it is very interesting to observe the planned scenario for the two last cited with 28,26% and 36,96%. So nearly 75% of respondents are using or have planned to use processes for the web-service identification and construction. Furthermore, the planned process-driven web service construction of 36,96% is the highest value for the planned usage scenarios in BPM. This is clearly the area with the biggest increasing potential of re-utilisation of BPM content.

Without process knowledge in a company, it is hardly imaginable to identify all relevant functions that might be candidates for services. Consequently, the implementation of loose coupling principle and the re-utilization of web-services is hardly feasible. Without any documentation, it is very hard to speak a common language. It is needless to stress the communication aspect of SOA project teams with business analysts, technical analysts and external consultants. The quality of the documentation should be high to avoid questions and waste of time regarding the correctness and the level of detail of modeled processes.

Therefore, BPM knowledge is rated as very important with 91,1% for SOA implementation. Only 8,9% of the respondents rate it neutral (6,7%) or as not important (2,2%).

Regarding the way SOA is implemented, 56,5% of respondents have chosen the top-down approach, 19,6% meet-in-the-middle and 15,2% decided for bottom-up. The remaining 8,7% were non applicable. The result shows a clear trend towards top-down approach and even more decide for meet-in-the-middle than for the bottom-up approach. This decision depends also on the project context and objectives.

In general, strategic model types such as e^3value, Balanced Scorecard (BSC) or Value Added Chain Model (VAC) are less known and used than business process requirement languages such as Business Process Modelling Notation (BPMN), Event driven Process Chain (EPC) and UML Activity Diagram or than technical process implementation languages (such as BPEL or WSDL).

Some modelling languages and notations are not known and used at all[1] : Archimate, BOP, EEML, EKS, Grai/Gim, IEM/Mo2Go, JPDL, Memo, Metis, Meml, Pim4SOA, PIF, PSL Core, SADT, SPEM, Testbed, UEML and Yawl.

Clear trends are visible about modelling languages usage on the three different levels of abstraction (Strategy, Processes, IT). For Strategy, the most known and used model type is the BSC model and Value Added Chain model. Most of business requirements at the process level are captured through BPMN, BPML, EPC, IDEF, UML Activity Diagram. For IT or implementation languages, BPEL, WSDL, WPDL are particularly often known and used. Again, the respondents' choice is showing a clear trend towards notations seeming to be good candidates for a model driven and process-oriented SOA project. We will in the multiple case studies evaluate why specific notations are more promising than others and identify which notation is applied for what specific context.

---

[1] Meaning that more than 85% of respondents do not know nor use it.

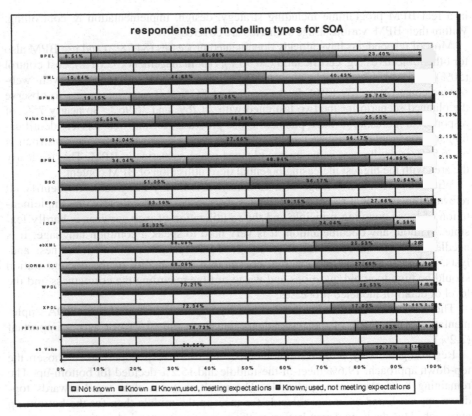

Fig. 2. Respondents and modelling types for SOA

5 Related Research

To our knowledge, empirical studies similar in scope and objectives to the one presented in this paper have not been done so far in academia. Industry studies exist e.g. [27], but not as detailed as ours. A common conclusion is summarizing a process oriented approach as a critical success factor for SOA methodologies.

6 Conclusions

In this paper, we presented the results of a survey on the knowledge and practice of SOA in industry. From the results obtained in chapter 4, we can draw some general conclusions knowing that the questionnaire will be opened for a second phase to increase statistical relevance and remove shortcomings in the survey research design. However, the so far obtained results show first trends. The validation of the questions have confirmed the need for the presented research of process-driven SOA implementation. For the future research this might have an impact as these principles were considered as important issue to address. We will furthermore in our future work ensure interlocking the developed SOA Domain Model in industrial application scenarios' and refine the model appropriately.

References

[1] Henderson, J.C., Venkatraman, N.: Strategic Alignment: Leveraging Information Technology for transforming organisations. IBM Systems Journal 32(1) (1993)

[2] Terlouw, J., Terlouw, L., Jansen, S.: An Assessment Method for Selecting an SOA Delivery Strategy: Determining Influencing Factors and Their Value Weights. In: 4th International Workshop on BUSITAL, Amsterdam (June 2009)

[3] Erl, T.: Service Oriented Architecture: Concepts, Technology and Design. Prentice Hall PTR, Englewood Cliffs (2005)

[4] Channabasavaiah, K., Holley, K., Tuggle, E.: Migrating to Service Oriented Architecture – part 1, IBM Developer Works (2003)

[5] Papazoglou, P.M., Traverso, P., Dustdar, S., Leymann, F., Krämer, B.J.: Service oriented computing: a Research Roadmap. In: Cubera, F., Krämer, B.J., Papazoglou, M.P. (eds.) Dagstuhl Seminar Proceedings 05462, March (2006), ISSN 1862 – 4405

[6] Luthria, H., Rabhi, F.: Service Oriented Computing in Practice – An Agenda for Research into Factors Influencing the Organizational Adoption of Service Oriented Architectures. Journal of Theoretical and Applied Electronic Commerce Research 4(1) (April 2009)

[7] Ricken, J., Petit, M.: Characterization of Methods for Process-Oriented Engineering of SOA. In: Ardagna, D., et al. (eds.) BPM 2008 Workshops. LNBIP, vol. 17, pp. 621–632. Springer, Heidelberg (2009)

[8] Zdun, U., Dustdar, S.: Model-Driven Integration of Process-Driven SOA Models. International Journal of Business Process Integration and Management 2(2), 109–119 (2007)

[9] Kaplan, R., Norton, D.: The Balanced Scorecard – Measures That drive Performance. Harvard Business Review, 71–79 (January/February 1992)

[10] Porter, M.: Competitive Advantage: Creating and Sustaining superior Performance. Free Press (1985)

[11] Arsanjani, A.: Service-Oriented Modelling and Architecture (SOMA), IBM developerWorks (2004)

[12] IEEE,
http://standards.ieee.org/reading/ieee/std_public/description/se/1471-2000_desc.html (access 22.4.2008)

[13] Ricken, J.: Results on Testing a SOA Domain Model through an empirical study – Executive Summary, Technical Report, University of Namur, Computer Science Faculty (July 2009),
https://www.fundp.ac.be/universite/personnes/page_view/00008362/cv.html

[14] Kruchten, P.: The 4+1 View Model of Architecture. IEEE Software 12(6) (1995)

[15] Vernadat, F.B.: Enterprise Modeling and Integration: principles and applications, 1st edn. Chapman & Hall, Boca Raton (1996)

[16] Yvanov, K.: ARIS Value Engineering for SOA, IDS Scheer AG (2006)

[17] Woods, D., Mattern, T.: Enterprise SOA: Designing IT for Business Innovation. O'Reily Media, NC (2006)

[18] Tran, H., Zdun, U., Dustdar, S.: View-based Integration of Process-driven SOA Models At Various Abstraction Levels. In: Kutsche, R.-D., Milanovic, N. (eds.) Proceedings of First International Workshop on Model-Based Software and Data Integration MBSDI 2008, Berlin, Germany. CCIS, vol. 8, pp. 55–66. Springer, Heidelberg (2008)

[19] Benguria, G., Larrucea, X., et al.: A Platform Independent Model for Service Oriented Architectures. In: I-ESA conference 2006, Bordeaux, March 22-24. Springer, Heidelberg (2006)

[20] Papazoglou, P., van der Heuvel, W.J.: Service-oriented Design and Development Methodology. Int. J. of Web Engineering and technology, IJWET (2006)
[21] Shum, A., et al.: SOA practitioners guide, BEA Systems (September 2006), http://dev2dev.bea.com/pub/a/2006/09/soa-practitioners-guide.html (access 2.2.2007)
[22] Jick, T.D.: Mixing qualitative and quantitative Methods: Triangulation in Action. Administrative Science Quarterly 24(4), 602–611 (1979)
[23] Mingers, J., Brocklesby, J.: Multimethodology: Towards a framework for Mixing Methodologies. International Journal of Management Science 25(5), 489–509 (1997)
[24] Ragin, C.C.: Constructiong Social Research. Pine Forge Press, Thousand Oaks (1994)
[25] Benbasat, I., et al.: The Case Research Startegy in Studies of Information Systems. MIS Quartely 11(3), 369–386 (1987)
[26] http://www.informationweek.com/news/software/soa/show.art.9904293 (access 19.8.2008)
[27] Harmon, H., Wolf, C.: Business Process Management and Service Oriented Architecture, http://www.bptrends.com/surveys_landing.cfm (access 2.4.2008)

On Measuring the Understandability of Process Models

Joachim Melcher[1], Jan Mendling[2], Hajo A. Reijers[3], and Detlef Seese[1]

[1] Institut AIFB, Universität Karlsruhe (TH), Germany
{melcher,seese}@aifb.uni-karlsruhe.de
[2] Humboldt-Universität zu Berlin, Germany
jan.mendling@wiwi.hu-berlin.de
[3] School of Industrial Engineering, Eindhoven University of Technology,
The Netherlands
h.a.reijers@tue.nl

Abstract. Much efforts are aimed at unveiling the factors that influence a person's comprehension of a business process model. While various potential factors have been proposed and studied in an experimental setting, little attention is being paid to reliability and validity requirements on measuring a person's structural understanding of a process model. This paper proposes the concepts to meaningfully argue about these notions, for the sake of improving future measurement instruments. The findings from an experiment, involving 178 students from three different universities, underline the importance of this topic. In particular, it is shown that the *coverage* of model-related questions is important. This paper provides various recommendations to properly measure structural model comprehension.

Keywords: Process understandability, process metric, experiment.

1 Introduction

Process models are often used as a communication vehicle among people, for example to clarify how a new information system is expected to support operations or to explain a new employee's duties in a particular field. These examples motivate the importance of process models being clearly understandable. It has been suggested that various factors play a role in the sense-making of a process model, like a reader's expertise [1], the used modeling notation [2], the visual layout of the model [3,4] and the structural attributes of the process model [5,6].

While certain insights can be derived from relevant theories, for example [7], it is clear that empirical research is required to substantiate and adapt these for the process modeling domain. A common set-up for that kind of research, and one that has been applied in earlier work [8,9,10], is to proceed as follows. One selects an independent variable, for example, a process reader's familiarity with a notation, and aims to study the relation between its variation and that of a particular measure for the reader's structural understanding of a model,

S. Rinderle-Ma et al. (Eds.): BPM 2009 Workshops, LNBIP 43, pp. 465–476, 2010.

the dependent variable. Typically, respondents are asked to study one or more process models and then provide answers to questions related to these. The answers can then be used to quantify their structural comprehension of the process models in question.

The main research question that this paper addresses is how to develop a *reliable* and *valid* measurement instrument to determine the extent to which a respondent structurally understands a process model. The importance of this question is this: If we cannot be certain that we correctly capture a person's understanding of a process model, we cannot hope to uncover the factors that influence that comprehension level. For example, we need to know about the type and the number of model questions that need to be asked to conclude that someone really understands the model in question.

Previously, Melcher and Seese have approached this issue by giving formal definitions for measuring structural process understandability [10,11]. They also investigated some empirical properties of this measure using a small sample size. This paper substantially extends this work, as it provides the hypotheses involving the reliability and validity of these notions. Furthermore, this paper reports on a large-scale, online experiment involving 178 students from three different universities that was used to put the various hypotheses to the test. Because of space restrictions, some detailed experimental results can only be presented in [12].

This paper is organized as follows: Section 2 discusses the background of our work. Our foundations of measuring structural process model understandability are shown in Section 3. These include hypotheses about empirical properties of the measures. Section 4 presents an experiment for examining these hypotheses and the respective results. Section 5 concludes with a summary and future work.

2   Background

A group including Mendling *et al.* investigate empirical relationships between personal, process specific (structural) properties and structural process understandability [8]. They use a questionnaire with 12 process models (each with 25 tasks) for recording structural process model understanding of 73 students. As operationalization of structural process understandability, they created the SCORE metric—essentially the sum of correct answers to eight closed questions about order, concurrency, exclusiveness or repetition of tasks as well as one open question about possible errors for each process model. In [9], the influence of content related factors on structural process understandability is additionally considered. In this latter experiment, six yes/no questions about process model structure and behavior are presented to the participants. The metric PSCORE (sum of correct answers about the six process models of the questionnaire) quantifies in how far a person can catch the content of a model.

In [10,11], Melcher and Seese point to a potential issue in these works with respect to reliability and validity for the proposed structural understandability metrics. *Reliability* requires that metric values obtained by different observers of the same phenomenon have to be consistent. For instance, if one wants to measure the height of a person, the measurements should be taken at a special time of day (e. g., in the morning) and always barefooted [13, pp. 70–71]. Otherwise, the values of the same person can vary significantly. *Validity* can be subdivided into *construct validity* and *content validity* [13, pp. 71–72]. The first checks whether the metric really represents the theoretical concept to be measured (e. g., is church attendance a good metric for religiousness?). The second checks whether the metric covers the range of meanings included in the concept (e. g., a test of mathematical ability for elementary pupils cannot be limited to addition but should also include subtraction, multiplication, division and so forth). Melcher and Seese point out that these issues have not been explicitly addressed in the existing research.

3 Measuring Structural Process Understandability

3.1 Aspects of Process Understandability

As we already discussed in Section 2, it is important to cover the different aspects of structural process understandability[1] in order to meet the content validity requirement for metrics. Our definitions formalize the aspects *concurrency*, *exclusiveness*, *order* and *repetition* which are identified by Mendling *et al.* in [8, p. 52][2]. While these notions are thought to cover a broad array of understandability aspects, we do not deny the possible existence of other aspects.

Our definitions are based on the concept of an activity period.

Definition 1 (Activity Period). *An activity period of task t is the period between a point in time when t becomes executable and the next point in time when the actual execution of t terminates.*

Using this concept, we can define relations for the four aspects of process understandability we mentioned.

Definition 2 (Concurrency). *For the questions about task concurrency, the relations $c_{\sharp}, c_{\exists}, c_{\forall} \subseteq T \times T$ with the following meanings are used.*

$(t_1, t_2) \in c_{\sharp} \Leftrightarrow$ *There is no process instance for which the activity periods of tasks t_1 and t_2 overlap.*

$(t_1, t_2) \in c_{\exists} \Leftrightarrow$ *There is a process instance for which the activity periods of tasks t_1 and t_2 overlap at least once (several executions of t_1 and t_2 per process instance are possible). But there also exists a process instance for which this does not hold.*

$(t_1, t_2) \in c_{\forall} \Leftrightarrow$ *For each process instance, the activity periods of tasks t_1 and t_2 overlap at least once.*

---

[1] For the sake of simplicity, we use the term "process understandability" instead of "*structural* process understandability" in the rest of this paper.

[2] Note that the process understandability metrics, other definitions and hypotheses presented in this section (except Subsection 3.3) are adapted from [10,11].

Definition 3 (Exclusiveness). *For the questions about task exclusiveness, the relations $e_\nexists, e_\exists, e_\forall \subseteq T \times T$ with the following meanings are used.*
$(t_1, t_2) \in e_\nexists \Leftrightarrow$ *There is* no *process instance, for which tasks t_1 and t_2 are both executed.*
$(t_1, t_2) \in e_\exists \Leftrightarrow$ *There is a process instance, for which tasks t_1 and t_2 are both executed. But there also exists a process instance for which this does not hold.*
$(t_1, t_2) \in e_\forall \Leftrightarrow$ *For each process instance, the tasks t_1 and t_2 are both executed.*

Definition 4 (Order). *For the questions about task order, the relations $o_\nexists, o_\exists, o_\forall \subseteq T \times T$ with the following meanings are used.*
$(t_1, t_2) \in o_\nexists \Leftrightarrow$ *There is* no *process instance for which an activity period of task t_1 ends before an activity period of task t_2 starts.*
$(t_1, t_2) \in o_\exists \Leftrightarrow$ *There is a process instance for which an activity period of task t_1 ends before an activity period of task t_2 starts. But there also exists a process instance for which this does not hold.*
$(t_1, t_2) \in o_\forall \Leftrightarrow$ *For each process instance, an activity period of task t_1 ends before an activity period of task t_2 starts.*

Definition 5 (Repetition). *For the questions about task repetition, the relations $r_{=1}, r_?, r_*, r_+ \subseteq T$ with the following meanings are used.*
$t \in r_{=1} \Leftrightarrow$ *For each process instance, task t is executed exactly once.*
$t \in r_? \Leftrightarrow$ *For each process instance, task t is executed not once or exactly once. Both cases really occur.*
$t \in r_* \Leftrightarrow$ *For each process instance, task t is executed not once, exactly once or more than once. There exists a process instance for which t is executed not once and another one for which t is executed more than once.*
$t \in r_+ \Leftrightarrow$ *For each process instance, task t is executed at least once. There exists a process instance for which t is executed more than once.*

We constructed these definitions in such a way that we get the properties of Corollary 1, which are beneficial for the measurement process.

Corollary 1 (Properties of relations). *The relations have the following properties:*

1. *The relations $c_\nexists, c_\exists, c_\forall$ and $e_\nexists, e_\exists, e_\forall$ are symmetric.*
2. *For all possible task combinations, exactly one relation per aspect is true.*

Because of property 2 of Corollary 1, we can group the different relations for an aspect to questions about the process model: The question $q_r(t)$, for example, asks which of the relations $r_{=1}, r_?, r_*, r_+$ holds for task t. Because of property 1 of Corollary 1, $q_c(t_1, t_2) = q_c(t_2, t_1)$ and $q_e(t_1, t_2) = q_e(t_2, t_1)$ hold.

Corollary 2 (Maximum number of questions). *The maximum number $|Q_{a,max}(p)|$ of possible different questions of aspect $a \in \{c, e, o, r\}$ about process model p with n tasks is*

$$|Q_{c,max}(p)| = |Q_{e,max}(p)| = \frac{n(n-1)}{2} \tag{1}$$

$$|Q_{o,max}(p)| = n(n-1) \tag{2}$$

$$|Q_{r,max}(p)| = n \ . \tag{3}$$

As one can see, the maximum number of questions for *concurrency*, *exclusiveness* and *order* grows quadratically with the number of tasks, while the maximum number of questions for *repetition* grows only linearly.

We can now define process understandability.

Definition 6 (Personal process understandability). *The personal process understandability $U_a(p, s)$ of aspect a of process model p by subject s is defined as the fraction of correct answers given by s to the $|Q_{a,max}(p)|$ different questions of aspect a about p.*

$$U_a(p, s) := \frac{\# \ correct \ answers \ to \ Q_{a,max}(p)}{|Q_{a,max}(p)|} \quad , a \in \{c, e, o, r\} \tag{4}$$

Hypothesis 1. *The personal process understandability metric values $U_a(p, s_i)$ of a process model p are normally distributed.*

The different values of personal process understandability can be seen as outcomes of a random variable. The expected value can be estimated as follows.

Definition 7 (Estimated process understandability). *The estimated process understandability $\widehat{U}_a(p, S)$ of aspect a of process model p and subjects S is defined as the average personal process understandability of p by the subjects of S.*

$$\widehat{U}_a(p, S) := \frac{1}{|S|} \sum_{s \in S} U_a(p, s) \quad , a \in \{c, e, o, r\} \tag{5}$$

Hypothesis 2. *The different aspects of process understandability result in different values of the $\widehat{U}_a(p, S)$ of a process model p.*

Consequently, it is important to measure at least all of these aspects to achieve an insight into one's "overall understandability" of a model.

3.2 Partial Process Understandability

In order to reduce the effort for measuring process understandability, only a subset of all possible questions about the different aspects can be selected for being answered by the subjects. This approach was also used in [8,9].

Definition 8 (Personal partial process understandability). *The personal partial process understandability $U_a(p, s, Q_a)$ of aspect a, process model p, subject s and questions $Q_a \subseteq Q_{a,max}(p)$ is defined as the fraction of correct answers given by s to the questions Q_a of aspect a about p.*

$$U_a(p, s, Q_a) := \frac{\#\ correct\ answers\ to\ Q_a}{|Q_a|} \quad , a \in \{c, e, o, r\} \tag{6}$$

Here again, the different values of personal partial process understandability can be seen as outcomes of a random variable. The expected value of this variable can be estimated according to Definition 9.

Definition 9 (Estimated partial process understandability). *The estimated partial process understandability $\widehat{U}_a(p, S, Q_a)$ of aspect a, process model p, subjects S and questions Q_a is defined as the average personal partial process understandability of p and Q_a by the subjects of S.*

$$\widehat{U}_a(p, S, Q_a) := \frac{1}{|S|} \sum_{s \in S} U_a(p, s, Q_a) \quad , a \in \{c, e, o, r\} \tag{7}$$

For measuring the number of asked questions Q_a relative to the number of possible questions $Q_{a,max}(p)$ about process model p, we define *coverage rate*.

Definition 10 (Coverage rate). *The coverage rate of a set of questions $Q_a \subseteq Q_{a,max}(p)$ about aspect a of process model p is defined as*

$$r_a(Q_a, p) := \frac{|Q_a|}{|Q_{a,max}(p)|} \quad , a \in \{c, e, o, r\} \quad . \tag{8}$$

Hypothesis 3. *The different questions of $Q_{a,max}(p)$ are not equally difficult. This has two consequences: (1) For the same coverage rate, one gets different values for estimated partial process understandability depending on the selected questions Q_a. (2) The smaller the coverage rate, the bigger the standard deviation of the different values of estimated partial process understandability for that coverage rate.*

As a consequence, the coverage rate should not be selected too small. Furthermore, the questions for the set Q_a should be chosen randomly in order to minimize the risk of intentionally or unintentionally selecting especially easy or difficult questions. The two recommendations shall assure that the estimated partial process understandability does not differ that much from the true value of process understandability.

3.3   Process Understandability Using Virtual Subjects

As the number of possible questions soon becomes so high for larger process models (see Corollary 2), not all of them can be asked to one single subject. Besides using partial process understandability (Subsection 3.2), there is a second approach—virtual subjects—which is based on the following hypothesis.

Hypothesis 4. *Randomly dividing a set of questions answered by a group of subjects into two subsets of approximately same size results in a strong correlation between the rates of correct answers given by the same subject to the questions of the two subsets.*

Roughly speaking that means that a subject with good results for one subset of questions will also be good for the second subset. This is used by us in inverse direction in order to "construct" a new virtual subject's answers out of the answers given by several real subjects:

The set of all possible questions of one aspect is divided into different subsets which are each answered by different groups of subjects. Afterwards, in each group the subjects are ordered by their personal partial process understandability values. Now, new virtual subjects are "created" by combining the answers of one subject from each group. For this step, the best subjects from each group are combined to the best new virtual subject, the second best subjects to the second best new virtual subject—and so on.

4 Experimental Evaluation and Results

4.1 Experimental Design

For our experimental evaluation, we used the process model depicted in Figure 1. We used the same top-to-bottom layout as in [10,11,8,9].

As the process model has 12 tasks, the number of possible questions about the four aspects are $|Q_{c,max}(p)| = |Q_{e,max}(p)| = 66$, $|Q_{o,max}(p)| = 132$ and $|Q_{r,max}(p)| = 12$. Since the number of possible questions per aspect is too high, we could not present them all to each participant. Instead, we used the virtual subjects approach (Subsection 3.3) and divided the questions for *concurrency*,

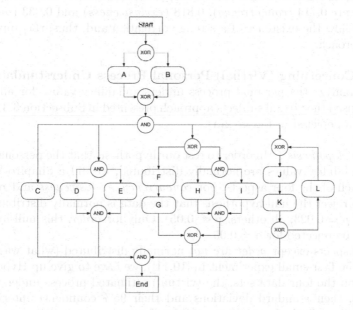

Fig. 1. Process model used in experiment

exclusiveness and *order* into different subsets. Accordingly, we created a questionnaire with nine groups (groups 1 to 4 with questions about *order* [*o1-o4*]; groups 5 to 8 with questions about *concurrency* [*c5-c8*] and *exclusiveness* [*e5-e8*]; group 9 with questions about *repetition* [*r9*])—resulting in 13 data sets. In each group, we used 33 questions (group 9 was filled by 21 "dummy questions").

We asked students attending courses on workflow management at Humboldt-Universität zu Berlin, Eindhoven University of Technology and Universität Karlsruhe (TH) to participate in the experiment. Participation was voluntary. Students from Berlin and Eindhoven got a bonus for their final exam—students from Karlsruhe could use it as training for their exam. Altogether, 178 students completed the questionnaire. The participants were randomly assigned to one group of the questionnaire.

4.2   Results

Results Concerning Virtual Subjects Approach

Regarding Hypothesis 4. In order to show that there is really a strong correlation between the results for two subsets of questions and that, thus, the virtual subjects approach is legitimate, we did the following analysis: Using the data about the aspects *concurrency, exclusiveness* and *order* from the experiment in [10,11], we randomly divided the questions for each aspect into two halves of the same size. In the next step, the Spearman rank correlation coefficient [14, pp. 42–45] between the personal partial process understandability values from the two halves was computed. This was repeated 5,000 times for each aspect. The medians were 0.714 (*concurrency*), 0.818 (*exclusiveness*) and 0.933 (*order*). So, we could show the existence of a strong correlation and, thus, the applicability of the approach.

Results Concerning (Virtual) Personal Process Understandability. In order to analyze the personal process understandability values for all four aspects, we used the virtual subjects approach presented in Subsection 3.3 resulting in the data depicted in Figure 2(a).

Regarding Hypothesis 1. In order to test our hypothesis that the personal process understandability values are normally distributed, we did a Shapiro-Wilk test [15] for each of the four aspects. For *concurrency, exclusiveness* and *repetition*, we had to reject the null-hypothesis that the data is normally distributed (*concurrency*: $p = 0.023$; all others: $p \ll 0.05$). Only for *order*, this null-hypothesis could not be rejected for $\alpha = 0.05$.

As all aspects except *order* are *not* normally distributed (what was also the result of the first small experiment in [10,11]), we have to give up Hypothesis 1.

Based on the four data sets, the (virtual) estimated process understandability values, their standard deviations and their 95% confidence intervals were computed (see Table 1 and Figure 2(b)). For *order*, we used the method for

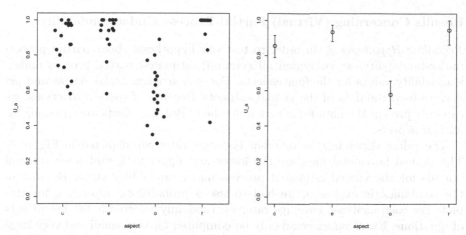

(a) (Virtual) personal process understandability values for the four aspects

(b) (Virtual) estimated process understandability values and 95% confidence intervals for the four aspects

Fig. 2. Some results of the virtual subjects approach

Table 1. (Virtual) estimated process understandability values, standard deviations
and 95% confidence intervals for the four aspects

	concurrency	exclusiveness	order	repetition
(virtual) est. process underst.	0.856	0.934	0.578	0.945
standard deviation	0.140	0.109	0.157	0.153
lower confidence interval bound	0.790	0.881	0.499	0.861
upper confidence interval bound	0.915	0.974	0.656	1.000

estimating confidence intervals for means of normal distributions [14, pp. 446–447]. For the other three aspects, we used the bootstrap approach [16], which does not require normally distributed data.

One can notice that aspect *order* has the lowest values. This is quite counter-intuitive and should be further examined in future research.

Regarding Hypothesis 2. For testing our hypothesis that the process understand-ability values for the four aspects are different, we used Wilcoxon rank-sum tests for independent values [14, pp. 590–597]. This test does not require nor-mally distributed data. Only for the combination *exclusiveness-repetition*, the null-hypothesis (data belongs to same distribution) could not be rejected on the $\alpha = 0.05$ level ($p = 0.110$).

So, we could show that there are really differences between the aspects (ex-cept between *exclusiveness* and *repetition*). Consequently, all aspects have to be measured to get "overall understandability".

Results Concerning (Virtual) Partial Process Understandability.

Regarding Hypothesis 3. In order to test our hypothesis about partial process understandability, we computed all (virtual) estimated partial process understandability values for the four aspects. For *concurrency, exclusiveness* and *order*, we used the data of the virtual subjects. Because of space restrictions, we can only present the data for aspect *order* here. But the effects are the same for all four aspects.

The values depending on different coverage rates are depicted in Figure 3. The dashed horizontal lines are the lower and upper 95% confidence interval bounds for the virtual estimated process understandability value. Because of the combinatoric explosion, we had to use a probabilistic algorithm for this plot: For each analyzed coverage rate, we randomly selected 5,000,000 subsets of questions. Exact values could only be computed for very small and very large coverage rates.

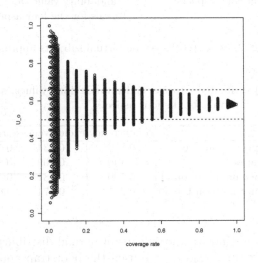

Fig. 3. Virtual estimated partial process understandability values for aspect *order* depending on coverage rate

Figure 3 supports our hypothesis: For the same coverage rate, many different virtual estimated partial process understandability values exist. The smaller the coverage rate, the higher the standard deviation and the number of values outside the confidence interval. Consequently, only asking very few questions is not advisable. Note that for the process model used in this experiment, a coverage rate of 0.25 produces less than 1% lower or upper outliers for all four aspects.

5   Conclusion and Future Work

In this paper, we have introduced considerations on reliability and validity of operational definitions of structural process understandability which have not been addressed so far. We have formally defined different matters of structural understanding, described statistical formulas for estimating the respective measures and identified hypothetical properties of these measures.

The findings from an experiment involving 178 students support our hypothesis that different aspects of structural process understandability are related to different levels of complexity (only *exclusiveness* and *repetition* are quite similar for our process model). Also, it turns out that using only a small part of the set of possible questions can cause values for structural process understandability differing substantially from the real value. Therefore, all different aspects have to be included and the coverage rate of asked questions should not be too small. With respect to the process model in our experiment, a coverage rate of 0.25 resulted in less than 1% outliers (higher or lower than 95% confidence interval) for all four aspects. Finally, the asked questions should be selected at random as to minimize the risk of choosing particularly easy or difficult questions.

Our work also points to open issues that need to be addressed by future research. In our experiment, only *order* was normally distributed. This aspect also had the lowest values which is not directly intuitive. Arguably, *concurrency* and *exclusiveness* are more complicated matters than *order*. Presumably, we have to consider further characteristics of the process model in order to get an overall picture, in particular, where certain aspects matter and to what extent they can be observed in isolation when observing them in the model.

Another future issue is the selection of suitable coverage rates minimizing the measuring effort *and* the differences from the real structural process understandability value. We need to investigate whether the ideal coverage is indicated relative or absolute to the process model size and whether it depends on other (structural) process properties. It should also be examined whether there are other relevant aspects of structural understandability. Finally, once reliable and valid metrics for structural process understandability are in place, the examination of influencing factors as part of a prediction system is an important task of research.

Acknowledgment. The authors want to thank Kerstin Schmidt for her technical assistance as well as the participating students.

References

1. Recker, J., Dreiling, A.: Does it matter which process modelling language we teach or use? An experimental study on understanding process modelling languages without formal education. In: Proceedings of the 18th Australasian Conference on Information Systems (ACIS 2007), pp. 356–366 (2007)
2. Sarshar, K., Loos, P.: Comparing the control-flow of EPC and Petri net from the end-user perspective. In: van der Aalst, W.M.P., Benatallah, B., Casati, F., Curbera, F. (eds.) BPM 2005. LNCS, vol. 3649, pp. 434–439. Springer, Heidelberg (2005)

3. Moher, T.G., Mak, D.C., Blumenthal, B., Leventhal, L.M.: Comparing the comprehensibility of textual and graphical programs: The case of petri nets. In: Cook, C.R., Scholtz, J.C., Spohrer, J.C. (eds.) Empirical Studies of Programmers: Fifth Workshop: Papers Presented at the Fifth Workshop on Empirical Studies of Programmers, pp. 137–161 (1993)

4. Reijers, H.A., Mendling, J.: Modularity in process models: Review and effects. In: Dumas, M., Reichert, M., Shan, M.-C. (eds.) BPM 2008. LNCS, vol. 5240, pp. 20–35. Springer, Heidelberg (2008)

5. Mendling, J.: Metrics for Process Models: Empirical Foundations of Verification, Error Prediction, and Guidelines for Correctness. LNBIP, vol. 6. Springer, Heidelberg (2008)

6. Vanderfeesten, I., Reijers, H.A., Mendling, J., van der Aalst, W.M.P., Cardoso, J.: On a quest for good process models: The cross-connectivity metric. In: Bellahsène, Z., Léonard, M. (eds.) CAiSE 2008. LNCS, vol. 5074, pp. 480–494. Springer, Heidelberg (2008)

7. Green, T.R.G., Petre, M.: Usability analysis of visual programming environments: A 'cognitive dimensions' framework. Journal of Visual Languages and Computing 7(2), 131–174 (1996)

8. Mendling, J., Reijers, H.A., Cardoso, J.: What makes process models understandable? In: Alonso, G., Dadam, P., Rosemann, M. (eds.) BPM 2007. LNCS, vol. 4714, pp. 48–63. Springer, Heidelberg (2007)

9. Mendling, J., Strembeck, M.: Influence factors of understanding business process models. In: Abramowicz, W., Fensel, D. (eds.) BIS 2008. LNBIP, vol. 7, pp. 142–153. Springer, Heidelberg (2008)

10. Melcher, J., Seese, D.: Towards validating prediction systems for process understandability: Measuring process understandability. In: Negru, V., Jebelean, T., Petcu, D., Zaharie, D. (eds.) Proceedings of the 10th International Symposium on Symbolic and Numeric Algorithms for Scientific Computing (SYNASC 2008), pp. 564–571 (2008)

11. Melcher, J., Seese, D.: Towards validating prediction systems for process understandability: Measuring process understandability (experimental results). Research report, Universität Karlsruhe (TH), Institut AIFB (2008), http://digbib.ubka.uni-karlsruhe.de/volltexte/1000009260

12. Melcher, J., Mendling, J., Reijers, H.A., Seese, D.: On measuring the understandability of process models (experimental results). Research report, Universität Karlsruhe (TH), Institut AIFB, Humboldt-Universität, Berlin, Eindhoven University of Technology (2009), http://digbib.ubka.uni-karlsruhe.de/volltexte/1000011993

13. Kan, S.H.: Metrics and Models in Software Quality Engineering, 2nd edn. Addison-Wesley, Reading (2002)

14. Panik, M.J.: Advanced Statistics from an Elementary Point of View. Elsevier Academic Press, Amsterdam (2005)

15. Shapiro, S.S., Wilk, M.B.: An analysis of variance test for normality (complete samples). Biometrika 52(3-4), 591–611 (1965)

16. Efron, B., Tibshirani, R.J.: An Introduction to the Bootstrap. Chapman & Hall, Boca Raton (1993)

Declarative versus Imperative Process Modeling Languages: The Issue of Maintainability

Dirk Fahland[1], Jan Mendling[1], Hajo A. Reijers[2], Barbara Weber[3],
Matthias Weidlich[4], and Stefan Zugal[3]

[1] Humboldt-Universität zu Berlin, Germany
fahland@informatik.hu-berlin.de, jan.mendling@wiwi.hu-berlin.de
[2] Eindhoven University of Technology, The Netherlands
h.a.reijers@tue.nl
[3] University of Innsbruck, Austria
barbara.weber@uibk.ac.at, stefan.zugal@uibk.ac.at
[4] Hasso-Plattner-Institute, University of Potsdam, Germany
matthias.weidlich@hpi.uni-potsdam.de

Abstract. The rise of interest in declarative languages for process modeling both justifies and demands empirical investigations into their presumed advantages over more traditional, imperative alternatives. Our concern in this paper is with the ease of maintaining business process models, for example due to changing performance or conformance demands. We aim to contribute to a rigorous, theoretical discussion of this topic by drawing a link to well-established research on maintainability of information artifacts.

Keywords: Process model maintainability, declarative versus imperative modeling, cognitive dimensions framework.

1 Introduction

The ongoing release of new modeling languages is an important challenge for process modeling. How should we weigh the claims in favor of new languages that relate to "ease of use"? In [1] a new process modeling language is proposed that is claimed to be "easily human-readable". UML Activity Diagrams, EPCs, IDEF3, and YAWL, in contrast, are considered in that work to be too difficult to apply for capturing real-life processes, leading to models that would be difficult to interpret. Our intent is not to repudiate such claims, nor to dispute the need for new process modeling languages. Rather, our point is that quality issues cannot be addressed by formal research alone. We are in need of theories – either by finding or establishing them – that explain how people interact with information artifacts like process models. Furthermore, an empirical research agenda is required to put the explanatory powers of such theories to the test.

In this paper, we zoom in on the spectrum of imperative[1] versus declarative process modeling languages. This distinction is arguably one of the most prominent

---

[1] Computer scientists prefer the term "procedural"; the term "imperative" is popular in other communities [2]. In this paper, we will be using the terms as synonyms.

S. Rinderle-Ma et al. (Eds.): BPM 2009 Workshops, LNBIP 43, pp. 477–488, 2010.
© Springer-Verlag Berlin Heidelberg 2010

in the development of new modeling languages. For example, with respect to the recent development of ConDec (first published as "DecSerFlow"), a declarative process modeling language, it is claimed that "many problems described in literature (e.g., the dynamic change bug and other problems for procedural languages) can be avoided, thus making change easy" [3].

In an earlier paper [4], we focused on the *understandability* of a process model as an important point of comparison between languages. The motivation for the current paper is an insight that we encountered from cognitive research into programming languages: *design is redesign* [5]. It turns out that software programs are created iteratively, i.e., any attempted solution to any goal may be subject to later change [6]. Like software programs, business processes are subject to change too (e.g., to address the need for process optimization, organizational engineering, compliance issues and market dynamics) [8]. So, the constant need for process evolution makes *maintainability* another important quality factor, just as it is in comparing programming languages. Both *understandability* issues, which we discussed in [4], and *modifiability* of process models are important factors influencing the ease of maintaining a process model along evolving needs.

Against this background, our paper aims to propose how different process modeling languages affect the *maintainability* of the models that are created with these. Its contribution is a set of theoretically grounded propositions about the differences between imperative and declarative process modeling languages with respect to modification issues. As such, this paper is an essential stepping stone to an empirical evaluation of these languages, which is planned by the authors as future research. It should be noted that the focus of this paper is on build-time modifications of process models and does not consider run-time aspects of changes (e.g., ad-hoc changes or instance propagation [9,10]). Moreover, the paper deals with the question to what extent a particular language embraces changes and fosters maintainability, whereas the effect that the used environment has on ease of change is not considered.

To argue and support the proposed hypotheses, this paper is structured as follows. Section 2 provides a theoretical background for our work. Section 3 characterizes the notational spectrum of process modeling languages. Section 4 derives propositions on when a process modeling language could be superior to another one, based on the cognitive dimensions framework. Finally, Section 5 describes the empirical research agenda for validating the propositions.

2 Background

To the best of our knowledge, no explicit explorations have taken place of differences in the *modifiability* of process models as linked to the language that was used to create them. Limited research has looked into the impact on *understandability* [11], and found a slightly better performance of models created with EPCs than with a Petri net variant.

In lack of a theoretical basis or earlier relevant results for the process modeling domain, we turn our attention to the field of software engineering. Various authors have noted the similarities between process models and software programs

[12,13]. For example, a software program is usually partitioned into modules or functions, which take in a group of inputs and provide some output. Similar to this compositional structure, a business process model consists of activities, each of which may contain smaller steps (operations) that may update the values of data objects. Furthermore, just like the interactions between modules and functions in a software program are precisely specified using various language constructs, the order of activity execution in a process model is defined using logic operators. For software programs and business process models alike, *human agents* are concerned with properly capturing and updating their logic content. This stresses the importance of sense-making for both types of artifacts, both during the construction process and while modifying artifacts at later stages.

In the past, heated debates have taken place about the superiority of one programming language over the other, e.g. with respect to expressiveness [14] or effectiveness [15]. During the 1970s and 1980s, alternative views were proposed on how programmers make sense of code as to provide a theoretical explanation of the impact of programming languages on this process. In [4], we summarized this debate and the opposing views that were brought forward.

An important outcome of this debate, and one that has been postulated and empirically validated in [16,17,5], is that different tasks that involve sense-making of software code are supported differently by the *same* programming language. For example, the overall impact of a modification of a single declaration may be difficult to understand in a PASCAL program, but it is relatively easy to develop a mental picture of the control-flow for the same program. The implication of this view is that a programming language may provide superior support with respect to one comprehension task, while it may be outperformed by other languages with respect to a different task.

The latter view has been the basis for the "mental operations theory" [5], which in essence states that a notation that requires fewer mental operations from a person for any task is the better performing one. In other words, a "matched pair" between the notational characteristics and a task gives the best performance. This view has evolved and matured over the years towards the "cognitive dimensions framework" (CDF)[6,7], which contains many different characteristics to distinguish notations from each other. This framework has been highly influential in language usability studies [18]. The CDF extends the main postulate of the mental operations theory towards a broad evaluation tool for a wide variety of notations, e.g. spreadsheets, style sheets, diagrams, etc. As such, and in absence of other competing, domain-specific theories, it appears the best available candidate for our purposes. As far as we know, no other work in the process modeling domains has built on the CDF, with the exception of [19].

The relevance of the CDF is particularly evident when in [20] Green and Blackwell elaborate on the relation between activity types and cognitive dimensions. Figure 1 shows that several cognitive dimensions are fostering modifications (e.g., role expressiveness or abstraction hunger), while others are hindering them (e.g., viscosity, hidden dependencies, premature commitment).

	transcription	incrementation	modification	exploration
viscosity	acceptable	acceptable	harmful	harmful
role-expressiveness	desirable	desirable	essential	essential
hidden dependencies	acceptable	acceptable	harmful	acceptable for small tasks
premature commitment	harmful	harmful	harmful	harmful
abstraction barrier	harmful	harmful	harmful	harmful
abstraction hunger	useful	useful (?)	useful	harmful
secondary notation	useful (?)	–	v. useful	?
visibility / juxtaposability	not vital	not vital	important	important

Table 2 Suggested relationship between activities types and cognitive dimensions
(from Green and Blackwell, 1998)

Fig. 1. Relationships between activity types and cognitive dimensons

Adapting a software program to evolving needs involves both sense-making tasks (i.e., to determine which changes have to be made) and action tasks (i.e., to apply the respective changes to the program). An important result that has been established in the development of the CDF regarding the sense-making of information artifacts relates to the difference between the tasks of looking for sequential and circumstantial information in a program. While *sequential* information explains how input conditions lead to a certain outcome, *circumstantial* information relates to the overall conditions that produced that outcome. Empirical evidence supports the hypothesis that procedural programming languages display sequential information in a readily-used form, while declarative languages display circumstantial information in a readily-used form [16,5]. The reverse is also true: Just as procedural languages tend to obscure circumstantial information, so do declarative languages obscure sequential information.

When considering "modifiability" of a software program (or an information artifact in general) several competing factors have to be considered. Most notably is the cognitive dimension of "viscosity": A "low" viscosity for a particular language means that a change can more easily be achieved with that language. Green [6] distinguishes between *repetitive viscosity* (i.e. referring to the "resistance of change") and *knock-on viscosity* (i.e. to what extent once having made a change entails further actions to restore consistency). Sidiqqi et al. [21] extend the work of Green [6] comparing the viscosity of procedural and declarative programming languages. Both the results of Green and Siddiqi et al. point at a relatively low repetitive viscosity for BASIC compared to PROLOG in the domain of programming languages. In turn, the results for knock-on viscosity are inverse (i.e., PROLOG has a lower knock-on viscosity compared to BASIC). These results point to the fact that "resistance to change" involves a variety of competing factors. The role of tool support that is available to someone manipulating an information artifact must not be underestimated.

While viscosity is affected by both the *entity* being manipulated (notation) and the *tools* that enable the manipulation (environment) [21], other dimensions in the CDF, like "premature commitment", rather relate to the environment that is imposing restrictions on the ordering in which things can be inserted. Green [6] states that "No problems can arise in an environment where the statements may be inserted in any convenient order - paper and pencil, for instance.". This is highly relevant for any experimental design to test our hypotheses.

The implications for the formulation of our hypotheses are as follows:

(a) we will adopt a relativist starting point, characteristic for the CDF, with respect to the superiority of any process modeling language,
(b) we will consider both understandability and modifiability of process models as important sub-characteristics for maintainability,
(c) we will consider modifications within the sequential and circumstantial spectrum, and
(d) we will build on viscosity to conjecture about declarative and imperative process modeling languages with respect to maintainability.

3   The Declarative-Imperative Spectrum

Given the insights from programming language research, this section analyzes to what extent an analogy can be established between procedural and declarative programming and respective approaches to process modeling. Section 3.1 elaborates on the difference between imperative and declarative programming and Section 3.2 discusses to which extent the distinction of sequential and circumstantial information is appropriate for process modeling.

3.1   Imperative versus Declarative Programming

Assuming that the reader has an intuitive understanding of what an imperative (or procedural) program is, we approach the topic from the declarative angle. According to Lloyd "declarative programming involves stating what is to be computed, but not necessarily how it is to be computed"[22]. Equivalently, in the terminology of Kowalski's equation [23] 'algorithm = logic + control', it involves stating the logic of an algorithm (i.e. the knowledge to be used in problem solving), but not necessarily the control (i.e. the problem-solving strategies). While the logic component determines the meaning of an algorithm, the control component only affects its efficiency [23].

Roy and Haridi [24] suggest to use the concept of a *state* for defining the line between the two approaches more precisely. Declarative programming is often referred to as stateless programming as an evaluation works on partial data structures. In contrast to that, imperative programming is characterized as stateful programming [24]: a component's result not only depends on its arguments, but also on an internal parameter, which is called its "state". A state is a collection of values being intermediate results of a desired computation (at a specific point in time). Roy and Haridi [24] differentiate between implicit (declarative) state and explicit state. Implicit states only exist in the mind of the programmer without requiring any support from the computation model. An explicit state in a procedure, in turn, is a state whose lifetime extends over more than one procedure call without being present in the procedure's arguments. Explicit state is visible in both the program and the computation model.

3.2 Imperative versus Declarative Process Modeling

Process modeling is not concerned with programs, variables, and values, but aims at describing processes. In general, a *process* is a collection of observable actions, events, or changes of a collection of real and virtual objects. A *process modeling language* provides concepts for representing processes. Discussions of declarative versus imperative process modeling are scarce and so are precise distinctions. A description is given in Pesic's PhD thesis [3, p.80]: "[Imperative] models take an 'inside-to-outside' approach: all execution alternatives are explicitly specified in the model and new alternatives must be explicitly added to the model. Declarative models take an 'outside-to-inside' approach: constraints implicitly specify execution alternatives as all alternatives that satisfy the constraints and adding new constraints usually means discarding some execution alternatives." Below, we relate declarative and imperative modeling techniques to the notion of state.

An *imperative* process modeling language focuses on the aspect of *continuous* changes of the process' objects which allows for two principal, dual views. The life of each object in the process can be described in terms of its *state space* by abstractly formulating the object's *locations* in a real or virtual world and its possibilities to get from one location to another, i.e. state changes. The dual view is the *transition space* which abstractly formulates the distinct actions, events, and changes of the process and how these can possibly succeed each other. Based on topological considerations of Petri [25], Holt formally constructs a mathematical framework that relates state space and transition space and embeds it into the theory of *Petri nets* [26]. Holt deducts that Petri net places (or states in general) act as "grains in space" while Petri net transitions (or steps in general) act as "grains in time" providing dedicated concepts for structuring the spatial and the temporal aspect of a process. A directed flow-relation defines pre- and post-places of transitions, and corresponding pre- and post-transitions of places. Thus, in a Petri net model, beginning at any place (state) or transition, the modeler can choose and follow a *continuous* forward trajectory in the process behavior visiting more places (states of objects) and transitions. This interpretation positions Petri nets as a clear imperative process modeling language.

A *declarative* process modeling language focuses on the *logic* that governs the overall interplay of the actions and objects of a process. It provides concepts to describe *key qualities* of objects and actions, and how the key qualities of different objects and actions relate to each other in time and space. This relation can be arbitrary and needs not be continuous; it shall only describe the logic of the process. In this sense, a declarative language only describes *what* the essential characteristics of a process are while it is insensitive to *how* the process works. For instance, a possible key quality of a process can be that a specific action is "just being executed". Formalizing this quality as a predicate ranging over a set of actions, one can use the temporal logic LTL to model how executions of actions relate to each other over time. The logical implication thereby acts as the connective between cause and effect: Each action is executed a specific number of times (e.g. at least once, at most three times); the execution of one action requires a subsequent execution of some other action (at some point); the execution of two given actions is mutually exclusive; etc. Thereby state and step are not explicated in the model, but they are constructed when *interpreting* predicates and formulas. This kind of description relies on an *open-world assumption* leaving room for how the process' changes are continuously linked to each other. Any behavior that satisfies the model is a valid behavior of the process. This approach was formalized for modeling processes in the language ConDec [30].

The probably most notable difference between imperative and declarative modeling is how a given behavior can be classified as satisfying a model or not. In an imperative model, the behavior must be reconstructible from the description by finding a continuous trajectory that looks exactly like the given behavior or corresponds to it in a *smooth* way. For instance, the linear runs of a Petri net are not explicitly visible in the net's structure, but states and steps can be mapped to places and transitions preserving predecessor and successor relations. In a declarative model, all requirements must be satisfied by the given behavior; there is no smooth correspondence required between behavior and model.

The reason for this difference between imperative and declarative modeling is the *degree* to which these paradigms make states and transitions explicit. An imperative process model like a Petri nets explicitly denotes states or transitions or both and their direct predecessor-successor relations. Thus enabled transitions and successor states can be computed locally from a given state or transition; runs can be constructed inductively. In a declarative model like an LTL formula states and transitions are implicitly characterized by the predicates and the temporal constraints over these predicates. Any set of states and transitions that are "sufficiently distinct" and relate to each other "sufficiently correct" are a valid interpretation of the model. This prohibits a construction of runs, but allows for characterizing states and transitions as satisfying or not.

Despite these differences, declarative and imperative models can be precisely related to each other. While a direct transformation of declarative models into well-conceivable imperative models implies overhead, the resulting imperative model is operational and allows for executing declarative ones [30].

4 Propositions

Having elaborated on the characteristics of imperative and declarative process modeling languages, this section aims to discuss the notion of process change in the context of both imperative and declarative process modeling languages.

Process change is the transformation of an initial process model S to a new process model S' by applying a set of change operations. A change operation modifies the initial process model by altering the set of activities and their order relations [27]. For imperative process models typical change primitives are *add node, add edge, delete node* or *delete edge* [28]. In turn, for declarative process modeling languages like ConDec typical change primitives are *add activity, add constraint, delete activity* or *delete constraint* [29].

To conduct such a change to a process model the process designer 1.) needs to determine which changes have to be made to the model (i.e., to identify the necessary change operations) and 2.) apply the respective changes to the process model. Consequently, the effort needed to perform a particular process model change is on the one hand determined by the cognitive load to determine which changes have to be made to the model, which is a comprehension and sense-making task. On the other hand, the effort covers the number of edit operations required to conduct these changes, which is an action task. While the cognitive load is largely related to understandability issues of process models [4], the second issue can be related to the *viscosity* dimension of the CDF.

For the remainder, we explore to what extent repetitive viscosity and knock-on viscosity – the theoretical constructs from CDF – may apply to process model changes by discussing some well-chosen examples. Since we cannot hope to cover all existing process modeling notations, we restrict ourselves to two notations that seem characteristic for the poles of the imperative-declarative spectrum. For the imperative side we refer to workflow nets, a Petri net variant. For the declarative side, we refer to ConDec.

4.1 Repetitive Viscosity

The effect of repetitive viscosity can be measured in terms of the *process edit distance* of the initial process model S and the new process model S'. This is the minimum number of operations needed to transform S to S' [27]. Siddiqi defines repetitive viscosity exactly along these lines [21].

Fig. 2 shows a simple business process comprising five distinct activities which are all to be executed exactly once in arbitrary order. The respective process is both modeled in an imperative manner using the workflow net notation and in a declarative manner using ConDec. Let us assume that this business process should be modified such that an additional activity F is inserted in parallel to the 5 already existing activities. To implement this change in the imperative process model seven change primitives are required (add node (3x), add add edge (4x)). The modification in the declarative model, in turn, requires 2 change primitives (add activity and add cardinality constraint). Consequently, repetitive viscosity for this particular change is lower for the declarative process model compared to its imperative counterpart. Consider another change scenario where an additional activity G should be inserted directly after activities A-E. For the imperative process model this change is relatively easy and only requires 4 change primitives (add node (2x) and add edge (2x)). For the declarative model this change turns out to be more complicated needing 7 change primitives (add activity, add cardinality constraint, and add precedence constraint (5x) – each of A-E "must precede G"). For this change repetitive viscosity is lower for the imperative process model compared to the declarative process model.

Obviously, tool support plays a fundamental role in reducing repetitive viscosity. To foster process changes and to hide the complexity from the end users adaptive process management systems like ADEPT combine change primitives to high-level change operations [28,9]. Obviously, the usage of high-level change operations (often referred to as *change patterns*) reduces repetitive viscosity.

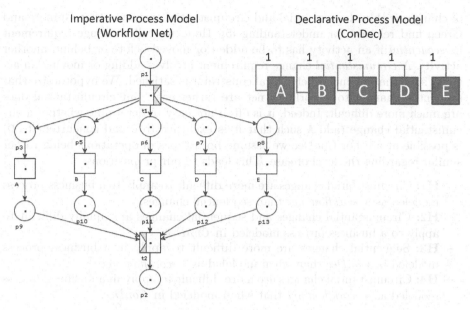

Fig. 2. Process Change: Imperative versus Declarative

However, our focus is to investigate the differences between different process modeling languages and we consequently consider change primitives only.

4.2   Knock-on Viscosity

Knock-on viscosity, in turn, becomes relevant when a particular process change entails further actions to restore consistency [6]. In the context of process model changes the deletion of an activity might require additional modifications to ensure data availability. In addition, changes of an activity interface might require changes of other activities as well. At this stage we abstract from the observation that higher coupling of activities in a model might result in a higher knock-on viscosity (see [12]), and focus on general language features.

Assume that activity B should be moved behind activity C in Fig. 2. In the ConDec model, this only involves adding a precedence constraint. In the workflow net, on the other hand, this operation requires several knock-on operations. Once B is connected with the path behind C there are different clean-up deletions to be made, e.g. deleting the place p5 that served as a precondition to B. Apparently, ConDec is more robust to such clean-up actions that relate to knock-on viscosity.

Altogether, we can conclude that the process edit distance implied by a change requirement is a major factor for viscosity. We have discussed that the set of change operations offered by the modeling environment has a significant impact on this edit distance. At this stage, we have considered elementary change operations, e.g. adding or deleting nodes and edges in a workflow net. We have noted that these elementary change operations seem to imply less knock-on viscosity for ConDec models. Furthermore, it might be reasonable to discuss types of changes within the sequential and circumstantial spectrum that Gilmore and Green find relevant for understanding [5]. Here, we call a change requirement as *sequential* if an activity has to be added or moved before or behind another activity. A *circumstantial* change requirement involves adding or moving an activity such that a general behavioral constraint is satisfied. We hypothesize that sequential changes to a workflow net are rather easy, but circumstantial ones are much more difficult. Indeed, it is often not easy to determine whether a circumstantial change (add A such that it is exclusive to C and concurrent to D) is possible at all. For ConDec we assume both types of operations being rather similar regarding the level of ease. This leads to our propositions:

- **H1:** Circumstantial changes are more difficult to apply to a business process modeled as a *workflow net* than sequential changes.
- **H2:** Circumstantial changes and sequential changes are equally difficult to apply to a business process modeled in *ConDec*.
- **H3:** Sequential changes are more difficult to apply in a business process modeled in *ConDec* than when modeled as a *workflow net*.
- **H4:** Circumstantial changes are more difficult to apply in a business process modeled as a *workflow net* that when modeled in *ConDec*.

Recall that at the start of this section we have distinguished for process changes a phase of sense-making, the cognitive task, and a phase of actually performing a number of change operations, which is an action task. Since there is no understanding of the relative importance of both phases in applying process changes or their exact interaction, we aim to study these phases isolated from each other to the best of our ability.

We have discussed the aspects of understandability in an earlier paper [4], which arguably affect the first phase. Because our interest in this paper is with the second part of process change, the action task, we explicitly prefer to determine the presence or absence of the hypothesized differences in terms of measures that do not relate to time. After all, the overall modification time is affected by the duration of both phases. Rather, we prefer to rely on the *number of errors* that are induced by applying a change, assuming that a higher number of change primitives will inevitably lead to more mistakes.

Additionally, since it is impossible to rule out that sense-making is an important matter *during the action task*, we will prepare our experimental set-up such that we can control for differences in the understanding of the same business process modeled in the two notations under consideration. For example, we can use control questions on the understanding of the models before actual process changes are requested. By taking these measures, we hope to arrive at the best possible understanding of differences in the actual change effort that the different notations require from modelers in case of modifications.

5   Conclusion

In this paper, we presented a set of propositions that relate to the maintainability of process modeling languages. Specifically, these propositions focus on the distinction between declarative and imperative languages, formulating relative strengths and weaknesses of both paradigms. The most important theoretical foundation for these propositions is the cognitive dimensions framework including the results that are established for programming languages.

This paper is characterized by a number of limitations. First of all, there is a strong reliance on similarities between process modeling languages on the one hand and programming languages on the other. Differences between both ways of abstract expression may render some of our inferences untenable. At this point, however, we do not see a more suitable source of inspiration nor any strong counter arguments. Another limitation that is worth mentioning is that this paper primarily focuses on the effect the selection of the process modeling language has on maintainability of process models. However, resistance to change is also affected by the tools used for modification.

As follows from the nature of this paper, the next step is to challenge the propositions with an empirical investigation. We intend to develop a set of experiments that will involve human modelers carrying out a set of modification tasks on process models. Such tasks will involve both repetitive and knock-on viscosity including more and less declarative (imperative) languages. The cooperation of various academic partners facilitates extensive testing and replication of such experiments. Ideally, this empirical investigation will lead to an informed voice in the ongoing debate on the superiority of process modeling languages.

References

1. Svatoš, O.: Conceptual Process Modeling Language: Regulative Approach. In: 9th Undergraduate and Graduate Students eConf. and 14th Business & Government Executive Meeting on Innovative Cross-border eRegion, Univ. of Maribor (2007)
2. Boley, H.: Declarative and Procedural Paradigms - Do They Really Compete? In: Boley, H., Richter, M.M. (eds.) PDK 1991. LNCS, vol. 567, pp. 383–385. Springer, Heidelberg (1991)
3. Pesic, M.: Constraint-Based Workflow Management Systems: Shifting Control to Users. PhD thesis, Eindhoven University of Technology (2008)
4. Fahland, D., Lübke, D., Mendling, J., Reijers, H.A., Weber, B., Weidlich, M., Zugal, S.: Declarative versus Imperative Process Modeling Languages: The Issue of Understandability. In: BPMDS 2009 and EMMSAD 2009. LNBIP, vol. 29, pp. 353–366. Springer, Heidelberg (2009)
5. Gilmore, D.J., Green, T.R.G.: Comprehension and recall of miniature programs. International Journal of Man-Machine Studies 21(1), 31–48 (1984)
6. Green, T.: Cognitive dimensions of notations. In: Sutcliffe, A., Macaulay, L. (eds.) People and Computers V, Proceedings, pp. 443–460 (1989)
7. Green, T., Petre, M.: Usability Analysis of Visual Programming Environments: A Cognitive Dimensions Framework. J. Vis. Lang. Computing 7(2), 131–174 (1996)
8. Mutschler, B., Reichert, M., Bumiller, J.: Unleashing the Effectiveness of Process-oriented Information Systems: Problem Analysis, Critical Success Factors, Implications. IEEE Trans. Sys., Man, and Cybernetics (C) 38(3), 280–291 (2008)
9. Reichert, M., Dadam, P.: ADEPT$_{flex}$ – Supporting Dynamic Changes of Workflows Without Losing Control. J. of Intelligent Inf. Systems 10(2), 93–129 (1998)
10. Rinderle, S., Reichert, M., Dadam, P.: Correctness Criteria for Dynamic Changes in Workflow Systems – A Survey. Data Knowl. Eng. 50(1), 9–34 (2004)

11. Sarshar, K., Loos, P.: Comparing the Control-Flow of EPC and Petri Net from the End-User Perspective. In: van der Aalst, W.M.P., Benatallah, B., Casati, F., Curbera, F. (eds.) BPM 2005. LNCS, vol. 3649, pp. 434–439. Springer, Heidelberg (2005)

12. Vanderfeesten, I., Reijers, H.A., Van der Aalst, W.M.P.: Evaluating workflow process designs using cohesion and coupling metrics. Comp. in Ind. 59(5), 420–437 (2008)

13. Guceglioglu, A., Demirors, O.: Using Software Quality Characteristics to Measure Business Process Quality. In: van der Aalst, W.M.P., Benatallah, B., Casati, F., Curbera, F. (eds.) BPM 2005. LNCS, vol. 3649, pp. 374–379. Springer, Heidelberg (2005)

14. Felleisen, M.: On the Expressive Power of Programming Languages. Science of Computer Programming 17(1-3), 35–75 (1991)

15. Prechelt, L.: An Empirical Comparison of Seven Programming Languages. Computer 23–29 (2000)

16. Green, T.: Conditional program statements and their comprehensibility to professional programmers. Journal of Occupational Psychology 50, 93–109 (1977)

17. Green, T.: Ifs and thens: Is nesting just for the birds? Software Focus 10(5), 373–381 (1980)

18. Blackwell, A.: Ten years of cognitive dimensions in visual languages and computing. J. Vis. Lang. Computing 17(4), 285–287 (2006)

19. Vanderfeesten, I., Reijers, H.A., Mendling, J., Van der Aalst, W.M.P., Cardoso, J.: On a Quest for Good Process Models: The Cross-Connectivity Metric. In: Bellahsène, Z., Léonard, M. (eds.) CAiSE 2008. LNCS, vol. 5074, pp. 480–494. Springer, Heidelberg (2008)

20. Green, T., Blackwell, A.: A Tutorial on Cognitive Dimensions (1998), http://www.ndirect.co.uk/~thomas.green/workStuff/Papers/index.html

21. Siddiqi, J.I., Roast, C.R.: Viscosity as a metaphor for measuring modifiability. lEE Proc. Software Engineering. 144(4), 215–223 (1997)

22. Lloyd, J.: Practical advantages of declarative programming. In: Joint Conference on Declarative Programming, GULP-PRODE 1994 (1994)

23. Kowalski, R.: Algorithm = logic + control. Commun. ACM 22(7), 424–436 (1979)

24. Roy, P.V., Haridi, S.: Concepts, Techniques, and Models of Computer Programming. MIT Press, Cambridge (2004)

25. Petri, C.A.: Concepts of net theory. In: Mathematical Foundations of Computer Science: Proc. of Symposium and Summer School, High Tatras, September 3-8, pp. 137–146. Math. Inst. of the Slovak Acad. of Sciences (1973)

26. Holt, A.W.: A Mathematical Model of Continuous Discrete Behavior. Massachusettes Computer Associates, Inc. (November 1980)

27. Li, C., Reichert, M., Wombacher, A.: On Measuring Process Model Similarity based on High-level Change Operations. In: Li, Q., Spaccapietra, S., Yu, E., Olivé, A. (eds.) ER 2008. LNCS, vol. 5231, pp. 248–264. Springer, Heidelberg (2008)

28. Weber, B., Reichert, M., Rinderle-Ma, S.: Change Patterns and Change Support Features -Enhancing Flexibility in Process-Aware Information Systems. Data and Knowledge Engineering 66(3), 438–466 (2008)

29. Pesic, M., Schonenberg, M.H., Sidorova, N., Van der Aalst, W.M.P.: Constraint-Based Workflow Models: Change Made Easy. In: Meersman, R., Tari, Z. (eds.) OTM 2007, Part I. LNCS, vol. 4803, pp. 77–94. Springer, Heidelberg (2007)

30. Van der Aalst, W.M.P., Pesic, M.: DecSerFlow: Towards a truly declarative service flow language. In: Bravetti, M., Núñez, M., Zavattaro, G. (eds.) WS-FM 2006. LNCS, vol. 4184, pp. 1–23. Springer, Heidelberg (2006)

Tangible Business Process Modeling – Methodology and Experiment Design

Alexander Grosskopf[1], Jonathan Edelman[2], and Mathias Weske[1]

[1] Hasso Plattner Institute, University of Potsdam, Germany
alexander.grosskopf@hpi.uni-potsdam.de, mathias.weske@hpi.uni-potsdam.de
http://bpt.hpi.uni-potsdam.de
[2] Centre for Design Research, Stanford University, CA, USA
edelman2@stanford.edu
http://www-cdr.stanford.edu

Abstract. Visualized business process models are the central artifacts to communicate knowledge about working procedures in organizations. Since more organizations take the process perspective to share knowledge and make decisions, it is worth investigating how the processes are elicited.

In current practice, analysts interview domain experts and translate their understanding to process models. Domain experts, often unfamiliar with process thinking, have problems understanding the models and providing meaningful feedback.

It is our desire to improve process elicitation and strengthen the role of the domain expert. To do so, we propose to complement interviews with a toolkit and a methodology to engage the domain experts in process modeling. We call this Tangible Business Process Modeling (TBPM). In this paper, we outline our approach and present the design of an experiment for empirical validation. Through the use of TBPM, pracitioners are expected to achieve better understanding, higher consensus and a higher rate of adoption of the results.

Keywords: Process Modeling, Structured Interviews, Media-Models, BPMN, TBPM.

1 Introduction

Visualized process models serve as a communication vehicle in business process management. These processes are the starting point for shared understanding, improvements, measurements and automation of the procedures that run organizations. At present only a small group of method experts can create and read process models. We observed that domain experts who have the required business knowledge can only give limited feedback, because they lack expertise in process modeling.

The starting point of our research was process elicitation. Structured interviews conducted with the domain expert are widely used and seen as a very effective technique [1]. In a subsequent step a process modeling expert creates

S. Rinderle-Ma et al. (Eds.): BPM 2009 Workshops, LNBIP 43, pp. 489–500, 2010.
© Springer-Verlag Berlin Heidelberg 2010

a process model based on the interview. The model is handed back to the domain expert who is asked to provide feedback. That usually leads to additional communication effort to explain the model and to resolve misunderstandings. Sometimes domain experts reject process models because they don't understand them, having concluded that their knowledge is not appropriately represented.

We looked for a way to get better information upfront, instant feedback and a shared understanding of the process. We believe that this can be accomplished by modeling the process together with the domain expert during the elicitation phase. Based on these considerations, we developed a tool and methodology to complement structured interviews with a strong participative component. Doing so has significant effects on the interview situation, such as:

- **Increased User Engagement**
  Using a tool and creating something actively involves the interviewees and results in an increased engagement to complete the task.
- **Two-Dimensional Representation of Processes (Non-Linearization)**
  Modeling the process de-linearizes the story told in spoken language. It allows to jump between different phases of the process during the discussion, while maintaining the big picture.
- **Immediate Feedback**
  The process model embodies a shared understanding. Examining the model helps to reveal misunderstandings and fosters feedback about the process.

While these effects are obvious it is not clear how to achieve them. Our goal is to enable the domain experts during a one hour interview to model her process. Through a couple of iterations we developed a toolkit and a methodology for interview situations.

We introduce our toolkit in Section 2 and relate our ideas to other research in Section 3. In Section 4 we present findings from pilot studies and subsequently formulate our hypotheses in Section 5. The core of the paper in Section 6 outlines an experiment design to assess our hypotheses. We discuss our research method in Section 7 and conclude the paper in Section 8 with a discussion of future research.

2 The Toolkit

The use of low-resolution physical prototypes has been very successful in innovative practices for product design [2]. Especially the early and repetitive involvement of users is responsible for the success of these methods. Repetitive user involvement with prototypes is well known as a patterns in agile software development [3]. The use of low-resolution physical representations for software engineering models is less popular. We decided to investigate whether this approach could be fruitfully used to elicitate business processes.

To follow this path, we created elements of business process models that are tangible. Things you can hold in your hand and move around the table. Something with which everybody can easily be engaged. In particular, we built a

Fig. 1. TBPM Toolkit - BPMN shapes cut out of pexiglas

tangible BPMN modeling toolkit (see Figure 1). We produced the four basic BPMN shapes which can be transformed to all BPMN elements for control and data flow. Flow itself and resource allocation (pools and lanes) are drawn directly on the table. The shapes are relatively large and thick to provide a comfortable haptic experience.

The semantics associated with the different shapes focus the discussion and push the participants to frame their output to fit into the concepts of control flow, data flow and resources. The analogy to children's blocks dramatically lowers the barrier for non-process modelers to use the toolkit and participate in process modeling. They can easily create, delete, arrange and rearrange objects.

3   Related Research

User participation in software engineering is widely seen as a crucial factor for success [4]. However, the type of participation varies significantly. As an extreme example, agile software engineering approaches [3] favor customer feedback to running software in short term iteration cycles. On the other extreme participation might also be seen as listening to all stakeholders to become aware of their problems, demonstrate interest and reduce resistance to the final solution. In large scale projects current best practice is to listen, e.g. in interviews, and to give limited influence to predefined design decisions, e.g. in workshops [5]. Model building together with the end user usually happens in moderated groups [6,7,8] in which a modeling expert translates the input into a model that is discussed with the audience. In the framework of Rautenberg [6] our approach is a semi-formal simulation with a (semi-formal) model as a result. But we aim to let the user drive this with support from the modeling expert and instead of hours to weeks we expect to create a fast result due to the eased changeability of the model.

For elicitation techniques in requirements engineering, Davis et al. [1] found that structured interviews work best. This was concluded by review and synthesis of other research on the comparison of elicitation techniques. These involved structured and unstructured interviews, card sorting and thinking aloud but no mapping technique similar to TBPM.

Mapping information, however, is considered to have a significant impact on the elicitation. Research conducted on cognitive load theory [9] indicates that humans have limitations with respect to their role as information processors. People have been shown to remember seven plus or minus two items without context. Unloading information to external objects eases the cognitive load. Additionally the visual impression adds context (dimensions), such as color and position, which expands the bandwidth for memories [10]. Research on software requirements analysis and knowledge acquisition is aware of this issue [8,11] as one of many obstacles that exist within, between and among people [11].

We make use of these effects but also frame the output to a particular concept type, a process. According to the cognitive fit theory, the way the problem is represented determines the thinking model applied [12]. This was also shown to hold true for process-oriented vs. object-oriented problems in computer science [13]. Techniques that structure the user's mental models are recommended [8,14] for elicitation. We do that by framing the output to fit into the schema of the process model to be elicited.

4   Learnings from Pilot Studies

We began a series of investigations with different interview situations. In summary, we conducted nine different interviews with university assistants. We used the same interview guide for all situations starting with a high-level overview, drilling down into particular process steps and concluding with a 'what else..?' question. Two interviews were done without tooling, two more with post-its and five with different stages of the TBPM toolkit. We desired to get a feeling for the way that the tool influences the interview situation.

In structured interviews without additional aid the interviewees tended to tell a compact narrative to describe their process. There was little response to the last question, 'What else...?'. When using post-its in interviews we encouraged the interviewee to map as much knowledge to post-its a they liked. The result was a stream of post-its along the story that the interviewee told. Mapping knowledge to post-its was quite fast because every thought was mapped without reflection. In the two interviews conducted with post-its the resulting stream included events, activities, hand-overs, artifacts and notes. When asking the last question, people read their story again from the post-its and added detailed information. However, the result was not framed as a process. A similar effect was reported by Stirna et.al. [15] for participative enterprise modeling. Post-its offer fast-mapping but do not foster framing and reflection.

Mapping knowledge was very different when we used the TBPM toolkit. As described in Section 2 the toolkit represents concepts from process modeling. A proper usage of these concepts is the goal. We did not explicitly introduce the concept of control flow, alternatives and parallelism. Intuitively, subjects accepted a logical order if steps were laid out from left to right. Parallelism and

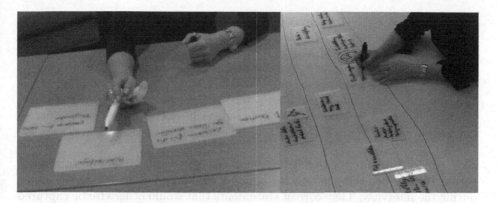

Fig. 2. Two interview situations: process modeling driven by domain experts

alternatives were both captured by putting activities one over another. Only in processes where both concepts occurred together, gateways were introduced. In general, we introduced as little concepts as possible to reduce distraction from the problem (distraction by language overhead was also reported by [15]).

Interviewees were reluctant to use the tool in the first place. Through iterations, we found that it works best if the interviewer listens to the high-level process summary at first and then models the first steps of the process. Using this as an example, the interviewer explains the concepts behind the objects. From that point on subjects accepted the tool as the thinking model and started using it themselves.

The initial process creation with TBPM was relatively slow because subjects had to find appropriate activity names and write them down on a tangible object. Once the process was modeled, it functioned as a map through which interviewees navigated confidently. We observed subjects jumping around in the storyline. They added details, rearranged objects or created additional ones. Pointing at the activities made it easy for the interviewer to follow their explanations. Figure 2 shows two interview situations with the TBPM toolkit at different stages of our development.

5   Hypotheses

Based on Section 3 and 4 we hypothesize higher consensus, more adoption, higher self-correction and a better understanding of the result by complementing structured interviews with our methodology and toolkit. We also hypothesize that interviewers will remember more details based on the additional cognitive dimensions. We explain our hypotheses here and formalize them in Section 6.3.

Higher consensus and adoption. We believe that modeling with the domain expert leads to a consensus about the results. The resulting process is an agreed upon artifact. The domain expert may recognize the model that she co-designed as her work and thereby identify with the result.

Participation is widely seen as a critical success factor to increase acceptance of results [4,6] for software engineering projects. For participation in enterprise modeling Stirna et al. [15] also reported less objections and change requests leading to less iteration cycles and more efficient elicitation.

A domain expert feeling misunderstood may get distrustful and therefore may question the elicited model as a whole. The use of visual artifacts as a common language is suggested [8,6] to reduce misunderstandings inherent in natural languages. We hypothesize that TBPM addresses these issues.

Self-correction during the interview. We believe that domain experts will correct information they claimed beforehand and apply the changes to the model during the interview. They correct statements that would otherwise be captured as inconsistent information.

Spoken language alone is ambiguous and might cover misunderstandings [8]. To overcome this it is suggested to complement discussions with visual artifacts [6]. The artifacts reduce misunderstandings by embodying the shared knowledge. Interview situations that create intermediate artifacts [16,17] report instant feedback and corrected information. We observed this to be true in our pilot studies. Interviewees that created the process have a notion of ownership and responsibility that makes them correct the model if they find a mistake. The use of TBPM affords domain experts the ability to easily correct and amend statements.

Better understanding of process and notation. We believe that the domain experts learn the basics of process modeling and notation by the hands-on experience. We hypothesize that they are not only able to read their own models but also to modified models or even unknown models because they can distinguish the different concepts and relate them to their process example.

Given that the domain experts have no previous experience in process oriented thinking and modeling, any modeling experience is better than nothing. Stirna et. al. also report [15] that people adopt knowledge quite well by hands-on experience. We observed a fast adoption of the process modeling concepts by explaining the example. We believe this experience can help to improve the general understanding of process models.

Interviewers remember more details. We believe that interviewers can remember many more details about the process if it is mapped on the table. That will help to document the interview results after the interview situation.

Humans are limited in terms of their ability to remember details [9,10]. But it was also shown that additional dimensions can help to recall more details [10]. The visual mapping is such a dimension which provides a fatter bandwidth of memories. The haptic experience of the tactile toolkit is an additional dimension. An important factor for recall is the cognitive fit of the representation to the problem domain [12,18]. The additional dimension and the fitness of process models for the application domain let us hypothesize a better recall of the process information by the interviewer.

6   Experiment Design

Experiments are not as popular as case studies and surveys in recent BPM research [19] but they provide the environment needed to support or falsify hypotheses [20]. We choose a laboratory experiment over alternatives [21] to gain the most control over intervening and confounding variables. A significant variable is subjects selection. We see describe this in Section 6.1.

Our independent variable is the TBPM method and toolkit that is applied (or not) in different interview settings. The different situations to be compared are described in Section 6.2. How we measure the effect, the dependent variables, is described in Section 6.3. Considerations about the actual implementation of the experiment is done in Section 6.4. The decision for a laboratory experiment and the remaining validity threats are discussed in Section 6.5.

6.1   Subject Selection

To ensure a homogeneous subject group we fix the following requirements.

· no process modeling background
· part of the same organization
· equivalent knowledge about the domain process

Moreover, we plan to capture variables such as sex, age, field experience and education by means of a questionnaire. We do not expect those variables to have a significant effect on the results but we'll trace them to monitor this assumption. In our experiment, we expect to test more than twenty subjects.

6.2   Experiment Group and Control Group

To compare TBPM and structured interviews, we randomly assign subjects to one of two groups. Each group receives a different treatment during the interview. Structured interviews for the control group (CG) and TBPM for the experiment group (EG).

Control Group. The process is elicited by means of a structured interview. No visual mapping tools are provided. The interviewer follows the interview guide (a list of pre-determined questions) and asks clarifying questions to learn about the process steps that are conducted, the roles that are involved and the documents that are used. In the beginning, the process is framed by clarifying the starting point and the end point of the process. After all process steps were named, questions are asked about particular process steps to collect deeper knowledge. At the end of the interview, the interviewer summarizes his understanding verbally to get feedback on his understanding of the process.

Experiment Group. The interview uses the same interview guide that is used for the control group *(CG)*. In addition, the TBPM toolkit is provided as a visual mapping tool.

The interview is guided by the same list of guiding questions. After a first overview the interviewer maps the initial steps using the TBPM toolkit. The interviewer explains the concepts, such as activities and responsibilities, using the example steps. From thereon the interviewee is encouraged to drive the process modeling. The interviewer my intervene to ensure the correct usage of the process modeling concepts.

6.3   Formalized Hypotheses

After having set the terms experiment group *(EG)* and control group *(CG)* we now state our hypotheses in a more formal way. The three letter acronyms used in this section always represent a function that returns a value for each group. Using them, we state our hypotheses as equations. We also describe how we intend to calculate the values for the functions.

Hypothesis 1

Subjects in EG show higher consensus (CON) and adoption (ACC) of the resulting process than subjects in CG.

$$ACC(EG) > ACC(CG)$$
$$CON(EG) > CON(CG)$$

To measure this we create a follow-up questionnaire that contains a digital version of the elicited process model and questions. Subjects shall decide on a Likert scale whether they *accept (ACC)* this model as correctly elicited. Also we ask subjects to raise objections against the represented knowledge. The amount of objections indicates the level of *consensus (CON)*.

Hypothesis 2

Subjects in EG self correct (SCR) themselves more often during the interview than subjects in CG.

$$SCR(EG) > SCR(CG)$$

All subjects can correct or clarify previously made statements. Given both groups have the same amount of time for the interview, the amount of corrections/clarifications results in the *self correction rate (SCR)* during the interview. This will be quantified using video coding analysis.

Hypothesis 3

Subjects in EG have a better understanding (PMU) of the process model and the notation than the subjects in CG.

$$PMU(EG) > PMU(CG)$$

We use the same follow-up questionnaire as in **Hypothesis 1**. The subjects are asked questions about modified and unknown models. Each question gives a statement about the model. Subjects answer with yes/no. The accuracy with which they answer the questions is equivalent to the *process model under-standing (PMU)*.

Hypothesis 4

After an interview with EG, the interviewers can proportionally remember many more correct details ($\frac{NSR}{TNS}$) about the process than after an interview with CG.

$$\frac{NSR(EG)}{TNS(EG)} > \frac{NSR(CG)}{TNS(CG)}$$

All interviewers are asked to recall the process steps in the correct order directly after the interview. The *number of process steps recalled (NSR)* correctly is related to the *total number of process steps (TNS)* stated in the interview.

6.4   Conducting the Experiment

Location, Setup and Preparations. The interview is done in a separate room. Subjects should feel comfortable in a private setting. A video camera captures the movements on the table with a birds-eye view. The interviews are always conducted in a one to one situation. Thus, the interviewer has to be the process modeling expert and camera operator as well. Before the interview, the subjects are familiarized to the technical setup and the capturing angle but not with the goal of the experiment.

The Interview. The interview is conducted with a standardized interview guide. It requests the subject to run briefly through the process first. Then questions about all named process steps are asked to gain deeper knowledge. Subjects are asked what they like and dislike about the process. In the last quarter the interviewer summarizes his understanding of the interview and asks wether he missed something, misunderstood something or whether there is any kind of other information that the subject would like to share. All interviews are strictly bound to one hour.

Post-interview Activities. Directly after the interview each subject fills in a questionnaire that captures the subject specific variables (see Section 6.1). Additionally, we try to determine the subjects emotions about the interview situation and get feedback about the interview technique. This shall help us to get a better feeling for future directions.

Within one hour after the interview, the interviewer recalls the process and notes it down. This is the basis to assess **Hypothesis 4**. The video is coded to determine the self-correction rate during the interview (**Hypothesis 2**). One week after the interview, each subject gets an email with the link to an online questionnaire. The questionnaire contains the individually elicited process. As outlined in Hypotheses 1 and 3 the questions determine the acceptance of the model and the degree of process model understanding.

6.5   Validity Threats for the Experiment

We decided for a laboratory experiment to control as many variables as possible. The most vital variable is the subject selection [21]. While we fix some aspects in Section 6.1, others are open: The performance of requirements elicitation interviews is significantly influenced by the personality and inter-personal sympathy of interviewee and the interviewer. We try to average that out by random subject assignment and a total number of 20+ interviews.

Likewise the interviewer is a threat to the internal validity. He is aware of the hypotheses and part of the system to be investigated. Additionally, there is a learning effect to be expected which is a threat to hypothesis 4. The interviewer might recognize and understand the process much better upfront after some interviews. We try to minimize the impact on the interview by standardized questions. Alternatively, we could interview about different processes or use interviewers. However, we expect that changing these variables would have an even bigger impact on the internal validity.

To achieve a higher external validity and therefore generalizability one could (re)run the experiment in the field. That would require an organization with a real project and a large process elicitation effort. This was not yet found. Nevertheless, we want to apply our findings in an industry setting at a later stage. That can be captured as a field experiment with an expected lower number of subjects and a lowered internal validity.

7   Discussion of the Research Method

Our research was driven by principles of *create* and *test* in a high frequency of iterations. This was adopted from the CDR[1] which is mostly concerned with teaching product design principles to mechanical engineering students [22] and investigating design innovation cycles [23]. In the light of the design science discussion [24,25] this can be seen as a high frequency of the core processes *build* and *evaluate* whereas the evaluation is informal and driven by the need to receive immediate feedback to ideas. Once the artifacts get more stable we move towards a proper evaluation which this paper is a first humble step towards. We see our approach as consistent with the design science research principles by Hevner [25] and his framework as suited to further structure our research.

The experiment design was guided by Creswell [20]. According to his framework our work is a mixed-method approach, a combination of quantitative and qualitative methods. Quantitative techniques aim to create numbers to be analyzed with statistical techniques. These allow researchers to quantify effects and use functions to express hypotheses. We do that, see Section 6.3, and in addition we use qualitative techniques to capture data and leave room for new insights, see Section 6.4. For example, open questions are asked, yielding answers which are difficult, if not impossible to quantify. Video is used to capture the interview. The video is coded to quantify the number of self-corrections, see hypothesis 3,

---

[1] Centre for Design Research at Stanford University.

but can also be used as a qualitative tool to investigate further topics that are not yet on our agenda.

8   Conclusion and Outlook

Structured interviews are considered state of the art for process elicitation. In this paper, we discussed the problems that arise with spoken language in structured interviews. We presented a toolkit and a methodology (TBPM) to complement interviews with a participative modeling. The novelty lies in empowering the end user to quickly adopt and apply process modeling. We shared our observations from pilot studies, derived hypotheses and proposed an experiment design to empirically validate our ideas. We want to understand how the TBPM toolkit changes interview outcomes in order to develop refinements of the method.

In the future we aim to refine the TBPM practices and the TBPM toolkit for interview situations. We envision the potential to expand the use of TBPM toolkits for process improvement sessions with groups of process modeling experts. Tangible building blocks lower the barrier for interaction and change the way people think address the problems at hand.

References

1. Davis, A., Dieste, O., Hickey, A., Juristo, N., Moreno, A.: Effectiveness of requirements elicitation techniques: Empirical results derived from a systematic review. In: 14th IEEE International Conference Requirements Engineering, pp. 179–188 (2006)
2. Buxton, W., Service, S.O.: Sketching user experiences: getting the design right and the right design. Morgan Kaufmann, San Francisco (2007)
3. Martin, R.: Agile software development: principles, patterns, and practices. Prentice Hall PTR, Upper Saddle River (2003)
4. Krallmann, H., Schönherr, M., Trier, M.: Systemanalyse im Unternehmen. Oldenbourg Verlag (2007)
5. Gabrielli, S.: Sap bpm methodology (September 2008), https://wiki.sdn.sap.com/wiki/display/SAPBPX/BPM (last checked 11/07/09)
6. Rauterberg, M.: Partizipative Modellbildung zur Optimierung der Softwareentwicklung. Informationssysteme und Künstliche Intelligenz 24, 26 (1992)
7. Persson, A.: Enterprise modelling in practice: situational factors and their influence on adopting a participative approach. PhD thesis, Dept. of Computer and Systems Sciences, Stockholm University (2001)
8. Byrd, T.A., Cossick, K.L., Zmud, R.W.: A synthesis of research on requirements analysis and knowledge acquisition techniques. Mis Quarterly, 117–138 (1992)
9. Sweller, J., Chandler, P.: Evidence for cognitive load theory. Cognition and Instruction, 351–362 (1991)
10. Miller, G.: The magical number seven, plus or minus two. Psychological review 63, 81–97 (1956)
11. Valusek, J., Fryback, D.: Information requirements determination: obstacles within, among and between participants. In: Proceedings of the twenty-first annual conference on Computer personnel research, pp. 103–111. ACM, New York (1985)

12. Vessey, I., Galletta, D.: Cognitive fit: An empirical study of information acquisition. Information Systems Research 2(1), 63 (1991)
13. Agarwal, R., Sinha, A., Tanniru, M.: Cognitive fit in requirements modeling: A study of object and process methodologies. Journal of Management Information Systems 13(2), 137–162 (1996)
14. Kettinger, W.J., Teng, J.T.C., Guha, S.: Business Process Change: A Study of Methodologies, Techniques, and Tools. Management Information Systems Quarterly 21, 55–80 (1997)
15. Stirna, J., Persson, A., Sandkuhl, K.: Participative Enterprise Modeling: Experiences and Recommendations. In: Krogstie, J., Opdahl, A.L., Sindre, G. (eds.) CAiSE 2007 and WES 2007. LNCS, vol. 4495, pp. 546–560. Springer, Heidelberg (2007)
16. Schneider, K.: Generating fast feedback in requirements elicitation. In: Sawyer, P., Paech, B., Heymans, P. (eds.) REFSQ 2007. LNCS, vol. 4542, pp. 160–174. Springer, Heidelberg (2007)
17. Brooks, A.: Results of rapid bottom-up software process modeling. Software Process: Improvement and Practice 9(4), 265–278 (2004)
18. Tversky, B.: Some ways that maps and diagrams communicate. In: Habel, C., Brauer, W., Freksa, C., Wender, K.F. (eds.) Spatial Cognition 2000. LNCS (LNAI), vol. 1849, pp. 72–79. Springer, Heidelberg (2000)
19. Bandara, W., Tan, H.M., Recker, J., Indulska, M., Rosemann, M.: Bibliography of process modeling: An emerging research field. Technical report, QUT (January 2009)
20. Creswell, J.W.: Research design: Qualitative, quantitative, and mixed methods approaches. Sage Pubns., Thousand Oaks (2008)
21. Sjøberg, D., Hannay, J., Hansen, O., Kampenes, V., Karahasanovic, A., Liborg, N., Rekdal, A.: A survey of controlled experiments in software engineering. IEEE Transactions on Software Engineering 31(9), 733–753 (2005)
22. Dym, C., Agogino, A., Eris, O., Frey, D., Leifer, L.: Engineering design thinking, teaching, and learning. IEEE Engineering Management Review 34(1), 65–92 (2006)
23. Beckman, S., Barry, M.: Innovation as a learning process: Embedded design thinking. Harvard Business Publishing, Boston (2007)
24. March, S., Smith, G.: Design and natural science research on information technology. Decision Support Systems 15(4), 251–266 (1995)
25. Hevner, A., March, S., Park, J., Ram, S.: Design science in information systems research. Management Information Systems Quarterly 28(1), 75–106 (2004)

A Comparison of Soundness Results Obtained by Different Approaches

Volker Gruhn and Ralf Laue

Chair of Applied Telematics / e-Business*
Computer Science Faculty, University of Leipzig, Germany
{gruhn,laue}@ebus.informatik.uni-leipzig.de

Abstract. Business processes are often modelled using a language for which no semantics is standardized in a formal way. Examples for such languages are BPMN or Event-Driven Process Chains. The common way for reasoning about the soundness of such models is to define a formal semantics first by translating the model into a well-founded formalism (for example Petri-nets). Afterwards, formal reasoning methods can be applied on the obtained formal model. In the past years, several such semantics that give a formal meaning to BPMN or EPC models have been published.

In this paper, we used a repository of almost 1,000 real-world EPC models and computed their soundness using three different tools. Those tools build on different semantics definitions: Kindler's fixed-point semantics, Mendling's state/context semantics and the YAWL semantics. While the soundness results for the majority of models were the same for all three tools, we identified a few interesting cases where the results differ. The results of our comparative study can lead to a better understanding of the differences between the semantics.

Keywords: Business process models, formal semantics, OR-join.

1 Introduction

Business processes are often modelled using a language for which no semantics is standardized in a formal way, for example the Business Process Modeling Notation or Event-Driven Process Chains (EPC). The first challenge on the way to a tool that verifies the correctness of such a model is to define a formal semantics of the model. The usual way is to map the model to a semantically well-founded formalism. In particular, Petri nets, Pi calculus or formal automata have been used for this purpose.

Different semantics definitions for modelling languages like BPMN or EPC have been suggested. An overview is given in Sect. 2. The aim of this paper is to analyse a large number of real-world models using different semantics in order to gain insight into the differences between the approaches. Sect. 3 describes the origin of the models used in our experiment. We selected three tools that

---

* The Chair of Applied Telematics / e-Business is endowed by Deutsche Telekom AG.

S. Rinderle-Ma et al. (Eds.): BPM 2009 Workshops, LNBIP 43, pp. 501–512, 2010.
© Springer-Verlag Berlin Heidelberg 2010

build on different semantics defintions and used them to validate the soundness property for the models from our repository. An overview of the tools used is given in Sect. 4. The results are presented and discussed in Sect. 5. Finally, Sect. 6 summarizes and discusses the findings from our comparative study.

2   Semantics Definitions from the Literature

For the basic modelling constructs used in languages like BPMN, the mapping to a well-founded formalism like Petri-nets is rather straightforward. However, for some modelling constructs such a mapping is difficult. In particular, it has been shown in [1] that it is impossible to define a semantics for the OR-join in a satisfactory manner.

The OR-join is used to model the "Synchronizing Merge" workflow pattern. This pattern is described in [2] as "a point in the workflow process where multiple paths converge into one single thread. If more than one path is taken, synchronization of the active threads needs to take place. If only one path is taken, the alternative branches should reconverge without synchronization".

Informally, an OR-join has to wait until all previously started control flows that can arrive on its incoming arcs have been completed. This means that before processing an OR-join, it has to be decided whether the flow of control can reach one more of its incoming arcs. In [1], some counterexamples have been given that show the impossibility to define a formal semantics of an OR-join which corresponds to the concept of a synchronizing merge. Problems can occur in models with multiple OR-joins in a loop where the possibility to process one OR-join depends on the possibility to process another one.

From a theoretical point of view, the OR-join problem has been solved by the work of Kindler [3]. In [3], the concept of a fixed-point semantics has been used for developing an algorithm that decides whether a satisfying semantics can be defined for a model. Models that have such a semantics are called clean and others (like the counterexamples from [1]) unclean. An algorithm has been presented that computes efficiently the fixed-point semantics (if it exists) or shows that there is no fixed-point semantics [4,5].

Nevertheless, the calculation of a fixpoint-semantics has also been criticized as too difficult and time-consuming by some authors. For this reason, several other semantics definitions have been proposed that claim to have certain advantages over the computation of a fixed-point semantics[6,7,8,9,10].

Some work has been done on comparing different semantical approaches. In [11], some of the earlier approaches to define a semantics for EPCs are discussed in comparision. All those approaches impose some additional well-formedness requirements on the models. Wehler [12] also compared two such semantics - the one defined by van der Aalst [13] for models without loops and the semantics proposed by Langner, Schneider and Wehler [14] that is based on Boolean Petri nets and restricts the modeller to use loops in a certain well-structured way only. Mendling [9] discusses five semantics definitions and identifies disadvantages of those semantics. Some semantics can be used for a certain class of "structured" models only. For others, a "well-strucutred refinement" (inserting a well-structuring construct into a model) can change the semantics of OR-joins in the original model.

Some differences among the definitions for OR-join semantics have been discussed in [7]. The authors of [7] propose a new semantics which does not impose any restrictions on the structure of the model and requires a lower computational complexity than other known approaches.

All papers mentioned above used mainly a small number of constructed examples for comparing the different semantics definitions. To our best knowledge, there has been no attempt so far to use a large number of real-world models for identifying differences among different semantics and the validation tools based on them. We used the "soundness validation" analysis that is included in three different tools for analysing 984 models. By comparing the results from those tools, some advantages and disadvantages of the tools and its underlying approaches can be found.

3   Models Used for Our Comparative Study

For the purpose of this comparative study, we collected a repository of 984 business process models which have been modelled as EPCs. EPCs consist of functions (activities which need to be executed, depicted as rounded boxes), events (pre- and postconditions before / after a function is executed, depicted as hexagons) and connectors (which can split or join the flow of control between the elements). Arcs between these elements represent the control flow. The trigger for starting the execution of an EPC is that certain start events (i.e. events without incoming arc) happen.

Table 1. Connectors in different modelling languages

	AND-join	XOR-join	OR-join	AND-split	XOR-split	OR-split
BPMN						
YAWL						
EPC						

Table 1 shows the different connectors that can be found in EPC models and the corresponding symbols for the connectors in YAWL and BPMN[1] in order to assist those readers who prefer another language.

---

[1] In BPMN, the connectors are called gateways.

The models in our repository have been collected from 130 sources. These sources can be categorized as follows: We took 531 EPCs from the SAP R/3 reference model, 112 EPCs from 31 bachelor and diploma thesises, 25 EPCs from 7 PhD thesises, 13 EPCs from 2 technical manuals, 82 EPCs from 48 published scientific papers, 12 EPCs from 6 university lecture notes, 4 EPCs from sample solutions to university examination questions, 88 EPCs from 11 real-world projects, 88 EPCs from 7 textbooks and 29 EPCs from 14 other sources.

Among the models in our repository, there is a great variation in size of the models, purpose of modelling, business domain and experience of the modellers. For this reason, we think that the models represent a reasonable good sample of real-world models.

4   Tools Used for Our Comparative Study

For analysing the models, we used three open source tools that are freely available: *EPCTools*, the *ProM plugin for EPC soundness analysis* and the *YAWL Editor*. All of them offer a feature "analyse soundness". What makes the comparision of the analysis results interesting is the fact that the tools use different definitions of semantics.

All the tools run as a Java program. We executed the tools on an Intel Core2 Duo CPU running at a speed of 3 GHz. By starting the Java virtual machine with the option -Xmx1536m, we allowed a heap size of 1.5 GB to be used.

EPCTools[4,5] calculates a fixed-point semantics for a model. If such a fixed-point semantics exists, a temporal model-checker is used by *EPCTools* for deciding about the soundness property. For the majority of models from our repository, an analysis result was given in a few seconds. There was only one model for which the analysis took more than 10 minutes. This model was validated in 63 minutes. For 28 models, *EPCTools* had to stop the computation because of an *Out of Memory* error. We applied soundness-preserving reduction [15,9] on these models. For 6 of the reduced models EPCTools still ran into a *Out of Memory* error, the others have been analysed.

The *ProM plugin for EPC soundness analysis* [16] uses the semantics defined by Mendling [9] for constructing a transition system for the model. Mendling's semantics combines the concept of a state (represented by tokens attached to arcs of the model) with the concept of a context (represented by additional binary tokens attached to the arcs). The context can be either "wait" (i.e. the arc still has to wait for more tokens to arrive) or "dead" (no tokens are expected to arrive). Both kinds of tokens are propagated in a four-staged process.

For 31 models, ProM failed to deliver a result because of an *Out of Memory* error. For 5 models, the computation took more than 10 minutes, the longest computation time was 26 minutes.

The third tool, *YAWL Editor*[17,18], originally has been constructed for analysing YAWL models. Our EPC models had to be translated into YAWL in order to analyse them. While the mapping of EPC modelling elements to YAWL is straightforward, there is an important difference between EPC and

YAWL: YAWL does not support process models with more than one start event. In order to avoid the problems that arise from the different instantiation semantics for EPC and YAWL models[19], we ran the YAWL soundness validation only for those 737 models for which the EPC model has exactly one start event after applying soundness-preserving reduction rules as described in [15,9]. YAWL Editor has a built-in restriction that stops the execution of the analysis if the calculated state-space exceeds 10,000 states. This is necessary, because the YAWL semantics allows an infinite state space[17]. This restriction was enforced for 22 models, meaning that no analysis result was available for them. The computation was very fast for the majority of the models. 628 have been analysed in less than 1 second, the longest computation took 23 sec. However, it took much longer to detect that a model cannot not be analysed because the state space exceeds 10,000 states. For only one model this fact could be realized in less than 5 minutes. The longest computation took more than 5 hours before the program terminated with the information that the state space exceeds 10,000 states.

5   Soundness Analysis Results

Soundness is an important and widely used correctness criterion for business process models. It has been originally introduced by van der Aalst for workflow nets[20,21] and later adapted to the EPC notation[13,9].

The formal definition of soundness can be found in the mentioned literature. Informally, a business process model is sound, if:

1. In every state that is reachable from a start state, there must be the possibility to reach a final state *(option to complete)*.
2. If a state has no subsequent state, then it must be a final state *(proper completion)*.
3. There is no element of the model that is never processed in any execution of the model *(no needless elements)*.

We used the tools described in Sect. 4 for testing the soundness property of the models from our repository.

Table 2. Result of the soundness analysis of those models which could be analyed by all three tools

ProM plugin for EPC soundness analysis	EPCTools	YAWL Editor	Models found
unsound	unsound	unsound	32
unsound	unsound	sound	0
unsound	sound	unsound	1
unsound	sound	sound	12
sound	unsound	unsound	(4)
sound	unsound	sound	0
sound	sound	unsound	0
sound	sound	sound	663

712 models could be analysed by all three tools. The results of their analysis is shown in Tab. 2.

The 4 cases in the 5th line of Tab. 2 (sound/unsound/unsound) could clearly be traced to a bug in the ProM plugin which is of no interest for our comparision of the theory behind the tools. The interesting cases are the ones where the results from the tools differ, i.e. one case "unsound/sound/unsound" and the 12 cases "unsound/sound/sound", highlighted by gray background.

In the next sections, we will present the results for the different tools. In particular, the differences shown in the gray lines of Tab. 2 will be discussed.

5.1   EPCTools (Using Fixed-Point Semantics)

EPCTools tries to compute a fixed-point semantics for each model. From the 984 models in our repository, exactly 3 did not have such a semantics, i.e. EPCTools identified them as not being clean.

As all tools used in our survey, EPCTools defines the state of an EPC by placing tokens on modelling elements. An initial state is one for which only start events carry a token. EPCTools than computes soundness based on the following definition:

An EPC is sound in a given initial state if, from all reachable states, a proper terminal state can be reached; where a proper terminal state is a state in which only end events carry a token[2].

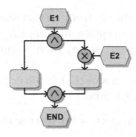

Fig. 1. Regarded as sound by EPCTools when execution is triggered by E1

This means that it is assumed that the initial state (i.e. combination of start events that can trigger the execution of the model) is known. As this information is in most cases not part of the model, we considered all possible combinations of start events and let EPCTools check for which of these combinations the EPC is sound. Afterwards, we classified an EPC as sound iff there is an initial state for which it is sound. This is the same approach that has been used in the EPC soundness definition by Mendling [9] which is implemented by the ProM plugin.

However, by comparing EPCTools' soundness results defined this way with the ones computed by the ProM plugin, we found 46 models that were reported

---

[2] This definition has been slightly simplified, in reality the tokens are placed on the arcs instead of the modelling elements.

as being sound by EPCTools while ProM identified them as unsound. The reason for this difference lies in the fact that EPCTools did not take the third property of the soundness definition (no needless elements) into account. For example, the model in Fig. 1 has a proper execution when triggered by start event E1. However, if triggered by start event E2, a deadlock at the AND-join will occur. Hence, the model should be regarded as unsound, because E2 never contributes to a proper execution of the model. The conclusion is that for models with more than one start event, EPCTools fails to detect problems that result from needless elements.

5.2 ProM Plugin (Using Mendling's Semantics Based on State and Context)

The ProM plugin for EPC soundness analysis is based on the state/context semantics defined by Mendling [9].

The plugin uses the soundness definition by Mendling [9]. In short, for an EPC to be sound, it is required that

1. There is at least one initial state (i.e. a combination of start events which are marked at the beginning of the execution) that leads to an execution ending in a state where only events without outgoing arcs are marked.
2. Every start event belongs to such an initial state.
3. From the selected initial states, it is not possible to reach a state other than an end state (where only events without outgoing arcs are marked) that does not have a successing state.

ProM found that all three EPCs that have computed to be unclean by EPCTools are not sound under Mendling's semantics.

For the majority of EPCs, the soundness results from the ProM plugin coincided with the soundness results of EPCTools. However, we have identified one class of models where a model which is sound according to the fixed-point semantics runs into a deadlock under Mendling's semantics. All those models for which the result from EPCTools differs from the result by the ProM plugin contain a pattern where an OR join is the entry into a loop.

Fig. 2 (a) shows the most basic variant of such a pattern. For this model, Mendling's semantics would lead to a deadlock at the OR-join. In our opinion, this is an undesirable property of this semantics. The statement "an OR-join can always replace any XOR-join or AND-join" which holds for the behaviour of models under other semantics is not true for Mendling's semantics.

Fig. 2 (b) shows a variant of this pattern. This model would also deadlock at the OR-join. The interesting point here is that the reduction rules published in [9] (which are assumed to be soundness-preserving) would completely reduce the model in Fig. 2 (b) which would lead to the wrong result that the model is sound. As a consequence, the reduction rule that removes a control block starting with an XOR-split and ending with an OR-join should be removed from the set of reduction rules in [9], because it does not necessarily preserve soundness.

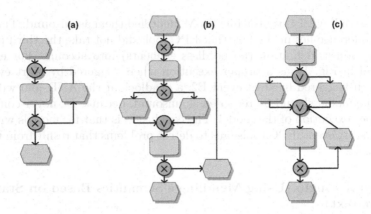

Fig. 2. Models that have a deadlock under Mendling's semantics

Finally, the EPC in Fig. 2 (c) is a third variant of the same pattern. Here the OR-join at which the deadlock occurs would have to be replaced by a combination of an OR-join (which ends the block started by the OR-split) and another XOR-join (as a loop end point) in order to make the model sound.

5.3   YAWL Editor (Using YAWL Semantics)

In order to avoid problems of OR-joins depending on each other, the YAWL semantics computes the ability to forward tokens for each OR-join separately. Other OR-joins are assumed to act like XOR-joins with a non-local semantics, i.e. they forward every incoming token. The computation whether an OR-join can forward tokens is performed by computing the predecessor markings of the current marking (see [17] for details).

For the models from our repository, the soundness results delivered by YAWL were almost identical to the soundness results computed by EPCTools. The differences will be discussed below.

Other than the semantics definitions used by EPCTools and ProM, the semantics definition of YAWL allows elements marked with more than one token. Such a definition allows the state space of a model to become infinite. However, the analysis presented in [17] works for models with a finite state space only, and no algorithm is given that can decide whether the state space will become infinite. The YAWL editor stops the computation when a threshold of 10,000 states is reached. Such a situation most likely indicates that the state space becomes infinite and the model is not sound (although it is not an absolute indicator).

From the 737 EPCs that have been validated by YAWL, the mentioned restriction for 10,000 states was enforced for 22 models. From the 3 models which are unclean according to EPCTools, two could be reduced to models with a single start event and hence analysed by YAWL. For both, the state space exceeded 10,000 states.

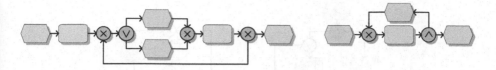

Fig. 3. Models with an infinite state space in the YAWL analysis

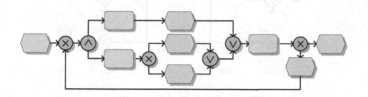

Fig. 4. Two OR-joins depending on each other

All other models for which YAWL stopped after the threshold of 10,000 markings was reached were unsound under the fixed-point semantics used by EPC-Tools. This result supports the expectation that an increase above 10,000 markings indicates an error in the model.

However, a drawback of the YAWL analysis is that even in simply-looking cases like the ones shown in Fig. 3 the error cannot be found. Combining the YAWL approach with techniques like invariants [22] or reduction rules with error cases [9] could help to improve the results.

Another interesting case is shown in Fig. 4. This model contains two OR-joins in a feedback loop. EPCTools computes a fixed-point semantics (where both OR-joins forward a token without having to wait). However, the YAWL semantics concludes that both OR-joins block while waiting for another token to arrive. Hence, this model is sound according to EPCTools but unsound according to YAWL[3]. In our opinion, in this case the fixed-point semantics meets the expectation of the modeller better than the YAWL semantics.

6   Findings

In this section, we want to summarize the findings of our analysis:

6.1   Unclean Models

Three models that do not have a fixed-point semantics have been found among our real-world examples. Although they are rare (3 out of 984), such models exist, i.e. the discussion about their semantics is not just an academic pastetime. To

---

[3] Because of an error in the implementation of the reduction rules, YAWL has to be started without applying YAWL reduction rules for coming to this result. Note that removing the loop is not soundness preserving.

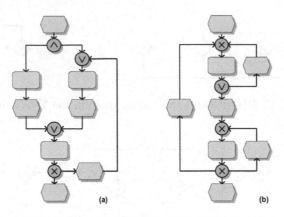

Fig. 5. Two unclean models

our surprise, we even found an instance of a model that was almost identical to the original vicious circle published in [1]. Other examples for unclean models are the "partial redo" pattern (see Fig. 5 (a), discussed in [23] and [7]) and the pattern shown in Fig. 5 (b).

6.2 Soundness Definitions

The soundness definition used by EPCTools differs from van der Aalst's definition [20,21]: It does not take into accout the requirement that there must not be elements in the model which do not contribute to a proper completion of the model. This way, some models are classified as being sound (for a certain initial state) even if such useless elements are present. We recommend to prefer Mendling's definition [9] (as used in the ProM plugin) which pays attention to the "no needless elements" requirement.

6.3 Mendling's Semantics

While Mendling's semantics based on state and context performes well for most models, we have identified a class of models for which it leads to unexpected results. OR-joins that are a loop entry will lead to a deadlock. While Mendling's semantics has several desirable properties (as discussed in [9]), it does not have the property that any AND- or XOR-join can be replaced by an OR-join without affecting the semantics of the model. We have shown an example for which the reduction rules given in [9] are not soundness-preserving as assumed.

6.4 YAWL Semantics

For most models, the analysis using YAWL semantics lead to the same results as the EPCTools analysis using fixed-point semantics. We found exactly one model for which YAWL computes the soundness property differently from EPCTools (which uses fixed-point semantics). A drawback is that for models with an infinite state-space some kinds of errors cannot be located.

7   Conclusion and Directions of Future Research

In our comparative study of soundness results computed by three different tools, we found some differences that can lead to interesting insights on advantages and disadvantages of semantics definitions. A by-product of our analysis of a large number of models was that some bugs in YAWL (in particular in the reduction rules) could be detected. We would like to thank the YAWL community and in particular A. ter Hofstede, M. Adams and E. Verbeek for the fruitful discussion and for fixing the bugs very quickly. From the fact that we found several bugs in YAWL and one in the ProM plugin, we have learned the lesson that testing with a large repository of real-world models is very useful for assuring a high quality of tools that validate business process models. As a next step, we will look into the question for which category of models the execution of the soundness analysis by the tools takes an unusual long time. We hope that this can help to improve the algorithms used for the validation.

References

1. van der Aalst, W.M.P., Desel, J., Kindler, E.: On the semantics of EPCs: A vicious circle. In: EPK 2004, Geschäftsprozessmanagement mit Ereignisgesteuerten Prozessketten, pp. 71–79 (2002)
2. van der Aalst, W.M.P., ter Hofstede, A.H.M., Kiepuszewski, B., Barros, A.: Workflow patterns. Distributed and Parallel Databases 14(3) (2003)
3. Kindler, E.: On the Semantics of EPCs: A Framework for Resolving the Vicious Circle. In: Desel, J., Pernici, B., Weske, M. (eds.) BPM 2004. LNCS, vol. 3080, pp. 82–97. Springer, Heidelberg (2004)
4. Cuntz, N., Kindler, E.: On the semantics of EPCs: Efficient calculation and simulation. In: Proceedings of EPK 2004: Geschäftsprozessmanagement mit Ereignisgesteuerten Prozessketten, pp. 7–26 (2004)
5. Cuntz, N., Freiheit, J., Kindler, E.: On the Semantics of EPCs: Faster calculation for EPCs with small state spaces. In: EPK 2005, Geschäftsprozessmanagement mit Ereignisgesteuerten Prozessketten, pp. 7–23 (2005)
6. Wynn, M.T., Edmond, D., van der Aalst, W.M.P., ter Hofstede, A.H.M.: Achieving a General, Formal and Decidable Approach to the OR-Join in Workflow Using Reset Nets. In: Ciardo, G., Darondeau, P. (eds.) ICATPN 2005. LNCS, vol. 3536, pp. 423–443. Springer, Heidelberg (2005)
7. Dumas, M., Großkopf, A., Hettel, T., Wynn, M.T.: Semantics of standard process models with or-joins. In: Meersman, R., Tari, Z. (eds.) OTM 2007, Part I. LNCS, vol. 4803, pp. 41–58. Springer, Heidelberg (2007)
8. van Hee, K.M., Oanea, O., Serebrenik, A., Sidorova, N., Voorhoeve, M.: History-based joins: Semantics, soundness and implementation. In: Dustdar, S., Fiadeiro, J.L., Sheth, A.P. (eds.) BPM 2006. LNCS, vol. 4102, pp. 225–240. Springer, Heidelberg (2006)

9. Mendling, J.: Detection and Prediction of Errors in EPC Business Process Models. PhD thesis, Wirtschaftsuniversität Wien (2007)
10. Börger, E., Sörensen, O., Thalheim, B.: On defining the behavior of OR-joins in business process models. J. Universal Computer Science 14, 1–22 (2008)
11. Rittgen, P.: Quo vadis EPK in ARIS? Wirtschaftsinformatik 42(1), 27–35 (2000)
12. Wehler, J.: Boolean and free-choice semantics of event-driven process chains. In: EPK 2007, Geschäftsprozessmanagement mit Ereignisgesteuerten Prozessketten, pp. 77–96 (2007)
13. van der Aalst, W.M.P.: Formalization and verification of event-driven process chains. Information & Software Technology 41(10), 639–650 (1999)
14. Langner, P., Schneider, C., Wehler, J.: Relating event-driven process chains to Boolean Petri nets. Technical Report 9707, München (December 1997)
15. van Dongen, B.F., van der Aalst, W.M.P., Verbeek, E.: Verification of EPCs: Using reduction rules and Petri nets. In: Proceedings of the International Conference on Advanced Information Systems 2005, pp. 372–386 (2005)
16. Barborka, P., Helm, L., Köldorfer, G., Mendling, J., Neumann, G., van Dongen, B.F., Verbeek, E., van der Aalst, W.M.P.: Integration of EPC-related tools with ProM. In: EPK 2006, Geschäftsprozessmanagement mit Ereignisgesteuerten Prozessketten. CEUR Workshop Proceedings, vol. 224, pp. 105–120 (2006)
17. Wynn, M.T.: Semantics, Verification, and Implementation of Workflows with Cancellation Regions and OR-joins. PhD thesis, Queensland University of Technology Brisbane, Australia (2006)
18. Wynn, M.T., Verbeek, E., van der Aalst, W.M.P., Edmond, D.: Business process verification - finally a reality! Business Process Management Journal 15(1), 74–92 (2009)
19. Decker, G., Mendling, J.: Instantiation semantics for process models. In: Dumas, M., Reichert, M., Shan, M.-C. (eds.) BPM 2008. LNCS, vol. 5240, pp. 164–179. Springer, Heidelberg (2008)
20. van der Aalst, W.M.P.: Verification of workflow nets. In: Azéma, P., Balbo, G. (eds.) ICATPN 1997. LNCS, vol. 1248, pp. 407–426. Springer, Heidelberg (1997)
21. van der Aalst, W.M.P.: Structural characterizations of sound workflow nets. Computing Science Reports/23 (96) (1996)
22. Verbeek, E., van der Aalst, W.M.P., ter Hofstede, A.H.M.: Verifying workflows with cancellation regions and or-joins: An approach based on relaxed soundness and invariants. Comput. J. 50(3), 294–314 (2007)
23. Gruhn, V., Laue, R.: Good and bad excuses for unstructured business process models. In: Proceedings of 12th European Conference on Pattern Languages of Programs, EuroPLoP 2007 (2007)

Empirical Analysis of a Proposed Process Granularity Heuristic

Joachim Melcher and Detlef Seese

Institut AIFB, Universität Karlsruhe (TH)
76128 Karlsruhe, Germany
{melcher,seese}@aifb.uni-karlsruhe.de

Abstract. Choosing the adequate size of process activities (process granularity) is a problem during process design. Vanderfeesten *et al.* have proposed a heuristic based on a process granularity metric and postulated a hypothesis concerning error probability about its use. The heuristic prefers process designs with high cohesion and low coupling—a principle originating in software engineering.

In this paper, we present an experimentation system consisting of a small web-based workflow engine for empirically analyzing the error probability hypothesis. Furthermore, the results of a conducted experiment with 165 students using this experimentation system are reported. The experiment does not support the hypothesis. Instead, an alternative error probability model explaining the results is suggested.

Keywords: Process granularity, heuristic, process metric, experimental system, experiment.

1 Introduction

During the design phase of a workflow, one has to choose the adequate size of process activities (process granularity). Recently, Vanderfeesten *et al.* have proposed a process granularity metric inspired by software engineering [1, 2]. This metric measures the ratio between process coupling and cohesion. Based on this metric, Vanderfeesten *et al.* have suggested a heuristic for selecting between different process designs which prefers designs with high cohesion and low coupling. They have also postulated the hypothesis that those process designs are less error-prone during process execution. As they do not give an empirical validation of their heuristic and hypothesis, it is still no valid prediction system as explained in [3].

In this paper, we present an experimentation system for analyzing the hypothesis and report the results of a conducted experiment with 165 students using this experimentation system. Additionally, we suggest an alternative error probability model. Because of space restrictions, some experimental details can only be presented in [4].

The remainder of this paper is organized as follows: In Section 2, we give a short introduction into the process granularity heuristic proposed by Vanderfeesten *et al.* Our experimentation system for analyzing the hypothesis about

S. Rinderle-Ma et al. (Eds.): BPM 2009 Workshops, LNBIP 43, pp. 513–524, 2010.
© Springer-Verlag Berlin Heidelberg 2010

error probability postulated by Vanderfeesten *et al.* is presented in Section 3. The conducted experiment and its results are shown in Section 4. The paper gives a conclusion and presents possible future work (Section 5).

2 Process Granularity Heuristic

2.1 Information Element Structure

The proposed process metrics and the suggested granularity heuristic of [1, 2] are based on the methodology of product-based workflow design [5, 6, 7]. In this approach, a process is not originally represented by a process graph (e. g., using event-driven process chains, Petri nets or workflow nets). Instead, modeling starts one step earlier with a so called *information element structure* (see Figure 1).

The nodes of this graph are *information elements* which represent data that is needed during process execution. The directed edges stand for *operations* on information elements. Each operation has one or more input information elements and one output information element. The output of an operation can be the input of another one.

There are different types of operations: The simplest one has exactly one input information element (e. g., only element 18 is needed for computing element 38 in Figure 1). The second type is an AND construct which has at least two input nodes (e. g., elements 12 and 13 for the computation of element 18). The last type is an XOR construct. Here, several possible operations for the computation of an information element exist. Each operation has a boolean constraint so that only exactly one alternative is executable during each process execution. Looking at Figure 1, element 42 can be either computed by an operation using elements 39, 40 and 41 as inputs or by another operation with element 27 as input.

During the next modeling step, the information element structure is partitioned into different *activities* (consisting of a number of operations on information elements) which together form a traditional process graph. The activities A to G depicted in Figure 3, for example, are a partition of the information element structure of Figure 1 and can be combined to the process shown in Figure 2(a).

In [8], Kress *et al.* present an algorithm for directly executing the information element structure.

2.2 Process Granularity Metric

In this paper, we use the definitions of [2, pp. 426–429]—omitting the references to resource classes or roles which are able to execute the operations and activities as they are not relevant for our analysis.

Definition 1 (Operations structure). *An operations structure is a tuple* (D, O) *with*

- *a set D of information elements which are processed and*
- *a set $O \subseteq D \times \mathcal{P}(D)$ of operations on these information elements, such that there are no "dangling" information elements and no value of an information element depends on itself (also not indirectly).*

Based on a operations structure, the contained information elements and operations are partitioned into different activities.

Definition 2 (Activitiy). *An activity $T \subseteq O$ on an operations structure (D, O) is a set of operations.*

As a shorthand, the notation $\hat{T} := \bigcup_{(p,cs) \in T}(\{p\} \cup cs)$ for the information elements processed in an activity T is introduced.

The different activities can be combined to a process which processes and computes the information elements of the operations structure in a valid sequence. For details on how to specify the control flow or how to check the correctness and soundness of the process, the reader is referred to [7]. For our purpose, the following definition is sufficient.

Definition 3 (Process). *A process on an operations structure (D, O) is a set S of activities on this operations structure.*

Based on these notations, metrics for *process cohesion* and *coupling* can be defined.

Process cohesion consists of two components. The first one, *activity relation cohesion*, quantifies how much the operations of an activity are related. For that purpose, it measures the average overlap of operations. Two operations overlap if they share input or output information elements.

Definition 4 (Activity relation cohesion). *For an activity T on an operations structure (D, O), the activity relation cohesion $\lambda(T)$ is defined as*

$$\lambda(T) := \begin{cases} \frac{|\{((p_1, cs_1), (p_2, cs_2)) \in T \times T | ((\{p_1\} \cup cs_1) \cap (\{p_2\} \cup cs_2)) \neq \emptyset \wedge p_1 \neq p_2\}|}{|T| \cdot (|T|-1)} & for \ |T| > 1 \\ 0 & for \ |T| \leq 1 \end{cases} \quad (1)$$

The second cohesion component, *activity relation cohesion*, measures which fraction of information elements of an activity are used in more than one operation.

Definition 5 (Activity information cohesion). *For an activity T on an operations structure (D, O), the activity relation cohesion $\lambda(T)$ is defined as*

$$\mu(T) := \begin{cases} \frac{|\{d \in D | \exists ((p_1, cs_1), (p_2, cs_2)) \in T \times T : (d \in ((\{p_1\} \cup cs_1) \cap (\{p_2\} \cup cs_2)) \wedge p_1 \neq p_2\}|}{|\hat{T}|} & for \ |\hat{T}| > 0 \\ 0 & for \ |\hat{T}| = 0 \end{cases} \quad (2)$$

The total cohesion of an activity is simply the product of its relation and information cohesion.

Definition 6 (Activity cohesion). *For an activity T on an operations structure (D, O), the activity cohesion $c(T)$ is defined as*

$$c(T) := \lambda(T) \cdot \mu(T) \quad . \tag{3}$$

The overall cohesion of a process is computed by the average activity cohesion.

Definition 7 (Process cohesion). *For a process with set S of activities on an operations structure (D, O), the process cohesion ch is defined as*

$$ch := \frac{\sum_{T \in S} c(T)}{|S|} \quad . \tag{4}$$

Process coupling quantifies how strong the activities of a process are connected to each other. Two activities are connected if they share at least one information element. The coupling metric measures the fraction of connected activity pairs.

Definition 8 (Process coupling). *For a process with set S of activities on an operations structure (D, O), the process coupling cp is defined as*

$$cp := \begin{cases} \frac{|\{(T_1, T_2) \in S \times S | T_1 \neq T_2 \wedge (\hat{T}_1 \cap \hat{T}_2) \neq \varnothing\}|}{|S| \cdot (|S| - 1)} & \text{for } |S| > 1 \\ 0 & \text{for } |S| \leq 1 \end{cases} \quad . \tag{5}$$

Finally, Vanderfeesten *et al.* define a process coupling/cohesion ratio which serves as a process granularity metric.

Definition 9 (Process coupling/cohesion ratio). *For a process with set S of activities on an operations structure (D, O), the process coupling/cohesion ratio ρ is defined as*

$$\rho := \frac{cp}{ch} \quad . \tag{6}$$

2.3   Process Granularity Heuristic

According to Vanderfeesten and Reijers, an important issue in process design is "the proper size of the individual activities in a process (the process granularity)" [1, p. 290]. The heuristic presented in [1,2] is thought to help designers "to select from several alternatives the process design that is strongly cohesive and weakly coupled" [2, p. 420].

Vanderfeesten *et al.* state that the proposed metrics and the heuristic are inspired by software engineering "where an old design aphorism is to strive for *strong cohesion, and loose coupling*" [2, p. 421].

Consequently, the statement of the heuristic is that a workflow design with a smaller value of the process granularity metric (process coupling/cohesion ratio) of Definition 9 is to be preferred over another one with a larger value. Yet, it does not describe how different alternative workflow designs can be found. [2, p. 429]

Vanderfeesten *et al.* establish the following hypothesis about the implications of their heuristic [2, pp. 425–426]:

Hypothesis 1. *The smaller the value of the process granularity metric of a workflow design, the smaller the probability of run-time mistakes.*

Instead of an empirical validation of this hypothesis, they only give some arguments as a motivation [2, p. 426]:

- "A *loose coupling* of activities will result in few information elements that need to be exchanged between activities [...], reducing the probability of run-time mistakes."
- "*Highly cohesive* activities [...] are likely to be understood and performed better by people than large chunks of unrelated work being grouped together."

3   Experimentation System

In order to analyze the hypothesis of Vanderfeesten *et al.* about their heuristic, we created a computer-based experimentation system.

The main goal was to ensure comparability and repeatability of experiments (also with different subjects). Consequently, no special domain knowledge of the subjects shall be necessary. We decided to use very abstract operations structures for the experimentation system: Each information element represents a single variable of type boolean, integer or double. Operations are functions with the variables corresponding to the operation's input information elements as input parameters. According to the variable types, these functions consist of addition, subtraction, multiplication or logical AND, OR, XOR and negation. Activities consist of sets of corresponding functions which can depend on each other in a non-cyclic manner. Examples of these functions can be found in [4].

Core of the experimentation system is a small web-based workflow engine. It controls the execution of process instances. Each experimental subject is assigned to a resource role[1]. When an activity becomes executable, it is delegated in first-come, first-served order to the next free subject with the corresponding role. The functions of that activity together with the values of the input parameters of the basic functions[2] are displayed on the subject's screen. The subject has to enter the computed values into special text fields. By clicking a button, the computed values are sent to the workflow engine for further processing. At XOR splits, the workflow engine routes automatically by evaluating the boolean constraint expressions for the different branches.

---

[1] Consequently, one needs at least as many subjects as resource roles in the executed process instances.
[2] Basic functions are functions for which the values of its input parameters are not computed by other functions of the same activity.

During execution, the following data is logged: start and end time of each activity and each process instance, correct or incorrect activity execution[3] and correct or incorrect process instance execution[4].

4   Experimental Analysis and Results

4.1   Experimental Design

In order to test Hypothesis 1 (error probability), we conducted an experiment using the experimentation system described in Section 3.

In the experiment, the independent variable is the process granularity metric value of a process design, the response variables are the rates of incorrectly executed process instances and activities.

For this experiment, we used the information element structure depicted in Figure 1, which is presented as an example in [1, 2]. The structure was used in the abstract fashion described in Section 3. So, only the structural properties—and consequently the process metric values—stayed unchanged. Because of space restrictions, we can only present the functions used for the operations in [4].

Based on the information element structure, the three different process design alternatives (Figure 2) already proposed in [1, 2] were used. The respective partition into activities is shown in Figure 3.

The process metric values for process coupling (cp), cohesion (ch) and granularity (ρ) of the process design alternatives are listed in Table 1. So, there are three levels of the independent variable in the experiment. According to the heuristic, alternative 1 should be preferred as it has the smallest value of ρ. Following Hypothesis 1, it should also have the smallest error probability.

Table 1. Metric values for the three process alternatives

	cp	ch	ρ
alternative 1	0.714	0.183	3.9
alternative 2	0.611	0.105	5.8
alternative 3	0.8	0.114	7.0

We created a set of ten process instances which was used for all process design alternatives. All these process instances were executable from the start of the experiment and were processed in the same order. The instances had different

---

[3] The correctness of an activity execution is assessed based on the values of its input parameters. So, if the values of the input parameters are incorrect—caused by an earlier activity—but the output value of the function is correctly computed based on these input values, the activity execution is assessed as correct.

[4] A process instance execution is assessed as incorrect if at least one of its activities was executed incorrectly.

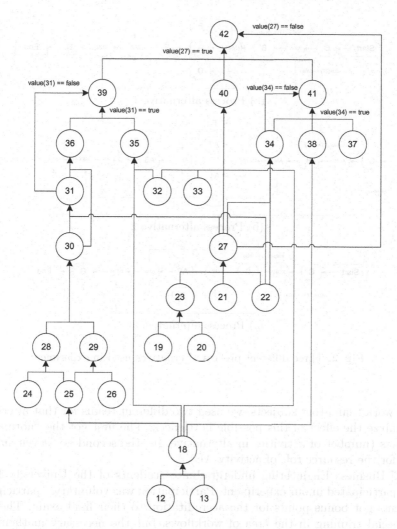

Fig. 1. Information element structure used in experiment

values for its basic information elements[5]. If they were correctly executed, the first and last instances of the set were routed directly from activity C to G at the XOR split—the others had to take the branch with all the other activities.

For each process design alternative, we used several teams which each processed that same set of process instances in order to average the team results. Each team consisted of exactly as many subjects as there are activities in its process alternative. As the subjects executing activity AE in alternative 3 have much

---

[5] Basic information elements are information elements whose values are not computed by any operation. Instead, their values have to be given for each process instance before the execution.

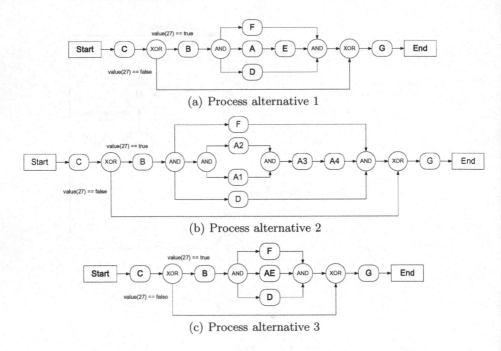

(a) Process alternative 1

(b) Process alternative 2

(c) Process alternative 3

Fig. 2. Three different process alternatives used in experiment

more work than other subjects, we used two different teams for that alternative to analyze the effect of this possible bottleneck: The first got the "normal" six subjects (number of activities in alternative 3)—the second got seven subjects (two for the resource role of activity AE).

165 Business Engineering undergraduate students of the University Karlsruhe participated in our experiment. Participation was voluntary—participating students got bonus points for the accreditation to their final exam. They had no special training in the area of workflows, but the necessary mathematical knowledge for the used abstract functions (cf. Section 3). As the subjects were randomly assigned to the resource roles within the different teams for the different process alternatives, individual differences should be balanced. Finally, there were six teams for alternative 1, alternative 3 with six subjects and alternative 3 with seven subjects, respectively, as well as five teams for alternative 2.

4.2   Results

The number of incorrect process instances and activities (over all teams) for the different process alternatives are shown in Table 2.

First, we checked whether there is a significant difference between alternative 3 with six and seven subjects. For that purpose, we used Pearson's chi-square test [9, pp. 643–648]. The null-hypothesis that the numbers belong to the same

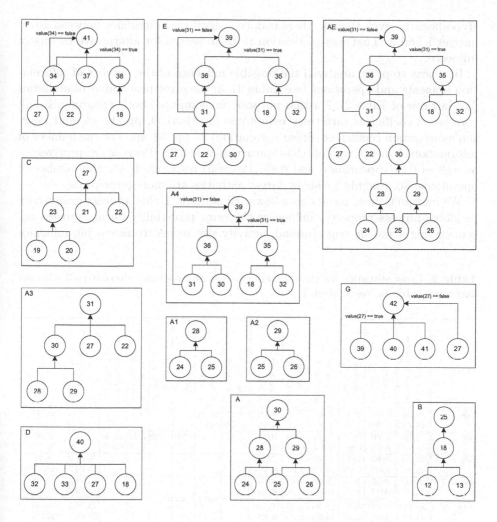

Fig. 3. Partitioning of the information element structure in smaller activities

distribution could not be rejected on the $\alpha = 0.05$ level. Consequently, both cases were mixed together for the further analysis (row "sum alt. 3" in Table 2).

Afterwards, we look at the actual hypothesis. As one can see in Table 2, alternative 1, which should be the best process design according to Hypothesis 1, has the highest ratio of incorrect process instances closely followed by alternative 3, which should be the worst design. Again, we did a chi-square test to test the alternatives for significant differences. Only for the pair alternative 1 and 2, the null-hypothesis (no difference) could be rejected ($p \approx 0.030$). So, the results of our experiment do not support Hypothesis 1.

Next, we did an analysis on activity level. The results of pairwise chi-square tests are shown in Table 3. Looking at Table 2, one sees that the error probabilities of activities A–AE have exactly the opposite order than predicted by

Hypothesis 1—even though, there is only a significant difference between alternatives 1 and 3. That was motivation to us to search for alternative factors of influence.

In a next step, we analyzed the possible influence of the number of information elements and operations (see Table 4) on the error probability of activities (see last row of Table 2). For that purpose, we computed both Spearman's rank correlation coefficient (arbitrary monotonic function) [9, pp. 42–45] and Pearson's correlation coefficient (linear correlation) [9, pp. 38–40]. For the number of information elements, we got 0.95 (Spearman) and 0.78 (Pearson) respectively— as well as 0.97 (Spearman) and 0.85 (Pearson) respectively for the number of operations. So, roughly speaking, larger activities are more error-prone.

We interpret these results as follows: Hypothesis 1 that process granularity (a global process property) influences the error probability during process execution might not be true. Instead, activity size seems to have a big influence

Table 2. Error statistics for the different process alternatives (alternative 3 with six and seven subjects, respectively)

	# incorrect process instances	# incorrect activities C	# incorrect activities B	# incorrect activities F	# incorrect activities D	# incorrect activities G	# incorrect activities A	# incorrect activities E	# incorrect activities A1	# incorrect activities A2	# incorrect activities A3	# incorrect activities A4	# incorrect activities AE	# process instances with at least one of A–AE incorrect
alt. 1	29/60 48.3%	9/60 15.0%	1/41 2.4%	3/41 7.3%	1/41 2.4%	0/60 0.0%	5/41 12.2%	14/41 34.1%	-	-	-	-	-	18/41 43.9%
alt. 2	14/50 28.0%	0/50 0.0%	0/40 0.0%	2/40 5.0%	0/40 0.0%	0/50 0.0%	-	-	0/40 0.0%	1/40 2.5%	2/40 5.0%	10/40 25.0%	-	13/40 32.5%
alt. 3, 6 s.	26/60 43.3%	3/60 5.0%	3/47 6.4%	9/47 19.1%	1/47 2.1%	7/60 11.7%	-	-	-	-	-	-	9/47 19.1%	9/47 19.1%
alt. 3, 7 s.	24/60 40.0%	0/60 0.0%	2/48 4.2%	9/48 18.8%	1/48 2.1%	4/60 6.7%	-	-	-	-	-	-	15/48 31.3%	15/48 31.3%
sum alt. 3	50/120 41.7%	3/120 2.5%	5/95 5.3%	18/95 18.9%	2/95 2.1%	11/120 9.2%	-	-	-	-	-	-	24/95 25.3%	24/95 25.3%
sum		12/230 5.2%	6/176 3.4%	23/176 13.1%	3/176 1.7%	11/230 4.8%	5/41 12.2%	14/41 34.1%	0/40 0.0%	1/40 2.5%	2/40 5.0%	10/40 25.0%	24/95 25.3%	

Table 3. Results of chi-square tests for error statistics on activity level ($\alpha = 0.05$). For cells marked with "+", the null-hypothesis (no difference) was rejected.

	activity C	activity B	activity F	activity D	activity G	activities A–AE
# alt. 1 vs. 2	+	-	-	-	-	-
# alt. 1 vs. 3	+	-	-	-	+	+
# alt. 2 vs. 3	-	-	+	-	+	-

Table 4. Number of information elements and operations per activity

	activity C	activity B	activity F	activity D	activity G	activity A	activity E	activity A1	activity A2	activity A3	activity A4	activity AE
# information elements	6	4	7	5	5	6	9	3	3	6	7	14
# operations	2	2	4	1	2	3	5	1	1	2	4	8

on the error probability of an activity. From the point of view of a subject, the remaining process is some kind of "black box". It only sees its own activity with the contained operations. This fact motivates the following alternative error probability model.

Error Probability Model. If the probabilities p_i that activity i is executed erroneously for a process instance are stochastically independent, then the probability P_{err} that the process instance is executed erroneously is

$$P_{err} = 1 - \prod_i (1 - p_i) \ . \tag{7}$$

If one further assumes for simplicity that all error probabilities p_i of the n activities of a process are equal with value p, one gets

$$P_{err} = 1 - (1 - p)^n \ . \tag{8}$$

Now, one can compare the error probabilities P_{err_A} and P_{err_B} of two alternative process designs. Let us look at the following example: Alternative B has larger but less activities than alternative A. So, while alternative B has n activities with error probability $p_B = 0.075$, alternative A has $2n$ activities with error probability $p_A = 0.05$. One can show that $P_{err_B} < P_{err_A}$ for all values of n. Generally, one finds many parameters for the above model so that the process design with the larger but less activities has a smaller error probability than the alternative design.

These findings about the error probability model are consistent with our interpretation of the results of our experiment. Hypothesis 1 could be wrong. Instead of process granularity, the size (and consequently error probability) and the number of activities in a process could be the main reasons for different error probabilities of alternative process designs.

5   Conclusion and Future Work

In this paper, we gave a short introduction into the process granularity heuristic of Vanderfeesten *et al.* We presented a web-based experimentation system for analyzing the hypothesis of Vanderfeesten *et al.* that process designs with smaller process granularity metric values are less error-prone. Furthermore, we reported the results of an experiment involving 165 students.

The experiment does not support the hypothesis. Instead, we presented an alternative error probability model which is able to explain the results.

For future work, we suggest to conduct further and even larger experiments to re-check our results about the heuristic of Vanderfeesten *et al.* as well as our proposed alternative error probability model.

Acknowledgment

The authors want to thank Roland Küstermann for his technical assistance as well as the participating students.

References

1. Reijers, H.A., Vanderfeesten, I.T.P.: Cohesion and coupling metrics for workflow process design. In: Desel, J., Pernici, B., Weske, M. (eds.) BPM 2004. LNCS, vol. 3080, pp. 290–305. Springer, Heidelberg (2004)
2. Vanderfeesten, I., Reijers, H.A., van der Aalst, W.M.P.: Evaluating workflow process designs using cohesion and coupling metrics. Computers in Industry 59(5), 420–437 (2008)
3. Melcher, J., Seese, D.: Process measurement: Insights from software measurement on measuring process complexity, quality and performance. Research report, Universität Karlsruhe (TH), Institut AIFB (2008), http://digbib.ubka.uni-karlsruhe.de/volltexte/1000009225
4. Melcher, J., Seese, D.: Empirical analysis of a proposed process granularity heuristic (experimental details). Research report, Universität Karlsruhe (TH), Institut AIFB (2009), http://digbib.ubka.uni-karlsruhe.de/volltexte/1000012016
5. van der Aalst, W.M.P., Reijers, H.A., Limam, S.: Product-driven workflow design. In: Shen, W., Lin, Z., Barthès, J.P., Kamel, M. (eds.) Proceedings of the 6th International Conference on Computer Supported Cooperative Work in Design, pp. 397–402 (2001)
6. Reijers, H.A., Limam, S., van der Aalst, W.M.P.: Product-based workflow design. Journal of Management Information Systems 20(1), 229–262 (2003)
7. Reijers, H.A. (ed.): Design and Control of Workflow Processes : Business Process Management for the Service Industry. LNCS, vol. 2617. Springer, Heidelberg (2003)
8. Kress, M., Melcher, J., Seese, D.: Introducing executable product models for the service industry. In: Sprague, R.H. (ed.) Proceedings of the 40th Annual Hawaii International Conference on System Sciences (HICSS 2007), p. 46 (2007)
9. Panik, M.J.: Advanced Statistics from an Elementary Point of View. Elsevier Academic Press, Amsterdam (2005)

BPMNCommunity.org: A Forum for Process Modeling Practitioners – A Data Repository for Empirical BPM Research

Alexander Grosskopf, Jan Brunnert, Stefan Wehrmeyer, and Mathias Weske

Hasso-Plattner-Institute, Potsdam 14482, Germany
{alexander.grosskopf,mathias.weske}@hpi.uni-potsdam.de,
{jan.brunnert,stefan.wehrmeyer}@student.hpi.uni-potsdam.de
http://bpt.hpi.uni-potsdam.de

Abstract. This short paper reports on an online platform where modelers can gather, share and discuss knowledge around BPMN. The models, ratings, comments and discussions are no longer based on pictures but related to actual process models that can be edited in the web browser. After two months 97 registered users developed and shared 166 process models and 372 revisions. In this paper we introduce the platform, show its architecture and provide samples for data extraction and analysis. We invite researchers to use the available data to conduct further empirical studies.

Keywords: Online Communities, Oryx, Process Modeling, BPMN.

1 Introduction

Business process modeling is at the heart of modern organizations, since process models capture how work is performed in the organization and how business goals are reached. Recently, the Business Process Modeling Notation (BPMN) became the de facto standard in process modeling. We observed that, dealing with this new language, people desire to discuss the best or most adequate model to represent a common real-world situations. We want to support these discussions.

In this paper we introduce BPMNCommunity.org, a web collaboration platform that supports discussions about process models. Other than traditional wikis, the process modeling environment Oryx [1] is embedded, so that process models can be created and modified with standard web browsers. All models in the community are public knowledge. Together with tags, ratings, descriptions, comments, and the revision history, it creates a diverse data pool that can be leveraged for empirical research in business process management.

This paper is organized as follows. Section 2 introduces the major use cases supported by the platform, before Section 3 sketches its software architecture. Section 4 looks at the available data for empirical research, before the paper concludes with project information.

S. Rinderle-Ma et al. (Eds.): BPM 2009 Workshops, LNBIP 43, pp. 525–528, 2010.

2   Use Cases and Functionality for the Community

We started with the goal to create a user-driven community. Following the wiki principle all content can be read and changed by all users. Models can be described, tagged, rated, and comments can attached to modeling elements. This allows discussions to take place directly at the models. We tailored the platform to meet three main use cases: learn BPMN, jointly create a processes, and discuss good modeling style.

BPMN novices can learn the language using the tutorial section. Tutorials and exercises are created by users for users. Solutions to exercises can be submitted and rated. To create models together users can use the groups section of the platform. One group can have multiple members and processes that relate to the topic. At present, groups have formed, e.g. to show the Workflow Patterns [2] modeled in BPMN, discuss reference processes or the relation of EPC and BPMN. Discussions about modeling alternatives and good style are captured in the best practice modeling section. Users can start a topic similar to a group. Alternative solutions can be modeled and marked as a good or bad sample to model a given situation in BPMN. By now, best practices were created on topics such as multiple start events, reactive processes and batch processing of events.

Additionally, the platform provides a dash board with widgets that aggregate information from the platform and the internet. Widgets show new or most active users, recent news, blog posts or twitter messages related to BPMN, and more information that can be customized by the user to have a cockpit into the BPMN world.

3   Platform Architecture

The web platform was built with Django, a Python Web framework. As mentioned before, we integrate the Oryx Editor [1], a web modeling tool. The process models are stored in the Oryx data base. They are accessible through HTPP interfaces in various formats, such as ERDF, JSON, PNML (Petri Nets Markup Language), and picture formats. For BPMNCommunity.org we created an API to easily access, navigate and comment models in websites.

To edit a model, users are redirected to the Oryx modeling environment. Upon saving a new model is created and this information is passed back to the

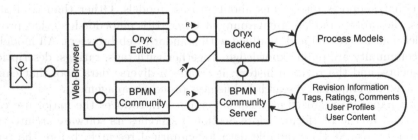

Fig. 1. System architecture of the BPMN Community

community platform. There we manage the revision links, the user profiles and all other content, except for the process models themselves. Figure 1 depicts available information in the community database.

4 Community Data Analysis - An Example

We assume that the data created in the community is interesting to researchers for analysis. As an example, we used the Kettle ETL tool[1] and custom scripts to load and transform the data from the community database into an analysis database. We extracted the models as ERDF and PNML format using existing Oryx web interfaces. This model data can be used to calculate process metrics.

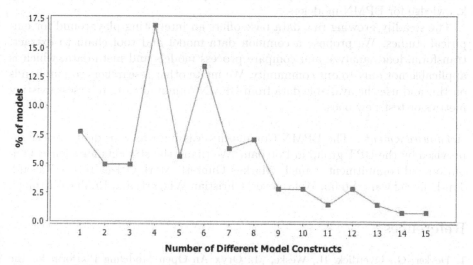

Fig. 2. Syntax Complexity Graph for 166 head revision models (26th of June 2009)

To demonstrate this we created a sample script that counts the number of model elements.Then we replicated Figure 5 from the 2008 paper 'How much language is enough' [3] using the community data, see Figure 2. The other graphics from the same paper can be replicated alike. For sophisticated metrics calculation, we used the PNML exported models and a modified version of ProM [4] that can bulk-process PNML models. This allows us to reuse the existing Petri-Net complexity calculation implementations in the ProM framework yielding metrics such as Density [5] or CFC [6].

These formal metrics could be related to the ratings, comments, revision history and other information given in the community. This is yet to be investigated. As an example, one could relate structural complexity metrics to the number of distinct editors, the editor experience or some kind of editor trust metric. Furthermore, as a process model is a result of a social process, meta-data gathered during the evolutionary development in a community context may prove valuable in a holistic approach to researching the characteristics of process models.

---

[1] http://kettle.pentaho.org

5   Conclusion and Future Directions

This paper introduced BPMNCommunity.org a web platform to learn BPMN, co-create models and discuss them. We outlined the functionality and architecture. We believe that the gathered information is valuable not only for BPMN practitioners but also for empirical research. By example, we showed how data can be accessed and used for calculations.

Within the first two month the platform attracted more than ninety registered users. We aim to expand its reach and get more people involved in the discussions around BPMN modeling. With the new standard revision, BPMN 2.0[7], to be finalized soon we expect even more need for a place to meet, discuss, and develop knowledge for BPMN modelers.

The steadily growing raw data base offers an interesting playground for empirical studies. We propose a common data model and tool chain to extract, transform, load, analyze and compare process models and meta-data, which is applicable not only to our community. We invite other researchers to join hands on this and use the available data from BPMNCommunity.org to assess existing metrics or test new ones.

Acknowledgements. The BPMN Community was built as a student project supervised by the BPT group in Potsdam. We thank the students for their contribution and commitment, namely Markus Güntert, Mark Oelze, Tobias Rawald, Jan-Felix Schwarz, Stefan Wehrmeyer, Christian Wiggert, and Emilia Wittmers.

References

1. Decker, G., Overdick, H., Weske, M.: Oryx–An Open Modeling Platform for the BPM Community. In: Dumas, M., Reichert, M., Shan, M.-C. (eds.) BPM 2008. LNCS, vol. 5240, pp. 382–385. Springer, Heidelberg (2008)
2. Russell, N., Ter Hofstede, A., van der Aalst, W., Mulyar, N.: Workflow control-flow patterns: A revised view. BPM Center Report BPM-06-22, BPMcenter. org, pp. 06–22 (2006)
3. Zur Muehlen, M., Recker, J.: How much language is enough? theoretical and practical use of the business process modeling notation, pp. 465–479
4. van Dongen, B., de Medeiros, A., Verbeek, H., Weijters, A., van der Aalst, W.: The proM framework: A new era in process mining tool support. In: Ciardo, G., Darondeau, P. (eds.) ICATPN 2005. LNCS, vol. 3536, pp. 444–454. Springer, Heidelberg (2005)
5. Mendling, J.: Testing density as a complexity metric for EPCs. In: German EPC workshop on density of process models (2006)
6. Cardoso, J.: Complexity analysis of bpel web processes. Software Process: Improvement and Practice 12(1) (2007)
7. OMG: Business Process Model and Notation (BPMN) Specification 2.0 V.0.9.12 (May 2009)

From ADEPT to AristaFlow BPM Suite:
A Research Vision Has Become Reality

Peter Dadam[1], Manfred Reichert[2], Stefanie Rinderle-Ma[1], Andreas Lanz[1],
Rüdiger Pryss[1], Michael Predeschly[1], Jens Kolb[1], Linh Thao Ly[1],
Martin Jurisch[2], Ulrich Kreher[2], and Kevin Göser[2]

[1] Institute of Databases and Information Systems, University of Ulm, Germany
[2] AristaFlow GmbH, Ulm, Germany

1 Introduction

During the last decade we have developed the ADEPT next generation process
management technology. Its features and its different prototype versions attracted a
number of companies. However, an enterprise cannot base the implementation of its
process-aware information system (PAIS) on an experimental prototype, especially if
maintenance and further development are not assured. At the beginning of 2008,
therefore, we founded a spin-off as joint venture with industrial partners to transfer
ADEPT into an industrial-strength product version called *AristaFlow BPM Suite*, and
to provide maintenance support for it. The product version is now available for
academic and industrial use.

The work done in the ADEPT project on ad-hoc deviations at the process instance
level and process schema evolution has been documented in many research papers,
and is therefore rather well-known. Much less known, however, is another
fundamental aspect of the ADEPT project which significantly influenced and guided
our research work, namely *ease of use*. Although this may sound like the typical lip
service, we consider ease of use as being fundamental for the broad usage of process
management technology in different domains. It needs not only be achieved for end
users, but should be provided to process implementers and application developers as
well. Obviously, ease of use does not come for free; i.e., somebody has "to pay the
price". Supporting ad hoc changes at the process instance level, for example,
requires a profound understanding of basic PAIS concepts as well as deep
knowledge about PAIS internals. If such system-near knowledge is required for
process administrators or application programmers, however, the battle will be lost
before it will have begun.

We all know: "There ain't no such thing as a free lunch." Regarding the user
groups for which ease of use shall be achieved, however, we can observe that one
party is missing: the implementers of the fundamental PAIS technology. When
developing ADEPT we have had one shining example in mind which has enabled
ease of use by hiding complexity beneath the surface: relational database technology.
Our basic belief was that we would be able to achieve a similar effect for PAIS if we
were able to develop the adequate underlying theory. One of our basic challenges was
to develop a technology which supports "correctness by construction" during process
composition and which guarantees correctness in the context of dynamic process
changes. This was probably the most influential challenge for our research activities.

S. Rinderle-Ma et al. (Eds.): BPM 2009 Workshops, LNBIP 43, pp. 529–531, 2010.

It had also significant impact on the development of the AristaFlow BPM Suite. In particular, we had to hide the inherent complexity of process-orientation (especially in conjunction with process flexibility) as far as possible from system administrators and application programmers; i.e., we have to perform all complex things "beneath the surface" in the process management system.

2 Ease of Use Aspects

To speed up process implementation, AristaFlow pursues the idea of process composition in a "plug & play" style supported by comprehensive correctness checks. These checks are accomplished in such a way that runtime errors during process execution can be excluded to a large extent. As prerequisite, implicit data flow and other dependencies among application services, being relevant for their execution order, have to be made known to AristaFlow to be incorporated in the correctness checks. AristaFlow provides an intuitive graphical editor to process implementers, and it applies a *correctness by construction principle* by providing at any time only those operations to the user which allow to transform a structurally correct process schema into another one; i.e., change operations are enabled or disabled according to which region in the process graph is marked for applying the respective operation. Deficiencies not prohibited by this approach (e.g., concerning data flow) are checked on-the-fly and are reported continuously in the problem window of the *Process Template Editor*.

Another goal was to make the assignment of application functions to process steps as simple as possible; i.e., a process implementer should not need to know details about the implementation of these application functions. However, this should not be achieved by undermining the correctness by construction principle. Both goals have been achieved. All kinds of executables, that may be associated with process activities, are first registered in the *Activity Repository* as activity templates. An activity template provides all information to the *Process Template Editor* about mandatory or optional input and output parameters, as well as information about data dependencies to other activity templates. The process implementer just drags and drops an activity template from the *Activity Repository Browser* window of the *Process Template Editor* onto the desired location in the process graph.

A developer who wants to provide a new application function must implement a corresponding activity template and add it to the *Activity Repository*. This way it becomes available and accessible within the *Process Template Editor* during process modelling. To simplify implementation of such activity templates, we support several levels of abstraction. At the lowest one, we provide an *Execution Environment* for each kind of supported basic operation; e.g., AristaFlow offers execution environments for SQL statements, web services, EXE files, BeanShell scripts, basic file operations, and system-generated forms. Based on them one can rather easily develop customized activity templates for specific purposes like, for example, retrieving a set of tuples from the database which satisfy a certain predicate.

Enabling ease of use for end users is mainly the task of application developers. They decide how "manual" process activities interact with the end user. They also decide whether the standard workflow client is used or whether a dedicated one shall be provided. An important prerequisite for realizing adapted user interfaces is to provide the appropriate methods to the application developer; e.g., to enable him to realize end user interactions in the context of ad-hoc changes. To implement clients with such capabilities, the application developer can make use of the powerful system functions provided by the AristaFlow API. To move, for example, an activity to another position within the process graph is rather simple to implement: After having identified an activity x to be moved, the application receives a list of activities *after* which x could be inserted. Having selected one or more activities, it receives a list of activities *before* which x could be completed. After having selected one or more activities from that list, the AristaFlow system will execute the operation "insert between node sets". That's it!

3 The AristaFlow Community Platform

Due to its "correctness by construction" principle, AristaFlow is ideally suited to teach the implementation of PAIS because one can very quickly compose robustly executable processes. AristaFlow supports also rapid prototyping of PAIS. One can at first, for example, only model the control and data flow among activities, and not assign any "executables" to them. Nevertheless, the process becomes already test-wise executable, because the *AristaFlow TestClient* will automatically assign forms to them so that one gets already a rather realistic impression how the final process will look like. Also the idea of service-oriented process development is very easy to communicate due to the plug & play style outlined above as well as the provided repository services.

We, therefore, have established a community platform to support the utilization of the AristaFlow BPM suite in higher level education and research projects. The intention is that users (including ourselves) help other users in using the system in these areas but providing, e.g., sample processes, auxiliary activity templates, organization models, auxiliary tools, and share experiences.

For an extended version of this paper see:
Dadam, Peter and Reichert, Manfred (2009) The ADEPT Project: A Decade of Research and Development for Robust and Flexible Process Support - Challenges and Achievements. Springer, Computer Science - Research and Development, Vol. 23, No. 2, pp. 81-97

For further information please visit the following web sites:
    www.AristaFlow-Forum.de − for the community platform
    www.AristaFlow.com   − for obtaining the AristaFlow BPM Suite
    www.uni-ulm.de/dbis   − for information on our research activities

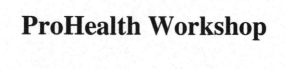

ProHealth Workshop

Introduction to the Third International Workshop on Process-Oriented Information Systems in Healthcare (ProHealth 2009)

Healthcare organizations and providers are facing the challenge of delivering high quality services to their patients, at affordable costs. High degree of specialization of medical disciplines, prolonged medical care for the ageing population, increased costs for dealing with chronic diseases, and the need for personalized healthcare are prevalent trends in this information-intensive domain. The emerging situation necessitates a change in the way healthcare is delivered to the patients and healthcare processes are managed.

BPM technology provides a key to implement these changes. Though patient-centered process support becomes increasingly crucial in healthcare, BPM technology has not yet been broadly used in healthcare environments. This workshop shall elaborate both the potential and the limitations of IT support for healthcare processes. It shall further provide a forum wherein challenges, paradigms, and tools for optimized process support in healthcare can be debated. We want to bring together researchers and practitioners from different communities (e.g., BPM, Information Systems, Medical Informatics, E-Health) who share an interest in both healthcare processes and BPM technologies.

The success of the first two ProHealth Workshops, which were held in conjunction with the 5th and 6th International Conferences on Business Process Management (BPM'07 and BPM'08), demonstrated the potential of such an interdisciplinary forum to improve the understanding of domain specific requirements, methods and theories, tools and techniques, and the gaps between IT support and healthcare processes that are yet to be closed.

The 3d International Workshop on Process-oriented information systems in healthcare (ProHealth '09) was held in Ulm in conjunction with the 7th Int'l Conf. on Business Process Management (BPM 2009) dealt with different facets of process-oriented healthcare information systems, and gave insights into the social and technological challenges, applications, and perspectives emerging for BPM in this context.

Enterprise-wide process-oriented information systems have been demanded by healthcare institutions for over 20 years and terms like "continuity of care" have even been discussed for over 50 years. Yet, healthcare organizations are currently using a plethora of specialized nonstandard information systems and continue to focus on development of systems for specialized departments that frequently only focus on their internal processes. Many of the successful existing information systems focus on non-process oriented systems, such as imaging, drug order-entry, laboratory test result storage, storage of diagnoses and progress notes in electronic medical records, alerts and reminders, and billing applications.

Information systems and decision-support systems for managing *patient care processes*, however, are still scarcely developed; most often only by a small number of university-led teams. Such patient care management systems are highly complex

S. Rinderle-Ma et al. (Eds.): BPM 2009 Workshops, LNBIP 43, pp. 535–538, 2010.
© Springer-Verlag Berlin Heidelberg 2010

and pose many challenges: they require availability of encoded data coming from different sources, flexibility in deviating from the encoded process at the discretion of the physician user, and may involve a team of clinical users that together take care of a patient in a coordinated way.

The recent trend towards healthcare networks and integrated care even increases the need to effectively support interdisciplinary cooperation along with the patient treatment process. Recent studies discussing the preventability of adverse events in medicine recommend the use of information technology, since insufficient communication and missing information turned out to be among the major factors contributing to adverse events. Yet, there is still a discrepancy between the potential and the actual usage of IT in healthcare.

The ProHealth 2009 workshop focused on IT support of high-quality healthcare processes. IT addressed topics included the modeling of healthcare processes, process-oriented system architectures in healthcare, workflow management in healthcare, IT support for guideline implementation and medical decision support, flexibility in healthcare processes, process interoperability in healthcare and healthcare standards, clinical semantics of healthcare processes, healthcare process patterns, best practices for design of healthcare processes, healthcare process validation, verification, and evaluation.

The workshop received 21 papers from Germany (6), The Netherlands (3), Austrai (2), Norway (2), The United States (2), Canada (1), Denmark (1), Israel (1), Italy (1), Portugal (1), Spain (1), and Switzerland (1). Three modalities of papers were allowed: full length papers describing either advanced or finished works, position papers introducing works with preliminary promising results, and tool reports. Papers had to clearly establish their research contribution as well as their relation to healthcare processes. Eleven papers (8 full length papers, 2 position papers, and 1 tool report) were selected and presented in the workshop according to their relevance, quality, and originality.

In his keynote paper "A hybrid multi-layered approach to the integration of Workflow and Clinical Guideline approaches", Prof. Paolo Terenziani from the Informatics Department, University degli Studi di Torino suggests using a hybrid approach in which a computer-interpretable guideline approach is used to focus on "physician-oriented" issues, a Workflow approach is used to cope with the related "business-oriented" issues, and the integration of them is obtained at the underlying semantic level (modeled using Petri Nets), where also general inferential mechanisms operate.

The following four papers focus on utilizing clinical semantics for IT support. The paper entitled "Learning the Context of a Clinical Process" by Johny Ghattas, Mor Peleg, Pnina Soffer and Yaron Denekamp propose an approach which helps with identifying and categorizing the clinical contexts that need to be taken into account within a clinical care process. In their two papers "A Light-Weight System Extension Supporting Document-based Processes in Healthcare" and "alpha-Flow: A Document-based Approach to Inter-Institutional Process Support in Healthcare", Christoph P. Neumann and Richard Lenz target document-based process support in healthcare. The first paper by these authors advocates the application the classic diagnostic-therapeuthic cycle as the model for a document-oriented information exchange allows to foster inter-institutional information exchange in healthcare. The α-Flow approach adopts electronic documents as the primary means of information exchange, suggesting a paradigm wherein workflow schemas are represented as documents that can be shared. The paper entitled "An Approach for Managing Clinical Trial Applications using Semantic Information Models" by Hans-Georg Fill and Ilona Reischl presents a modeling approach based on semantic information models that supports the management of clinical trial applications including the generation of user-centric visualizations, performance and compliance analyses and the distribution of the contained knowledge within an organization and to third parties.

The next three papers focus on healhcare process design and quality assessment. Teh paper entitled "Workflow for Healthcare: A Methodology for Realizing Flexible Medical Treatment Processes" by Nick Russell, Hajo Reijers, Simone Van der Geer and Gertruud Krekel presents a methodology for realizing processes that possess the required degree of flexibility that makes them suitable for the healthcare domain. To demonstrate the methodology's feasibility, it is applied to the processes that are found in a Dutch outpatient clinic. The paper entitled "BPR Best Practices for the Healthcare Domain" by Mariska Netjes, Ronny Mans, Hajo Reijers and Wil van der Aalst present a list of historically successful improvement tactics, the BPR best practices, and via an analysis of 14 case studies argue that thes practices are a highly suitable to optimize healthcare processes more effeciently and in a more patient-focused way. In the paper entitled "User-oriented Quality Assessment of IT-supported Healthcare Processes – a Position Paper" Elske Ammenwerth, Ruth Breu and Barbara Paech provides a first collection of process quality indicators that capture the user view of the quality of IT-supported health care processes.

The last three papers focus on verification and testing of healthcare process models. The paper entitled "Verification of Careflow Management Systems with Timed BDI-CTL Logic" by Keith Miller and Wendy MacCaull presents a prototype next-generation multi-threaded model checker to reason about timed processes in careflows sensitive to patient preferences and the goals of the care team using a temporal logic extended with modalities of beliefs, desires and intentions. The paper entitled "Process-Aware Information System Development for the Healthcare Domain - Consistency, Reliability, and Effectiveness" by R.S. Mans, Wil van der Aalst, Nick Russell, Piet Bakker and Arnold Moleman proposes an approach in which the same model is used for specifying, developing, testing and validating the operational performance of a new system. This approach has been applied to a schedule-based workflow system developed for the AMC hospital in Amsterdam. The tool report entitled "An Integrated Collection of Tools for Continuously Improving the Processes by Which Health Care is Delivered: A Tool Report" by Leon Osterweil, Lori Clarke and George Avrunin presents an integrated collection of tools that supports the precise definition, careful analysis, and execution of processes that coordinate the actions of humans, automated devices, and software systems for the delivery of health care. It is intended to support the continuous improvement of health care delivery processes.

We would like to thank the invited speaker as well as the members of the Program Committee and the reviewers for their efforts in selecting the papers (in alphabetical order): Wil van der Aalst, Elske Ammenwerth, Joseph Barjis, Oliver Bott, Dominic

Covvey, Stefan Jablonski, Silvia Miksch, Bela Mutschler, Øystein Nytrø, Silvana Quaglini, Manfred Reichert, Hajo Reijers, Danielle Sent, Yuval Shahar, Ton Spil, Annette ten Teije, Paolo Terneziani, Lucineia Thom, Samson Tu, Dongwen Wang, and Barbara Weber. They helped us to compile a high-quality program for the ProHealth 2009 workshop. We would also like to acknowledge the splendid support of the local organization and the BPM 2009 Workshop Chairs.

We hope you will find the papers of the ProHealth 2007 workshop interesting and stimulating.

September 2009

Mor Peleg
Richard Lenz
Paul de Clercq

A Hybrid Multi-layered Approach to the Integration of Workflow and Clinical Guideline Approaches

Paolo Terenziani

Dipartimento di Informatica, Univ. Piemonte Orientale "A. Avogadro", Italy
terenz@mfn.unipmn.it

Abstract. In BPM, several formalisms have been proposed to model Workflows. Almost independently, several formalisms have been developed to model clinical practice guidelines (CPG). Since the increasing informatization of healthcare processes is demanding for an integrated treatment of medical activities, some approaches have started to fill the gap between the Workflow and CPG areas. In most cases, such approaches have tried to adapt and/or extend one of the formalisms (either a Workflow or a CPG formalism) in order to cope with the whole set of phenomena. In this position paper, we argue in favor of an alternative hybrid approach, in which a CPG approach is used to focus on "physician-oriented" issues, a Workflow approach is used to cope with the related "business-oriented" issues, and the integration of them is obtained at the underlying semantic level, where general inferential mechanisms operate.

Keywords: Clinical Practice Guidelines, Workflows, Integration.

1 Introduction

This position paper sketches the viewpoint of the author about how research in the domains of BPM (and, specifically, in Workflow management) and CPG could impact each other in the medical informatics context. This paper is not aimed to enter into any specific technical issue. Instead, it argues in favor of a new position regarding the integration of Workflow and CPG approaches to cope with clinical guidelines and their execution environment. The author and his group have already obtained some preliminary results along the line of research proposed in this paper (see [1]), but, due to space constraints, such technical results are not reported here.

There is a growing consciousness of the advantages of providing computer support to healthcare processes [2]. Different perspectives have been followed by current approaches. In the Workflow context, the focus is mostly on the flow of operations that describe the organizational structure, and/or on resources (i.e., on *organizational processes* [2]). In many cases, the goal is to model the organization of activities, in order to analyze and improve them (e.g., to discover and remove bottlenecks). In this sense, a workflow model of hospital activities can be

S. Rinderle-Ma et al. (Eds.): BPM 2009 Workshops, LNBIP 43, pp. 539–544, 2010.

seen as the representation of such activities from the viewpoint of a manager, or of an analyst. On the other hand, CPGs can be roughly defined as frameworks for specifying the best clinical procedures (i.e., *medical treatment processes* [2]) and for standardizing them. CPGs are mostly aimed at providing user-physicians the recommendations of *evidence-based* medicine, usually providing support for therapeutic and diagnostic decisions. In this sense, CPGs reflect the viewpoint of a specific physician, dealing with a given patient affected by a given disease (the one coped with by the CPG). Physicians only want to focus on such clinical procedures, so that an integrated model coping with both evidence-based guidelines and organizational processes is likely not to be accepted/used by them. In summary, it seems to us that Workflows and CPGs, when applied to the health-care domain, act as *complementary* frameworks looking at different aspects of the same reality, and having different focuses and purposes.

Both in the area of Workflow Management and CPG, many different formalisms and management approaches have been developed in the last two decades or so. Recently, a structured survey of the state of the art in CPG research has been proposed in [3]. On the other hand, van der Aalst et al. have proposed an extensive analysis of Workflow patterns proposed in the literature [4]. In past years, several CPG formalisms have been tested to model also the organization of processes in a hospital. More recently, the capability of several CPG formalisms to express control-flow patters has been analysed considering typical workflow patterns, and the declarative language CIGDec, which is deeply rooted in the Workflow tradition, has been proposed to enhance their expressiveness and flexibility [5]. Other approaches have been proposed to make Workflows more data-oriented, declarative, and/or adaptive (consider, e.g., [6]). In this position paper, we focus on the knowledge representation and reasoning issues, suggesting that an alternative way of integrating the contributions of CPG and Workflow areas can be investigated.

2   Preliminaries: Parameters to Choose a Representation Formalism

Our viewpoint originates from the consideration that, although important, *expressiveness is not at all the only parameter that should be used in order to evaluate a formalism*, or an approach. Indeed, in a computer, everything finally turns out to be expressed by binary code. Thus, if expressiveness would be the only worth criteria, programmers and computer scientists would still work using just binary code! And most of the work done in Computer Science (e.g., to design high-level programming languages or data/knowledge representation formalisms) would we worthless or vain! But, hopefully, this is not the case. This fact means that other parameters, different from expressiveness, have motivated the work of the Computer Science area, and must be used in order to evaluate formalisms and approaches. Three of such parameters are particularly relevant to support our point of view:

1. **User-oriented.** There is a large variety of formalisms in Computer Science, ranging from formalisms for "technical" users (e.g., programming languages), which can only be used by specialists, to formalisms for "naïve" (with respect to Computer Science) users, intended to be used by non-specialists. Anyway, it is always important to remember that formalisms have, indeed, to be used. Thus, each formalism has to fit the expectations of its potential users.

2. **Domain/goal-oriented.** There are quite general formalisms (e.g., logics), and domain or goal-oriented ones. Specifically, both CPG and Workflow formalisms can be regarded as Domain/Goal oriented formalisms, since they are deliberately suited to model a specific range of phenomena (by the way, notice that, in some cases, some degree of expressiveness may be deliberately lost in domain/goal-oriented languages, simply because it is not needed for the specific domain/goal).

3. **Inference and Semantics.** In Computer Science, formal languages are usually equipped with inferential mechanisms operating on them. Indeed, representation without inference is, in several cases, quite useless (for instance, inference is needed to discover whether a knowledge base or a domain model is inconsistent). And such inferential mechanisms should operate on (or, at least, must be consistent with) the semantics of the formalisms. Needless to say, in most cases there is a trade-off between the expressiveness of formalisms and the computational complexity of inferential mechanisms operating on them.

It is important to stress that the above parameters are not independent of each other. Even worst, they seem to be *in contrast* which each other! As a matter of fact, from the point of view of users, "naïve" (more user-oriented) and domain/goal-oriented languages are preferable, since they support the users' view of the phenomena to be modeled, and make the task of modeling the application domain/goals easier. On the other hand, from the point of view of the inferences, more "technical" and "general" languages (e.g., logics) are usually more suited.

3 Integrating Workflow and CPG Approaches

Now, let us contextualize the above general discussion to the problem at hand. First, let us consider only the parameters (1) and (2) above. Workflow and CPG formalisms are, in our viewpoint, formalisms for generally "naïve" users. This is particularly true for CPG formalisms, that have to be used by physicians. And, obviously, both are quite domain and task oriented, since they have been deliberately designed in order to easily capture specific aspects of reality. Going into the detail of what can be represented and how in each formalism is obviously outside the goals of this position paper. But, given the above discussion, it seems uncontestable to us that:

- **CPG formalisms are the best suited formalisms to cope with clinical guidelines in a "physician-oriented" way.** The way CPGs are modeled in such formalisms is, in most cases, as close as possible to the way physicians are used to look at them. Notice that, for instance, physicians usually want to neglect as much as possible problems such as resource management, laboratory examination scheduling, personnel and resource scheduling, and so on. Physicians want to just focus on the diagnostic and therapeutic treatment of the specific patient at hand. And this is exactly what CPG formalisms and tools are aimed to provide them, with a specific focus on modeling and supporting diagnostic and therapeutic decisions.

– **Workflow formalisms are the best suited formalisms to cope with organizational processes.** They usually want to capture the workflow of processes in an organization (e.g., in the hospital, or in a department of the hospital), and are used to analyze and optimize it. They are biased toward different intended users with respect to CPG formalisms. Analysts and managers can take advantage of them in order, e.g., to identify and eliminate bottlenecks, or to optimize the overall throughput of the organization. On the other hand, problems related to, e.g., diagnostic decisions are mostly out of scope in this context.

Does this mean that, in our viewpoint, CPG and Workflow formalisms/approaches must be independent and unrelated areas of work? The answer is no, and the reason roots back in the consideration of the parameter (3) above: inferences. Suppose that our goal is that of modeling both CPGs and their execution environment (e.g., a hospital). I.e., one is interested in modeling both the diagnostic and the therapeutic treatments of patients, and the personnel and laboratory resources and activities in the hospital in which guidelines are executed. In short, one aims at modeling the "whole" activities in a hospital (or hospital department). Hopefully, such modeling is not just a theoretical exercise, but it is aimed, e.g., to discover the feasibility and cost of activities and/or bottlenecks, or to optimize the resource allocation, and so on. All such tasks require performing inferences on the represented model(s). And, as discussed above, inferences are based on the semantics of the models themselves. Thus, in our opinion, **inference and semantics are the bridge where the CPG and Workflow approaches may meet**. In other words, we advocate the approach graphically shown in Figure 1 (which is the abstract architecture of the system we aim at developing in our future work). In Figure 1, a Workflow approach is used to model and cope with "business oriented" aspects of the problem (the guideline "execution environment"); a CPG approach is used to cope with clinical guidelines; both models are mapped onto a common semantic representation, and inferences are performed at the semantic level. Specifically, we think that Petri Nets (and their extensions) are very good candidates to cope with both Workflow and CPG formalisms, and to provide suitable and efficient inferential mechanisms. As a matter of fact, Petri Nets constitute the underlying semantics of several Workflow formalisms (consider, e.g., [7]), and, recently, they have been also used in order to model the semantics of CPGs [1,8]. Last, but not least, they provide composition as a primitive operation, which is a crucial one for achieving the goal of integrating the semantics of the Workflow and CPG models into a unique overall semantic model. Of course, different families of Petri Nets are

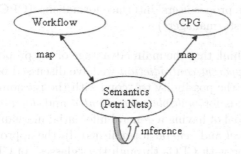

Fig. 1. A hybrid multi-layered approach integrating Workflow and CPG

available, and the problem of choosing the one best suited to the above goal is not a trivial one. In particular, we think that Well-formed Net [9] are well suited, since they can provide a more compact and readable representation of the system, and the possibility of using efficient solution techniques.

4   Concluding Remarks

To conclude, it is worth to point out some of the most critical issues in the realization of the proposed approach (which highlights open problems for future research), and some of its merits (at least from our viewpoint).

- **Modeling complex aspects.** Expressiveness is not the only issue, but it is a major one. For instance, CPGs usually contain complex qualitative and quantitative temporal constraints between actions, including periodicity or repetition constraints (see, e.g., [10]), for which specific extensions of the basic Petri Net models are needed (e.g., Timed Petri Nets [11]).
- **Composition.** The task of integrating the (translation into Petri Nets of the) model of the physician activities in the CPG with the (translation into Petri Nets of the) model of the organizational activities in the hospital provided in the Workflow model is not trivial at all. Common processes must be identified, as well as overlaps, and refinements. The adoption of a common vocabulary/ontology by both the knowledge engineers building the CPG and the Workflow model, is, in our opinion, just a first crucial step in order to make this difficult task feasible.
- **Scalability.** In real hospitals (hospital departments), hundreds of guidelines can be concurrently executed on patients. The dimension of the resulting Petri Net, modeling the hospital daily activities, is likely to rise temporal complexity problems for the underlying inferential mechanism.
- **User-oriented output.** The architecture sketched in Figure 1 is aimed to allow each user (physician or manager/analyst) to look at the phenomena through her/his preferred "glasses". However, in order to consistently support such a goal, one should also transform the output of the inferential mechanism (which is provided at the internal leyer, i.e., at the level of

Petri Nets) into the proper users' interface formalisms (CPG for physicians, Workflow for analysts/managers).

As regards merits, we think that the main advantage of the proposed approach is that it *reconciles the apparent contradiction* we have discussed between the goal of providing users with the possibility to "cope with the phenomena as they are used to" (which demands for *multiple user-oriented* and *domain /task-oriented* approaches), and the goal of having a general inferential mechanisms (which demands for more *technical* and *general* formalisms). In the approach we suggest, physicians can still cope with CPGs through the "glasses" of CPG approaches, analysts and managers can look at organization processes and resources with the "glasses" provided by Workflow approaches, and nevertheless general inferential mechanisms can be provided on the integration of the whole knowledge. We thus propose an approach in which the best features of CPG, Workflow and Petri Nets approaches are grasped and merged together, for the sake of providing a **(multiple-)user-oriented approach with a strong semantics and enhanced inferential capabilities**.

References

1. Beccuti, M., Bottrighi, A., Franceschinis, G., Montani, S., Terenziani, P.: Modeling and verifying clinical guidelines through Petri Nets. In: Combi, C., Shahar, Y., Abu-Hanna, A. (eds.) Artificial Intelligence in Medicine. LNCS, vol. 5651, pp. 61–70. Springer, Heidelberg (2009)
2. Lenz, R., Reicher, M.: IT support for healthcare processes - premises, challenges, perspectives. Data & Knowledge Engineering 61, 39–58 (2007)
3. Ten Teije, A., Miksch, S., Lucas, P.: Computer-based Medical Guidelines and Protocols: A Primer and Current Trends. Studies in Health Technology and Informatics, vol. 139 (2008) ISBN: 978-1-58603-873-1
4. van der Aalst, W.M.P., ter Hofstede, A.H.M., Kiepuszewski, B., Barros, A.P.: Workflow Patterns. Distributed and Parallel Databases 14(3), 5–51 (2003)
5. Mulyar, N., Pesic, M., van der Aalst, W.M.P., Peleg, M.: Towards the Flexibility in Clinical Guideline Modelling Languages. BPM Center Report BPM-07-04, BPMcenter.org (2007)
6. Rinderle, S., Rreicher, M., Dadam, P.: Flexible support of team processes by adaptive workflow systems. Distributed Parallel Databases 16(1), 91–116 (2004)
7. van der Aalst, W.M.P.: The Application of Petri Nets to Workflow Management. The Journal of Circuits, Systems and Computers 8(1), 21–66 (1998)
8. Peleg, M., Tu, S., Manindroo, A., Altman, R.B.: Modeling and analyzing biomedical processes using workflow/petri net models and tools. In: Proc. MedInfo., pp. 74–78 (2004)
9. Chiola, G., Dutheillet, C., Franceschinis, G., Haddad, S.: Stochastic Well-formed Coloured nets for symmetric modelling applications. IEEE Transactions on Computers 42(11), 1343–1360 (1993)
10. Terenziani, P., German, E., Shahar, Y.: The temporal aspects of clinical guidelines. In: [3], pp. 81–100 (2008)
11. Vicario, E.: Static Analysis and Dynamic Steering of Time-Dependent Systems. IEEE Trans. on Software Engineering 27(8), 728–748 (2001)

Learning the Context of a Clinical Process

Johny Ghattas[1], Mor Peleg[1,2], Pnina Soffer[1], and Yaron Denekamp[3]

[1] Department of Management Information Systems, University of Haifa, Israel, 31905
[2] Center of Biomedical Informatics, Stanford University, Stanford, CA, 94305
[3] Carmel Medical Center, Haifa, Israel
GhattasJohny@gmail.com, {morpeleg,pnina}@mis.hevra.haifa.ac.il,
Yarondp@clalit.org.il

Abstract. Clinical guidelines provide recommendations to assist clinicians in making decisions regarding appropriate medical care for specific patient situations. However, characterizing these situations is difficult as it requires taking into account all the variations that patients may present. We propose an approach which helps with identifying and categorizing the contexts that need to be taken into account within a clinical process. Our methodology is based on a formal process model and on a collection of process execution instances. We apply machine-learning algorithms to group process instances by similarity of their paths and outcomes and derive the contextual properties of each group. We illustrate the application of our methodology to a urinary tract infection management process. Our approach yields promising results with high accuracy for some of the context groups that were identified.

Keywords: Clinical guidelines, context, business process learning, process goals, soft-goals, process model adaptation, flexibility.

1 Introduction

Clinical guidelines are systematically developed statements to assist practitioner and patient decision making about appropriate health care for specific clinical circumstances [1]. They aim to improve patient care, limit unjustified treatment variation, and reduce costs. However, a clinical guideline cannot possibly address the variations in patient populations that occur in different healthcare institutions who try to apply the guideline. For example, the guideline may recommend that a certain conventional antibiotic should be given to patients with urinary tract infection (UTI) but that for patients who are resistant to the antibiotic (i.e., the pathogens which caused UTI in the patient are resistant to the antibiotic), a different antibiotic should be provided. Since giving a patient a non-effective treatment has many risks, in particular, that the patient's condition would deteriorate, the goal is to know under what context a patient is likely to be resistant to the conventional antibiotic. Guidelines often leave the conditions under which a patient is likely to be resistant to antibiotic undefined.

In this paper we propose to learn the different contexts relevant to UTI treatment in a local hospital, by mining electronic healthcare records (EHRs) of UTI patients. To

S. Rinderle-Ma et al. (Eds.): BPM 2009 Workshops, LNBIP 43, pp. 545–556, 2010.
© Springer-Verlag Berlin Heidelberg 2010

this end, we apply a context based process learning methodology which we have developed. We postulate that the context [2, 3] of a process, namely, information about the properties and environmental events of each medical case, affect the process' execution and outcomes. However, the significant affecting variables and their effect are not necessarily known. Our approach aims at categorizing possible environmental conditions and case properties into context categories which are meaningful for the process execution. The context learning algorithm is part of a business process learning framework that we are developing, in which the best path would be proposed for each context group.

The remainder of the paper is structured as follows. Section 2 explains what a clinical context is and provides the motivation for the context learning framework. Section 3 describes our context learning framework and section 4 illustrates the application of context learning to a clinical process - the Urinary tract infection management process. Finally Section 5 discusses the implications of the model and compares it to models proposed in the past that have some similarity to our model.

2 Clinical Contexts

Clinical processes (anamnesis, diagnosis, treatment) highly depend on the characteristics of each patient as well as on environmental conditions (e.g., availability of medical equipment and expertise in a healthcare facility).

Clearly, different contextual conditions should be handled by different paths for the process to achieve its goals. To facilitate this, three main challenges need to be met. First, normally there is no obvious way to establish a full repository of all possible context variations that are yet to appear. Second, while it is possible to have information about an (almost) unlimited amount of case properties, we should be able to identify which specific properties have an effect on the process. Third, medical organizations need to know how to select their process paths per each one of these situations in order to achieve the best outcome.

In this work, we focus on the second challenge and demonstrate via a case study of a UTI process the application of a context-learning framework that we developed. Context groups cluster together process instances that at the same time have similar path and outcome and can be grouped by sets of shared contextual properties, thereby limiting the number of context variations to be dealt with. This can be a first step towards defining process paths for each context group, such that taking that path would lead to desired process outcomes (goals). For this purpose, we target an active process, namely, a process which has already been executed for a while, and acquired past execution data. Our basic assumption is that in these past executions, some cases were addressed "properly" according to their relevant contextual properties (although a relation between context and path selection was not necessarily formally specified). Other cases were not properly addressed, and this should be reflected in the performance achieved by the process for these cases, which should be lower when compared to the properly addressed cases. Hence, the proposed methodology is based on clustering process instance data of past executions, relating to their context, path, and outcomes.

3 An Approach for Learning Context Groups of Business Processes

In this section, we briefly describe our context learning framework [4].

A business process instance (PI) is completely defined given its context, path, and attained termination state (goal or exception). In addition, our initial knowledge of the business process model provides us with the criteria necessary to identify when we reach our goal or when the process terminates in an exception. The information of the business process model and its execution data enable us to learn the relevant context groups. In this paper, we consider only goal states as outcomes, and not exceptions.

However, it is not uncommon *not* to have a completely defined process model or complete contextual information of the recorded process instances. Our context learning approach can use partial knowledge of the process model and approximate similarity measurements of different process instances.

Rather than estimating the similarity of paths separately from the similarity of outcomes, we apply machine learning algorithms to existing path and goal state data together. We developed a clustering strategy constructed of the following stages.

(1) We partition our process instances based on existing domain knowledge. For example, existing UTI guidelines partition patients into populations that depend on age, gender, catheter usage, etc.
(2) We estimate the similarity between all process instance paths and goal states, establishing a measure of the similarity of these instances, and grouping them into clusters. Technically, this is done by representing the process instance path and outcome data as vectors of values of state variables and using a clustering algorithm, to find clusters based on vector proximity. Then we use feature selection to omit state variables that are not important for determining the clusters.
(3) Once the clusters of PIs (PICs) have been identified, we apply supervised-learning algorithms (algorithms that build decision trees and prune them) to determine the meaning of the context groups that correspond to these groups. To do so, we focus only on the context information of the PIs of each PIC and express the meaning of the corresponding context group as a logical condition over the set of context variables. The context groups learning procedure is schematically shown in Figure 1.

4 Context Group Learning in Urinary Tract Infection (UTI) Management Process

We apply the context learning framework to a clinical process dealing with urinary tract infection (UTI) patients.

4.1 UTI- A Brief Overview

Different healthcare organizations have developed their own guidelines for diagnosing and managing UTI. These guidelines indicate different care paths for different partitions of the population, partitioned by age, gender, and other conditions,

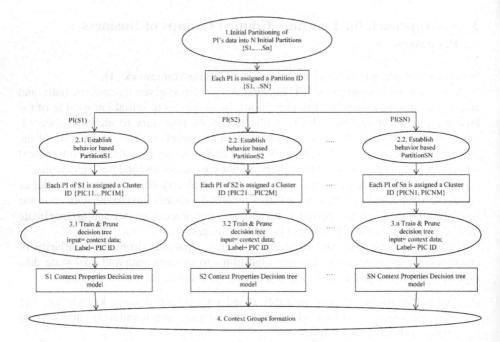

Fig. 1. Architecture of the context groups learning algorithm. PI- process instance; S- Initial partition.

including the use of catheters and existence of complications related to arterial, heart and kidney diseases, and diabetes mellitus. The most important partition is the one concerning elderly women, which constitute more than two thirds of the impacted population.

4.2 UTI Process Instances and Context Data

The data for our case study was collected at a general internal medicine department in Carmel Medical Center, Haifa, Israel, and includes 297 patient records. Most patients in our database are elderly persons (above 50 years old), who arrived first at the emergency room, where they were diagnosed as potentially having UTI. Then they were admitted into the general internal medicine department. Most of the context data is known from the medical record of the patient (either electronically (EHR) or paper-based) and is further collected from the patient as a first step of the process. This step is known as "anamnesis". In it, the physician questions the patient to identify chronic illnesses, medications that the patient is taking for other conditions, symptoms he is having, whether UTI is a recurring problem, historical illnesses related to UTI (such as calculi existence, reflux problems, kidney problems, etc.), general test results (urinalysis), and physical examination results. A partial list of context data includes: (1) age, (2) gender, (3) race, (4) vital signs, such as fever, blood pressure, and heart rate, (5) symptoms, (6) physical examination results, (7) chronic illnesses, such as diabetes mellitus (DM), hypertension (HTN), coronary arterial disease (CAD), congestive heart failure (CHF), cancer/hematological disorder, chronic pulmonary disease (CPD), chronic renal failure (CRF), cerebro-vascular disease (CVD), (8) medications, such as beta-blockers (BB), (9) previous UTI, (10) existence of a permanent catheter, (11) general mental and overall state of the patient, (12) whether UTI was acquired in the hospital, and (13) residence (e.g., nursing home).

Following the anamnesis and physical examination, the patient is diagnosed. Several diagnoses may be given and registered in the medical record; we consider up to ten different diagnoses, which impact the further diagnosis and treatment of UTI, including, among others, fever, hypertension, chronic renal failure, depression, anxiety, and pneumonia.

Following the initial diagnosis, initial treatment may be provided (e.g., antibiotics or other medications) and additional tests may be ordered to further diagnose the patient's condition and evaluate the expected outcomes (prognosis). Tests may include urine culture tests, ultrasound, prostate examination for men, etc. The tests depend on the patient's context. The test results may arrive several days after the patient has been initially diagnosed and has undergone initial treatment. After the test results become available, the treatment may be changed and additional tests may be ordered.

Hence, the main activities in the UTI management process path and the main outcome state variables that we expect to be reflected in the patients' records include the following 6 data items: (1) the ten diagnosis terms (mentioned above), (2) initial treatment (with 27 kinds of antibiotics), (3) three categories of medical tests (urine culture, blood tests, ultrasound), (4) modified treatment (after test results return), (5) additional tests ordered after treatment has been modified (three possible tests), and (6) four possibilities of final status: death, cured, partially cured, follow up needed by other specialists. A partial sample of path data is provided in Table 1.

Table 1. Path data structure

Process instance ID	253467
Initial Treatment	< Augmentin>
Diagnosis	<CVD, CRF, UTI>
Urine Culture test results	<...>(1 field for each measure), <ESBL+= Y>
Blood test results	<...> (1 field for each measure)
Ultra sound	<OK>
Modified treatment	< ZINACEF>
Additional tests	<<CT, OK>, <ESBL, +>
Final Patient status	<Partially cured- require home care >

4.3 Establishing Context Groups for the UTI Data

Different patients may have different initial conditions, such as different symptoms and different chronic illnesses. Hence, the UTI diagnosis and treatment process may vary from one patient to another. The question we are trying to answer using our context learning framework is: can we group patients' data into context groups in such a way that consistent outcomes are achieved for a defined set of process paths for each group?

We describe how our context learning algorithm follows the three steps defined in Section 3 for the UTI case.

Step 1: Initial partitioning of context data. We partition the data based on different populations addressed in UTI clinical guidelines. Through a review of existing guidelines, we saw that UTI guidelines distinguish between the following partitions: (1) New born; (2) Children; (3) Pregnant women; (4) Young women; and (5) Elderly Men and women. Some guidelines distinguish between patients with permanent catheters and without catheters. Since most of the patients in our database are elderly men and women (above 50 years old) we will focus on analyzing partition #5.

Step 2: For the 297 patients, we recoded the process activities (e.g., medications, tests, procedures, diagnosis) and outcome state variables discussed in Section 4.2. Using a modification of the two-step clustering offered as part of the SPSS package [5], we clustered process instances (PIs) according to similar path and outcome data and assigned each PI to a PIC ID. To find a set of clusters that achieves good clustering results, we generated 15 cluster sets, consisting of 1 to 15 clusters, respectively. Using the Akaike information criterion (AIC) [6] as a measure of the goodness of fit of an estimated statistical model and is grounded in the concept of entropy, we identified the set of clusters that achieves the best results. The best cluster set partitioned the 297 samples into five clusters (PIC1 through ...PIC5) of size 54, 27, 51, 80, and 85 samples, respectively.

After the process instance data was clustered, we used the chi-square statistical test as a method for feature selection. Using the chi-square statistic, we analyzed the significance of each variable to each one of the five clusters in order to omit from the cluster features that are non-significant. For example, the variable "Urinary Cancer" is most significant for Cluster #3 but could be omitted from the context variables of the rest of the clusters. The variable "Renal Failure not including CRF" is highly significant for Cluster #2 and #3, but could be omitted from the context variables of clusters #1, #4, #5. Performing feature selection for each one of the variables reduced the number of variables representing the clusters' context by an average of 20 %.

Step 3: We partitioned the context variables of the PIs into 35 variables, categorizing the values of each variable into discrete ranges of values that would be significant for a medical expert. For example, the age was partitioned into the following ranges: 45-55, 55-65, 65-75, 75-85, 85-90 and 95-105 years. Based on the context data of the PIs clustered in each cluster, we used a modified Chi-squared Automatic Interaction Detection (CHAID) growing decision tree algorithm [7] to construct the decision tree that represents the context groups and their relationships (see Figure 2). We provide CHAID with the context data of the PIs and with the PIC ID of each PI, which was deduced in step 2 according to the path and outcome data of the PIs. The PIC ID serves as the dependent label. CHAID tries to split the context part of the PI data into nodes that contain PIs that have the same value of the dependent variable (i.e., which were labeled in step 2 by the same PIC ID). The root of the tree shown in Figure 2 is partition #5 (Male and Female patients over 50 years), selected in Step 1. From there, the tree-building algorithm hierarchically partitions the nodes further, using at each split a context variable that is most important for segmenting the tree node, importance being estimated by chi-square. For example, nodes 0 is split based on age. The semantics of the nodes are criteria over the state variables. Node 4, for example, corresponds to age in the range 45-55.

Although CHAID aims to split the root node into *clean* nodes, each containing PIs that received a single PIC ID label in step 2, not all nodes formed are clean. For example, in Figure 2, nodes 21 and 23 are clean, containing PIs that were labeled as PIC #4 and PIC #3, respectively, as seen by the single column in the bar graph for these nodes. On the other hand, node 8 is less clean than nodes 21 and 23 as it contains similar levels of PIs with different labels and hence it is hard to select the most probable value for this node when trying to classify instances through it. Therefore, we state that this node has a high level of prediction error, while nodes 21 and 23 have very low prediction error. The predicted PIC ID for each node in the tree is the PIC ID that minimizes the prediction error. A common way of minimizing the prediction error is choosing the most dominant PIC ID for the node. For instance, considering node 17 or node 21, the output would be PIC = 4 with a probability of 98%, for node 23 it would be PIC =3 with a probability of almost 100%, while for node 8 it is not possible to predict the value of the output.

We used a cross-validation procedure [8] to find the misclassification (prediction) error we may expect for future PIs that we would classify with the tree. Cross validation divides the sample into a number of subsamples, or folds. Tree models are then generated, excluding the data from each subsample in turn. The first tree is based on all of the cases except those in the first sample fold, the second tree is based on all of the cases except those in the second sample fold, and so on. For each tree, misclassification risk is estimated by applying the tree to the subsample excluded in generating it. Cross validation produces a single, final tree model. The cross-validated risk estimate for the final tree is calculated as the average of the risks for all of the trees. In Table 2, we cross-tabulate the actual PIC ID (column 1) that was used to train the tree with the predicted PIC ID of the final tree. For example, of the 54 PIs that were originally labeled in PIC #1, 37 were predicted by the tree to have label of PIC #1, but 7 PIs were predicted to have label #2, and 10 PIs to have label #5.

Our objective is that the tree model would provide the predicted PIC for every new PI that we would submit to it. The ideal case would be that each leaf node of the tree would contain instances from one single PIC. However, this is not feasible due to the inherent errors of machine learning classification, and in addition, due to data completeness and correctness issues that arise despite our best to have the data validated and corrected. Therefore, we cannot be sure that we have all the context-related variables neither can we be sure that the data source is 100 % correct.

More importantly, we assume that when the analysis is performed there is no definition of path per context group. So we cannot expect all instances of the same context to follow the same path; the process is performed differently for different instances, even if they belong to the same context group, simply because there are no defined decision rules that relate path to context. Therefore we are not expecting our learning approach to find perfect correspondence between context groups and PICs.

Moreover, it is very likely to see different levels of success, measured via the classification error ratio, for different clusters, as seen in Table 2. For example, we see that for PIC ID #1 and #2 we have less than 70% successful prediction rate, for PIC ID #3 and #4 we have a prediction rate of 74-78%, and for PIC #5 we have a success rate of over 90%. The overall classification success rate for the provided set of data is 72%.

Table 2. Tree cross-validations results for the UTI process, considering the elderly males and females partition

PIC ID used to train the tree	PIC ID predicted by the decision-tree					
	1	2	3	4	5	% Correct
1	37	7	0	0	10	67.7%
2	13	13	20	0	5	39.7%
3	1	21	0	0	5	78.2%
4	11	9	0	60	0	74.6%
5	7	1	0	1	76	90.0%
Overall %	23.3%	17.1%	6.9%	20.5%	32.2%	72.0%

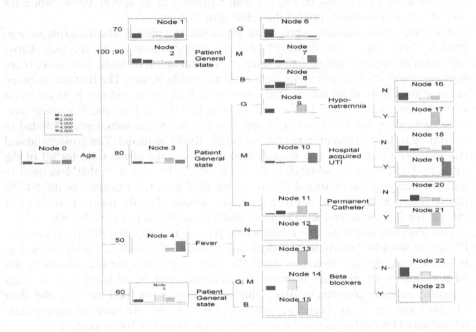

Fig. 2. Decision tree resulting from applying Step 3 to the UTI process data. The initial node (Node 0 at the left) is the starting point of the process of growing the tree, corresponding to partition 5 obtained in Step 1. The variables that are used to split n nodes are written to the right of each node. The thresholds of the variable that determines the criteria representing each node are marked at each split. For example, Node 0 is split over the variable age into 6 different splits (50, 60, 70, 80, 90-100), indicating the age ranges 45-55, 55-65, 65-75, 75-85, 85-90 and 95-105. Patient_General_state has values Bad (B), Medium (M), and Good (G). The other variables are Boolean. The histogram shown at each tree node represents the number of vectors in the tree node that were labeled with a specific label.

4.4 Identifying Context Groups

Once we have built the decision tree, we define the context groups' logical conditions using the following steps. First, we label the tree's leaf nodes by walking through the tree from its root, collecting state variables and variable values used to split nodes. For example, tree node #23 is labeled as "55 <age < 65 AND (General_state = Medium or General_state = Good) AND Beta Blockers= Y". In this way we label the other 14 leaf nodes (1, 6, 7, 8, 10, 12, 13, 15-23).

Then, we examine the population of labels for each node; the different colors given for a single tree node represent the five PIC labels that were used to train the tree. The histogram shown at each tree node represents the number of vectors in the tree node that were labeled with a specific label. For example, the PIs in tree node #23 are all labeled with PIC #3, whereas the PIs in tree node #6 are labeled mostly with PIC #1. Of the 15 tree nodes, 9 are predominantly labeled by a single PIC. We use them to determine the logical condition that defines the PIC. The results are shown in Table 3.

As a measure of *sensitivity* [9], we calculated how many (percentage) of PIs that belonged to a given PIC also belonged to the tree nodes in the CG from which the semantic label for the CG was derived. As a measure of *specificity* [9], or "cleanness" of the semantic label, we calculated the number (percentage) of PIs in a tree node that received the predominant label for the node. We noticed that we had 3 categories (CGs 3, 4, and 5) that had specificity above 95%. These groups included 47.5% of the sample.

5 Discussion and Conclusions

In this paper we addressed the identification of context groups of a clinical process. A clinical process would be executed differently for different context groups. Hence, the identification of context groups helps in defining decision-support for clinical processes. In the medical informatics literature, ideas similar to context have been used for decision-support for clinical processes. Tu et al. [10]proposed the consideration of usage scenarios in order to identify opportunities for providing decision support, the roles and information needs of care providers, events that may activate the guideline system, and guideline knowledge relevant in these scenarios. The usage scenarios are derived by mapping of generic guidelines to specific medical institutions and drive the whole process of clinical process design by providing the process with all necessary inputs: "who is doing what, where and when". A similar idea of context is also used in the definition of Act classes in Health Level 7's Reference Information Model (RIM) [11]. Taking an action-centered view, Act classes identify the kind of action (what happens), the actors who accomplish the action, the objects or targets whom the action influences. Adverbs of location (where), time (when), manner (how), and other information about circumstances, such as reasons (why) or motives (what for) are additional pieces of information that may be required or optional in given situations.

Process mining has been applied to healthcare processes [12]. The objective of process mining is to discover out of the process data the process model that has been followed. In our work we depart from the assumption that the current business process model is known, or has been discovered though process mining, and apply our framework to discover out of the process path and events the context of each instance. We consider that our context learning framework can be used by process mining algorithms in order to first establish groups of instances which are similar at the path and outcomes level and then discover the associated paths. This would provide process mining frameworks with two main capabilities: first, taking process outcomes into account when discovering the path, which, as we show, is an essential element for distinguishing between similar and non-similar instances; second, focusing the discovery on groups instead of mining all instances, which should improve notoriously the performance and the quality of the mining results.

Table 3. Resulting context groups for the UTI management process. The logical criteria are given for each relevant tree node. When a context group contains more than one tree node, the logical conditions of the nodes are combined with an OR to obtain the context group definition.

CG#	Tree Node	Logical Criterion	Sensitivity	Specificity	% of total sample
1	6	85 <age < 105 AND General state =Good	53.1%	58.6 %	6.6%
	22	55 < age < 65 AND (General state = Medium or General_state = Good) AND Beta- Blockers="N"	46.9%	66.7%	5.1%
2	--				
3	23	55 <age < 65 AND General state = Medium or Good AND Beta Blockers= Y	100%	100%	6.9%
4	13	45 <age <55 and Fever =Y	22.7%	100%	4.6%
	15	55 <age <65 AND General state = Bad	25.6%	100%	5.1%
	17	75 <age <85 AND General state = Good AND Hyponatremia=Y	23.9%	95.8%	4.8%
	21	75 <age <85 AND General state = Bad AND Permanent Catheter=Y	27.8%	98.0%	5.6%
5	12	45 <age < 55 AND Fever=N	33.3%	100%	13.7%
	19	75 <age <85 AND General state = Medium AND hospital acquired UTI =Y	66.7%	100%	6.9 %
Total and weighted averages			45.5%	92%	59.2%

We have demonstrated the context learning framework by applying it to a clinical process in order to automatically deduce context groups. We postulate that the process path and outcomes are highly dependent on the process context, which specifies the inputs of the external environment to the process and hence constrains the adopted path and the reached termination state. Our approach is based on clustering similar process instances and then using the cluster IDs as labels for a decision-tree learning algorithm from which semantic labels are extracted. The semantic labels are logical predicates over process state variables. This procedure renders the task of identification of contexts easier for a medical expert, enabling him to focus on analyzing the required paths for each context group without needing to deal with hundreds of samples. When a context group contains more than one tree node, we combined the logical conditions of the nodes with an *or* relation to obtain the context group definition. For each context group we will recommend one path. However, the different tree nodes that belong to the same context group are kept distinct, as they belong to different patient populations. It is important to keep them separated in this way so that the domain experts would relate to them clearly.

The resulting decision tree not only provides semantic labels for context groups; it may also be used to identify the context group of future instances automatically.

We note that our knowledge and definition of contexts is usually limited. Establishing a fully-accurate context definition would require having all the state variable data collected, which is impractical. We also need to expect some level of error in the provided data. All this, in addition to the inherent error of classification, which is in the nature of machine learning, implies that we always need to account for some level of classification error. Before applying our technique for deducing semantic labels from the clean nodes of the decision tree, the overall prediction level of the tree was 72% (Table 2) but it was not uniform. For example, in our study, the prediction level for PIC #2 was low - we did not have enough PIs in PIC #2 to learn a semantic definition for it. On the other hand, the results that we obtained for PIC # 3 were excellent – 100% specificity and sensitivity (Table 2 and Table 3). Comparing Table 2 and Table 3, we see that the method that we used for deducing the semantic labels produced high specificity (higher than the prediction rate observed in Table 2) because we used only clean nodes to provide the semantic labels but low sensitivity, because we dropped the PIs belonging to nodes that were not clean. These preliminary results, based on only 297 patients, are encouraging and show promise for our approach. We believe that when we collect more data, these results could be improved.

Our algorithm is a first component of a process learning architecture [2]that we have started to develop. The purpose of that approach is to learn, based on an initial process model schema and the outcomes of PIs, the process paths that should best be adopted for a PI that is awaiting execution. It is our goal to modify the initial process model schema based on the learned knowledge and achieve a better process model schema. Our approach differs from case-based reasoning (CBR) [8, 13], which uses a case-base of PIs to propose for a given PI awaiting execution a similar PI from the case-base that achieved good outcomes. CBR has been applied to the domain of business process management [14].

Since our approach is generic and is based on a formal conceptual model definition of the process model, process context, and process outcomes [4], it could potentially be applicable to other domains. Future research directions would examine this prospect.

References

1. Field, M.J., Lohr, K.N.: Guidelines for Clinical Practice: Directions for a New Program. Institute of Medicine, National Academy Press, Washington (1990)
2. Ghattas, J., Soffer, P., Peleg, M.: A Goal-based approach for business process learning. In: Workshop on Business Process Modeling, Development, and Support (BPMDS 2008), in conjunction with CAISE 2008, Montpellier, France (2008)

3. Ploesser, K., Peleg, M., Soffer, P., Rosemann, M., Recker, J.: Learning from Context to Improve Business Processes. In: BPtrends 2009 (1), pp. 1–9 (2009)
4. Ghattas, J., Soffer, P., Peleg, M.: A formal model for Process context learning. In: 5th workshop on Business process intelligence, Ulm, Germany (2009)
5. SPSS corporation. SPSS statistics software, version 16 (2009), http://www.spss.com
6. Akaike, H.: A new look at the statistical model identification. IEEE Transactions on Automatic Control 19(6), 716–723 (1974)
7. Kass, G.V.: An Exploratory Technique for Investigating Large Quantities of Categorical Data. Journal of Applied Statistics 29(2), 119–127 (1980)
8. Geisser, S.: Predictive Inference. Chapman and Hall, New York (1993)
9. Simon, D., Boring, J.R.: Sensitivity, Specificity, and Predictive Value. In: Clinical Methods: The History, Physical, and Laboratory Examinations, 3rd edn. (1990)
10. Tu, S.W., Campbell, J.R., Glasgow, J., Nyman, M.A., McClure, R.J., McClay, J.P.C., Hrabak, K.M., Berg, D., Weida, T., Mansfield, J.G., Musen, M.A., Abarbanel, R.M.: The SAGE Guideline Model: achievements and overview. J. Am. Med. Inform. Assoc. 14(5), 589–598 (2007)
11. Russler, D.C., Schadow, G., Mead, C., Snyder, T., Quade, L.M., McDonald, C.J.: Influences of the Unified Service Action Model on the HL7 Reference Information Model. In: Proc. AMIA Symp., pp. 930–934 (1999)
12. Mans, R.S., Schonenberg, M.H., Song, M., van der Aalst, W.M.P., Bakker, P.J.M.: Application of Process Mining in Healthcare - A Case Study in a Dutch Hospital. BIOSTEC 25, 425–438 (2008)
13. Aamodt, A.E.: EP. Case based reasoning: foundational issues, methodological variations and system approaches. AI Communications 7(1), 39–59 (1994)
14. Weber, B., Rinderle, S., Wild, W., Reichert, M.: CCBR-Driven Business Process Evolution. In: Muñoz-Ávila, H., Ricci, F. (eds.) ICCBR 2005. LNCS (LNAI), vol. 3620, pp. 610–624. Springer, Heidelberg (2005)

A Light-Weight System Extension Supporting Document-Based Processes in Healthcare

Christoph P. Neumann and Richard Lenz

Friedrich-Alexander University,
Erlangen-Nuremberg, Germany
christoph.neumann@cs.fau.de
http://www6.cs.fau.de/

Abstract. Inadequate availability of patient information is a major cause for medical errors and affects costs in healthcare. Traditional information integration in healthcare does not solve the problem. Applying the classic diagnostic-therapeuthic cycle as the model for a document-oriented information exchange protocol allows to foster inter-institutional information exchange in healthcare. The goal of the proposed architecture is to provide information exchange between strict autonomous healthcare institutions, bridging the gap between primary and secondary care, following traditional paper-based working practice. The combination of a RESTful architecture with a distributed light-weight workflow model provides minimized requirement for participating systems.

Topics: Process oriented system architectures in healthcare, process interoperability & standards in healthcare, context-aware healthcare processes, inter-institutional healthcare information systems, document-oriented integration.

1 Introduction

In a systems analysis of adverse drug events, 18% of the medical errors were associated with inadequate availability of patient information [1]. The problem of inadequate availability of patient information as a major cause for medical errors is aggravated by the rise of healthcare networks and the increasing number of healthcare parties that are involved in a treatment: The aging of western society affects the public health sector, chronic diseases and multimorbidity become the focus of interest, and the cost pressure rises. For example, cancer, diabetes, asthma, or cardiac insufficiency require more healthcare parties than common diseases. Coevally, the rapid advance in medicine leads to an advancing specialization of physicians that is an additional cause for the increasing number of involved parties regarding a single patient's treatment. For improving the treatment quality and in order to avoid unnecessary costs, an effective information and communication technology is vital for the support of inter-institutional patient treatment.

S. Rinderle-Ma et al. (Eds.): BPM 2009 Workshops, LNBIP 43, pp. 557–568, 2010.

In order to foster the continuity of care, the inter-institutional cooperation needs to bridge the current gap between institutions of the primary and secondary care. Such effort must not instrument regional standards, as it is done in *regional healthcare information networks* (RHIN) [2], but *transregional standards*. Accomplishing information exchange in distributed healthcare scenarios requires the integration of heterogeneous and *strict autonomous IT systems*. To allow for *inter-institutional cooperation* the support of distributed and seamless flow of information is required, thus changing paradigms from closed and hegemonic to open and distributed architectures. The proposed architecture adheres to these boundary conditions.

2   Idea and Objectives

This paper outlines the goal to focus on a document-oriented paradigm [3] for healthcare system integration following the paper-based clinical work practice as reference model. There are two prime objectives of the proposed solution. The first is the abdication of any central server, like joint databases, transaction monitors, and central context managers, as adherence to the strict autonomy of the institutions. The second objective is the application of document-oriented integration with lightweight interfaces instead of service-oriented integration with semantically rich interfaces. Document-orientation favors local autonomy by adhering to the design goal of loose coupling.

A subsequent design objective is to aim for minimal standards in order to yield minimal requirements to the participating systems. Favoring local autonomy over central hegemony requires, for example, that distribution of information will not be enforced, but is voluntary and process participation can be supplemented on demand. Platform independence and the avoidance of vendor lock-ins require that the basic architecture is decoupled from any specifically instrumented middleware and components off-the-shelf. Loose coupling, as desirable property of the proposed system extensions [4], particularly means that it should be possible to add and remove participants without any modification of other participants. Thus, without previously interconnecting two participants, it should be possible to interchange information[1].

A risk in instrumenting a central content storage, like German D2D or Google Health[2], is an information leak that potentially involves all patients. This is not comparable to any possible abuse scenario in today's paper-based infrastructure: No current healthcare institution hoards information about so many patients as will do any centralized solution for inter-institutional scenarios. The distributed approach mirrors the current state in paper-based working practice and provides *information locality*: The patient information is available only to the directly involved healthcare systems. As a result, the consequences of a security breach are limited to a fraction.

---

[1] Excluding considerations for a federated, large-scale security infrastructure which might still impose coupling on certain levels.

[2] http://www.google.com/health

3   Methods

This section will motivate the document-oriented integration approach with its capacity to support loose coupling and deferred system design. For implementation, a REST[3] architecture will be instrumented which provides document-orientation naturally.

3.1   Foundations of Semantic Compatibility

Exchange of patient information among institutions requires data compatibility. *Data integration* achieves data compatibility either by common standards or by data transformation. Data integration for medical processes requires standards for medical terminology that have to deal with volatile medical concepts [5]. Over the intervening years numerous standards for medical ontologies have been created on *type level* for system implementers at design-time and on *instance level* primarily for end-users as a semantic reference at run-time.

At instance level, standards like ICD , SNOMED , and LOINC exist which unremittingly evolve over time. The HL7[4] v2 is a well-established standard for clinical message specification [6]. It is a standard on type level, and incorporates coding schemes and terminologies on instance level. The HL7 v2 standard allows for the specification of self-defined messages, which has lead to incompatibilities. The relatively new HL7 v3 standard is based on the HL7 v3 *reference information model* (RIM) and is radically different from the v2 standard: It allows for new types to be derived from a limited number of core classes, enabling RIM-based systems to handle even unknown message-types in a generic way.

Electronic medical record (EMR) and *electronic health records* (EHR), e.g. [7], are popular approaches to share patient related information among institutions. They typically contain data that can be extracted on demand. Yet, it is unclear how these systems scale and how direct communication between institutions can be effectively supported in large-scale scenarios. A conceptual change from messages and records to documents is provided by the HL7 v3 *clinical document architecture* (CDA). CDA provides a framework for XML-structured medical documents. EMRs and EHRs fit in the notion of our approach by specifications like the *continuity of care document* (CCD), a U.S.-specific standard, which is a constraint on HL7 and focuses on document-oriented medical content types. In Germany, based on HL7 v3 CDA, the SCIPHOX[5] working group develops specific document content types for German healthcare; for example, referral vouchers and discharge letters[6]. The CCD and SCIPHOX standards do not consider process history or coordination information. Any new standards should respect the ones

---

[3] REpresentational State Transfer.
[4] Health Level 7, http://www.hl7.org
[5] Standardized Communication of Information Systems in Physician Offices and Hospitals using XML.
[6] Particularly "eArztbrief SCIPHOX CDA R1" and its advancement "eArztbrief VHitG CDA R2".

already in practice for backwards-compatibility and to achieve and maximize acceptance. Therefore, the exchanged documents of the proposed system extension are motivated by the increasing importance of HL7 v3 CDA. Yet, the proposed infrastructure does not depend on CDA.

3.2   Interface- vs. Document-Orientation

System integration in healthcare is traditionally based on interface-orientation. Three-tier network-based architectures with remote procedure calls are yet the dominant architectural style for information systems. The most common technological occurrence of remote invocations is based on SOAP with WSDL. The *interface-oriented integration* focuses on available functionality, and the integration method affects semantically rich interfaces. An invocation uses parameters to detail its synchronous service request to a target system. In interface-oriented integration the information being passed is not necessarily viable on its own but often in the context of the service request only.

Even if a service is triggered event-oriented using asynchronous messaging, like it is done in HL7 v2-based systems, such parameters or messages essentially represent transient fine-grained information that is assimilated by the targeted system. The three main problems in information integration projects, including healthcare systems, are insufficient synchronization of redundant data, problems with data consistency, and functional overlapping [8]. Therefore, interface-oriented and message-oriented integration between distinct institutions is complex and custom-designed.

In contrast, documents are coarse-grained, self-contained, and viable. A document can exist independently from the system it stems from. Changes are not propagated by update information, but by creating an updated document that replaces its predecessor. The *document-oriented integration* focuses on available information, and the integration method affects the semantic scalability of document models, using standardized and minimal interfaces for hand-over. Redundancy in data distribution is not critical with documents because, due to the self-containedness, a synchronization in the classical sense is not required. Instead, document versioning and variant management solutions are effective. Likewise are traditional data consistency checks confined to the scope of the document, inconsistencies between documents represent logical errors or divergence in opinion on such semantically high level that a conflict can only be detected or solved by specialized decision support systems or humans.

3.3   Loose Coupling and Deferred System Design

The *deferred system design* principle of evolutionary systems [9] requires semantic decisions not to be frozen in an interface schema because they are hard to revise. Applying a document-oriented approach improves the adaptability of the information systems by deferring schema decisions from design-time to deploy- or run-time.

HL7 v3 CDA provides semantic scalability for healthcare documents, both because this has been an inherent feature of the underlying RIM and because CDA is particularly structured in three levels of semantic abstraction: CDA level 1 is the unconstrained CDA specification. CDA level 2 applies section-level templates. CDA level 3 applies entry-level templates. For example, CDA level 1 simply ensures the ability to display a document like a PDF file. Any CDA document can be accepted without immediate support for processing. Advanced semantic processing support of CDA level 2 or 3 can be added to the system, seamlessly enhancing the information value of already stored CDA documents. HL7 v3 CDA supports deferred system design by its semantic scalability. The proposed solution applies CDA as primary document type, extending the CDA header with information exchange protocol and process participant information.

As an architectural style which implies minimal requirements to be supported by participating systems, the REST paradigm is applied in DMPS. The REST architectural style is the generalization of the architecture of the web, proposed by Fielding [10], the co-author of the original HTTP[7] with Berners-Lee. REST provides a paradigm for decentralizing applications in which applications are decomposed into resources with various representations and links between them. The RESTful approach does not require an additional marshaling layer as do interface-oriented remote invocation approaches. The focus of REST lies in the explicit modeling of the representation; in the interface-oriented approach the representation is often generated implicitly by vendor-specific development environment tools. The benefits of a REST architecture are its minimal requirements and its coarse-grained resource/representation approach which compels loose-coupling and allows for a document-oriented architecture.

4 Proposed Solution

The proposed exchange protocol and system extension is named *distributed medical process support* (DMPS). DMPS targets a document-oriented process support between strictly autonomous institutions. It follows the paper-based work practice as reference model, focusing on referral vouchers and result reporting by letters of referral. The DMPS exchange protocol is deduced from the traditional diagnostic-therapeutic cycle [11] in fig. 1.

The basic technological DMPS adoption of the diagnostic-therapeutic cycle will provide remote information exchange for the edges of the cycle. It is based on the REST architectural style, requiring only HTTP and support of HL7 v3 CDA documents as well as the implementation of the procotol statechart as it will be described in sect. 4.2.

In contrast to clinical environments, in which the focus of process support often relates to decision support (which is e.g. based on rule-based artificial intelligence) and process control (to guarantee process quality), the inter-institutional process support only supplements coordination information and enables coordination guidance instead of control. At the moment our approach focuses on sharing a distributed process identifier and managing a merged process history of participating institutions. To provide context awareness in form of a process

---

[7] HyperText Transfer Protocol.

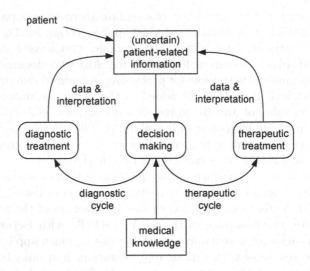

Fig. 1. The traditional diagnostic-therapeutic cycle

history is one of several most important challenges for inter-institutional information system integration in healthcare [12].

4.1 Scenario

The basic scenario of the intended DMPS system extension is outlined in fig. 2. Document transportation can be done *online* by REST access or *offline* by transporting documents with the aid of an external medium like an eGK smart card or a flash drive. Another dimension of transport classification is the *counterpart accessibility*: the delivery can be done by *direct* communication or by a *mediated* approach. The direct approach delivers documents directly from the source DMPS node to the sink DMPS node using online or offline mechanisms, whereas the mediated approach uses a third DMPS node as intermediator, for example a DMPS node that hosts DMPS accounts for patients. The third classification dimension, which is not visualized in fig. 2, is the *counterpart identity availability*: the counterpart can be known at the time of document shipping (*addressed* communication) or the counterpart can yet be unknown (*unaddressed* communication).

The DMPS scenario considers three communication variations: *direct/online*, *direct/offline*, and *mediated*. The mediated approach is a composite of directed communications, and arbitrarily uses online or offline transport for each of its atomic edges. The distinction due to the counterpart identity availability is motivated by most basic examples: Letters of referral are addressed communication scenarios, but referral vouchers are unaddressed ones because the voucher lists only the medical specialty, while the patient can arbitrarily choose the actual institution and medical specialist. A referral voucher or a prescription can, for example, be delivered in a mediated/online fashion using a patient-centered third-party DMPS node which hosts patient DMPS accounts, enabling the patient to collect documents

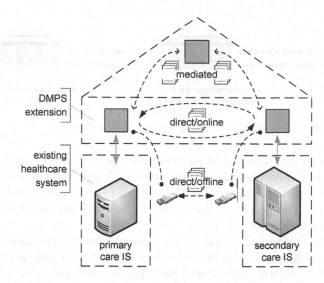

Fig. 2. The DMPS scenario

inside his or her account history and to delegate initially unaddressed vouchers or prescriptions to a healthcare institution of his or her choice. If the patient does not want to use an own DMPS account, e.g. because the necessary IT education is not present, the referral voucher or prescription can still remain unaddressed using a direct/offline fashion, e.g. instrumenting an eGK smart card. A mutual exclusion exists only between direct/online and unaddressed because every direct/online communication requires a known delivery endpoint.

Introductorily, the direct/online approach is outlined: Each existing *healthcare information system* (HCIS)[8] that participates in the DMPS information exchange posts documents that are to be delegated to another institution to its local DMPS extension using a REST/HTTP endpoint of the DMPS. The DMPS extension manages the process instance and delivery protocol by a statechart implementation and forwards the documents to the DMPS extension of the receiving HCIS (called "downstream" as it is outlined in fig. 3). The delivery instruments an intra-DMPS REST endpoint. An independent local process instance is created and managed by the downstream DMPS extension and the documents are delivered to the local HCIS by a third REST endpoint, which has to be provided by the local HCIS. Once the diagnostic or therapeutic treatment has been accomplished, the downstream HCIS reports its result documents to its DMPS extension which will return them to its upstream DMPS correspondent. The upstream DMPS extension delivers the result documents, e.g. CDA-based letters of referral, pictures, or PDF documents, to its local HCIS.

In the whole process, each HCIS is free to delegate diagnostic-therapeutic treatments to one or many downstream institutions. The DMPS subsystem creates

---

[8] The information systems in primary care are abbreviated either HIS (hospital) or CIS (clinical). To avoid any clash, healthcare information systems in general (of the primary and the secondary care) have been abbreviated as HCIS.

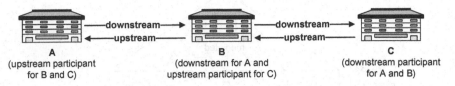

Fig. 3. Downstream and upstream relationships

a document that contains the global process information, or propagates this process document to the downstream DMPS correspondents. The process status information consists of a shared process ID and the process history with any involved institutions. The process history provides information about the pre-treatment or mutual treatment providers.

The process status information that is sent downstream or upstream by the DMPS and can be configured to be filtered by each institution individually: It is neither necessary to inform downstream institutions about preceding institutions nor to inform the upstream institution about self-conducted delegations. The local DMPS extension manages all available historic information that has been provided by the upstream and downstream institutions together with its own actions, but can reduce or eliminate this information for each own delegation. This is necessary because DMPS also targets generalized scenarios where in complex hospital environments there exists a DMPS endpoint for information exchange with external institutions, but in addition the internal delegation between hospital subsections is just as well supported by intra-institutional DMPS extensions. Therefore an arbitrary control of a HCIS over the globally observable process history is required.

4.2   Leight-Weight Protocol for Inter-institutional Exchange

The statechart that is deduced form the traditional and essential diagnostic-therapeutic cycle (fig. 1) to facilitate inter-institutional treatment delegation is shown in fig. 4 and named *pandiagnostic-pantherapeutic protocol*[9].

There are two entry points, the first is the leadoff patient entry: the patient visits the first healthcare professional which internally cycles diagnostic-therapeutic phases until a delegation to an external institution is decided. The second entry point into the statechart is an incoming treatment request from an upstream institution that is accepted. The documents are subsequently delegated to the local HCIS while the process waits for the decision either to reply a result report from its local HCIS to the upstream DMPS or to initiate a successive delegation to another downstream institution. The statechart comprises the four combinations of from/to and upstream/downstream.

Encapsulating the exchange and process support mechanism into a distinct component allows to extend DMPS by a public-key infrastructure (PKI). In terms of security, cryptographic measures have to be distinguished into the ones for

---

[9] Greek "pan-" as a prefix: "of everything", "involving all members" of a group.

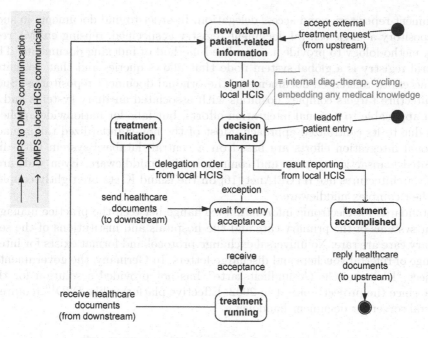

Fig. 4. The pandiagnostic-pantherapeutic protocol

expressing declarations of intent (equal to paper-based signatures) and technical ones for documenting information origin (securing exchange independently of human signatures). Signatures for declarations of intent are object to the HCIS, documents that are delegated to the DMPS extension for delivery are either signed or not. Integrating PKI mechanisms for technically securing the information origin could be plugged into the REST/HTTP endpoints. The DMPS project does not focus on PKI but is designed to fit into existing security frameworks like German eGK [13], PaDok [14] or IHE ATNA [15]. Yet, in order to build authentication and authorization during the establishment of DMPS-to-DMPS relationships a generalized PKI component integration is required, being applicable independently of national PKI specifications.

In DMPS a broad spectrum of document exchange scenarios is supported. First and foremost DMPS is compliant to traditional paper-based working practice, provides process history, and enables process support. It additionally intends to allow for patient-centered document management, fostering cross-sectional life-long patient-centered healthcare documentation.

5   Related Work

Existing protocol standards for information exchange in healthcare focus on hospitals of the secondary care, commonly instrumenting centralized system functionality for tailor-made integration purposes: For example, the *cross-enterprise document sharing* (XDS) [15] standard from IHE allows for distributed document repositories and access delegation. In order to find documents in such a repository a single central document registry is specified, reusing ebXML registry methodology to provide a centralized method of indexing documents. The central registry is a global system node that allows queries and that delegates the access to referenced documents to the original document repositories. Such architecture targets complex hospitals with associated ancillary systems and is even applicable to regional integration efforts, but fails for nationwide application due to its centralized approach. Most of the non-standardized tailor-made regional integration efforts are based on a central database system with distributed transaction systems and communication middleware. Even wide-area RHIN architectures like HYGEIAnet [16] on the island Kreta are tightly-coupled by their complex middleware.

Standards for electronic information exchange between the practice management systems of the primary care and the hospitals and institutions of the secondary care are rare. No universal exchange protocol and format exists for interchange of referral vouchers and discharge letters. In Germany, the governmental project "Elektronische Gesundheitskarte" has not provided a solution for the issue since the project's outset in 2002. Effective platforms like D2D[10] require a central server for document handover.

6 Future Work

In DMPS, the shared information is the global process ID, being created during leadoff delegation and propagated among the involved DMPS nodes. The patient identity has to reside in the transported documents which are not evaluated by DMPS. Providing distributed process support of multiple process instances for an individual patient in the context of a patient identity requires a distributed master patient index. Traditional federated master patient index systems like IHE PIX[11] or OMG[12] PIDS[13] instrument hierarchical federation with central system nodes and are not applicable in distributed environments like the DMPS scenario. Therefore, a loosely-coupled distributed patient identification service for interinstitutional purpose is required.

Whereas DMPS supports unidirectional transport for traditional healthcare supply chains, closely cooperating dynamic teams require mechanisms for team publication. With the DEUS mediated publish-subscribe infrastructure [17] we are implementing a distribution system for document-oriented integration purposes. At the moment, neither the process identifier nor the merging of process history is integrated into DEUS but both efforts will converge into a unified platform.

The document-oriented information exchange is a foundation for interinstitutional process support. At the moment, the DMPS extends the transported documents with process history information within its distributed light-weight

---

[10] Doctor to Doctor, www.d2d.de, based on PaDok cryptographic infrastructure [14].
[11] Patient Identifier Cross-Referencing.
[12] Object Management Group.
[13] Patient IDentification Service.

workflow layer, and provides an exchange protocol that adheres to the diagnostic-therapeutic cycle as coarse-grained intuitional reference from working practice. In DMPS, a workflow status model for cooperative but distributed medical treatment processes is not yet available. Such workflow model must further formalize the activities that take place inside each institution, being represented by the central state "decision making" in the pandiagnostic-pantherapeutic protocol. Yet, extending documents with process information can be considered as a preparation to achieve such workflow support in form of *active documents* [18].

7 Conclusion

For inter-institutional process support, there exists a semantic gap that is not covered by standards, concerning the functional integration of autonomous healthcare information systems. The initial goal of the proposed DMPS architecture is to foster the availability of patient information in order to bridge the gap between primary and secondary care. The prime objectives in design are the document-oriented integration approach and the abdication of any central servers. The essential argument for document-oriented integration over interface-oriented integration lies in its capacity to support deferred system design. Deferred system design supports demand-driven system evolution which is needed for healthcare information systems.

The DMPS architecture achieves a document-oriented process support between strict autonomous institutions following the paper-based work practice as reference model. The document exchange includes propagation of the process history which provides information about the pre-treatment or mutual treatment providers. It is oriented at traditional healthcare communication directly between healthcare institutions without patient involvement. Additionally, it intends to allow for patient-centered document management by optionally mediating document transport through a patient DMPS account. The combination of a REST architecture with a distributed light-weight workflow model provides a minimal set of requirements to be supported by participating systems.

References

1. Leape, L.L., Bates, D.W., Cullen, D.J., Cooper, J., Demonaco, H.J., Gallivan, T., Hallisey, R., Ives, J., Laird, N., Laffel, G.: Systems analysis of adverse drug events. ADE Prevention Study Group. JAMA 274(1), 35–43 (1995)
2. Williams, M.H., Venters, G., Marwick, D.: Developing a regional healthcare information network. IEEE Transactions on Information Technology in Biomedicine 5(2), 177–180 (2001)
3. Beyer, M., Kuhn, K., Lenz, R.: Potential der CDA in verteilten Gesundheitsinformationssystemen. In: Lenz, R., Hasenkamp, U., Hasselbring, W., Manfred, R. (eds.) EAI, Marburg, Germany, July 2005. CEUR Workshop Proceedings, vol. 141 (2005), CEUR-WS.org
4. Lenz, R.: Information Systems in Healthcare – state and steps towards sustainability. In: Geissbuhler, A., Kulikowski, C. (eds.) IMIA Yearbook of Medical Informatics, Stuttgart, Schattauer (2009) (accepted for publication)

5. McDonald, C.J., Marc Overhage, J., Dexter, P., Takesue, B., Suico, J.G.: What is done, what is needed and what is realistic to expect from medical informatics standards. International Journal of Medical Informatics 48(1-3), 5–12 (1998)
6. HL7v2. ANSI/HL7 V2.6-2007, http://www.hl7.org/Library/standards_non1.htm
7. Powell, J., Buchan, I.: Electronic Health Records Should Support Clinical Research. Journal of Medical Internet Research 7(1) (2005)
8. Lenz, R., Kuhn, K.A.: A strategic approach for business-IT alignment in health information systems. LNCS, pp. 178–195 (2003)
9. Patel, N.V.: Adaptive Evolutionary Information Systems. Idea Group Inc., USA (2002)
10. Fielding, R.T.: Architectural Styles and the Design of Network-based Software Architectures. PhD thesis, University of California (2000)
11. Lenz, R., Reichert, M.: IT Support for Healthcare Processes. In: van der Aalst, W.M.P., Benatallah, B., Casati, F., Curbera, F. (eds.) BPM 2005. LNCS, vol. 3649, pp. 354–363. Springer, Heidelberg (2005)
12. Lenz, R., Beyer, M., Meiler, C., Jablonski, S., Kuhn, K.A.: Informationsintegration in Gesundheitsversorgungsnetzen. Informatik-Spektrum 28(2), 105–119 (2005)
13. Gematik. Einführung der Gesundheitskarte - Gesamtarchitektur - Version 1.5.0, Revision 2.3.4 (September 2008)
14. Fraunhofer Institute for Biomedical Engineering (IBMT). PaDok – Patientenbegleitende Dokumentation (2000), http://www.ibmt.fraunhofer.de/fhg/Images/ MT_padoknetzkonzept_de_tcm266-68980.pdf
15. ACC, HIMSS, and RSNA. IHE IT Infrastructure Technical Framework, vol. 1 (ITI TF-1): Integration Profiles, Rev 4.0 (August 2007)
16. Tsiknakis, M., Katehakis, D.G., Orphanoudakis, S.C.: An open, component-based information infrastructure for integrated health information networks. International Journal of Medical Informatics 68(1-3), 3–26 (2002)
17. Neumann, C.P., Rampp, F., Daum, M., Lenz, R.: A Mediated Publish-Subscribe System for Inter-Institutional Process Support in Healthcare. In: Proc of the 3rd ACM International Conference on Distributed Event-Based Systems (July 2009)
18. LaMarca, A., Edwards, W.K., Dourish, P., Lamping, J., Smith, I., Thornton, J.: Taking the work out of workflow: mechanisms for document-centered collaboration. In: Proc. of the 6th conference on European Conference on Computer Supported Cooperative Work, pp. 1–20. Kluwer Academic Publishers, Norwell (1999)

α-*Flow*: A Document-Based Approach to Inter-institutional Process Support in Healthcare

Christoph P. Neumann and Richard Lenz

Friedrich-Alexander University,
Erlangen-Nuremberg, Germany
{christoph.neumann,richard.lenz}@cs.fau.de
http://www6.cs.fau.de/

Abstract. Inter-institutional collaboration requires clean task boundaries and the separation of responsibilities. In addition, healthcare processes are intrinsically fluid. Traditional activity-oriented workflow models or content-oriented workflow models do not provide adequate support for the paper-based working practice in healthcare. The α-*Flow* approach adopts electronic documents as the primary means of information exchange, fusing both paradigms into a combined workflow schema model, wherein workflow schemas are represented as documents which are shared coequally to content documents.

Topics: Process modeling in healthcare, workflow management in healthcare, context-aware healthcare processes, inter-institutional healthcare information systems, document-oriented integration.

1 Motivation and Challenges

The patient treatment process increasingly changes from isolated treatment episodes towards a continuous process incorporating multiple organizationally independent institutions and different professions. Effective treatment of unclear symptoms or multimorbid patients increasingly leads to the need for establishing and managing dynamic teams of cooperating specialists. Independent electronic health records are discussed as a basis for inter-organizational cooperation, but despite of existing standards like openEHR, reality is still far away from this vision, and IT-support for inter-organizational patient treatment processes is an open issue. Today, IT support for healthcare processes is typically limited to intra-institutional approaches, and systems in different organizations are heterogeneous and rarely integrated.

Semantic scalability is an important requirement for a distributed IT application in healthcare. Therefore, we are looking for an evolutionary and decentralized approach to support inter-institutional processes in healthcare. The traditional approach to manage inter-institutional processes is based on documents with a dedicated semantics, such as a referral or a discharge letter. We pick

S. Rinderle-Ma et al. (Eds.): BPM 2009 Workshops, LNBIP 43, pp. 569–580, 2010.

up this interaction paradigm and try to extend it to support more complex cooperation scenarios. The basic idea is to use electronic documents as self-contained units of information interchange which also carry process related information. As an illustrative application example one might consider disease management programs which are managed by paper-based documents that carry checklists.

2   Objectives

The goal of the α-*Flow* project is to develop a concept for an document-based workflow with loosely coupled heterogeneous systems at the participating sites. This particularly incorporates a meta-model for document-based process management, which provides the fundamental artifacts for process specification.

The α-*Flow* approach fuses the activity-oriented workflow paradigm with the content-oriented workflow paradigm into a combined model, wherein workflow schemas are represented as documents which are shared coequally to content documents. The intent is to allow access, viewing, and editing of the original content documents in standard ways like general editors without corrupting the workflow semantics. This paper will present the necessary artifacts and the resulting requirements to the infrastructure that is needed for an α-*Flow* implementation.

3   Background

The two basic aspects for collaborative activities are the support for content manipulation and the support for coordination. An information system traditionally focuses on the *manipulation of content*. Support is given for the gathering, the storage, access control, structuring, classification, and presentation of the information as well as the reaction to new information. Collaboration extends this focus with the concern of *coordination*. The information system must support the "articulation work" [1] as it is part of Computer Supported Cooperative Work (CSCW) [2]. Articulation support must enable cooperating actors to partition work into units, to divide it amongst themselves, and to schedule, mesh and interrelate their collective activities.

In *activity-oriented workflows* the central point is a task. Process definitions describe tasks with states and transitions (like Petri Nets) or with actors and activities (like BPMN[1]). At any given moment at run-time, the workflow is in a well-defined state and it moves to a different state when certain conditions are met. In Petri Nets the workflow engine enacts a set of actions during transitions, in BPMN the actions are internal part of an activity. Although each task is characterized by preconditions, postconditions, and possible exceptions, any required or generated artifacts, documents for example, are not necessarily considered by the workflow schema.

Content-oriented workflow systems, in contrast, place a content artifact in the center of the workflow process, focusing on its creation and manipulation phases.

---

[1] Business Process Modeling Notation.

Each workflow step alters the content object. At the end of each step, the state of the document reflects the step's result. The workflow definitions for content-oriented workflows have their origin in write-and-review processes in publishing companies.

Both approaches, the activity-oriented workflows and the content-oriented, are commonly based on predefined workflow schemas that can be instantiated by an enactment engine. For example, a content-oriented workflow schema will prospectively specify actors like "author", "reviewer", and "publisher" as well as any steps and content states like "private", "submitted", "reviewed", and "published". Ad-hoc workflows with an initially unknown set of actors and state/transitions are not considered, traditionally.

4 The α-*Flow* Approach

The α-*Flow* approach focuses on the relationship between content and coordination aspects of collaborative and large-scale environments. The collaboration is considered as a feature of the artifact and not of the application system. The α-*Flow* model adopts electronic documents, called α-*Docs*, as the primary means of information exchange and coordination.

4.1 Content vs. Coordination

In order to support heterogeneous systems, we need to decouple collaboration functionality from the application. Therefore we have to distinguish between content documents and coordination documents.

The *content documents* conduct medical information and are of arbitrary type, like Adobe PDF files, Microsoft Word documents, or HL7[2] CDA[3] documents. Content documents belong to the healthcare applications which generate them. The healthcare applications provide them to the distributed workflow engine by an export or by an universal resource identifier.

The *coordination documents* are independent of the application system and belong to the distributed workflow. They conduct information about actors, roles, and institutions, as well as system topology information, workflow reports or summaries, and control structures.

4.2 Artifacts: α-*Docs* and α-*Cards*

For applying a document-based workflow, the overall treatment process must be represented by a document. This document is a *treatment status artifact* and its state represents the overall state of the treatment process. Several documents, both further coordination documents and arbitrary content documents, will accompany the treatment process. Later, we will elaborate on the relationship between the treatment status artifact, the supporting coordination artifacts, and the involved content artifacts. In this section, we will only focus on the structure of the α-*Doc* documents.

---

[2] Health Level 7, http://www.hl7.org
[3] Clinical Document Architecture.

Motivating two granularity levels of document artifacts. α-*Docs* are the units of information interchange, but the unit of validation must be smaller. Parts of a singular α-*Doc* should be validated while others remain in a preliminary state and are filled as the workflow continues. For example, in a process to generate a report the report is represented by an α-*Doc*. The report consists of a form. The form will be filled by different organizations. It is necessary to structure the form schema and its later values into separate units such that it is possible to assign them to different organizations.

Inter-institutional healthcare example. The initial episode of breast cancer treatment is outlined in fig. 1. The goal of this treatment episode is to find out whether or not a knot in a breast is actually malignant cancer.

The treatment begins with a patient visiting her gynecologist, who writes the anamnesis documentation. After the anamnesis, the gynecologist conducts a sonography with an according report as its result. In fig. 1, the participant's superscript A stands for ambulant (office-based, primary care) in contrast to C for clinical (secondary care).

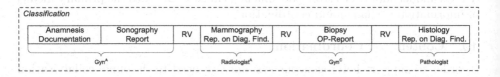

Fig. 1. The initial breast cancer treatment episode: classification

If the result is either malignant or dubious he/she will send the patient to a radiologist for mammography, using a referral voucher RV. After the radiologist's treatment,the mammography report on diagnostic findings is sent back to Gyn^A. The gynecologist evaluates the mammography report, primarily the medical indicator BI-RADS[4], and decides whether the patient has to be send to a hospital for a biopsy. The biopsy involves a clinic's Gyn^S, accordingly a referral voucher is created. The tissue is taken by Gyn^S and sent to a pathologist for histological diagnosis. The histology report is sent back from the pathologist to the clinical Gyn^S, who bundles the report with a short report about the biopsy operation and finally delivers the reports back to Gyn^A. The histology provides definite evidence, yet, the Gyn^A is the one who takes the histology result and is responsible for informing the patient. In the malignant case, another episode begins now by sending the patient to a breast cancer treatment center for primary therapy.

For α-*Flow*, the traditional paper-based reports in fig. 1 can be considered as one report, that is successively filled by the participating institutions. Each such distributed treatment episode can be characterized by a common goal of the collaborating participants. Considering both the institutional and collaborative view on a treatment episode two kinds of granularity can be distinguished.

---

[4] Breast Imaging – Reporting and Data System.

α-Docs versus α-Cards. The units of validation and organizational account-ability are named α-Cards. One α-Doc consists of one or more α-Cards. On the one hand an α-Card is quite larger than single database fields. On the other hand the intended granularity of an α-Card is a more fine-grained one than the one that is experienced from paper-based working practice in healthcare. A single α-Card contains, for example, a diagnostic finding, clinical evidence, a diagnosis, a therapeutic measure, an order, or a prescription. This improves the structure of the patient files, and provides higher selectivity in retrieval and display. In fact, an α-Card is required to fulfill the fundamental feature of a document, to be self-contained on its own. To ensure this property of an α-Card rests with the institutional healthcare information systems.

Difference and coherence between α-Docs and α-Cards. In the document-based α-Flow approach for inter-institutional process support, each individual α-Doc is a collection of α-Cards. The α-Docs are the atomic units of informa-tion interchange. An α-Card is the atomic unit of validation, clearance, shared visibility, and cryptographic signatures.

α-Cards in the context of content vs. coordination. α-Cards are not only used for structuring content documents but also to consolidate coordina-tion information. For example an α-Card might collect information about process participants, their institutional information, or treatment role models. Others provide information about system topologies or access control lists. The treat-ment status information is also consolidated in an α-Card conducting the overall workflow schema.

4.3   Fusing Activities into α-Flow

A distributed process as a structure of distributed activities is called an *episode*, or an α-Episode to accentuate the α-Flow context. One α-Episode is character-ized by a particular goal and represented by one α-Doc. By using the term of an α-Episode in contrast to α-Doc we point out that the α-Flow approach is not blind to the necessary activities.

Yet, α-Flow tries to eliminate any modeling of activities in its coordination model. Activities are fused into the α-Flow approach by completely represent-ing them by their results, the α-Cards as part of the α-Doc. This is necessary, because any decisions for process routing requires either a domain- and section-specific decision support system (e.g. based on rule-based artificial intelligence) or a human decision. No conditional model element like in activity-orientation is sufficient for most decision modeling and process routing in healthcare. Fur-thermore, most activities are human tasks or require a complex local health-care information system. Due to the heterogeneity and complexity of the existing systems, they are essentially factored out of the coordination layer but remain integrated by document-orientation.

The basic α-Flow assumption for inter-institutional workflows is that human or computer supported decisions can always be represented in a newly occurred demand for further information, e.g. patient-related information as it is well-known by the diagnostic-therapeutic cycle [3] in healthcare. An episode ends when no further information is required for the particular goal. Any decision that is made in the course of an α-*Episode* can be represented by the creation of a record keeping α-*Card*.

4.4   Workflow Progress by the Notion of Active Documents

An *active document* [4] is a document that allows a direct interaction with itself. Therefore, documents become active documents if they are assigned with *active properties*. In case of the α-*Flow* approach only the α-*Cards* are assigned with active properties. An α-*Doc* artifact becomes active if it contains at least one α-*Card* that has an active property. Not every α-*Card* necessarily has active properties but each can be assigned one.

The "*alpha*" in our artifact names relates to the active properties: By their active properties, α-*Cards* are triggers for workflow progress. Activities are not modeled explicitly but, instead, an newly demanded α-*Card* placeholder is created in the coordination list of the treatment status artifact. Workflow progress means successive fulfillment of requested content α-*Cards*. Workflow schema change means editing the list of required α-*Cards* and adopting the progress actions that occur at state change.

The active properties do not implement activities. They support the state change and exchange of the α-*Doc*/α-*Cards*. By propagating the α-*Doc* state change, the requests for α-*Card* fulfillment are delegated to the cooperating participants, indirectly triggering their institutional activities.

Active properties in regard to process, function, and data. In conclusion, the active properties' logic drive the progress of the *process*, but the *functions* that are equal to the notion of activities are subordinate to their results in form of *data*. The data is required in form of *documents* because α-*Flow* targets large-scale scenarios. Such require a document-oriented integration approach as we have detailed in [5]: Interface- or service-orientated integration approaches suffer from various shortcomings in order to provide a large-scale electronic health record infrastructure. In contrast, document-orientation is suitable to support the *deferred system design* principle [6] enabling evolutionary systems [7]. In α-*Flow*, a process definition basically consists of a set of α-*Card* documents and their control flow being expressed in active properties.

5   The α-*Flow* Meta-model

The α-*Flow* approach is a dual workflow paradigm that aims at a unification of content-oriented workflows with activity-oriented workflows. In activity-orientation the activities' artifacts, either required or produced, are resistant to change and are inferior workflow elements. In content-orientation the information document is changed through collaboration with the focus on role models and notification mechanisms. The actual activities' tasks are commonly hard-coded, initially unknown sets of actors and state/transitions are not considered.

The α-Flow approach fuses both paradigms into a combined model. Workflow schemas are represented as *intelligent to-do lists*, in which each list item is an α-Card document that is either available or that is requested in order to progress the α-Episode process. The intelligent to-do list is represented by an α-Card generically named *treatment status artifact*. The intelligence is provided by its active properties. As outlined in sect. 4.2 the treatment status artifact is one of several coordination α-Card documents that are shared coequally to the involved content documents.

The state of an individual α-Card and an α-Doc has to be distinguished from the state of the treatment. The treatment process and its state will progress with the creation or the change of α-Cards, but each α-Card has its own properties independent of a treatment. Furthermore, it should be possible to use the original documents, which are basically the payload of an α-Card, in standard ways like general editors without corrupting the workflow semantics.

The state of an α-Card is based on what we call *adornment models*. Before we describe the adornment models in more detail, it is necessary to introduce what we call *collaboration resource models*.

5.1 The Collaboration Resource Models

Collaboration resources are illustrated as the who, where, with whom, and with what. The collaboration resource models contain the information about actors, roles, institutions, and systems. They are part of the coordination system and form a cross-cutting infrastructure being used by several of the α-Card adornment models.

5.2 The α-Card Adornment Models

The validity and visibility of α-Cards have to be considered separately. In traditional database-centric approaches, visibility is strictly coupled to validity. Information is only visible if it is committed, and the commit has to ensure the integrity constraints. In contrast, for document-centric approaches it is common to share documents preliminarily, by making them visible, although guarantees of validity are not provided just yet for the content.

The document-centric approach supports the separation between validity and visibility. The validity has to be distinguished into the *intent validity*, for expressing declarations of intent by humans being related to paper-based signatures, and *technical validity*, which is essentially defined by specifying how versions and variants are consolidated. Yet, providing electronic signatures for declarations of intent is subject to the local healthcare information systems. The α-Flow approach does not focus on PKI but is designed to fit into existing security frameworks like German eGK [8], PaDok [9] or IHE ATNA [10]. Contemporary workflow approaches, in regard to their artifact model, do not distinguish between the four aspects of intent validity versus visibility and versioning versus variants.

The introduction of α-Cards as an explicit unit of validation has been motivated by the need for flexibly dealing with intent validity and visibility. The *intent validity model* might simply consist of the classifiers "invalid" and "valid", whereas the *visibility model* might simply consist of the classifiers "private" and "public". Private α-Cards are for non-collaborative purposes or to prepare and configure collaborative purpose. An invalid public α-Card is interim information. A valid public α-Card is not allowed to change without versioning. Validity does not imply visibility: Valid private α-Cards are allowed, e.g. they are required if access control has yet to be configured for an α-Card before it is advertised by setting its visibility to public.

A *versioning model* is required both for content and coordination α-Cards. Versioning is mandatory for public and valid α-Cards because the individual systems require a global version for the tracking of changes. Any other α-Cards (in terms of visibility and validity) are equally allowed to use versioning as it seems appropriate. There is always exactly one current version of any α-Card.

A *variants model* is additionally required. In contrast to versions, there may exist several valid variants of an α-Card coequally at any given time. This concerns content α-Cards, especially but not solely public invalid α-Cards. It might as well be required for coordination α-Cards, for example if an ad-hoc medical consensus on further workflow activities is negotiated by different institutions by exchanging extended or modified variants of the treatment status artifact. Both the versioning model and the variants model contribute to the α-Card identity.

The *authentication model* and *authorization model* are augmenting the visibility with access control. The visibility is a general property of the α-Card. If access privileges have to be differentiated according to actors, roles, institutions, or arbitrary groups, a kind of access control mechanism is required. While the visibility state transition from private to public triggers a notification or a content advertising, the access control mechanism filters the audience of a notification or authorizes content access.

The *syntactic payload type model* describes the format of an α-Card. For example, PDF, Microsoft Word, or HL7 CDA for content artifacts. It would even be possible to exchange jPDL or BPEL files as coordination artifacts that are documenting intra-institutional processes. The MIME[5] types provide a common standard for the syntactic types.

With the *semantic payload type model* an α-Card is classified semantically. We distinguish the fundamental semantic type from the domain-specific semantic type, and eventually the user-specific semantic type. The *fundamental semantic type* classifies artifacts into "content" vs. "coordination". The *domain-specific semantic type*, for example, classifies content artifacts as "diagnostic finding", "therapeutic measure", or "prescription". For coordination artifacts, there exist predefined semantic types like the "treatment status artifact", the α-Card carrying the workflow schema, or the "treatment team artifact", the α-Card carrying the information about participating collaboration resources.

---

[5] Multipurpose Internet Mail Extensions.

The *subject model* describes the authors of an α-*Card*. For example a doctor for content α-*Cards* or a workflow-engineer for coordination α-*Cards*. In contrast, the *object model* describes the object of an α-*Card*. For example the patient for most content α-*Cards*, or a treatment process name for coordination α-*Cards*. Both the subject model and the object model contribute to the α-*Card* identity.

A *linkage model* is required to associate α-*Cards* arbitrarily among each other. The linkage model is also the basis for the navigation between the α-*Cards*. The linkage model could be based on XLink and XPointer technology, but is an adornment, allowing to associate even non-XML artifacts with other artifacts.

5.3 The α-*Doc* Adornment Models

An α-*Doc* is a named collection of α-*Cards*. Any progress of a treatment process will essentially change such a collection by the creation or change of α-*Cards* from distinct process participants and institutions. The *collection model* for α-*Docs* must provide an overview over all α-*Cards*. It enables the process participants to gain shared knowledge about each other's activities.

A *transfer model* for the α-*Docs* is required. It references the transfer capabilities of particular institutions. Model elements are service endpoint declarations of the participating sites and applied communication protocols. The transfer model is based on the infrastructure that is provided by the collaboration resource models.

5.4 Active Property Model

The *active property model* has to provide mechanisms to assign active code to an α-*Card*. The active code of an active property is called a *progress action*. The active property model encompasses several sub-models: the ordering model, the activation condition model, and the evaluation phase model. Support for an *ordering model* of multiple active properties is required because there will exist several active properties for a single α-*Card*. The *activation condition model* must allow to describe conditions under which the active property is triggered, supporting both event-triggers and periodical triggers.

The *evaluation phase model* describes a three-phased evaluation cycle of active properties: The *verification phase* ensures the applicability according to any boundary conditions that are provided by the access control conditions of the adornment models or any conditions of the workflow model. The *operation phase* carries out the active code. The *finalization phase* carries out notifications and handles error or abort situations.

The modeling of a workflow schema can fulfill two very different intentions in loosely-coupled inter-institutional scenarios: a retrospective modeling for documentation and further delegation or a prospective modeling for enactment automation. For *retrospective modeling*, the focus lies on providing end-users with workflow schema editors to allow them to keep record of their latest process step and to allow them a process delegation to another institution. For *prospective modeling*, the focus lies on providing ad-hoc mechanisms for consensus finding if two participants have divergent notions of the treatment process articulated as variant treatment status artifacts. Both use-cases for workflow schema modeling have to be considered in the overall α-*Flow* approach.

6   Related Work

This section is separated into approaches related to active documents and approaches related to workflow models.

6.1   Active Document Technology

The X-Folders project [11] instruments WebDAV folders which can react to the insertion or modification of a document by starting a task. Because WebDAV folders can be distributed, multiple X-Folders can be combined to a site-spanning workflow. Yet, the guards and triggers are hard coded for each X-Folder, e.g. one folder to accept new forms, another folder with pending forms, and a last folder with accepted forms. The X-Folders project neither provides a formal representation of the workflow schema nor a dynamic adaptation; and it does not provide a distributed institution or role management.

The Placeless documents project [12] from Xerox PARC provides an infrastructure to implement active properties for arbitrary documents. It seemingly provides abstraction from existing document- and file-management interfaces.

With the DEUS mediated publish-subscribe infrastructure [5] we are implementing a distribution system for α-*Cards*. For implementing the α-*Flow* approach, we need a technical foundation that allows to assign active properties to an artifact like an α-*Card*. In the future, we will evaluate both the X-Folders and the Placeless documents system as partner to the DEUS platform to combine transfer features with active property features in α-*Flow*.

6.2   Related Workflow Approaches

There exist several related workflow approaches. The case-handling paradigm focuses on workflows like clinical pathways and requires semantic integration of medical data in form of data objects and forms. In [13], the authors acknowledge that the case handling creates an integration problem, because the state of a "case" is derived from "data objects" with a well-known schema which cannot be separated from the process. In addition, data objects are still product of a modeled activity, whereas α-*Flow* tries to separate an explicit model of intra-institutional activity from the inter-institutional model.

The object-aware workflow systems [14], focusing on write-and-review processes like job applications, the artifact-centric approach [15], and the data-driven process structures [16] all represent advanced solutions to the content-oriented approach. The *object*, respectively the *business artifact* or *data*, needs a structured and predefined content schema. All approaches allow to model life-cycle state-charts for the records. The coordination is provided by state-changes in the life-cycle model, as explained for content-oriented workflows which has been part of the inspiration for α-*Flow*. Yet, a fine-grained project-specific life-cycle and information model is required and cannot be changed ad-hoc. A more comprehensive comparison of these types of workflow modeling is contained in [14].

From these approaches stem models to describe consistency between the process model and the object life-cycle. Both the artifact life-cycle language [17] and the work of Ryndina et al [18] seem promising and could eventually be adopted as formalism to α-*Flow*.

The primary boundary condition in the inter-institutional scenario is the integration of autonomous systems by loose coupling and respecting the manifold document standards which comprise arbitrary taxonomies and ontological standards for healthcare. The existing workflow approaches fail these conditions but provide sophisticated solutions for a homogeneous system environment with canonical information models. The core motivation of α-*Flow* is to support decentralized, large-scale scenarios in which semantically heterogeneous and even informal content types drive the distributed, collaborative workflow. Such requires the utter decoupling of content from coordination.

7 Conclusion

The α-*Flow* approach adopts electronic documents as the primary means of information exchange. The collaboration is considered as a feature of the artifact and not of the application system. Our artifacts themselves take on the active role in managing coordination. In order to support heterogeneous systems, we need to decouple collaboration functionality from the application.

This paper provides a systematic classification of the required elements for a document-based approach for inter-institutional process support in healthcare. Healthcare processes are intrinsically fluid and require clean task boundaries, separation of responsibilities, and multiple versions or variants of a document as well as initially unknown sets of actors and state/transitions. Neither activity-oriented workflow models nor traditional content-oriented workflow models provide adequate support for the paper-based working practice in healthcare. Only the fusion of both paradigms will enable a seamless enhancement of existing healthcare information systems with inter-institutional collaboration facilities.

References

1. Schmidt, K., Bannon, L.: Taking CSCW seriously: Supporting Articulation Work. Computer Supported Cooperative Work (CSCW) 1(1), 7–40 (1992)
2. Greif, I.: Computer-supported cooperative work: A book of readings. Morgan Kaufmann, San Francisco (1988)
3. van Bemmel, J.H., Musen, M.A., Helder, J.C.: Handbook of medical informatics. Bohn Stafleu Van Loghum (1997)
4. LaMarca, A., Edwards, W.K., Dourish, P., Lamping, J., Smith, I., Thornton, J.: Taking the work out of workflow: mechanisms for document-centered collaboration. In: Proc. of the 6th conference on European Conference on Computer Supported Cooperative Work, pp. 1–20. Kluwer Academic Publishers, Norwell (1999)

5. Neumann, C.P., Rampp, F., Daum, M., Lenz, R.: A Mediated Publish-Subscribe System for Inter-Institutional Process Support in Healthcare. In: Proc of the 3rd ACM International Conference on Distributed Event-Based Systems (July 2009)
6. Patel, N.V.: Adaptive Evolutionary Information Systems. Idea Group Inc., USA (2002)
7. Lenz, R.: Information Systems in Healthcare – state and steps towards sustainability. In: Geissbuhler, A., Kulikowski, C. (eds.) IMIA Yearbook of Medical Informatics, Stuttgart. Schattauer (2009) (accepted for publication)
8. Gematik. Einführung der Gesundheitskarte - Gesamtarchitektur - Version 1.5.0, Revision 2.3.4 (September 2008)
9. Fraunhofer Institute for Biomedical Engineering (IBMT). PaDok – Patientenbegleitende Dokumentation (2000),
   http://www.ibmt.fraunhofer.de/fhg/Images/
   MT_padoknetzkonzept_de_tcm266-68980.pdf
10. ACC, HIMSS, and RSNA. IHE IT Infrastructure Technical Framework, vol. 1 (ITI TF-1): Integration Profiles, Rev 4.0 (August 2007)
11. Rossi, D.: Orchestrating document-based workflows with X-Folders. In: Proc of the ACM symposium on Applied computing, pp. 503–507. ACM, NY (2004)
12. Dourish, P., Edwards, W.K., Howell, J., LaMarca, A., Lamping, J., Petersen, K., Salisbury, M., Terry, D., Thornton, J.: A programming model for active documents. In: Proc. of the 13th annual ACM symposium on User interface software and technology, pp. 41–50. ACM, New York (2000)
13. van der Aalst, W.M.P., Weske, M., Grünbauer, D.: Case handling: a new paradigm for business process support. Data & Knowledge Engineering 53(2), 129–162 (2005)
14. Künzle, V., Reichert, M.: Towards Object-Aware Process Management Systems: Issues, Challenges, Benefits. In: Halpin, T., et al. (eds.) BPMDS 2009 and EMMSAD 2009. LNBIP, vol. 29, pp. 197–210. Springer, Heidelberg (2009)
15. Cohn, D., Hull, R.: Business Artifacts: A Data-centric Approach to Modeling Business Operations and Processes. Bulletin of the IEEE Computer Society Technical Committee on Data Engineering
16. Muller, D., Reichert, M., Herbst, J.: Data-driven modeling and coordination of large process structures. In: Meersman, R., Tari, Z. (eds.) OTM 2007, Part I. LNCS, vol. 4803, pp. 131–149. Springer, Heidelberg (2007)
17. Gerede, C.E., Su, J.: Specification and verification of artifact behaviors in business process models. In: Krämer, B.J., Lin, K.-J., Narasimhan, P. (eds.) ICSOC 2007. LNCS, vol. 4749, pp. 181–192. Springer, Heidelberg (2007)
18. Ryndina, K., Kuster, J.M., Gall, H.: Consistency of business process models and object life cycles. In: Kühne, T. (ed.) MoDELS 2006. LNCS, vol. 4364, pp. 80–90. Springer, Heidelberg (2007)

An Approach for Managing Clinical Trial Applications Using Semantic Information Models

Hans-Georg Fill[1] and Ilona Reischl[2]

[1] University of Vienna, 1210 Vienna, Austria
hgf@dke.univie.ac.at
[2] AGES PharmMed, Schnirchgasse 9, 1030 Vienna, Austria
ilona.reischl@ages.at

Abstract. The management of clinical trial applications by public authorities is a complex process involving several regulations, actors, and IT systems. In this paper we present a modeling approach based on semantic information models that supports this process. In particular, the approach can be used for the generation of user-centric visualizations, performance and compliance analyses and the distribution of the contained knowledge within an organization and to third parties. The approach has been developed together with AGES PharmMed and applied to their core processes.

Keywords: Clinical trials, process management, semantic information, visualization.

1   Introduction

The preservation of a high standard of public health is today one of the major challenges of the industrialized countries. This involves both the efficient use of public resources for all types of health services as well as the provision of regulations that foster the development of new medical treatments and products cf. [1]. The development of new methods and new drugs in particular is a long, costly and risky process primarily conducted by pharmaceutical companies [2]. The translation of recent discoveries in basic biomedical research such as in human genomics, stem cell biology, molecular biology or immunology into knowledge that ultimately affects clinical practice and human health requires *clinical research* [3]. Thereby, new understandings of disease mechanisms that are gained in the laboratory are translated into methods for diagnosis, therapy, and prevention. In the course of *clinical trials* these methods are then tested in humans. The results are translated into clinical practice and health decision making, thus leading to the potential improvement of human health care [3].

In the heavily regulated pharmaceutical industry it is thus essential that the involved parties cooperate effectively to ensure both a high quality of service and regulatory compliance [4]. The application for clinical trials has to be approved by *public authorities*. Thereby formal, pre-clinical, and clinical aspects

S. Rinderle-Ma et al. (Eds.): BPM 2009 Workshops, LNBIP 43, pp. 581–592, 2010.

are evaluated. In parallel, ethics committees assess the ethical impact of the prospective trial, the pre-clinical and clinical aspects and the standard of care. The basis for all these tasks are a number of national and European legal regulations. After the clinical trial phase, the licensing applications may either be submitted on a national level, in the course of a mutual recognition procedure (MRP) if a substance is already approved in one member country, by a decentralised procedure (DCP) for gaining approval in several countries in parallel or, for selected substances, via a central procedure by the European Medicines Agency (EMEA). During the stage of clinical trial evaluation there is usually a tight interaction between the applicant and the public authorities. During these tasks several national and European IT systems and databases are accessed to exchange information with authorities in other EU countries. Based on the legal regulations set time frames have to be kept for informing the applicant of the acceptance or rejection of the application.

In the following we will describe a modeling approach for the administration of clinical trial applications on the side of public authorities that has been developed together with AGES PharmMed[1]. In this context, a combination of meta modeling and semantic modeling techniques were used for three purposes: a. to create user-centric visualizations for managing the complexity of the processes, b. to support management in the analysis of the performance and compliance of their processes, c. to make the knowledge contained in the processes accessible to other stakeholders.

The remainder of the paper is structured as follows: In section two we will outline the foundations used for our modeling approach. Section three presents the modeling approach and the meta model. In section four the concrete scenario of managing clinical trials at AGES PharmMed and the application of the modeling approach are described. The paper is concluded in section four by giving an outlook on future work.

2   Foundations

This section gives a brief introduction to the fields of meta modeling and the relation of semantic business process modeling and semantic information models.

2.1   Meta Modeling

Today it can be chosen from a large variety of different modeling methods and corresponding modeling languages, each with its particular advantages and pitfalls. Besides the selection of a single modeling language it is also possible to

---

[1] AGES PharmMed and the the Federal Office for Safety in Health Care (BASG), the Austrian Competent Authority, went operative on January 2, 2006 following a reorganization and out-sourcing from the Federal Ministry for Health. Legal responsibilities of the BASG center around issues pertinent to drug development and licensing. The purpose of AGES PharmMed, which is fully owned by the Republic of Austria is to support the BASG by providing services, personnel and location.

create a new domain or purpose specific language, modify an existing language to meet particular needs or use a combination of these options. For our approach we will therefore revert to the concepts and terminology of *meta modeling*.

In this terminology modeling methods are divided into a modeling technique and mechanisms and algorithms [5] (see figure 1). The modeling technique comprises a modeling language and a modeling procedure. The modeling language is used to describe the models and is itself split into syntax, semantics, and notation. The semantics of the modeling language contain a semantic schema and a mapping of the syntax of the modeling language to the schema. The notation is separated from the syntax of the modeling language and thus allows for an independent modification of the visual representation [6]. The modeling procedure defines the way how to apply the modeling language. Mechanisms and algorithms are used by the modeling procedure. A meta model can now be viewed as a model of a modeling language [7]. Meta models may also be graphically represented themselves and can thus provide a means to discuss the concepts of a modeling language also with non-technical users.

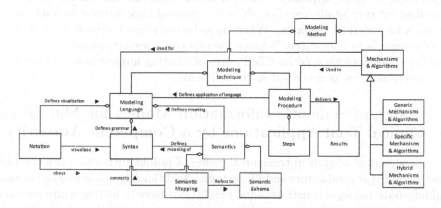

Fig. 1. Components of Modeling Methods [5]

2.2 Semantic Business Process Modeling and Semantic Information Models

The use of business process modeling can today be regarded as the defacto standard approach for analyzing complex organizational relationships and enabling IT-based management. Several modeling languages are available for this purpose. In general, it can be differentiated between two types of languages: On the one side modeling languages that are explicitly directed towards business processes such as event driven process chains [8], Adonis [9] or BPMN [10]. And on the other side modeling languages that are also suitable for business process modeling but that have not originally been conceived for this application such as UML activity diagrams [11] or Petri nets [12].

Recent attempts have been made to investigate how the *inherent semantics* of the elements, i.e. the inner meaning of the elements can be made explicit [13].

Thereby, the information contained in the description of the model elements shall be made processable by machines. In several publications this approach is denoted as *semantic business process modeling* (SBPM) e.g. [14,15]. Through SBPM several benefits may be gained: By annotating or lifting model elements with concepts from a formal semantic schema, functionalities such as semantic similarity measures and transformations between models [15], automated re-use of process fragments [14], semantic service discovery [16] or auto-completion during the creation of the models may be realized [14]. Similar results for measuring syntactic, linguistic, and structural similarity can be achieved through the transformation of business process models to a formal semantic schema [12].

Besides business process management, model annotation has also been used for other types of models, e.g. interaction and workflow models [17]. Additionally, semantic annotation may also be applied on the level of meta models [14], for the assignment of graphical notations [6] or for mechanisms and algorithms. We will therefore denote the combinations of traditional models with formal semantic schemata through annotation as *semantic information models*. The application of these approaches to real-world scenarios has so far only been described for very small cases [18]. It is therefore of high interest to apply these methods to practical scenarios. When introducing these methods to practice a central issue is to adequately balance technological opportunities and business benefits. Therefore we used modified parts of existing approaches together with new functionalities as described in the following.

3   Design of Semantic Information Models for Managing Clinical Trial Applications by a Competent Authority

The management of clinical trials on the side of public authorities is a complex issue involving several actors and IT systems. Additionally, a number of national and international legal constraints and regulations have to be taken into account. These are not invariant but are subject to frequent changes based on advancements in scientific methods and new organizational requirements. Derived from these regulations is the importance of time constraints and the appropriate planning of available resources. For these purposes we derived a modeling framework using semantic information models.

3.1   Setup of the Modeling Framework

In the first step it had to be decided which types of models should be included in the framework (see figure 2). As the management of clinical trials is basically a complex sequence of activities, the use of business process models seemed obvious. Therefore, Adonis as an established process modeling language was chosen based on its intuitive notation and extensive configuration options [9]. Several extensions were used compared to the pure process modeling configuration: *swimlanes* to represent the interaction between human actors and IT systems, *simulation elements* to allow for stochastic simulations of the duration time and capacity analyses, and *IT resource elements* to depict concrete

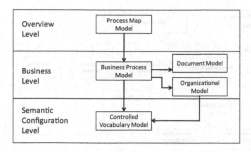

Fig. 2. Modeling Framework for Managing Clinical Trials using Semantic Information Models

IT applications during the process flow. For the representation of organizational structures a model type including *actors, role definitions* and *organizational units* was added. To be able to document the relation to legal regulations a document model was used and linkages from the activity elements of the business process model were defined.

To take advantage of some of the benefits arising from semantic annotation a *controlled vocabulary model* completes the modeling framework. It contains *terms* and relations to express *is broader* relationships between terms. To keep the semantic models manageable also by standard users further semantic relations are currently not included. The controlled vocabulary model is linked both to activites of business processes as well as role elements in the organizational model. By using *view definition elements* in the business process and the organizational model term instances may be selected for each instance. All model types were defined in the form of meta models and linked to each other (see figure 3). The meta model was then implemented using the Adonis meta modeling platform[2].

3.2   User-Centric Semantic Visualizations

A particular advantage of using meta modeling techniques together with semantic information models can be yielded in regard to the visualization of the models [6]. Through using the information contained in the models to influence their visualization, additional insights into the structure and relationships of a model can be gained. In our approach the visualization of elements in the process models and the organizational models can be modified based on the view definition elements and the semantic annotations through terms in the sense of *semantic visualization* [6]. By selecting terms in the view definition element other elements that are annotated with the same or related terms can be highlighted. This allows to visualize semantic relationships in the model that could otherwise not be investigated at first sight. Especially for very large models containing huge numbers of elements this functionality directly supports model analyses.

---

[2] Adonis is a commerical product by BOC AG. A free community edition is available at http://www.adonis-community.com/

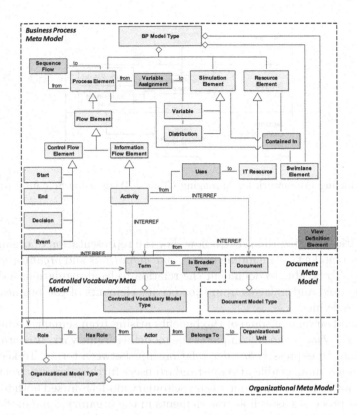

Fig. 3. Excerpt of the used Meta Model

3.3 Performance and Compliance of Processes

As the compliance to legal regulations and time constraints is of particular concern for the management of clinical trial applications, special attention was given to this subject. Based on the formal definition of the model syntax by meta models several types of analyses and simulations can be applied. Examples include the evaluation of durations and cycle times of process paths, capacity analyses for the planning of what-if scenarios or the analysis of interactions with IT systems during different process stages. Based on the linkage with document models activities relevant to certain changes of legal regulations can be directly identified and adapted if necessary. Again, the use of semantic annotations by using the controlled vocabulary model type can additionally support these analyses by integrating user-specific information. It is thus e.g. possible to annotate certain process activities with terms defining their priority in case of legal changes.

3.4 Knowledge Distribution

Due to the numerous actors and stakeholders involved in the processing of applications for clinical trials the efficient and specific distribution of knowledge marks an important aspect. On the one side the existing staff as well as new employees of the public authority require personalized information about their embedding in the overall process structure. On the other side also third parties such as other public authorities, pharmaceutical companies or quality auditors may demand information about the processes. By reverting to the formal representation of the meta models and models transformations to other formats, e.g. HTML, word-processors or spreadsheets can be immediately realized. With the help of the semantic annotation also visualizations that are customized to a specific user group are possible. An example is the highlighting of activities in a large process that are related to a certain overall subject such as the filing of documents.

4 Management of Clinical Trial Applications at AGES PharmMed

In the following we will describe how the approach of semantic information models has been applied to the management of clinical trial applications at the Austrian public service authority AGES PharmMed.

4.1 Function and Responsibilities of AGES PharmMed

The Austrian medicines and medical devices agency (PharmMed) area of activity of AGES provides service responsibilities related to the life-cycle of medicinal products and devices. AGES PharmMed is concerned with eight tasks: (a) the approval of pharmaceuticals; (b) pharmacovigilance, i.e. the systematic logging of new adverse reactions; (c) the monitoring of the market of medicincal products; (d) the inspection of pharmaceutical companies; (e) haemovigilance, i.e. the monitoring of blood donations and transfusions; (f) the provision of scientific advice for pharmaceutical companies; (g) the official medicines control laboratory (OMCL); and (h) the official international representation of Austria in several pharmaceutical bodies.

4.2 Focus Area: Registration and Approval of Clinical Trials

The management of clinical trial applications is subject to several legal regulations. The European Clinical Trials Directive that is applicable to all EU member countries aims to harmonize clinical research practice within the EU and align Europe with international standards in the following way [19]: The role of central and local ethics committes is clearly defined. A central ethics committee should provide a single opinion for a country. The parallel submission of clinical trial applications to a central ethics committee and the country's competent authority has to be put in place. Both ethics committees and competent authorities at the country level should give an opinion on the trial within 60 days from the receipt of the application. As the the duration of the regulatory approval process has been supposed to directly affect the competitive position of a country in clinical research this time schedule is today of particular concern [19]. Additional challenges that have to be met by government agencies involved in the administration of clinical research are [3]: to provide mechanisms whereby regulatory information can be accessed and understood by both investigators and the general public; to evaluate and improve standards in clinical trials that maintain an appropriate level of privacy while ensuring enough freedom for research; and the standardization of information systems in the health care area, in particular the development of standards to facilitate the collection and sharing of information in clinical research. Furthermore, constant adaptations of national and international procedures require a high degree of flexibility. An example are the recent developments in regard to a *voluntary harmonization procedure* that aims for an optimization of multi-national clinical trials applications [20].

4.3   Application of Modeling Approach

At AGES PharmMed the following steps were taken to apply the modeling approach. At first, the main processes related to the administration of clinical trial applications were identified. These were depicted using the process map model type to provide a first overview (see figure 4).

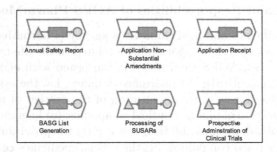

Fig. 4. Excerpt of the Process Map Model

In a second step, each of the processes has been detailed - for an overview of the main process see figure 5. For each process the involved organizational units and IT systems have been assessed. For the administration of clinical trials four main entities have been identified at AGES PharmMed: the evaluators and management staff of the department for science and information at AGES PharmMed, the ethics committees or institutional review boards (IRB), PharmMed service units such as mailpoint or finance, the Eudra-CT system, and the national clinical trials database (CTN). Eudra-CT is a European database of all clinical trials since May 2004[3]. It provides unique identifiers (Eudra-CT numbers) to track clinical trials all over Europe and log their status. The CTN provides the same service on a national level. These four main entities have been modeled using the swimlane element.

---

[3] https://eudract.emea.europa.eu/

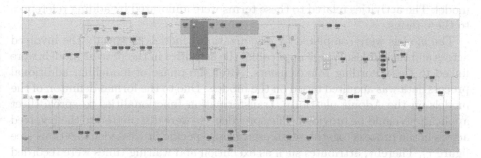

Fig. 5. Prospective Main Process for the Future Management of Clinical Trials

As shown in figure 6 the use of swimlanes directly allows to model parallel flows and task responsibilities for several actors. Especially the interaction with different IT systems can be clearly shown. For activities that are related to legal regulations links to elements of the document model have been created. From the document elements references to electronic documents and websites were stored to allow for a direct access when analyzing the process. After the modeling of the processes a number of terms were declared using the controlled vocabulary

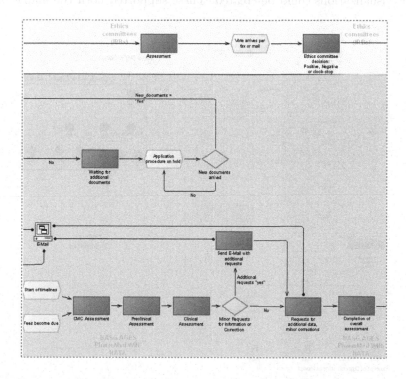

Fig. 6. Excerpt of the Prospective Main Process from Figure 5 for Managing Clinical Trial Applications at AGES PharmMed

model. The activities related to these terms were annotated by adding references to these terms.

The models were completed by organizational models to specify the involved actors and their roles. Where applicable, the activities in the process models were linked to the according role elements. After the phase of modeling, additional process data was acquired based on the models. Due to the formal definiton of the models on the Adonis plattform, transformation functionalities to spreadsheet applications could be provided. The spreadsheets were distributed to the involved actors in the process together with user-group specific process visualizations (see figure 7). Thereby, attributes such as execution and waiting times were recorded for several process executions. Together with existing data about the number of applications analyses and simulations of the cycle times for selected process paths could then be conducted. Due to confidentiality these results are not included here. From the models on the Adonis platform other distribution formats such as HTML-pages were generated and made available for involved parties.

4.4   Evaluation of the Approach

Although the application of the approach is currently limited to one organization first results can be reported. Based on the annotation of the process models user-centric visualizations could be created. These supported both the management

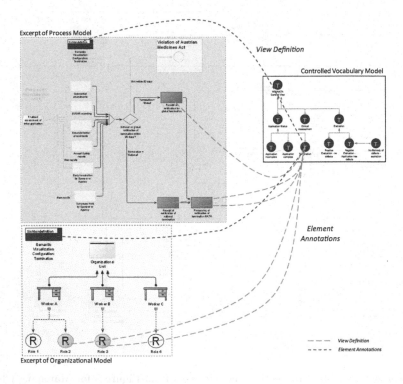

Fig. 7. Example for a Semantic Visualization for higlighting process parts

staff of AGES PharmMed in analyzing specific parts and relationships of complex processes and helped staff involved in the process executions to better understand their embedding in the overall structure. Furthermore, the possibility to analyze the duration times of the processes directly allowed to check process parts for the compliance to legal regulations. In addition, a first basis for the management of resources along the processes was established. Through the clear depiction of the currently involved IT systems requirements for the future IT support could be formulated and candidates of activities for additional automation identified.

By distributing the process models and their visualizations to the management staff and the workforce of AGES PharmMed as well as to external stakeholders the knowledge about the application processes could be easily made available. Thereby precise feedback on possible process optimizations and future interfaces to other departments and involved parties could be given. A particular advantage was also the availability of intuitive process descriptions for newly hired personnel.

5   Conclusion and Future Work

With the presented approach it could be shown how semantic information models can be used for real-world scenarios. The approach is estimated to be directly applicable to public authorities working in health care management of other EU countries. Future work will include the derivation of a reference process for the administration of clinical trials in the EU and the further evaluation of the approach.

References

1. Kyle, M.: Pharmaceutical Price Controls and Entry Strategies. The Review of Economics and Statistics 89(1), 88–99 (2007)
2. Sauer, C., Sauer, R.: Is it possible to have cheaper drugs and preserve the incentive to innovate? The benefits of privatizing the drug approval process. Journal of Technology Transfer 32, 509–524 (2007)
3. Sung, N., et al.: Central Challenges Facing the National Clinical Research Enterprise. The Journal of the American Medical Association 289(10), 1278–1287 (2003)
4. Himmelreich, J.: A compliance office for heavily regulated enterprises – a best practice approach meeting US FDA requirements. BT Technology Journal 25(1), 41–49 (2007)
5. Karagiannis, D., Kuehn, H.: Metamodeling platforms. In: Bauknecht, K., Min Tjoa, A., Quirchmayer, G. (eds.) EC-Web 2002. LNCS, vol. 2455, p. 182. Springer, Heidelberg (2002)
6. Fill, H.G.: Visualisation for Semantic Information Systems. Gabler (2009)
7. Favre, J.-M.: Foundations of meta-pyramids: Languages vs. metamodels - episode ii: Story of thotus the baboon. In: Bzivin, J., Heckel, R. (eds.) Language Engineering for Model-driven Software Development, Dagstuhl, Germany, IBFI Dagstuhl (2005)

8. Keller, G., Nuettgens, M., Scheer, A.W.: Semantische Prozessmodellierung auf der Grundlage Ereignisgesteuerter Prozessketten (EPK). Veroeffentlichungen des Instituts für Wirtschaftsinformatik (IWi), Universität des Saarlandes Heft 89, 29 p. (1992),
http://www.iwi.uni-sb.de/nuettgens/Veroef/Artikel/heft089/heft089.pdf
9. Herbst, J., Karagiannis, D.: Integrating machine learning and workflow management to support acquisition and adaptation of workflow models. Intelligent Systems in Accounting, Finance & Management 9(2), 67–92 (2000)
10. Wohed, P., Van der Aalst, W.M.P., Dumas, M., Ter Hofstede, A., Russell, N.: On the suitability of bpmn for business process modelling. In: Dustdar, S., Fiadeiro, J.L., Sheth, A.P. (eds.) BPM 2006. LNCS, vol. 4102, pp. 161–176. Springer, Heidelberg (2006)
11. Russell, N., Van der Aalst, W.M.P., Ter Hofstede, A., Wohed, P.: On the Suitability of UML 2.0 Activity Diagrams for Business Process Modelling. In: Third Asia-Pacific Conference on Conceptual Modelling (APCCM 2006), Australia (2006)
12. Ehrig, M., Koschmider, A., Oberweis, A.: Measuring similarity between semantic business process models. In: Roddick, J.F., Hinze, A. (eds.) Proceedings of the Fourth Asia-Pacific Conference on Conceptual Modelling (APCCM 2007). Australian Computer Science Communications, vol. 67, pp. 71–80. ACM, New York (2007)
13. Karagiannis, D., Hoefferer, P.: Metamodels in action: An overview. In: Filipe, J., Shishkov, B., Helfert, M. (eds.) ICSOFT 2006 - First International Conference on Software and Data Technologies, pp. IS–27 – IS–36. Insticc Press, Setùbal (2006)
14. Lautenbacher, F., Bauer, B., Seitz, C.: Semantic Business Process Modeling - Benefits and Capability. In: AAAI Spring Symposium, Stanford University, California. AAAI, Menlo Park (2008)
15. Hoefferer, P.: Achieving Business Process Model Interoperability Using Metamodels and Ontologies. In: Oesterle, H., Schelp, J., Winter, R. (eds.) Proceedings of the 15th European Conference on Information Systems (ECIS 2007), pp. 1620–1631. University of St. Gallen, St. Gallen (2007)
16. Hepp, M., Leymann, F., Domingue, J., Wahler, A., Fensel, D.: Semantic business process management: a vision towards using semantic web services for business process management. In: IEEE International Conference on e-Business Engineering, 2005. ICEBE 2005, pp. 535–540 (2005)
17. Fill, H.G.: Design of Semantic Information Systems using a Model-based Approach. In: AAAI Spring Symposium, Stanford University, CA. AAAI, Menlo Park (2009)
18. Stein, S., Stamber, C., El Kharbili, M., Rubach, P.: Semantic Business Process Management: An Empirical Case Study. In: Loos, P., Nuettgens, M., Turowski, K., Werth, D. (eds.) MobIS Workshops, vol. 420, pp. 165–177 (2008)
19. Heerspink, H., Dobre, D., Hillege, H., Grobbee, D., De Zeeuw, D.: Does the European Clinical Trials Directive really improve clinical trial approval time? British Journal of Clinical Pharmacology 66(4), 546–550 (2008)
20. Canary Ltd.: Voluntary harmonisation procedure pilot begins. CRAdvisor - A newsletter for those involved in clinical trials (236) (2009)

Workflow for Healthcare: A Methodology for Realizing Flexible Medical Treatment Processes

Hajo A. Reijers[1], Nick Russell[1],
Simone van der Geer[2], and Gertruud A.M. Krekels[3]

[1] School of Industrial Engineering, Eindhoven University of Technology,
The Netherlands
n.c.russell@tue.nl, h.a.reijers@tue.nl
[2] Department of Dermatology, Erasmus Medical Center, Rotterdam, The Netherlands
s.vandergeer@erasmusmc.nl
[3] Department of Dermatology, Catharina Hospital Eindhoven, The Netherlands
gertruud.krekels@catharina-ziekenhuis.nl

Abstract. While workflow management technology is applied in many industrial domains to improve the operational efficiency of business process execution, its usage in the healthcare domain is limited. One possible cause is that healthcare processes are often considered to be more whimsical and less predictable than procedures found in industry. Extending previous work on *workflow* and *flexibility patterns*, this paper presents a methodology for realizing processes that possess the required degree of flexibility that makes them suitable for the healthcare domain. To demonstrate the methodology's feasibility, it is applied to the processes that are found in a Dutch outpatient clinic. Interestingly, the flexibility demands of the investigated processes match quite well with the capabilities of current workflow management technologies, further motivating their increased usage in the healthcare domain.

Keywords: Workflow management technology, healthcare processes, flexibility patterns, dermatology.

1 Introduction

It is clear that healthcare organizations are under pressure from a wide variety of market and demographic forces. These drive the many ongoing initiatives to improve the efficiency of healthcare operations while still maintaining an acceptable level of quality of care. Yet, the impression we get from our collaboration with various healthcare professionals and managers is that a palpable uncertainty exists in regard to selecting appropriate methods, techniques, and tools on which to base their improvement initiatives.

In this context, one of the attractive options from the IT domain is *workflow management technology*. A workflow management system (WfMS) is a software system that supports the specification, execution, and control of business processes. WfMSs have been widely and successfully applied in various industries to

S. Rinderle-Ma et al. (Eds.): BPM 2009 Workshops, LNBIP 43, pp. 593–604, 2010.

streamline process execution, lower cycle times, and liberate human actors from routine coordination work, see e.g. [1,2,3]. What is surprising, however, is that this technology is rarely applied in the healthcare domain [4,5].

Perhaps this is due to the predominant concern of IT projects in the healthcare domain with the storage, retrieval, and uniformization of patient data for high-profile Electronic Patient Record (EPR) initiatives, as for example noted in [6]. This selective view on *data* usage obstructs a more comprehensive *process perspective* on healthcare operations. It is the focus on the latter perspective that has been instrumental in other domains in achieving significant efficiency improvements. Without it, the application of workflow management technology may not even be considered, or at best becomes hard to implement [7].

This paper is concerned with another possible reason for workflow's limited track record in healthcare settings: the belief – justified or not – that health-care processes (or *careflows*) are intrinsically different from those found in other domains. The recent literature highlights the ability to deal with exceptions as a major success factor for applying workflow technology in any context [8] and "this is particularly true in healthcare applications, where flexibility is a condition sine-qua-non for using a computerized system"[4]. For many, it is un-clear whether workflow technology provides the support for a crucially important requirement in medical processes: the ability to flexibly deviate from the stan-dardized procedure for a category of patients with the same diagnosis. Other work that relates to this issue is reported, for example, in [9,10].

In this paper, we propose a methodology for realizing processes that possess the degree of flexibility required for deployment in the healthcare domain. This instrument is intended to reduce the uncertainty surrounding the suitability of workflow technology in the medical domain and to facilitate a rational decision-making process regarding its application. Primarily, the instrument builds on the flexibility taxonomy as published in [11]. Also, it incorporates earlier re-search into control-flow, data, and resource patterns that can be distinguished in workflow processes [12,13,14]. To demonstrate the feasibility of the instru-ment, this paper contains a case study of its application in an outpatient clinic of the Catharina Hospital Eindhoven.

The structure of the paper is as follows. We start with providing a background on the relevant ingredients for the proposed methodology in Section 2. The main contribution of this paper, the flexible process realization methodology, is described in Section 3. Next, our case study is presented in Section 4. We end this paper with a summary and a discussion.

2   Background

2.1   Flexibility Patterns

Flexibility patterns [11] describe a series of approaches for enhancing the flex-ibility of a business process. Flexibility is considered to be the ability to deal with changes in the operational environment through the pursuit of alternate execution paths which may not have been foreseen at design-time and are not explicitly catered for by the process model. The flexibility patterns are based on the *Taxonomy of Process Flexibility* [15] which recognizes five distinct approaches to incorporating flexibility in a process: (1) *flexibility by design* involves the explicit incorporation of flexibility mechanisms into a process at design-time using available process modelling constructs such as splits and joins, (2) *flexibility by deviation* involves allowing individual process instances to temporarily deviate from the prescribed process model at runtime in order to accommodate identified changes, (3) *flexibility by underspecification* is the ability to deliberately underspecify parts of a process model at design-time in anticipation of the fact that the required execution details will become known some future time, (4) *flexibility by momentary change* involves changing the process model for a specific process instance at runtime and (5) *flexibility by permanent change* involves changing the process model for all process instances at runtime. Thirty four flexibility patterns have been proposed as summarized in Table 1. These are divided into eight distinct groups depending on the specific intent of the pattern.

Table 1. Flexibility patterns in summary

Pattern Focus	Flexibility Type				
	Design	Deviation	Underspecification	Momentary Change	Permanent Change
Flexible initiation	Alternative entry points	Entrance skip	Undefined entry	Momentary entry change	Permanent entry change
Flexible termination	Alternative exit points	Termination skip	Undefined exit	Momentary exit-point change	Permanent exit-point change
Flexible selection	Choice	Task substitution	Late selection	Momentary choice insertion	Permanent choice insertion
Flexible reordering	Interleaving	Swap		Momentary reordering	Permanent reordering
Flexible elimination	Foreseen bypass path	Task skip		Momentary task elimination	Permanent task elimination
Flexible extension		Task invocation	Late creation	Momentary task insertion	Permanent task insertion
Flexible concurrency	Parallelism			Momentary task parallelization	Permanent task parallelization
Flexible repetition	Iteration	Redo		Momentary loop insertion	Permanent loop insertion

2.2 Workflow Patterns

The Workflow patterns are a collection of 126 patterns identified as part of the *Workflow Patterns Initiative*, a multi-year collaborative research effort focused on providing a conceptual basis for process technology. Workflow patterns describe *desirable* properties of business processes and provide a comprehensive source book of the requirements and scenarios commonly encountered during their modelling and enactment. In common with other patterns initiatives, the workflow patterns were identified on an experiential basis through surveys of commercial and open-source offerings, standards and modelling formalisms and comprehensive literature reviews. Patterns are described in an imperative form identifying a specific problem that arises in a business process context that is both recurrent and has generic applicability, and offer one or more possible solutions by which it can be addressed. Workflow patterns have been identified in a number of orthogonal process perspectives including the control-flow [12], data [13] and resource [14] dimensions. Since their release, the workflow patterns have been used for a wide variety of purposes including evaluation of process technology, tool selection, process design, education and training. They have been enthusiastically received by both industry practitioners and academics alike. Further details can be found at http://www.workflowpatterns.com.

3   Methodology

The healthcare domain is an area that has the potential to benefit markedly from the appropriate deployment of workflow technology. However the difficulty when developing suitable process support in this area is in determining what aspects of existing careflows should be captured and how they can be catered for from a technological standpoint. A pre-eminent consideration in this regard is in ensuring that the flexibility requirements of existing careflows are fully recognized and retained and where possible augmented further so as to maximize the utility of the automated process.

The *Flexible process realization methodology* is a four stage technique designed to guide healthcare practitioners through the process of readying their existing careflows for workflow deployment and in doing so it seeks to maximize the flexibility embodied in a given process. It is composed of four distinct stages: *discovery, exploration, selection* and *realization* as illustrated in Figure 1. Each of these stages are discussed in more detail in the following sections.

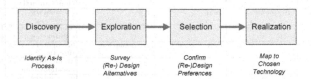

Fig. 1. Flexible process realization methodology

3.1   Discovery

The first step in automating a healthcare process is to determine what form the process takes. In many situations, including those encountered at the Catharina Hospital, there is no existing process support in place or even any documented procedures that dictate the way in which the careflow is undertaken. Consequently there is the need to *discover* the process from first principles. During this phase of the methodology, the aim is both to gain a thorough understanding of the current (As Is) healthcare process and to document it in a form that allows for subsequent evaluation and enhancement. Key steps in the discovery process include:

– Systematic observation of careflow execution, including diagnostic activities, surgical and treatment procedures and consultation meetings both between medical staff members and also those involving medical practitioners and the patient;

- Structured interviews with key staff members to gain an understanding of their role in overall careflow delivery;
- Documenting the discovered process in a form that captures the key sequences of events and decision points, the flow of information during the careflow and the staff responsibilities and involvement in individual tasks within the overall careflow; and
- Validating the identified process with key staff members to ensure it is both complete and correct.

Once the candidate careflow process has been delineated, it is possible to move onto examining how existing flexibility requirements are met by the discovered process and what additional opportunities might exist for enhancing its capabilities in this area.

3.2 Exploration

The second stage in the methodology is the *exploration* of alternative approaches to augmenting current flexibility support in the candidate careflow process. This is based on the use of the flexibility patterns discussed in Section 2.1. These are used in two distinct ways during this stage: (1) as a means of stimulating input from domain experts as to conceivable deviations from the documented As-Is process and (2) as a way of precisely describing the changes to be made to the As-Is process.

The basic conduct of the exploration stage involves a facilitated discussion amongst a group of domain experts who have experience in conducting tasks within the careflow under consideration. It comprises four distinct phases:

1. Briefing domain experts about the operation of the As-Is process model revealed during the discovery stage;
2. Identification of potential operational scenarios that are not captured by the As-Is model;
3. Consideration of the various flexibility patterns in the context of the As-Is model as a means of seeding other possible operational scenarios; and
4. Identification of the specific flexibility patterns that can assist in catering for the additional operational scenarios revealed during steps 2 and 3.

At the conclusion of this stage of the methodology, the knowledge contained in the As-Is process model is augmented with a series of additional operational scenarios that need to be catered for and a set of flexibility patterns that may assist in this effort. The next stage of the methodology takes these various items as input and determines what the ultimate form of the careflow to be realized will be.

3.3 Selection

This stage of the methodology focuses on selecting the specific flexibility patterns and operational scenarios that it is feasible to support and modifying the As-Is model to incorporate them. Two distinct types of decisions need to be made during this phase: (1) which of the additional operational scenarios identified are to be realized and (2) which of the identified flexibility patterns will be utilized. The first of these decisions typically requires stakeholder input in order to assess the feasibility of supporting the additional operational scenarios identified. Determining which flexibility patterns will be supported involves consideration of the corresponding flexibility types. Typically there are organizational factors that will influence which of these flexibility types are acceptable, e.g. often flexibility by deviation is not acceptable if a concrete process model is required against which operational compliance can be assessed. At the conclusion of this stage of the methodology, the To-Be process model is revealed.

3.4   Realization

The final stage of the method involves selecting the technology which will realize the To-Be process model. For this purpose the various classes of workflow patterns are utilized as a means of benchmarking the control-flow, data and resource requirements of the To-Be process model. Based on the required pattern support that is identified, the results can be correlated with those from other patterns-based technology evaluations to identify a suitable implementation offering on which to base the careflow deployment.

4   Case Study

4.1   Background

The case study focuses on the treatment of patients with skin cancer and premalignant skin lesions in the outpatient dermatology clinic of the Catharina Hospital. It is the largest specialized provider of skin cancer treatment in the Netherlands. The treatment of skin cancer, which may involve various interventions and therapies, accounts for roughly 50% of the time of the dermatologists' working in this clinic, and involves the treatment of 5,000 patients per year.

What can be noted on a worldwide scale, can also be observed at the Catharina Hospital: the incidence of skin cancer is rising dramatically [16]. However, the steady, yearly increase of 5-10% in patient numbers cannot be matched with a similar increase of resources. To maintain the required quality level of care and still allow for the treatment of other dermatology patients, the Catharina Hospital has initiated the development of a *disease management system for skin cancer*. This is an extensive program that covers a variety of elements, such as intensified prevention activities, training of specialized dermato-oncology nurses, and smart interweaving of medical treatments (see [17] for more details). The consideration to apply workflow technology, the subject of this section, fits within this overall disease management system.

4.2   Discovery

This phase focused on identifying the existing process, commencing with the observation of 17 patients undergoing various types of surgery and 15 patients during consultation meetings, over a two week timeframe. During the consultation meetings, it was possible to ask for clarification on follow-up activities and the reasons why dermatologists decided to carry out certain activities or skip them. Further details were also uncovered in interviews with the dermatologists and nurses. In particular, to find out the exact differences between all possible treatments, three dermatologists and two nurses were interviewed. As the last two of these five interviews showed such a high level of correlation with established earlier information it was decided that further ones were unnecessary.

A high-level overview of the process model emerging from this phase can be seen in Figure 2. It is modeled using the YAWL notation [18], making it convenient for identifying the various patterns in the successive evaluation steps.

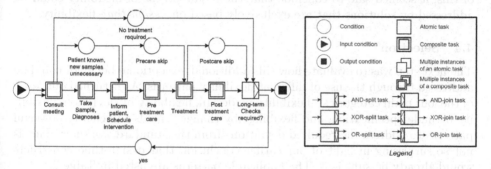

Fig. 2. High-level overview of the As-Is process

In essence, the process consists of a diagnosis phase (consult meeting, take sample, diagnoses, inform patient, schedule intervention), a treatment phase (pre-treatment care, treatment), and after care (post treatment care, long-term checks required). Parts of the process can be skipped for individual patients, and the process can be repeated time and again, e.g. for chronic patients. Because of space restrictions, we cannot present the full process, the accompanying resource classification, or details on the data usage but these were all mapped.

For validating the process models it was decided to perform structured walkthroughs with the three most experienced dermatologists, preceded by a familiarization phase with the notation and the model. During the validation meeting with the first physician, a number of changes were made to the detailed model and some decision constructs were added. The second and third dermatologist asserted that the corrected models adequately reflected the *standard* process adequately. This, in their estimations, accounts for 80% of the population.

4.3   Exploration

To establish the process flow for complex patients and assess other unanticipated process behavior, two separate meetings with two dermatologists were scheduled.

It turned out that the differences for the 20% of complex patients with the standard flow can explained by differences in the type of treatment interventions, i.e. the middle part of the overall process as depicted in Figure 2. For normal patients, there is an exclusive choice between five different interventions. For complex patients, however, any finite sequence of interventions is possible that have zero or more occurrences for each, e.g. treatment of type (2) followed by a treatment of type (3), or two successive treatments of type (2). At the same time, there is strong preference in the ordering of such treatments. For example, a type (3) treatment should only be commenced out after treatment type (2) has been completed.

Despite extensive brainstorming and the explicit discussion of scenarios not covered by the above description, no further deviations from the standardized flow could be conceived by the dermatologists involved. It should be taken into account that their experience extends to over 20,000 different cases. On the basis of this, it seemed safe to conclude that the required type of flexibility could be addressed by solutions that are exclusively based on *design-time* flexibility.

4.4   Selection

The next step was to evaluate how this additional, exceptional behavior could be addressed through the use of different flexibility patterns. As it turned out, each of the four main categories – flexibility by design, flexibility by deviation, flexibility by underspecification, and flexibility by change – holds sufficiently powerful patterns to address the required deviations from the standard workflow. This is not so surprising in light of our earlier conclusion that design-time constructs would already be sufficient. The applicable patterns are listed in Table 2.

Table 2. Flexibility patterns addressing the requirements for exceptional cases

Flexibility by	Addressed by Patterns
Design	Interleaving, Iteration
Deviation	Task Invocation
Underspecification	Late Selection
Change	Momentary Task Insertion, Momentary Loop Insertion, Permanent Choice Insertion, Permanent Task Insertion, Permanent Loop Insertion

Due to space restrictions, we do not present the complete solutions for each of the pattern sets. For the sake of illustration, the relevant fragment of the process model, the part that specifies the treatment phase, is shown in Figure 3 for both the flexibility by design (a) and flexibility by underspecification (b) solutions. In the case of the latter, the treatment task is shown as a placeholder for the late selection of a pre-specified sequence of treatments (not displayed).

Which of the flexibility categories offers the most effective means of supporting the process in question depends on a number of different factors. In this case,

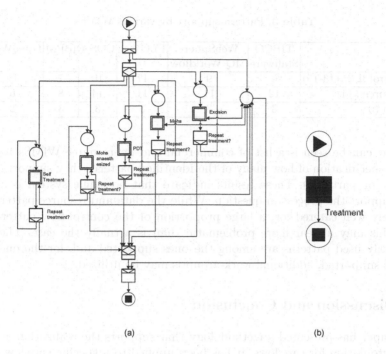

(a)   (b)

Fig. 3. Alternative solutions: (a) flexibility by design, and (b) flexibility by underspecification

we discussed the differences between each of the possible solutions with the stakeholders with a specific focus on (1) the ease of enforcing compliance to the specific process, (2) comprehensibility of the process to stakeholders, (3) skills required to implement and maintain the solution (e.g. adding new treatments) and (4) the time and effort required to make modifications. By working through this sequence of events, it was possible to arrive at a decision as to the most effective solution. In this case, the solution offered by flexibility by design proved to be most aligned with the stakeholder's requirements and they were able to confidently reject the ones that did not meet with their needs, e.g. the solution as offered by flexibility by change was not preferred because it seemed too difficult to apply in field, whilst that based on flexibility by deviation was not useful as it did not provide a means of ensuring process compliance.

4.5   Realization

The four complete solutions were assessed with respect to the control-flow, data and resource patterns that they cover. Depending on the exact solution, between 13 and 15 control-flow patterns can be identified as being necessary. In addition, regardless of the solution, three data-patterns and 14 resource patterns were identified. When these were matched against the evaluations that have been published in [12,13,14], a picture emerges that is summarized in Table 3.

Table 3. Pattern support by various WfMSs

	TIBCO Staffware	WebSphere MQ Workflow	FLOWer	COSA	jBPM	OpenWFE
control flow (13-15)	6	9	11	10	7	11
resource (14)	12	11	11	14	8	6
data (3)	3	3	3	3	3	2

What can be seen is a list of commercial and open-source WfMSs together with a specification of how many of the identified patterns they support (either directly or partially). These results indicate that no single system is able to fully support the process in question. While the data and resource patterns are relatively well catered for, a large proportion of the control-flow patterns are not. This may appear more problematic than is actually the case. The most frequently used patterns are among the ones supported and, for the ones that are not supported, additional work-arounds may be utilized.

5   Discussion and Conclusion

This paper has presented a methodology that supports the realization of workflow automation for careflows. It has been applied to a specific careflow at the Catharina Hospital. The methodology incorporates four steps, including a detailed flexibility assessment of the As-Is process using the flexibility and workflow patterns. Our assessment on the basis of our case study is that the method is feasible in practice.

This work is subject to several limitations. First of all, it is questionable to what extent the applicability of our proposed method can be generalized. This can only be established by subsequent work, which we intend to conduct with our partners. Secondly, it should be noted that the proposed method by its focus on *flexibility* only takes into account one of the many aspects that should be considered when realizing process support. Technical aspects (e.g. integration with legacy systems), the political context (e.g. management support), and cultural factors (e.g. acceptance) are also known to play an important role in making a workflow implementation a success [19].

This study once again demonstrates the tangible support offered by the *Workflow Patterns Initiative* for technology assessments in the process support domain. The patterns have been extremely useful in our discussions with healthcare professionals, as well as in the evaluation of actual technologies.

The most important observation arising from our work is the resounding confirmation of the potential of workflow technology to embody the range flexibility requirements encountered in a healthcare setting. This observation is consistent with earlier positive findings in this domain [5]. Several reasons for this result in this particular context may be considered.

First of all, acute care of critically ill patients where patient conditions change rapidly is *not* delivered at the outpatient clinic we considered. In line with a paper that we presented at the previous ProHealth workshop, it can be conjectured that acute care will require an entirely different level of flexibility support.

Secondly, and perhaps more importantly, the healthcare professionals involved in this study have shown themselves to be surprisingly process-aware and, in many cases, already consider their work practices in terms of processes comprised of constituent tasks with alternate pathways between them depending on the circumstances encountered. This form of thinking appears to be independent of the extent of (or even the lack of) existing technology support and to stem from more general factors inherent in this field, such as the general adoption of standard treatment schedules, the high degree of correlation between individual patient treatment trajectories, and the understanding that there are important decision points at various stages of a given treatment that may necessitate deviations from standard treatment practices.

If similar conditions can be established for other careflows, we sincerely hope that our results will foster the consideration of workflow technology as a powerful means of improving operational efficiency.

Acknowledgement

We wish to acknowledge the help of Robert de Groot and all involved dermatologists, nurses, and administrative staff of the Catharina Hospital Eindhoven.

References

1. Doherty, N.F., Perry, I.: The uptake and application of workflow management systems in the UK financial services sector. Journal of Information Technology 14(2), 149–160 (1999)
2. Liu, J., Zhang, S., Hu, J.: A case study of an inter-enterprise workflow-supported supply chain management system. Information & Management 42(3), 441–454 (2005)
3. Reijers, H.A., Poelmans, S.: Re-configuring workflow management systems to facilitate a "smooth flow of work". International Journal of Cooperative Information Systems 16(2), 155–175 (2007)
4. Quaglini, S., Stefanelli, M., Lanzola, G., Caporusso, V., Panzarasa, S.: Flexible guideline-based patient careflow systems. Artificial Intelligence in Medicine 22(1), 65–80 (2001)
5. Lenz, R., Reichert, M.: IT support for healthcare processes–premises, challenges, perspectives. Data & Knowledge Engineering 61(1), 39–58 (2007)
6. Van Hee, K.M., Schonenberg, H., Serebrenik, A., Sidorova, N., van der Werf, J.M.: Adaptive Workflows for Healthcare Information Systems. In: ter Hofstede, A.H.M., Benatallah, B., Paik, H.-Y. (eds.) BPM Workshops 2007. LNCS, vol. 4928, pp. 359–370. Springer, Heidelberg (2008)
7. Reijers, H.A.: Implementing BPM systems: the role of process orientation. Business Process Management Journal 12(4), 389–409 (2006)
8. Weber, B., Reichert, M., Rinderle-Ma, S.: Change patterns and change support features–enhancing flexibility in process-aware information systems. Data & Knowledge Engineering 66(3), 438–466 (2008)

604   H.A. Reijers et al.

9. Greiner, U., Ramsch, J., Heller, B.: Adaptive guideline-based treatment workflows with AdaptFlow. In: Proceedings of the Symposium on Computerized Guidelines and Protocols (CGP 2004), pp. 113–117. IOS Press, Amsterdam (2004)
10. Han, M., Thiery, T., Song, X.: Managing exceptions in the medical workflow systems. In: Proceedings of the 28th international conference on Software engineering, pp. 741–750. ACM, New York (2006)
11. Mulyar, N., Russell, N., Van der Aalst, W.M.P.: Process flexibility patterns. Working paper WP 251, Beta Research School (2008)
12. Russell, N., ter Hofstede, A.H.M., Van der Aalst, W.M.P., Mulyar, N.: Workflow control-flow patterns: A revised view. BPM Center Report BPM-06-22, BPM Center (2006)
13. Russell, N., ter Hofstede, A.H.M., Edmond, D., van der Aalst, W.M.P.: Workflow data patterns: Identification, representation and tool support. In: Delcambre, L.M.L., Kop, C., Mayr, H.C., Mylopoulos, J., Pastor, Ó. (eds.) ER 2005. LNCS, vol. 3716, pp. 353–368. Springer, Heidelberg (2005)
14. Russell, N., Van der Aalst, W.M.P., ter Hofstede, A.H.M., Edmond, D.: Workflow resource patterns: Identification, representation and tool support. In: Pastor, Ó., Falcão e Cunha, J. (eds.) CAiSE 2005. LNCS, vol. 3520, pp. 216–232. Springer, Heidelberg (2005)
15. Schonenberg, M., Mans, R.S., Russell, N., Mulyar, N., van der Aalst, W.M.P.: Process flexibility: A survey of contemporary approaches. In: Dietz, J.L.G., et al. (eds.) CIAO! 2008 and EOMAS 2008. LNBIP, vol. 10, pp. 16–30. Springer, Heidelberg (2008)
16. De Vries, E., van de Poll-Franse, L.V., Louwman, W.J., De Gruijl, F.R., Coebergh, J.W.W.: Predictions of skin cancer incidence in the Netherlands up to 2015. British Journal of Dermatology 152(3), 481 (2005)
17. Van der Geer, S., Reijers, H.A., Krekels, G.A.M.: How to run an effective and efficient dermato-oncology unit. Journal of the German Society of Dermatology (2009) (in press)
18. Van der Aalst, W.M.P., ter Hofstede, A.H.M.: YAWL: yet another workflow language. Information Systems 30(4), 245–275 (2005)
19. Parkes, A.: Critical success factors in workflow implementation. In: Terano, T., Myers, M.D. (eds.) Proceedings of the Sixth Pacific Asia Conference on Information Systems, Jasmin, pp. 363–380 (2002)

BPR Best Practices for the Healthcare Domain

Mariska Netjes, Ronny S. Mans, Hajo A. Reijers, Wil M.P. van der Aalst,
and R.J.B. Vanwersch

Eindhoven University of Technology,
P.O. Box 513, NL-5600 MB, Eindhoven, The Netherlands
{m.netjes,r.s.mans,h.a.reijers,w.m.p.v.d.aalst}@tue.nl

Abstract. Healthcare providers are under pressure to work more efficiently and in a more patient-focused way. One possible way to achieve this is to launch Business Process Redesign (BPR) initiatives, which focus on changing the structure of the involved processes and using IT as an enabler for such changes. In this paper, we argue that a list of historically successful improvement tactics, the *BPR best practices*, are a highly suitable ingredient for such efforts in the healthcare domain. Our assessment is based on the analysis of 14 case studies. The insights obtained by the analysis also led to an extension of the original set of best practices.

Keywords: Healthcare, Business Process Redesign, best practices.

1 Introduction

Healthcare providers need to reduce operational costs while improving the quality of care [9]. Since in various countries the healthcare sector is reorganized on a free-market basis, it makes sense for patients to visit the provider with the shortest access time or the lowest costs. The healthcare domain is responding to this trend with a focus on efficiency and process improvement. One dominant form of improvement initiatives that results from these developments is known as Business Process Redesign (BPR). In a BPR initiative, the focus is on the improvement of an entire, cross-functional business process. Typically, such an effort consists of describing the *as-is* situation, performing an analysis of the *as-is* to find bottlenecks, and constructing the *to-be* process [7].

In the BPR field, the use of so-called BPR best practices [16] is one way to support the creation of one or more *to-be* processes from the *as-is* process. A BPR best practice – or best practice, for short – is a solution that has been applied previously and seems worthwhile to replicate in another situation or setting. By going through this set of best practices, practitioners can find inspiration to generate evolutionary, local updates to an existing process. The use of a set of best practices can be easily integrated in existing redesign methodologies, such as the one in [18]. Furthermore, an evolutionary approach using best practices is probably the most appropriate for improvement efforts in the healthcare domain [3]. When applying best practices in the healthcare domain, the focus is on the

S. Rinderle-Ma et al. (Eds.): BPM 2009 Workshops, LNBIP 43, pp. 605–616, 2010.

organization and structure of the involved processes and not on improving the medical practice itself. In this sense, a best practice describes a pattern for improvement. In [14], a pattern-based analysis is applied on clinical guideline modeling languages to evaluate their support of the control-flow patterns.

While one earlier application of the best practices in the healthcare domain has been reported in [10], no convincing argument has been made yet about the potential of their application. Clearly, this is an important issue if successful and appropriate usage of best practices could help to move the healthcare domain to higher levels of performance. Against this background, we aim to further investigate the use of best practices in the healthcare domain by addressing the following questions:

1. To what extent are the best practices suitable for redesigning healthcare processes?
2. Is the use of best practices effective in the healthcare domain?
3. Is it possible to extend the set of best practices with the lessons learned from redesigning healthcare processes?

The outline of this paper is as follows. In Section 2, we provide some background information on the best practices and their application. Section 3 presents the methodology that has been followed in this paper to answer the research questions. In Section 4, we address the first research question, i.e., the suitability of the best practices to the healthcare domain. Section 5 deals with the second research question and in Section 6 the third research question is addressed. This paper concludes with a discussion and concluding remarks.

2   Background

In this section we present the best practices, which are embedded in a conceptual framework, and we provide a method for the application of best practices.

Although many methodologies, techniques and tools are available to facilitate a BPR effort, little concrete support is provided on how to create the *to-be* situation from the *as-is* [15]. For the guidance and support of the redesign process itself, we earlier defined a BPR framework [16] (see Figure 1). The various components of the framework help to distinguish the different aspects that can be addressed in a BPR initiative. These aspects guide users to the most appropriate subset of best practices that are relevant to improve a certain aspect. In [16], we have identified best practices related to the topics in the framework by conducting a literature review and evaluating the successful execution of BPR implementations. For each best practice, a qualitative description, its potential effects, and possible drawbacks are given. The identified best practices are considered to be applicable across a wide range of domains, such as governmental, industrial, and financial processes. For an overview of the 29 best practices we refer the reader to Appendix A. The framework and its associated best practices have been validated among a wide group of BPR practitioners in the UK and the Netherlands. The main conclusion is that the framework is helpful in supporting

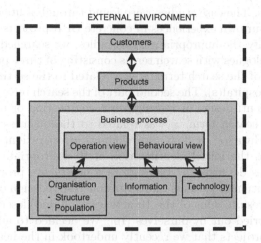

Fig. 1. The BPR framework

process redesign and that its core elements are recognized and frequently put to practice by the BPR practitioner community [13].

To provide methodological support for the application of the best practices, we described in [10] a sequence of successive phases that a BPR initiative may go through:

1. The process is *modeled* in such a way that it is a realistic image of the real process and that it can be used for *simulation* purposes. The process model and the simulation results for this initial model have to be *validated* with the process owner.
2. For each *best practice* it is considered which part(s) of the process, i.e., set of tasks, may potentially benefit from this particular best practice. The result of this step is (a) a list of applicable best practices, and (b) a list of process parts that may be changed by one or more best practices.
3. For each process part, the redesign consultant and the process owner decide which (combination of) best practice(s) is interesting. This step results in a number of *to-be* scenarios.
4. For each scenario a *new process model is created* by adapting the initial model. A simulation study is used to evaluate the effect of a scenario and the simulation results are compared with the results of the initial model. The models and results are validated with the process owner.
5. The final step is to *decide* which scenarios are taken into account when actually redesigning the process.

3 Methodology

To investigate the suitability and effectiveness of best practices for the redesign of healthcare processes, we mainly build on a set of case studies to address our research questions. The case studies were found through a literature review and augmented with our own experiences in concrete BPR projects in the healthcare domain. To identify the appropriate case studies, we searched the ABI/Inform and INSPEC catalogues with search terms consisting of three parts (x and y and z). The first part of the search term, x, was related to the setting: health or care or healthcare or hospital(s). The second part of the search term, y, was related to the redesign element: design or redesign or reengineering or management. The third part of the search term, z, was related to the business process element: process(es) or pathway(s) or flow(s) of chain(s) or operation(s) or operational. This search led to the initial identification of 10 appropriate case studies. All the related articles describe the redesign of a healthcare process that involves the close participation of patients and state concrete redesign options and quantitative redesign results. One of the 10 articles we found describes a case study that has been carried out by ourselves [10]. We decided to add two more case studies on BPR projects that we recently undertook in the health care domain, and decided to include two more case studies that we were aware of through our cooperation with the Dutch Academic Medical Center (AMC). The latter two have been carried out and described by Elkhuizen [6]. In total, this brings the number of case studies that were considered for this paper to a total of 14.

4   Suitability of Best Practices

As stated before, the described redesign approach with best practices has been tested earlier within the context of a single case study [10]. This leads to the preliminary insight that some of the best practices seem applicable, but we wish to confirm that a large part of the best practices is applicable to a wide range of healthcare settings. In particular, we explore in this section the following question "To what extent are the best practices suitable for redesigning healthcare processes?". To answer this question, we make a distinction between the case studies that explicitly applied the best practices, and the case studies in which the participants did not use our particular set of best practices to create *to-be* scenarios.

4.1   Explicit Use of Best Practices

We have conducted three BPR initiatives in a healthcare setting that explicitly reflect on and use the set of best practices. In Table 1, these are listed as case studies 1 to 3. Each case study includes 5 to 7 feasible *to-be* scenarios and each scenario involves the combined application of multiple best practices. These best practices are also listed in Table 1 (see Appendix A for the meaning of the abbreviations). Case study 1 involved the improvement of the intake procedure that processes new requests for non-urgent treatment of elderly patients at a Dutch mental healthcare institute. One identified *to-be* scenario consists of asking the referring family doctor at referral for the medical file of the patient. This scenario combines the following best practices: *contact reduction* (REDUC), *exception* (EXCEP), *resequencing* (RESEQ) and *triage* (TRI). Another identified *to-be* scenario consists of giving the intakers the full responsibility for the determination of the treatment plan. This empowerment of the intakers is prescribed by the *empower* (EMP) best practice. Case study 2 and 3 are performed at a Dutch hospital in the southern part of the Netherlands. Case study 2 evaluates the procedure for processing elective and semi-urgent Percutaneous Coronary Intervention (PCI) requests at the cardiology department. Examples of *to-be* scenarios that the process owner classified as successful are the use of an electronic registration form to add information at once to the central information system (a combination of ELIM, RESEQ, AUTO, SPLIT and TECH), and combining two intake meetings (COMPOS and REDUC). Case study 3 investigates the treatment processes at the dermatology oncology department including consultations, pre treatment care, treatment and post treatment care. Examples of proposed *to-be* scenarios are the immediate analysis of a biopsy while the patient is waiting (a combination of PAR, REDUC and ELIM) and combining the scheduling and informing of the patient (REDUC and ASSIGN). For case studies 1, 2 and 3 it can be concluded that for each study a substantial number of best practices is applicable.

Table 1. Case studies and applicable BPR best practices

Nr.	Subject	Applied best practices
		Explicit use of best practices
1	patient intake in mental healthcare institute [10]	COMPOS, TECH, CASEB, XRES, REDUC,EXCEP, RESEQ, TRI, AUTO, ELIM, INTG, PAR, EMP
2	invasive cardiologic therapeutic procedure in cardiology department	ELIM, RESEQ, AUTO, SPLIT, TECH, RELOC, CASEB, COMPOS, REDUC, XRES, SPEC
3	treatment process in dermatology oncology outpatient clinic	ASSIGN, INTG, PAR, REDUC, ELIM, RELOC, SPLIT, SPEC
		Implicit use of best practices
4	diagnosis process in outpatient gynecological oncology department [6]	TRUST, RESEQ, REDUC, XRES, TYPE, EMP
5	diagnosis in pulmonology outpatient clinic [6]	REDUC, RESEQ, TYPE, EXCEP, EMP
6	process at Walk-in Centre (multi-service facility) [1]	TRI, SPEC, ADD, XRES
7	operation cycle for emergency and hospitalized patients [2]	SPEC, CENTR, TRI, XRES
8	process at Magnetic Resonance Imaging (MRI) department [5]	TYPE, CASEB, ELIM
9	the outpatient consultation process in internal medicine department [11]	RELOC, REDUC, COMPOS, TECH, PAR, RESEQ, XRES, AUTO
10-14	other healthcare case studies	XRES

4.2 Implicit Use of Best Practices

The majority of the 14 case studies did not rely on an explicit consideration of our set of best practices to create *to-be* scenarios. In Table 1, these case studies are listed as case studies 4 to 14. However, because the related papers specifically describe the interventions that have been proposed, it is possible to determine retrospectively which of the best practices that we distinguished were used after all. We will refer to these as 'implicitly used' best practices. We conclude that a best practice is implicitly applied if part of the intervention is highly similar to the description of a best practice as published in [16]. In case study 4, for instance, part of the intervention consists of redesigning the diagnostic process such that a uniform set of examinations is provided for patients with dyspnea. A receptionist triages new patients to see whether they are referred for dyspnea. In this description we recognize, among others, the implicit use of the *case types* (TYPE) best practice and the *trusted party* (TRUST) best practice. The *case types* best practice "distinguishes separate processes and case types" which has been done for patients with dyspnea. The *trusted party* best practice suggests to "replace a decision task by the decision of an external party", i.e., trust the referral with dyspnea. Another example can be found in case study 7, which describes the redesign of an operating theater by changing the degree of specialization / generalization of the involved resources. Here, we derive the implicit use of the *specialist-generalist* (SPEC) best practice which is "consider making resources more specialized or generalized". Table 1 lists the best practices that we consider to be implicitly applied in case studies 4 to 14. Note that the number of best practices per case study is less than the number in the case studies we performed ourselves. The main reason for this is that in the papers that relate to case studies 4 to 14 only the implemented *to-be* scenario is described, while our case studies have included several possible *to-be* scenarios.

Based on this analysis, the answer to the question "To what extent are the best practices suitable for redesigning healthcare processes?" is that almost three quarters of the total number of available best practices has been applied, across a wide variety of healthcare settings. In the case studies that explicitly applied best practices, 17 different best practices have been used. In the case studies that implicitly used best practices, we distinguished 18 different best practices. Altogether, Table 1 covers 21 best practices out of the available 29. This indicates that our small test sample suggests that the existing set of best practices is suitable for application in healthcare. This does not necessarily mean that its application leads to improved performance. In the next section, we address the second research question and discuss the effectiveness of the application of best practices.

5 Effectiveness of Best Practices

In the previous section, our findings suggested that our best practices are applied in the healthcare domain. The next question, then, is "Is the use of best practices effective?". We consider the use of best practices to be effective, if the *to-be* process created with the best practices shows an improved performance on the chosen performance indicators, i.e., the improvement goals of the redesign effort have been achieved. First, we evaluate the effectiveness of the best practices applied in case studies 1 to 3. In these case studies simulation studies are used to predict whether a *to-be* scenario may be effective. However, a simulation study cannot give the ultimate proof that a certain *to-be* scenario indeed performs better than the *as-is* process. Fortunately, in case studies 4, 5 and 8 the performance of the *as-is* process (before intervention) and the *to-be* process (after intervention) has been measured and compared.

5.1   Simulation-Based *To-be* Evaluation

The *to-be* scenarios of case studies 1 to 3 are evaluated in conformance with the fourth phase of the redesign approach. On the one hand, the process owner decides which *to-be* scenarios are most suitable and which performance dimensions, i.e., costs or throughput time, (s)he finds most important. On the other hand, a simulation study is used to determine the key performance indicators for each scenario. For case studies 1 to 3, the simulation results of most of the *to-be* scenarios show an improvement with respect to the chosen performance indicators. In case study 1, for instance, the *to-be* scenario involving the request of the medical file of the patient at referral predicts a throughput time reduction of 13%. The *to-be* scenario of case study 1 involving the empowerment of the intakers to determine the treatment plan predicts a 20% reduction of the throughput time, decreasing the average throughput time from 10 to 8 days [10]. It can, however, not be guaranteed that in real life a certain *to-be* scenario indeed performs as the simulation results indicate. This can only be tested by the implementation of a *to-be* scenario and a measurement of the effect of the change. Based on case studies 1 to 3, therefore, we can only tentatively state that best practices have the potential to be effective.

5.2   *To-be* Evaluation by Post-intervention Measurement

Case studies 4, 5 and 8 include information on the performance of the implemented *to-be* process. The effects of the intervention are evaluated with a before-after design including post-intervention measurements. The post-intervention measurements of case study 4 show that the percentage of patients that can access treatment within 7 days is increased from 60% to 100%. Furthermore, waiting times in the process and the total throughput time are significantly reduced [6]. Case study 5 shows a significant reduction of throughput time (from 37 to 9 days) and the number of visits (from 4 to slightly more than 2) [6]. Case study 8 also describes a before-after comparative study with the goal to maximize MRI capacity. The measurements indicate that the average MRI examination time was shortened by five minutes per patient resulting in an 18% increase in patient throughput for MRI examinations [5]. For the sake of completeness, we note that case studies 6, 7 and 9-14 include mathematical and/or simulation results.

The answer to the question "Is the use of best practices effective?" is that it is *plausible*. Process owners find *to-be* scenarios created with best practices suitable and simulation studies show that such *to-be* scenarios may result in an improvement in performance. Furthermore, post-intervention measurements in case studies 4, 5 and 8 give an improvement in performance which can primarily be attributed to the (implicit) application of best practices. In the next section, we address the third research question and derive additional, specific best practices from the healthcare domain.

6   Derivation of Best Practices

In this section, we address the last research question "Is it possible to extend the set of best practices with the lessons learned from redesigning healthcare processes?". An evaluation of the *to-be* scenarios proposed in the case studies reveals that not all changes are covered by the current set of best practices. Therefore, we revisit the case studies from Table 1 to find the lessons learned and discover new potential best practices. Note that the components of the redesign framework remain unchanged. For each identified potential best practice that we describe next, we include its name and abbreviation, a motivation why it should be included, a qualitative description, its potential effects, and references to related literature beyond the healthcare domain.

Customer Involvement. Hospitals are putting increasing effort into making healthcare more patient-centered. Most improvements, however, have been based on assumptions made by professionals. Therefore, the patient's view should be taken into account when making decisions on redesign priorities [6]. The patient is one of the customers of a healthcare provider. We propose to add the following best practice to the *customer* element of the BPR framework.

INVOL: *Obtain insight in the demands of customers and the added value and bottlenecks as perceived by customers.*

Application of this best practice improves the quality of *to-be* scenarios. The *Customer Involvement* best practice is also mentioned in BPR literature. Harmon [8], for instance, explicitly suggests to ask the customer if it is unclear whether a task adds value or not.

Scheduling. In line with making healthcare providers more patient-centered is the improvement of the scheduling of patients. This is the main conclusion of the review performed by Cayirli and Veral [4] who argue that further research should aim at finding the most suitable support for making appointments. We propose to extend the *behavioral view* element of the BPR framework with the following best practice.

SCHED: *Schedule the least variant patient categories at the beginning of the clinical sessions.*

The scheduling best practice results in a reduction of internal queueing times. Typically, this reduction significantly outweighs the increase in server idle time/ overtime [12].

Resource Joining. Case study 3 explains two situations in which patients leave the oncology dermatology department to go a long way through the hospital for some test and then return to the oncology department again. The *to-be* scenarios for these situations therefore propose to join the responsible resources and place them together in the oncology dermatology department. This best practice is added to the *organization-structure* element of the BPR framework.

JOIN: *Place resources responsible for adjacent tasks (geographically) close together.*

Resource joining reduces the throughput time of the process. Another way to use this best practice is presented by Reijers, Song and Jeong [17]. It would make sense to put human resources, who perform adjacent tasks, near to each other (for instance in the same corridor). Reijers *et al* show that there is a positive effect on the performance if resources are geographically close together [17].

The question "Is it possible to extend the set of best practices with the lessons learned from redesigning healthcare processes?" can be answered positively. We derived three additional, potential best practices of which two seem applicable to other domains as well. It has to be evaluated whether or not these potential best practices are generally applicable to the healthcare domain and beyond.

7   Discussion

The research questions in this paper are formulated in a positive way. It is also possible to formulate them as falsifiable propositions. The first question, for instance, would then be "To what extent are the best practices unsuited for redesigning healthcare processes?". According to our results only a small set of the best practices is not applicable to at least one of the studied processes. The formulation as falsifiable propositions would have led to the same conclusions. Also, a number of potential biases can be distinguished when having a closer look at the research and the used methodology. The first possible bias is a cognitive bias. The developers of the set of best practices are also the evaluators of the suitability of the best practices. This cannot be refuted. Even more so, they are also involved in some of the evaluated case studies. The bias is reduced because the best practices have been published before the case studies were conducted. Therefore, the results of the case studies can be verified by others. Another possible bias is a selection bias. In general, more studies with positive outcomes are published. This cannot be circumvented. A final issue is the small sample size. For our analysis we have used 14 case studies that are selected from the ABI/Inform and INSPEC catalogues and from our own experience. We acknowledge that many more reports on BPR studies in healthcare exist. Another literature review conducted by Elkhuizen [6] selected 86 studies in care process redesign from the Medline, Embase and Ebsco Business Source Premier databases. She categorized the interventions mentioned in the studies which led to 12 categories. In many of these categories we recognize a relation with one or more of our best practices.

8 Conclusion

In this paper, we have investigated whether the existing set of 29 best practices to support BPR initiatives are applicable to the healthcare domain. From the 14 healthcare case studies that we analyzed, we determined which best practices were applied. Almost three quarters of the total set of best practices was applied in one or more case studies, indicating that the best practices seem highly suitable for the healthcare domain. For three case studies, the outcomes of simulation studies were analyzed, all indicating that the application of the considered best practices would indeed improve most of the identified performance parameters. For three additional case studies, a before-after design study effectively showed a positive impact on the performance caused by the process change. Therefore, the use of best practices appears not only to be feasible but also an effective means to improve process performance. As a final contribution, we proposed an extension of the set of best practices with improvement practices we identified in the analyzed cases. We derived three additional, potential best practices that seem worthwhile to be considered for future BPR initiatives.

In our view, performance improvement initiatives in the healthcare domain can heavily benefit from relying on previous experiences. The best practices that are the focus of this paper form one example of how design knowledge can be re-used, and in such a way can contribute to improved performance. We therefore recommend the use of best practices in healthcare process redesign, while acknowledging the need for an ongoing reflection on and extension with similar heuristics.

Acknowledgement

This research is supported by the Technology Foundation STW, applied science division of NWO and the technology programme of the Dutch Ministry of Economic Affairs.

References

1. Ashton, R., Hague, L., Brandreth, M., Worthington, D., Cropper, S.: A Simulation-Based Study of a NHS Walk-In Centre. Journal of the Operational Research Society 56(2), 153–161 (2005)
2. Barkaoui, K., Dechambre, P., Hachicha, R.: Verification and Optimisation of an Operating Room Workflow. In: Proceedings of the 35th Hawaii International Conference on System Sciences (HICSS 2002), vol. 7, pp. 210–219. IEEE, Hawaii (2002)
3. Becker, J., Janiesch, C.: Restrictions in Process Design: A Case Study on Workflows in Healthcare. In: ter Hofstede, A.H.M., Benatallah, B., Paik, H.-Y. (eds.) BPM Workshops 2007. LNCS, vol. 4928, pp. 323–334. Springer, Heidelberg (2008)

4. Cayirli, T., Veral, E.: Outpatient Scheduling in Healthcare: a Review of Literature. Production and Operations Management 12(4), 519–549 (2003)
5. Chan, W.P., Chiu, W.-T., Chen, W.-M., Lin, M.-F., Chu, B.: Applying Six Sigma Methodology to Maximise Resonance Imaging Capacity in a Hospital. Int. Journal of Healthcare Technology and Management 6(3), 321–330 (2005)
6. Elkhuizen, S.G.: Patient Oriented Logistics. Studies on organizational improvement in an academic hospital. PhD thesis, University of Amsterdam, Amsterdam (2007)
7. Hammer, M., Champy, J.: Reengineering the Corporation: a Manifesto for Business revolution. Harper Business Editions, New York (1993)
8. Harmon, P.: Business Process Change. Morgan Kaufmann Publishers, San Francisco (2003)
9. Institute of Medicine: Crossing the Quality Chasm: A New Health System for the 21st Century. Academies Press, Washington, DC (2001)
10. Jansen-Vullers, M.H., Reijers, H.A.: Business process Redesign in Healthcare: Towards a Structured Approach. INFOR: Information Systems and Operational Research 43(4), 321–339 (2005)
11. Kim, H.-W.: Business Process versus Coordination Process in Organizational Change. Int. Journal of Flexible Manufacturing Systems 12, 275–290 (2000)
12. Klassen, K.J., Rohleder, T.R.: Outpatient Appointment Scheduling with Urgent Clients in a Dynamic, Multi-period Environment. Int. Journal of Service Industry Management 15(2), 167–186 (2004)
13. Limam Mansar, S., Reijers, H.A.: Best Practices in Business Process Redesign: Validation of a Redesign Framework. Computers in Industry 56, 457–471 (2005)
14. Mulyar, N., van der Aalst, W.M.P., Peleg, M.: A Pattern-based Analysis of Clinical Computer-interpretable Guideline Modeling Languages. Journal of the American Medical Informatics Association 14, 781–787 (2007)
15. Netjes, M., Vanderfeesten, I., Reijers, H.A.: "Intelligent" Tools for Workflow Process Redesign: A Research Agenda. In: Bussler, C.J., Haller, A. (eds.) BPM 2005. LNCS, vol. 3812, pp. 444–453. Springer, Heidelberg (2006)
16. Reijers, H.A., Limam Mansar, S.: Best Practices in Business Process Redesign: An Overview and Qualitative Evaluation of Successful Redesign Heuristics. Omega: The Int. Journal of Management Science 33(4), 283–306 (2005)
17. Reijers, H.A., Song, M., Jeong, B.: On the Performance of Workflow Processes with Distributed Actors: Does Place Matter? In: Alonso, G., Dadam, P., Rosemann, M. (eds.) BPM 2007. LNCS, vol. 4714, pp. 32–47. Springer, Heidelberg (2007)
18. Sharp, A., McDermott, P.: Workflow modeling: Tools for process improvement and application development. Arctech House (2001)

Appendix A: BPR Best Practices [16]

Customers		
RELOC	Control relocation	relocate control steps in the process to others
REDUC	Contact reduction	combine information exchanges
INTG	Integration	consider the integration with a process of client or supplier
Operation view		
TYPE	Case types	distinguish separate processes and case types
ELIM	Task elimination	delete tasks that do not add value from a client's viewpoint
CASEB	Case-based work	get rid of constraints that introduce batch handling
TRI	Triage	consider the division of a general task into alternative tasks
COMPOS	Task composition	combine small tasks into composite tasks or vice versa
Behavioral view		
RESEQ	Resequencing	move tasks to more appropriate places
PAR	Parallelism	introduce concurrency within a business process
KO	Knock-out	execute those checks first that have the most favorable ratio of expected knockout probability versus the expected effort
EXCEP	Exception	isolate exceptional cases from the normal flow
Organization-structure		
ASSIGN	Order assignment	let workers perform as many steps as possible for single cases
FLEX	Flexible assignment	assign resources in such a way that maximal flexibility is preserved for the near future
CENTR	Centralization	treat geographically dispersed resources as if they are centralized
SPLIT	Split responsibilities	avoid assignment of task responsibilities to people from different functional units
TEAM	Customer teams	consider assigning teams out of different departmental workers that take care of specific sorts of cases
NUM	Numerical involvement	minimize the number of departments, groups and persons involved in a process
MAN	Case manager	make one person responsible for the handling of a case
Organization-population		
XRES	Extra resources	increase capacity of a certain resource class
SPEC	Specialist-generalist	consider making resources more specialized or generalized
EMP	Empower	give workers most of the decision-making authority and reduce middle management
ADD	Control addition	check the inputs and outputs of a process
Information		
BUF	Buffering	subscribe to updates instead of complete info. exchange
Technology		
AUTO	Task automation	introduce technology to automate tasks
TECH	Technology	try to elevate physical constraints in a process by applying new technology
External environment		
TRUST	Trusted party	replace a decision task by the decision of an external party
OUT	Outsourcing	relocate work to a third party that is more efficient
INTF	Interfacing	consider a standardized interface with clients and partners

User-Oriented Quality Assessment of IT-Supported Healthcare Processes – A Position Paper

Elske Ammenwerth[1], Ruth Breu[2], and Barbara Paech[3]

[1] Institute for Health Information Systems, University for Health Sciences,
Medical Informatics and Technology (UMIT)
Elske.Ammenwerth@umit.at
[2] Institute of Computer Science, University of Innsbruck
ruth.breu@uibk.ac.at
[3] Institute of Computer Science, University of Heidelberg
paech@informatik.uni-heidelberg.de

Abstract. The user view of the quality of IT-supported health care processes is very important for a successful performance of these processes. Current approaches to process quality do not capture this point of view explicitly. This position paper provides a first collection of indicators for this view.

Classification: Process quality, Workflow management, Process optimization, Compliance, Process modelling.

1 Introduction

Health care is characterized by complex and interrelated processes. Often, these processes do not work well, with unnecessary duplication of tasks, high number of (computer-based) tools to be used in one process leading to media breaks and transcription of data, high efforts for coordination of tasks between professional groups, high efforts to search for required patient information, and limited usability and functionality of used tools. These problems can lead to severe disruption of workflow in a healthcare institution and to low stakeholder satisfaction both with regard to the overall organization and the IT tools used. This can contribute to IT failures and IT boycott. All of this indicates that in the healthcare area the stakeholder view of the processes is particularly important. Although the most important stakeholder is the patient, we focus on the medical actors. The satisfaction of the medical actors with the process directly influences the outcome of their work and thus has important effects on the patients. In the following we are interested in IT-supported processes. Thus, we call the medical actors in the process "users".

Healthcare processes typically aim at delivering a service. Therefore, it is difficult to capture the processes succinctly. Instead one has to take into account integration of external factors (patient or patient-related information and material), in particular high interaction, individuality, immateriality and intangibility (Health as the main "output"), and as for all service processes indivisibility, volatility and locality [2]:In particular, it is difficult to characterize the quality of a healthcare process. There are many proposals for the assessment of business processes. However, they typically

S. Rinderle-Ma et al. (Eds.): BPM 2009 Workshops, LNBIP 43, pp. 617–622, 2010.
© Springer-Verlag Berlin Heidelberg 2010

focus on the business aspect, such as time and cost and the contribution of the processes to the business goals [3]. So e.g. in the area of health care there is evidence on the overall effect of processes and their IT-support on health care, e.g. [1,4,6].The complexity of quality issues in healthcare processes and the point of view of the users are not sufficiently covered by those approaches. Similarly there are proposals for the definition and assessment of IT-supported processes [5]. They add an IT-perspective that focuses the general product and service assessment on the assessment of IT-systems (as products) and IT-services (e.g. ITIL [7] or COBIT [8]). These assessments also include codes for the satisfaction of the stakeholders involved such as the customer satisfaction or employee satisfaction. However, these assessments do not provide detailed insights into how well the processes and IT-systems support the users. They do not include characteristics of how the process and the IT-system need to provide the service to the stakeholders. Overall, a systematic and comprehensive approach to assess the quality of IT-supported processes in healthcare institutions from a users' point of view is not available at the moment.

The objective of this paper is to present a first approach to define and structure quality indicators for IT-supported processes from a users' point of view. Our approach consists of three views on process quality:

- the quality of the process in general
- the quality of data handling
- the quality of the used IT-system

These views are described in the following sections, followed by a short conclusion.

2 Quality of the Process

The process view captures the quality of the process definition and the process instances. We distinguish the categories: **definition, outcome and productivity, complexity and standardization** and **efficiency**.

In general, a process has to have a clear definition, that means a clear goal, a clear beginning and end, and clearly defined activities. For healthcare processes, we often find deficiencies here, as processes may be not clearly defined, do not have an agreed and documented goal, or do not terminate correctly. The outcome and productivity quality of a process can be characterized by looking at errors (e.g. where information does not reach the intended recipient) and the satisfaction or complaints of the process stakeholders or the process clients (e.g. the patients).The complexity of a process can be characterized by several aspects such as the duration, the structure complexity (e.g. number of actors or IT-systems involved, the number of AND/OR-splittings), the time flow complexity (e.g. number of parallel process instances) or the coordination complexity (e.g. number of interfaces between actors), as well as by the number of variants and exceptions. Within a process, efficiency is another important quality indicator. This can comprise e.g. the unnecessary repetition of tasks (e.g. multiple questioning of a patient on the same issues, e.g. patient anamnesis) or unnecessary waiting times or transportation times within the process.

Table 1 summarizes these major quality categories and proposes indicators for each of them. These indicators are not independent of each other, which is not considered a problem at this stage.

Table 1. Indicators for overall healthcare process quality

Quality category	Indicator
Definition	• Documentation and agreement of process goals • Availability of process description • Definition of process beginning and end
Outcome and productivity	• Number of instances that terminated correctly • Number of errors per instance • Number of complaints by process clients • Satisfaction of actors with process • Satisfaction of clients with process
Complexity and standardization	• Duration of process instances • Numbers of activities, actors or activities per actor • Number of IT-systems involved • Number of AND/OR splittings • Number of parallel process instances (overall or per actor) • Number of interfaces between actors • Number of interfaces between organizational units • Number of process variants • Number of exceptions handled within a process instance
Efficiency	• Unnecessary repetition of tasks • Unnecessary waiting, transportation or searching times

3 Data Handling Quality

The data handling view provides a view which is orthogonal to the process view. In the sequel we talk of *information objects,* meaning objects containing information at a business oriented and IT independent level. Examples of information objects in the healthcare domain are the various kinds of health related information (each one attached in a unique way to a citizen, but potentially also to a producer or a person responsible), staff information, medical device information or process related information (like calendars or referrals).

Information objects may be accessed across different processes by different actors and supported by different applications. This makes the data view indispensable for quality analysis. The term *application* is used to denote either an IT system with own data source and user interface or a paper-based system. This includes the possibility that an information object is stored on several different IT or paper-based systems (e.g. as a temporary notice, in a paper-based patient record and in an electronic patient record).

In order to capture the quality of information objects we propose three categories explained below. Table 2 lists selected indicators for each of the three categories.

Table 2. Indicators for data handling quality

Quality category	Indicator
Data quality	• Numbers of processes/work steps or process instances modifying an information object • Number of actors/actor instances modifying an information object • Number of applications storing an information object (persistently) • Is each health information attached with a unique patient?
Data access	• Is the actor warned at creation time if the object already exists in other applications? If yes, is this object accessible? • Is the information checked for completeness and correctness (at creation time/modification time/in certain time intervals)? • Does the executing actor know at deletion time whether the object is no longer used by any process? • Can information objects be found in an adequate way, be timely accessed if needed in a work step? • Is the data history available (if required)? • Are data modifications propagated to other applications in case of redundant storage?
Data security	• Are all actors reading, creating, modifying, or deleting an object authenticated and authorized? • Are all objects available in due time? • Are all actions performed on objects non repudiable? • Do all data access operations follow the rules of the data protection act? • Is data loss prevented?

Data quality assesses the semantic quality of the information objects. This comprises the following aspects:

- Is the information object correct throughout its lifetime?
- Is the information object up to date?
- Is the information stored redundantly?
- Can the information object be identified in a unique way?

Data access quality addresses the quality level of actions performed on information objects. These actions typically include: Creation of information objects, Modification, Deletion and archiving, Search and reading

Data access quality assesses the quality of data maintenance. However, it also considers aspects like the ergonomic and timely access to information.

Data security is particularly important in the healthcare domain due to the sensitivity of information. As usual we distinguish the aspects of data confidentiality, data integrity, data availability and non-repudiation of actions. In addition we consider compliance aspects, in particular the conformance to the data protection act.

4 Quality of IT-Support

Both, process execution and data handling should be alleviated through IT. In the following we distinguish the quality of an IT-system provided to a single user from the quality of the support provided by the whole IT-landscape in the process. The former is typically captured by standards such as ISO 9126 or the newer ISO/IEC 25000 [9]. The latter considers the overall support provided by IT to the users.

Table 3. Indicators for IT-support quality

Quality category	Indicator
IT-system efficiency	• Is the system function provided in adequate time? • Is the amount of system resources used adequate?
IT-system usability	• Effort required to understand, learn or operate the user interface • Attractiveness of the user interface • Adequacy of the IT-support to the task to be performed in the process step • User satisfaction
IT-system reliability	• Number of system failures due to internal errors or wrong user input in a specific period • Time needed to recover the system
IT-landscape variety	• Number of systems needed within one process • Number of different logins or authentications needed by one user within one process • Redundancy of functionality between these systems • Media breaks requiring repeated manual input
IT-landscape capacity	• Number of process steps supported by IT and degree of the automation • Up-to-dateness of the IT-systems • Additional services such as hotline • Mobility of system functionality in case of failures

IT-system quality comprises typically efficiency, usability, reliability, portability, changeability and a number of functionality-related categories such as security or interoperability. Portability and changeability refer to very technical qualities of the internal structures.These are not directly visible for for the users in the healthcare process and thus omitted here. Security is treated in the data handling section.

IT-landscape quality assesses the quality experienced by the user through the combination of several IT-systems. Here we distinguish on the one hand effects due to the complexity of using several systems in one process (**IT-landscape variety**) and on the other hand effects due to the integrated management of these systems (**IT-landscape capacity**). Typical indicators are the number of systems within one process, the number of steps supported by at least one system, the redundancy or media breaks between these systems or the up-to-dateness of the systems. These indicators are summarized in Table 3.

5 Conclusion

We have presented a first draft of user-oriented healthcare process assessment indicators. Several indicators can be found in some reference in the literature, but we are not aware of a systematic collection of the user-oriented assessment categories. In particular the data handling aspects are usually not treated explicitly.

As a next step we plan a more detailed literature search on process and data quality measurement, human-computer-interaction and work science as well as IT-service measurement in order to provide a more detailed list of user-oriented indicators. Furthermore, we want to apply the indicators to real healthcare processes in order to understand the difficulty of capturing the necessary data and to understand the usefulness of the results. For indicators capturing numbers we will look at possibilities for identifying reference values. In particular it is interesting to use such indicators to capture typical values in a given context and thus to detect outliers. In addition, we are looking for process modeling notations which support a quick overview of these user-oriented factors.

References

1. Chaudry, B., et al.: Systematic Review: Impact of Health Information Technology on Quality, Efficiency, and Costs of Medical Care. Annals of Internal Medicine 144(10), 742–752 (2006)
2. Ehlers, F.: Das Prozess-Potential-Screening, PhD Thesis, University of Heidelberg (2004) (in German)
3. Fischermans, G.: Praxishandbuch Prozessmanagement, Verlag Dr. Götz Schmidt (2009) (in German)
4. Gandjours, A., et al.: An evidence-based evaluation of quality and efficiency indicators. Qual. Manag. Health Care 10, 41–52 (2002)
5. Kütz, M.: Kennzahlen in der IT. dpunkt-Verlag (2009) (in German)
6. Shekelle, P.G., Morton, S.C., Keeler, E.B.: Cost and benefit of health care information technology. Evid. Rep. Technol. Assess (Full Rep.) (132), 1–71 (2006)
7. http://www.itil-officialsite.com/home/home.asp
8. http://www.isaca.org
9. http://www.iso.org/iso/iso_catalogue/catalogue_tc/catalogue_detail.htm?csnumber=35683

Verification of Careflow Management Systems with Timed BDI_{CTL} Logic

Keith Miller[*] and Wendy MacCaull[**]

Centre for Logic and Information
St. Francis Xavier University
Antigonish, NS B2G 2W5

Abstract. Health care workflows (careflows) involve complex, distributive processes with a high degree of variability. There are ubiquitous communication and massive data and knowledge management requirements and the processes are time sensitive, involve complex timing requirements, and are safety critical. Designing these processes and managing their performance is difficult and error prone. Using verification techniques, mathematical methods of proving correctness, we can reduce errors and ensure that the processes satisfy their specifications. We present a prototype next-generation multi-threaded model checker to reason about timed processes in careflows sensitive to patient preferences and the goals of the careteam using a temporal logic extended with modalities of beliefs, desires and intentions.

Keywords: Process Modeling, Workflow/Careflow Management, Tableau, Explicit-Time, Model Checking, BDI Logic, Computation Tree Logic.

1   Introduction

Complex processes are, by definition, difficult to describe, manage and analyze. Errors in the process definition or during execution are difficult to detect and determining the cause can require a tremendous amount of time and effort. Careflows have the added challenge of severe, probably expensive and possibly life-threatening, consequences of errors. While verification techniques have been used extensively in the design of hardware systems and more recently for software systems, to a large degree, verification is lacking in current workflow management systems (WfMSs).

WfMS increase the efficiency of processes but current WfMSs are only suited to well understood, stable environments, and are not equipped to handle a dynamic environment such as health care. While efficiency and completion time

[*] Keith Miller (kmiller@stfx.ca) is supported by a Natural Sciences and Engineering Research Council of Canada Industrial Postgraduate Scholarship.

[**] Wendy MacCaull (wmaccaul@stfx.ca) is supported by the Natural Sciences and Engineering Research Council of Canada and by the Atlantic Canada Opportunities Agency.

S. Rinderle-Ma et al. (Eds.): BPM 2009 Workshops, LNBIP 43, pp. 623–634, 2010.

are important factors in health care workflow, there is an added factor that the 'work' passing through the workflow includes humans with needs, goals, and preferences that a manufacturing or paper-pushing process does not need to consider. In addition, the variability of the processes is beyond that experienced in traditional workflow. The lack of verification in WfMSs leads to workflows being enacted without the certainty of correctness often resulting in errors that need to be handled in an ad hoc manner at runtime. This is unacceptable, in most cases, for careflow due to their time sensitive and safety critical nature.

This paper describes the design and development of a verification tool for healthcare workflows that integrates: (1) nonstandard logics to express complex behaviors, (2) ontologies to structure the data into a usable knowledge base and use the knowledge to guide the workflow, (3) verification tools to ensure processes are designed and executed in accordance with their specifications, (4) high performance computing methods.

The rest of the paper is outlined as follows. Section 2 presents a description of the techniques and methodologies used in the design of the verification tool. Section 3 describes the model checker that was developed. Section 4 discusses related work. The conclusion and future work are presented in Section 5.

This work is part of an ongoing effort to develop the next generation of Careflow Management Systems that integrate verification at design time, real-time monitoring at runtime and intelligence for guidance and adaption using healthcare ontologies which facilitate the organization and sharing of knowledge.

2   Overview of Techniques and Methodology Used

This section provides background information for the techniques and methods used for verification, modeling and knowledge management.

2.1   Verification

Our work focuses on model checking [1], which traverses every possible configuration of a system to determine if the design specifications are always satisfied. Both the description of a system, i.e., the model, and the specifications must have a formal mathematical representation. This allows the use of fully automated proof procedures, such as the tableau method we used. A model checker determines whether a specified property is satisfied by the model and, in general, generates a counter-example if the property is violated (which can be used for debugging). Model checking can provide quality assurance that goes beyond that which testing or simulation can achieve. A failed test conclusively proves the presence of an error but a successful test does not prove the absence of errors. Most current model checkers incorporate a temporal specification language, such as Computation Tree Logic (CTL) or Linear Temporal Logic (LTL). These are implicit time logics which allow the specification of qualitative properties. Qualitative properties include invariants, often called safety properties, e.g., "A patient must have an assigned Case Manager at all times." Other qualitative properties specify the relative ordering of events, e.g, "A patient must be evaluated by an oncologist before beginning chemotherapy," or that something happens at some future time, often called liveness properties, e.g., "A patient with symptoms eventually receives treatment." Verifying that a patient is "eventually" treated is not enough. Timed temporal logics, permitting the explicit reference to time, can specify quantitative properties e.g., "A patient must have been evaluated by an oncologist within three weeks of beginning chemotherapy." Logics with modalities for beliefs, desires and intentions (BDI Logics) permit reasoning about the mental state of actors (for healthcare theses include patients, caregivers, etc.). These modalities can be used to capture patient/caregiver preferences and priorities which is used to guide the decision making, for example, a patient who prefers not to travel may wait longer for a local service even if it is available sooner in another location.

Model checking requires the exhaustive search through all possible configurations, or states, of a system, which can require a very large amount of memory for even moderately complex systems. This search may take an unreasonable amount time, a critical issue in the very time-sensitive healthcare domain. High performance computing methodologies are employed to address this issue.

2.2   Timed Colored Petri Nets

Petri nets are a tool for modeling and analyzing asynchronous, distributed systems and have been used to model workflows [2]. Petri nets have a graphical notation yet are a formal mathematical representation [3]. A Petri net consists of places, transitions and directed arcs. Arcs are from places to transitions, called input places to the transition, or from transitions to its output places. Places may contain a finite number of tokens, representing resources. A transitions is enabled if there is a token in each of its input places. An enabled transition may fire, or occur, by removing a token from each of its input places and inserting a token into each of its output places. A marking is the number of tokens in each place of the net. Timed Colored Petri nets are an extension of Petri nets developed by Kurt Jensen [3]. Each place has an associated type, or color, that determines the kind of data which the place may contain. The token values may be complex data structures such as records, database states, or in our case, a structured knowledge base. A transition is color enabled if there is a token of the appropriate color in each of its input places. A global clock is used to represent the model time. Each token is given a time-stamp which describes the earliest time the token may be used. A transition is ready when there is a token in each of its input places that may be used. Tokens are consumed in a FIFO fashion. Transitions fire as soon as they are color enabled and ready: this is known as "eager firing." Transitions may have an associated delay and each token produced by the transition is given a time-stamp equal to the current time + the delay. Firing, itself, is instantaneous. Firing a transition may modify the token values and transitions may have guards, i.e., boolean expressions on the token values, that are further requirements for enabling based on the value of the token.

2.3   Ontologies and Description Logic

An ontology is a method of structuring knowledge in a usable format to allow reasoning about and the sharing of this knowledge. Ontologies have been used extensively in artificial intelligence to describe agents, agent attitudes and information sharing among agents. Ontologies provide an efficient method of managing medical/health and organizational knowledge. For example, an ontology for an organizational structure can be used to facilitate automatic communication and report generation and routing.

Description Logics (DLs) have been developed to provide formal way to describe and reason about the concepts of a domain. The syntax is designed to be readable by those not overly familiar with mathematical notation. DL is a fragment of First Order Logic and many DLs are decidable, making them convenient frameworks for automatic reasoning [4]. DLs are distinguished by the constructors they provide. Complex descriptions can be built from them inductively with concept constructors. A minimal DL language AL (attributive language), is defined as atomic concepts A, compliment of A, concept intersection, universal restriction and limited existential quantification [4]. Additional constructors include: C, negation of complex concepts, U, union of concepts, E, full existential quantification, H, role hierarchy, Q, qualified cardinality restrictions, and I, inverse properties. The language ALC, which is AL with arbitrary negation of concepts, or compliment, is very common and is often abbreviated to S. The popular Web Ontology Language (OWL) is based on $SHIQ$[5]. The ontology system used with our model checker is complete for SQ [6].

DL allows the extraction and use of implicit knowledge contained in the explicitly expressed knowledge base. As an example, there may be rules for all medications, other rules for pain medications and still more for ibuprofen, along with the fact that ibuprofen is a drug. For example, suppose there is a rule specifying that no drug be taken prior to some test. Then ibuprofen cannot be taken prior to that test, even though that rule is not explicitly stated. DL reasoners can be used to ensure consistency of the ontology.

2.4   Tableau-Style Model Checking

Tableau is a fully automated refutation proof system [7]. Tableau proof methods can be used for model checking when details of a model are fully articulated. A proof of a formula ϕ consists of showing that the negation of ϕ cannot be satisfied in the model. A tableau is a tree with a formula at the each node. This tree is built by expanding a formula using expansion rules. A branch represents the conjunction of the formulas occurring on it and the tree represents the disjunction of its branches. A branch is closed if both a formula, and its negation occur on the branch, and is open otherwise. A tableau is closed if and only if all of its branches are closed. A tableau proof of a formula ϕ is a closed tableau of the negation of ϕ. If a tableau contains an open branch then a counter-example can be built, that is, a valuation that satisfies $\neg\phi$.

2.5   High Performance Computing

Though the tableau method is easy to extend, it is often inefficient. Parallel methods offer a possible solution. Parallelizing a problem usually does not decrease the amount of work to be done, it just splits the work into smaller pieces that can be done simultaneously, and thereby reduces the time to completion [8]. The use of multiple cores also increases the available memory. Our model checker currently implements "or-parallelism" that exploits the structure of the tableau. The tableau rules act either conjunctively or disjunctively. Disjunctive rules create separate branches that share some information but closure of a branch is independent of the other branches. When a new branch is created, if the maximum number of threads has not been reached then a new thread is spawned to handle the branch. Otherwise the current thread adds the branch to the list of branches that it currently owns. Each thread continues to process the branches it owns, testing for closure and expanding as needed. The tableau is closed when all branches owned by all threads are closed. Our model checker also implements "and-parallelism" by computing the "transition successors" and "time successors" of a state concurrently.

3   A Tableau Model Checker for Timed BDI_{CTL}

The model checker is implemented in XSB prolog, a logic programming environment with a library for incorporating and managing ontology-style information. Logic programming is a natural fit for implementing the tableau proof method, which is easily extendible to the non-standard logics we use. Modeling was done using CPNTools, a graphical tool for designing, analyzing and simulating Colored Petri nets. The nets are exported as XML which is manually transformed to prolog predicates for use by the model checker.

Tableau rules specify how to break down a formula into its constituent parts, eventually resulting in a set of atomic formulas and their negations. By adding tableau rules to those for propositional logic we can check properties of more expressive logics. For Timed BDI_{CTL} we add temporal rules and rules for the BDI Logic used. The modeled system can change state by exactly one of the following: (a) an event, i.e., firing a transition, (b) a BDI revision/update, or (c) the advancement of the model time. We refer to the current sets of beliefs, desires, and intentions for agent i as the agent's knowledge base, KB_i, which may be structured using ontological principles. The KB_i can be updated by firing a transition, e.g., firing a transition "blood test", meaning the patient is given a blood test, should add the belief that a blood test was administered and remove any immediate desire, also known as a goal, for a blood test. Likewise, e.g., time related information can be updated by the advancement of time. We restrict the time advancement to a maximum time to ensure that all eventuality formulas are satisfied within a bounded time period. It is reasonable to assume that our BDI will change over time for reasons not directly related to the careflow (e.g., a service is no longer available). Thus, monitoring is vital to detect changes in the BDI that may invalidate previous verification results. For example, a change in preferences may affect which transitions are enabled.

We present details for a restricted Timed BDI_{CTL} logic where B,D,I, operators act on propositional formulas. A more complete proof system is found in [10] where BDI operators range over SQ. The syntax for Timed BDI_{CTL}, in Backus-Naur form is:

$$\phi ::= \top \mid \bot \mid p \mid \neg\phi \mid \phi \vee \psi \mid B_i(\alpha) \mid D_i(\alpha) \mid I_i(\alpha) \mid \text{succeeded}(e)$$
$$AX\phi \mid AG_n\phi \mid AF_n\phi \mid A_n(\phi \, U \, \psi) \mid EX\phi \mid EG_n\phi \mid EF_n\phi \mid E_n(\phi \, U \, \psi)$$

where p is an atomic formula, s is a state, n is an integer that specifies an upper bound on the time, i is an agent, ψ, ϕ are formulas, α is a propositional formula and $e \in \mathcal{E}$ a predetermined set of event types, AG, AF, EG, EF, AX, EX are the CTL temporal operators, B,D,I are modal operators, succeeded(e) is a boolean expressions. The following equivalence is assumed: $\neg B_i(\alpha) \equiv B_i(\neg\alpha)$, and similarly for desires and intentions and failed(e) $\equiv \neg$succeeded(e).

Models, M, are Kripke models arising from timed colored Petri nets. Hence, a model is a tuple $(S, \rightarrow, L(s))$, where S is a set of states, $\rightarrow$ is a transition relation on S such that for every $s \in S$ there exists at least one $s\prime$ such that $s \rightarrow s\prime$, and L is a labeling function specifying the set of atomic propositions true at s. The states correspond to the possible markings and times of a timed colored Petri net whose tokens contain agent knowledge bases. We denote the transition successor relation for the CPN by R. That is, sRs' iff the marking at s' is the result of firing some transition t in the CPN with the marking at s. Similarly we denote the time successor relation by R_t, i.e., sR_ts' iff $time(s')= time(s) + 1$, where $time(s)$ is the model time at state s. Finally, $\rightarrow = R \cup R_t$.

Given a model M, and state s, the satisfaction relation is given by:

$M,s \not\models \bot$

$M,s \models p$ iff $p \in L(s)$

$M,s \models \neg\phi$ iff $M,s \not\models \phi$

$M,s \models \phi \vee \psi$ iff $M,s \models \phi$ or $M,s \models \psi$ or both

$M,s \models AX\phi$ iff for all $s\prime$ such that $s \rightarrow s\prime$, M, $s\prime \models \phi$

$M,s \models AG_n\phi$ iff for all paths $s_0 \rightarrow s_1 \rightarrow s_2...$, where $s_0=s$,
         for all s_k along the path, M, $s_k \models \phi$ and $time(k) \leq n$

$M,s \models AF_n\phi$ iff for all paths $s_0 \rightarrow s_1 \rightarrow s_2...$, where $s_0=s$,
         and there exists some s_k along the path, M, $s_k \models \phi$ and $time(k) \leq n$

$M,s \models A_n(\phi \, U \, \psi)$ iff for all paths $s_0 \rightarrow s_1 \rightarrow s_2 ...$, where $s_0=s$,
         for some s_k along the path, $M,s_k \models \psi$ and $time(k) \leq n$ and
         for all s_j, $j < k$, $M,s_j \models \phi$

$M,s \models EX\phi$ iff for some $s\prime$ such that $s \rightarrow s\prime$, M, $s\prime \models \phi$

$M,s \models EF_n\phi$ iff for some path $s_0 \rightarrow s_1 \rightarrow s_2...$, where $s_0=s$,
         there exists some s_k along the path, M, $s_k \models \phi$ and $time(k) \leq n$

$M,s \models EG_n\phi$ iff for some path $s_0 \rightarrow s_1 \rightarrow s_2...$, where $s_0=s$,
         for all s_k along the path, M, $s_k \models \phi$ and $time(k) \leq n$

$M,s \models E_n(\phi \ U \ \psi)$ iff for some path $s_0 \rightarrow s_1 \rightarrow s_2 \ ...$, where $s_0 = s$,
      for some s_k along the path, $M,s_k \models \psi$ and $time(k) \leq n$ and
      for all s_j, $j < k$, $M,s_j \models \phi$
$M,s \models B_i(\alpha)$ iff $\alpha \sqsubseteq \beta$ (subsumption) and $B_i(\beta) \in KB_i$
$M,s \models D_i(\alpha)$ iff $\alpha \sqsubseteq \beta$ and $D_i(\beta) \in KB_i$
$M,s \models I_i(\alpha)$ iff $\alpha \sqsubseteq \beta$ and $I_i(\beta) \in KB_i$

We present a tableau-style proof system for the restricted Timed BDI_{CTL} logic. In the following tableau rules, formulas separated by a comma are placed on the same branch and formulas separated by | are placed on different branches. In addition to the rules presented here there are rules to move negation inward corresponding to equivalences, e.g., $\neg EG_n\phi \equiv AF_n\neg\phi$, $\neg EX\phi \equiv AX\neg\phi$, and so on. Details can be found in [10]

(1) $\dfrac{\neg\neg Z}{Z}$ (2) $\dfrac{\neg\top}{\bot}$ (3) $\dfrac{\neg\bot}{\top}$ (4) $\dfrac{\phi \vee \psi}{\phi \ | \ \psi}$ (5) $\dfrac{\neg(\phi \vee \psi)}{\neg\phi \ , \ \neg\psi}$

(6) $\dfrac{AX\phi^s}{\bigwedge \phi^{s'} \quad \forall s' : s \rightarrow s'}$ (7) $\dfrac{EX\phi^s}{\bigvee \phi^{s'} \quad \forall s' : s \rightarrow s'}$

(8) $\dfrac{AG_n\phi^s}{\phi^s \wedge time(s) \leq n \ , \ \bigwedge AG_m\phi^{s'} \quad \forall s' : s \rightarrow s'}$

(9) $\dfrac{AF_n\phi^s}{\phi^s \wedge time(s) \leq n \ | \ \bigwedge AF_m\phi^{s'} \quad \forall s' : s \rightarrow s'}$

(10) $\dfrac{A_n(\phi U \psi)^s}{\psi^s \wedge time(s) \leq n \ | \ (\phi^s \wedge A_m(\phi U \psi))^{s'} \quad \forall s' : s \rightarrow s'}$

(11) $\dfrac{EG_n\phi^s}{\phi^s \wedge time(s) \leq n \ , \ \bigvee EG_m\phi^{s'} \quad \forall s' : s \rightarrow s'}$

(12) $\dfrac{EF_n\phi^s}{\phi^s \wedge time(s) \leq n \ | \ \bigvee EF_m\phi^{s'} \quad \forall s' : s \rightarrow s'}$

(13) $\dfrac{E_n(\phi U \psi)^s}{\psi^s \wedge time(i) \leq n \ | \ (\phi^s \wedge E_m(\phi U \psi))^{s'} \quad \forall s' : s \rightarrow s'}$

(14) $\dfrac{BDI_i(a)^s}{\bigvee BDI_i(\beta)^s \quad \forall \beta \in KB_i : \alpha \sqsubseteq \beta}$

where BDI is one of B, D, or I, and $m = n - 1$ if $\rightarrow = R(t)$ and n otherwise (recall that firing a transition is instantaneous). "$\alpha \sqsubseteq \beta$" means that concept α is subsumed by concept β. The upper bound on time is handled as follows, $AF_0\phi^s \equiv \phi^s$, likewise for AG,EF,EG, and A_0 (or E_0) $(\phi U \psi)^s \equiv \psi^s$.

We refer to [10] for the proof of the following:

Theorem 1. (Soundness) If formula ϕ has a tableau proof then ϕ is a valid in the model. **(Completeness)** If formula ϕ is valid in the model then ϕ has a tableau proof.

3.1 Verifying Properties of a Sample Workflow

We now present an example clinical trial workflow, Figure 1, and example specification properties that can be checked on such a workflow. The example is fictitious but includes all the basic workflow constructs: sequence, parallel split, synchronization, exclusive choice and simple merge [23]. The tableau proofs can be found in [10]. Some details such as the arc expressions and delays on each transition have been removed to aid readability. A real clinical trial workflow includes many more states and conditions than this small example and verification by simple inspection is generally impossible. The model checker can verify that the workflow, or a particular task, can be successfully completed for a patient based on their current BDI. Thus the verification is relative to the specific

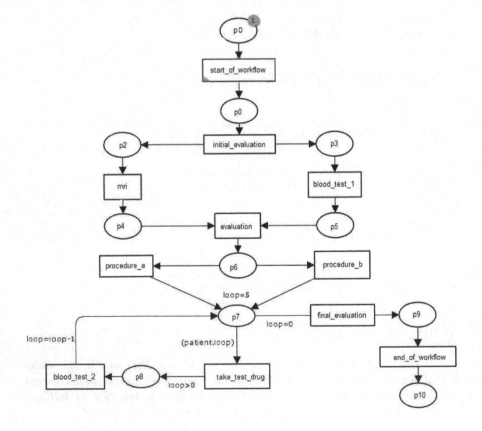

Fig. 1. Simple Drug Trial

patient and situation, however, the correctness of the protocol itself can be verified by using a patient with no specified priorities or preferences. The properties may refer to different levels of the taxonomy. for example, if the ontology defines "procedure_b" as a "noninvasive medical procedure," and a "noninvasive medical procedure" as a "medical procedure," then we can verify whether the patient can successfully complete a medical procedure, a noninvasive medical procedure, or if, in fact, he can complete the specific procedure. Drug or treatment contraindications are captured in the ontology and are processed when determining the enabled transitions. Properties involving time can be verified, e.g. "AF_6 succeeded(mri)" specifies that on all paths, starting in the current state, an MRI occurs within 6 time units. Looping constructs can be verified, e.g., "A_{100}"($\neg$succeeded(end_of_workflow) U loop=0)," specifies that the end of the workflow cannot be reached without the test drug loop occurring 5 times; the 100 denotes the upper bound on the paths considered. The model checker aids debugging by providing information to find where an error occurs. For example, verifying that there is no path on which procedure_b occurs will fail, generating a counter model, which is a sequence of transitions on which procedure_b does occur, e.g., [start_of_workflow, initial_evaluation, mri, blood_test_1, evaluation, procedure_b].

4   Related Work

Clinical guidelines identify decision points and possible courses of action which can be used to develop careflows by including assignment and flow of tasks. Much of the research on computer interpretable guideline modeling involves finding a middle ground between using a formalism expressive enough to describe all of the aspects of interest but simple enough for non-specialists to understand [9]. Asbru, for instance, defines clinical guidelines and protocols as time-oriented skeletal plans to provide a way to reuse existing domain-specific procedural knowledge while allowing for execution-time flexibility to achieve particular goals. [11]. The GuideLine Acquisition, Representation and Execution (GLARE) tool uses a small set of clearly defined primitives to represent guidelines as different types of actions linked by control relations to define the order of execution [12]. Model checking has been applied to Asbru using SMV to automatically verify properties of ACTL, which is CTL with no existential operators. ECTL properties, CTL with no universal operators, require human analysis [13]. Asbru also captures intentions, as temporal formulas, which are used to determine whether a care provider is still following most of a guideline or at least its spirit [14]. Initial work on model checking GLARE by translating the guideline to Promela, the modeling language for the popular SPIN model checker, is presented in [15]. Qualitative properties are automatically verified while timestamps are presented to the physician who determines if quantitative properties hold during execution.

The NewGuide Clinical Guideline Management System was developed at the Laboratory for Biomedical Informatics at the University of Pavia, Italy, for acute stroke care and is currently used in two hospitals [16]. It uses three independent modules: (1) a Guideline Management System that provides clinical decision support, (2) an Electronic Patient Record, and (3) a Workflow Management System that provides organizational support. The main focus is on process management, communication management, and organizational learning. The system uses a semi-automatic, knowledge-based approach to error handling but formal verification is not done [16]. The Electronic Patient Record is in a standard data base and can be queried using Structured Query Language (SQL) but does not allow the reasoning available with the query languages for ontologies.

Little-JIL is a graphical language for defining processes that coordinate the activities of autonomous agents and their use of resources during the performance of a task. A model checker for Little-JIL was able to detect errors in a blood transfusion protocol [17] and a chemotherapy process [18]. In [18], it is suggested that the modeling and analyzing of medical processes could benefit from an ontological structure to the domain knowledge but this was not implemented in their study. Initial efforts by our Centre to develop a model checker that interfaces with a medical ontology were presented in [19].

5   Conclusion and Future Work

We have described the design and implementation of a prototype model checker that automatically verifies quantitative and qualitative properties for workflows modeled as Timed Colored Petri nets and implemented in a high performance computing environment. Interfacing a workflow system with an ontology, coupled with a dynamic knowledge base provides intelligence to guide a workflow. A usable application in a real world setting would need to integrate with existing ontologies and/or to merge ontologies as in [20]. Such ontologies can be very large, e.g., SNOMED CT®, adopted by Canadian physicians, contains $310,311$ active elements and $1,218,983$ relations [21]. Efficient methods of reasoning about ontologies is a key consideration and the vast potential for parallel methods must be leveraged to achieve this.

Automatic translation of the XML representation of the workflow used by CPNTools to the prolog representation used by the model checker, needed to perform realistic simulation of the workflow or to allow a counter model of a nonvalid query to be visualized, has begun. These features are essential if the tool is to be used by non-logicians e.g., health care professionals. If non-logicians are to do the verification then a user-friendly interface to the logic must be provided. A distributed environment increases the memory and computing power available to perform the verification and should improve efficiency; recent work on explicit-time verification using un-timed model checkers has begun [22]. The model checker currently does not support nested beliefs, i.e., beliefs about beliefs or beliefs about other agents' beliefs and so on. Extending the model checker to reason about multiple agents is the next step to enable a practical workflow verification tool. The verification is relative to the current information. Therefore, the collecting and updating of information on, for instance, patient attitudes, is key. The use of emerging web technologies such as instant messaging is being explored [24] but for the present paper focuses on verification using the data at hand.

The development of next generation of CfMSs, as described here, is an ambitious undertaking. Such tools are essential to realize the full potential of emerging electronic health records systems and other emerging web-based technologies. Initial efforts have produced promising results. There are many areas for future investigation; we are working closely with our local health authority to model and verify workflows currently used in hospitals and for community care [24].

References

1. Clarke Jr., E.M., Grumberg, O., Peled, D.A.: Model Checking. MIT Press, Cambridge (1999)
2. van der Aalst, W.M.P.: The Application of Petri Nets to Workflow Management. The Journal of Circuits, Systems and Computers 8(1), 21–66 (1998)
3. Jensen, K.: Coloured Petri nets: A high level language for system design and analysis. In: Applications and Theory of Petri Nets, pp. 342–416 (1989)
4. Baader, F., et al. (eds.): Description Logic Handbook: Theory, Implementation and Applications. Cambridge University Press, Cambridge (2003)
5. Baader, F., Horrocks, I., Sattler, U.: Description logics as ontology languages for the semantic web. In: Hutter, D., Stephan, W. (eds.) Mechanizing Mathematical Reasoning. LNCS (LNAI), vol. 2605, pp. 228–248. Springer, Heidelberg (2005)
6. Swift, T., Warren, D.S.: Coherent Description Framework Programmers Manual Version 1 (beta)
7. Fitting, M.: First-order logic and automated theorem proving. Springer, New York (1990)
8. Johnson, R.: A Blackboard Approach to Parallel Temporal Tableaux. In: Proc. of Artificial Intelligence, Methodologies, Systems, and Applications. World Scientific, Singapore (1994)
9. OpenClinical: Knowledge Management for Medical Care, http://www.openclinical.org/gmmsummaries.html (last accessed, March 2009)
10. Miller, K.: Timed BDI_{CTL} Verification of Ontology Driven Workflow in a Shared Memory Environment. Master's Thesis. Saint Francis Xavier University (expected 2009)
11. Marcos, M., Roomans, H., ten Teije, A., van Harmelen, F.: Improving medical protocols through formalisation: a case study. In: Proceedings of the Sixth World Conference on Integrated Design and Process Technology (2002)
12. Terenziani, P., Carlini, C., Montani, S.: Towards a Comprehensive Treatment of Temporal Constraints in Clinical Guidelines. In: Proc. Ninth International Symposium on Temporal Representation and Reasoning (Time 2002). IEEE Computer Society Press, Manchester (2002)
13. Bäumler, S., Balser, M., Dunets, A., Reif, W., Schmitt, J.: Verification of Medical Guidelines by Model Checking – A Case Study. In: Valmari, A. (ed.) SPIN 2006. LNCS, vol. 3925, pp. 219–233. Springer, Heidelberg (2006)
14. Advani, A., Lo, K., Shahar, Y.: Intention-based critiquing of guideline-oriented medical care. In: Proc. AMIA Annual Symposium, pp. 483–487 (1998)

15. Giordano, L., Terenziani, P., Bottrighi, A., Montani, S., Donzella, L.: Model Checking for Clinical Guidelines: an Agent-based Approach. In: AMIA Annual Symposium Proceedings 2006, Washington, pp. 289–293 (2006)
16. Panzarasa, S., Madde, S., Quaglini, S., Pistarini, C., Stefanelli, M.: Evidence-based careflow management systems: the case of post-stroke rehabilitation. J. of Biomedical Informatics 35(2), 123–139 (2002)
17. Clarke, L., Chen, Y., Avrunin, G., Chen, B., Cobleigh, R., Frederick, K., Henneman, E., Osterweil, L.: Process Programming to Support Medical Safety: A Case Study on Blood Transfusion. Amherst, MA (2005)
18. Christov, S., Chen, B., Avrunin, G.S., Clarke, L.A., Osterweil, L.J., Brown, D., Cassells, L., Mertens, W.: Rigorously Defining and Analyzing Medical Processes: An Experience Report. In: Giese, H. (ed.) MODELS 2008. LNCS, vol. 5002, pp. 118–131. Springer, Heidelberg (2008)
19. Dallien, J., MacCaull, W., Tien, A.: Initial Work in the Design and Development of Verifiable Workflow Management Systems and Some Applications to Health Care. In: 3rd Workshop on Agents Applied in Health Care, 5th International Workshop on Model-based Methodologies for Pervasive and Embedded Software (MOMPES 2008), pp. 78–91 (2008)
20. Imam, F., MacCaull, W.: Integrating Healthcare Ontologies: An Inconsistency Tolerant Approach and Case Study. In: Ardagan, D., et al. (eds.) BPM 2008 Workshops. LNBIP, vol. 17, pp. 373–384. Springer, Heidelberg (2009)
21. Bodenreider, O.: Comparing SNOMED CT and the NCI Thesaurus through Semantic Web Technologies. In: Cornet, R., Spackman, K.A. (eds.) Proceedings of the 3rd international conference on Knowledge Representation in Medicine (2008)
22. Wang, H., MacCaull, W.: An Efficient Explicit-time Description Method for Timed Model Checking. In: Brim, L., van de Pol, J. (eds.) 8th International Workshop on Parallel and Distributed Methods in verification (PDMC 2009), EPTCS 14, pp. 77–91 (2009), doi:10.4204/EPTCS.14.6
23. van der Aalst, W.M.P., Hofstede, T.A.H.M.: Workflow Patterns: On the Expressive Power of (Petri-net-based) Workflow Languages. In: Jensen, K. (ed.) Proceedings of the Fourth Workshop on the Practical Use of Coloured Petri Nets and CPN Tools (CPN 2002), pp. 1–20 (2002)
24. Miller, K., MacCaull, W.: Toward Web-based Careflow Management Systems. Kuziemsky, C., Archer, N., Peyton, L. (eds.) Journal of Emerging Technologies in Web Intelligence (JETWI) Special Issue: E-health Interoperability 1(2), 137–145 (2009)
25. Terenziani, P., German, E., Shahar, Y.: The temporal aspects of clinical guidelines. In: Ten Teije, A., Miksch, S., Lucas, P. (eds.) Computer-based Medical Guidelines and Protocols: A Primer and Current Trends. Studies in Health Technology and Informatics, vol. 139 (2008)

Process-Aware Information System
Development for the Healthcare Domain -
Consistency, Reliability, and Effectiveness

R.S. Mans[1,2], W.M.P. van der Aalst[1], N.C. Russell[1],
P.J.M. Bakker[2], and A.J. Moleman[2]

[1] Department of Information Systems, Eindhoven University of Technology,
P.O. Box 513, NL-5600 MB, Eindhoven, The Netherlands
{r.s.mans,w.m.p.v.d.aalst,n.c.russell}@tue.nl
[2] Academic Medical Center, University of Amsterdam, Department of Quality
Assurance and Process Innovation, Amsterdam, The Netherlands
{p.j.bakker,a.j.moleman}@amc.uva.nl

Abstract. Optimal support for complex healthcare processes cannot be
provided by a single out-of-the-box Process-Aware Information System
and necessitates the construction of customized applications based on
these systems. In order to allow for the seamless integration of the new
technology into the existing operational processes of a healthcare organization, ensuring the correct operation and reliability of the developed
system are of the utmost importance. This paper proposes an approach
in which the same model is used for specifying, developing, testing and
validating the operational performance of a new system. The benefits
of using the same model for different purposes are decreased potential
for loss of user requirements and increased confidence in *reliability* and
correct operation of the resultant system before its deployment. This approach has been applied to a schedule-based workflow system developed
for the AMC hospital in Amsterdam.

Keywords: Workflow management, scheduling, testing, simulation.

1 Introduction

In healthcare organizations there is increasing pressure to improve medical and
organizational efficiency and effectiveness. The overall goal being to provide the
highest quality services at the lowest cost. Therefore, more attention is given to
the monitoring and control of healthcare processes.

Process-Aware Information Systems (PAIS), which are software systems that
operate on the basis of an underlying process model, present an attractive vehicle for the support and monitoring of healthcare processes. However, healthcare
processes tend to be both complex and of lengthy duration. Consequently, the
application of an out-of-the-box PAIS system does not directly deliver the required benefits. Additional functionality needs to be developed in order to satisfy
the specific needs imposed by the healthcare domain. Hence, a combination of

S. Rinderle-Ma et al. (Eds.): BPM 2009 Workshops, LNBIP 43, pp. 635–646, 2010.

different technologies need to be applied or developed in order to be able to deliver this additional functionality.

For the successful application of PAIS technology in the healthcare domain it is vital to precisely identify the required additional functionality and that a system is designed which addresses the existing needs in the healthcare domain. Unfortunately, although a candidate system may have been carefully designed, there still exists a "gap" between its deployment in a healthcare organization. This can easily be understood by the fact that healthcare processes are patient-centric, critical processes for which continuous operation must be guaranteed under all circumstances. Clearly, the introduction of a new technology system requires a seamless integration with the running operational processes of the hospital and no unexpected break-downs may occur. Additionally, it needs to be ensured that user expectations are met.

To address this "gap", we present an approach in which the same model is used for specifying, developing, testing and validating the operational performance of a new system. The different steps in this approach are as follows. First, during the *design* phase, a conceptual model is defined which is a *complete* and *formal* (i.e. executable) specification of the system to be developed. This model serves as a specification for the development of the system during the *implementation* phase. Finally, during the *testing* and *simulation* phase, the conceptual model and operational system are used to both test and validate the operational performance of the system.

The key characteristics of our approach are the *reuse* of the same model throughout the entire development process which *ensures there is minimal potential for loss of user requirements*. In addition, the approach leads to increased confidence in the *reliability* and *correct operation* of the resultant system which can be viewed as minimal requirements that need to be fulfilled before the deployment of such a system in a healthcare organization.

In this paper, we show the applicability of our approach in the healthcare domain. This is illustrated in the context of a schedule-aware workflow management system (WfMS), i.e. a particular type of PAIS, developed in conjunction with the Academic Medical Center (AMC) hospital, a large academic hospital in the Netherlands. In Section 2 we introduce both our conceptual model and a schedule-aware WfMS, and focus on its realization. In sections 3 and 4, we discuss the testing and validation of the operational performance of the resultant system. Finally, Section 5 discusses related work and Section 6 concludes the paper.

2   Schedule-Aware Workflow Management Systems

Deadlines and temporal constraints play an important role in the healthcare domain [7]. For example, many tasks are linked to appointments, e.g., a doctor cannot perform surgery without reserving an operating theater and making sure that the patient is present. Therefore, in this section, we focus on the design and implementation of a *schedule-aware WfMS*. First, some necessary concepts will be introduced. Afterwards, we elaborate on the conceptual model developed and

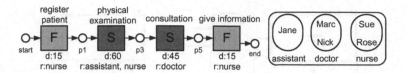

Fig. 1. Running example showing schedule (S) and flow (F) tasks. The prefix "d:" indicates the average time needed for performing the task and prefix "r:" indicates which roles are necessary for performing the task. For both schedule tasks, the patient is also required to be present.

discuss its functionality and how it has been realized. It is assumed that the reader is familiar with basic workflow management concepts, such as case and role [2].

2.1 Concepts

Figure 1 outlines a small example process for patient diagnosis. First the patient is registered by a nurse (task "register patient"). Then, the patient has an appointment with both an assistant and a nurse to check the physical condition of the patient (task "physical examination"), followed by an appointment with a doctor (task "consultation") to discuss the diagnosis. Finally, a nurse provides additional information to the patient (task "give information").

In this figure, we make a distinction between two kinds of tasks. The tasks labeled with an "F" in the figure are called *flow* tasks and can be performed *at an arbitrary point in time* when an available resource can undertake them. In order to do so, these flow tasks are presented in an ordinary *worklist* where a resource can start working on them at a time of their choosing. Only one role is defined for them as only a single resource is required to perform the task.

The other kind of tasks are called *schedule* tasks and are indicated by an "S" in the figure. They are performed by *one or more resources at a particular time*. Because such tasks are planned more than one role may be specified for this kind of task where for each role only *one* resource is involved in the actual performance of the task. Note that for a schedule task, the presence of the patient also might be required. The patient is considered to be a *passive* resource who should be present when the task is completed.

Each resource has its own *calendar* containing the appointments that have been made for schedule tasks. Where an appointment involves multiple resources, it is shown in the calendar for each of these resources. When determining the earliest time that an appointment can be started and the length of the appointment itself, the average duration of each task needs to be known. Despite this, sometimes appointments still need to be rescheduled because of anticipated delays in preceding tasks.

2.2 Conceptual Model

The main innovation of the system developed for the AMC is the incorporation of scheduling functionality. Therefore, the next challenge is to identify before the

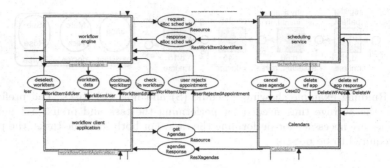

Fig. 2. The topmost level of the conceptual model realized in terms of CP Nets

implementation phase, how the new scheduling functionality being added should be integrated with existing workflow and calendar-based functionality. Therefore, *Colored Petri Nets (CPNs)* [10] have been chosen as the mechanism to identify and formalize the behavior of the system. CPNs provide a well-established and well-proven formal language suitable for describing the behavior of systems exhibiting characteristics such as concurrency, resource sharing, and synchronization.

In Figure 2 we see the topmost net of the conceptual model for the schedule-aware WfMS. Each substitution transition (represented as a rectangle) represents a component in the system. The places between two components (represented as circles) specify the interfaces between them. In total, the developed conceptual model consists of 30 nets, 250 transitions, and 634 places.

One of the main benefits of building a CPN model is that *experimentation* is possible. So, the model (or parts of it) can be executed, simulated and analyzed which leads to insights about the design and implementation of the system. Moreover, as can be seen in Figure 2, the conceptual model consists of several components. This allows for the incremental mapping of the model to an operational system mainly using available, third-party software.

2.3   Architecture

As can be seen in Figure 2, the resultant system consists of four main components. The functionality of each of them will now be explained together with a description of how they have been realized.

- **Workflow Engine:** The workflow engine is the "core" of the system and provides the standard facilities typical of this type of software [2]. For example, the engine takes care of the distribution of workitems and tracking their progress.

  Implementation: The engine is realized using both the open source WfMS YAWL [1] and a service which acts as an adaptor between the workflow client application and the scheduling service. The communication with these two components is based on the interchange of SOAP messages.

- **Scheduling Service:** The scheduling service provides the work scheduling facilities required by the system. Once a scheduling problem is received from the engine, it determines whether schedule tasks need to be (re)scheduled. Each scheduling problem is handled on a case-by-case base. A scheduling problem is represented as a graph which contains all the scheduling constraints for a case which are imposed by the engine (e.g. the ordering of tasks in the corresponding process definition for the case and the current state of the case).

  When scheduling appointments in a case, several issues are important. First, the appointments made for the (re)scheduled tasks need to be in the same order as they occur in the corresponding process definition and there should be sufficient time between them. Second, for the actual scheduling of an appointment multiple roles can be specified for a schedule task. For each role specified, precisely one resource needs to be selected and the corresponding appointment is booked in the calendar of these resources. If the patient also needs to be present, then this must also be taken into account.

  Based on these requirements several scheduling strategies for the booking of an appointment are possible. For example, one approach could be to search for the first opportunity where for each role specified, one resource is available.

  Implementation: The scheduling service is implemented in Java as an AXIS2 service. The communication with the calendar component takes place via a Java interface which exchanges information with this component.

- **Workflow Client Application:** the workflow client application offers a means of showing distributed workitems to a user. In the worktray, workitems corresponding to flow tasks can be seen. If a user is involved in the performance of a schedule task then the corresponding appointment can be found in their calendar. Once a workitem becomes available for the appointment, so that the task is ready to be executed, the corresponding workitem is completed via the calendar. For any appointments made in this way, a user can request their rescheduling.

  Implementation: A Microsoft Outlook 2003 client has been configured which acts as a full workflow client application. It provides both a view on a user's calendar and a view on the user's worktray.

- **Calendar:** The calendar component is responsible for providing display and manipulation facilities for user calendars. Both workflow and non-workflow related appointments can be created or deleted.

  Implementation: For this component, Microsoft Exchange Server 2007 has been selected as the system to support user calendars.

3 Testing

The complete system required the development of 13,692 lines of code (excluding pre-existing software such as YAWL, Outlook and Exchange). For the adaptor service in the workflow engine and the scheduling service, around 4.959 and

7.381 lines of code have been produced respectively. During its realization, the system or parts of it have been tested by executing a multitude of handcrafted scenarios and checking by visual inspection whether the produced output is correct. This approach revealed many programming errors. However, by nature, healthcare information systems should be highly reliable [7]. System failures will directly affect its acceptance by medical specialists. A complicating factor is that PAISs are more complex than traditional function- and data centric information systems. Obviously, a systematic approach for testing (parts of) the system is required to increase confidence in reliability of the resultant system.

3.1   Approach

The conceptual model provides a complete, formal description of the functionality of the system. As this model is executable, it also serves as a prototype implementation of the system. We can easily "replace" one or more components in the conceptual (CPN) model by its concrete implementation by making connections between the conceptual model and components in the actual system. This allows us to test the system on an incremental basis. Our focus is on the *black-box* testing of components where they can only be accessed and observed via their external interfaces. In addition, our focus is on identifying errors in the functionality of the system, also referred to as *functional testing*.

In order to fully automate the process of repeatedly testing one or more components of the realized system, we have built a test environment using Java. This environment consists of an *integration layer* which provides a connection between the CPN model and components in the actual system. Implemented components are tested by sequentially executing multiple tests. One test consists of a single, randomly generated, execution run of the conceptual model in which the implemented component(s) are tested. A test is considered to be complete if (1) an error is discovered in the implemented component or the integration layer, (2) a specified maximal number of steps have been executed in the conceptual model. For the execution of the conceptual model we use a Java interface which allows for loading and simulating CPN models created within CPN Tools.

3.2   Component(s) Testing

Once a testing framework is in place, one or more components of the implemented system can be tested. As for both the scheduling service component and the engine component, more lines of code have been developed in comparison to other components, we decided to (1) test the scheduling service component in isolation and (2) to test the workflow engine and the scheduling service together. In this way, we show that the approach works for both the testing of a single component and also when testing multiple components.

In order, to be able to run tests, the whole system first needs to be initialized. Therefore, a simple process definition has been added to the workflow engine so that cases can be started and workitems can be performed. Several users together with their corresponding calendars have also been added. In order to discover errors in the tested components and the integration layer it is determined whether during execution an exception occurs for one of them, i.e. it is tested whether a Java exception is generated. We will now discuss the different kind of errors that have been found when testing the workflow engine and the scheduling service.

- **Integration layer testing:** The integration layers between the scheduling service and the conceptual model and between the conceptual model and the workflow engine, contained in total 15 errors. All were conversion related.
- **Component testing:** For the workflow engine and the scheduling service component 12 errors have been identified. These ranged from simple coding errors to serious design flaws. For example, it was detected that a scheduling problem was sent to the scheduling service followed by a cancelation request, both for the same case, and that the latter request was handled first. This caused the scheduling service to crash. This issue could only be resolved by changing the corresponding interface.
- **Integration testing:** In total one error was identified which related to the integration of the workflow engine and the scheduling service component.
- **Conceptual model testing:** One challenge we faced was that no meaningful verification of the conceptual model was possible due to its size and complexity. Therefore, in the CPN model we added assertions to check whether certain invariants still hold. In total, 25 errors have been identified ranging from simple modeling errors to serious design flaws. These design flaws were all concurrency related and became visible as many different scenarios have been performed involving the conceptual model. For example, the state of two cases could become corrupted when checking in a workitem for each of them at the same time.

The majority of the identified errors were concurrency related. By using the CPN model for simulation, it is way easy to mimic arbitrary many user. Although our approach to testing revealed many errors which needed immediate attention, it does not guarantee that the tested components are error free as we did not actively check whether the output produced by each of the implemented components was correct. However, we discovered many errors that remained hidden during classical testing, thus increasing the confidence in the system.

4   Simulation

By testing the system more confidence has been gained and reliability increased. However, this is still not enough to know whether the system works properly. For example, in a hospital many critical patient-centric processes are carried out whose operational performance (e.g. waiting time for appointments) must not be negatively impacted by the introduction of the schedule-aware WfMS. If the operational performance is less, service levels offered to patients decrease as well. Obviously, this is not acceptable for a hospital. Therefore, we now elaborate on the use of *simulation* for assessing the impact of the system on the operational performance of the processes that it supports. This is investigated for several different configurations. Note that we use simulation for *operational decision making* and focus on the *transient* behavior of the system, also referred to as *short-term* simulation in [14].

4.1 Approach

In order to investigate the operational performance of our system, we take an existing healthcare process and consider several performance metrics specified for the process. As a candidate healthcare process, we take the diagnostic process for patients visiting the gynecological oncology outpatient clinic at the AMC hospital for which the schedule-aware WfMS was developed. This process deals with the diagnostic process that is followed by a patient, up to the point where the patient is diagnosed (see Figure 3). Given the space limitations, we only elaborate on the most important aspects of the simulation.

The whole process consists of 42 flow tasks and 6 schedule tasks. When a patient is registered, several administrative tasks need to be done before the first visit of the patient ("make conclusion" task). During such a visit, a doctor can request several diagnostic tests that are needed for the patient and for which an appointment needs to be made. These are a CT, MRI, a pre assessment test, and an examination under anesthetic which are all schedule tasks. However, it is also possible that these appointments are made at the beginning of the process, once it is known that they are needed.

In order to investigate the impact of the system on the operation performance of the healthcare process, for the period from 02-07-2007 to 19-03-2008, a group of 143 patients undertook the process. The flow tasks are performed by different actors in the process. For example, we have three nurses that perform all the tasks having prefix "N:". However, for the schedule tasks, corresponding appointments

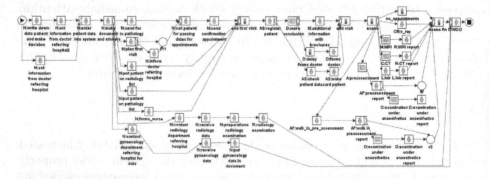

Fig. 3. Screenshot of the YAWL model showing the diagnostic process of the gynecological oncology healthcare process. The flow tasks are indicated by a person icon and the schedule tasks are indicated by a calendar icon. For all schedule tasks, the patient is required to be present.

will be made by our system. In order to ensure that the scheduling of these appointments matches reality as closely as possible, the contents of the calendars of the resources allowed to perform these tasks are based on historical data derived from the AMC electronic calendar system. These calendars are filled such that a resource is unavailable outside scheduled hours. In addition, during scheduled hours, a resource is also considered to be unavailable when a patient does not show-up for an appointment and when an appointment exists for a patient which is not in the group of patients we are considering.

One of the main challenges for the simulation is properly estimating the arrival of patients, the length of the appointments that need to be scheduled, and the selection of diagnostic tests that are chosen for each patient. As for all of these characteristics, real data exists in the AMC electronic calendar system, we decided to "replay" these events as they happened in reality. So, in the simulation, a patient arrives on exactly the same day as happened in reality, the same tests are chosen, and the length of the corresponding appointments are exactly the same as happened in reality. The same holds for a request to reschedule an appointment, triggered either by the hospital or the patient. Note that this does not imply that the simulation becomes deterministic. For example, the time spent by a resource on a flow task is determined by a stochastic distribution and the selection of a task is dependent on the availability of resources.

For the actual execution of the simulation experiments, we have used the same system configuration as has been used for testing both the workflow engine and scheduling service component in Section 3 which involves replacing both components with their implemented counterpart. Both the workflow client application and calendar component in the conceptual model have been configured such that the above mentioned aspects are included.

4.2 Results

Several sets of results have been obtained by performing various experiments. One experiment consists of 10 runs of the simulation model. A selection of these results are presented in Figure 4. Here we focus on the waiting time for the first appointment and the time between the first appointment and the CT, MRI, pre-assessment, and the examination under anesthetic respectively. For each of them, the color of the corresponding bars are indicated by the "GO", "MRI", "CT", "ANS", and "SU" text labels respectively. The average waiting times for these appointments experienced in reality are shown by the bars above the "REAL" text.

Experiment 1: Currently, for the first visit, the average waiting time experienced in reality is 11,333 minutes (7.9 days), which means that only 47% of the patients have an appointment within 7 calendar days. However, as the service level for the group of patients we are studying, it has been defined that for 90% of them, (1) the first visit should take place within seven calendar days of the registration of the patient, and (2) all diagnostic tests should be completed within 14 calendar days of their first visit. Clearly, for the average waiting time

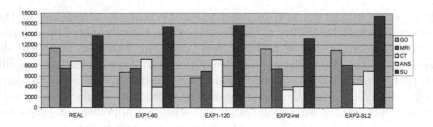

Fig. 4. Results of the experiments

for the first visit the required service level is not met. Note that for the other appointments, the required service level is met.

To examine how this situation might be remedied, the following two variations were examined: for a selected resource, every week, at the same day, an additional 60 and 120 minutes have been added for seeing patients respectively. The results of these experiments can be seen in Figure 4 by the bars above the "EXP1-60" and "EXP1-120" text respectively. Here it becomes clear that the average waiting time for the first visit already significantly drops when adding an additional 60 minutes per week for seeing patients. However, only in the situation where 120 minutes are added, is the service level met.

Experiment 2: Currently, the appointments for a CT, MRI, and pre-assessment may all be scheduled on a different day for a patient requiring multiple visits to the hospital.

In order to increase the service delivered to patients, the AMC likes to offer that the appointments for a CT, MRI, and pre-assessment are scheduled on the same day (although not when rescheduling) with a 1-4 hour gap between them. In order to be able to fully examine the impact of this rule, we simulated the situation in which an appointment for the CT, MRI, and pre-assessment is scheduled for the very first opportunity that all required resources are available. This is shown by the bars above the "EXP2-INIT" text. The bars above the "EXP2-SL" text show the results when applying this service level. Note that for both experiments a small delay of one day is added to the earliest opportunity that these appointments can be booked. In this way, the probability that these appointments need to be rescheduled is minimized which allows us to investigate the true impact of the rule as appointments are only scheduled once. When comparing the results for both experiments, it can be seen that applying this service level has quite some impact on the average waiting time for the pre-assessment and examination under anesthetic appointments. For the pre-assessment this can be explained by the fact that it is now often scheduled together with an MRI or CT test which both have a higher average waiting time. As the examination under anesthetic needs to be scheduled later than the pre-assessment test, this also explains the increased average waiting time for the examination under anesthetic appointment.

5 Related Work

The topic of appointment scheduling has received significant attention in healthcare, particularly the scheduling of appointments for outpatients. Most of this research only focuses on a single unit [9], whereas we take the scheduling of workitems into account for the whole workflow, together with its current state.

On the topic of management of time by WfMS, in [8], the satisfiability of time constraints and the enforcement of these at run-time is investigated. Another field of research is the scheduling of tasks itself [4,6]. Our approach does not present new scheduling algorithms, but instead focusses on augmenting a WfMS with scheduling facilities.

The advantages and disadvantages of using a conceptual model both for the design and testing of the same system have received quite some attention in the model-based testing literature [15]. The general thought is that although a development model typically contains too much detail for the testing phase, it does not describe the dynamic behavior well enough to enable automated test generation [15,12]. Where the dynamic behavior is described in sufficient detail it can be used for code generation. However, the goal of our conceptual model is not code generation. Rather, its level of abstraction is such that it describes precisely the requirements needed for implementing the system such that it can be concretized in many different ways.

Discrete-event simulation is often used in healthcare in order to improve efficiency and costs. However, most of these studies only focus on the analysis of individual units [11]. Our simulation considers the scheduling of appointments across several units. Within the workflow domain, the basic approach is to convert the process definition into a formal model, and then use simulation for optimization using the converted model [5]. A similar approach is described in [5] which focuses on embedding a simulation model within an existing business process management system. With regard to the use of simulation as a preliminary step for the subsequent implementation of a WfMS we are only aware of the work described in [13]. Related to this is [3], in which a business process model is constructed for requirements specification, animation, and validation of a complex software system to be built. Other than that, we are not aware of any approach which uses the same model for specifying, developing, testing, and validating the operational performance of the resultant system.

6 Conclusions

In this paper, we have presented a schedule-aware WfMS which augments a WfMS with scheduling facilities. During development, the same conceptual model is used for specifying, developing, testing, and validating the operational performance of the resultant system. For each of these steps, we have elaborated on the role and usefulness of the conceptual model and demonstrated how the overall development process is expedited through its use. In addition, the development approach pursued in this paper leads to increased confidence about the reliability and correct operation of the resultant PAIS and its ability to satisfy customer requirements. This is of the utmost importance for the deployment of the system in a healthcare organization and we believe that it leads to an increased uptake of the system by the medical specialists and the hospital.

References

1. van der Aalst, W.M.P., Aldred, L., Dumas, M., ter Hofstede, A.H.M.: Design and Implementation of the YAWL System. In: Persson, A., Stirna, J. (eds.) CAiSE 2004. LNCS, vol. 3084, pp. 142–159. Springer, Heidelberg (2004)
2. van der Aalst, W.M.P., van Hee, K.M.: Workflow Management: Models, Methods, and Systems. MIT Press, Cambridge (2002)
3. Barjis, J.: The importance of business process modeling in software systems design. Science of Computer Programming 71(1), 73–87 (2008)
4. Bettini, C., Wang, X.S., Jajodia, S.: Temporal Reasoning in Workflow Systems. Distributed and Parallel Databases 11(3), 269–306 (2002)
5. Choi, B.K., Lee, D., Kang, D.H.: DEVS Modeling of Run-time Workflow Simulation and Its Application. In: 22nd European Conference on Modeling and Simulation (2008)
6. Combi, C., Pozzi, G.: Architectures for a Temporal Workflow Management System. In: Haddad, H., Omicini, A., Wainwright, R.L., Liebrock, L.M. (eds.) Proc. of the 2004 ACM symposium on applied computing, pp. 659–666 (2004)
7. Dadam, P., Reichert, M.: The ADEPT project: a decade of research and development for robust and flexible process support: Challenges and Achievements. Computer Science - Research and Development 23(2), 81–97 (2009)
8. Eder, J., Panagos, E.: Managing Time in Workflow Systems. In: Workflow Handbook 2001. Future Strategies Inc. (2000)
9. Gupta, D., Denton, B.: Appointment scheduling in health care: Challenges and opportunities. IIE Transactions 40, 800–819 (2008)
10. Jensen, K., Kristensen, L.M., Wells, L.: Coloured Petri Nets and CPN Tools for Modelling and Validation of Concurrent Systems. International Journal on Software Tools for Technology Transfer 9(3-4), 213–254 (2007)
11. Jun, J.B., Jacobson, S.H., Swisher, J.R.: Application of discrete-event simulation in healthcare clinics: A survey. Journal of the Operational Research Society 50, 109–123 (1999)
12. Pretschner, A., Philipps, J.: Methodological issues in model-based testing. In: Broy, M., Jonsson, B., Katoen, J.-P., Leucker, M., Pretschner, A. (eds.) Model-Based Testing of Reactive Systems. LNCS, vol. 3472, pp. 281–291. Springer, Heidelberg (2005)
13. Quaglini, S., Caffi, E., Cavallini, A., Micieli, G., Stefanelli, M.: Simulation of a Stroke Unit Careflow. In: Studies in health technology and informatics (MED-INFO), pp. 1190–1194 (2001)
14. Reijers, H.A., van der Aalst, W.M.P.: Short-Term Simulation: Bridging the Gap between Operational Control and Strategic Decision Making. In: Proceedings of the IASTED International Conference on Modelling and Simulation (1999)
15. Utting, M., Legeard, B.: Practical Model-Based Testing. Morgan Kaufman, San Francisco (2006)

An Integrated Collection of Tools for Continuously Improving the Processes by Which Health Care Is Delivered: A Tool Report

Leon J. Osterweil, Lori A. Clarke, and George S. Avrunin

Department of Computer Science
University of Massachusetts, Amherst, MA 01003
{ljo,Clarke,avrunin}@cs.umass.edu

Abstract. This report will present a collection of tools that supports the precise definition, careful analysis, and execution of processes that coordinate the actions of humans, automated devices, and software systems for the delivery of health care. The tools have been developed over the past several years and are currently being evaluated through their application to four health care processes, blood transfusion, chemotherapy, emergency department operations, and identity verification. The tools are integrated with each other using the Eclipse framework or through the sharing of artifacts so that the internal representations generated by one might be used to expedite the actions of others. This integrated collection of tools is intended to support the continuous improvement of health care delivery processes. The process definitions developed through this framework are executable and intended for eventual use in helping to guide actual health care workers in the performance of their activities, including the utilization of medical devices and information systems.

1 Introduction

Many reports (e.g., [1]) have suggested that manifest shortcomings in the delivery of health care could be addressed by the application of appropriate information technologies. Because health care is often delivered through complex processes, involving the coordination of several different types of agents, process technologies should be useful in addressing some of these shortcomings. Our interest in the application of process technology to various domains is longstanding and has resulted in the creation of a growing collection of tools that have been of value in addressing problems in such diverse areas as software development, dispute resolution, and digital government. Our preliminary results in applying them to health care have been encouraging.

2 Our Approach

Broadly speaking our approach entails applying the notion of Continuous Process Improvement (CPI) to human-centric processes, such as those that often arise in health care. For such processes, our approach to CPI requires 1) defining a process

S. Rinderle-Ma et al. (Eds.): BPM 2009 Workshops, LNBIP 43, pp. 647–653, 2010.

precisely, 2) analyzing the process definition to determine the presence or absence of defects or vulnerabilities, 3) modifying the process definition to address identified defects as well as possible, and 4) observing the execution of the modified process to determine whether past defects have been removed or whether new defects are revealed. The last three steps may be repeatedly revisited.

This view has led us to develop process technologies that address needs in the areas of

- Process elicitation and definition
- Requirements specification and process analysis
- Process execution, simulation, and monitoring

3   Our Toolset

3.1   Process Elicitation and Definition Tools

The tools in this category revolve around the Little-JIL process definition language. Little-JIL incorporates features that are seldom found in current process modeling languages, but that seem important for the clear and precise definition of health care processes.   Thus, for example, Little-JIL provides powerful support for exception management, which has been important in the clear, concise, and complete definition of processes as diverse as emergency division management and chemotherapy delivery.   Language support for specifying concurrency and synchronization has been useful in representing interactions among doctors, nurses, and blood banks in blood transfusion processes. Little-JIL's emphasis on the use of abstraction and modularity has led to process definitions that foster reuse, clarity, and conciseness.   The language's support for precise specification of artifact flow and resource utilization to complement specifications of activity coordination has been particularly useful in defining emergency division processes.   A full description of Little-JIL can be found in [2]. Language features such as those just summarized seemed to us to offer advantages over existing process modeling languages that justified our extra work in defining and implementing the language, and in building tool support needed to make good use of it. bu

Little-JIL is rigorously defined by means of finite-state machine semantics, is supported by a visual interface, and has been used extensively to support the definition of processes in diverse domains. The development of health care processes is described in several papers (e.g. [3-5]), and will be demonstrated with the support of the Visual-JIL screen editor, which facilitates the creation and editing of Little-JIL process definitions. In recognition of the value of complementary forms of these process definitions, our toolset also includes facilities for displaying these definitions as linear trees and as natural language hypertext, both of which will be shown along with other tools that support the creation and display of various cross-reference reports and summaries.

In recent work we have been comparing detailed patient identification process definitions to determine how well these process definitions actually reflect the way that these processes are actually performed by real medical practitioners. We are doing this by comparing observed traces of actual patient identification process executions to Little-JIL process definitions hoping to improve the process definitions, and also improve our process elicitation procedures as well.

3.2 Analysis

A major goal of our work has been to demonstrate the feasibility of doing rigorous analysis of process definitions. This is possible only when processes are defined in a rigorously defined language. In defining our own process language we were also able to define its semantics. Little-JIL's semantics are sufficiently well-defined to support a variety of static analyses, of which two types will be demonstrated.

Finite-state Verification. We will demonstrate how our FLAVERS finite-state verification tool [7] can be used to determine the presence or absence of defects in Little-JIL process definitions (at least up to a fixed bound loop iterations) [8]. FLAVERS compares all possible execution traces through a Little-JIL process definition to a Finite-state Automaton (FSA) definition of a property. When the FSA defines a desirable property (e.g. a safety property), then the FLAVERS analysis determines whether it is possible for there to be an execution of the process that violates the desirable property. When such a violation occurs, FLAVERS provides a counter example trace that demonstrates how the property can be violated. We have used FLAVERS to look for such process defects as allowing the possibility that a blood transfusion may be done without prior to obtaining informed consent, and administering chemotherapy without confirming that dosages have been computed with up-to-date height and weight information.

We will also demonstrate how our PROPEL tool [9] can be used to define FSAs that are then suitable for use by FLAVERS. PROPEL supports the specification of FSAs in three formats, disciplined natural language, question trees, and FSA depictions. The user can work with any one of the formats and have the results displayed in the others, or can work with the three formats simultaneously. We have used PROPEL to create properties such as the two described above that were the basis for actual finite state verifications [4].

Fault Tree Analysis. We will also demonstrate how Fault Trees can be generated from Little-JIL process definitions [10], and show how their analysis can be used to complement the finite-state verifications generated using FLAVERS. Finite-state verification can be used to identify defects in a process definition that result from the occurrence of undesired sequences of process events (e.g. beginning a transfusion before patient consent has been obtained). But these analyses assume that all process steps have been carried out correctly. We will demonstrate two types of analyses, Fault Tree Analysis (FTA) and Failure Mode and Effects Analysis (FMEA), that are centered on Fault Trees, and that explore the ramifications of incorrect performance of process steps.

We have generated an FTA from a Little-JIL definition of a blood transfusion process, and a specification of a specific hazard (the delivery of an incorrect type of blood to the patient bedside). We then used our FTA generation tool to generate the minimal cut sets (MCSs) of this FTA, and used it to show how these MCSs can indicate vulnerabilities such as single points of failure, namely single steps whose incorrect performance can lead directly to specified hazard. We also support FMEA, using it to show the consequences of a step (e.g. getting a blood type) being performed incorrectly. FTA and FMEA are complementary analyzes; one shows the possible clusters of failures that could lead to a hazard and the other shows the hazards that could result from a particular failure.

3.3 Execution, Simulation, and Monitoring

We will also demonstrate some of the dynamic analysis capabilities in our toolset, including tools that support the actual execution of processes and tools that support simulations of process executions.

Process Execution tools. Little-JIL processes are defined hierarchically. Each step can be thought of as an instance of a procedure to which arguments and resources are bound at runtime. Child steps of a parent step should be thought of as subprocedures that can be invoked by the parent. When a leaf step is invoked, the actions associated with that step are to be performed by agents in any way that the agent may desire. Thus, in an important sense, the Little-JIL process definition is a specification of the order in which steps are to be executed, the assignment of specific agents to the execution of steps, and the flow of artifacts between agents as steps are assigned and executed. Our toolset contains a variety of tools needed to support such process execution. These tools include a manager of the resources that are to be used to perform process steps, an agenda manager that supports the distribution of tasks to (and back from) agents, and a subsystem that maintains effective communication between human participants and the other components of a running process. These tools and their coordination will be demonstrated.

Process discrete event simulation tools. We will also demonstrate how a Little-JIL process definition can be used to drive a discrete event simulation [11]. Many of the tools needed to support such simulations are already used to support process execution. But discrete event simulation also requires the creation of simulators of the behaviors of the agents that perform the various process steps. We will demonstrate the tools needed to simulate various agents. Perhaps of greatest interest are those tools that simulate the performance of humans in processes. Our demonstration will show how such human performance can be simulated at relatively basic levels, but still be sufficient to demonstrate the effects of varying resources. We have used this capability to begin explorations of how to vary the mix of human resources in a hospital Emergency Department in order to reduce patient waiting time, while keeping costs low.

Process-centered environment. Figure 1 is a conceptual view of how the capabilities of these tools can complement each other while supporting the overall goal of Continuous Process Improvement (CPI). The boxes in the middle of the figure represent different analyzers. Arrows to the left of these boxes represent the process definition artifacts (e.g. the Little-JIL coordination definition, and FLAVERS property specification) required by each of these analyzers. The arrows leaving these boxes represent the various analysis results produced. The figure indicates that these artifacts provide information whose consideration can be used to identify defects or shortcomings, which can then be taken as inputs to review processes that yield improvements (depicted as the long right-pointing arrows) to the process definition artifacts.

Note that this approach to process improvement amortizes the considerable cost of developing a process definition, by using that definition as input to several analyzers. Creating a detailed, accurate health care process model has in some cases taken several dozen meetings with domain experts. At a typical meeting, appropriate domain experts review the process definition for accuracy and the computer scientists prepare questions to flesh out incomplete, inconsistent, or erroneous aspects of the definition. It is most cost effective for such a large investment in time to yield the greatest return in benefits. Using the single articulate process definition to drive a number of different analyzes seems to improve the cost-benefit ratio of our approach.

4 Evaluation

The Little-JIL language has evolved through a series of modifications. Little-JIL version 1.5 is described in a generally available document [2]. The Visual-JIL screen editor is currently available for distribution, although some features of the 1.5 language version are not yet implemented. The FLAVERS finite-state verification system and PROPEL property elicitation system are both available for distribution. Thus it is possible to use publicly available tools to carry out finite-state verification of processes defined in Little-JIL against properties defined using PROPEL. The Fault Tree Analysis tools, the execution system, and discrete event simulation are not yet available for distribution.

Little-JIL and its toolset have undergone evaluation through their application to the definition and analysis of a range of health care processes. The language and tools have also been evaluated through their application to processes in such other domains as labor-management dispute resolution, elections [12], and scientific data processing [13]. These evaluations have resulted in modifications to Little-JIL, such as the creation of facilities to support preemption of tasks currently being executed. The evaluations have also led to changes to our analysis toolset.

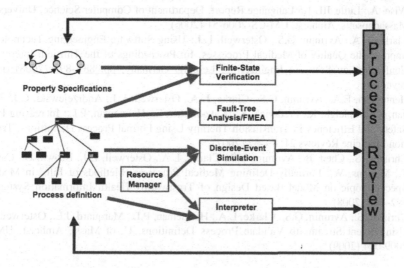

Fig. 1. Continuous Process Improvement Environment

5 Related Work

There has been some prior work in using process definition and analysis to improve medical processes. For example, the Protocure II project [14, 15] has goals that are quite similar to ours, but uses a rather different, AI-based, linguistic paradigm for defining processes. Noumeir has also pursued similar goals, but using a notation like UML to define processes [16]. Others (eg. [17]), view medical processes as work-flows and use a workflow-like language to define processes and drive their execution. But, we note that these projects seem to place less emphasis on analysis.

There have been other approaches to improving medical safety, as well, but much of the emphasis of this work has been targeted towards quality control measures [18], error reporting systems [19], and process automation in laboratory settings [20], such as those where blood products are prepared for administration. In other work, Bayesian belief networks have been used as the basis for discrete event simulations of medical scenarios, and to guide treatment planning (eg. [21]).

Acknowledgements. The Little-JIL language and the suite of support tools described above are the products of a great deal of work by dozens of participants who are too numerous to be listed here. This work has been supported by numerous grants, including by the National Science Foundation under Award(s) CCF-0427071, CCF-0820198, and IIS-0705772. Any opinions, findings, and conclusions or recommendations expressed in this publication are those of the author(s) and do not necessarily reflect the views of the National Science Foundation.

References

1. Kohn, L.T., Corrigan, J.M., Donaldson, M.S. (eds.): To Err is Human: Building a Safer Health System. National Academy Press, Washington (1999)
2. Wise, A.: Little-JIL 1.5 Language Report. Department of Computer Science, University of Massachusetts, Amherst, UM-CS-2006-51 (2006)
3. Clarke, L.A., Avrunin, G.S., Osterweil, L.J.: Using Software Engineering Technology to Improve the Quality of Medical Processes. In: Proceedings of the Thirtieth International Conference on Software Engineering, Leipzig, Germany, pp. 889–898 (2008) (invited keynote)
4. Henneman, E.A., Avrunin, G.S., Clarke, L.A., Osterweil, L.J., Andrzejewski, C.J., Merrigan, K., Cobleigh, R., Frederick, K., Katz-Basset, E., Henneman, P.L.: Increasing Patient Safety and Efficiency in Transfusion Therapy Using Formal Process Definitions. Transfusion Medicine Reviews 21, 49–57 (2007)
5. Christov, S., Chen, B., Avrunin, G.S., Clarke, L.A., Osterweil, L.J., Brown, D., Cassells, L., Mertens, W.: Formally Defining Medical Processes. Methods of Info, in Medicine. Special Topic on Model-Based Design of Trustworthy Health Information Systems 47, 392–398 (2008)
6. Christof, S., Avrunin, G.S., Clarke, L.A., Henneman, P.L., Marquard, J.L., Osterweil, L.J.: Using Event Streams to Validate Process Definitions. U. of Mass., Amherst, UM-CS-2009-004 (2009)

7. Dwyer, M.B., Clarke, L.A., Cobleigh, J.M., Naumovich, G.: Flow Analysis for Verifying Properties of Concurrent Software Systems. ACM Transactions on Software Engineering and Methodology 13, 359–430 (2004)
8. Chen, B., Avrunin, G.S., Henneman, E.A., Clarke, L.A., Osterweil, L.J., Henneman, P.L.: Analyzing Medical Processes. In: Proceedings of the Thirtieth International Conference on Software Engineering, Leipzig, Germany (2008) (to appear)
9. Cobleigh, R.L., Avrunin, G.S., Clarke, L.A.: User Guidance for Creating Precise and Accessible Property Specifications. In: Proceedings of the 14th ACM SIGSOFT International Symposium on Foundations of Software Engineering, pp. 208–218. ACM Press, Portland (2006)
10. Chen, B., Avrunin, G.S., Clarke, L.A., Osterweil, L.J.: Automatic Fault Tree Derivation from Little-JIL Process Definitions. In: Proceedings of the Software Process Workshop and Process Simulation Workshop, Shanghai, China. LNCS, pp. 150–158. Springer, Heidelberg (2006)
11. Raunak, M.S., Osterweil, L.J., Wise, A., Clarke, L.A., Henneman, P.L.: Simulating Patient Flow through an Emergency Department Using Process-Driven Discrete Event Simulation. In: Proceedings of the 31st International Conference in Software Engineering Workshop on Software Engineering and Health Care, Vancouver, Canada (2009) (to appear)
12. Simidchieva, B.I., Marzilli, M.S., Clarke, L.A., Osterweil, L.J.: Specifying and Verifying Requirements for Election Processes. In: Proceedings of the 9th Annual International Conference on Digital Government Research, Montreal, Canada (2008) (to appear)
13. Osterweil, L.J., Clarke, L.A., Podorozhny, R., Wise, A., Boose, E., Ellison, A.M., Hadley, J.: Experience in Using a Process Language to Define Scientific Workflow and Generate Dataset Provenance. In: Proceedings of the ACM SIGSOFT 16th International Symposium on Foundations of Software Engineering, Georgia, Atlanta, pp. 319–329 (2008)
14. Marcos, M., Galán, J.C., Wittenberg, J., van Croonenborg, J., Rosenbrand, K., Martínez-Salvador, B.: Construction of a Process Model for the Integration of Formal Methods in the Development of Medical Guidelines. In: eChallenges e-2006 Conference (October 2006)
15. ten Teije, A., Marcos, M., Balser, M., van Croonenborg, J., Duelli, C., van Harmelen, F., Lucas, P., Miksch, S., Reif, W., Rosenbrand, K., Seyfang, A.: Improving medical protocols by formal methods. Art. Intell. in Medicine 36(3), 193–209 (2006)
16. Noumeir, R.: Radiology interpretation process modeling. Journal of Biomedical Informatics 39(2), 103–114 (2006)
17. Ruffolo, M., Curio, R., Gallucci, L.: Process Management in Health Care: A System for Preventing Risks and Medical Errors. In: van der Aalst, W.M.P., Benatallah, B., Casati, F., Curbera, F. (eds.) BPM 2005. LNCS, vol. 3649, pp. 334–343. Springer, Heidelberg (2005)
18. Mintz, P.D.: Quality assessment and improvement of transfusion practices. Transfusion Med. 9, 219–232 (1995)
19. Kaplan, H.S., Battles, J.B., Van der Schaaf, T.W., et al.: Identification and Classification of Events in Transfusion Medicine. Transfusion 38, 1071–1081 (1998)
20. Jensen, N.J., Crosson, J.T.: An Automated System for Bedside Verification of the Match Between Patient Identification and Blood Unit Identification. Transfusion 36, 216–221 (1996)
21. van der Gaag, L.C., Renooij, S., Witteman, C.L.M., Aleman, B.M.P., Taal, B.G.: Probabilities for a probabilistic network: A case-study in oesophageal cancer. Artificial Intelligence in Medicine 25(2), 123–148 (2002)

RefMod Workshop

Introduction to the 12th International Workshop on Reference Modeling (RefMod 2009)

In the past decades, conceptual models have proven to be a useful means to support information systems engineering. Nevertheless, due to the usual complexity of information systems, creating and especially maintaining conceptual models is quite challenging and costly.

A common strategy to reduce cost is reuse. Reference models represent a special class of conceptual models, which are designed with the explicit aim of being reused. These models provide recommendations how to build specific conceptual models for a given problem area. The problem areas addressed by reference models reach from particular business areas, such as invoice auditing, to entire economic sectors, for instance trade.

Due to their claim of representing "best practice" or "common practice" solutions, the main objective of reference models is to realize cost savings in the construction process of purpose-specific models on the one hand. Through reuse of business knowledge stored in the reference models, they accelerate the modeling process. On the other hand, modelers aim at increasing the quality of their models through reuse of reference models, since these claim to contain proven concepts.

Reference modeling research addresses the question how to design conceptual models in order to make them notably reusable and how to apply them efficiently without any loss of quality. In particular, it includes the topics

- methods and modeling languages for the development of reference models
- adaptation of reference models
- evaluation of reference models
- semantic aspects of reference modeling
- cconomic aspects of reference modeling
- reference models for manufacturing, retailing, service, and (public) administration
- reference modeling tools.

In 2009, we could accept four high-quality papers whose topics reached from methodical basics to reference modeling applications in particular business domains:

Based on an approach towards adapting reference models automatically to requirements of different user groups, SEBASTIAN HERWIG and ARMIN STEIN develop a generic XML format being able to exchange configurable reference model data. They aim at supporting distributed construction of reference models with different modeling tools and different modeling languages, yet allowing using a unified configuration approach. JAN VOM BROCKE and BIRGIT HOFREITER apply universal design techniques of reference modeling to the United Nation's Centre for Trade Facilitation and e-business (UN/CEFACT) modeling methodology and show their applicability in the field of international trade. WERNER ESSWEIN, SINA LEHRMANN and JEANNETTE STARK demonstrate the potential of reference modeling for simulating mobile construction machinery. They apply reference models to engineering, construction, sales and marketing, and service. It is shown how these conceptual models can be aligned with different application scenarios and how they are to be connected to the according

S. Rinderle-Ma et al. (Eds.): BPM 2009 Workshops, LNBIP 43, pp. 657–658, 2010.
© Springer-Verlag Berlin Heidelberg 2010

formal simulation models. Finally, VOLKER HOYER, KATARINA STANOEVSKA-SLABE-
VA and JAN VOM BROCKE outline the contribution of reference models for organizing
Enterprise Mashup environments. In contrast to most research focusing on the tech-
nical implementation, they point the organizational aspect of setting up Enterprise
Mashup environments.

The contributions of the workshop have been selected in a rigorous, double blind
peer-review process. We would like to thank all authors, organizers and involved
persons that have made the workshop and this book section possible. Finally, we
thank the organizers of BPM 2009 who have provided a professional and competent
environment for RefMod 2009.

Münster, Germany, September 2009   Jörg Becker
                                                                Patrick Delfmann

Enabling Widespread Configuration of Conceptual Models – An XML Approach

Sebastian Herwig and Armin Stein

European Research Center for Information Systems,
Westfälische Wilhelms-Universität Münster
Leonardo-Campus 3, 48149 Münster, Germany
{sebastian.herwig,armin.stein}@ercis.uni-muenster.de

Abstract. The manual adaptation of conceptual models in general and reference models in particular is a time consuming and error prone task, which has to be carefully conducted. The configurative reference modeling approach promises support for the model developer as well as for the model user, as certain parts of a model can be automatically removed with respect to the requirements of a certain perspective. By this automation, the risk of creating faulty models during adaptation can be highly reduced. However, up to now this approach exists in terms of its conceptual specification, leaving software support to a proprietary prototype, not providing support for widespread modeling tools, which is necessary for acceptance and applicability of the approach. To face this gap, our approach proposes an XML schema, enabling the configuration of serialized conceptual model data of virtually any modeling language and any modeling tool capable of XML export.

Keywords: Conceptual Modeling, Configuration, XML, Interchange.

1 Introduction

Conceptual information models can serve as a means for knowledge management and as a starting point for the construction of information systems (see e.g., [1], p. 16). Reference information models provide a comprehensive and complete view on the subject it is intended to cover (see e.g., [2]). As usually all required perspectives are included into the reference model, the downside often is its high complexity, which makes it hard to understand for those users not requiring all the information. On the one hand, users might require perspectives hiding certain *aspects* like information about data, processes or organizational structures. Those aspects might be whole models of certain types, model sections or certain element types. On the other hand, independent from their type, certain *parts* (i.e., branches or single model elements) of models might not be required for a specific model user because they belong to a process not in the scope of the user's demand. Thus, to generate stakeholder specific variants of the reference model, parts of it have to be removed consistently, depending on the user's requirements. The manual configuration of a reference model tends to be an exhaustive task, as the modeler has to take care for the consistency of the models

S. Rinderle-Ma et al. (Eds.): BPM 2009 Workshops, LNBIP 43, pp. 659–670, 2010.
© Springer-Verlag Berlin Heidelberg 2010

derived. Neither too many model elements may be removed, nor should elements remain in the models, which are not required. Furthermore, the compliance of the models has to be regarded with respect to their meta models, if applicable. The Event-Driven Process Chain (EPC) [3] modeling language for example does not allow two events to succeed each other.

Configurative Reference Modeling [4] is regarded as a promising approach to face the problem of the complexity of model configuration. However, for our approach, we do not semantically distinct between models and reference models, hence we speak of *models* in its general meaning throughout this paper. By attaching meta information to model elements within modeling tools, their relevance for certain perspectives can be determined. Those meta information can either be related to specific characteristics of a certain element (like `automation = manual`, called *attributes*) or to certain perspectives (like `transaction type = (warehouse business ∨ third-party deal)`, called *terms*). By doing so, the model base can be automatically manipulated in a way that only those elements remain in the derived model collection that carry the respective attributes and/or terms. So far, wide spread modeling tools like the ARIS Suite (IDS Scheer), Adonis (BOC-Group) or the Corporate Modeler (Casewise) support the attachment of meta information to model elements, yet none of the tools enables the subsequent configuration. Apart from this, all of the tools that are known to us have the ability to serialize and export models to a proprietary XML (Extensible Markup Language) format, which we use for our approach. We propose a schema that enables and simplifies the configuration of serialized model data on an XML basis. For this, we discuss current approaches of configurative (reference) modeling and the lack of applicable implementations in Section 2. Concerning the serialization of conceptual models, we discuss restrictions of widespread modeling tools and limitations of present serialization formats. In Section 3, we present our research method, which follows the Design Science approach. Section 4 deals with decisions for the design of an XML schema in the sense of our approach and presents suggestions for its realization. Section 5 exemplifies the application of our approach. Section 6 concludes the paper, list identified limitations and gives an outlook on our next research steps.

2   Related Work

Methodical support for the configuration of conceptual information models is addressed by several approaches (cf. Soffer, Golany and Dori [5]; Rosemann and van der Aalst [2]; Becker, Delfmann and Knackstedt [4]; la Rosa, Gottschalk, Dumas and van der Aalst, W. [6]). All these approaches have in common, that they operate on an integrated model base, which comprise relevant aspects of the application contexts the model is developed for. In order to perform the configuration, attributes are used to define the assignment of model elements to the relevant application contexts. Based on this, the model that fits best to a specific application context can be derived by the evaluation of the attributes. In comparison to the approaches proposed by [5], [2] and [6], the configurative information modeling approach of [4] varies in the possibilities of influencing the model base. In order to fit the model base to a specific application context, different configuration mechanisms (*Model Type Selection, Element Type Selection, Model and Element Selection by Attributes or by Term*, see [7] for further details) are provided by this approach, that are able to adapt a model basis concerning relevant types of models as well as particular relevant models, model sections and model elements. These mechanisms can be performed automatically. Considering the comparatively extensive and language independent set of configuration mechanisms and the possibility to serialize all configuration relevant model data, we decided to base our approach upon the configuration concept proposed by [4].

To take the advantages of the configurative information modeling approach, an appropriate tool support is desirable. Empirical evaluations of widespread modeling tools revealed that an adequate configuration support is not provided by those tools or only available as research prototypes (cf. [8]). To face the demand of modeling tool support, existing modeling tools can be enhanced by implementing functionality for model configuration into the tools, or a new configurative modeling tool can be developed from scratch. In this context, it must be particularly pointed out that expandability is not sufficiently given in most modeling tools (cf. again [8]) and new developments have to stand up to well-established modeling tools. To enable widespread functionalities for model configuration, the development of an external as well as modeling tool independent configuration module is considered as a promising approach. Hence, a format for model data interchange is needed, that is independent in terms of modeling tools and modeling languages and simplifies the configuration.

Almost all of the established modeling tools which are known to us provide an XML-based but proprietary format for model data interchange (e.g. AML of the ARIS Suite, ADL of Adonis, and Corporate Modeler's XML). Moreover, open interchange formats have been defined for specific modeling languages. Based on the Meta Object Facility (MOF) [9], the Object Management Group (OMG) has specified the XML Metadata Interchange (XMI) format [10] and concretize this for the Unified Modeling Language (UML) [11]. In the field of business process modeling, specific interchange formats are proposed for particular process modeling languages like PNML [12] for Petri Nets, EPML [13] for EPCs, or XPDL [14] for the Business Process Modeling Notation (BPMN) [15]. The authors make use of techniques like XSLT [16] or XPath [17] to transform serialized models from proprietary formats of modeling tools to their proposed format and vice versa.

For the design of XML schemas, the Accredited Standards Committee (ASC) X12 proposes four high level design principles (cf. [18], p. VIII), which we chose to consider for our approach: *Alignment*: A schema should reference to existing standards, which are proposed by organizations like the OMG, the Organization for the Advancement of Structured Information Standards (OASIS), the World Wide Web Consortium (W3C) or UN/CEFACT. In the context of our analysis, we also considered de facto standards provided by modeling tools like the ARIS Suite, Casewise Corporate Modeler or Adonis. *Simplicity*: This item, which is specified in a very general manner by ASC X12, is rewritten by Mendling and Nüttgens in terms of *readability* (cf. [19], p. 51; [20], p. 170), expecting "[...] components, interactions, use of features, choices, etc. [...] to be kept [...] to a reasonable minimum". *Prescriptiveness*: This principle expects schemas to be precise enough to fulfill their expected purpose. It should not be generalized. *Limit randomness*: Aligned with *simplicity* and *prescriptiveness*, randomness of data should be kept to a minimum.

As mentioned above in the context of *readability*, Mendling and Nüttgens complement these principles with respect to their EPML approach [19]: *extensibility* deals with the provision of different perspectives of a serialized model, *Tool orientation*, which – in terms of [19] – deals with the graphical representation of models, and *syntactical correctness*.

Up to now, an *tool and language independent* interchange format for conceptual models is missing. Existing open interchange formats are defined in relation to a particular modeling language (e.g., EPML, PNML, XPDL) or have to be concretized for a certain modeling language (e.g., XMI). However, a (reference) model base can consist of different types of models, so that exiting interchange formats are not able to cover the overall model base. To enable established modeling tools to perform model configuration, we make use of their proprietary XML interfaces and propose an open and modeling language independent XML schema. This schema is aligned to the requirements of configuration of conceptual models and serves as medium for the exchange between modeling tools and a configuration module, and for the model configuration itself. Therefore, the proposed XML schema is able hold model data of more than one type of model. Furthermore, it will be as much as possible be aligned with the requirements for XML schema generation.

3 Research Method

The research method followed here complies with the design science approach [21] that deals with the construction of scientific *artifacts* like methods, languages, models, and implementations. Following the Design Science approach, it is necessary to assure that the research addresses a *relevant problem*. To solve the relevant problem of lacking tool support for the configuration of information (reference) models (cf. Section 1), a scientific artifact is developed in the presented research in terms of an XML schema, which serves as medium for the configuration of conceptual models. For this purpose, related work does not provide satisfactory solutions up to now (cf. Section 2). Hence, the approach presented here (cf. Section 4) complies with the Design Science approach by representing an *innovative contribution* to the existing knowledge base. Subsequent to the construction of the artifact, it has to be *evaluated* in order to prove its fulfillment of the research goals. To show the generals applicability of the developed approach, we have prototypically implemented a configuration tool. The configuration tool is based on the proposed XML schema and facilitates the configuration of serialized models. To show the interoperability of the approach we connected the configuration tool with two widespread modeling tools (cf. Section 5). Further evaluations concerning feasibility and efficiency will be conducted in empirical studies (cf. Section 6).

4   Concept of the XML Schema

4.1   Design Decisions

The approach presented in this paper fills the gap motivated in Section 2, as it is independent from any modeling tool as well as the modeling language. It is based on the manipulation of XML files, thus its only obligatory requirement is a modeling tool that at least is able to serialize its model data into a certain XML dialect. Furthermore, to simplify the attachment of configuration parameters, the modeling tool should provide means to enrich model elements with meta information. Another requirement is the compliance with the idea of model element definitions and their respective model element occurrences. This enables the modeler to reuse existing element definitions throughout the modeling project. Renaming one element of a certain definition then leads to the synchronous renaming of all occurrences (see e.g., [7], p. 86).

Concerning the creation of their proprietary XML schema, the model tool developer's intentions differ from the purpose of efficient model configuration. Understandably enough, their requirement first and foremost is the *interchange* of model data between the vendor's modeling tool. To enable *easy configuration* of serialized model data, different aspects come to the fore. This is the direct access to configuration attributes or configuration terms has to be granted, as well as the possibility to consistently remove whole sections of the XML file which correspond to certain model types, models, element definitions or element occurrences. Thus, transformations have to take place that convert tool specific XML files into XML files that are aligned to model configuration and vice versa. The configuration has to be conducted by a software tool, providing the business logic required for evaluating the attributes and terms (see Fig. 1). To support the above described process and for best compliance with the XML schema design principles (see again Section 2), we tried to consider them as good as possible for the schema we propose. For *alignment*, we analyzed de facto standards provided by the before mentioned modeling tools in the context of our analysis in Section 2. Concerning *simplicity*, we followed this proposal by choosing names for the XML elements and attributes that are as much self explaining as possible. By this, developers should be able to intuitively create translations for schemas

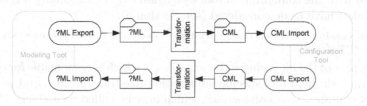

Fig. 1. Process of Interchange and Configuration

of modeling tools not yet considered. Regarding *prescriptiveness*, we developed the schema in regard to its purpose, namely enabling the configuration of serialized information models. For this aspect – and with respect to *simplicity* – the schema has to offer possibilities to store data relevant for configuration in a meaningful and consistent way. This has to be considered by the positioning of the elements. However, certain parts have to be kept generalized, which has to be done in account with the requirements of the approach. As the approach should be independent from the modeling tool, it has to allow for saving tool specific data, which is not immediately relevant for the configuration. This shall be done by passing through the unchanged structure of the original tool specific XML schema into the so-called *miscellaneous area* and their *child elements*. In this area and underlying elements, information about the version of the tool the XML file was generated with, the timestamp the model was serialized, or the author's name can be stored. To *limit randomness*, we try to provide a schema structure that is clear and understandable enough for the developer of the translator. Where necessary, the developer of the XML translator, transforming the proprietary XML dialect into our proposed schema, should not be able to store data in the wrong position. Besides this, we offer a handbook that describes each element and each attribute in detail. *Extensibility* is not explicitly being regarded within our approach, as the generation of perspectives of the respective models lies in the hand of the business logic which configures the XML file, we do not incorporate this here. However, we support the subsequent configuration by providing means in terms of special configuration relevant elements (configuration attributes and terms), describing the respective perspectives. Due to the fact that the approach explicitly is tool independent, *tool orientation* is not being regarded by our approach. Furthermore, *syntactical correctness* is not being considered in our approach, as it should be language independent. Moreover, the correctness of translation initially lies in the developer's responsibility. Afterwards, during the configuration process, the configuration tool has to take care not to offend against the model's syntactical correctness, if a meta model is provided. However, by offering a well structured schema, we provide means to *store* the serialized data syntactically correct.

4.2   Implementation

The following snippets exemplary describe the structure of CML. After the obligatory XML definition, the schema expects information about the modeling tool the file was created with (line 2). This should be stored for the subsequent configuration with the configuration tool (see again Fig. 1), especially if tool specific meta models have to be considered (see Section 6):

```
1 <?xml version="XMLVersion" encoding="Encoding" standalone="BOOL"?>
2 <CML Tool="Tool">
```

The next part of the file includes the <MiscArea>, which is responsible for collecting and handing through tool specific information like time, author, and so on. This area may contain <MiscChildElements>, which may be called recursively. "*" at the end of a line indicates that multiple instances of this element might follow.

```
3    <MiscArea>
4      <MiscChildElement MiscCEName="MiscCE">*
5        <MiscCEAttribute MiscCEAName="MiscCEA" MiscCEAValue="MischCEAV"/>*
6      </MiscChildElement>
7    </MiscArea>
```

In regard to the concept of definitions and occurrences, the following XML section <DefinitionArea> holds all definitions of elements, independent from the model they are used in. A definition is identified by its *type*, an *ID* and a *symbol* (see line 9). The type might be *"epc function"*, the symbol a value the modeling tool uses for graphical representation of an element. Again, a definition can hold several <DefChildElements> for handing through tool specific data (lines 10–15). In contrast to the <MiscArea>, these information are being stored here for simplification purposes, as the detachment of tool specific data from nested elements would contradict to the *Simplicity* principle.

```
8    <DefinitionArea>
9      <Definition DefType="DefType" DefID="DefID" DefSymbol="DefSymbol">*
10       <DefChildElement DefCEName="DefCE">*
11         <DefCEAttribute DefCEAName="DefCEA" DefCEAValue="DefCEAV" />*
12         <DefChildElement DefCEName="DefCE" DefCEValue="DefCEV">*
13           <DefCEAttribute DefCEAName="DefCEA" DefCEAValue="DefCEAV" />*
14         </DefChildElement>
15       </DefChildElement>
```

With respect to the principle of *prescriptiveness*, certain elements were positioned on the same level, such as the *label of the definition* (line 16) and the *IDs* of the element's occurrences (line 17). For configuration purposes (e.g. to find preceding or succeeding elements), incoming (<InDefCxn>, line 18) and outgoing connections (<OutDefCxn>, lines 19–21, with the respective target occurrence, line 20) have to be stored as well.

```
16       <DefLabel DefLabelLang="Lang" DefLabelValue="DefLabelValue" />
17       <OccRef OccRefID="OccID" />*
18       <InDefCxn InDefCxnID="InDefCxnID" />*
19       <OutDefCxn OutDefCxnID="OutDefCxnID"
                  TargetObjDef="TargetObjDefID">*
20         <OutCxnOccRef OutCxnOccRefID="OutCxnOccRefID" />
21       </OutDefCxn>
22     </Definition>
23   </DefinitionArea>
```

The <ModelArea> holds information about models and the included occurrences of the elements defined in the <DefinitionArea>. The model area can hold several models, which is useful for the configuration of reference models, which often include a variety of models of different types.

```
24   <ModelArea>
25     <Model ModID="ModID" ModType="ModType">*
26       <ModLabel ModLabelLang="Lang" ModLabelValue="ModLabelValue" />
27       <ModAttribute ModAName="ModAName" ModAValue="ModAValue" />*
28       <ConfigAttribute CAID="CAID" CAName="CAName" CAParam="CAParam"
                  CAValue="BOOL" />*
```

```
29        <ConfigTerm CTID="CTID" CTName="CTName" CTValue="CTValue"/>
30        <ModChildElement ModCEName="ModCEName">*
31          <ModCEAttribute ModCEAName="ModCEAName"
                 ModCEAValue="ModCEAValue" />*
32          <ModChildElement ModCEName="ModCEName2"
                 ModCEValue="ModCEValue2">*
33            <ModCEAttribute ModCEAName="ModCEAName2"
                 ModCEAValue="ModCEAValue2" />*
34          </ModChildElement>
35        </ModChildElement>
```

Similar to element definitions, <Models> are identified by an *ID* and its *type*, which might be something similar to "EPC" or "ERM" (Entity Relationship Model, see [22], line 25). Beside the model's name (line 26), multiple <ModAttributes> (e.g., line 27) and <ModChildElements> can be stored, again relevant for modeling tool peculiarities. Configuration parameters and their respective values are stored within the elements <ConfigAttribute> or <ConfigTerm> (line 28, 29). If either one of the equations CAParam == CAValue or one of the terms CTValue evaluates true, the business logic has to remove the <Model> and all enclosed element <Occurrences>.

Finally, the file holds information about element occurrences. To keep a basic ability of representing the serialized models inside a configuration tool, and to support the variation of representational aspects (cf. [4], p. 41), related information are directly stored inside the <Occurrence> element.

```
36        <Occurrence DefRef="ObjDefID" OccID="OccID" OccSymbol="OccSymbol"
             OccColor="OccColor" BorderStyle="BorderStyle"
             BorderColor="BorderColor" BorderWidth="BorderWidth"
             ElemSizeX="ElemSizeX" ElemSizeY="ElemSizeY">*
```

Additional information can again be stored inside the elements <OccCEAttribute> or <OccChildELement>.

```
37          <OccAttribute OccAName="OccAName" OccAValue="OccAValue" />*
38          <OccChildElement OccCEName="OccCEName">*
39            <OccCEAttribute OccCEAName="OccCEAName"
                 OccCEAValue="OccCEAValue" />*
40          </OccChildElement>
```

As for <Models>, the configuration parameters and their respective values are stored within the elements <ConfigAttribute> or <ConfigTerm>. Again, if either one of the equations CAParam == CAValue or one of the terms CTValue evaluates true, the business logic has to remove the occurrence from the model.

```
41        <ConfigAttribute CAID="CAID" CAName="CAName" CAParam="CAParam"
             CAValue="BOOL" />*
42        <ConfigTerm CTID="CTID" CTName="CTName" CTValue="CTValue"/>
```

As the removal of a single element would leave the model in an inconsistent state, the business logic needs means to follow the paths in and out of the element, pointing to the succeeding and preceding element(s). Hence, information about the respective elements have to be stored as well (TargetObjOccID, line 43).

```
43        <OutCxnOcc OutCxnOccID="OutCxnOccID" OutCxnDefID="OutCxnDefID"
             TargetObjOccID="TargetObjOccID">*
```

Information about incoming connections are being stored inside the related definition, which is referenced by DefRef (line 36). The reference to the definition is required for deleting the definition once no more of its occurrences are present in any of the models.

```
44            <OutCxnOccCEAttribute OutCxnOccCEAName="OutCxnOccCEAName"
                 OutCxnOccCEAValue="OutCxnOccCEAValue" />*
45            <OutCxnOccChildElement OutCxnOccCEName="OutCxnOccCEName">*
46               <OutCxnOccCEAttribute OutCxnOccCEAName="OutCxnOccCEAName"
                    OutCxnOccCEAValue="OutCxnOccCEAValue" />*
47            </OutCxnOccChildElement>
48         </OutCxnOcc>
49      </Occurrence>
```

This concludes the structure of serialized model data inside our XML file with the closure of the remaining elements (lines 50–52).

```
50      </Model>
51   </ModelArea>
52 </CML>
```

5 Sample Application

As motivated in Section 2, we followed the configurative reference modeling approach of Becker et al. [4]. Fig. 2 conceptually illustrates how the application of selected mechanisms effects a serialized model. On the left side, an excerpt of a retail reference model as it is organized in ARIS is presented. Besides several *EPCs*, the reference model holds models of the type *Functiontree* and *ERM*. The *EPC* model "Rearrangement" holds several model elements of different types (*XOR, AND, Event, Role* and *Function*). On the right side, excerpts from the CML file illustrate how the reference model got serialized using CML. The pictographs in the middle represent the configuration mechanisms and point to the elements on which they have an effect.

For the mechanism *Model Type Selection*, all <Models> of a certain type – which can be identified by the ModType="ModType" attribute – have to be removed from the file. When removing a certain model, its <Occurrences> have to be removed as well. By following the DefRef="ObjDefID" attribute, the reference inside the <Definiton>, can also be removed. The example in Fig. 2 assumes the removal of all ERM models. *Model Selection* removes <Models> holding certain <ConfigAttributes> or a <ConfigTerm>, if the user configuring the model chooses the corresponding configuration parameter. Once a <Model> is to be removed, the same procedures as those for the *Model Type Selection* apply. The example assumes the removal of models where the **Transaction Type** is not **Warehouse Business OR Third-Party Deal**. *Element Type Selection* removes all elements of a certain type in a certain language (e.g., all Organizational Units or Entity Types of the EPC language). Here, all <Definition> elements with the corresponding <Occurrences> in the <Models> have to be removed. The <Occurrences> can be found by following the <OccRef OccRefID="OccID"/> elements inside the <Definitions>. The example assumes the removal of all elements of the type *Role*. Comparable to

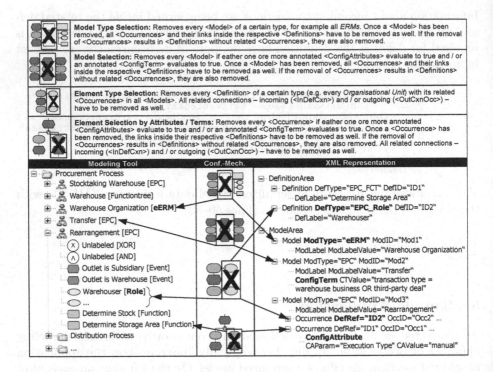

Fig. 2. Configuration Mechanisms and their Effects on CML

the *Model Selection*, the mechanism of *Element Selection by Attribute or Term* removes <Occurrences> due to their <ConfigAttributes> and/or their <ConfigTerm>. The Definitions remain inside the model as long as at least one <Occurrences> exists. The example assumes the removal of all elements tagged with **manual execution type**.

The feasibility of the approach has been examined with serialized models of two widespread modeling tools: the ARIS Business Architect and the Adonis Business Process Management Toolkit. For this, the original AML (ARIS) and ADL (Adonis) files were transformed to our schema using XSLT (see again Fig. 1). Afterwards, the prototype **adapt(X)** was used to configure the XML files, before transforming them back to their respective format. By this, we successfully configured EPC, ERM, Function Tree and Organization Chart models during a research project. The approach was tested in cooperation with a small IT company, thus supporting our initial evaluation step of design science research. The IT company uses conceptual models for presenting their modular ERP solutions to their customers during the requirements analysis. Each of the modules is described in detail by conceptual models, the processes of using the modules are described via EPCs. During presentations with clients, the field service persons were able to configure the models to the client's needs, automatically removing models of the respective modules, and the not relevant elements and model parts.

6 Summary and Outlook

The approach presented in this paper is able to complement widespread modeling tools like ARIS, Adonis or Casewise with means for automatic model configuration in conjunction with a lightweight configuration tool. As none of the modeling tools supports configuration out of the box, the ability to use their XML export interface and a subsequent transformation seems promising. Required XSLT style sheets up to now exist for ARIS and Adonis. Beside the successful evaluation during the research project, we identified several limitations.

In general, the serialization of model data into XML files solely *stores* this data in a machine-readable format. To *perform* the configuration, it is still necessary to provide means for configuration in terms of an application. In contrast to heavyweight modeling tools, this application can be specialized in its purpose and can thus be realized as lightweight solution. Besides the removal of certain elements due to the equation of the configuration terms and attributes, the application has to provide business logic to transfer the file into a then again consistent state. This indicates that those elements, between which other elements have been removed, have to be connected consistently. As our approach solely provides means for exchanging model data and the respective information relevant for configuration, its only chance to support the required succeeding consistency check is the placement of the information required in elements on a prominent position. Afterwards, the business logic of a configuration module has to implement algorithms like those provided for the EPC by [7]. Furthermore, the naming of tool specific conventions like the naming of element types, colors (black vs #000000) or positioning (absolute vs. relative) has to be considered. The configuration tool has to be able to identify whether an element for instance is a function of an EPC model or an activity of a BPMN model. Thus, a lexicon has to be provided that translates the tool specific namings into standardized ones. It has to be decided whether the translation is done during the XML transformation or inside the tool. Another aspect that we did not cover in this paper is the serialization of stateful modeling languages like Petri Nets [23]. However, approaches presented in Section 2 give starting points on how to incorporate these features. Future research is intended to face the above mentioned limitations, evaluate the feasibility with partners during research projects and to try to incorporate its usage in day-to-day operations.

References

1. vom Brocke, J.: Referenzmodellierung: Gestaltung und Verteilung von Konstruktionsprozessen. PhD thesis, University of Münster (2002)
2. Rosemann, M., van der Aalst, W.M.P.: A configurable reference modelling language. Information Systems 32, 1–23 (2007)
3. Scheer, A.-W.: ARIS: Business Process Modeling, 3rd edn. Springer, Heidelberg (2000)
4. Becker, J., Delfmann, P., Knackstedt, R.: Adaptive reference modeling: Integrating configurative and generic adaptation techniques for information models. In: Becker, J., Delfmann, P. (eds.) Reference Modeling – Efficient Information Systems Design Through Reuse of Information Models, pp. 27–58. Physica-Verlag, Heidelberg (2007)

5. Soffer, P., Golany, B., Dori, D.: Erp modeling: a comprehensive approach. Information Systems 9(28), 673–690 (2003)
6. Rosa, M.L., Gottschalk, F., Dumas, M., van der Aalst, W.M.: Linking domain models and process models for reference model configuration. In: ter Hofstede, A.H.M., Benatallah, B., Paik, H.-Y. (eds.) BPM Workshops 2007. LNCS, vol. 4928, pp. 417–430. Springer, Heidelberg (2008)
7. Delfmann, P.: Adaptive Referenzmodellierung. Methodische Konzepte zur Konstruktion und Anwendung wiederverwendungsorientierter Informationsmodelle. PhD thesis, University of Münster (2007)
8. Delfmann, P., Knackstedt, R.: Konfiguration von informationsmodellen – untersuchungen zu bedarf und werkzeugunterstützung. In: Oberweis, A., Weinhardt, C., Gimpel, H., Koschmider, A., Pankratius, V., Schnizler, B. (eds.) eOrganisation: Service-, Prozess-, Market-Engineering, vol. 2, pp. 127–144 (2007)
9. OMG: Meta object facility (mof) core specification, version 2.0. (2006), http://www.omg.org/docs/formal/06-01-01.pdf
10. OMG: Xml metadata interchange (xmi), version 2.1.1. (2007), http://www.omg.org/docs/formal/07-12-01.pdf
11. OMG: Unified modeling language (uml), version 2.2. (2009), http://www.omg.org/docs/formal/09-02-04.pdf
12. Billington, J., Christensen, S., van Hee, K., Kindler, E., Kummer, O., Petrucci, L., Post, R., Stehno, C., Weber, M.: The petri net markup language: Concepts, technology, and tools. In: van der Aalst, W., Best, E. (eds.) Proceedings of the 24th International Conference on Applications and Theory of Petri Nets, Eindhoven, pp. 483–505. Springer, Heidelberg (2003)
13. Mendling, J., Nüttgens, M.: Epc markup language (epml) - an xml-based interchange format for event-driven process chains (epc). Technical Report JM-2005-03-10, Vienna University of Economics and Business Administration (2005)
14. WfMC: Xml process defintion language (xpdl) specification, version 2.1 (2008)
15. OMG: Business process modeling notation (bpmn) specification, version 1.2. (2009), http://www.omg.org/docs/formal/09-01-03.pdf
16. W3C: Xsl transformations (xslt) version 2.0. (2009), http://www.w3.org/TR/xslt20/
17. W3C: Xml path language (xpath) 2.0 (2009), http://www.w3.org/TR/xpath20/
18. ANSI: Asc x12 reference model for xml design (2002), http://www.x12.org/x12org/comments/ X12Reference_Model_For_XML_Design.pdf
19. Mendling, J., Nüttgens, M.: Xml-based reference modelling: Foundations of an epc markup language. In: Becker, J., Delfmann, P. (eds.) Proc. of the 8th GI Workshop Referenzmodellierung 2004 at MKWI 2004, Essen, Germany, pp. 51–72 (2004)
20. Mendling, J., Nüttgens, M.: Xml-basierte geschäftsprozessmodellierung. In: Uhr, W., Esswein, W., Schoop, E. (eds.) Wirtschaftsinformatik 2003/Band II, pp. 161–180. Physica-Verlag, Heidelberg (2003)
21. Hevner, A.R., March, S.T., Park, J., Ram, S.: Design science in information systems research. MIS Quarterly 28(1), 75–105 (2004)
22. Chen, P.P.: The entity-relationship model – toward a unified view of data. ACM Transactions on Database Systems 1(1), 9–36 (1976)
23. Peterson, J.L.: Petri Net Theory and the Modeling of Systems. Prentice-Hall, Englewood Cliffs (1981)

On the Contribution of Reference Modeling to e-Business Standardization – How to Apply Design Techniques of Reference Modeling to UN/CEFACT's Modeling Methodology

Birgit Hofreiter and Jan vom Brocke

University of Liechtenstein,
Martin Hilti Chair of Business Process Management,
Institute of Information Systems, Principality of Liechtenstein
{birgit.hofreiter,jan.vom.brocke}@hochschule.li

Abstract. Reference Modeling has evolved as a strong discipline especially driven by the German speaking community. Great achievements have been made in finding ways to leverage the potentials of reuse in business modeling. However, the perception of reference modeling as such is still limited to a rather small group of scholars. This is surprising as the phenomenon of "re-use" is very much in the center of various current topics in the international information systems and business process management discipline. In this paper, we set out exploring the contribution of findings in the field of reference modeling for business standardization. We show that in particular design techniques for reference modeling perfectly apply to solve conflicts of globalization and localization in business standards. As an example, we study the UMM as a specific standard developed within the United Nations CEFACT group.

Keywords: Reference Modeling, Re-use, Construction Concepts, Standardization, UN/CEFACT Modeling Methodology (UMM).

1 Introduction

With its roots in the early 1990s reference modeling has predominantly been driven by the German speaking IS community. The essential idea behind it may be seen in "not wanting to re-invent the wheel" whenever engaging in a new modeling process. It is intended to provide some kind of "reference" to start with in order to increase both the efficiency and effectiveness of modeling processes [1, 2, 4, 8, 10]. However, despite of this kind of common understanding, we can observe quite an intensive discussion on the very characteristics of reference models and reference modeling respectively. (For an overview see e. g. [3, 13]).

Considering this discussion, we hold that putting the concept of re-use at the core of reference modeling enables the use of synergies by combining them with corresponding fields of research in IS. Accordingly, reference models are referred to as special information models that serve to be reused in the design process of other information models [19, 20] as outlined in Fig. 1.

S. Rinderle-Ma et al. (Eds.): BPM 2009 Workshops, LNBIP 43, pp. 671–682, 2010.
© Springer-Verlag Berlin Heidelberg 2010

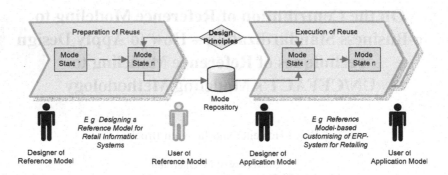

Fig. 1. Reuse-oriented Concept of Reference Modeling [20]

In this paper we study the potential of reference modeling and its phenomenon of "re-use" in the field of business standardization. In particular we focus on the standardization of inter-organizational business processes. In this case business standardization has to focus on the business activities that require communication between the partners. This results in standardized interface processes that allow an easy integration of new business partners or the easy creation of virtual enterprises. Instead of describing these inter-organizational business processes for a specific platform like Web Services or ebXML we prefer to specify platform independent models that are later transformed to platform specific processes.

Such an approach is envisioned by the United Nation's Centre for Trade Facilitation and e-business (UN/CEFACT) by the UN/CEFACT Modeling Methodology (UMM) [17], which we have co-authored. We have defined the UMM as a UML profile specifying a set of stereotypes, tagged values and constraints that put UML in a very strict corset resulting in well-defined artifacts. These artifacts may be transformed to BPEL [5, 6] or BPSS [7] in a next step.

In this paper we use the UMM as our modeling language of choice. In order to guarantee acceptance of the UMM, it must be both effective and easy to understand for business process modelers and software architects. Re-use is vital for efficiently managing the complexity of standard models on different levels of application. In particular, techniques of model re-use that have been subject to intensive research in reference modeling may well be applicable here. Thus, we set out to demonstrate and further analyze the synergies between reference modeling and e-business standardization by means of UMM. We introduce some well accepted design techniques in reference modeling in section 2. In section 3 we analyze the potential of these design techniques when creating a UMM model. The conclusion in section 4 summarizes the benefits that reference modeling offers to UMM.

2   An Overview of Design Techniques in Reference Modeling

In order to facilitate re-use, various design techniques are subject to research in reference modeling (see Fig. 2). These techniques provide rules describing the way in which the content of one model is reused in constructing another model. The rules describe ways of taking over contents as well as of adapting and extending it in the resulting model. With each design techniques, specific sets of rules are differentiated.

In former studies on reference modeling, the design of configurative reference models was focused on, in order to support the derivation of multiple variants of a reference model for a certain application [1, 10, 13]. This work intends to encounter all relevant variants of prospective applications during build-time of the model in order to facilitate adaptability by means of choices [18]. Considering the variety of requirements to be faced in today's business engineering, the design techniques of configuration illuminates specific limitations. In particular, it is increasingly hard to take into account the various requirements that may be relevant, and to incorporate them in the reference model.

	Definition	Situation
Analogy ~ by creativity	An original model "A" serves as a means of orientation for the construction of a resulting model "a" The relation between the models is based on a perceived similarity of both models regarding a certain aspect	The application domain can be described by certain patterns recurring in each application ; the entire solution however has to be replenished in an indefinite manner
Specialisation → by revising	Derivation of a resulting model "S" from a general model "G" That way all statements in "G" are taken over in "S" and can either be changed or extended (but generally not deleted)	The application domain can be covered by a core solution ; but this solution has to be extended and modified (without deleting, in an indefinite manner for various applications
Aggregation → by combination	The combination of one or more original models "p" that build "a" resulting model "T" with the models "p" forming complete parts of "T"	The application domain can be described partly; each part can fully be specified whereas their combination for replenishing the entire coverage of an application cannot be foreseen when building the reference model
Instantiation → by embedding	The creation of a resulting model "I" by integrating one or multiple original models "e" into generic place holders of the original model "G" The model "I" incorporates the integrated construction results of "e" in "G"	The application domain can be covered by a general framework; this framework however has to be adapted in regard to selected aspects that can not fully be described while building the reference model
Configuration → by selection	The technique of configuration is characterised by deriving a configured model c out of a configurative model C by means of making choices from a greater variety of alternatives offered in C	The application domain can be described fully in design time including all relevant adaptations that have to be considered in various applications

Fig. 2. Design Techniques of Reference Modeling according to [20]

Hence, supplementary design techniques have been developed in order to enlarge the "tool-kit" of reference modeling. Particularly referring to software-engineering [9, 12] the techniques aggregation, specialization, instantiation, and analogy are presented in this paper [19, 20]. According to instantiation, general aspects of a domain are designed as a framework providing generic placeholders for plugging in models considering special requirements of an application. Specialization enables the take-over of the entire contents of a general model into a specific model allowing for modification and individual extending. Aggregation enables the take-over of contents delivered by various part models that are composed in and extended according to special requirements of application. Analogy, finally, employs seemingly similar solutions in a creative way in order to tackle new problems.

Studies show that each of the technique has different economic effects in regard to context situation of the modeling process. Looking at the derivation of costs, it becomes apparent that configuration and analogy form two opposite techniques for reference modeling. Whereas configuration implies that most of the work on reusing content is done by building the reference model, this work is left for the application using analogy. Consequently, configuration comes along with relatively high costs for building the reference model on the one hand, but with low costs for applying it on the other. The principle of analogy, on the contrary, causes a minimum cost for building the model and yet a maximum for applying it. The other techniques gradually lie in between the two first ones. Applying instantiation, prospective applications do not need specification entirely while building the reference model. Saying that, a minimum of certain generic aspects have to be identified and specified for embedding special solutions. In aggregation, only certain parts of the application domain definitively require description that may be combined and extended in various ways. However, modifications of each part model to be aggregated are not provided. This is possible thanks to the principle of specialization giving way to rather flexible modifications without eliminating parts of the reference model. With the techniques of analogy, finally, unlimited ways of adapting the content are given.

Assumingly, these techniques may well be used in order to manage different variants of a standard within a global business standardization initiative. This will be further analyzed in the next chapter.

3 Applying Design Techniques to the UMM

The UMM is a methodology that guides the modeler through a development process of well defined tasks in order to create a UMM compliant model. The methodology itself and the resulting artifacts are structured in three main phases and views, correspondingly. The first phase gathers domain knowledge and existing process knowledge of the business domain under consideration. The resulting artifacts are captured in the business requirements view and its subviews. Based on these requirements, the second phase is used to describe the resulting inter-organizational business processes as a choreography from an observer's perspective. Consequently, the artifacts are kept in the business choreography view, which comprises the subviews business transaction view, business collaboration view and business realization view. The last phase is used to model the business document types which are used in the exchanges between business partners. Its artifacts are part of the business information view.

Due to space limitations we are not able to demonstrate how the design techniques of reference modeling apply to all of the UMM artifacts. Thus, we limit ourselves to the task of specifying an agreed choreography between the business partners, which is also the core focus of the UMM. Consequently, we focus on the artifacts of the business choreography view. In the following two subsections we analyze the potential of reference modeling for the subviews business transaction view and business collaboration view.

3.1 Business Transaction View

The basic building blocks of a UMM choreography are business transactions. The goal of a business transaction is synchronizing the business entity states between two parties. Synchronization of states is either required in a uni-directional or in a bi-directional way. In the former case, the initiator of the business transaction informs the other party about an already irreversible state change the other party has to accept - e.g., the notification of shipment. It follows, that responding in such a scenario is neither required nor reasonable. In the latter case, the initiating party sets a business entity to an interim state and the responding party decides about its final state - consider a *request for quote* that the responder might either refuse or accept when returning a *quote*.

The synchronization takes place by exchanging business information. According to the definitions above, an exchange always takes place between exactly two parties. It is either a uni-directional exchange or a bi-directional exchange including a response. Due to this strict setting, business transactions no matter what business goal they try to achieve always follow the same basic structure. Thus, the design technique of analogy is appropriate for constructing business transactions.

Exploring Analogy

The design technique of analogy is realized in UMM by providing a basic pattern for UMM transactions which has to be used when creating a new business transaction. An activity diagram stereotyped as business transaction always includes two partitions, one for each participating role. Each partition includes exactly one activity, the requesting business activity and the responding business activity, correspondingly. The activity diagram starts off with the requesting business activity.

Exactly one requesting business document is exchanged. This is notated by an object flow from the output pin of the requesting business document to the input pin of the responding business activity. In case of a one-way business transaction, no document is returned, i.e. no object flows are modeled in the reverse direction. In case of a two-way transaction at least one document is exchanged from an output pin of the responding business transaction to an input pin of the requesting business transaction. If alternative responses are allowed, additional object flows are added to the reverse direction.

A business transaction must always lead to a well-defined business entity state. The requestor is able to recognize the resulting state by receiving the responding document or by an acknowledgment in case of a one way transaction. As a consequence, the resulting business entity states are model by transitions from the requesting business activity to the end states. There must be at least one business entity state. Further alternative business entity states may be added, but must be well distinguished by mutually exclusive transition guards.

This analogy has to be followed whenever a new business transaction is created, no matter whether *quote requests*, *purchase orders*, *notification of shipment*, etc., are modeled. Fig. 3. depicts an example of a business transaction for *quote requests*.

Since we talk about standardized business transactions, a model library should only include one business transaction for a specific business goal, i.e. there should be only one business transaction for *quote requests*. However, the UMM concept of a business transaction comes also with a set of tagged values. The requesting/responding business activities are described by values for *is authorization required, is non-repudiation required, time to perform, time to acknowledge receipt*, and *time to respond*. The values for *is non-repudiation of receipt required* and for *retry count* are only defined for the requesting business activity. Most of these attributes are self-explanatory. An *acknowledgment of receipt* is usually sent after grammar validation, sequence validation, and schema validation. However, if the *is intelligible check required* flag is set to false, the acknowledgment is sent immediately after receipt without any validation. An acknowledgment of processing is sent after validating the content against additional rules to ensure that the content is processable by the target application. *Retry count* is the number of retries in case of control failures.

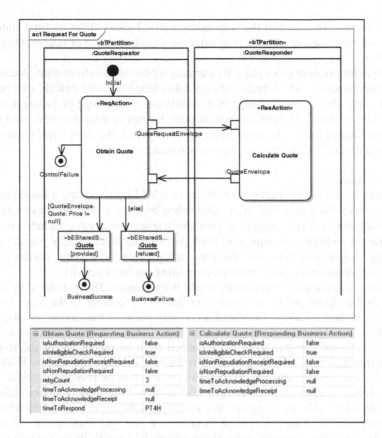

Fig. 3. Business Transaction: Request For Quote

In practice, it is realistic that an existing standardized business transaction, e.g. for *quote requests*, fits to needs of a specific business partnership. However, it is rather unlikely that the values for the tagged values are acceptable for all business partnerships using this business transaction. For example, one partnership expects the quote to be returned (time to respond) within four hours and the other one within a day. To overcome this problem of different tagged values the design technique of configuration may be used.

Exploring Configuration

The design technique of configuration is realized for UMM business transactions by providing a master business transaction for each business goal, e.g. for a request for quote in the model library. This master business transaction does not specify any predefined values for the tagged values. If this master business transaction is used in a specific scenario for a to-be created partnership, a new business transaction is created based on the master business transaction, but which sets the tagged values. Thereby, it is guaranteed that standardized process and document interfaces are re-used, but with different timings and security parameters.

3.2 Business Collaboration View

The main artifact of the business collaboration view is the business collaboration protocol. Whereas the business transaction models a simple inter-organizational business process exchanging one document and optionally returning another one, the business collaboration protocol models complex business collaboration usually including many activities between the involved parties. For the purpose of re-use, a business collaboration protocol uses the design technique of aggregation.

Exploring Aggregation
It follows that a business collaboration protocol is built by aggregating existing models, either existing business transactions or other existing business collaboration protocols which are nested within the to-be created business collaboration protocol. Accordingly, a business collaboration protocol includes two kinds of actions. A business transaction action calls the sub-process of an existing business transaction, whereas a business collaboration action calls the sub-process of another existing business collaboration protocol. The call of sub-processes is noted in UML in general by the rake symbol in the action.

In Fig. 4 we show the example of a simple business collaboration protocol for *order from quote*. The resulting activity graph is built by two business transaction actions. The first one calls the sub-process of the business transaction *request for quote* which we have outlined in Fig. 3. The second one is a call to the business transaction *place order* which we omit to depict. The transitions in the business collaboration protocol are guarded by entity states. Each business entity state of a business transaction must lead to a transition starting from the business transaction action in the business collaboration protocol For example, the business transaction *request for quote* sets the state of the business entity quote either to provided or refused. Accordingly, the business transaction action *request for quote* has two outgoing transitions: If the quote is provided the business collaboration protocol continues with *place order* and if the quote is refused the business collaboration terminates.

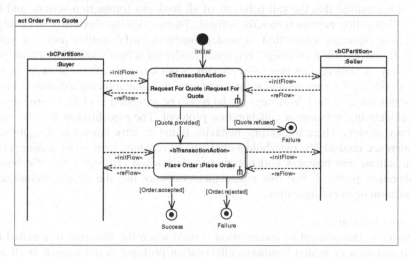

Fig. 4. Fig. 4: Business Collaboration Protocol: Order From Quote

In order to foster the re-use of an existing business transaction in different business collaboration protocols, it is not desired to mandate that the roles on the two different levels of abstraction must be identical. In other words, one and the same business transaction may be re-used in different business collaboration protocols each performed by a different set of partners. In order to cope with this requirement UMM has to consider the design technique of specialization.

Exploring Specialization
In order to allow the specialization of roles, one has to use the concept of partitions in the business collaboration protocols. However, the partitions are not used to cover the actions – which are by definition inter-organizational ones. The partitions serve the purpose of role mapping. This is rather unusual in UML, but this concept is adopted from BPMN [11]. A business transaction action is linked with the partitions of the involved parties by the concept of init flow and in case of an underlying two way transaction also by a re-flow. Thereby, the role of the partition that is the source of an init flow performs the initiating role of the called business transaction. Vice versa, the role of the partition that is the target of an init flow performs the responding role of the called business transaction.

For a better understanding, consider our example. The business transaction *request for quote* is performed between the roles *quote requestor* and *quote responder*. The business collaboration protocol defines the collaboration between a *buyer* and a *seller*. In case of the business transaction action *request for quote*, the init flow starts from the buyer's partition and leads to the seller's partition. Consequently, the buyer plays the *quote requestor* (initiating role) and the seller acts as *quote responder* (responding role) in the underlying business transaction.

3.3 Extension to the Business Collaboration View

All the design techniques we have described so far do not require any changes to the UMM meta model. In order to develop a UMM compliant business collaboration view it is required that the call behavior of all business transaction actions and business collaboration actions is exactly defined. There exists no flexibility in calling the underlying business transaction or nested business collaboration protocol, respectively. However, when creating a reference model for a business collaboration protocol it may be desired that this call behavior is not exactly defined in order to reach some flexibility for variants and at the same time still guaranteeing a common base.

For this purpose the UMM meta model has to be extended in order to provide some placeholders in the business collaboration protocol. The placeholders may be used in reference models where the calling behavior is not exactly known at design time of the reference model. The placeholders have to be replaced later on by business transaction actions and business collaboration models when creating a specific business collaboration protocol. For this replacement on may use the design techniques of instantiation or of configuration.

Exploring Instantiation
Accordingly, the concept of instantiation is used when the structure of a called business transaction or nested business collaboration protocol is not known at all at the design time of the reference model. Whereas the concept of configuration is applied

in case different alternative already existing business transactions or nested business collaboration protocols may be used. Evidently, we need new UMM stereotypes to cope with the two kinds of placeholders. In analogy, to the design technique we call these stereotypes *instantiation action* and *configuration action*. Since a configuration action must later on be replaced one out of a set of alternative business transactions / nested business collaboration protocols, it is required that UML dependencies are established between the configuration action and the members of this set.

In order to demonstrate the need for placeholders in UMM reference models we continue our *order from quotes* example which finally results in the business collaboration protocol of Fig. 5. At the design time of the reference model is known that after an order is accepted, the process continues with tracking and tracing the shipment of the order as well with the billing, which may occur in parallel. However, it is not yet known how tracking and tracing as well as billing are realized exactly. In case of billing one may consider two alternatives, either classical invoicing or the self-billing approach. Thus, billing is modeled in the business collaboration protocol of Fig. 5 as a configuration action. The dependencies of this configuration action to the two alternative business transactions must be conceptually defined, but are not part of the business collaboration protocol. It should be noted that classical invoicing is usually initiated by the seller, whereas self-billing is initiated by the buyer. Thus, it does not make sense to specify init flows and re-flows in the reference model. Since the structure of tracking and tracing is not defined in any ways, i.e. no pre-defined alternatives exist, it is modeled by an instantiation action.

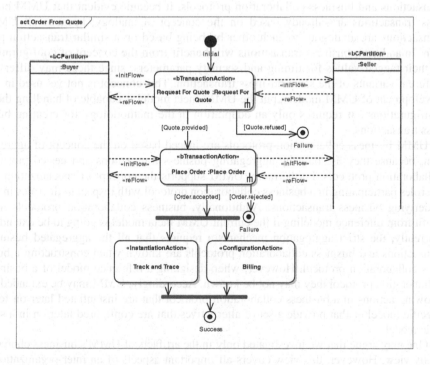

Fig. 5. Business Collaboration Protocol: Order From Quote (incl. new stereotypes)

4 Conclusion

When developing a new model one may start from scratch, or one may have a look on an already existing model that was developed in a "similar" context to speed up the development process and to leverage quality. Reference modeling is an IS field that intends at providing consistent design techniques for developing reference models and customizing them when creating new models. In this paper we evaluated how the standardization of inter-organizational business process models may benefit from the concepts of reference modeling. These concepts seem to be of particular interest since it is rather unlikely that all companies as well as public administrations will be able to work with a single standardized process. It is much more likely that different variants of the same base process are accepted. For example, there does not exist a one-for-all procurement process that serves the needs of all companies and agencies all over the world in any industry sector. However, it is expected that many different inter-organizational procurement processes share a common ground that may be modeled in a reference model.

For our evaluation we use the UN/CEFACT modeling methodology (UMM) which is a common approach to model inter-organizational business processes from an observer's perspective. We investigated how the five design techniques of reference modeling – configuration, instantiation, specialization, aggregation, and analogy – may be adopted when developing UMM models. In particular, we demonstrated the use of these techniques for the business choreography view which comprises business transactions and business collaboration protocols. It became evident that UMM business transactions are already based on the concept of analogy, because all UMM transactions are analogous to each other by being based on a similar transaction pattern. In addition, business transactions will benefit from the concept of configuration of their tagged values for timing and security parameters, since these may differ for different variants of the same business transaction. This concept is not yet used in the development of UMM models, but the UMM meta model is capable of handling these configurations - it requires only an adaptation in the methodology for creating business transactions.

UMM business collaboration protocols are indeed based on the concept of aggregation, because they are built by aggregating business transactions and nested business collaboration protocols. Furthermore, UMM supports the concept of specialization for the roles participating in a business collaboration protocol with respect to the roles in the underlying business transactions. Additionally, business collaboration protocols may profit from reference modeling if the current UMM meta model is going to be extended. Currently, the strict aggregation mechanism requires that all the aggregated business transactions and business collaboration protocols are known when constructing a business collaboration protocol. However, when designing a reference model of a business collaboration protocol they may not be known. Accordingly, UMM may be extended by allowing actions in a business collaboration protocol that are instantiated later on for a specific model or that provide a set of alternatives that are configured later on in a specific model.

One may argue that we investigated only in the artifacts of UMM's business choreography view. However, this view covers all important aspects of an inter-organizational process choreography. The business requirements view, which precedes the business choreography view, targets at capturing the requirements of to-be constructed collaboration. Thus, this view is always context specific and will not benefit much from more general, context-independent reference model. In contrary, the business information view models the document types being exchanged that may differ for different variants of business partnerships. Thus, this view may benefit as well from reference modeling. Whereas this paper concentrates on the process, future work will address the structural aspects of the business documents.

References

1. Becker, J., Delfmann, P., Dreiling, A., Knackstedt, R., Kuropka, D.: Configurative Process Modeling - Outlining an Approach to Increased Business Process Model Usability. In: Information Resources Management Association Conference, New Orleans (2004)
2. Fettke, P., Loos, P.: Classification of reference models - a methodology and its application. Information Systems and e-Business Management 1(1), 35–53 (2003)
3. Fettke, P., Loos, P. (eds.): Perspectives on Reference Modeling, Hershey, PA, USA. Reference Modeling for Business Systems Analysis, pp. 1–20 (2007)
4. Frank, U.: Evaluation of Reference Models. In: Fettke, P., Loos, P. (eds.) Reference Modeling for Business Systems Analysis, Hershey, PA, USA, pp. 118–140 (2007)
5. Hofreiter, B., Huemer, C.: Transforming UMM Business Collaboration Models to BPEL. In: Meersman, R., Tari, Z., Corsaro, A. (eds.) OTM-WS 2004. LNCS, vol. 3292, pp. 507–519. Springer, Heidelberg (2004)
6. Hofreiter, B., Huemer, C., Liegl, P., Schuster, S., Zapletal, M.: Deriving executable BPEL from UMM Business Transactions. In: International Conference on Services Computing. IEEE Computer Society, Salt Lake City (2007)
7. Huemer, C., Kim, J.: From an ebXML BPSS choreography to a BPEL-based implementation. ACM SIGecom Exchanges 5(2), 1–11 (2004)
8. Huschens, J., Rumpold-Preining, M.: IBM Insurance Application Architecture (IAA). An Overview of the Insurance Business Architecture. In: Bernus, P., Mertins, K. (eds.) Handbook on Architectures of Information Systems, 2nd edn., pp. 669–692. Springer, Berlin (2006)
9. Karhinen, A., Ran, A., Tallgren, T.: Configuring designs for reuse. In: 19th international conference on Software engineering, Boston, Massachusetts, United States (1997)
10. Meinhardt, S., Popp, K.: Configuring Business Application Systems. In: Bernus, P., Mertins, K., Schmidt, G. (eds.) Handbook on Architectures of Information Systems, 2nd edn., pp. 705–721. Springer, Berlin (2006)
11. OMG - Object Management Group: Business Process Modeling Notation Specification 1.0 (2006)
12. Peterson, A.S.: Coming to terms with software reuse terminology: a model-based approach. SIGSOFT Software Engineering Notes 16(2), 45–51 (1991)
13. Recker, J., Rosemann, M., van der Aalst, W.M.P., Mendling, J.: On the Syntax of Reference Model Configuration. In: First International Workshop on Business Process Reference Models (BPRM 2005), Nancy, France (2005)
14. Scheer, A.-W.: Business Process Engineering: Reference Models for Industrial Enterprises. Springer, New York (1994)
15. Scheer, A.-W., Nüttgens, M.: ARIS Architecture and Reference Models for Business Process Management. In: van der Aalst, W.M.P., Desel, J., Oberweis, A. (eds.) Business Process Management - Models, Techniques, and Empirical Studies, Berlin, pp. 376–389 (2000)

16. Thomas, O.: Understanding the Term Reference Model in Information System Research. In: Bussler, C.J., Haller, A. (eds.) BPM 2005. LNCS, vol. 3812, pp. 484–496. Springer, Heidelberg (2006)
17. UN/CEFACT: UN/CEFACT's Modeling Methodology (UMM), UMM Meta Model - Foundation Module. Technical Specification – Candidate for V2.0 (2006), http://www.untmg.org/wpcontent/uploads/2009/01/specification_umm_foundation_module_v20_implementationdraft_20090130.pdf
18. van der Aalst, W.M.P., Dreiling, A., Gottschalk, F., Rosemann, M., Jansen-Vullers, M.H.: Configurable process models as a basis for reference modeling. In: Bussler, C.J., Haller, A. (eds.) BPM 2005. LNCS, vol. 3812, pp. 512–518. Springer, Heidelberg (2006)
19. vom Brocke, J.: Reference Modeling, Towards Collaborative Arrangements of Design Processes, Berlin (2003) (in German)
20. vom Brocke, J.: Design Principles for Reference Modeling. Reusing Information Models by Means of Aggregation, Specialisation, Instantiation, and Analogy. In: Fettke, P., Loos, P. (eds.) Reference Modeling for Business Systems Analysis, Hershey, PA, USA (2007)

The Potential of Reference Modeling for Simulating Mobile Construction Machinery

Werner Esswein, Sina Lehrmann, and Jeannette Stark

Technische Universität Dresden, Department of Business Management and Economics,
Chair of Systems Engineering
{Werner.Esswein,Sina.Lehrmann,Jeannette.Stark}@tu-dresden.de

Abstract. This research-in-progress paper summarizes first results of the INPROVY project by applying reference modeling to the simulation of mobile construction machinery. Four Business cases for a potential application of reference modeling are derived by an expert interview. For these four business cases this paper discusses principles of reference modeling can be applied best and how reference modeling can be used to support Simulation of Mobile Construction Machinery economically.

Keywords: Reference model principles, Design for Reuse, Design with Reuse, Virtual Prototyping.

1 Introduction

Increasing competitive pressure on products in mobile construction machinery forces producers to design their products more efficiently. For an efficient design of products producers use virtual prototypes to assess and improve their products not only for validating technical features but also for assessing man-machine interactions in an early stage. Prior research in mechanical engineering has broached the issue of technologies for constructing real time capable and multi-domain simulation models combining hydraulic, mechanical and electrical aspects of a machine [11].

In practice, however, simulation models are still designed from scratch for each simulation problem at hand. As the design of simulation models and the related configuration of virtual environment are expensive and time-consuming, prior research of mechanical engineering has proposed reuse approaches for simulation models [4][6][10]. Yet, these approaches are characterized by two problems – structure and application of reusable simulation models: First, prior research follows a bottom-up approach for reuse and does not structure its simulation models for reuse systematically. That way, component models are assessed towards their potential to be reused and stored within a database but do not offer mechanisms for their application. Secondly, prior research does not consider that reusable simulation models can be applied in different stages of a product life cycle. Different requirements, however, can be derived when using a simulation model in different stages of the product life cycle. To exploit the potential of simulation in different business case, like research and development, construction or sales, the development of virtual prototypes has to become more efficient by the reuse of existing simulation models and parts of it.

S. Rinderle-Ma et al. (Eds.): BPM 2009 Workshops, LNBIP 43, pp. 683–694, 2010.

These two problems are addressed in a BMBF-funded research project INPROVY (for further project details see [2]). This project aims to systemize the application of interactive machine simulations within business processes and the provision of methodical support for it in the area of mobile construction machinery. The methodical support is model-based and comprises the development of a modular design of the simulation models to enable a flexible replacement and variation of components for a comparative assessment of the behavior of machine. Based on the modular design we discuss the contributions of reference modeling principles for virtual engineering.

To put it shortly, INPROVY addresses the two problems, structure and application, of the engineering domain by analyzing different business cases for an application of reusable models and by integrating prior research of reference modeling to facilitate a top-down approach for reuse in simulation of mobile construction machinery.

This research contributes to reference modeling by discussing the application of reference modeling for different business cases of mobile construction machinery. Furthermore it provides a use case in which reference models are not used to derive models that are applied for process improvement, understanding of an application domain or documentation in business systems analysis but models that are directly transformed into the simulation process.

The article is structured as follows: Section two and three present ideas how to address the two above-mentioned problems. In section two reference modeling will be introduced to support mechanical engineering assuring a top-down approach and the structuring of the domain. In section three we present the results of an expert interview that was conducted to identify business cases offering potential for simulation in mobile construction machinery. Based on these business cases we discuss the application of reference modeling to mobile construction machinery in section four. Section five concludes the discussion and pinpoints to future research of the project.

2   Reference Modeling

Reference modeling is a part of information modeling that deals with reuse [7]. Reference models 'are referred to as special information models that serve to be reused in the design process of other information models' [9], p. 49. VOM BROCKE identified two dimensions of reference modeling: 1) stages of reference modeling and 2) principles for reference modeling [9][8][7]. These dimensions are summarized in figure 1.

The first dimension deals with the reference modeling process. Before a reference model can be applied to the construction of models the reference model has to be designed. The design of the reference model and its application comprises two stages within the reference modeling process. These stages are summarized as 'Design for Reuse' and 'Design with Reuse' [9]. Within a typical Design for Reuse process a designer of the reference model creates a model based on user's requirements, including cost and time of a future application of the reference model and required quality of the derived information model. The reference model is then used by the designer of the information model for the process Design with Reuse. Subsequently, the information model can be applied by the user of the information model [7].

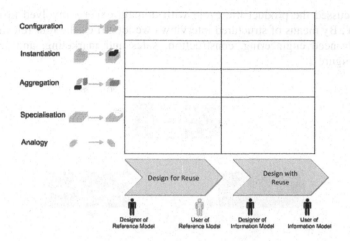

Fig. 1. Reference Model Framework [9]

The second dimension of reference modeling deals with different reference modeling principles. Prior research has identified five principles. According to VOM BROCKE configuration is used for an application domain that can be described in total in the reference model and can be applied to the construction of an information model by selecting elements from the reference model. These elements will subsequently form the elements of the information model. Instantiation covers the application domain generally, but has still to be adapted for selected aspects that can't be described in fully in the reference model. A reference model that allows instantiation comprises generic placeholders and a number of elements that can be integrated into the placeholders. The reference model that allows aggregation consists of elements that can be fully specified, but whose contribution for the whole is not predictable. Applying this reference model requires the selection of elements of the reference model and their combination. Reference models that can be used by specialization, cover only a core solution and need to be extended and modified when applied by revising elements or combining certain elements. A reference model that can be used by analogy describes the application domain by using patterns. These patterns can be adapted and changed in the information model [7][9].

Principles and stages of reference modeling will be discussed for the different business cases of mobile construction machinery. These business cases are subject of the next section.

3 Situation-Analysis for Reuse-Potential

For identifying suitable business cases, which could gain benefit from using virtual prototypes, we have analyzed the technical product life cycle [5][12]. Three identified stages relevant for information flows, manufacturing, usage and disposal [5] form the basis for the aggregation of the very detailed product stages relevant for mechanical engineers, product research, product planning, product construction, product proving, product production, product distribution, product usage, product disposal ([12], pp. I1ff.).

We discussed the product life cycle with domain experts involved in the project INPROVY. By means of structured interviews we identified the four relevant product stages, advanced engineering, construction, sales and marketing, and service presented in Figure 2.

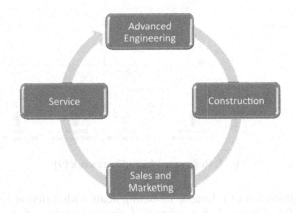

Fig. 2. INPROVY Business Cases for Machine Simulation

The product production and product disposal are not considered in our approach due to the lack of meaningful applicability of virtual prototypes. The product production comprises the manufacturing of components, their assembling and the quality inspection of products. These tasks as well as the product disposal are not influenced by the behavior of machine. Therefore, an interactive machine simulation does not contribute to decision support for this kind of problems.

Advanced Engineering
The Advanced Engineering stage comprises product research and product planning. For product research new products and new markets are explored and analyzed. It should be detected where products could be placed and what machine functions have to be provided. Thereon a systematic planning of new products and the development of an innovative product policy takes place. Virtual prototypes are used for proving novel and innovative technical solutions. The interactive simulation with virtual prototypes is only applied for proof of concept and the assessment of the impact on the behavior of machine. Restrictions resulting from the construction of a physical prototype, e.g. the nature of the installation space, do not have to be considered. Therefore, it is possible to try out innovative ideas at a very early stage without entering subsequent processes, like construction and manufacturing. Virtual prototypes enable a creative research process. Therefore, the high expenses are already accepted by a large number of machine manufacturers.

Construction
The purpose of the Construction stage is the determination of machine functions and the structure of realizable modules and components. The result of the respective tasks is an overall design of the machine consisting of all relevant components and assemblies.

Mobile construction machinery is usually individual or of low volume production. In this context virtual prototypes are used to foster the construction of mature physical prototypes. The amount of iterations and the expenses for reconstructing the physical prototype could be reduced. But assembled vendor parts are a problem for the OEM due to insufficient information about the behavior of the sub-assembly documented in the product characteristic. The high expenses for the construction of related simulation models could be reduced by reusing available information from prior simulation projects or by simulation models delivered by the respective supplier. The application of virtual prototypes is profitable if the expenses for constructing a simulation model are lower than the additional costs of iterations and reconstructing.

Marketing and Sales
For selling customized mobile construction machinery virtual prototypes are used for product presentation. For this purpose the virtual environment has to meet several additional requirements like real-time behavior of machine, high quality graphic and working environment close to reality. The interactive simulation provides a good opportunity for specifying customer requirements. But to model the whole product catalog is not efficient and would exceed any benefit generated by the application of virtual prototypes.

Service
Service for mobile constructing machinery comprises maintenance and repairing of machinery. OEMs attach particular importance to this stage. On the one hand a significant share of sales is generated in this field but on the other hand important information can be provided for the development of successors. The machine simulation shall replicate problems, which customers had experienced. Engineers would like to detect the cause of the problem and to gain additional technical insight. Thereon solution possibilities can be proven also by means of machine simulation. Therefore the benefit of virtual prototypes is multifaceted. In the case of distant machine employment it could be efficient to find a problem solution by machine simulation before travelling to the site of operation. Furthermore novel expertise can be generated leading to product innovations. Business Cases identified in this section will subsequently be subject for a reference modeling discussion.

4 Discussion of Appropriate Reference Modeling Principles

Before discussing reference modeling for the business cases we will explain how reference models can be applied to a simulation process in general. For a holistic simulation of mobile construction machinery, information about components of the machine, its virtual environment, motion and sound is required. For a first discussion of reuse in mobile construction machinery we focus, however, on the components of the machine and thus leave the issue of virtual environment, motion and sound for future research of the project.

To facilitate reuse for the simulation of mobile construction machinery we ensure a top-down approach by using a reference model representing real product structures. The reference model contains various product variants whereas the derived configuration model represents a particular product specification. That way, the reference model is used to provide the general structure of the machine and offers diverse alternatives to combine its components. Possible elements for structure and component alternatives are stored in a reference model component library. The configuration model is then derived from the reference model. After having selected the actual configuration of a mobile construction machine a simulation model can be derived containing simulation relevant information about hydraulic, electric and mechanical characteristics of the machine's components. For this purpose a configuration model component has to be directly connected to the component description in the simulation model library.

For the development of the reference model as well as for the derivation of the configuration model, reference modeling principles will be discussed for each business case.

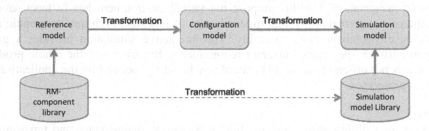

Fig. 3. Model transformation in Machine Simulation

Advanced Engineering
For product research and product planning, simulation is used for proving a novel and innovative technical solution and assessing it regarding its impact on the behavior of machine. For that reason the configuration model contains at least one novel component. The remainder of the machine model is constructed by using a reference model. By this means the efficiency and effectiveness of constructing simulation models should be improved. The former results from the reuse of existing information and avoiding duplication of work. The latter is due to the application of tested and improved simulation models.

The reference model for a specific machine type should provide a basic structure of the mobile construction machinery. The basic structure is facilitated by generic placeholders from the instantiation reference modeling principle. The generic placeholders, that build the framework of the machine type, have to be filled while deriving the configuration model. A library of model elements, representing product components, supports the completion of relevant placeholders. The product components could be described on different abstraction levels and should meet the design principle of aggregations. Due to the premise of at least one novel component, the application of configurable reference models is not meaningful for this business case. The availability of a suitable framework of a particular construction machinery and component descriptions, providing means for varied combinations and aggregations, are prerequisites for applying the identified design principles for reference modeling.

Both parts, the framework and the library of product components, compose the reference model, which has its source from machine modeling in prior Advanced

Engineering and Construction activities respectively. In this stage, Design for Reuse, a novel and innovative component is modeled analogously to existing components. Its state has to be marked as 'Idea' for distinguishing it from approved components. For extensive innovations regarding the basic structure of construction machinery, an analogy construction to existing machine models takes place, as well. But extensions of an existing framework of particular construction machinery by additional machine functions are more probable. For this purpose the design principle of specialization is applied. The results of reference modeling for Advanced Engineering are summarized in figure 4.

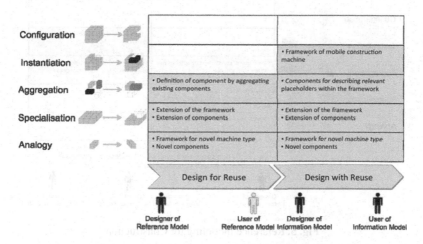

Fig. 4. Reference modeling for Advanced Engineering

Construction
For specifying the overall design of mobile construction machinery, all relevant components and assemblies have to be selected. While Advanced Engineering occurs only when at least a new component is involved, Construction also includes the development of a new composition of components into a framework.

Simulation is a well-established means for assuring mature physical prototypes. Yet, the high expenses for constructing an adequate simulation model can be reduced by reference modeling. Compared with Advanced Engineering activities, similar effects for efficiency and effectiveness of the modeling process within the Construction stage are expected. Beyond that, the possibility for knowledge transfer from subsequent activities, like feedback information from Marketing and Sales or systematic error causes detected within service tasks, is gaining additional benefit.

For constructing a customized machine the framework is determined by the related machine type. The reference model provides this framework, whose generic placeholders have to be instantiated by the combination of available product components, not having the state "Idea". New components could be entered into the library, e.g. a competitive product component should be assessed. Therefore reference model principles aggregation, specialization and analogy could be used. In Design for Reuse, the application of a particular principle depends on existing information captured by descriptions of product components stored in the reference modeling library. Apart from the development and extension of components the business case Construction provides the basis for the following business case Marketing and Sales. This will be discussed in the following scenario.

The basic structure of the machine is not allowed to be changed within the Process of Construction. Changes of the machine framework have to be made within the Process of Advanced Engineering. Figure 5 shows the result of the discussion for reference modeling for Construction:

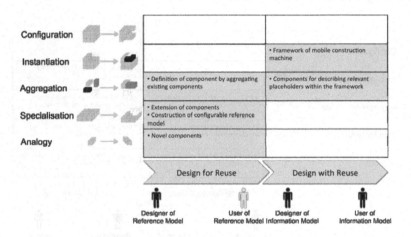

Fig. 5. Reference modeling for Construction

Sales and Marketing

Simulation in Sales and Marketing is used for product presentation of customized machinery. Thereby the customer can gain haptical, optical and acoustical impressions of the product. These impressions help specifying customer requirements. The deployment of simulation in this business case is advantageous if the expenses for simulation exceed those for reconstruction caused by insufficient requirements specification and the costs pertaining to loss of image.

If reference modeling in Sales and Marketing is used to present a small number of configuration variants and thus deals with little complexity, the configuration principle can be used to keep costs of the reference modeling application low. Hence, the reference model contains product configuration variants that can be used to define customer requirements. Further reference modeling principles such as instantiation, aggregation, specialization and analogy should not be applied, since they must be performed by a construction / engineering professional but not by a salesperson.

A prerequisite to use simulation in Sales and Marketing is a configurable reference model. This model is developed in the business case Construction after the configuration of a certain machine is approved. The development, in Design for Reuse, of a configurable reference model requires specialisation to provide alternatives. Figure 6 summarizes the results for Sales and Marketing.

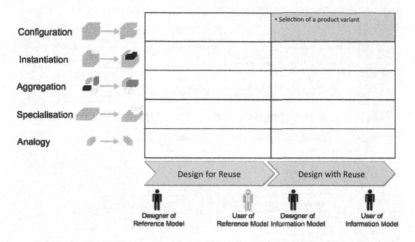

Fig. 6. Reference modeling for Sales and Marketing

Service

In Services simulation is applied for maintenance and repair. That way, simulation fosters efficiency if the simulation costs for finding the error and developing a solution are below the costs when using the real machine as a basis. Effectiveness can be increased by using an already tested and verified simulation model.

A reference model can be used in both stages of Services: error detection and solution development. For error detection the configuration model from the construction stage of the machine under consideration can be used. Parameters of the components can be changed within the simulation model until the error is localized. Neither the configuration nor the reference model is changed in this stage.

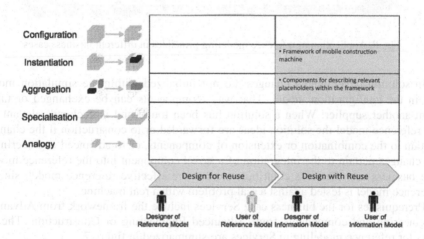

Fig. 7. Reference modeling for Services

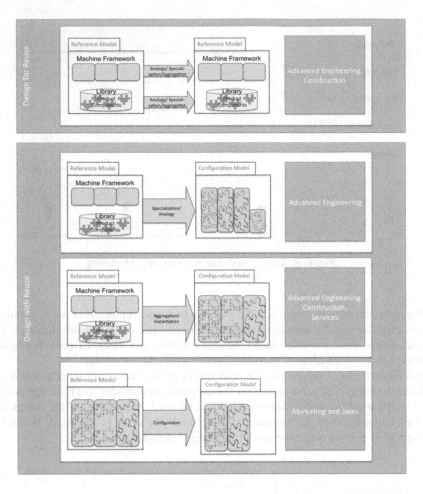

Fig. 8. Application of reference modeling principles in different business cases

In solution development changes are not initialized within the simulation model but in the configuration model. That way, components can be exchanged or taken from another supplier. When a solution has been found and is declared relevant for the reference model the solution ideas are forwarded or to construction if the changes pertain to the combination or extension of components, or to advanced engineering if the changes pertain to the integration of a novel component into the reference model. The business case Services contributes to a more effective reference model, since a reference model is tested against a real problem with a real machine.

Prerequisites for the business case Services include the framework from Advanced Engineering and components from Advanced Engineering or Construction. The results for reference modeling in Services are summarized in figure 7.

5 Conclusion

This research-in-progress paper has addressed problems of reuse of simulation models in mobile construction machinery. These problems comprise first the identification of the potential of reuse in the product life cycle and second the structure of reusable components that result from a bottom-up approach. For the first problem an expert interview has been conducted that has lead to four different business cases in which simulation is advantageous. These business cases comprise Advanced Engineering, Construction, Marketing and Sales and Services and were subject to a discussion of reference modeling stages and principles. As a result we identified that reference modeling is applicable, even though to a different degree, in all four business cases. The reference model principles that can be applied within the different business cases are summarized in figure 8.

As can be seen in figure 8 Design for Reuse is applied only in Advanced Engineering and Construction while Design with Reuse can be applied in all four business cases. Not only the stages of reference modeling differ among the business cases but also its principles. Instantiation and aggregation constitute the basis of deriving a configuration model from a reference model. Those principles are used in Advanced Engineering, Construction and Services. For a flexible application of reference modeling in mobile construction machinery principles should also include analogy and specialization to extend or modify components or frameworks. However, these principles should only be applied by a simulation expert. Sales and Marketing requires configuration as principle to derive a configuration model from a reference model since no expert is available in this business case but alternatives should be presented to derive customer requirements. Apart from integrating reference modeling in business cases we have focused on reference modeling principles for the construction of a configuration model that is directly transformed within a simulation process and have thereby provided a use case for reference modeling that is beyond the traditional focus of reference modeling. To elaborate this use case for reference modeling we will continue evaluating our selection of reference modeling mechanisms within discussed business cases with a prototypical implementation. By this means we are able to assess the appropriateness of particular design principles for reference modeling and the related constructs of modeling language. These prospective research results will contribute to the research in reference modeling by providing a real existing and complex modeling problem. And empirical investigation of quality characteristics of reference modeling language is considered necessary [3].

References

1. Becker, J., Delfmann, P., Knackstedt, R.: Adaption fachkonzeptueller Referenzprozessmodelle. Industrie Management 20(1), 19–21 (2004)
2. Esswein, W., Greiffenberg, S., Lehrmann, S.: Framework zur modellgestützten Simulation. In: Wissensportal baumaschine.de, 2 (2009), http://www.baumaschine.de
3. Fettke, P., Loos, P.: Referenzmodellierung – Langfassung eines Aufsatzes.16. Working Paper of the Research Group Information Systems & Management. Johannes Gutenberg-Universität Mainz (2004)

4. Hislog, D., Lacroix, Z., Moeller, G.: Issues in mechanical engineering design management. SIGMOD Record 33(2), 135–138 (2004)
5. Pahl, G., Beitz, W., Feldhusen, J., Grote, K.-H.: Konstruktionslehre: Grundlagen erfolgreicher Produktentwicklung, Methoden und Anwendung, 7th edn. Springer, Berlin (2007)
6. Summers, J.D., Vargas-Hernndez, n., Zhao, Z., Shah, J.J., Lacroix, Z.: Comparative Study of Representation Structures for Modeling Function and Behavior of Mechanical Devices. In: ASME DETC 2000 (2001)
7. Vom Brocke, J.: Referenzmodellierung. Gestaltung und Verteilung von Konstruktionsprozessen. Logos Verlag, Berlin, 2003, zugl. Diss., Universität Münster (2002)
8. Vom Brocke, J.: Verteilte Referenzmodellierung. Gestaltung multipersoneller Konstruktionsperspektiven. In: Dittrich, K., König, W., Oberweis, A., Rannenberg, K., Wahlster (eds.) Informatik 2003, Innovative Informatikanwendungen, Frankfurt. LNI (2003)
9. vom Brocke, J.: Design Principles for Reference Modeling: Reusing Information Models by Means of Aggregation, Specialisation, Instantiation, and Analogy. In: Fettke, P., Loos, P. (eds.) Reference Modeling For Business Systems Analysis, pp. 47–75. Idea Group, Hershey (2007)
10. Vornholt, S., Geist, I.: Flexible Integration Model for Virtual Prototype Families. In: 5th International Conference on Product Lifecycle Management (PLM 2008), Seoul, Korea (2008)
11. Vornholt, S., Geist, I.: Interface for Multidisciplinary Virtual Prototype Components. In: DEXA Workshop 1st International Workshop on Data Management in Virtual Engineering DMVE 2008 (2008)
12. Weidermann, F., Wieland, P.: Einführung in die Konstruktionsmethodik. In: Böge, A. (ed.) Handbuch Maschinenbau: Grundlagen und Anwendungen der Maschinenbau-Technik, 19th edn., pp. I1–I209. Vieweg + Teubner, Wiesbaden (2009)

On the Contribution of Reference Modeling for Organizing Enterprise Mashup Environments

Volker Hoyer[1,3], Katarina Stanoevska-Slabeva[1], and Jan vom Brocke[2]

[1] University of St. Gallen,
Institute for Media and Communications Management, MCM, Switzerland
[2] University of Lichtenstein, Martin Hilti Chair of Business Process Management,
Institute of Information Systems, Principality of Liechtenstein
[3] SAP Research St. Gallen, Switzerland
{volker.hoyer,katarina.stanoevska}@unisg.ch,
jan.vom.brocke@hochschule.li

Abstract. A new kind of Web-based applications, known as Enterprise Mashups, has gained momentum in the recent years. The vision is that business users with no or limited programming skills are empowered to leverage in a collaborative manner user friendly building blocks in the envisioned Enterprise 2.0. However, the transfer of this concept into practice is still a serious issue. Whereas most research focuses on technical aspects, we point the organizational dimension of implementing Enterprise Mashups. In particular, we claim that new capabilities are needed within the implementing organization that have yet to be discovered. For that purpose we propose a reference model for organizing Enterprise Mashup environments. We also report on two applications of this model within the projects SAP Research RoofTop Marketplace and FAST. In summary, we reflect on the usefulness of the reference model for making Mashups happen in enterprise environments.

Keywords: Reference Modeling, Enterprise Mashups, SAP Research RoofTop Marketplace, FAST Platform.

1 Introduction

1.1 Motivation

Since the beginning of the 1990s, companies have optimized their corporate Information Technology (IT) by introducing transactions systems. By following the management approach of business process engineering [1], in a first step, enterprises introduced the internal business process idea to overcome the functional-oriented organizational structure (i.e., by introducing an Enterprise Resource Planning system). In a second step, the process-oriented way of doing business was transferred to cross-organizational electronic transactions (i.e., Customer Relationship Management). This resulted in borderless enterprises [2] which are characterized by seamless cross-organizational business processes and real-time businesses [3]. The technological enabler is the Service-Oriented Architecture. Modular components defined by well-defined and standardized

S. Rinderle-Ma et al. (Eds.): BPM 2009 Workshops, LNBIP 43, pp. 695–706, 2010.

interfaces are loosely coupled and allow for flexible adaptation of business transaction systems by IT experts.

The next wave in corporate technology adoption promises further gains, although the capabilities differ from the first automation wave. It will exploit new productivity potential by means of a broad collaboration and a high degree of participation. In contrast to ERP or CRM systems, new technologies and tools from the Web 2.0 philosophy are interactive. They integrate users in order to generate new information or edit the work of others. Renowned management scholars such as McAfee and Tapscott envision an Enterprise 2.0 [5, 6]. It leverages these new consumer-driven technologies in order to put people in the center of the information-centric work.

At the interaction between the two corporate technology adoption waves, a new trend for a software development paradigm, known as Enterprise Mashups, has gained momentum in the recent years. It combines the characteristics of both technology adoption waves. At the core are two aspects: First, empowerment of the end users to cover ad-hoc needs by reusing and combining existing modular software artefacts from company's internal as well as external resources. Second, a broad involvement of users based on the peer production concept [7]. Thereby, the creative energy of a large number of people is used to reflect flexible on continuous and dynamic changes of the business environment. Instead of long-winded software development processes, existing and new enterprise-class application components are enhanced with interfaces (so called Application Programming Interfaces, APIs) and are provided as user friendly building blocks which can be combined individually.

1.2 Problem Statement and Research Question

Market research companies like Gartner [8], Forrester [9], or Economic Intelligence Units [10] and leading management consulting firms like McKinsey [11] forecast a growing relevance for the Mashup paradigm. Gartner sees Mashup applications at the mainstream adoption in less than two years in its hype cycle for Web and user interaction technologies 2008 [8]. Forrester also predicts that Enterprise Mashups will be coming to a $700 million market by 2013 [9]. In addition, BEA [13], EIU [10] and McKinsey [11], conducted surveys to analyze the current (2007) and planned use (2009) of Mashups within enterprises. The surveys show the intentions of enterprises to introduce the Mashup paradigm in the next several years. However, the market research institutes highlight that the sucessful transfer of the Mashup paradigm in corporate environments needs additional capabilities beyond those typically associated with consumer Mashup offerings. Even if traditional interoperability, portability, and security aspects are not solved so far, the main challenges to enterprise adoption of Mashups are related with the business and organization perspective [14]. In addition, the changing relationship and culture between users and the IT department in Enterprise Mashup environment require new concepts for organizing and managing the balance of top-down and user-self management [14, 15, 16].

However, the discussion of the Enterprise Mashup paradigm from an organizational perspective is still missing in the scientific community. The successful enterprise adoption of the Mashup paradigm requires a structure to understand the changing development model from an organizational perspective. The goal of this research paper is to fill this gap by elaborating and discussing of the contribution of reference modeling for organizing Enterprise Mashup environments. The general research question guiding this study is how reference modelling can contribute to understand these community-driven environments in order to design related Information Systems.

The remainder of this study is organized as follows: In section two, we introduce the Enterprise Mashup paradigm and related terms that build the foundation of this paper. Section three elaborates on the current research activities related to reference models. Section four presents a first scientific multi-view reference model and its successful application in the context of the SAP Research RoofTop Marketplace and the EU funded research project FAST. The contributions of reference modeling are presented in a lessons learned section. Finally, section five closes this paper with a brief conclusion and gives an outlook on future work.

2 Enterprise Mashups

2.1 Definition and Terminology

In literature, the definition of Enterprise Mashups is open to debate. In this work, we refer to the following definition: *"An Enterprise Mashup is a Web-based resource that combines existing resources, be it content, data or application functionality, from more than one resource by empowering end users to create individual information centric and situational applications"* [17]. By simplifying concepts of Service-Oriented Architecture (SOA) and by enhancing them with the Web 2.0 Philosophy of peer production, Enterprise Mashups focus generally on software integration on the user interface level instead of traditional application or data integration approaches. In contrast to SOA that is characterized by high technical complexity of the relevant standards and requiring specialists' technical knowledge, Mashups enable the integration of end users with no or limited programming skills in the development process.

The relevant architectural components of the Enterprise Mashup paradigm are resources, widgets, and Mashups [17] and can be structured in an Enterprise Mashup Stack comprising three layers (see Figure 1): Resources represent actual contents, data or application functionality that are the core building blocks of Mashups. They are encapsulated via well-defined public interfaces (Application Programming Interfaces; i.e., WSDL, RSS, Atom, etc.) allowing the loosely coupling of existing resources – a major quality stemming from the SOA paradigm [4]. These resources are provided by enterprise systems or by external Web providers (i.e., Amazon, Google, etc.) and are created by traditional developers who are familiar with the technical development concepts. On the second layer, widgets provide simple user interaction mechanism abstracting from the complexity of the underlying resources. For example a widget "Customer Data" might provide results for a predefined query requesting the data for all customers of a sales manager. The creation of these widgets can be done by consultants in the business units who understand the business requirements and know basic development concepts. Finally, end users with no programming skills are able to combine and configure visual widgets according to their individual needs, which results in a Mashup. For example, the sales manager wires the "Customer Data" with a map to show the location of the customers.

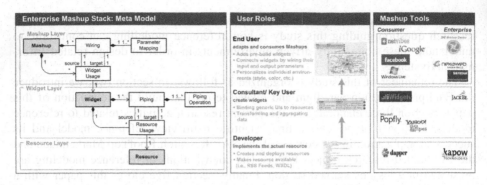

Fig. 1. Enterprise Mashup Stack – Meta Model, User Roles and Mashup Tools

2.2 Characteristics of the New Development Model

The shift from delivering finished applications created by the IT department toward delivering of user friendly building blocks that can be combined individually implicates a changing development model. This involves both managing the Mashup components and managing the relationships between the invovled people. To understand the changing development approach compared to traditional concepts such as SOAs, the table below summarizes our findings of a desk research [16, 19].

Table 1. SOA Development versus Enterprise Mashup Development

Criteria	Service-Oriented Architecture	Enterprise Mashups
Scope		
Time to Value	Many weeks, months or even years	Minutes, hours, or days
Life span	Long lived application	Variable, often short lived applications
Application Type	Strategic, standard applications	Backlog of simple, tactical, and individual applications ("Long Tail")
Functional Requirement	Defined by limited number of users, IT needs to freeze requirements to move to development	As requirements change, Enterprise Mashups usually changes to accommodate business changes
Non-Functional Requirement	Resources allocated to address concerns for performance, availabiltiy, and security, robust solutions	Little or no focus on scalability, maintainability, availability, etc.
Process		
Development Phase	Well defined and scheduled (requirement, specification, testing, deployment)	Ad-hoc or "good enough" solutions to address an immediate need
Governance	Formal, centralized	Decentralized, community driven
Evolution	Top-down, centrally	Organic
Users		
Application builders	IT department or external experts (developer skills)	Line of business, individuals, groups (limited or no programming skills)
Target Users	Large groups	Small teams or even individuals

In contrast to SOAs, Enterprise Mashups usually aren't constructed by a team of traditional software developers from the IT department. Instead, they are created by users from the business units characterized by no or limited programming skills. In that regard, Enterprise Mashups particularly serve as a means to address newly emerging requirements in the implementation process of service-oriented information systems. Just recently, studies have shown that – in contrast to the tendency towards a market-oriented exchange of services – the implementation process, rather calls for a move towards hierarchical (or at least hybrid) modes of governance [19, 20]. The rational behind this argumentation is that making use of the SOA-potentials, the specific business needs of a company have to be taken into account precisely. Here, the concept of Enterprise Mashups comes in, providing a promising means to involve users from the business engaging into the system design.

These users, however, desire specific functionality that mainstream SOA-based enterprise applications don't provide [19]. In this sense, the Enterprise Mashup paradigm aims at creating ad-hoc or "good enough" solutions which address daily and tactical user needs. According to the continuous changed business environment, they are often adapted and don't follow the traditional development phases. Instead, they evolve organically in a decentralized manner. Non-functional requirements like scalability, maintainability or availability play a minor role. In case created applications don't fulfill the user requirements from a functional and non-functional perspective, they are replaced immediately by the community. In this kind of grassroots computing [16] users share their customization efforts with a like-minded community. The focus on delivering a set of user friendly building blocks rather than finished enterprise applications enables to automate also tactical and opportunistic applications.

Another specific characteristic of Enterprise Mashup environments is their similarity to electronic markets [21]. Enterprise Mashup environments need to provide besides support for easy integration of software artefacts also support for efficient management and matching of supply and demand for Mashup components. [22] describes the trading of Web Services according to market transaction phases. [19] puts the discovery and sharing of mashable elements in the center of the development process to reuse existing assets in new combinations. However, it remains questionable in how far market-oriented mechanisms will prove to be efficient in the end. As we know from former work (e. g. in the field of component ware) a piece of software may well remain quite specific (e.g. in terms of its semantics). In addition, transaction cost theory for example exhibits that further characteristics are relevant choosing the most efficient governance mode, including i.e. characteristics such as frequency and strategic importance. So, we should to be aware of the fact that – despite the technological options – a market-based co-ordination may only be favorable for (a few) specific types of services. Anyway, even more so, we see that Enterprise Mashups raise several organizational questions and thus come with a comparable high risk that may turn out as hindrance for making use of the new concept in practice. In that regard, reference models may well be a means reducing this risk.

3 Reference Modeling

There has been quite a discussion on the concept of reference modelling, predominantly driven by the German speaking community. In this work we apply the "reuse-oriented" concept of reference modelling [26] that is establishing as a kind of common understanding [24, 25, 26]. Accordingly, reference models are referred to as a special kind of models that serve to be reused in the design process of artefacts [27]. Hence, reference models can be understood as blueprints, particularly used for information systems development. In the scientific community, particularly modeling guidelines [28] and evaluation criteria of reference models [24] are discussed.

By means of a literature review and by applying the classification framework of [29], we analysed existing reference models that are relevant for the Enterprise Mashups paradigm. Gartner proposes a practitioner reference model that specifies the technical architecture components in Enterprise Mashup environments [30]. A practitioner reference model of Forrester uses a similar layer structure like Gartner and the presented Enterprise Mashup Stack. In addition, a phase model is integrated specifying the inputs and information flow [9]. First, the actual content provided by the IT department is provisioned for the Enterprise Mashup environment from both internal and external resources. Second, users from the business units use a so-called Mashup composer to arrange and combine content, as well as to determine a visualization paradigm. Third, the mashable components are managed by a Mashup life-cycle manager and shared with others to use in new Mashups if desired. Even though both reference models provide first technical structures of Enterprise Mashup environments, a multi-view concept [31, 32] integrating the managerial perspective is missing. The existing reference models particularly miss support for the collaborative aspect of Enterprise Mashups development and do not provide sufficient support for the peer production process. In order to integrate the different aspects (community, processes, or technical), a multi-view reference model is necessary.

In reference modelling, multi-view models are well established. For example, the Architecture for Integrated Information Systems (ARIS) separates business processes into five views: organization, data, control, function, and service view [33] and thus provides a means for describing processes according to these different views. In Memo a strategy, organiation and information system perspective are differenciated just as well as different aspects such as resource, structure, process and goal [31]. Likewise, the Business Engineering reference model proposes a strategy, process, and information system layer for structuring enterprise architectures [34].

4   A Multi-view Scientific Reference Model for Enterprise Mashup Environments

4.1   Reference Model for Enterprise Mashups Environments

A comprehensive reference model for Enterprise Mashups is required that on the one hand considers technical requirements regarding the easy integration of mashable components and on the other hand support for matching of supply and demand for required Mashups based on the market paradigm. By incorporating the findings presented in the previous sections, we leveraged the St. Gallen Media Reference Model. The designed multi-view scientific reference model consists of three dimensions [21]: First, the architectural perspective with the three layer of the Enterprise Mashups

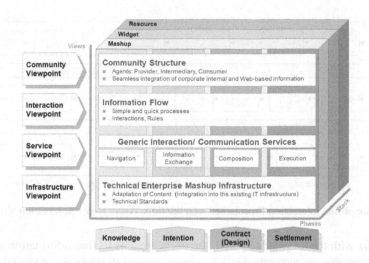

Fig. 2. Layers of the Reference Model for Enterprise Mashup Environments [21]

Stack (Mashup, widget, resource). Second, the four phases of a market transaction. Third, the four layer views structuring the different successive interation goals of interacting agents within the Enterprise Mashup medium.

The community view describes the participating agents, their roles and the organizational structure defining the relationships among roles together with their obligations and rights. The interaction view refers to the relevant processes and is based upon the underlying services. The service view comprises all services in the four market phases that need to be available on the platform. The four services are: First, the knowledge phase in which available mashable components (Mashup, widget, resource) are classified, rated and explained in different ways to the users of the Enterprise Mashup environment. Second, the intentions phase in which concrete offers are provided in a structured manner including the business model (payment mode, the price as well as the delivery conditions). In the contract (design) phase, users select the right mashable component based on the provided information, configure it according to their preferences and combine it with other components. Fourth, in the settlement phase the Enterprise Mashup is executed according to the underlying contract by using the platform's settlement services offered for this purpose. Finally, the infrastructure view contains communication protocols and standards which comprise the groundwork for the implementation of services.

In order to describe the interacting and connected users as well as their tasks, we refer to the following interaction model well known in SOAs and eletronic markets: A provider develops and publishes a mashable component via an intermediary, where a consumer can find it and subsequently may compose and consume it. For structuring Enterprise Mashup environments, we model a simplified interaction process covering the four phases of market transactions. The process itself is characterized by permanent loops between the converging design and runtime phases.

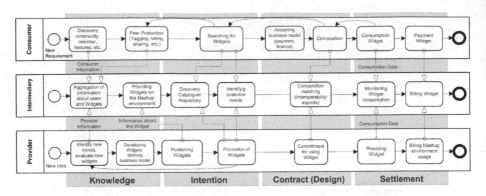

Fig. 3. Simplified Interaction Process between the three Agent Roles (Interaction View) [21]

Starting with the knowledge phase, the users are able to find information about the offered mashable components. Only if a huge amount of users is convinced of using the environment, it will exploit its actual potential. By following the intermediary role, the Enterprise Mashup platform aggregates information of the mashable components and provides it to the consumer in order to select a relevant widget. In addition to the annotations defined by the provider and consumers, the Enterprise Mashup environments monitor the behavior of the components. For example, the availability, reliability, or popularity indicates the quality of a mashable component. During the intentions phase, consumers are able to articulate their intentions and needs. Concepts from the Web 2.0 philosophy, like rating, tagging, or recommending are integrated for browsing through the growing number of available components. On the other side, providers can publish their created mashable components. Thereby, the provider defines the underlying business model such as fee, payment model, and consumption licence. After selecting a mashable component and accepting the underlying business model, consumers can compose the component with others by connecting their input and output parameters in the actual contract (design) phase. In alignment with the market principle, the usage requires a binding contract between consumers and the provider. Due to the dynamic characteristic, this commitment by the provider is done automatically. In contrast to the classical software development, the design of ad-hoc applications uses real data sources and no demo systems. In this sense the consumption in the settlement phase differs only from the hidden configuration capabilities in contrast to the design phase. In case a new business situation comes up, the consumer shifts quickly to the design or intention perspective to adapt the individual operational environment.

4.2 Application: SAP Research RoofTop Marketplace and FAST Platform

The reference model was applied to design and implement two Enterprise Mashup platforms: The SAP Research RoofTop Marketplace and the FAST platform.

The SAP Research RoofTop Marketplace is organized according to the modelled interaction process that guided the requirement analysis and technical design of the platform. The platform itself focuses on the Mashup architecture level and allows

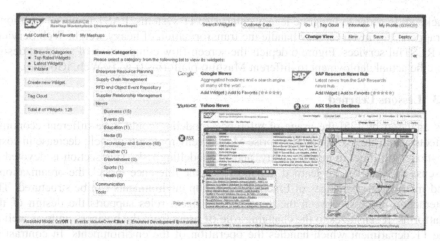

Fig. 4. SAP Research Rooftop Marketplace (Catalogue and Composition View)

creatig ad-hoc enterprise-class applications without any programming skills. An integrated catalogue manages all mashable components (Mashups and widgets) as depicted in the figure below. Community features like tagging, rating, sharing and recommending are also part of the catalogue. In the design environment, the user is empowered to combine the selected widgets from the catalogue by connecting their output and input ports with each others. By switching to the settlement view, the Mashup can be consumed immediately without changing the environment.

The second Enterprise Mashup platform, the EU-funded research project FAST, focuses on the integration of the architectural dimensions (Enterprise Mashups Stack) of the reference model. In particular, FAST allows creating complex enterprise-class widgets which can consist of a composition of several UI screens (screen-flow). These screens display the results of the piping composition of the resources from the

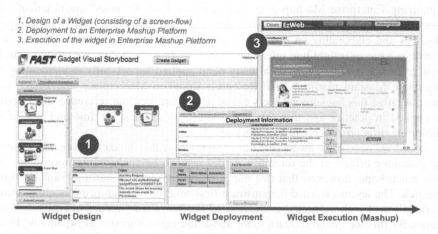

Fig. 5. FAST Platform (Design of Enterprise-Class Widgets)

backend. In order to integrate legacy enterprise IT systems, FAST provides additional wrappers. For instance, they handle the transformation of heavy weight Web Services to RESTful services. Figure 6 depicts the screen-flow composition of a widget design and the actual deployment to different Mashup platforms (i.e., EzWeb, iGoogle).

4.3 Lessons Learned

As analysed by [25] the usage of reference modeling could have different economic effects which are relevant in Enterprise Mashup environments as well: decrease in costs, in modelling time, in model quality, and in modelling risk. This section is devoted to discuss the first lessons learned. By means of the reference model, the organizational and managerial challenges of Enterprise Mashup environments can be structured. The interaction process between the three general agent roles supports the design of the platforms. It sensitizes to the changing role of users from the business units as well as the IT department which handles the operation of the envirionments. In contrast to existing Mashup platforms which try to transfer the consumer-oriented paradigm to enterprise environments without a relevant adaptation, the reference model highlights the importance of covering all market phases. So, the paradigm is not limited on the actual composition of mashable components. The community like navigation in the growing Mashup space as well as the converging design and runtime require a common integrated environment. In addition, the integration of existing legacy IT systems is a precondition for the success of Enterprise Mashups. The architectural dimension introduces a clear terminology and relationship between the various mashable components. Summing up, the reference model reduced the design time as well as the quality of the designed Enterprise Mashup platform.

5 Conclusion and Outlook

The aim of this paper is to analyse the benefits reference modeling might provide for organizing Enterprise Mashup environments. We first discussed the practical relevance of the emerging paradigm. After defining the main terms related to Enterprise Mashups and elaborating on the characteristics of the new development model, section three gave an insight into reference modeling. In section four, we present a multi-view reference model which has already been applied successfully implementing the Enterprise Mashup platform SAP Research RoofTop Marketplace and FAST platform. Against this background we were able to learn that the reference model could be applied in practice and that also positive effects in terms of time and cost of the implementation process could be observed.

Indeed we have to be aware that our research is still in an early stage. In particular the economic effects of the reference model need to be analyzed in more detail. We very much hope, however, that this paper might serves as a starting point for future research. The lessons learned demonstrate first benefits of reference modeling. Future work will deal with a detailed evaluation of the benefits by means of real-world scenarios. By this we intend to learn more about the various modes of organizing Enterprise Mashups for making this innovative concept happen in practice.

Acknowledgments. This work is supported in part by the European Commission under the first call of its Seventh Framework Program (FAST STREP Project, grant INFSO-ICT-216048).

References

1. Hammer, M., Champy, J.: Reegineering in Corporation, London, Bradley (1993)
2. Picot, A., Reichwald, R., Wigand, R.T.: Information Organization and Management: Expanding Markets and Corporate Boundaries. John Wiley and Sons, New York (1999)
3. Alt, R., Oesterle, H.: Real-Time Business. Springer, Berlin (2004)
4. McAfee, A.P.: Enterprise 2.0: The Dawn of Emergent Collaboration. MIT Sloan Management Review 47(3), 21–28 (2006)
5. Tapscott, D., Williams, A.D.: Wikinomics: How Mass Collaboration Changes Everythink, Portfolio, New York (2006)
6. Hoyer, V., Stanoevska-Slabeva, K.: Generic Business Model Types for Enterprise Mashup Intermediaries. In: Proceedings of the 15th Americas Conference on Information Systems (AMCIS), San Francisco, U.S. (2009)
7. Gootzit, D., Phifer, G., Valdes, R., Drakos, N., Bradley, A., Harris, K.: Hype Cycle for Web and User Interaction Technologies. Gartner Research G00159447 (2008)
8. Young, O.G.: The Mashup Opportunity: How to make Web 2.0 work, Forrester Resesarch, May 6 (2008)
9. The Economist Intelligence Unit, Serious Business – Web 2.0 goes Corporate, Report of the Economist Intelligence Unit (2008)
10. McKinsey Global Survey Results, Building the Web 2.0 Enterprise, The McKinsey Quarterly (2008)
11. BEA Systems, A Barometer of Web 2.0 Social Computing in Europe – A European Survey, BEA White Paper (2007)
12. Bradley, A.: Addressing the Seven Primary Challenges to Enterprise Adoption of Mashups, Gartner Research G00164390 (2009)
13. Chui, M., Miller, A., Roberts, R.P.: Six Ways to make Web 2.0 work. In: The McKinsey Quarterly (Feburary 2009)
14. Cherbakov, L., Bravery, A., Goodman, B.D., Pandya, A., Baggett, J.: Changing the Corporate IT Development Model: Tapping the Power of Grassroots Computing. IBM Systems Journal 46(4), 743–751
15. Hoyer, V., Stanoevska-Slabeva, K., Janner, T., Schroth, C.: Enterprise Mashups: Design Principles towards the Long Tail of User Needs. In: IEEE International Conference on Service Computing (SCC 2008), vol. 2, pp. 601–602 (2008)
16. Carrier, N., Deutsch, T., Gruber, C., Heid, M., Jarrett, L.L.: The Business Case for Enterprise Mashups, Web 2.0 Technology Solutions, IBM White Paper (2008)
17. vom Brocke, J., Schenk, B., Sonnenberg, C.: New Organizational Concepts for Implementing Service-Oriented ERP Systems. An Analysis Based on Transaction Cost Theory. Paper presented at the Pre-ICIS Workshop on Enterprise Systems Research in MIS (2008)
18. vom Brocke, J., Schenk, B., Sonnenberg, C.: Classification Criteria for Governing the Implementation Process of Service-oriented ERP Systems – An Analysis based on New Institutional Economics. Paper presented at the 15th Americas Conference on Information Systems (AMCIS 2009), San Francisco, USA (2009)

19. Hoyer, V., Stanoevska-Slabeva, K.: Towards a Reference Model for grassroots Enterprise Mashup Environments. In: Proceedings of the 17th European Conference in Information Systems (ECIS), Verona, Italy (2009)
20. vom Brocke, J.: Reference Modelling, Towards Collaborative Arrangements of Design Processes (in German). Berlin (2003)
21. Frank, U.: Evaluation of Reference Models. In: Fettke, P., Loos, P. (eds.) Reference Modeling for Business Systems Analysis, Hershey, PA, USA, pp. 118–140 (2007)
22. Becker, J., Knackstedt, R.: Construction and Application of Reference Models for Data Warehousing. In: Uhr, W., Esswein, W., Schopp, E. (eds.) Wirtschaftsinformatik/ Band II – Medien – Maerkte – Mobilitaet, pp. 415–433. Physica, Heidelberg (2003) (in German)
23. Thomas, O., Scheer, A.-W.: Tool Support for the Collaborative Design of Reference Models – A Business Engineering Perspective. In: Proceedings of the 39th Annual Hawaii International Conference on System Sciences. IEEE Computer Society Press, Los Alamitos (2006)
24. vom Brocke, J.: Design Principles for Reference Modeling. Reusing Information Models by Means of Aggregation, Specialisation, Instantiation, and Analogy. In: Fettke, P., Loos, P. (eds.) Reference Modeling for Business Systems Analysis, Hershey, PA, USA (2007)
25. Becker, J., Rosemann, B., Schuette, R.: Guidelines for Modeling. Wirtschaftsinformatik 37(5), 435–455 (1995) (in German)
26. Braun, R., Esswein, W.: Classification of Reference Models. In: Decker, R., Lenz, H.-J. (eds.) Studies in Classification, Data Analysis, and Knowledge Management, pp. 401–408. Springer, Berlin (2007)
27. Bradley, A.: Reference Architecture for Enterprise Mashups, Gartner Research G00151491 (2007)
28. Frank, U.: Multi-Perspective Enterprise Modeling (MEMO): Conceptual Framework and Modeling Languages. In: Proceedings of the Hawaii International Conference on System Sciences (HICSS-35), Honolulu (2002)
29. Rosemann, M.: Managing the Complexity of Multiperspective Information Models using the Guidelines of Modelling. In: Fowler, D., Dawson, L. (eds.) Proceedings of the 3rd Australian Conference on Requirements Engineering, 26-27, Geelong, pp. 101–118 (1998)
30. Scheer, A.W.: ARIS, Business Process Frameworks. Springer, Berlin (1999)
31. Oesterle, H., Back, A., Winter, R.: Business Engineering. Springer, Berlin (2004)

Author Index